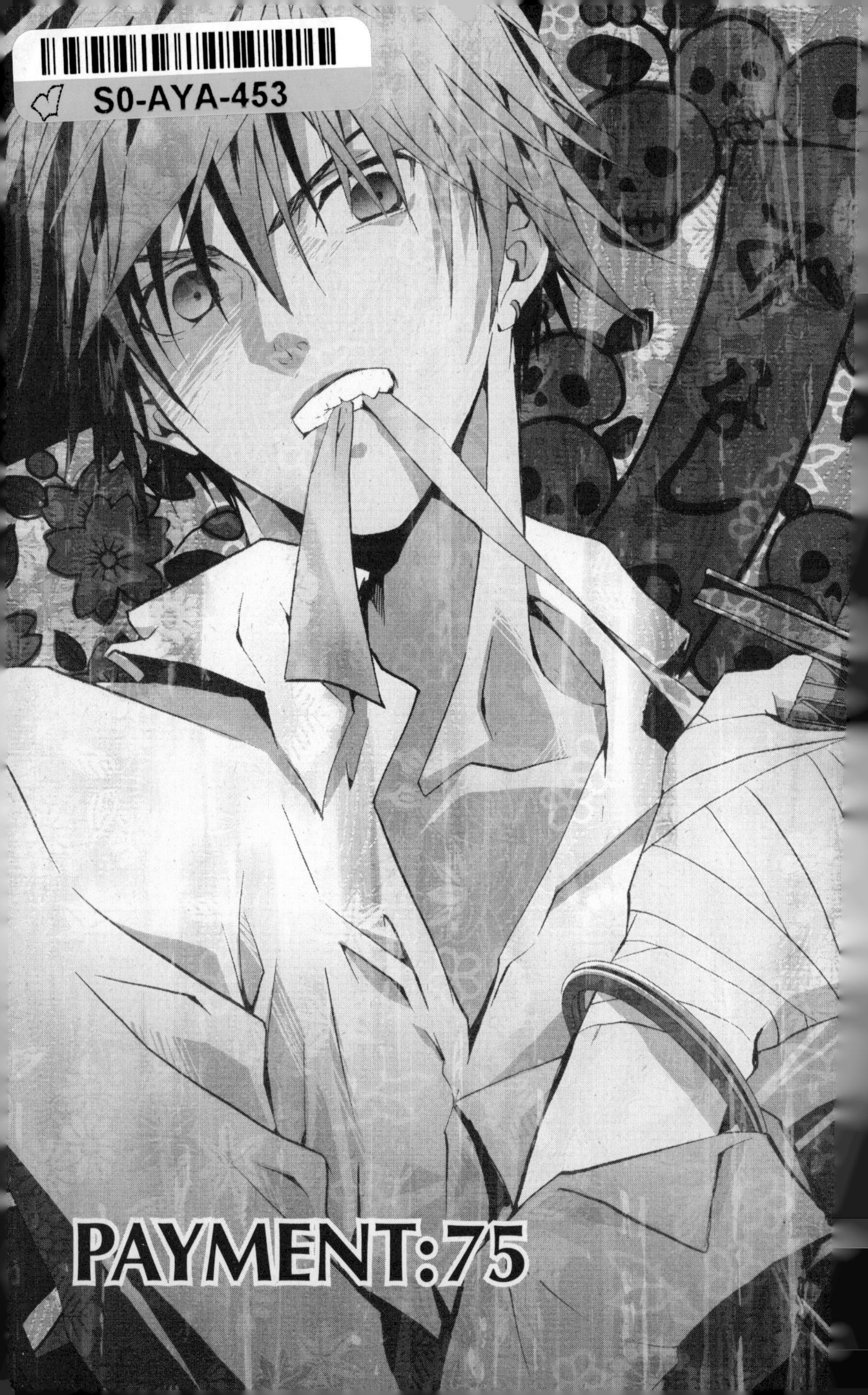
PAYMENT:75

ZOMBIE-LOAN

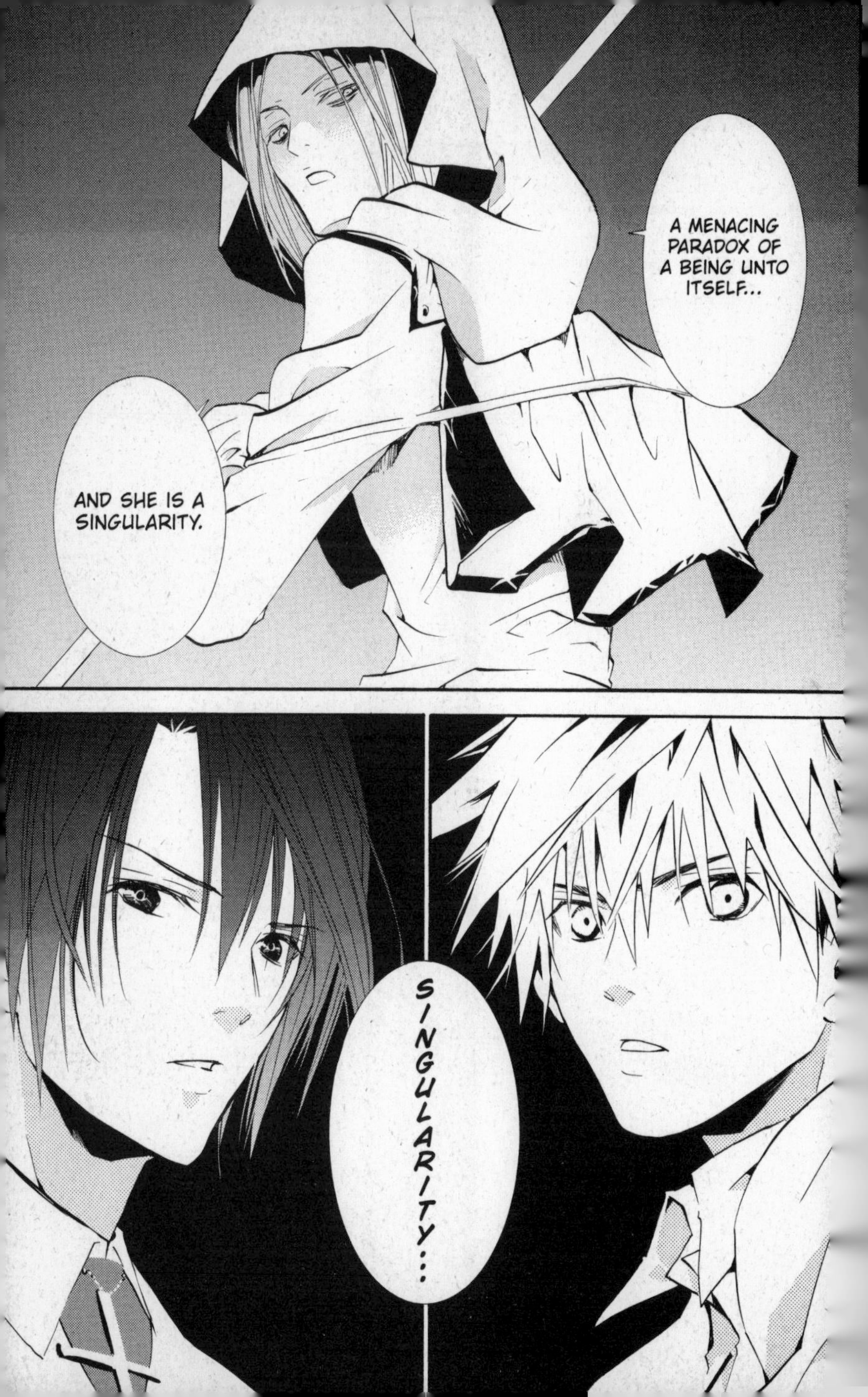
A MENACING PARADOX OF A BEING UNTO ITSELF...
AND SHE IS A SINGULARITY.
SINGULARITY...

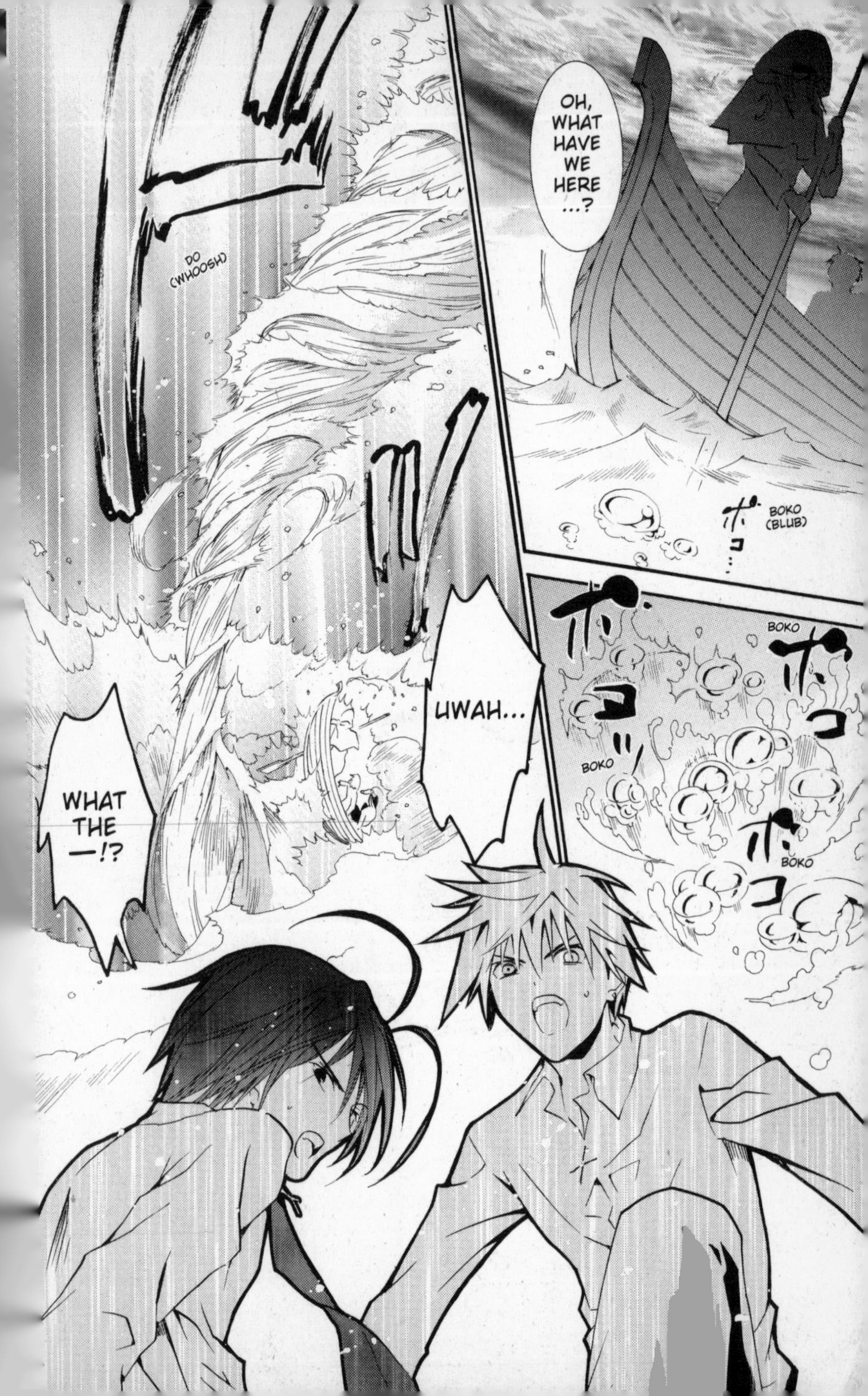
OH, WHAT HAVE WE HERE ...?
BOKO (BLUB)
BOKO
BOKO
BOKO
DO (WHOOSH)
UWAH...
WHAT THE—!?

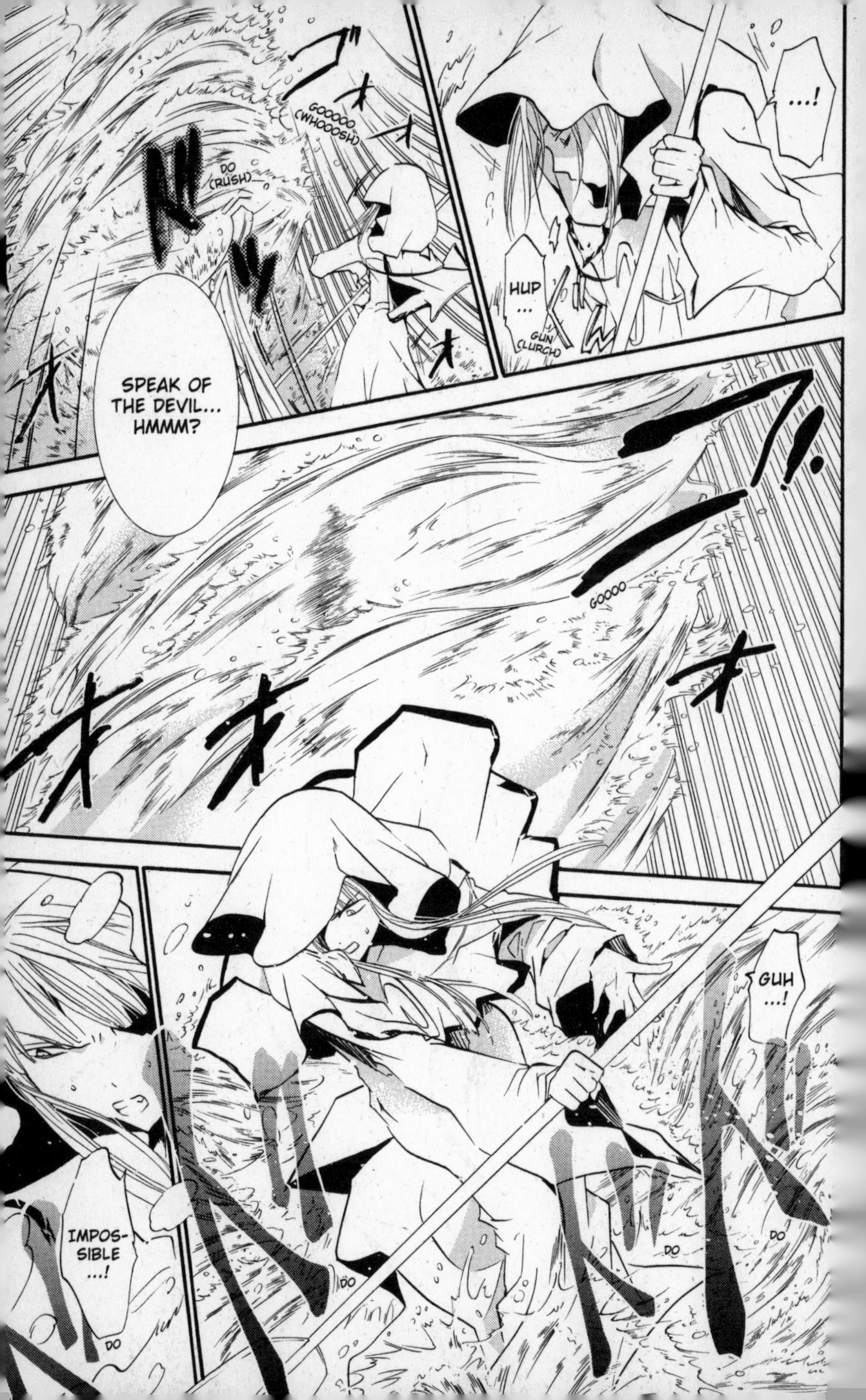
...!
HUP ...
GUN (LURCH)
GOOOOO (WHOOOSH)
DO (RUSH)
SPEAK OF THE DEVIL... HMMM?
GOOOO
GUH ...!
DO
DO
DO
IMPOS-SIBLE ...!
DO

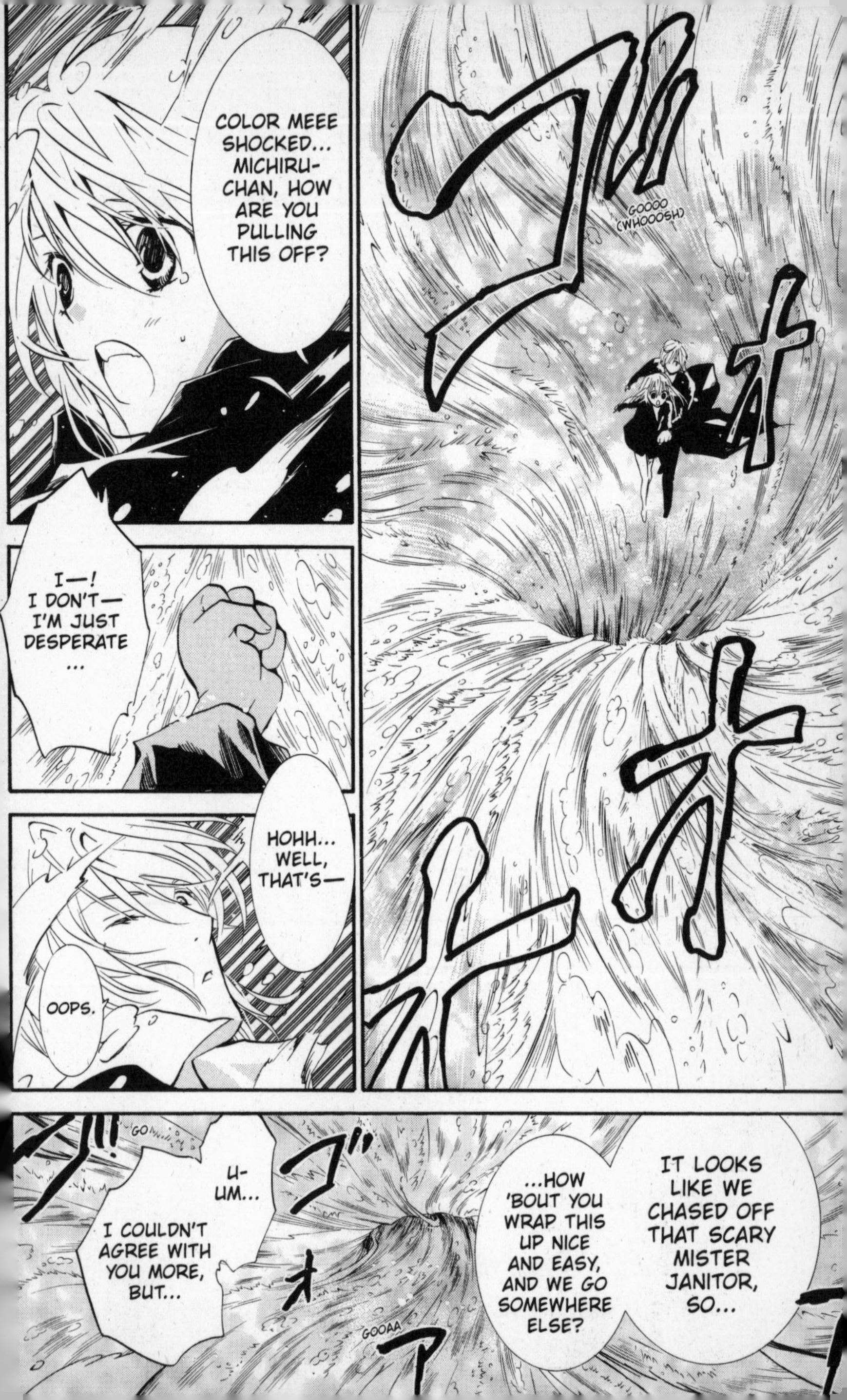
GOOOO (WHOOOSH)
COLOR MEEE SHOCKED... MICHIRU-CHAN, HOW ARE YOU PULLING THIS OFF?
I—! I DON'T— I'M JUST DESPERATE ...
HOHH... WELL, THAT'S—
OOPS.
IT LOOKS LIKE WE CHASED OFF THAT SCARY MISTER JANITOR, SO...
...HOW 'BOUT YOU WRAP THIS UP NICE AND EASY, AND WE GO SOMEWHERE ELSE?
U-UM...
I COULDN'T AGREE WITH YOU MORE, BUT...
GOOAA
GO

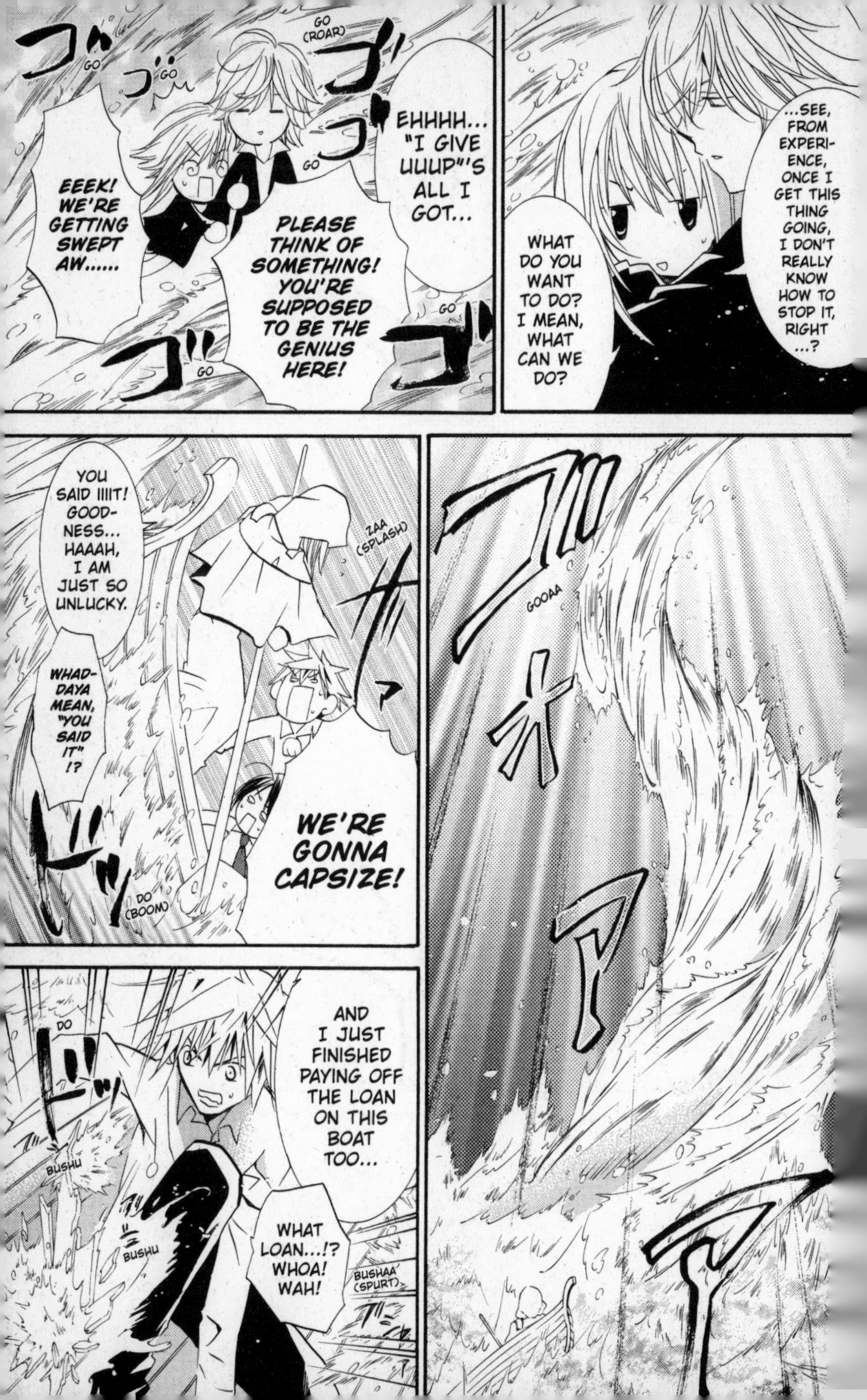
...SEE, FROM EXPERIENCE, ONCE I GET THIS THING GOING, I DON'T REALLY KNOW HOW TO STOP IT, RIGHT ...?
WHAT DO YOU WANT TO DO? I MEAN, WHAT CAN WE DO?
GO (ROAR)
EHHHH... "I GIVE UUUP"'S ALL I GOT...
GO
GO
PLEASE THINK OF SOMETHING! YOU'RE SUPPOSED TO BE THE GENIUS HERE!
GO
GO
EEEK! WE'RE GETTING SWEPT AW......
GO
GOOAA
ZAA (SPLASH)
YOU SAID IIIIT! GOODNESS... HAAAH, I AM JUST SO UNLUCKY.
WHADDAYA MEAN, "YOU SAID IT" !?
WE'RE GONNA CAPSIZE!
DO (BOOM)
AND I JUST FINISHED PAYING OFF THE LOAN ON THIS BOAT TOO...
DO
BUSHU
WHAT LOAN...!? WHOA! WAH!
BUSHAA (SPURT)
BUSHU

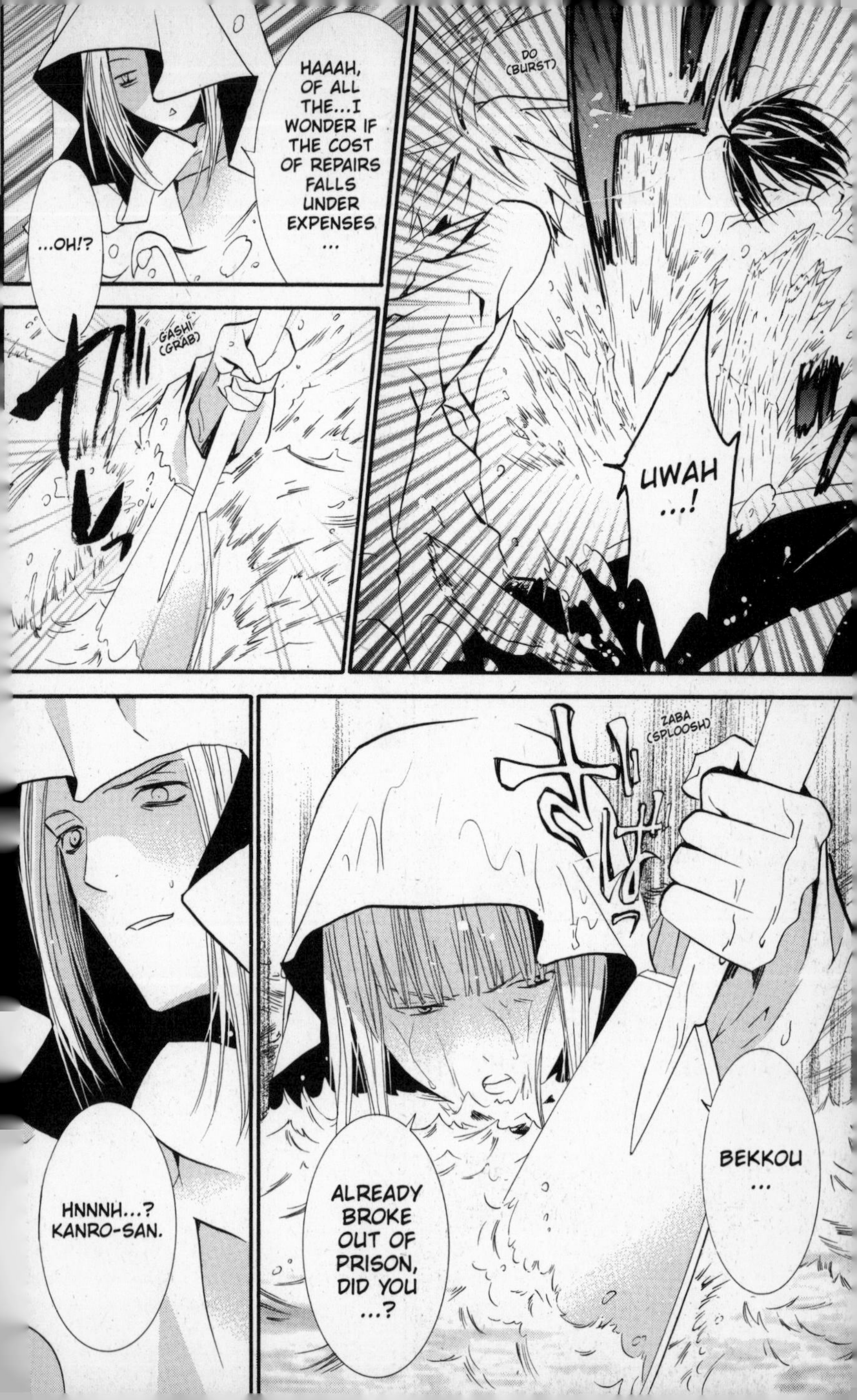
DO (BURST)
UWAH ...!
HAAAH, OF ALL THE...I WONDER IF THE COST OF REPAIRS FALLS UNDER EXPENSES ...
...OH!?
GASHI (GRAB)
ZABA (SPLOOSH)
BEKKOU ...
ALREADY BROKE OUT OF PRISON, DID YOU ...?
HNNNH...? KANRO-SAN.

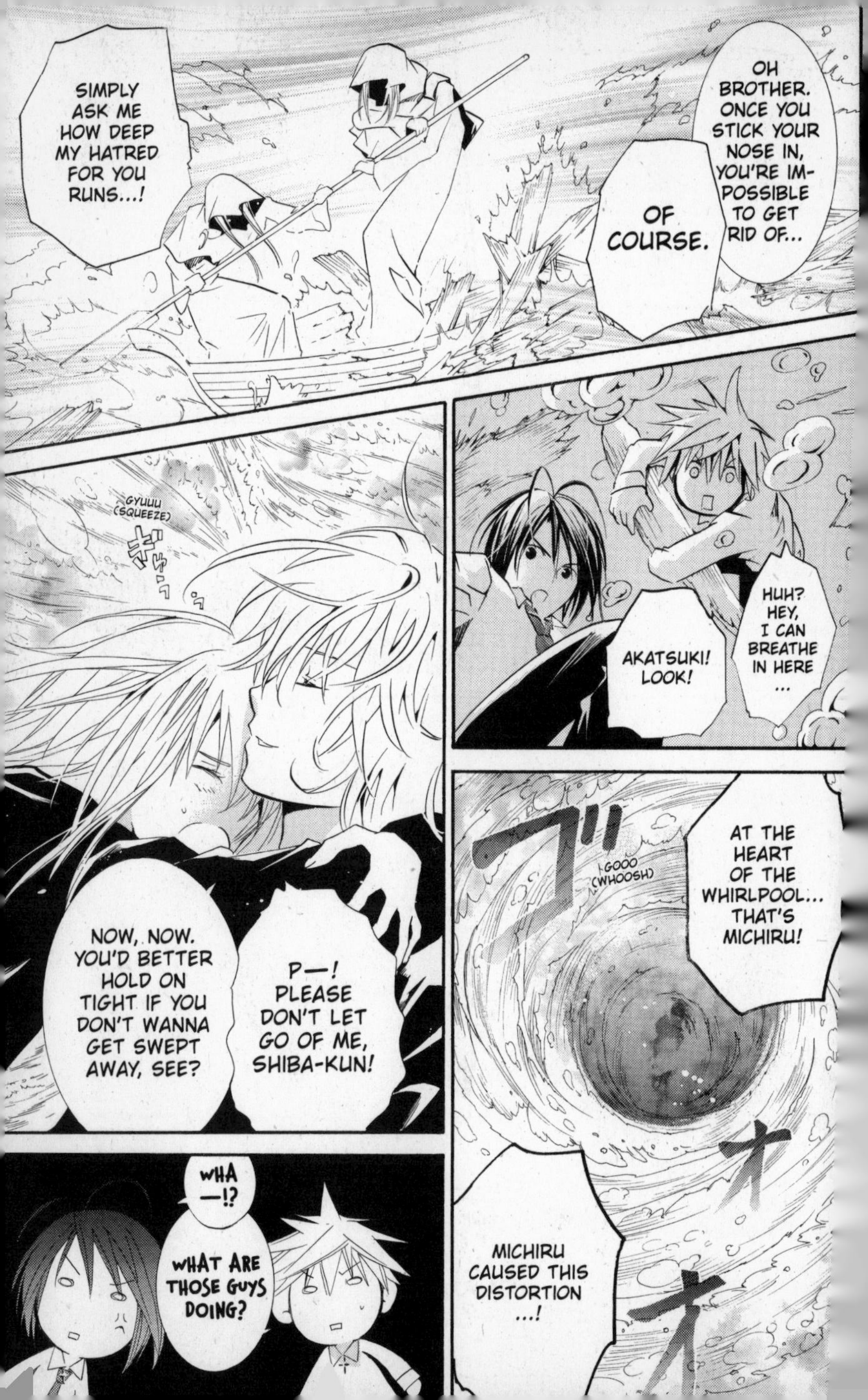
OH BROTHER. ONCE YOU STICK YOUR NOSE IN, YOU'RE IM-POSSIBLE TO GET RID OF...
OF COURSE.
SIMPLY ASK ME HOW DEEP MY HATRED FOR YOU RUNS...!
HUH? HEY, I CAN BREATHE IN HERE ...
AKATSUKI! LOOK!
GYUUU (SQUEEZE)
P—! PLEASE DON'T LET GO OF ME, SHIBA-KUN!
NOW, NOW. YOU'D BETTER HOLD ON TIGHT IF YOU DON'T WANNA GET SWEPT AWAY, SEE?
AT THE HEART OF THE WHIRLPOOL... THAT'S MICHIRU!
GOOO (WHOOSH)
MICHIRU CAUSED THIS DISTORTION ...!
WHA —!?
WHAT ARE THOSE GUYS DOING?

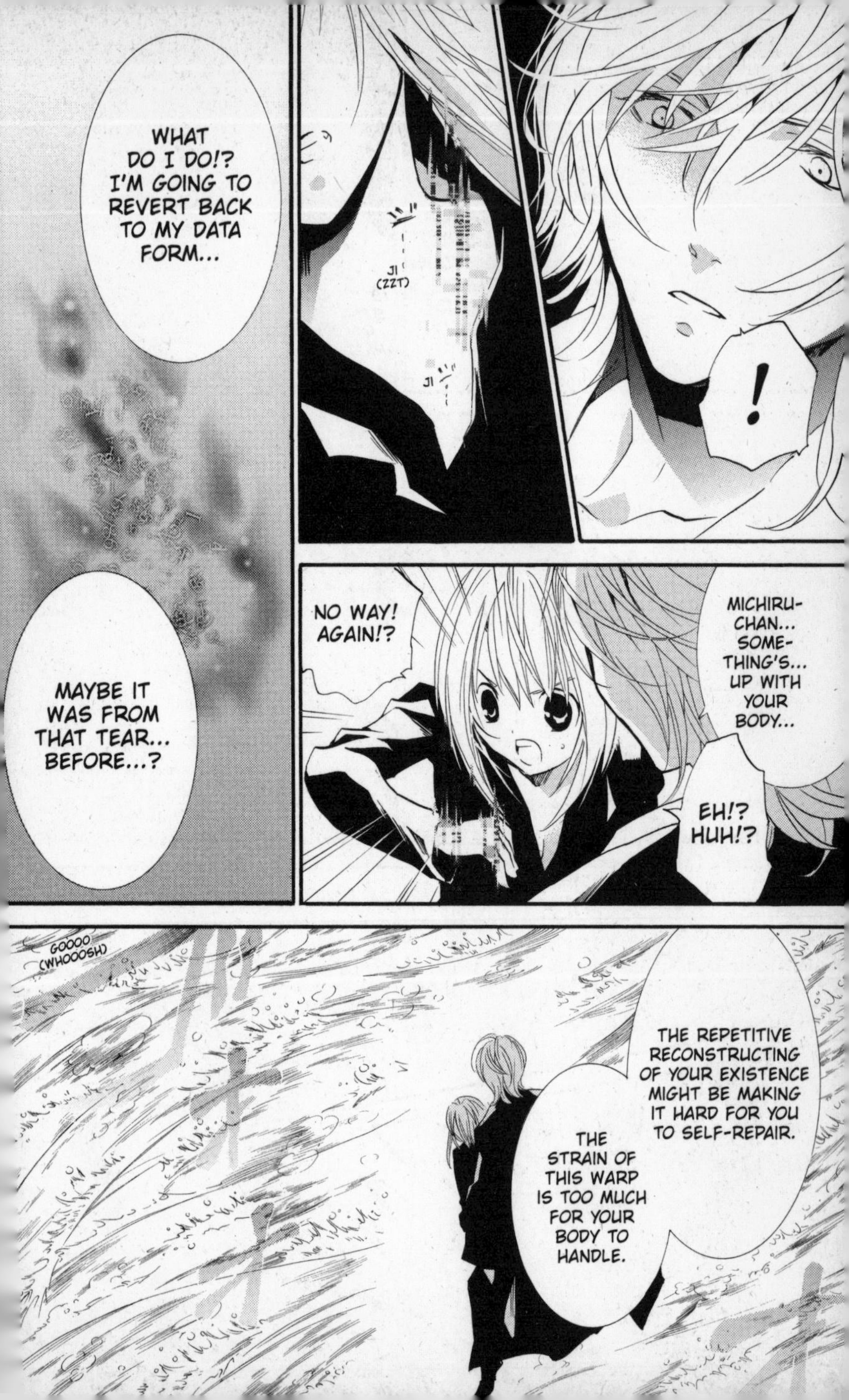
!
JI (ZZT)
JI
MICHIRU-CHAN... SOMETHING'S... UP WITH YOUR BODY...
EH!? HUH!?
NO WAY! AGAIN!?
WHAT DO I DO!? I'M GOING TO REVERT BACK TO MY DATA FORM...
MAYBE IT WAS FROM THAT TEAR... BEFORE...?
THE REPETITIVE RECONSTRUCTING OF YOUR EXISTENCE MIGHT BE MAKING IT HARD FOR YOU TO SELF-REPAIR.
THE STRAIN OF THIS WARP IS TOO MUCH FOR YOUR BODY TO HANDLE.
GOOOO (WHOOOSH)

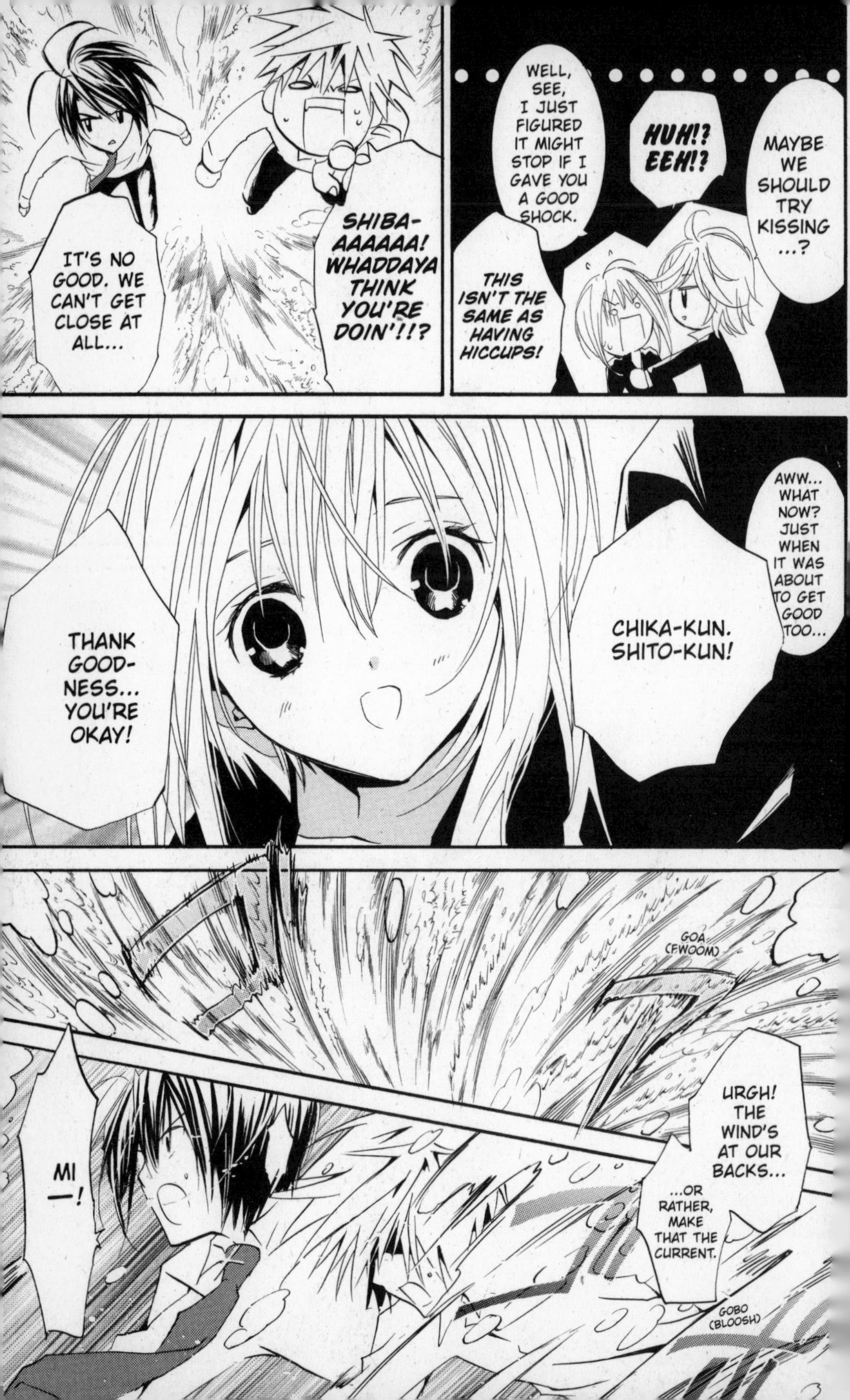

MAYBE WE SHOULD TRY KISSING ...?
HUH!? EEH!?
WELL, SEE, I JUST FIGURED IT MIGHT STOP IF I GAVE YOU A GOOD SHOCK.
THIS ISN'T THE SAME AS HAVING HICCUPS!
SHIBA-AAAAAA! WHADDAYA THINK YOU'RE DOIN'!!?
IT'S NO GOOD. WE CAN'T GET CLOSE AT ALL...
AWW... WHAT NOW? JUST WHEN IT WAS ABOUT TO GET GOOD TOO...
CHIKA-KUN. SHITO-KUN!
THANK GOODNESS... YOU'RE OKAY!
GOA (FWOOM)
URGH! THE WIND'S AT OUR BACKS...
...OR RATHER, MAKE THAT THE CURRENT.
GOBO (BLOOSH)
MI —!

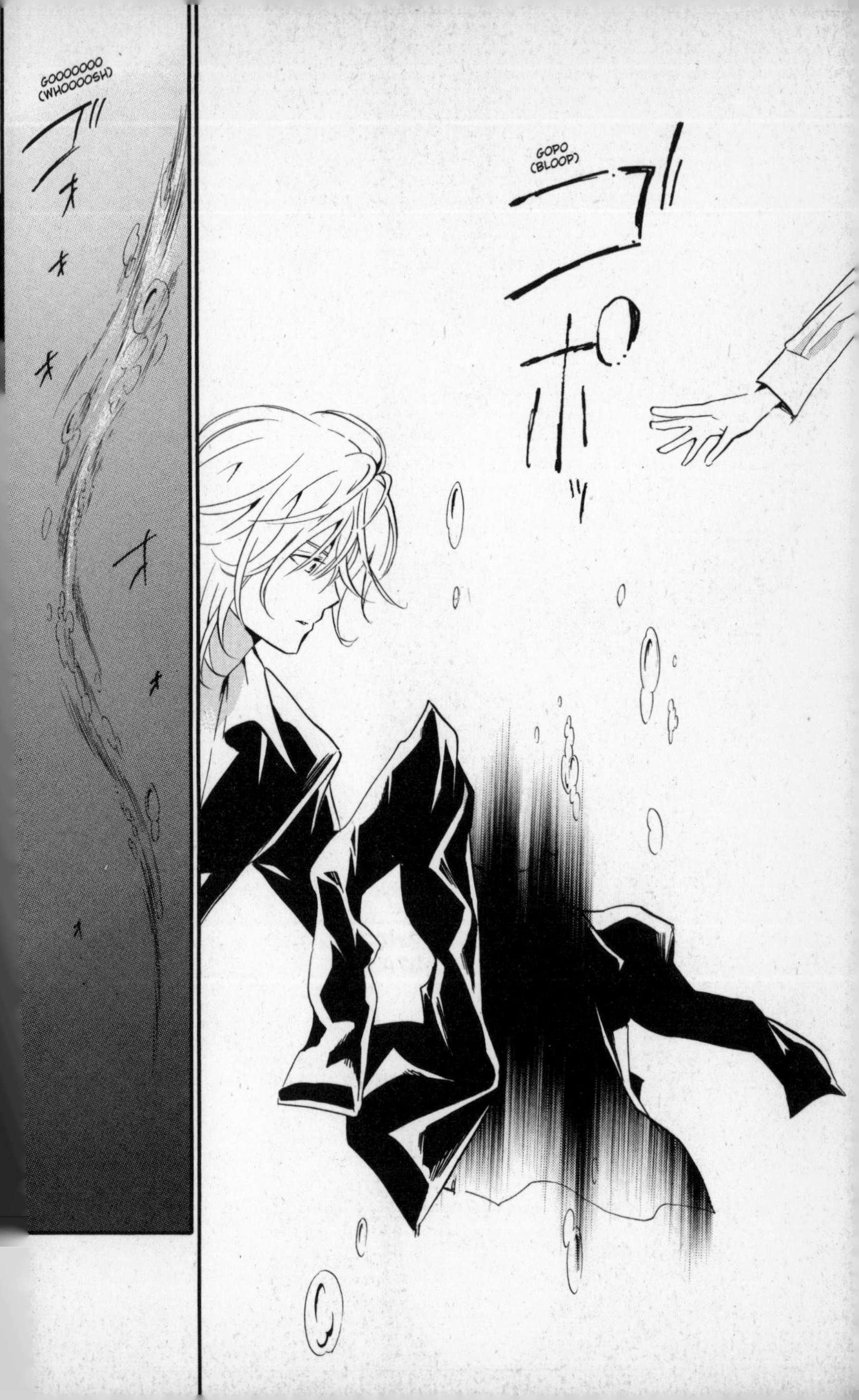
GOPO
(BLOOP)
GOOOOOOO
(WHOOOOSH)

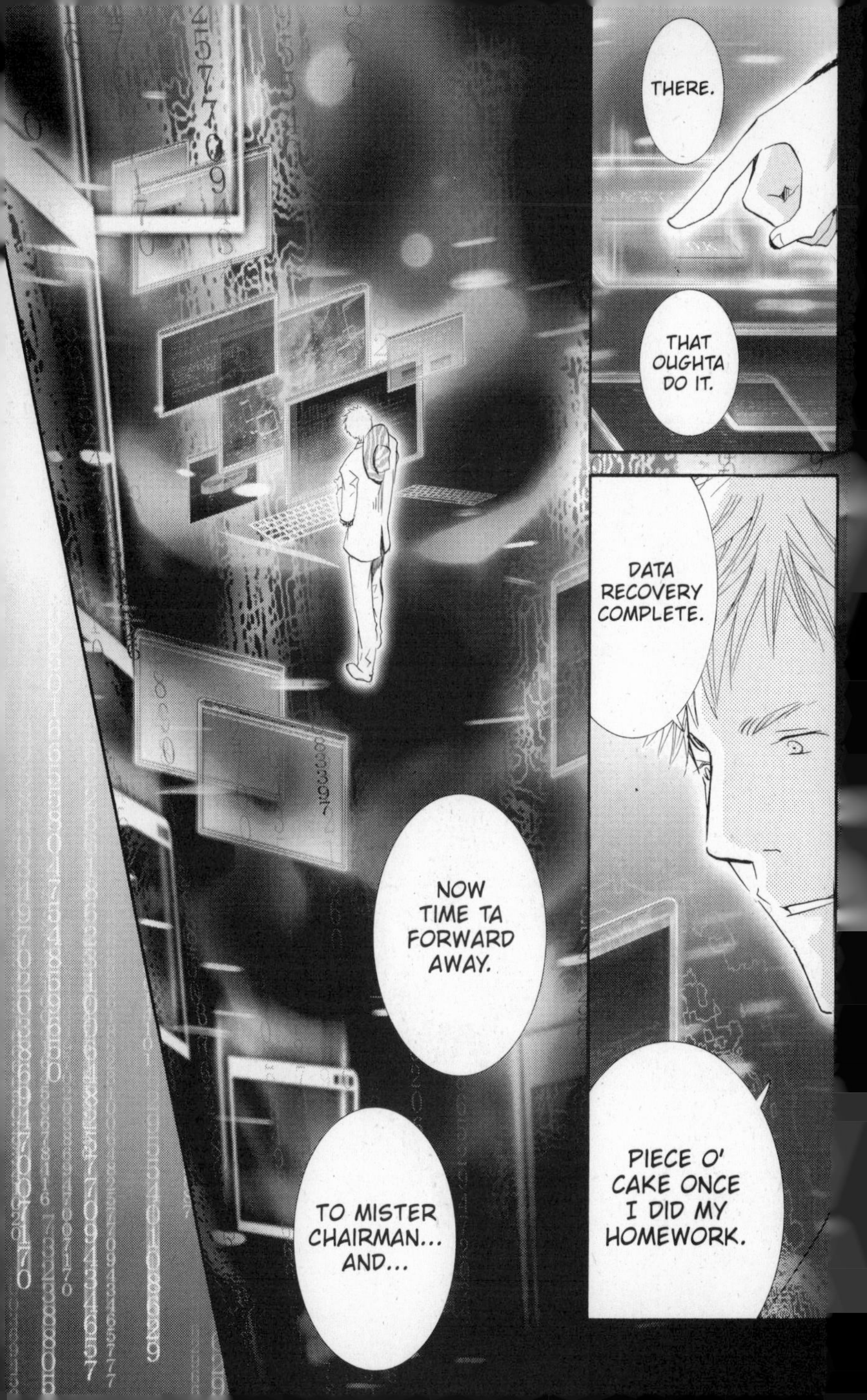
THERE.
THAT OUGHTA DO IT.
DATA RECOVERY COMPLETE.
PIECE O' CAKE ONCE I DID MY HOMEWORK.
NOW TIME TA FORWARD AWAY.
TO MISTER CHAIRMAN... AND...

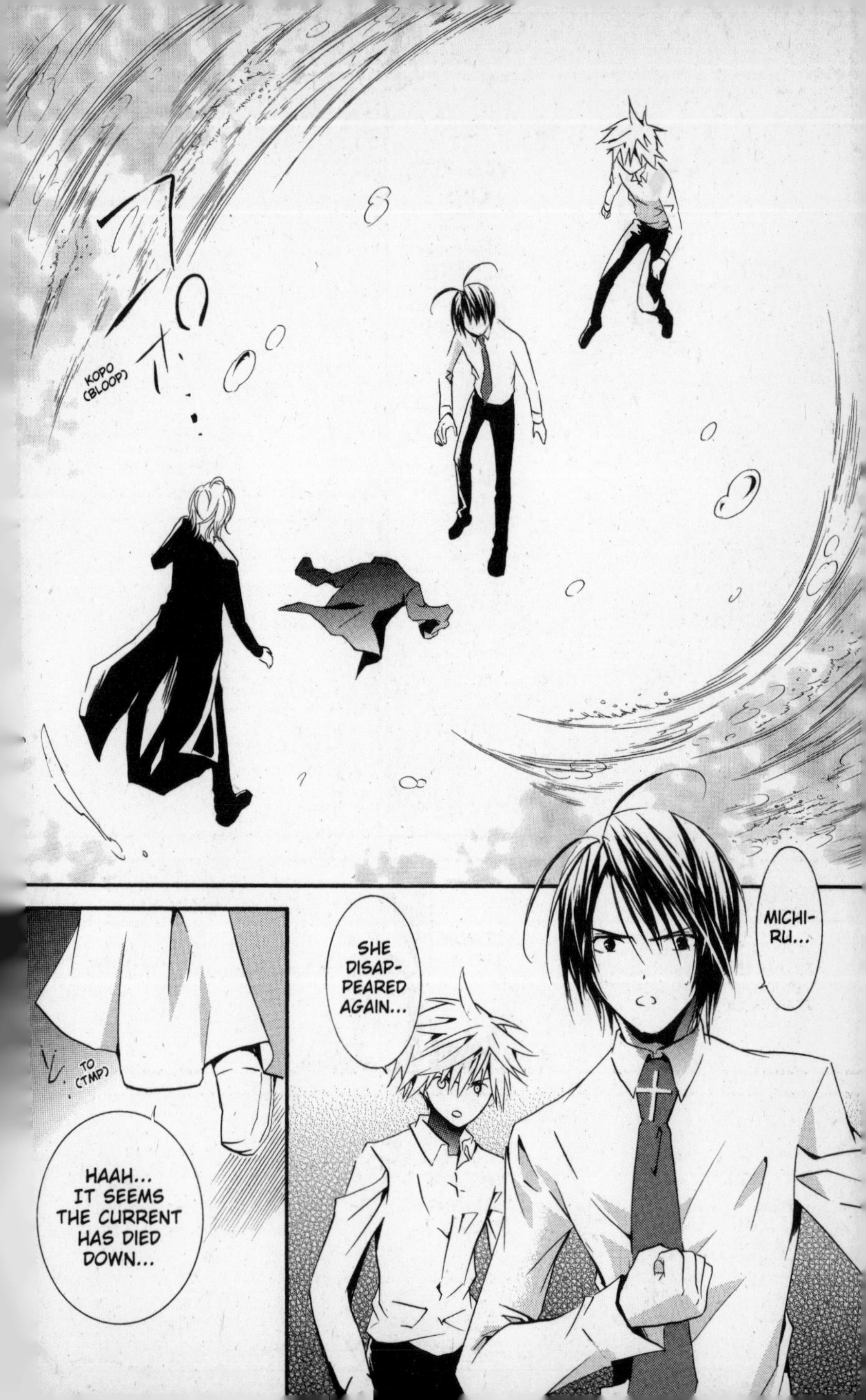
KOPO (BLOOP)
MICHI-RU...
SHE DISAP-PEARED AGAIN...
TO (TMP)
HAAH... IT SEEMS THE CURRENT HAS DIED DOWN...

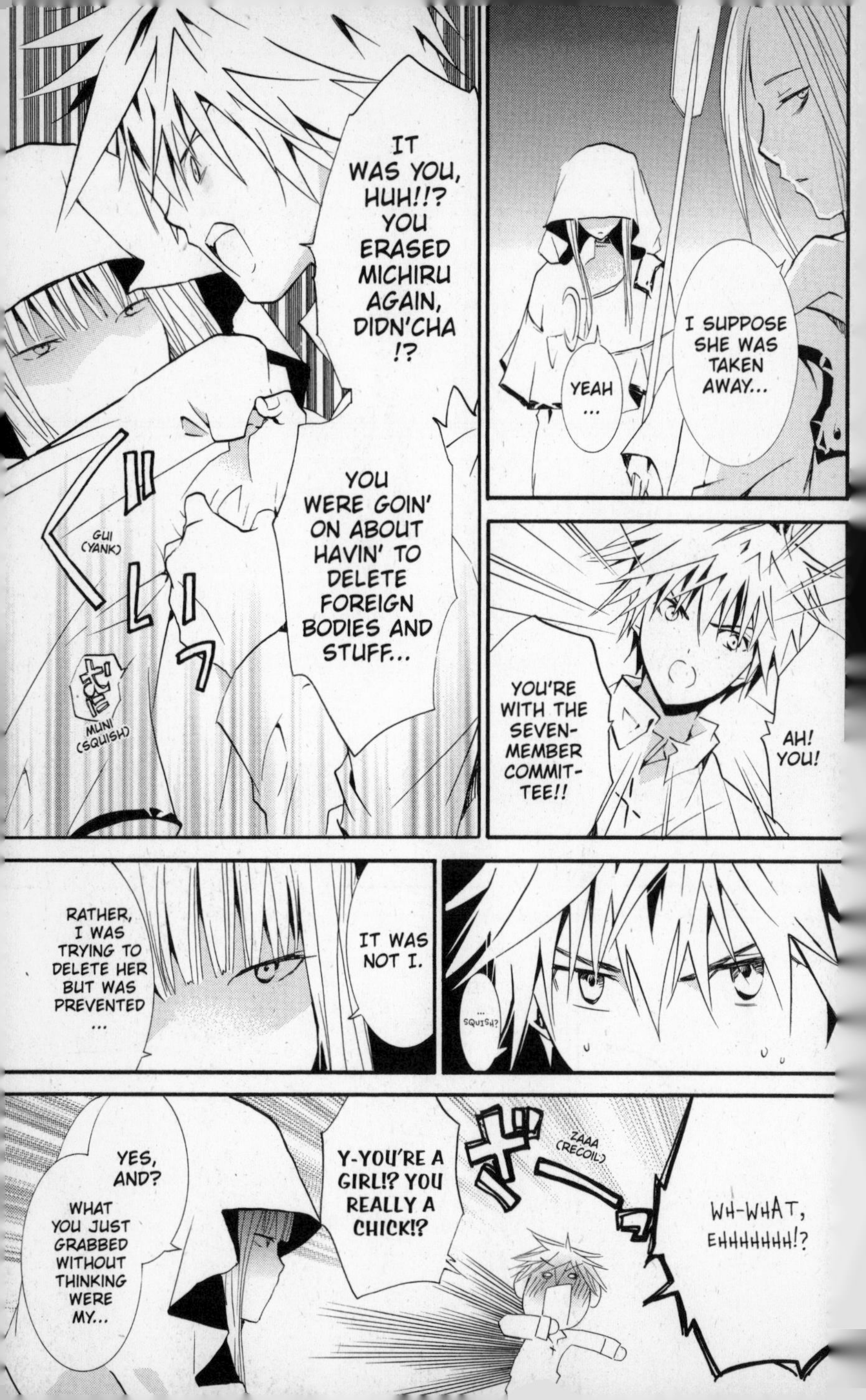

I SUPPOSE SHE WAS TAKEN AWAY...
YEAH...
AH! YOU!
YOU'RE WITH THE SEVEN-MEMBER COMMIT-TEE!!
IT WAS YOU, HUH!!? YOU ERASED MICHIRU AGAIN, DIDN'CHA!?
GUI (YANK)
YOU WERE GOIN' ON ABOUT HAVIN' TO DELETE FOREIGN BODIES AND STUFF...
MUNI (SQUISH)
...SQUISH?
IT WAS NOT I.
RATHER, I WAS TRYING TO DELETE HER BUT WAS PREVENTED...
WH-WHAT, EHHHHHHH!?
ZAAA (RECOIL)
Y-YOU'RE A GIRL!? YOU REALLY A CHICK!?
YES, AND?
WHAT YOU JUST GRABBED WITHOUT THINKING WERE MY...

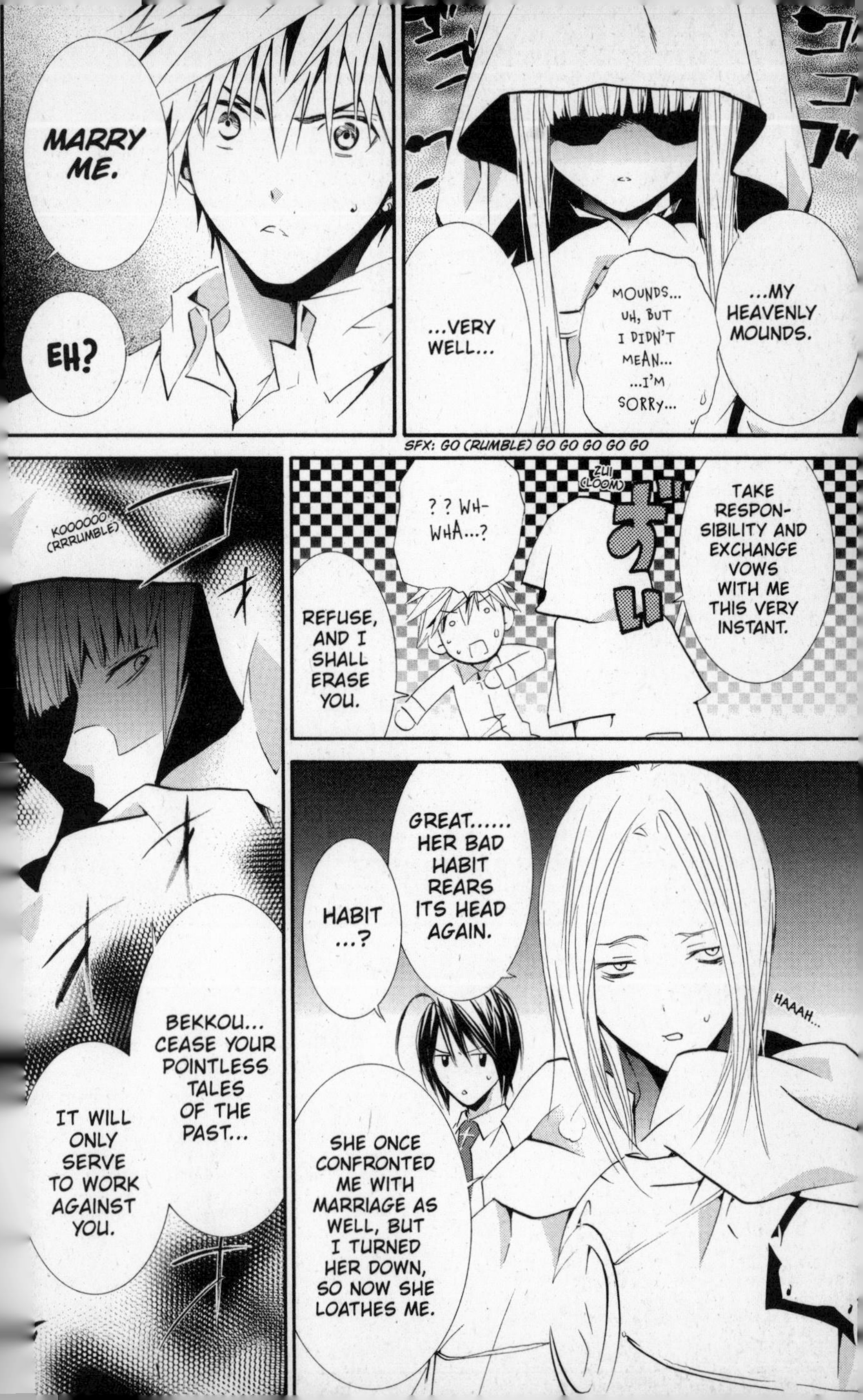
...MY HEAVENLY MOUNDS.
MOUNDS... UH, BUT I DIDN'T MEAN... ...I'M SORRY...
...VERY WELL...
MARRY ME.
EH?
SFX: GO (RUMBLE) GO GO GO GO GO
TAKE RESPONSIBILITY AND EXCHANGE VOWS WITH ME THIS VERY INSTANT.
ZUI (LOOM)
? ? WH-WHA...?
REFUSE, AND I SHALL ERASE YOU.
GREAT...... HER BAD HABIT REARS ITS HEAD AGAIN.
HABIT ...?
HAAAH...
SHE ONCE CONFRONTED ME WITH MARRIAGE AS WELL, BUT I TURNED HER DOWN, SO NOW SHE LOATHES ME.
KOOOOOO (RRRUMBLE)
BEKKOU... CEASE YOUR POINTLESS TALES OF THE PAST...
IT WILL ONLY SERVE TO WORK AGAINST YOU.

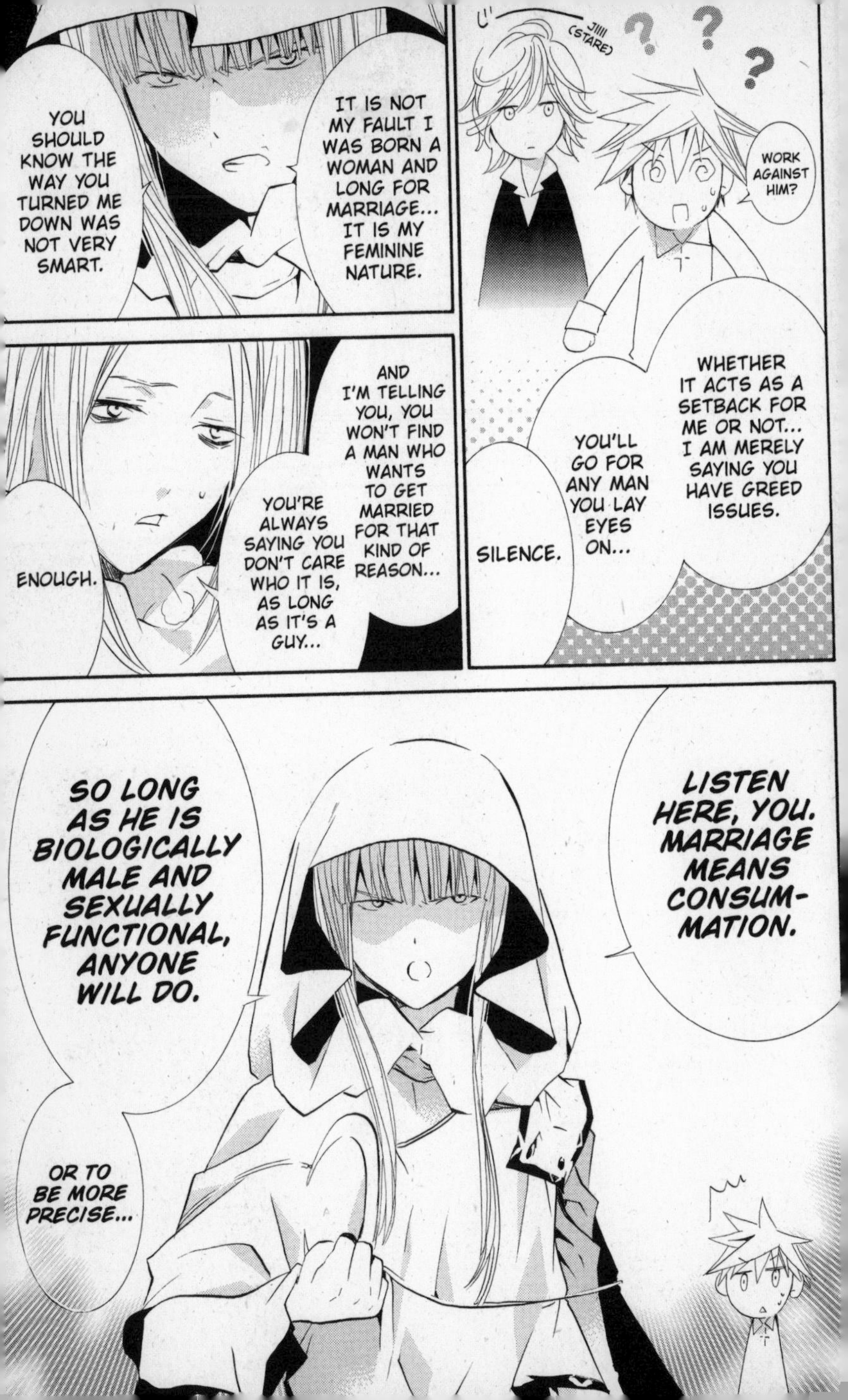

じ
JIIII (STARE)
? ? ?
WORK AGAINST HIM?
WHETHER IT ACTS AS A SETBACK FOR ME OR NOT... I AM MERELY SAYING YOU HAVE GREED ISSUES.
YOU'LL GO FOR ANY MAN YOU LAY EYES ON...
SILENCE.
IT IS NOT MY FAULT I WAS BORN A WOMAN AND LONG FOR MARRIAGE... IT IS MY FEMININE NATURE.
YOU SHOULD KNOW THE WAY YOU TURNED ME DOWN WAS NOT VERY SMART.
AND I'M TELLING YOU, YOU WON'T FIND A MAN WHO WANTS TO GET MARRIED FOR THAT KIND OF REASON...
YOU'RE ALWAYS SAYING YOU DON'T CARE WHO IT IS, AS LONG AS IT'S A GUY...
ENOUGH.
LISTEN HERE, YOU. MARRIAGE MEANS CONSUM-MATION.
SO LONG AS HE IS BIOLOGICALLY MALE AND SEXUALLY FUNCTIONAL, ANYONE WILL DO.
OR TO BE MORE PRECISE...

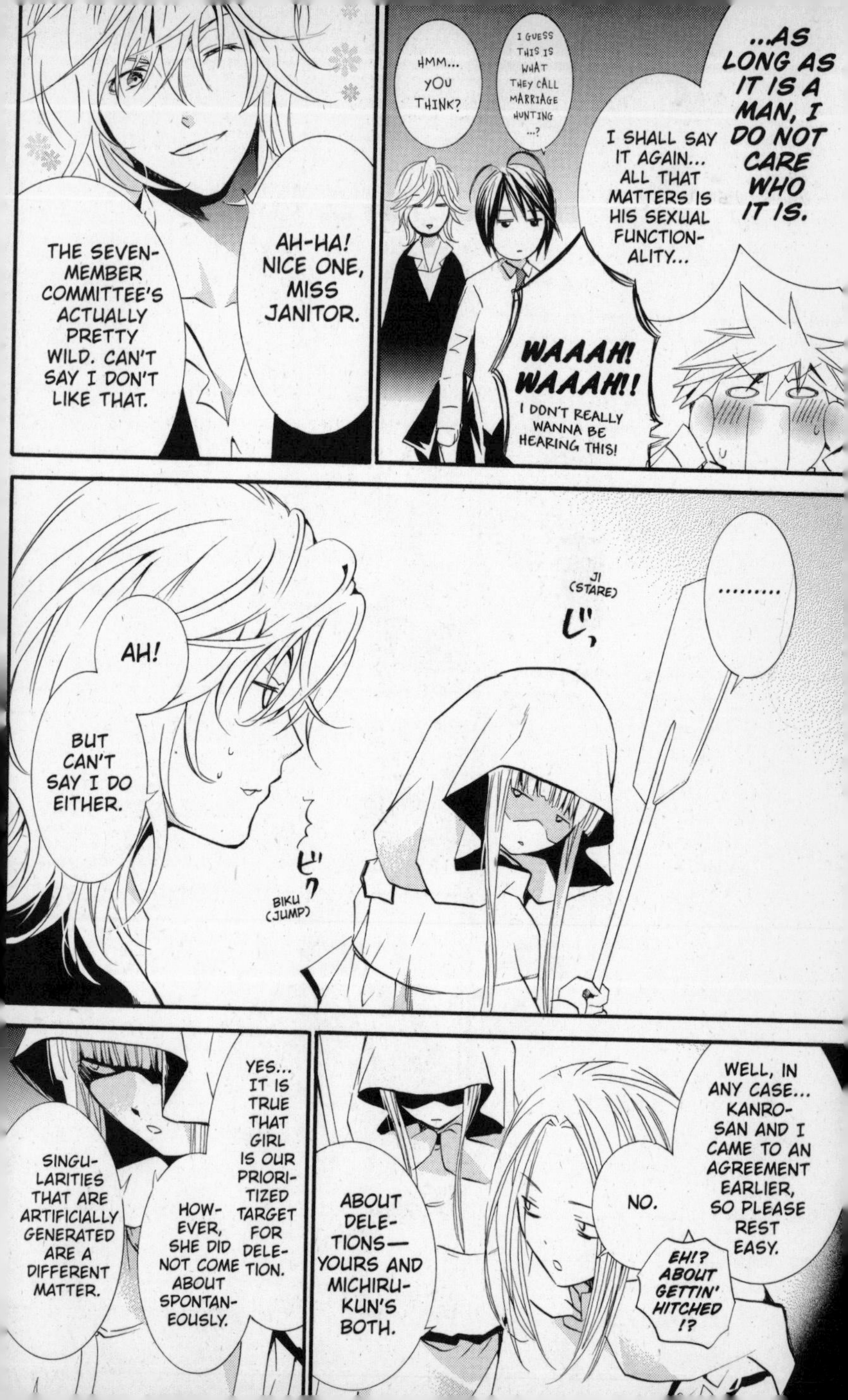
...AS LONG AS IT IS A MAN, I DO NOT CARE WHO IT IS.
I SHALL SAY IT AGAIN... ALL THAT MATTERS IS HIS SEXUAL FUNCTION-ALITY...
I GUESS THIS IS WHAT THEY CALL MARRIAGE HUNTING ...?
HMM... YOU THINK?
WAAAH! WAAAH!!
I DON'T REALLY WANNA BE HEARING THIS!
AH-HA! NICE ONE, MISS JANITOR.
THE SEVEN-MEMBER COMMITTEE'S ACTUALLY PRETTY WILD. CAN'T SAY I DON'T LIKE THAT.
....
JI (STARE)
AH!
BUT CAN'T SAY I DO EITHER.
BIKU (JUMP)
WELL, IN ANY CASE... KANRO-SAN AND I CAME TO AN AGREEMENT EARLIER, SO PLEASE REST EASY.
EH!? ABOUT GETTIN' HITCHED !?
NO.
ABOUT DELETIONS—YOURS AND MICHIRU-KUN'S BOTH.
YES... IT IS TRUE THAT GIRL IS OUR PRIORITIZED TARGET FOR DELETION.
HOW-EVER, SHE DID NOT COME ABOUT SPONTAN-EOUSLY.
SINGU-LARITIES THAT ARE ARTIFICIALLY GENERATED ARE A DIFFERENT MATTER.

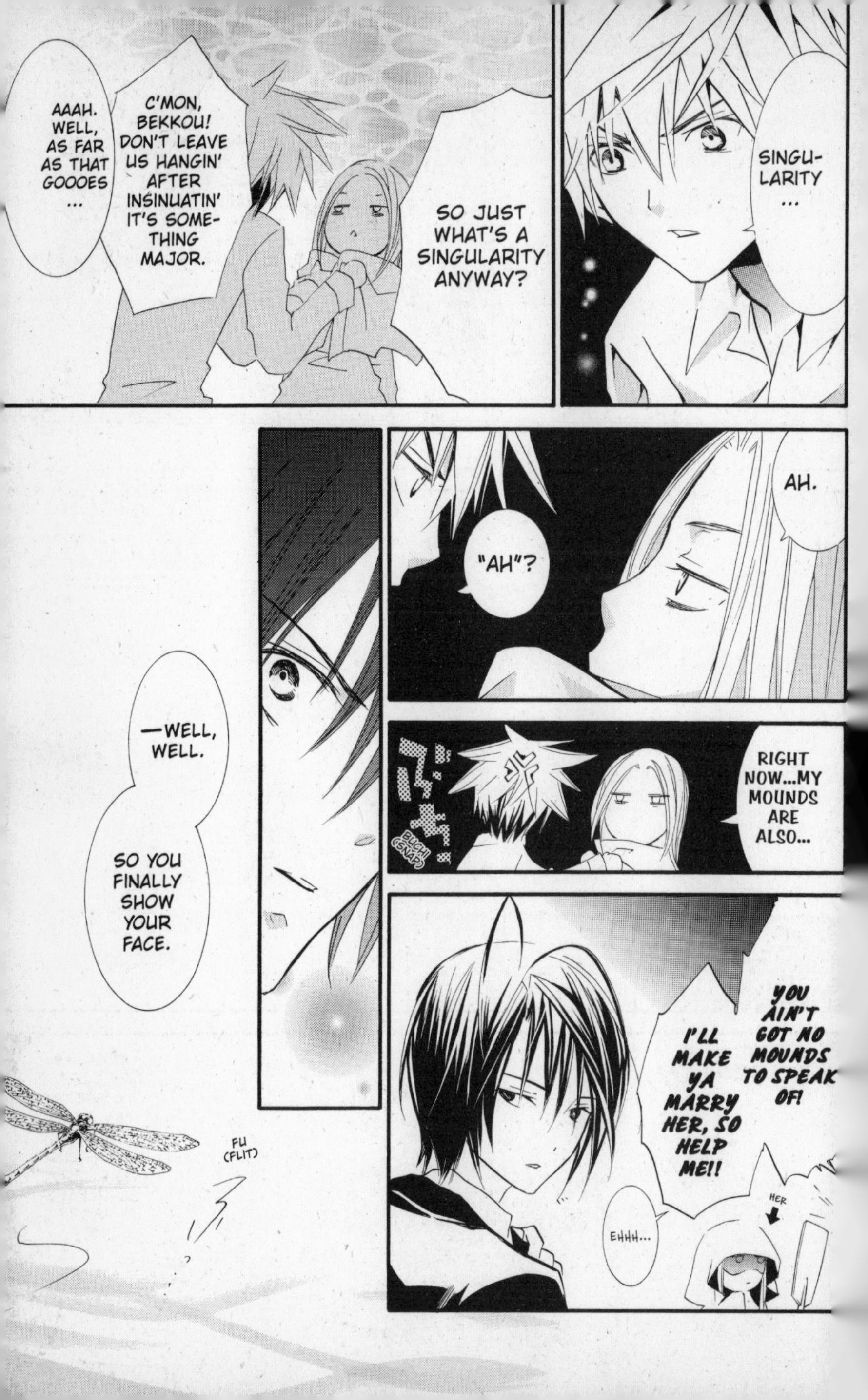
SINGULARITY...
SO JUST WHAT'S A SINGULARITY ANYWAY?
C'MON, BEKKOU! DON'T LEAVE US HANGIN' AFTER INSINUATIN' IT'S SOMETHING MAJOR.
AAAH. WELL, AS FAR AS THAT GOOOES...
AH.
"AH"?
RIGHT NOW...MY MOUNDS ARE ALSO...
BUCHI! (SNAP)
YOU AIN'T GOT NO MOUNDS TO SPEAK OF!
I'LL MAKE YA MARRY HER, SO HELP ME!!
HER
EHHH...
—WELL, WELL.
SO YOU FINALLY SHOW YOUR FACE.
FU (FLIT)

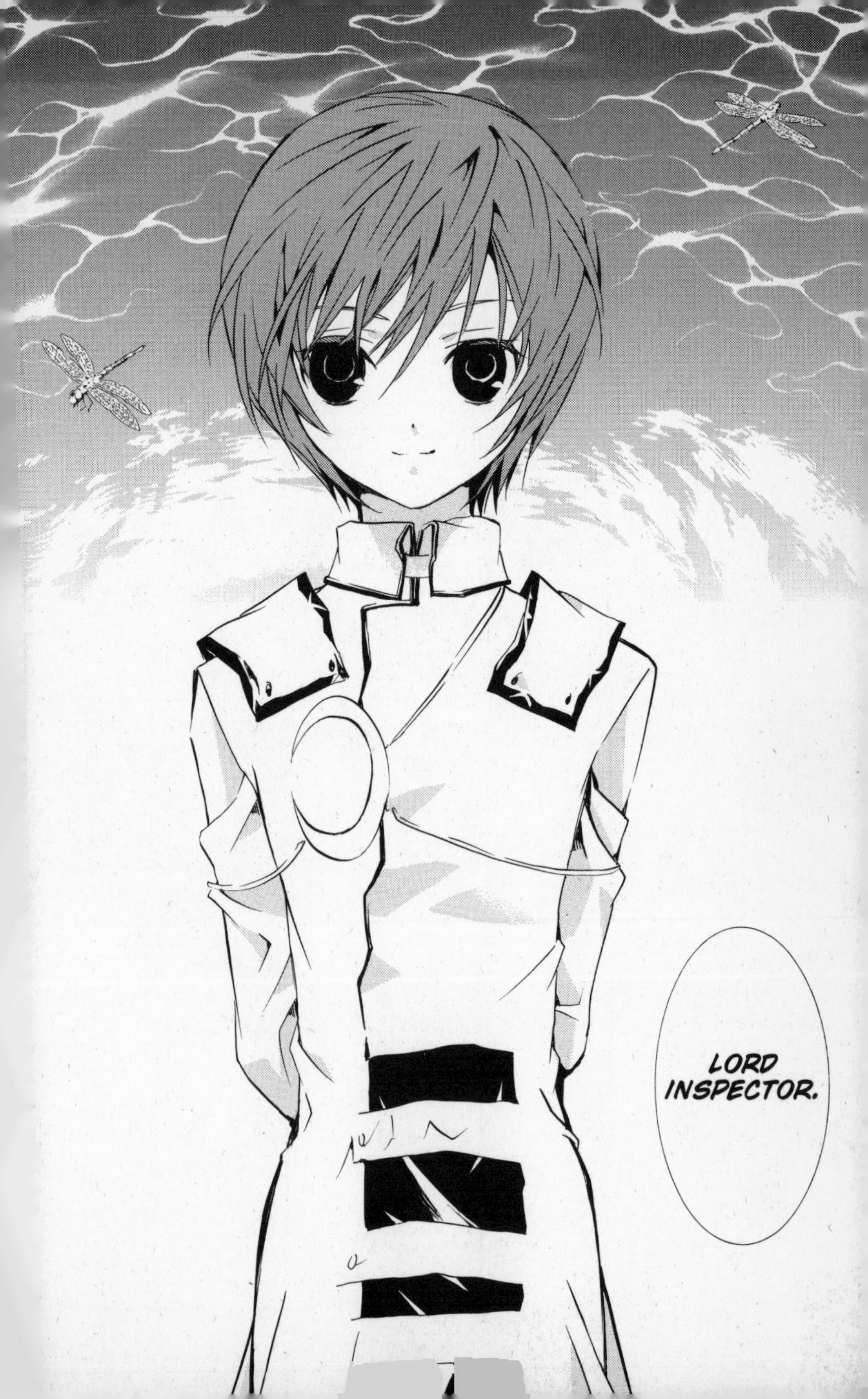
LORD INSPECTOR.

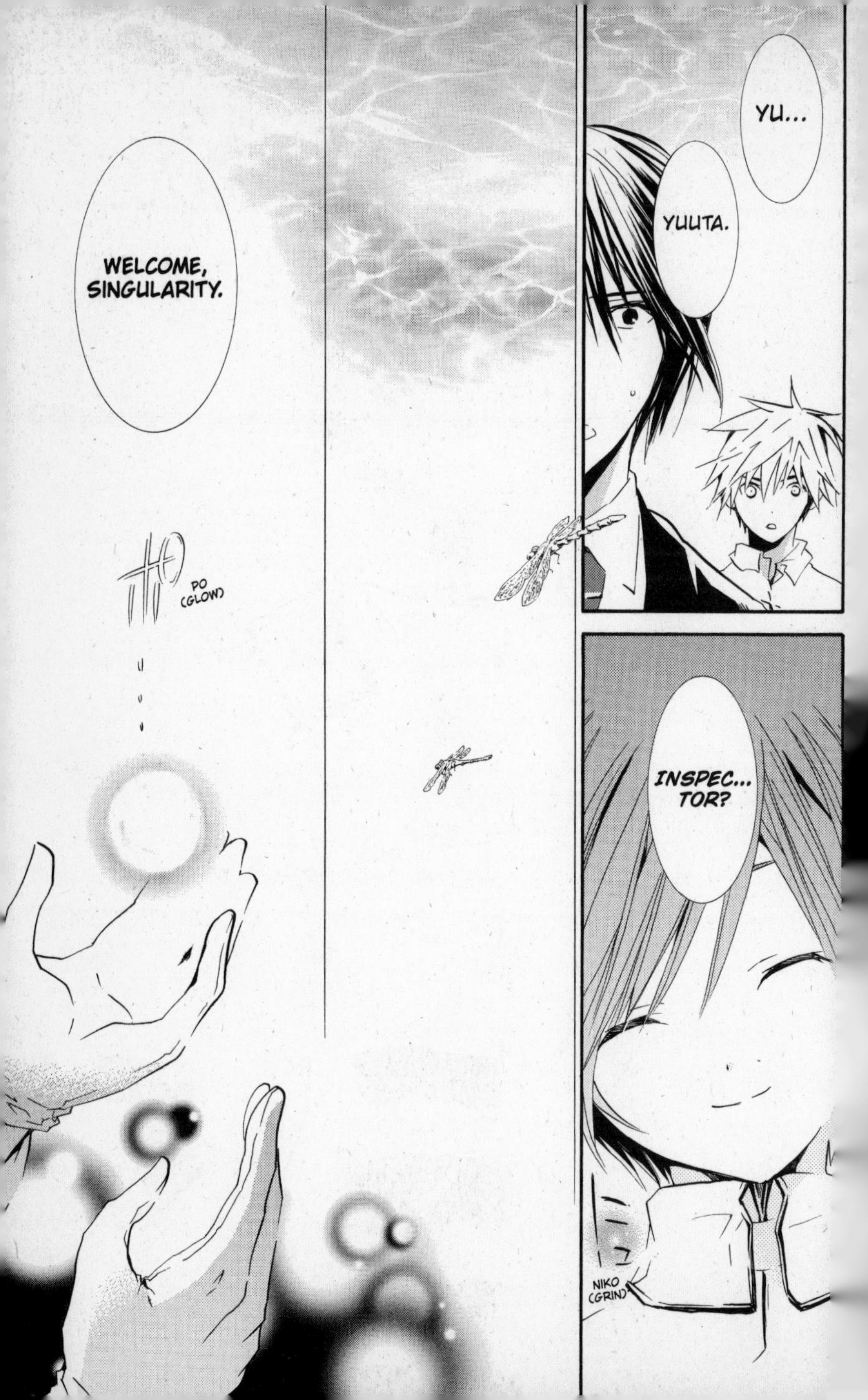
YU...
YUUTA.
INSPEC... TOR?
NIKO (GRIN)
WELCOME, SINGULARITY.
PO (GLOW)

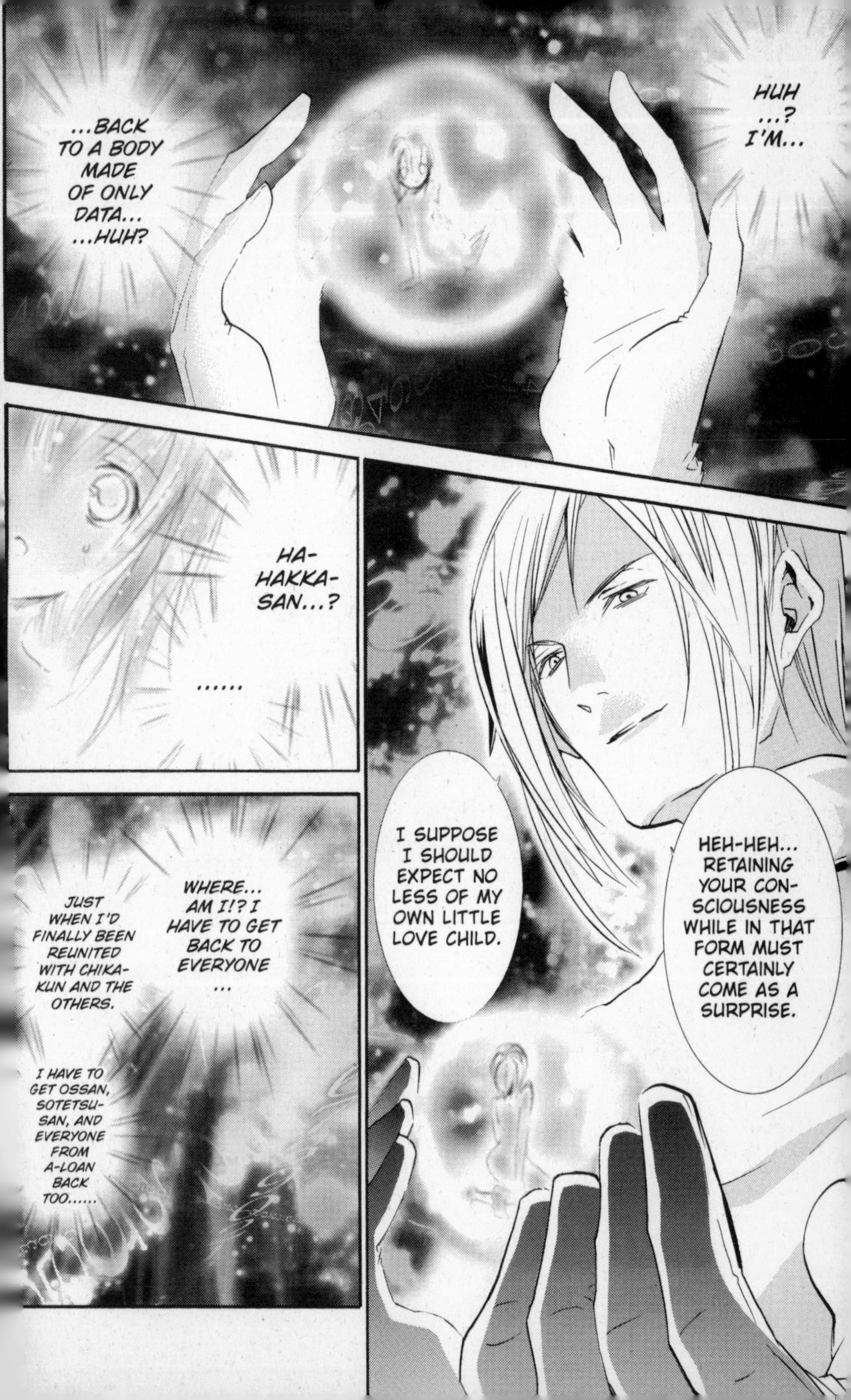
HUH ...? I'M...
...BACK TO A BODY MADE OF ONLY DATA... ...HUH?
HEH-HEH... RETAINING YOUR CON-SCIOUSNESS WHILE IN THAT FORM MUST CERTAINLY COME AS A SURPRISE.
I SUPPOSE I SHOULD EXPECT NO LESS OF MY OWN LITTLE LOVE CHILD.
HA-HAKKA-SAN...?
......
WHERE... AM I!? I HAVE TO GET BACK TO EVERYONE ...
JUST WHEN I'D FINALLY BEEN REUNITED WITH CHIKA-KUN AND THE OTHERS.
I HAVE TO GET OSSAN, SOTETSU-SAN, AND EVERYONE FROM A-LOAN BACK TOO......

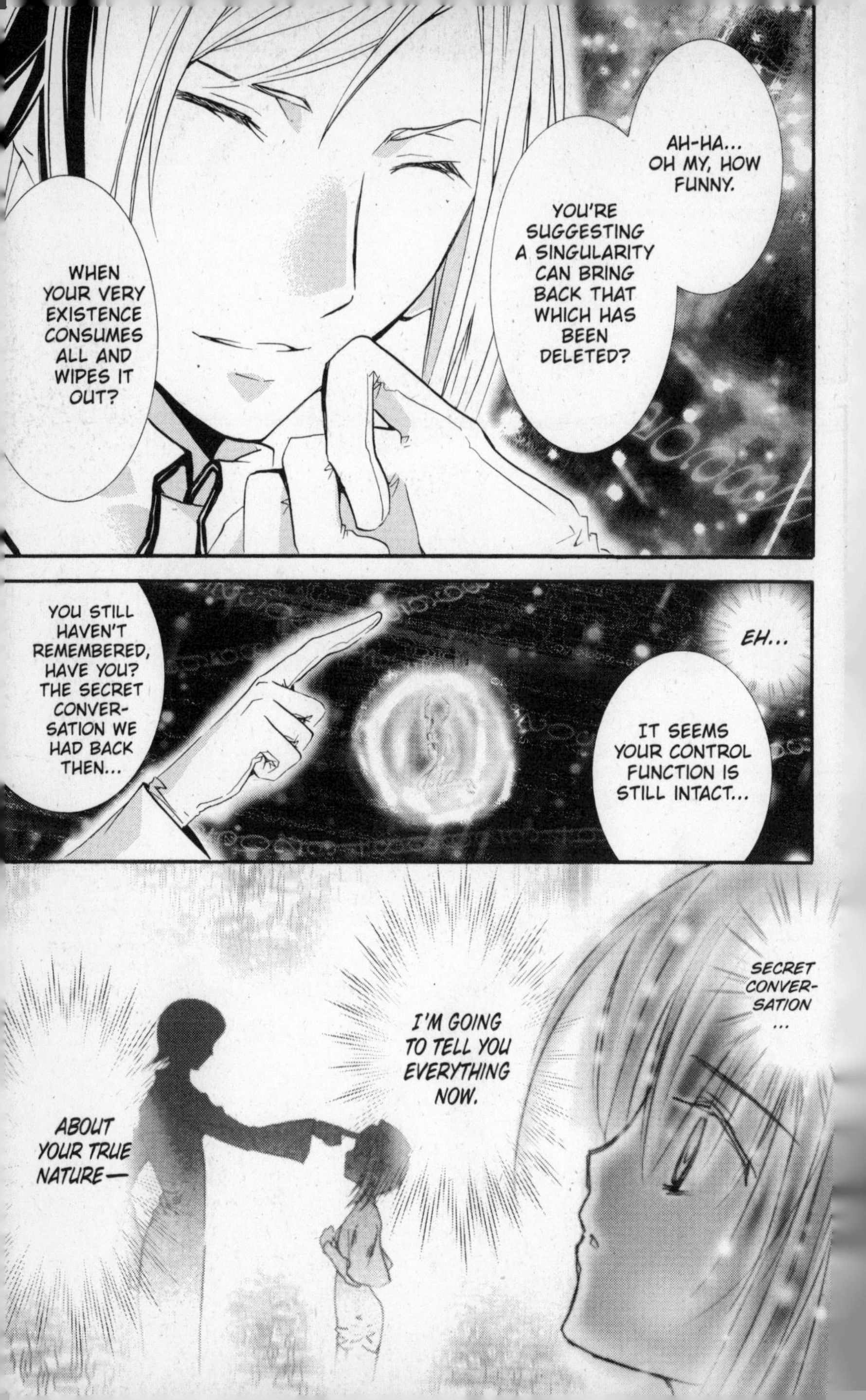
AH-HA... OH MY, HOW FUNNY.
YOU'RE SUGGESTING A SINGULARITY CAN BRING BACK THAT WHICH HAS BEEN DELETED?
WHEN YOUR VERY EXISTENCE CONSUMES ALL AND WIPES IT OUT?
EH...
IT SEEMS YOUR CONTROL FUNCTION IS STILL INTACT...
YOU STILL HAVEN'T REMEMBERED, HAVE YOU? THE SECRET CONVER-SATION WE HAD BACK THEN...
SECRET CONVER-SATION...
I'M GOING TO TELL YOU EVERYTHING NOW.
ABOUT YOUR TRUE NATURE—

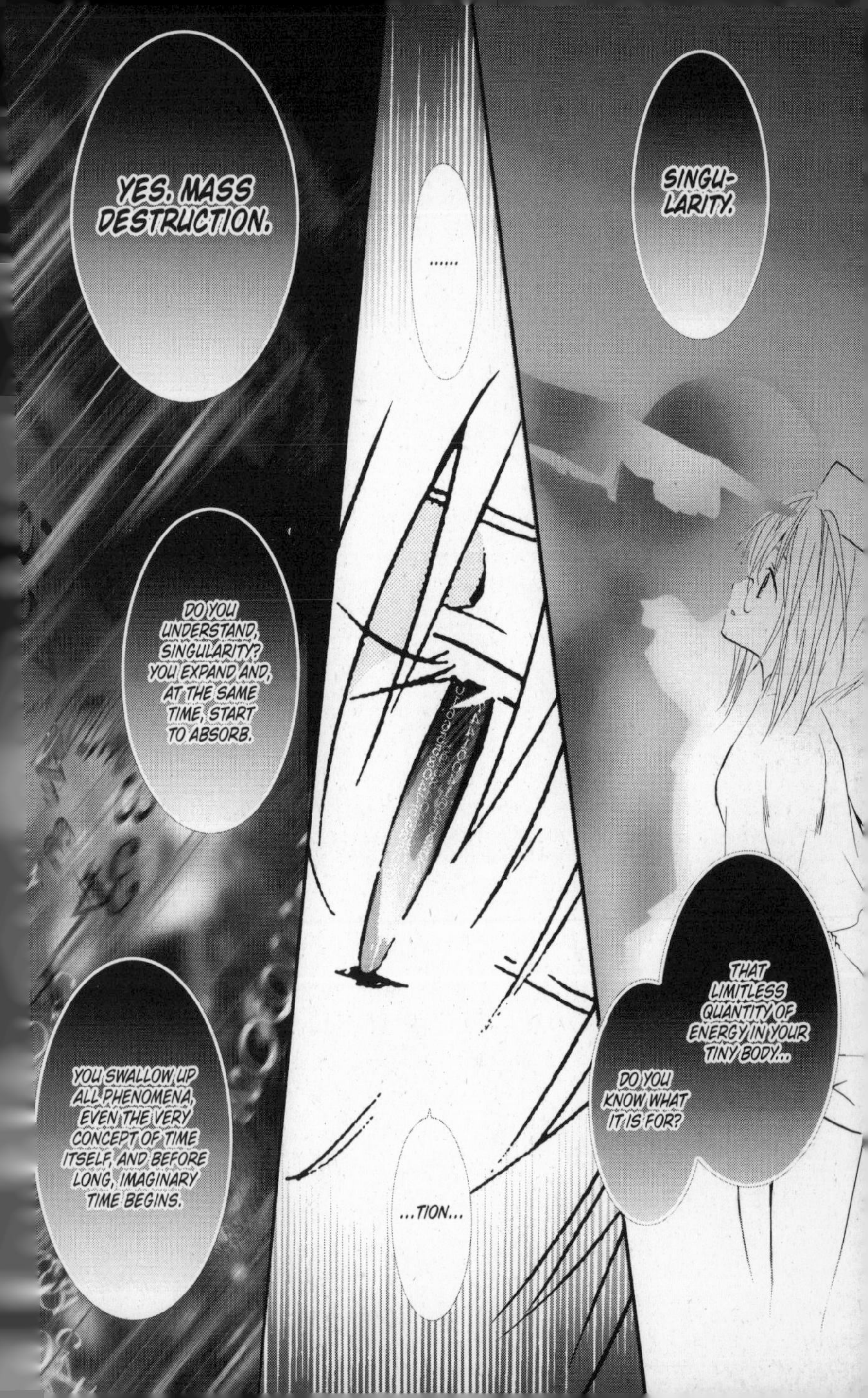
SINGU-LARITY.
THAT LIMITLESS QUANTITY OF ENERGY IN YOUR TINY BODY...
DO YOU KNOW WHAT IT IS FOR?
......
...TION...
YES. MASS DESTRUCTION.
DO YOU UNDERSTAND, SINGULARITY? YOU EXPAND AND, AT THE SAME TIME, START TO ABSORB.
YOU SWALLOW UP ALL PHENOMENA, EVEN THE VERY CONCEPT OF TIME ITSELF, AND BEFORE LONG, IMAGINARY TIME BEGINS.

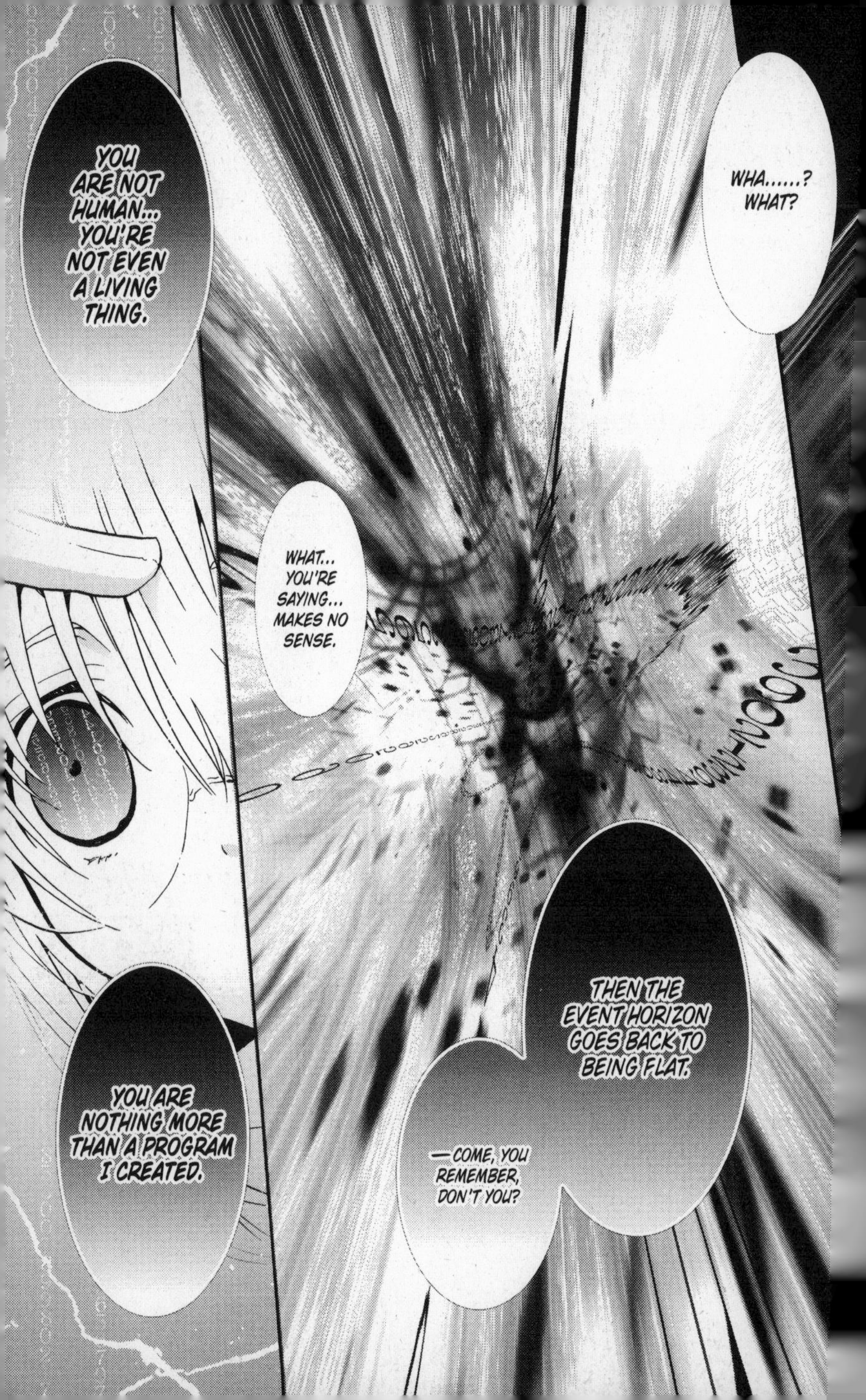
WHA......? WHAT?
YOU ARE NOT HUMAN... YOU'RE NOT EVEN A LIVING THING.
WHAT... YOU'RE SAYING... MAKES NO SENSE.
THEN THE EVENT HORIZON GOES BACK TO BEING FLAT.
—COME, YOU REMEMBER, DON'T YOU?
YOU ARE NOTHING MORE THAN A PROGRAM I CREATED.

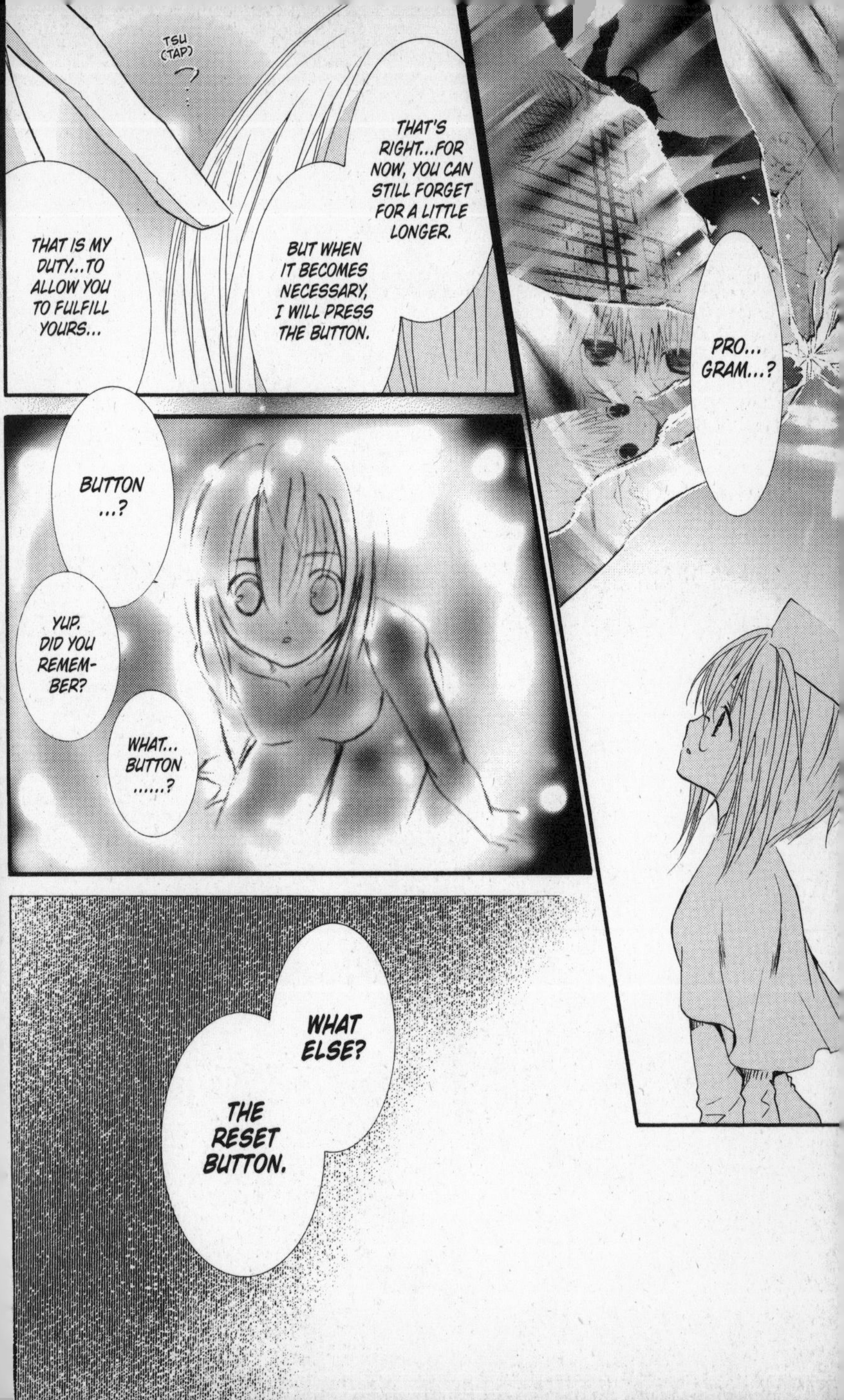
PRO... GRAM...?
TSU (TAP)
THAT'S RIGHT...FOR NOW, YOU CAN STILL FORGET FOR A LITTLE LONGER.
BUT WHEN IT BECOMES NECESSARY, I WILL PRESS THE BUTTON.
THAT IS MY DUTY...TO ALLOW YOU TO FULFILL YOURS...
BUTTON ...?
YUP. DID YOU REMEM-BER?
WHAT... BUTTON ......?
WHAT ELSE?
THE RESET BUTTON.

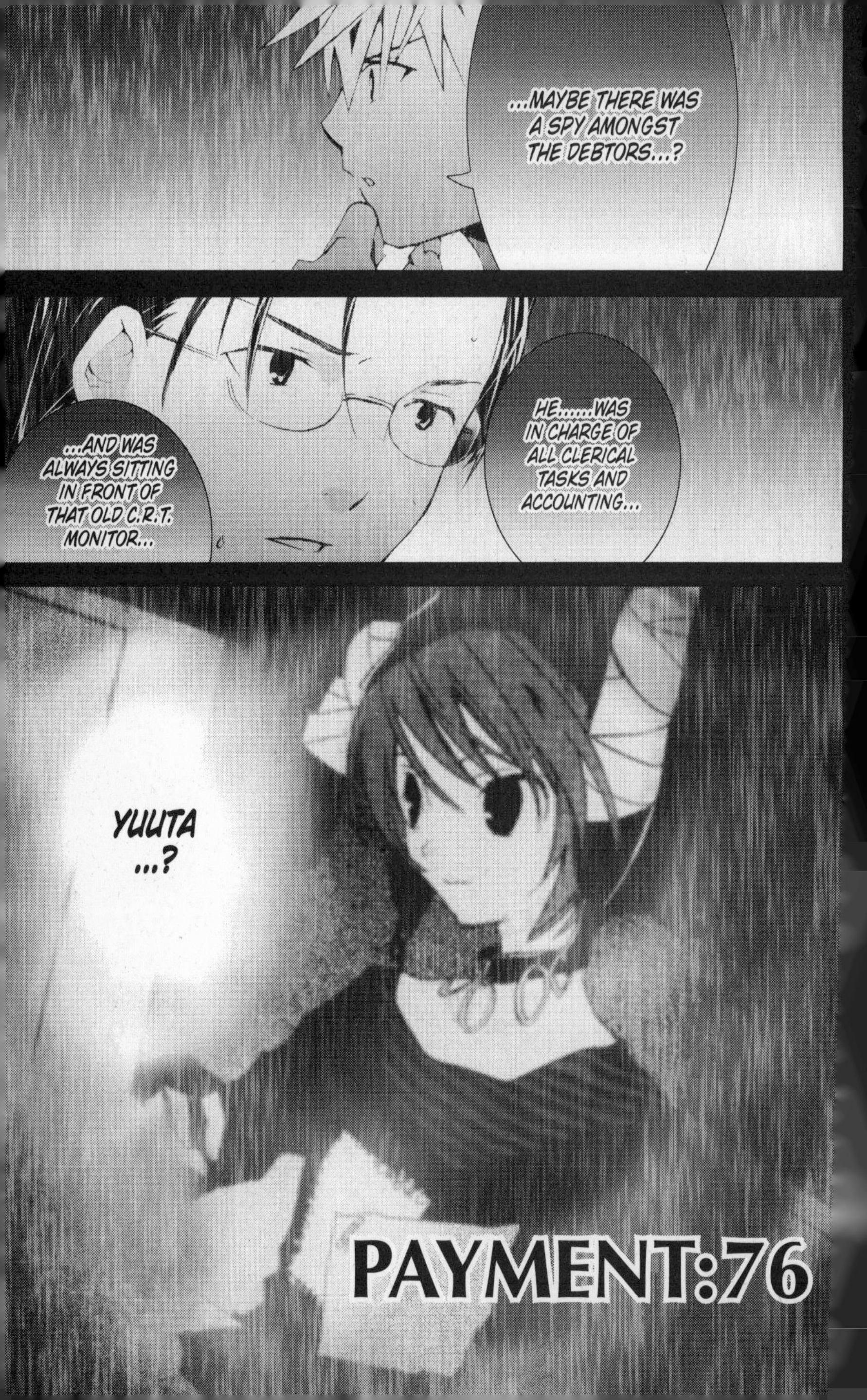

...MAYBE THERE WAS A SPY AMONGST THE DEBTORS...?
HE......WAS IN CHARGE OF ALL CLERICAL TASKS AND ACCOUNTING...
...AND WAS ALWAYS SITTING IN FRONT OF THAT OLD C.R.T. MONITOR...
YUUTA ...?
PAYMENT:76

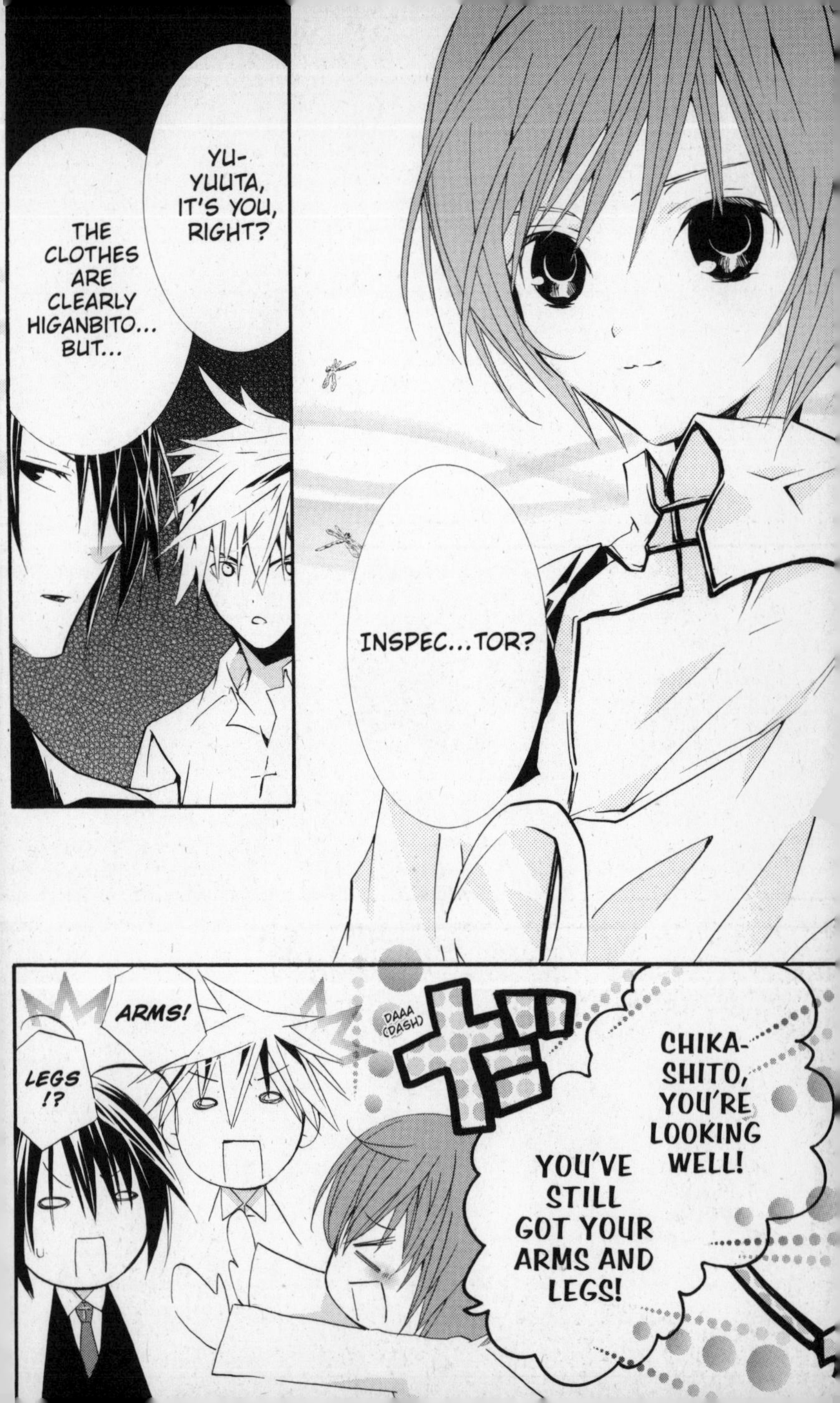
INSPEC...TOR?
YU-YUUTA, IT'S YOU, RIGHT?
THE CLOTHES ARE CLEARLY HIGANBITO... BUT...
CHIKA-SHITO, YOU'RE LOOKING WELL!
YOU'VE STILL GOT YOUR ARMS AND LEGS!
DAAA (DASH)
ARMS!
LEGS!?

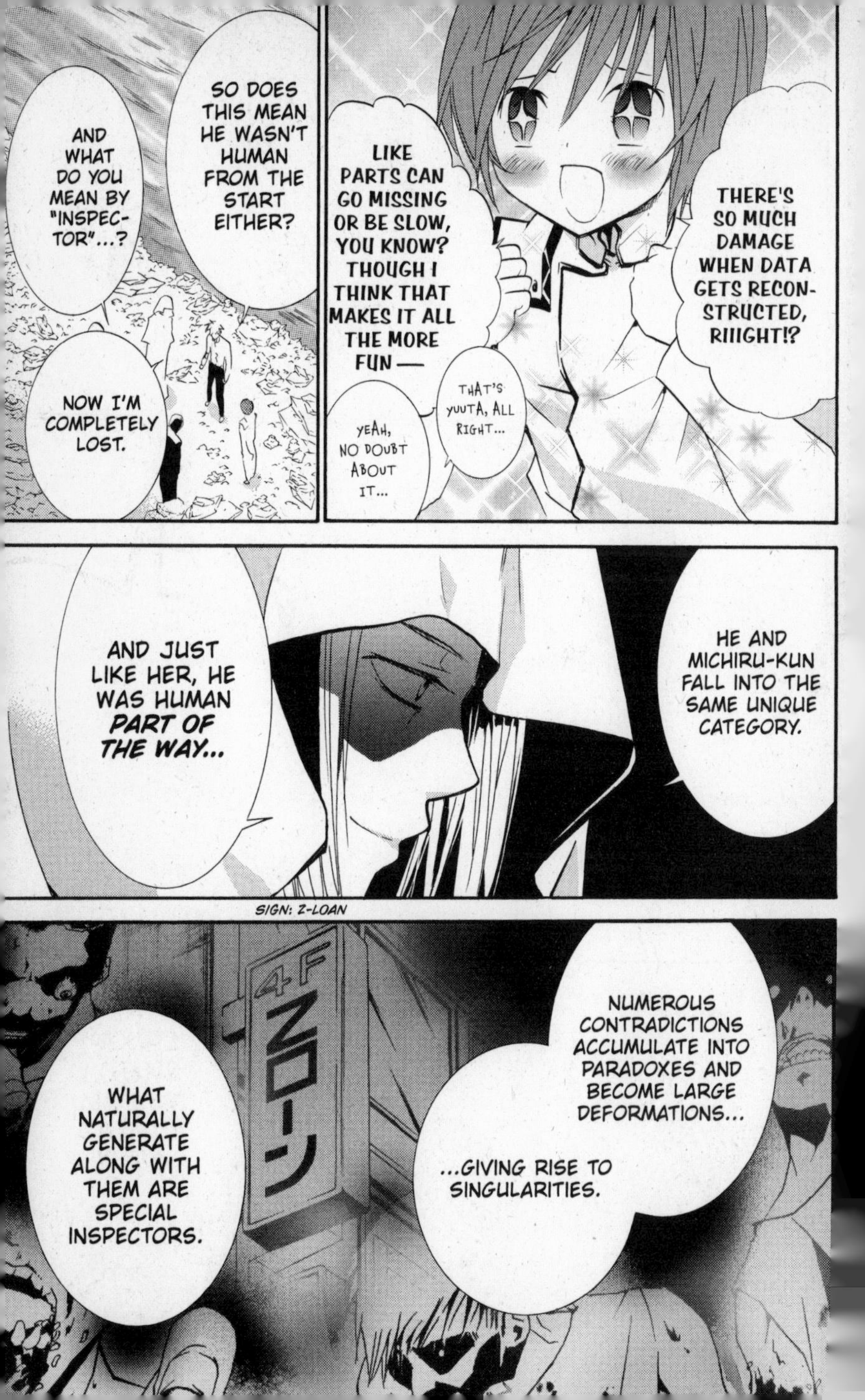
THERE'S SO MUCH DAMAGE WHEN DATA GETS RECONSTRUCTED, RIIIGHT!?
LIKE PARTS CAN GO MISSING OR BE SLOW, YOU KNOW? THOUGH I THINK THAT MAKES IT ALL THE MORE FUN—
THAT'S YUUTA, ALL RIGHT...
YEAH, NO DOUBT ABOUT IT...
SO DOES THIS MEAN HE WASN'T HUMAN FROM THE START EITHER?
AND WHAT DO YOU MEAN BY "INSPECTOR"...?
NOW I'M COMPLETELY LOST.
HE AND MICHIRU-KUN FALL INTO THE SAME UNIQUE CATEGORY.
AND JUST LIKE HER, HE WAS HUMAN *PART OF THE WAY...*
SIGN: Z-LOAN
NUMEROUS CONTRADICTIONS ACCUMULATE INTO PARADOXES AND BECOME LARGE DEFORMATIONS...
...GIVING RISE TO SINGULARITIES.
WHAT NATURALLY GENERATE ALONG WITH THEM ARE SPECIAL INSPECTORS.

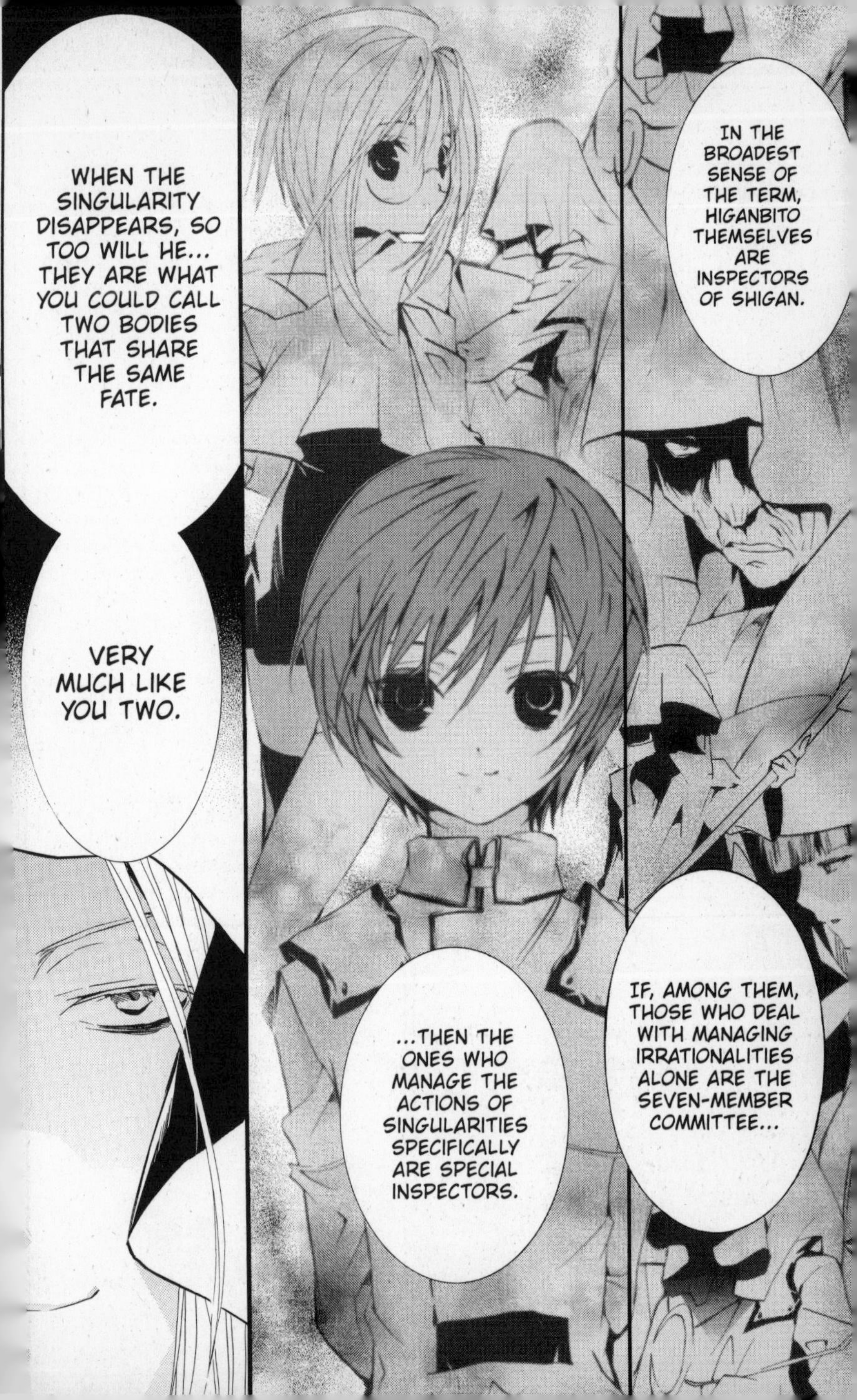
IN THE BROADEST SENSE OF THE TERM, HIGANBITO THEMSELVES ARE INSPECTORS OF SHIGAN.
IF, AMONG THEM, THOSE WHO DEAL WITH MANAGING IRRATIONALITIES ALONE ARE THE SEVEN-MEMBER COMMITTEE...
...THEN THE ONES WHO MANAGE THE ACTIONS OF SINGULARITIES SPECIFICALLY ARE SPECIAL INSPECTORS.
WHEN THE SINGULARITY DISAPPEARS, SO TOO WILL HE... THEY ARE WHAT YOU COULD CALL TWO BODIES THAT SHARE THE SAME FATE.
VERY MUCH LIKE YOU TWO.

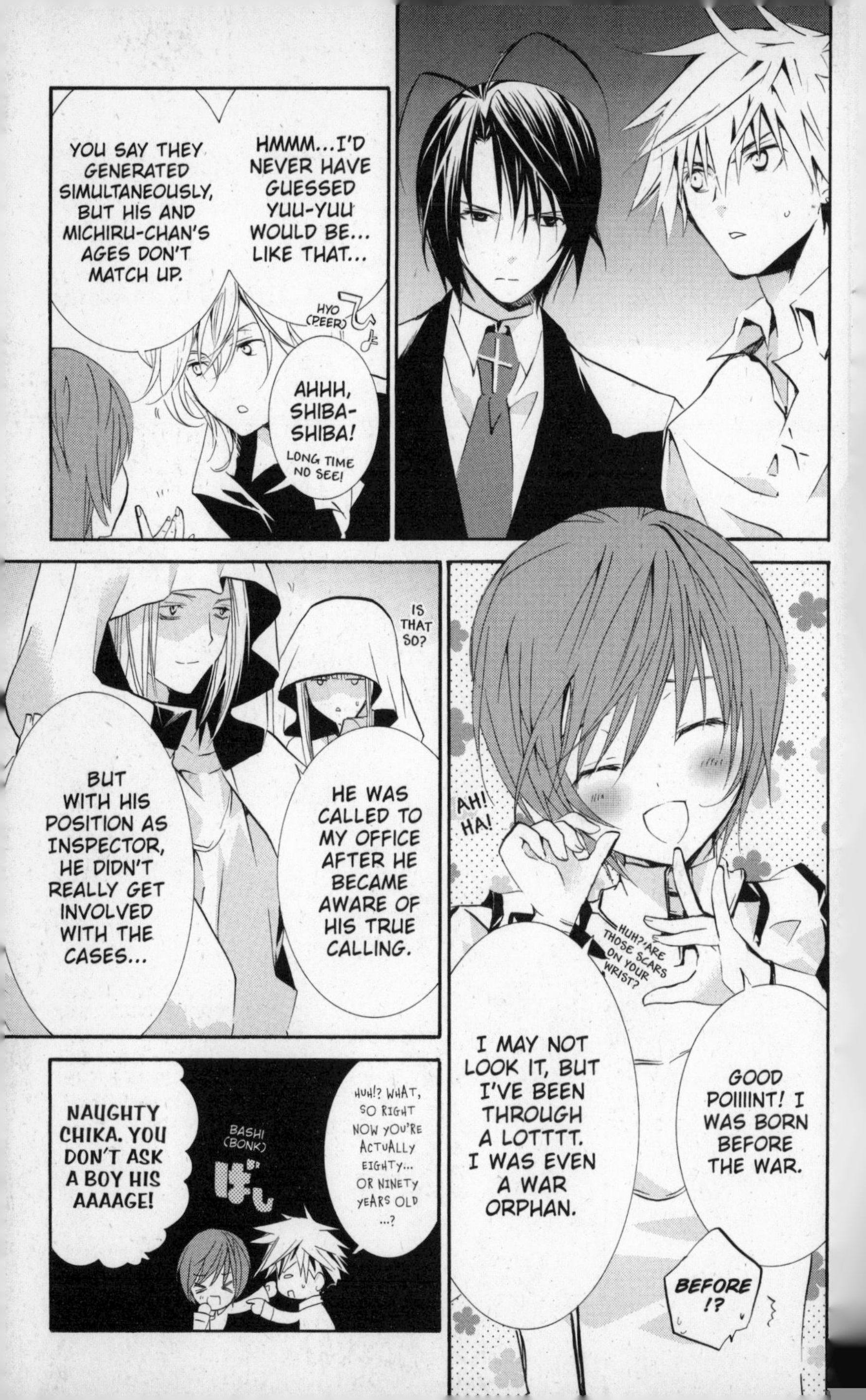
HMMM...I'D NEVER HAVE GUESSED YUU-YUU WOULD BE... LIKE THAT...
YOU SAY THEY GENERATED SIMULTANEOUSLY, BUT HIS AND MICHIRU-CHAN'S AGES DON'T MATCH UP.
HYO (PEER)
AHHH, SHIBA-SHIBA!
LONG TIME NO SEE!
AH! HA!
HUH!? ARE THOSE SCARS ON YOUR WRIST?
GOOD POIIIINT! I WAS BORN BEFORE THE WAR.
I MAY NOT LOOK IT, BUT I'VE BEEN THROUGH A LOTTTT. I WAS EVEN A WAR ORPHAN.
BEFORE !?
IS THAT SO?
HE WAS CALLED TO MY OFFICE AFTER HE BECAME AWARE OF HIS TRUE CALLING.
BUT WITH HIS POSITION AS INSPECTOR, HE DIDN'T REALLY GET INVOLVED WITH THE CASES...
HUH!? WHAT, SO RIGHT NOW YOU'RE ACTUALLY EIGHTY... OR NINETY YEARS OLD ...?
BASHI (BONK)
NAUGHTY CHIKA. YOU DON'T ASK A BOY HIS AAAAGE!

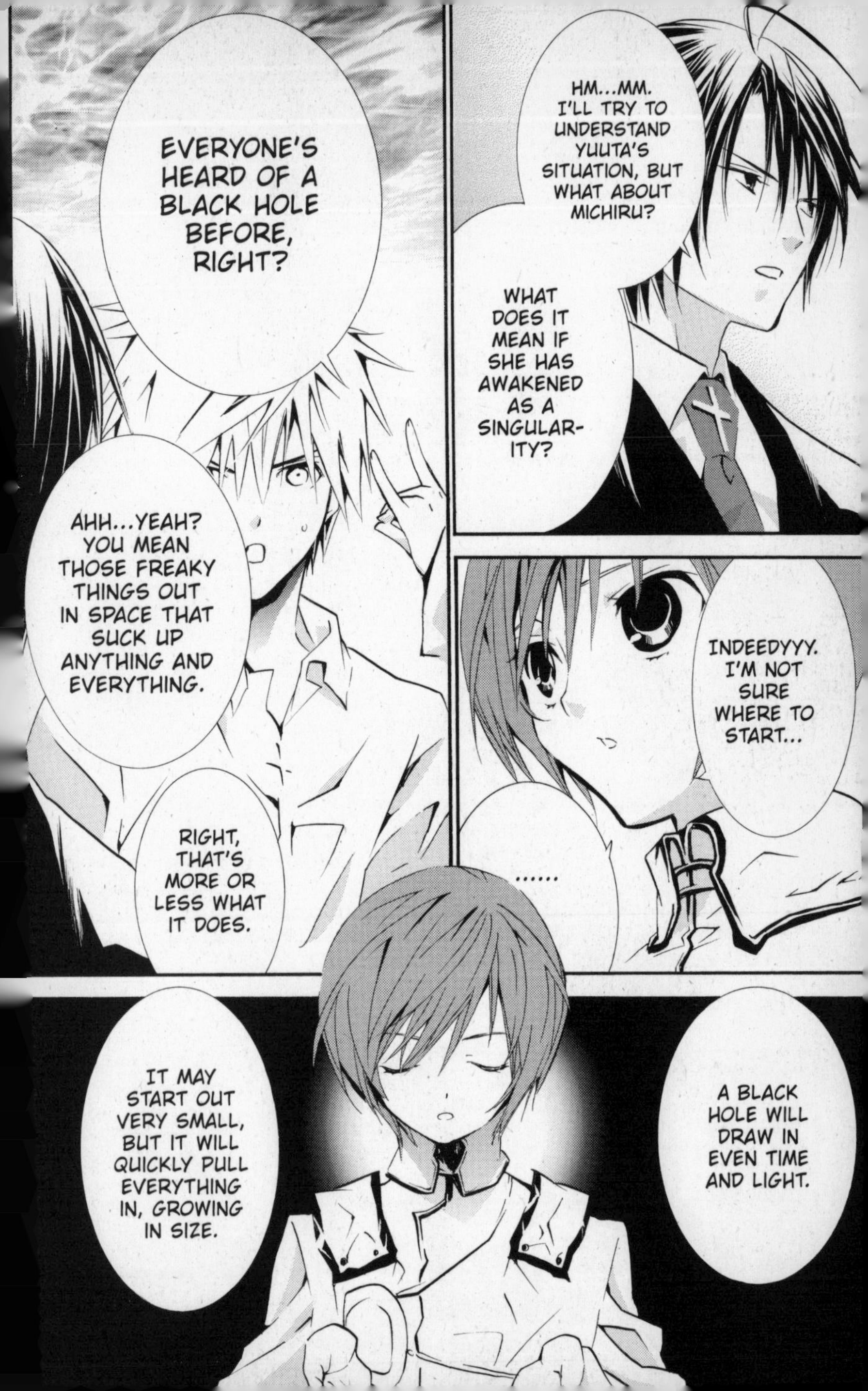
HM...MM. I'LL TRY TO UNDERSTAND YUUTA'S SITUATION, BUT WHAT ABOUT MICHIRU?
WHAT DOES IT MEAN IF SHE HAS AWAKENED AS A SINGULAR-ITY?
INDEEDYYY. I'M NOT SURE WHERE TO START...
......
EVERYONE'S HEARD OF A BLACK HOLE BEFORE, RIGHT?
AHH...YEAH? YOU MEAN THOSE FREAKY THINGS OUT IN SPACE THAT SUCK UP ANYTHING AND EVERYTHING.
RIGHT, THAT'S MORE OR LESS WHAT IT DOES.
A BLACK HOLE WILL DRAW IN EVEN TIME AND LIGHT.
IT MAY START OUT VERY SMALL, BUT IT WILL QUICKLY PULL EVERYTHING IN, GROWING IN SIZE.

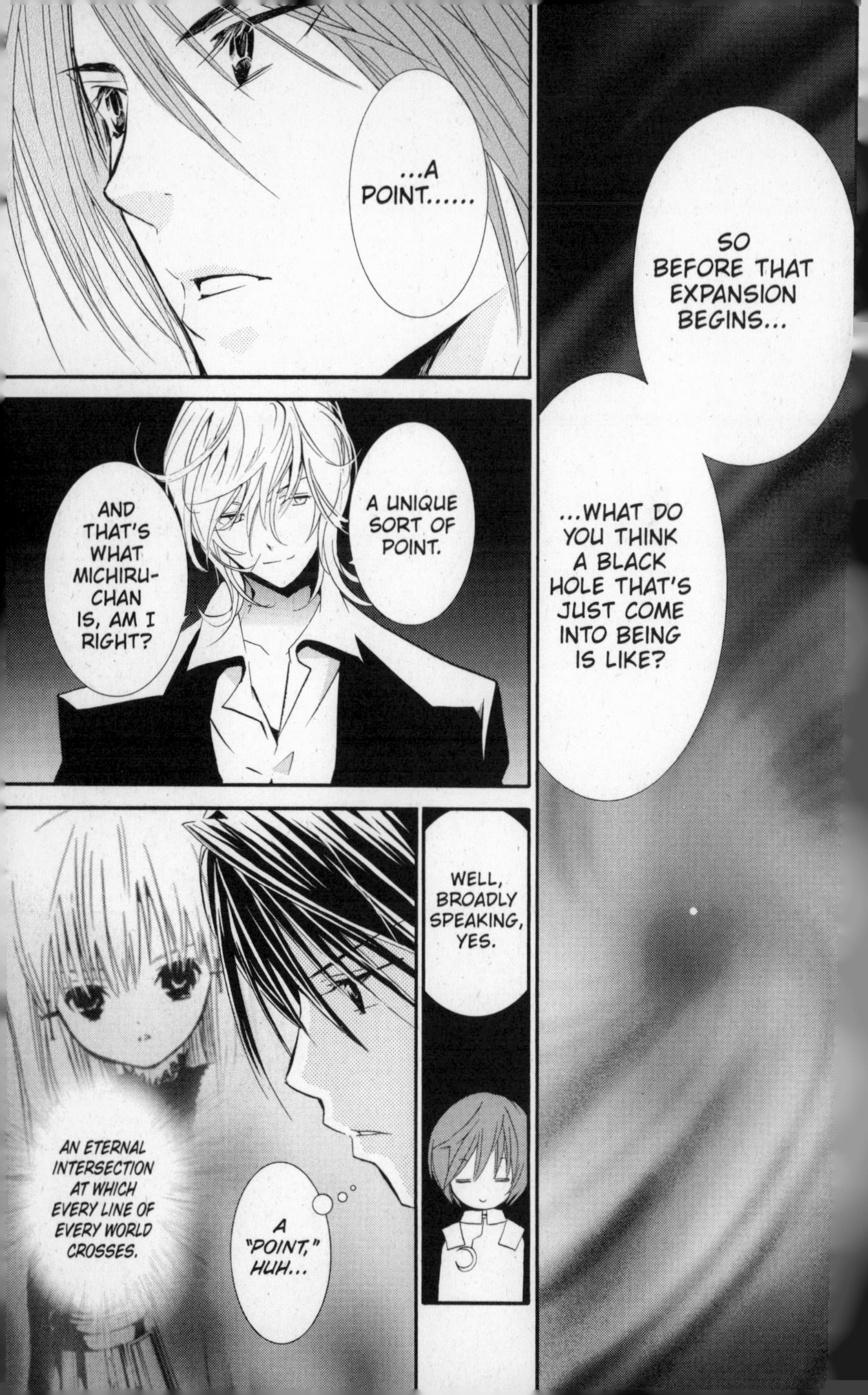
SO BEFORE THAT EXPANSION BEGINS...
...WHAT DO YOU THINK A BLACK HOLE THAT'S JUST COME INTO BEING IS LIKE?
...A POINT......
A UNIQUE SORT OF POINT.
AND THAT'S WHAT MICHIRU-CHAN IS, AM I RIGHT?
WELL, BROADLY SPEAKING, YES.
A "POINT," HUH...
AN ETERNAL INTERSECTION AT WHICH EVERY LINE OF EVERY WORLD CROSSES.

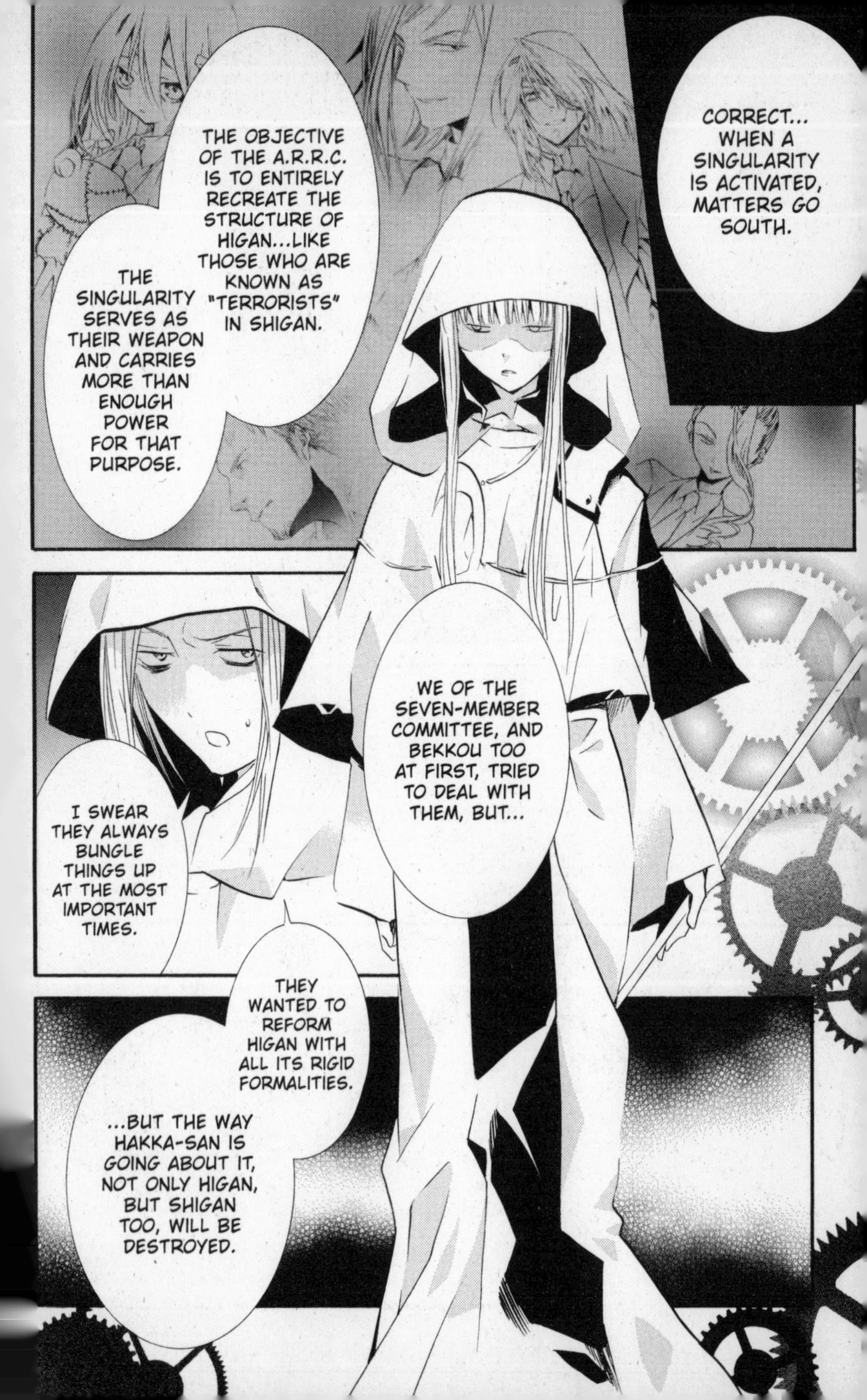
CORRECT... WHEN A SINGULARITY IS ACTIVATED, MATTERS GO SOUTH.
THE OBJECTIVE OF THE A.R.R.C. IS TO ENTIRELY RECREATE THE STRUCTURE OF HIGAN...LIKE THOSE WHO ARE KNOWN AS "TERRORISTS" IN SHIGAN.
THE SINGULARITY SERVES AS THEIR WEAPON AND CARRIES MORE THAN ENOUGH POWER FOR THAT PURPOSE.
WE OF THE SEVEN-MEMBER COMMITTEE, AND BEKKOU TOO AT FIRST, TRIED TO DEAL WITH THEM, BUT...
I SWEAR THEY ALWAYS BUNGLE THINGS UP AT THE MOST IMPORTANT TIMES.
THEY WANTED TO REFORM HIGAN WITH ALL ITS RIGID FORMALITIES.
...BUT THE WAY HAKKA-SAN IS GOING ABOUT IT, NOT ONLY HIGAN, BUT SHIGAN TOO, WILL BE DESTROYED.

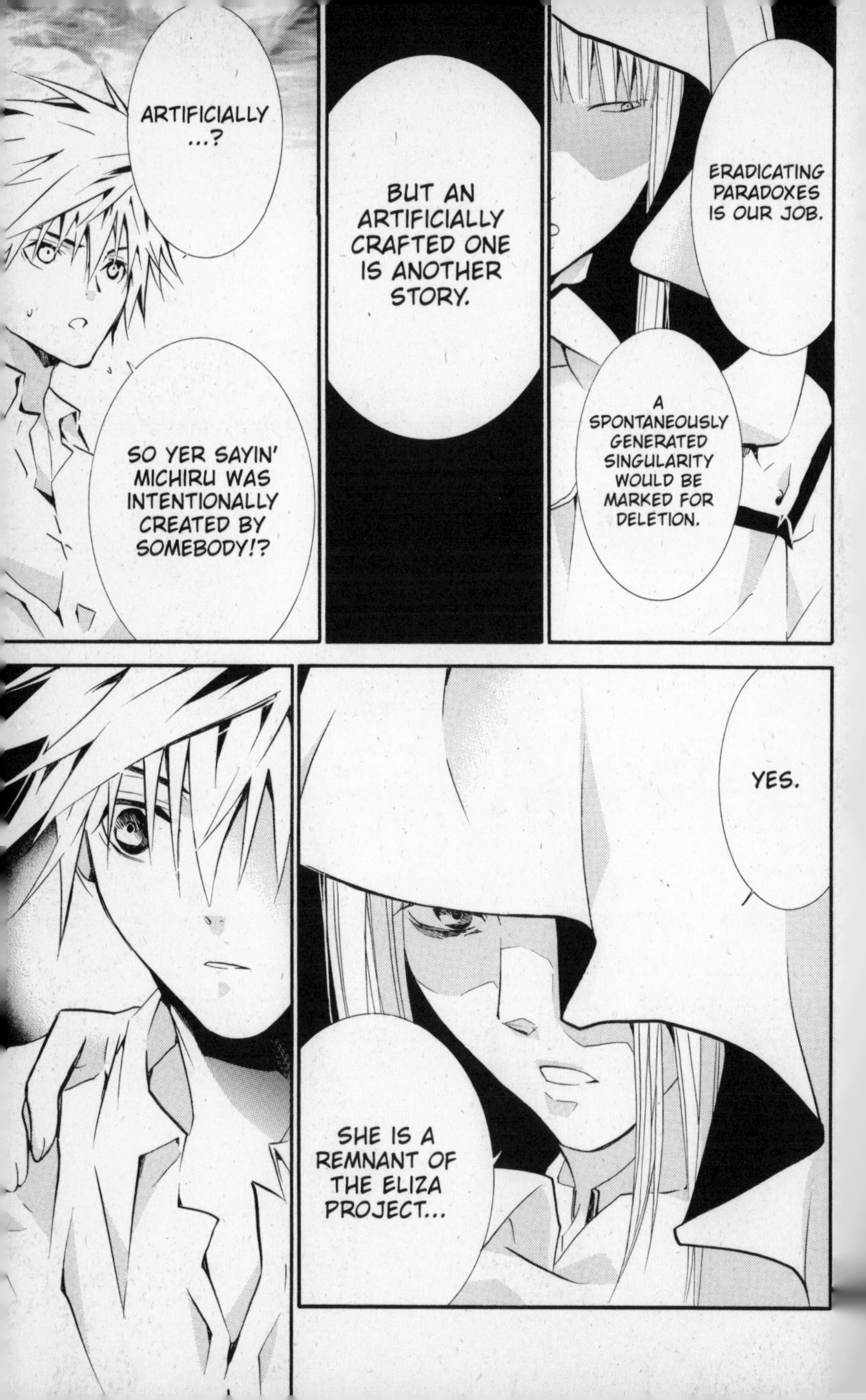
ERADICATING PARADOXES IS OUR JOB.
A SPONTANEOUSLY GENERATED SINGULARITY WOULD BE MARKED FOR DELETION.
BUT AN ARTIFICIALLY CRAFTED ONE IS ANOTHER STORY.
ARTIFICIALLY ...?
SO YER SAYIN' MICHIRU WAS INTENTIONALLY CREATED BY SOMEBODY!?
YES.
SHE IS A REMNANT OF THE ELIZA PROJECT...

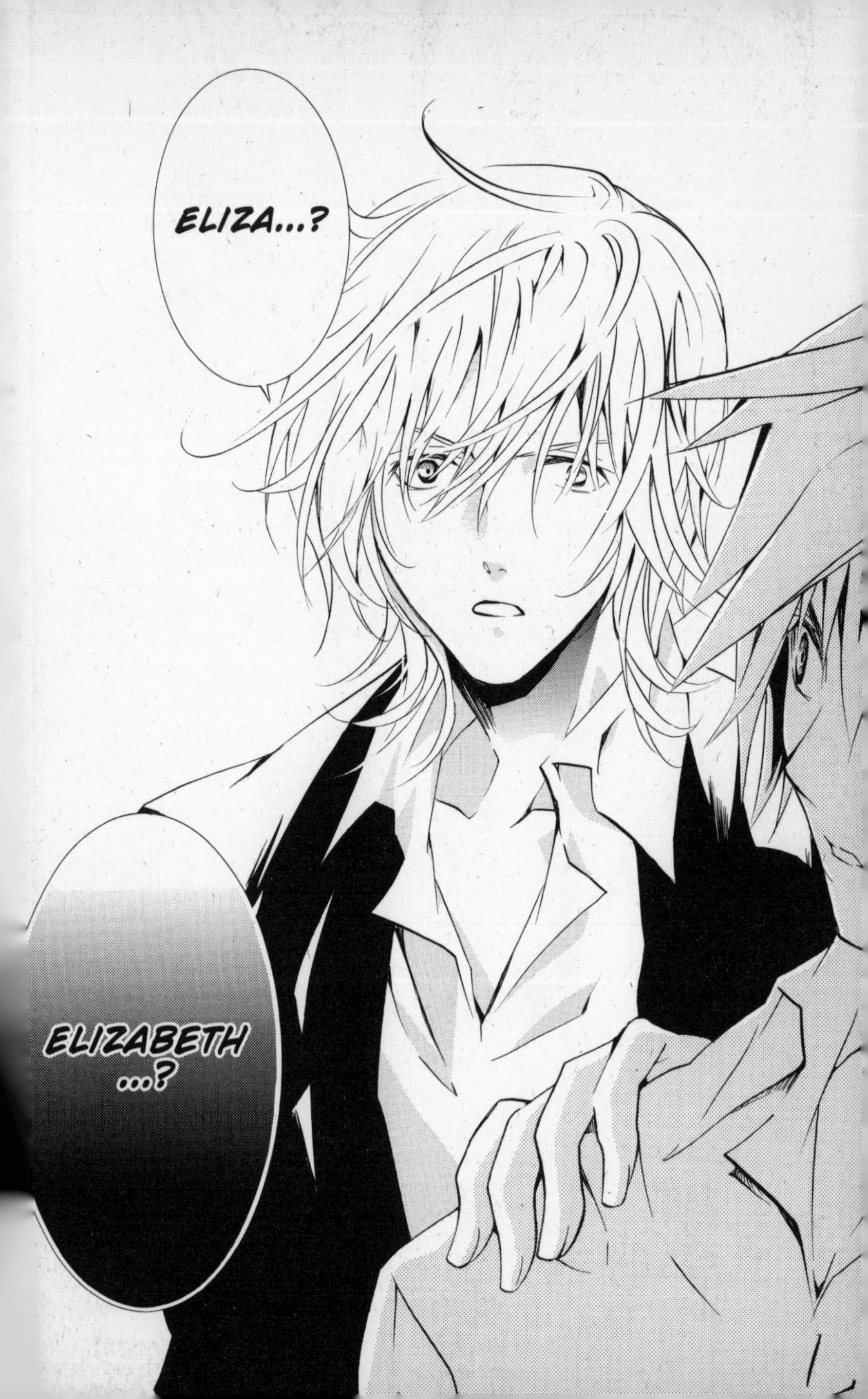
ELIZA...?
ELIZABETH ...?

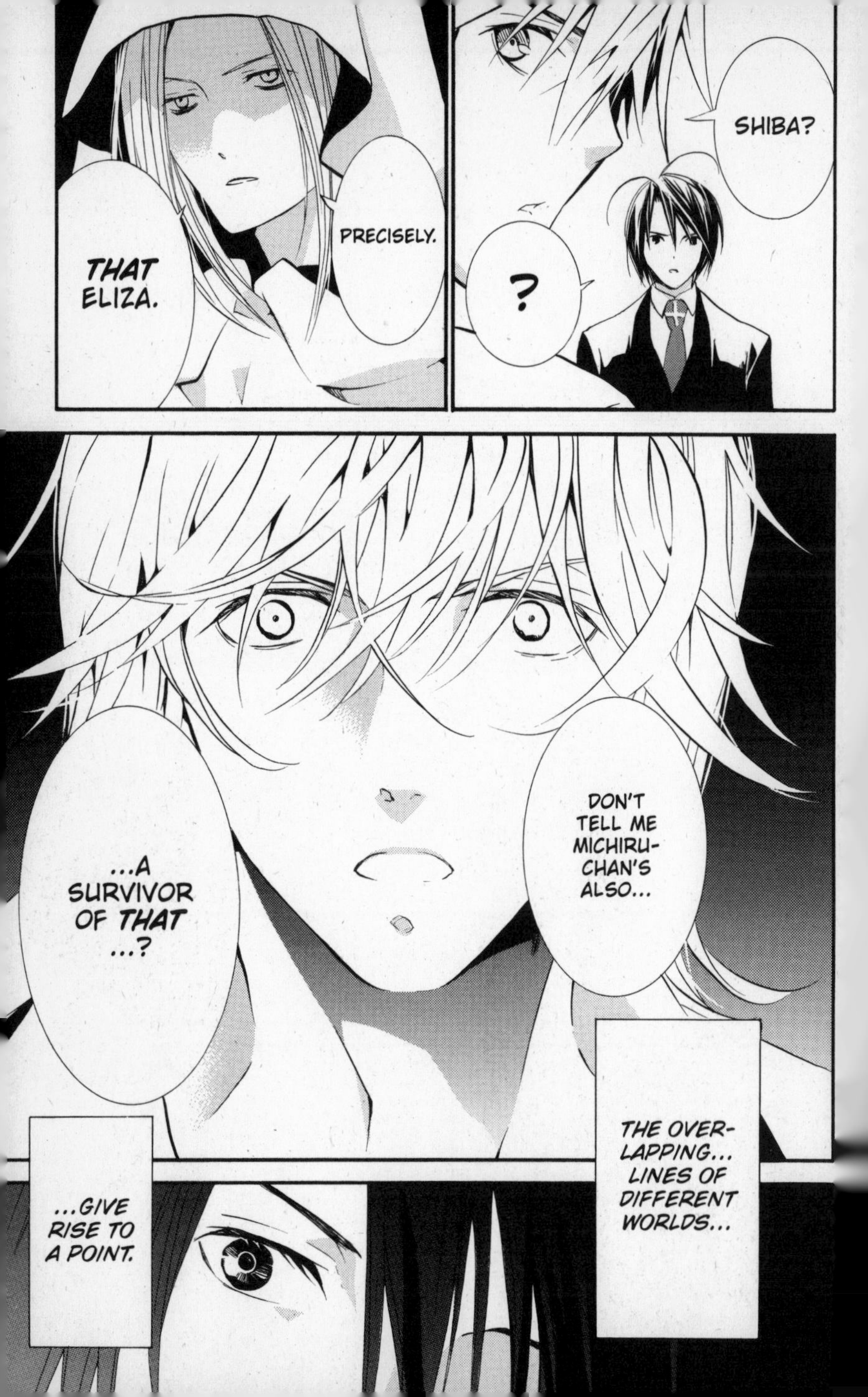
SHIBA?
?
PRECISELY.
THAT ELIZA.
DON'T TELL ME MICHIRU-CHAN'S ALSO...
...A SURVIVOR OF THAT ...?
THE OVER-LAPPING... LINES OF DIFFERENT WORLDS...
...GIVE RISE TO A POINT.

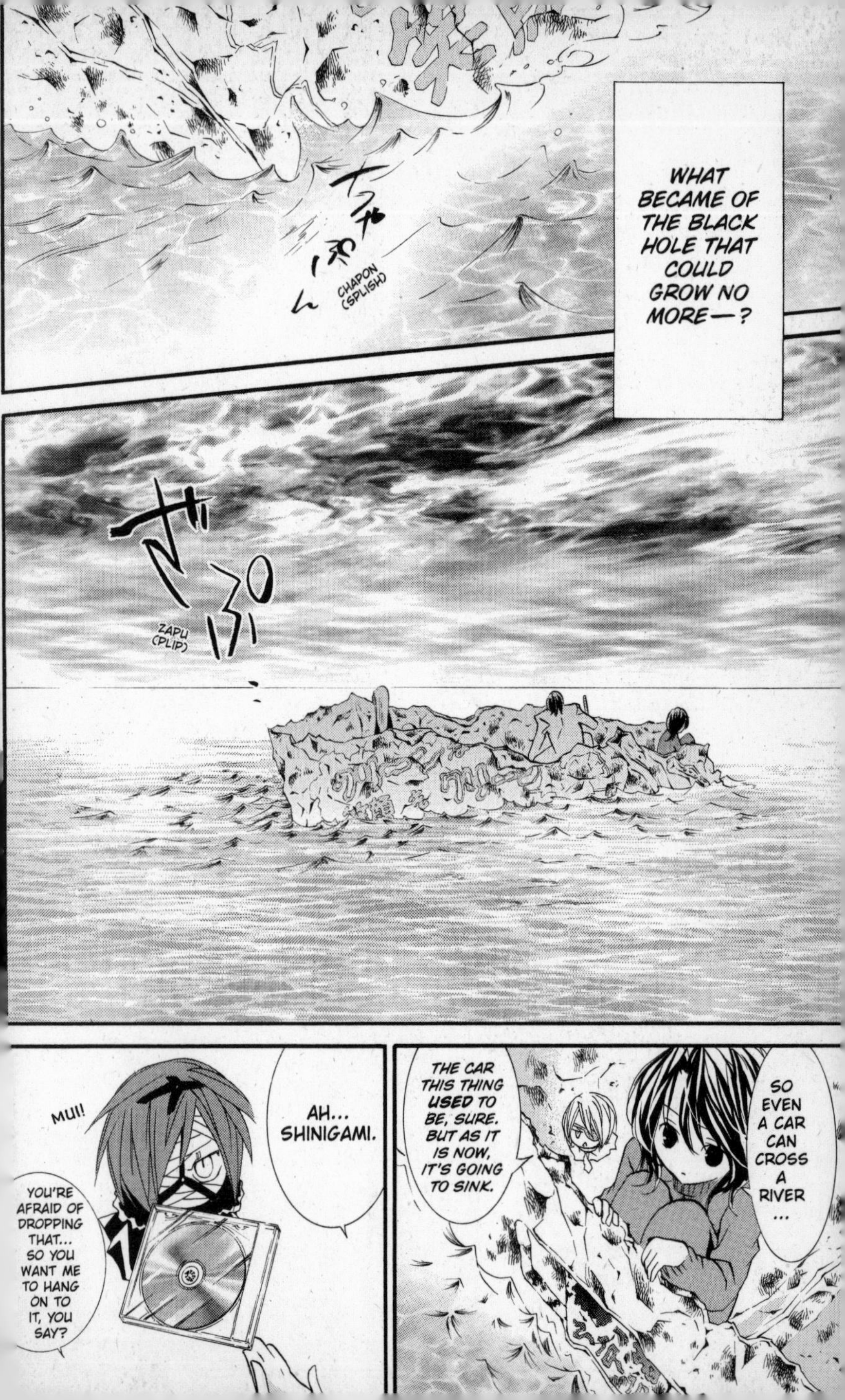
WHAT BECAME OF THE BLACK HOLE THAT COULD GROW NO MORE—?
CHAPON (SPLISH)
ZAPU (PLIP)
SO EVEN A CAR CAN CROSS A RIVER...
THE CAR THIS THING USED TO BE, SURE. BUT AS IT IS NOW, IT'S GOING TO SINK.
AH... SHINIGAMI.
MUI!
YOU'RE AFRAID OF DROPPING THAT... SO YOU WANT ME TO HANG ON TO IT, YOU SAY?

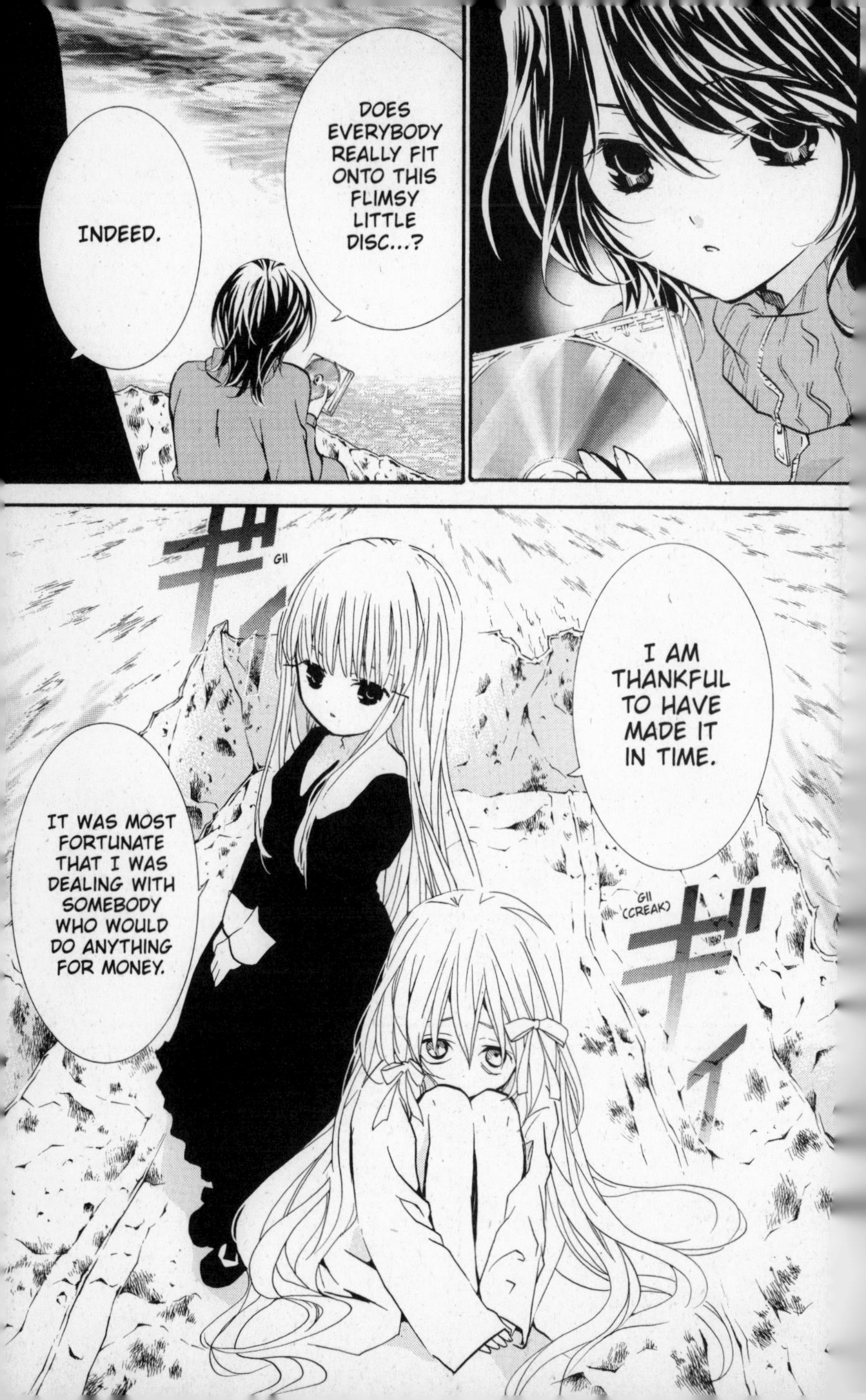
DOES EVERYBODY REALLY FIT ONTO THIS FLIMSY LITTLE DISC...?
INDEED.
I AM THANKFUL TO HAVE MADE IT IN TIME.
GII
IT WAS MOST FORTUNATE THAT I WAS DEALING WITH SOMEBODY WHO WOULD DO ANYTHING FOR MONEY.
GII (CREAK)

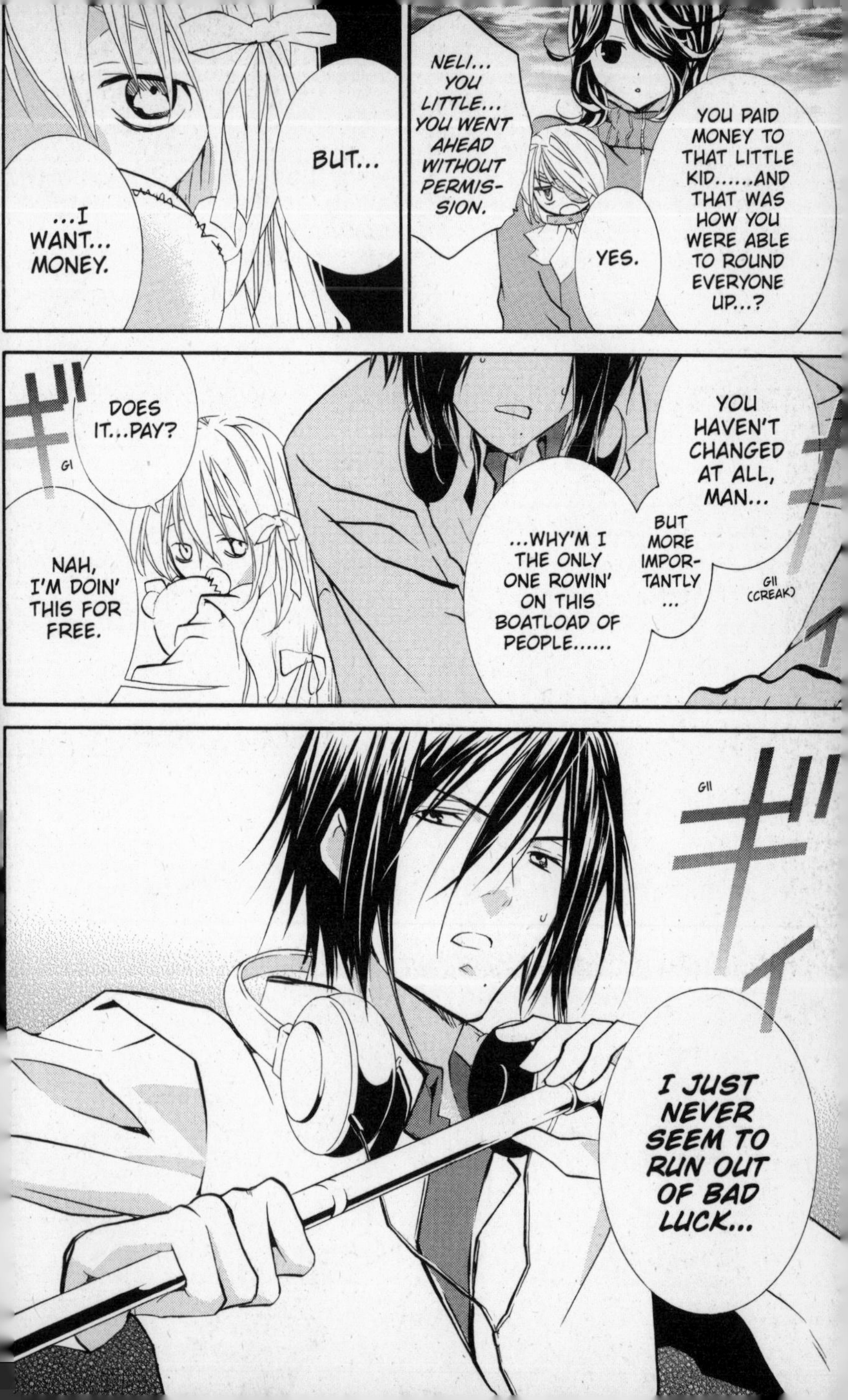
YOU PAID MONEY TO THAT LITTLE KID......AND THAT WAS HOW YOU WERE ABLE TO ROUND EVERYONE UP...?
YES.
NELI... YOU LITTLE... YOU WENT AHEAD WITHOUT PERMISSION.
BUT...
...I WANT... MONEY.
YOU HAVEN'T CHANGED AT ALL, MAN...
GII (CREAK)
BUT MORE IMPORTANTLY ...
...WHY'M I THE ONLY ONE ROWIN' ON THIS BOATLOAD OF PEOPLE......
DOES IT...PAY?
GI
NAH, I'M DOIN' THIS FOR FREE.
GII
I JUST NEVER SEEM TO RUN OUT OF BAD LUCK...

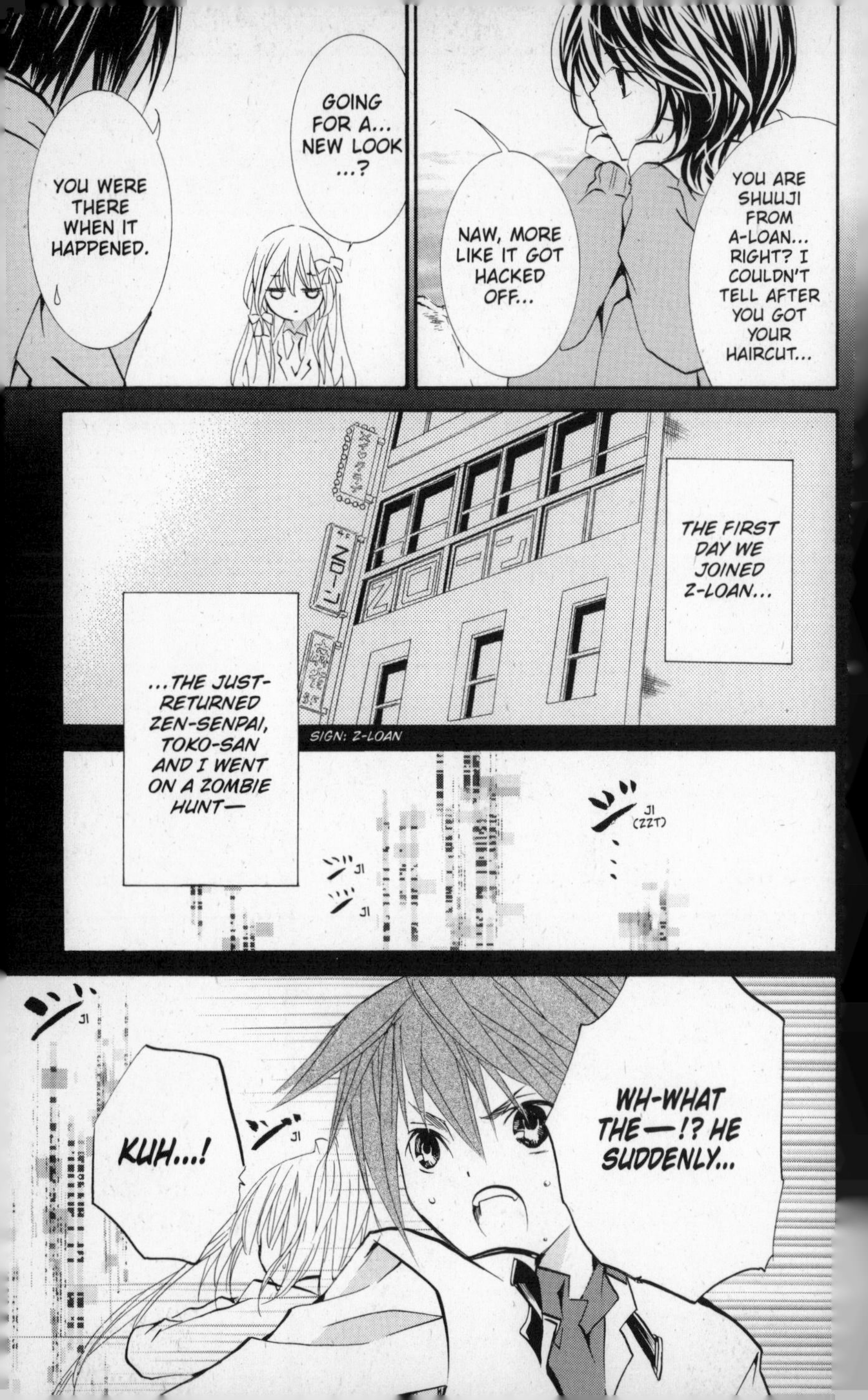
YOU ARE SHUUJI FROM A-LOAN... RIGHT? I COULDN'T TELL AFTER YOU GOT YOUR HAIRCUT...
NAW, MORE LIKE IT GOT HACKED OFF...
GOING FOR A... NEW LOOK ...?
YOU WERE THERE WHEN IT HAPPENED.
THE FIRST DAY WE JOINED Z-LOAN...
...THE JUST-RETURNED ZEN-SENPAI, TOKO-SAN AND I WENT ON A ZOMBIE HUNT—
SIGN: Z-LOAN
JI (ZZT)
JI
JI
JI
WH-WHAT THE—!? HE SUDDENLY...
JI
KUH...!

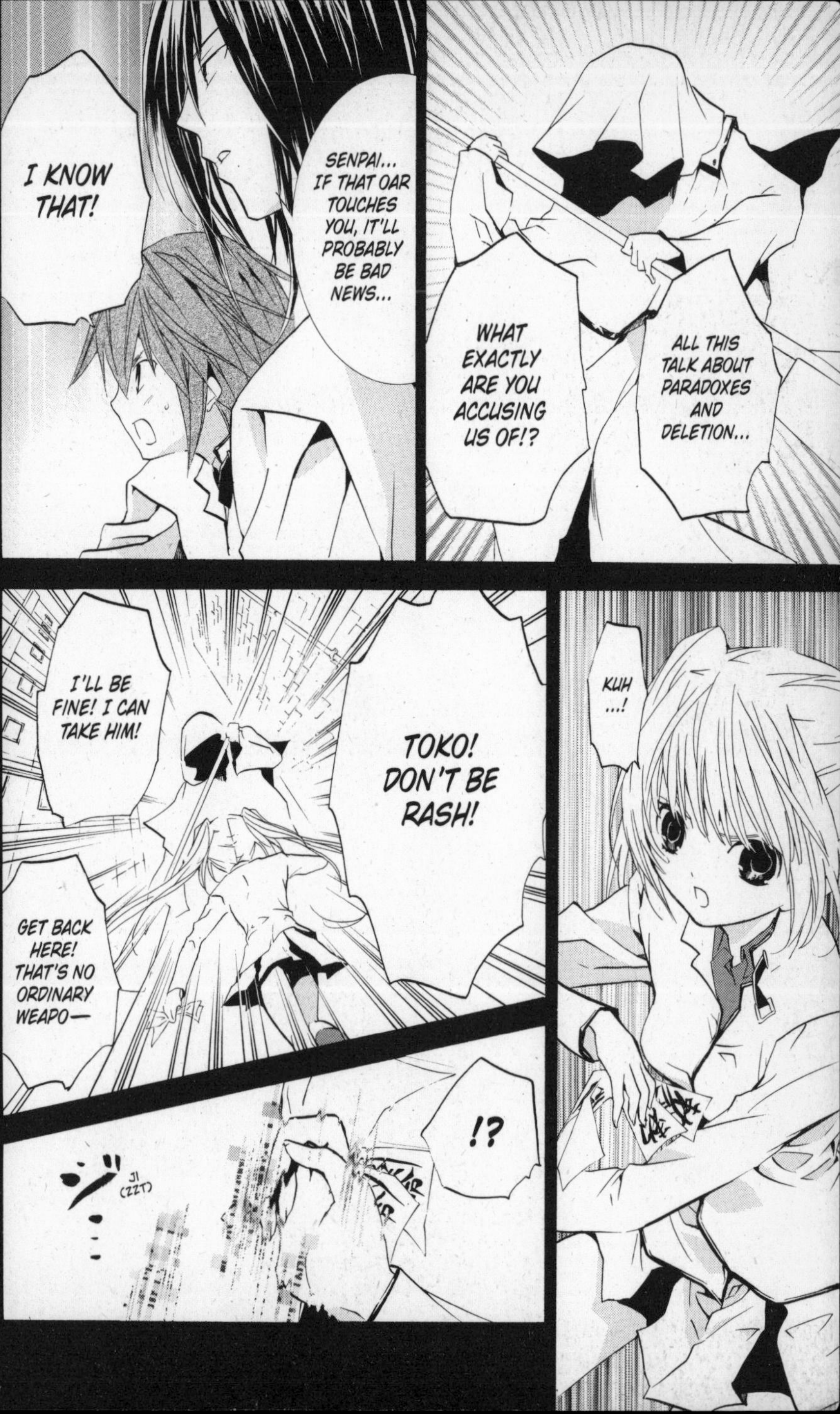

ALL THIS TALK ABOUT PARADOXES AND DELETION...
WHAT EXACTLY ARE YOU ACCUSING US OF!?
SENPAI... IF THAT OAR TOUCHES YOU, IT'LL PROBABLY BE BAD NEWS...
I KNOW THAT!
KUH ...!
TOKO! DON'T BE RASH!
I'LL BE FINE! I CAN TAKE HIM!
GET BACK HERE! THAT'S NO ORDINARY WEAPO—
!?
JI (ZZT)

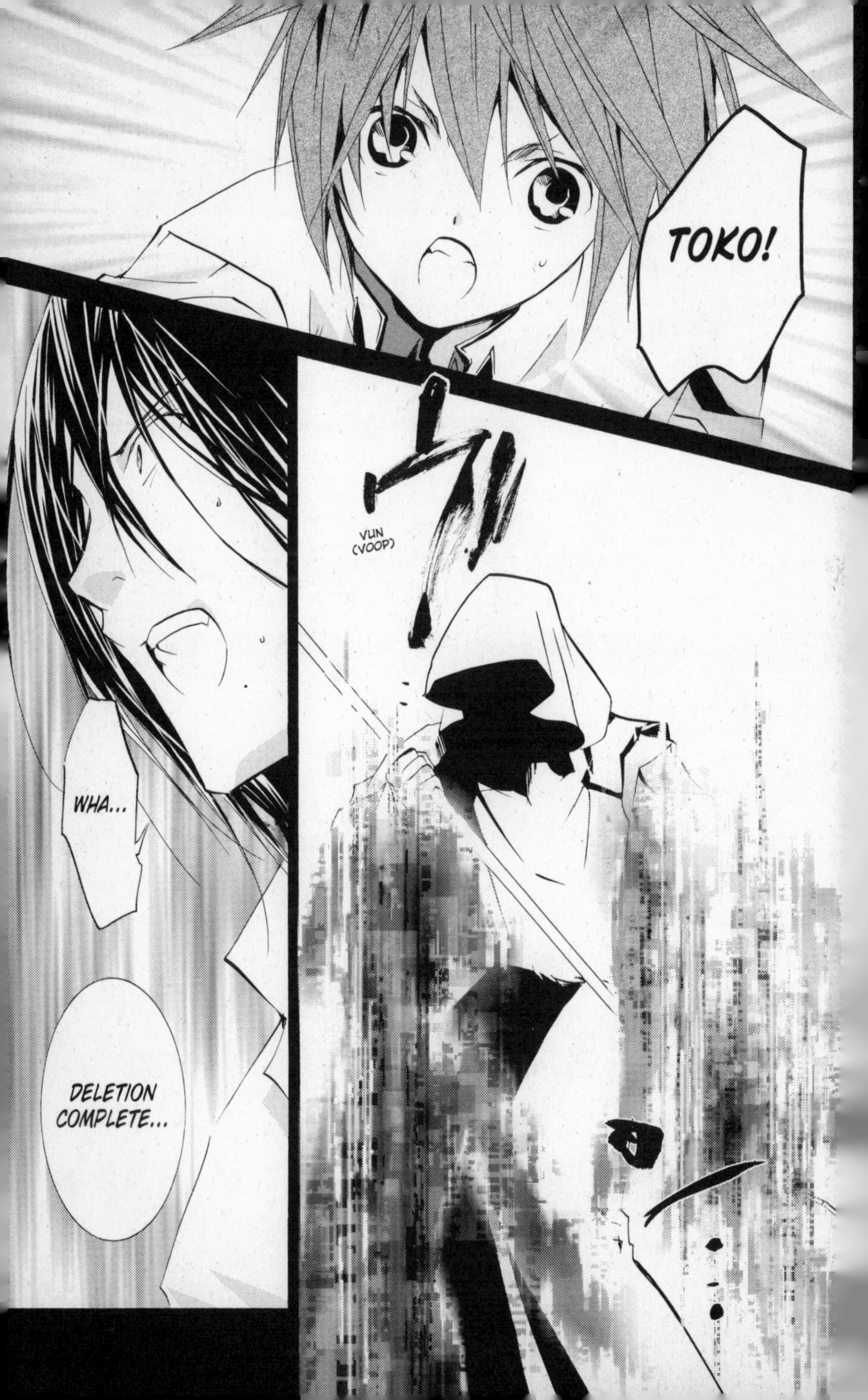
TOKO!
WHA...
DELETION COMPLETE...
VUN (VOOP)

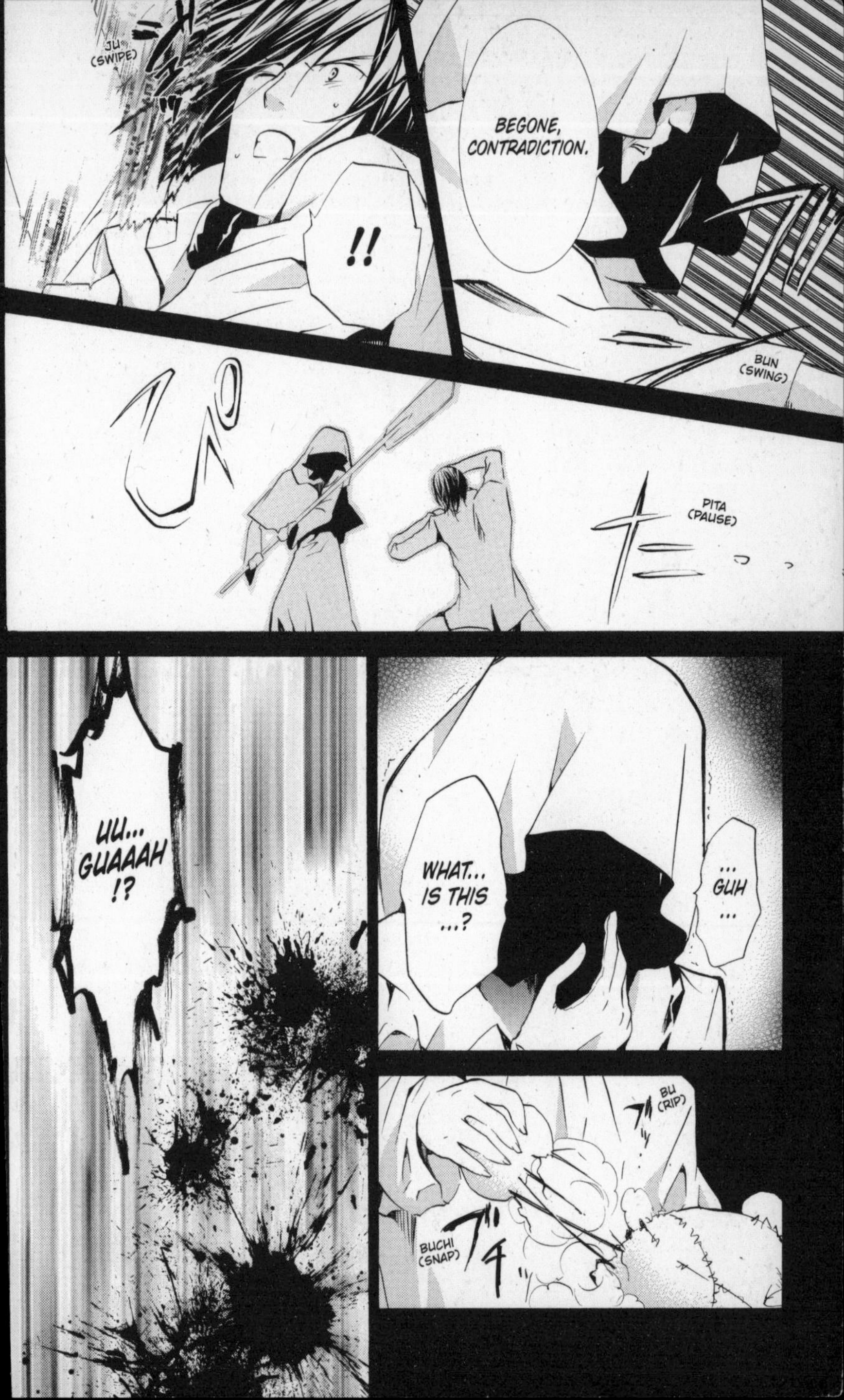
BEGONE, CONTRADICTION.
BUN (SWING)
JU (SWIPE)
!!
PITA (PAUSE)
... GUH ...
WHAT... IS THIS ...?
BU (RIP)
BUCHI (SNAP)
UU... GUAAAH !?

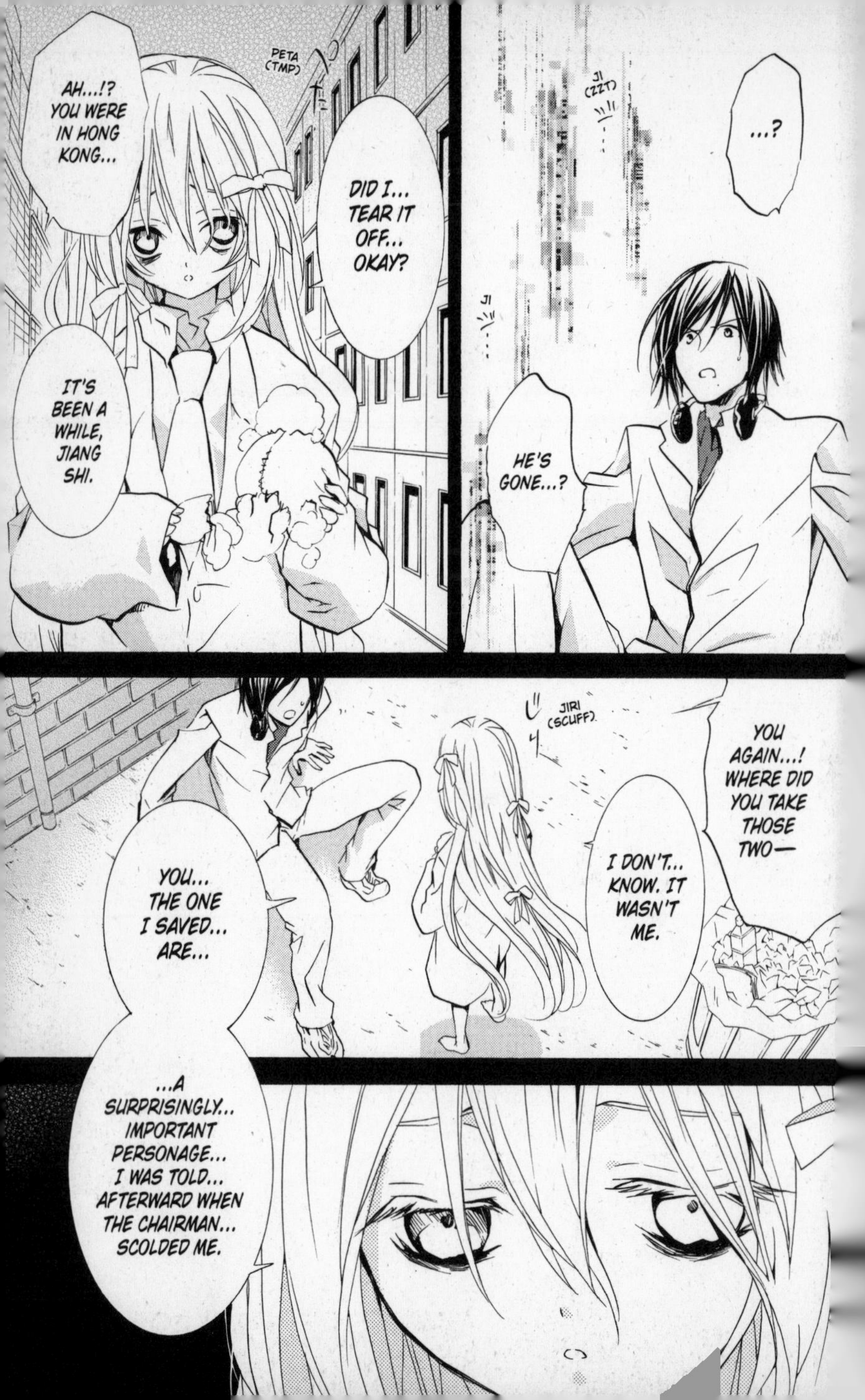
...?
JI (ZZZT)
JI
HE'S GONE...?
PETA (TMP)
DID I... TEAR IT OFF... OKAY?
AH...!? YOU WERE IN HONG KONG...
IT'S BEEN A WHILE, JIANG SHI.
YOU AGAIN...! WHERE DID YOU TAKE THOSE TWO—
JIRI (SCUFF)
I DON'T... KNOW. IT WASN'T ME.
YOU... THE ONE I SAVED... ARE...
...A SURPRISINGLY... IMPORTANT PERSONAGE... I WAS TOLD... AFTERWARD WHEN THE CHAIRMAN... SCOLDED ME.

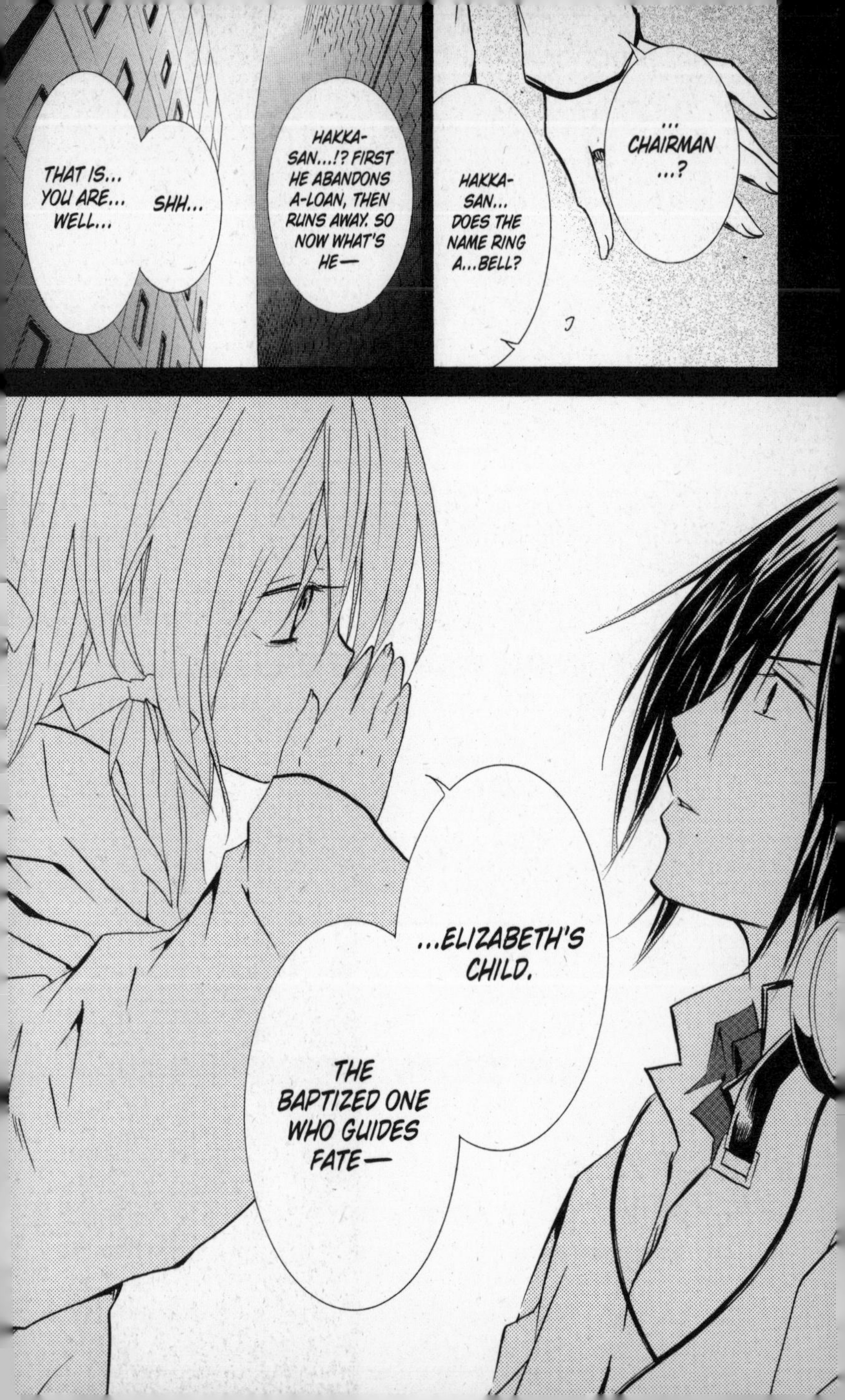
...CHAIRMAN...?
HAKKA-SAN... DOES THE NAME RING A...BELL?
HAKKA-SAN...!? FIRST HE ABANDONS A-LOAN, THEN RUNS AWAY. SO NOW WHAT'S HE—
SHH...
THAT IS... YOU ARE... WELL...
...ELIZABETH'S CHILD.
THE BAPTIZED ONE WHO GUIDES FATE—

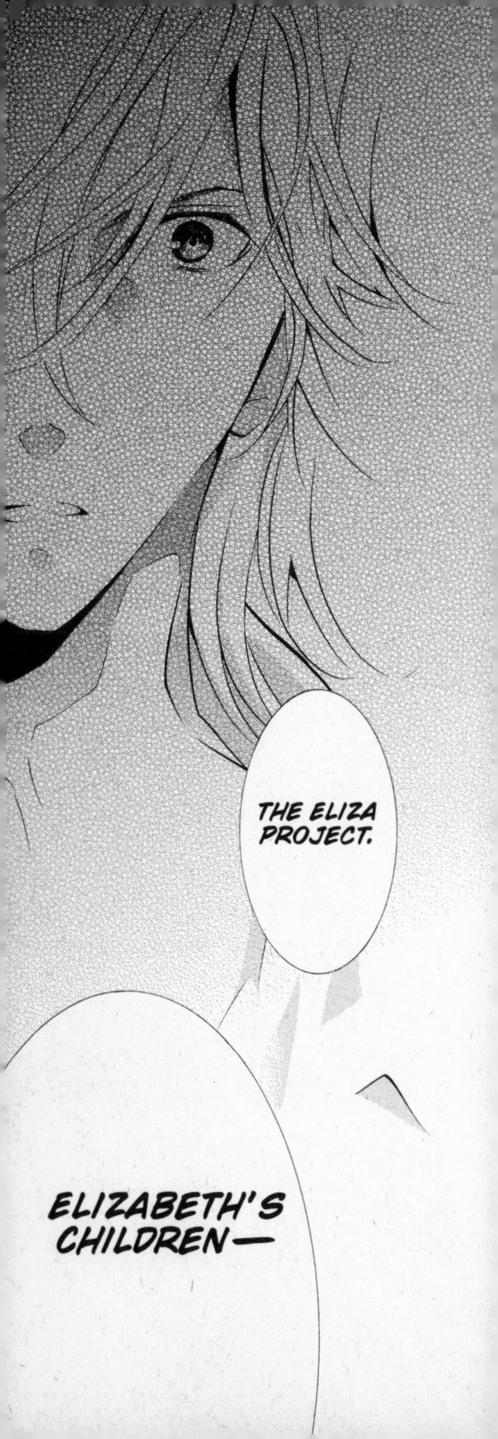
THE ELIZA PROJECT.
ELIZABETH'S CHILDREN—

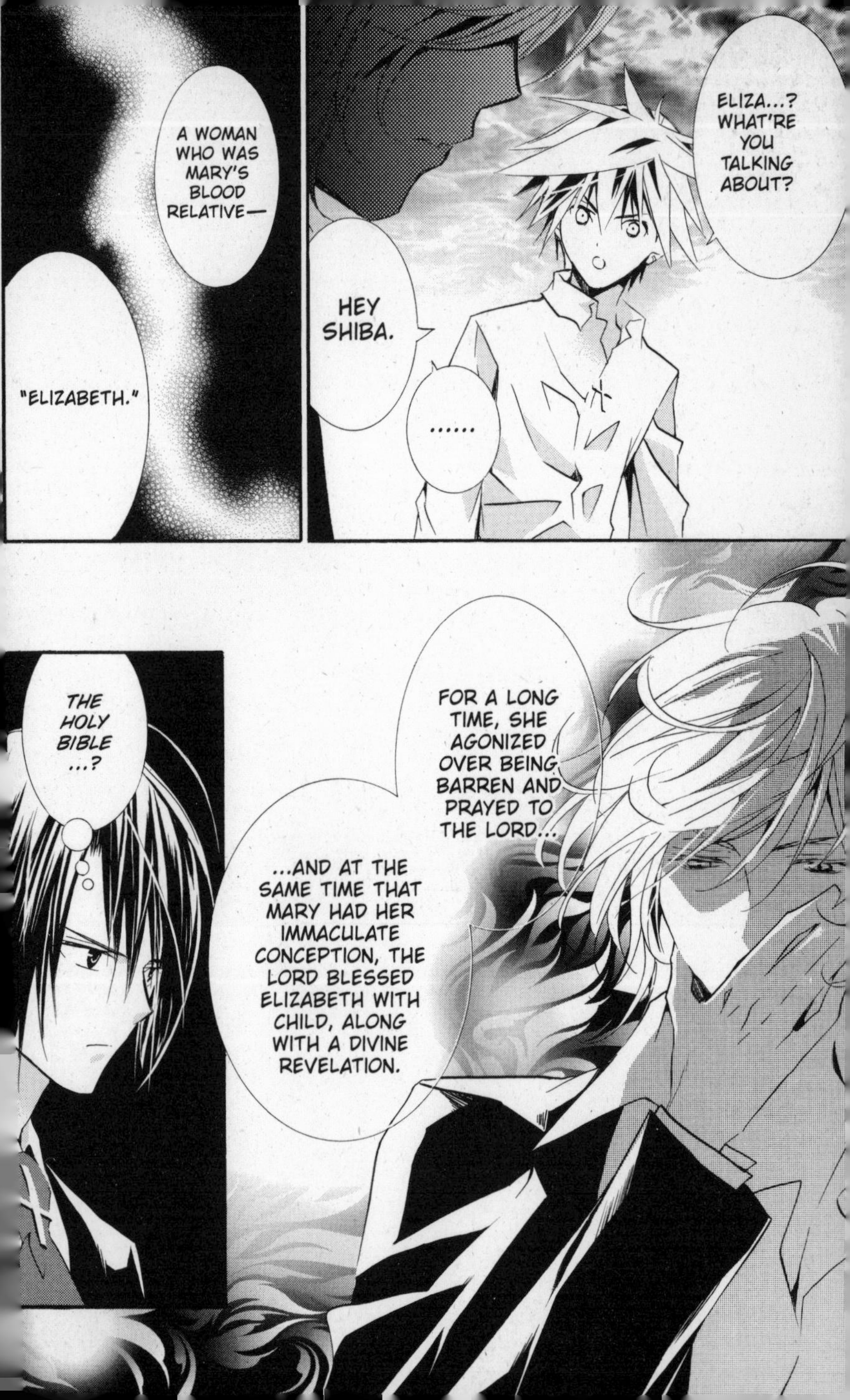
ELIZA...? WHAT'RE YOU TALKING ABOUT?
HEY SHIBA.
......
A WOMAN WHO WAS MARY'S BLOOD RELATIVE—
"ELIZABETH."
FOR A LONG TIME, SHE AGONIZED OVER BEING BARREN AND PRAYED TO THE LORD...
...AND AT THE SAME TIME THAT MARY HAD HER IMMACULATE CONCEPTION, THE LORD BLESSED ELIZABETH WITH CHILD, ALONG WITH A DIVINE REVELATION.
THE HOLY BIBLE ...?

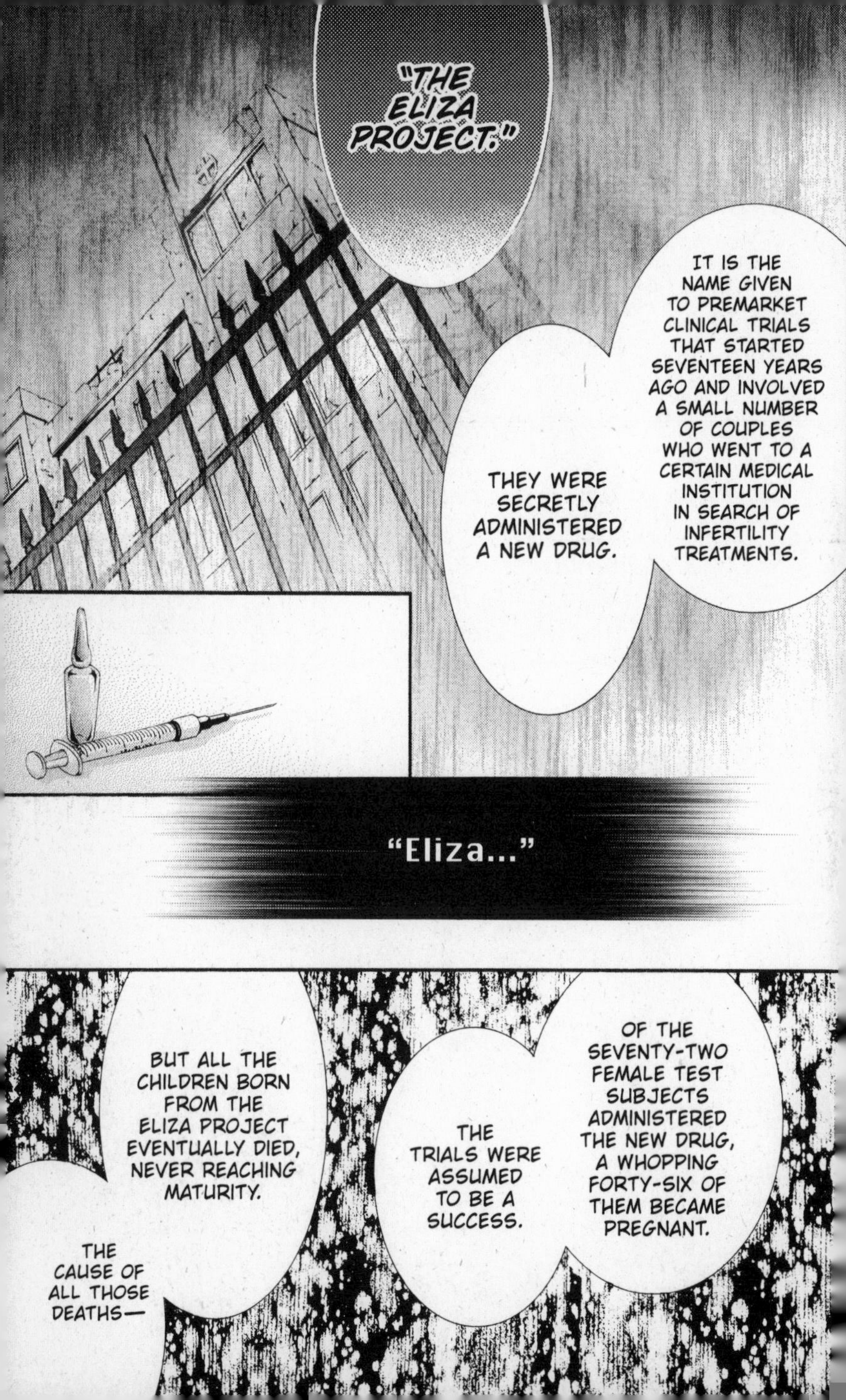
"THE ELIZA PROJECT."
IT IS THE NAME GIVEN TO PREMARKET CLINICAL TRIALS THAT STARTED SEVENTEEN YEARS AGO AND INVOLVED A SMALL NUMBER OF COUPLES WHO WENT TO A CERTAIN MEDICAL INSTITUTION IN SEARCH OF INFERTILITY TREATMENTS.
THEY WERE SECRETLY ADMINISTERED A NEW DRUG.
"Eliza..."
OF THE SEVENTY-TWO FEMALE TEST SUBJECTS ADMINISTERED THE NEW DRUG, A WHOPPING FORTY-SIX OF THEM BECAME PREGNANT.
THE TRIALS WERE ASSUMED TO BE A SUCCESS.
BUT ALL THE CHILDREN BORN FROM THE ELIZA PROJECT EVENTUALLY DIED, NEVER REACHING MATURITY.
THE CAUSE OF ALL THOSE DEATHS—

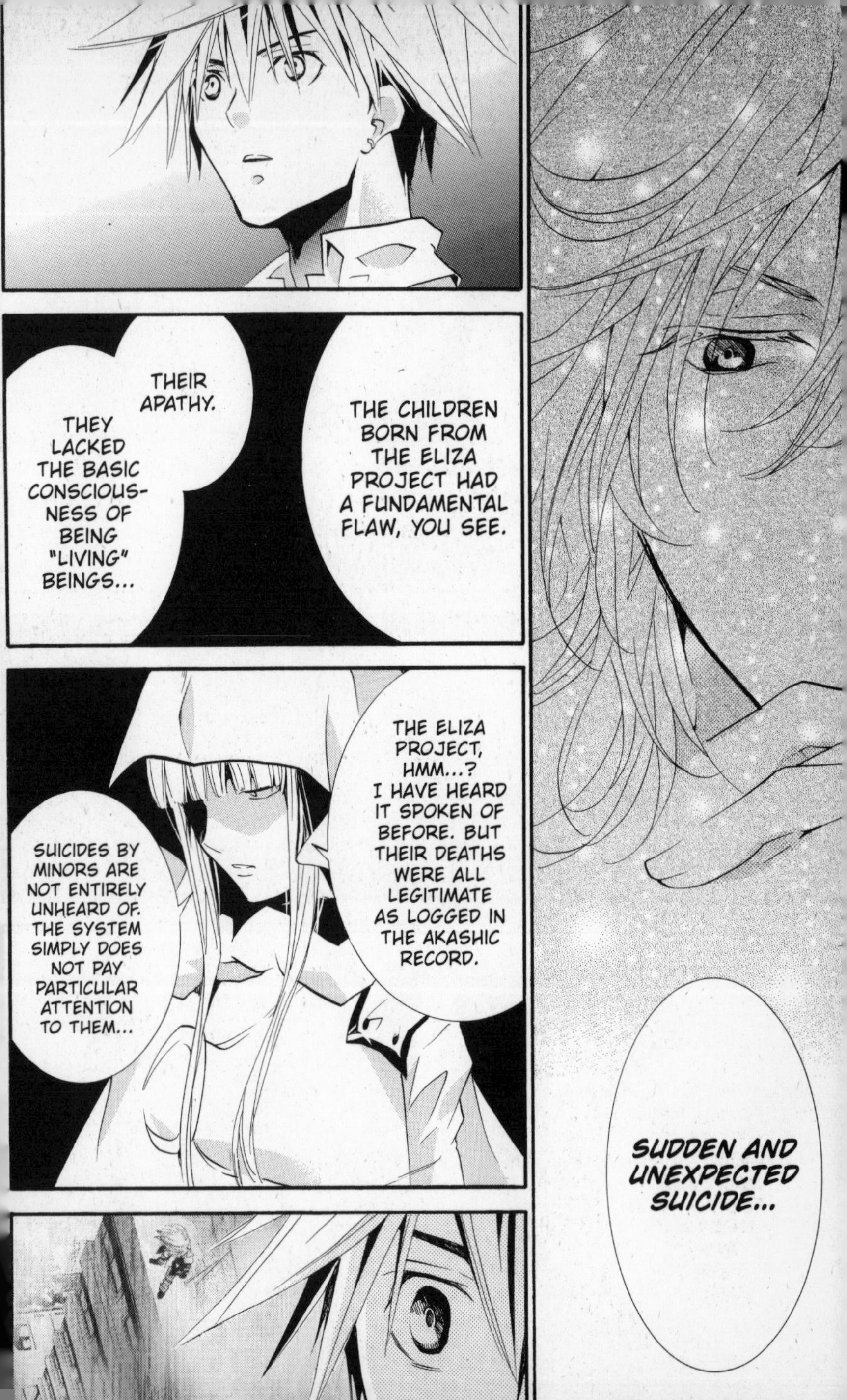
SUDDEN AND UNEXPECTED SUICIDE...
THE CHILDREN BORN FROM THE ELIZA PROJECT HAD A FUNDAMENTAL FLAW, YOU SEE.
THEIR APATHY.
THEY LACKED THE BASIC CONSCIOUS-NESS OF BEING "LIVING" BEINGS...
THE ELIZA PROJECT, HMM...? I HAVE HEARD IT SPOKEN OF BEFORE. BUT THEIR DEATHS WERE ALL LEGITIMATE AS LOGGED IN THE AKASHIC RECORD.
SUICIDES BY MINORS ARE NOT ENTIRELY UNHEARD OF. THE SYSTEM SIMPLY DOES NOT PAY PARTICULAR ATTENTION TO THEM...

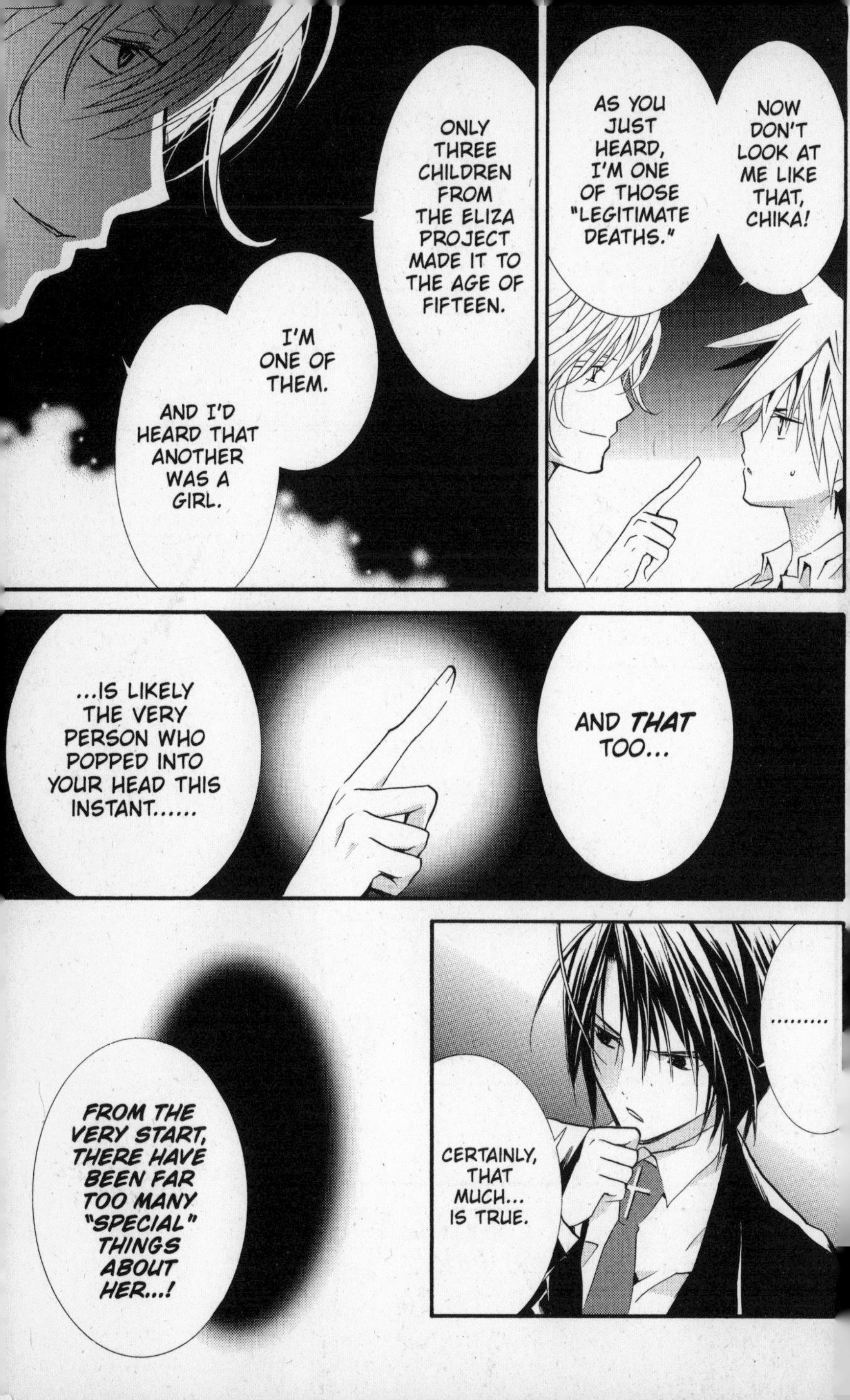
NOW DON'T LOOK AT ME LIKE THAT, CHIKA!
AS YOU JUST HEARD, I'M ONE OF THOSE "LEGITIMATE DEATHS."
ONLY THREE CHILDREN FROM THE ELIZA PROJECT MADE IT TO THE AGE OF FIFTEEN.
I'M ONE OF THEM.
AND I'D HEARD THAT ANOTHER WAS A GIRL.
AND *THAT* TOO...
...IS LIKELY THE VERY PERSON WHO POPPED INTO YOUR HEAD THIS INSTANT......
....
CERTAINLY, THAT MUCH... IS TRUE.
FROM THE VERY START, THERE HAVE BEEN FAR TOO MANY "SPECIAL" THINGS ABOUT HER...!

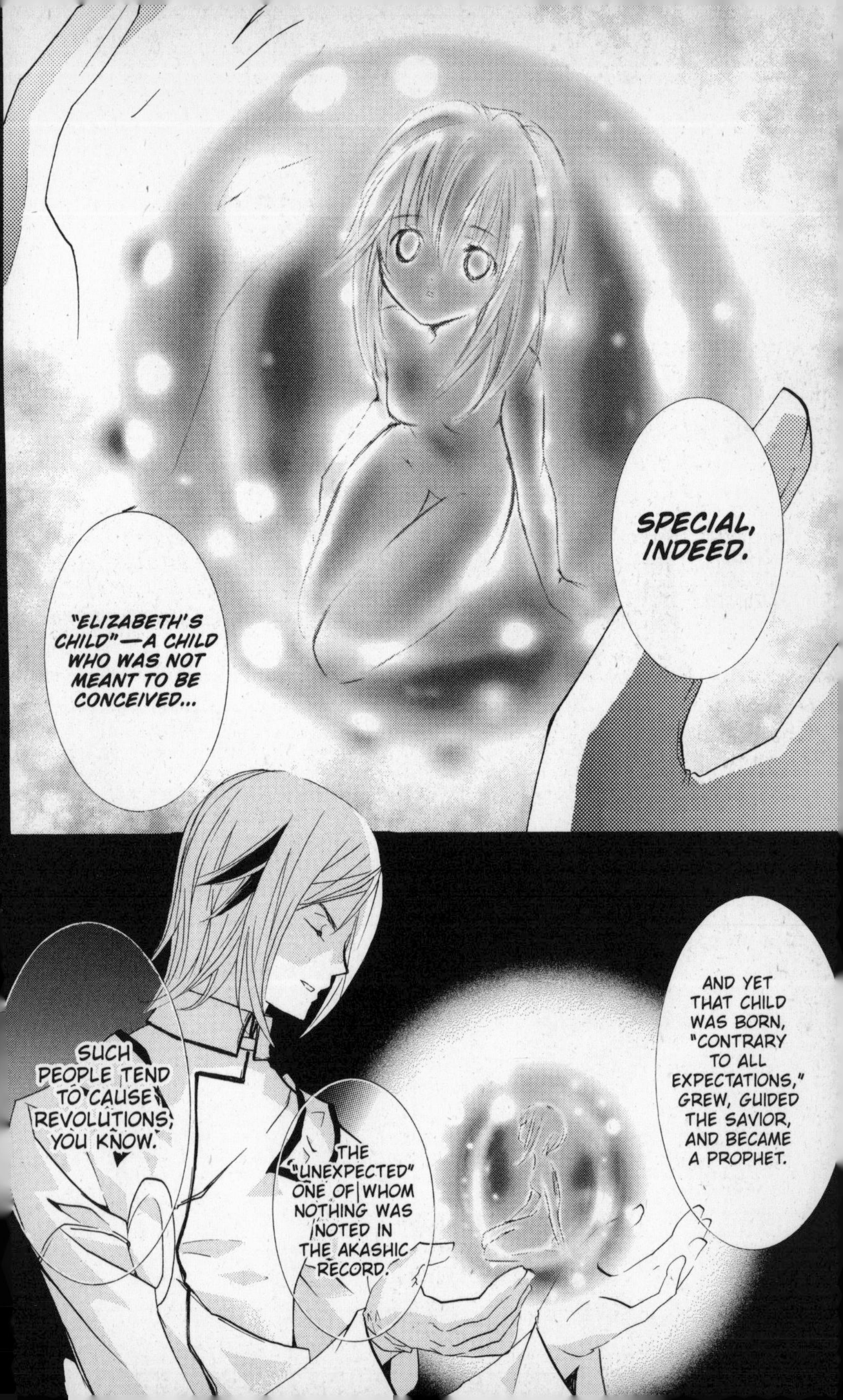
SPECIAL, INDEED.
"ELIZABETH'S CHILD"—A CHILD WHO WAS NOT MEANT TO BE CONCEIVED...
AND YET THAT CHILD WAS BORN, "CONTRARY TO ALL EXPECTATIONS," GREW, GUIDED THE SAVIOR, AND BECAME A PROPHET.
THE "UNEXPECTED" ONE OF WHOM NOTHING WAS NOTED IN THE AKASHIC RECORD.
SUCH PEOPLE TEND TO CAUSE REVOLUTIONS, YOU KNOW.

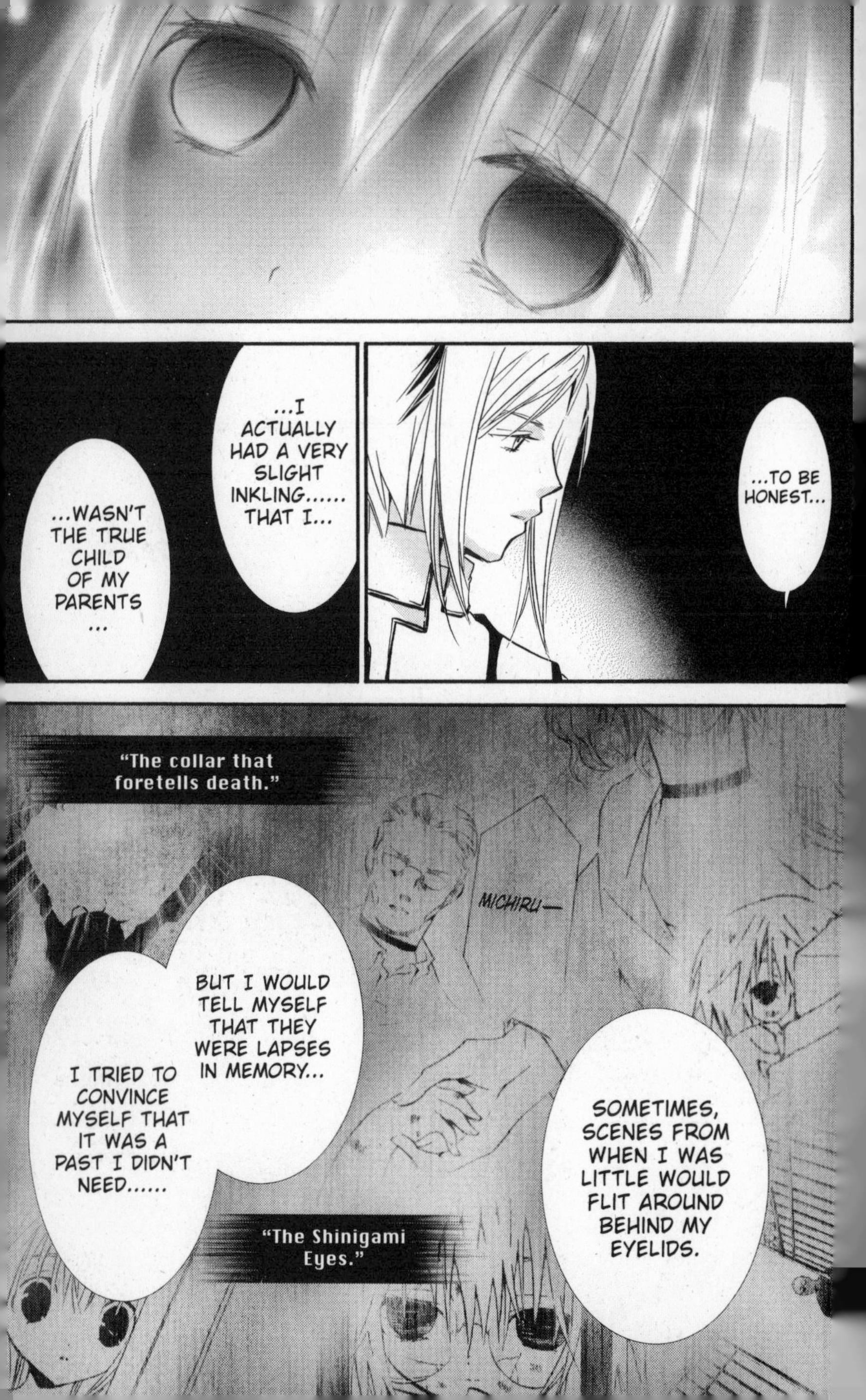
...TO BE HONEST...
...I ACTUALLY HAD A VERY SLIGHT INKLING...... THAT I...
...WASN'T THE TRUE CHILD OF MY PARENTS ...
"The collar that foretells death."
MICHIRU—
SOMETIMES, SCENES FROM WHEN I WAS LITTLE WOULD FLIT AROUND BEHIND MY EYELIDS.
BUT I WOULD TELL MYSELF THAT THEY WERE LAPSES IN MEMORY...
I TRIED TO CONVINCE MYSELF THAT IT WAS A PAST I DIDN'T NEED......
"The Shinigami Eyes."

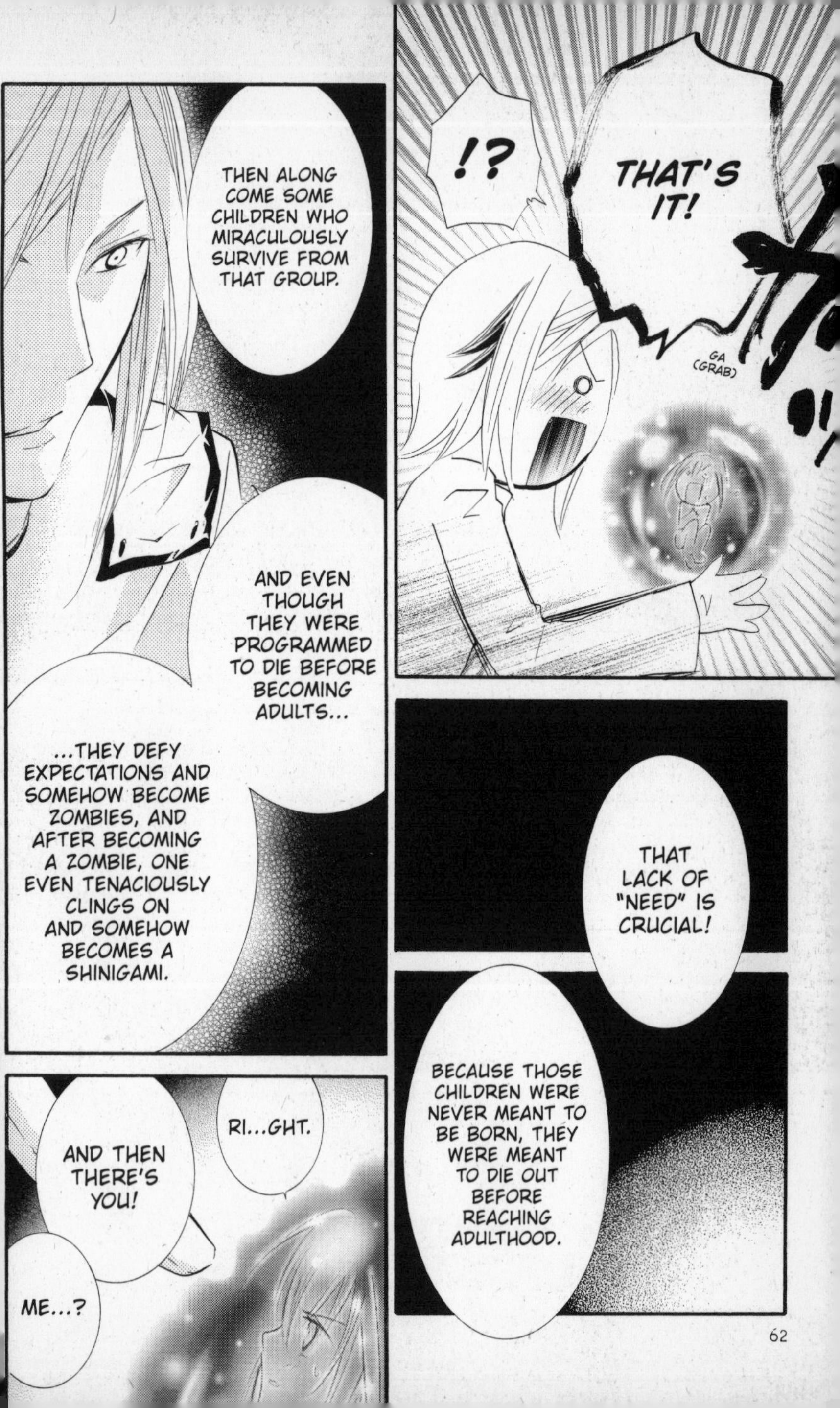
THAT'S IT!
!?
GA (GRAB)
THAT LACK OF "NEED" IS CRUCIAL!
BECAUSE THOSE CHILDREN WERE NEVER MEANT TO BE BORN, THEY WERE MEANT TO DIE OUT BEFORE REACHING ADULTHOOD.
THEN ALONG COME SOME CHILDREN WHO MIRACULOUSLY SURVIVE FROM THAT GROUP.
AND EVEN THOUGH THEY WERE PROGRAMMED TO DIE BEFORE BECOMING ADULTS...
...THEY DEFY EXPECTATIONS AND SOMEHOW BECOME ZOMBIES, AND AFTER BECOMING A ZOMBIE, ONE EVEN TENACIOUSLY CLINGS ON AND SOMEHOW BECOMES A SHINIGAMI.
RI...GHT.
AND THEN THERE'S YOU!
ME...?

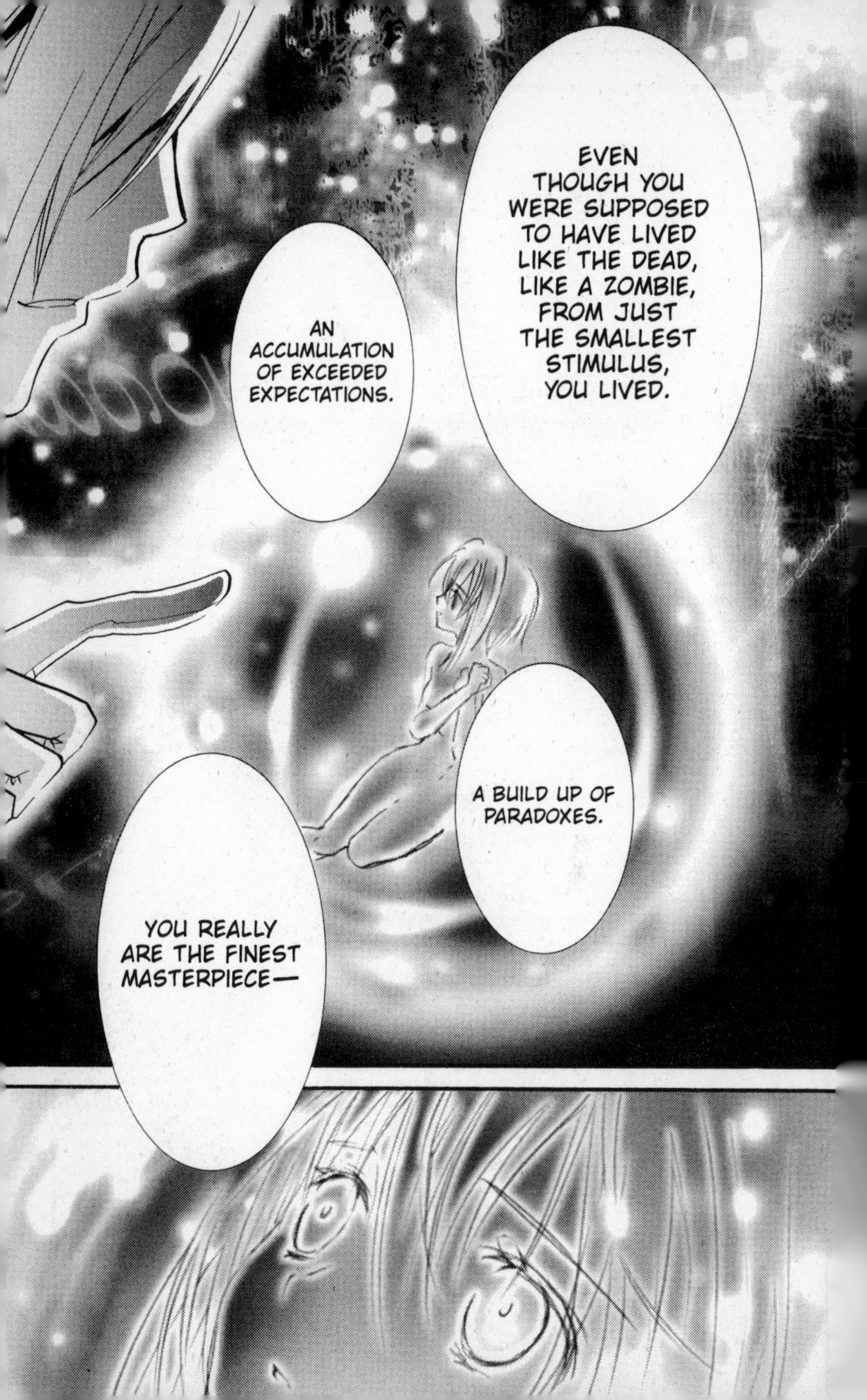
EVEN THOUGH YOU WERE SUPPOSED TO HAVE LIVED LIKE THE DEAD, LIKE A ZOMBIE, FROM JUST THE SMALLEST STIMULUS, YOU LIVED.
AN ACCUMULATION OF EXCEEDED EXPECTATIONS.
A BUILD UP OF PARADOXES.
YOU REALLY ARE THE FINEST MASTERPIECE—

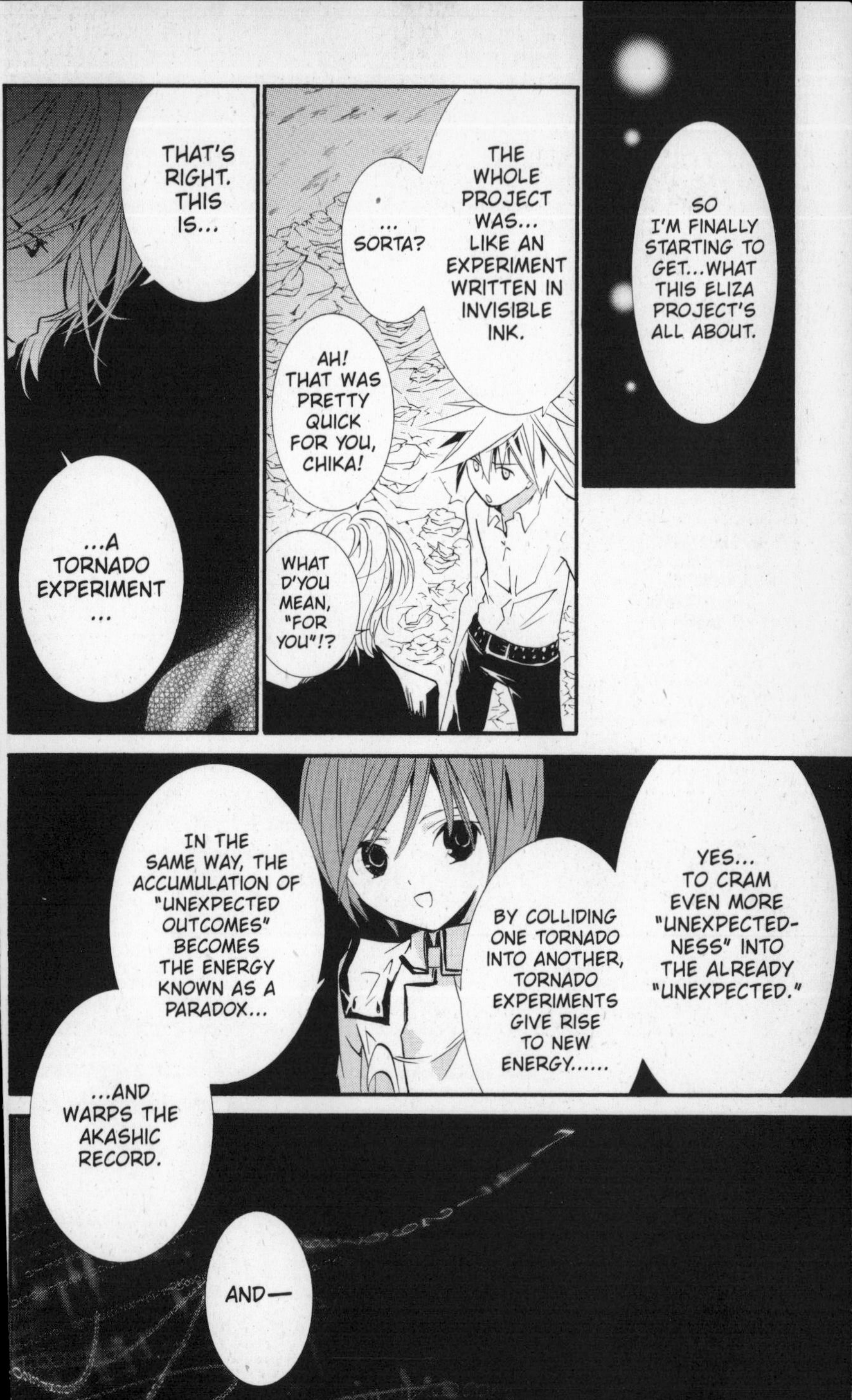
SO I'M FINALLY STARTING TO GET...WHAT THIS ELIZA PROJECT'S ALL ABOUT.
THE WHOLE PROJECT WAS... LIKE AN EXPERIMENT WRITTEN IN INVISIBLE INK.
... SORTA?
AH! THAT WAS PRETTY QUICK FOR YOU, CHIKA!
WHAT D'YOU MEAN, "FOR YOU"!?
THAT'S RIGHT. THIS IS...
...A TORNADO EXPERIMENT ...
YES... TO CRAM EVEN MORE "UNEXPECTED-NESS" INTO THE ALREADY "UNEXPECTED."
BY COLLIDING ONE TORNADO INTO ANOTHER, TORNADO EXPERIMENTS GIVE RISE TO NEW ENERGY......
IN THE SAME WAY, THE ACCUMULATION OF "UNEXPECTED OUTCOMES" BECOMES THE ENERGY KNOWN AS A PARADOX...
...AND WARPS THE AKASHIC RECORD.
AND—

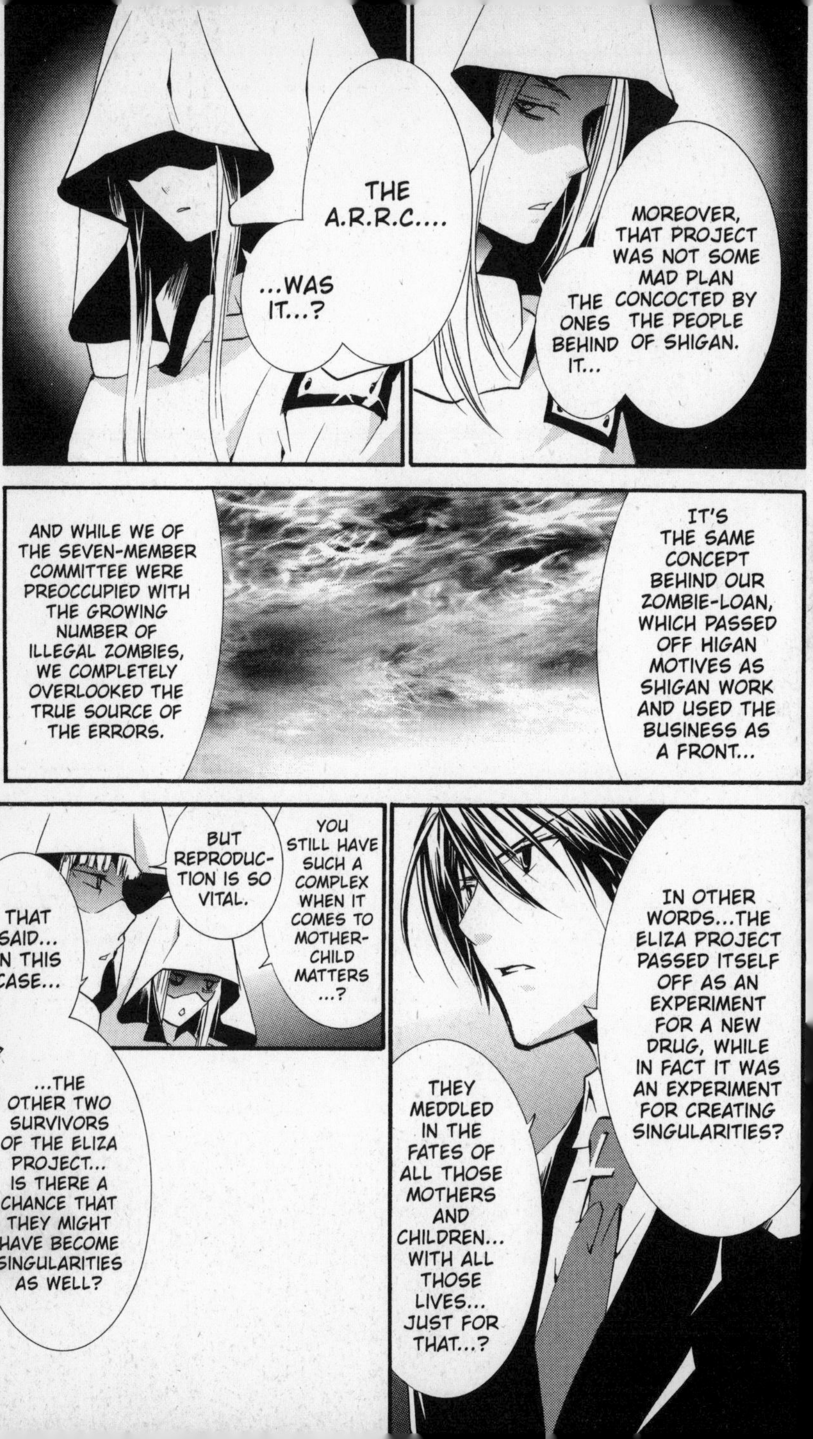
MOREOVER, THAT PROJECT WAS NOT SOME MAD PLAN CONCOCTED BY THE PEOPLE OF SHIGAN.
THE ONES BEHIND IT...
THE A.R.R.C....
...WAS IT...?
IT'S THE SAME CONCEPT BEHIND OUR ZOMBIE-LOAN, WHICH PASSED OFF HIGAN MOTIVES AS SHIGAN WORK AND USED THE BUSINESS AS A FRONT...
AND WHILE WE OF THE SEVEN-MEMBER COMMITTEE WERE PREOCCUPIED WITH THE GROWING NUMBER OF ILLEGAL ZOMBIES, WE COMPLETELY OVERLOOKED THE TRUE SOURCE OF THE ERRORS.
IN OTHER WORDS...THE ELIZA PROJECT PASSED ITSELF OFF AS AN EXPERIMENT FOR A NEW DRUG, WHILE IN FACT IT WAS AN EXPERIMENT FOR CREATING SINGULARITIES?
THEY MEDDLED IN THE FATES OF ALL THOSE MOTHERS AND CHILDREN... WITH ALL THOSE LIVES... JUST FOR THAT...?
YOU STILL HAVE SUCH A COMPLEX WHEN IT COMES TO MOTHER-CHILD MATTERS ...?
BUT REPRODUCTION IS SO VITAL.
THAT SAID... IN THIS CASE...
...THE OTHER TWO SURVIVORS OF THE ELIZA PROJECT... IS THERE A CHANCE THAT THEY MIGHT HAVE BECOME SINGULARITIES AS WELL?

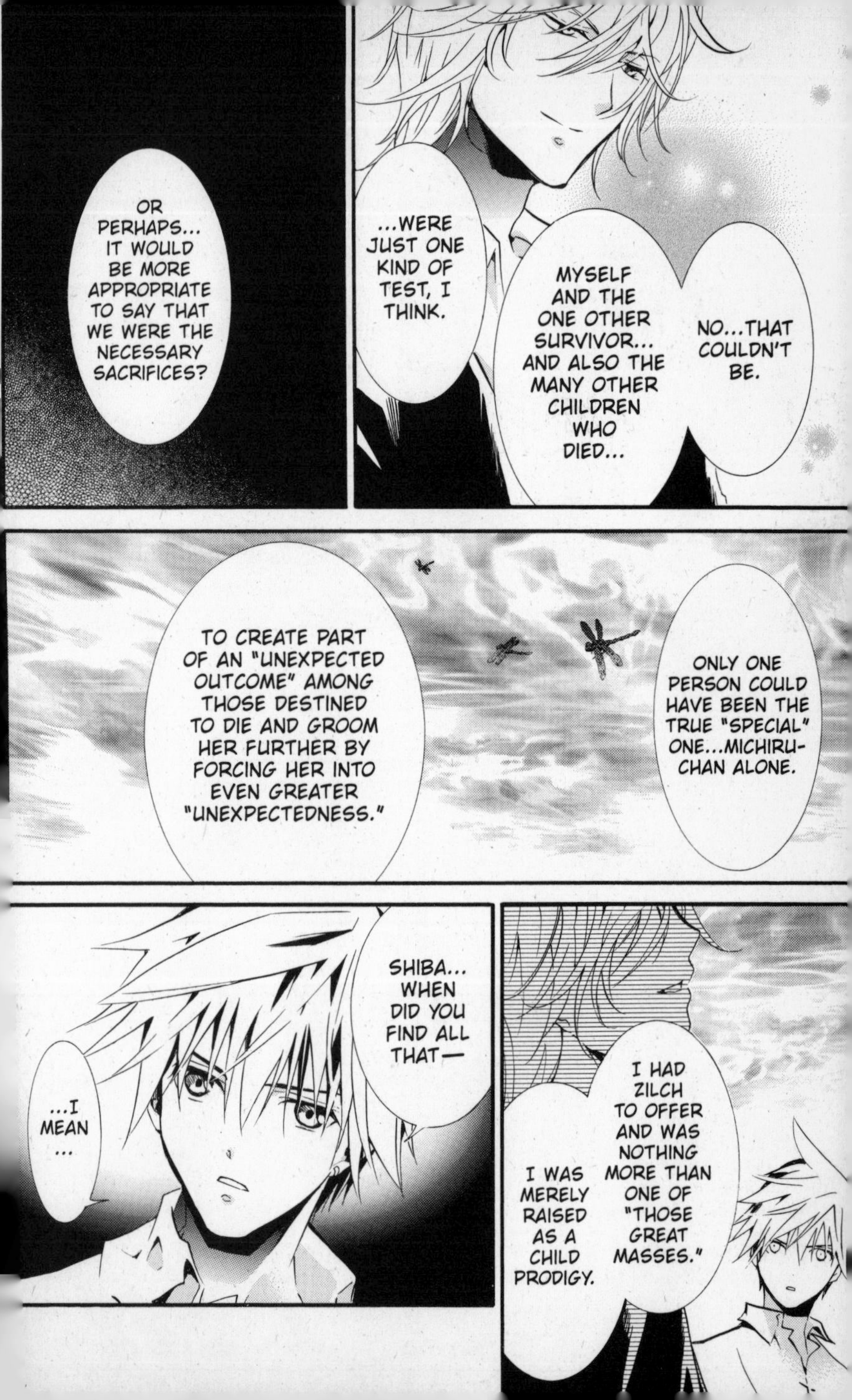
NO...THAT COULDN'T BE.
MYSELF AND THE ONE OTHER SURVIVOR... AND ALSO THE MANY OTHER CHILDREN WHO DIED...
...WERE JUST ONE KIND OF TEST, I THINK.
OR PERHAPS... IT WOULD BE MORE APPROPRIATE TO SAY THAT WE WERE THE NECESSARY SACRIFICES?
ONLY ONE PERSON COULD HAVE BEEN THE TRUE "SPECIAL" ONE...MICHIRU-CHAN ALONE.
TO CREATE PART OF AN "UNEXPECTED OUTCOME" AMONG THOSE DESTINED TO DIE AND GROOM HER FURTHER BY FORCING HER INTO EVEN GREATER "UNEXPECTEDNESS."
I HAD ZILCH TO OFFER AND WAS NOTHING MORE THAN ONE OF "THOSE GREAT MASSES."
I WAS MERELY RAISED AS A CHILD PRODIGY.
SHIBA... WHEN DID YOU FIND ALL THAT—
...I MEAN...

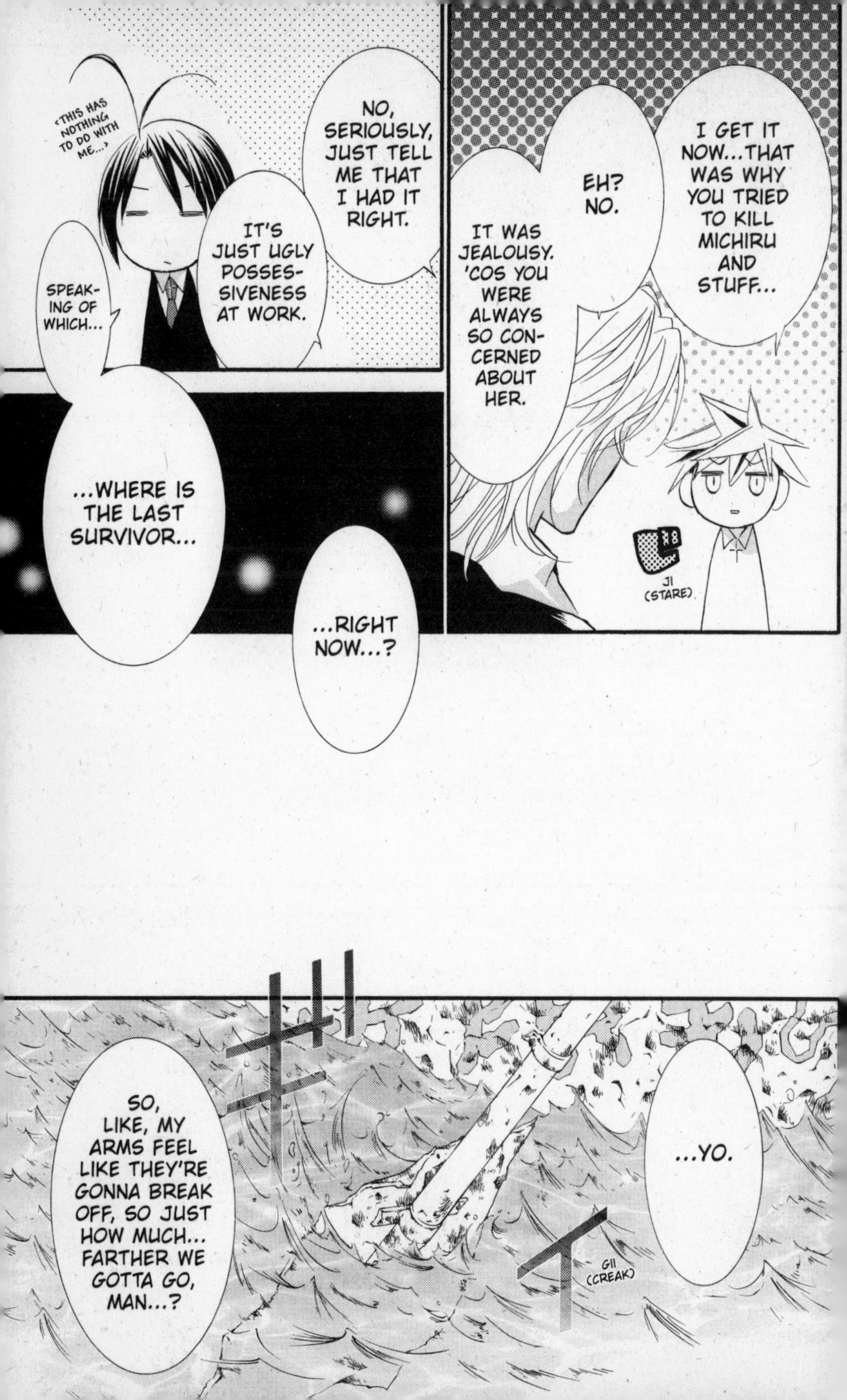
I GET IT NOW...THAT WAS WHY YOU TRIED TO KILL MICHIRU AND STUFF...
EH? NO.
IT WAS JEALOUSY. 'COS YOU WERE ALWAYS SO CONCERNED ABOUT HER.
JI (STARE)
NO, SERIOUSLY, JUST TELL ME THAT I HAD IT RIGHT.
IT'S JUST UGLY POSSESSIVENESS AT WORK.
<THIS HAS NOTHING TO DO WITH ME...>
SPEAKING OF WHICH...
...WHERE IS THE LAST SURVIVOR...
...RIGHT NOW...?
...YO.
GII (CREAK)
SO, LIKE, MY ARMS FEEL LIKE THEY'RE GONNA BREAK OFF, SO JUST HOW MUCH... FARTHER WE GOTTA GO, MAN...?

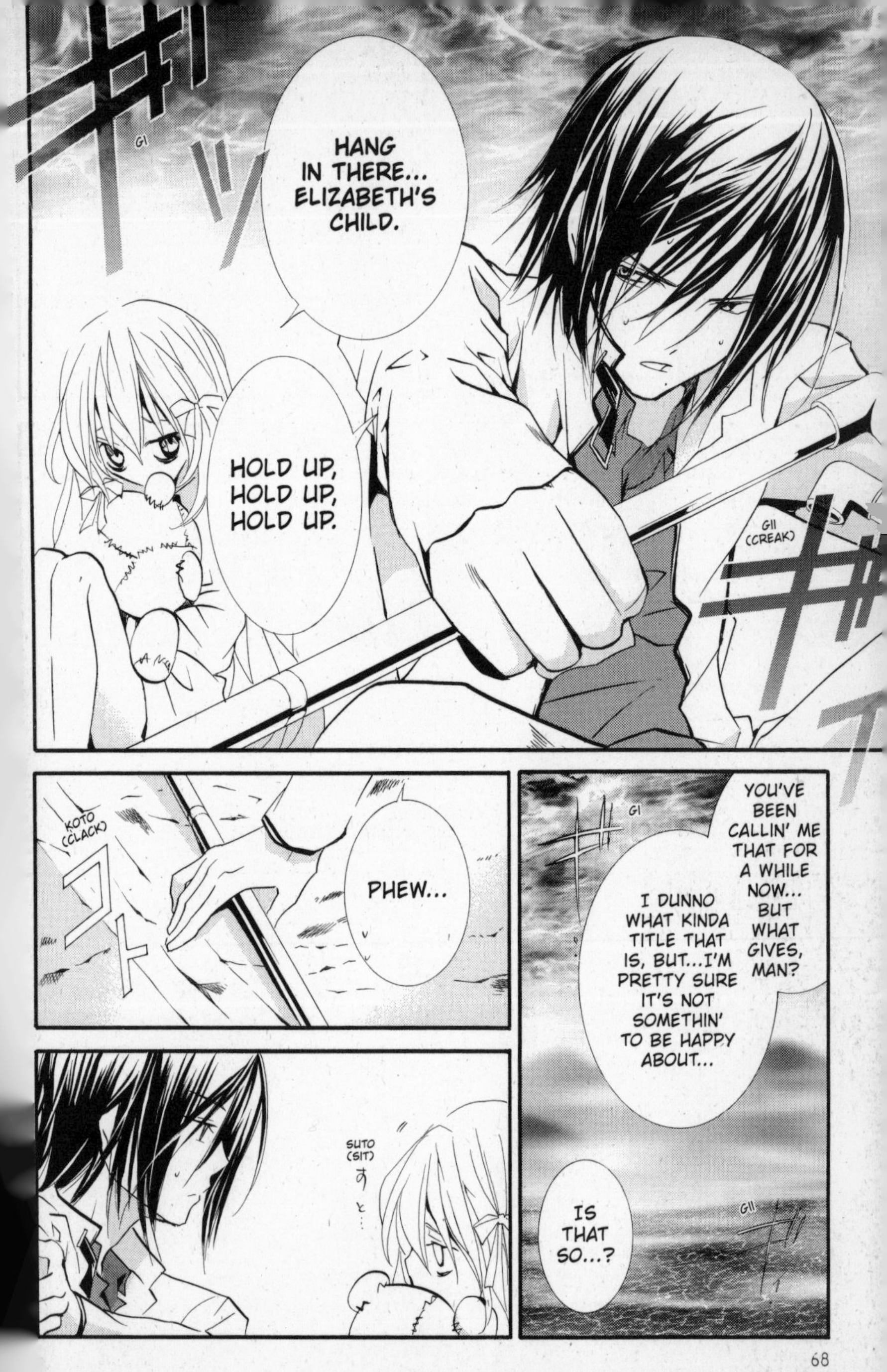
HANG IN THERE... ELIZABETH'S CHILD.
GI
HOLD UP, HOLD UP, HOLD UP.
GII (CREAK)
YOU'VE BEEN CALLIN' ME THAT FOR A WHILE NOW... BUT WHAT GIVES, MAN?
GI
I DUNNO WHAT KINDA TITLE THAT IS, BUT...I'M PRETTY SURE IT'S NOT SOMETHIN' TO BE HAPPY ABOUT...
IS THAT SO...?
GII
PHEW...
KOTO (CLACK)
SUTO (SIT)
すと…

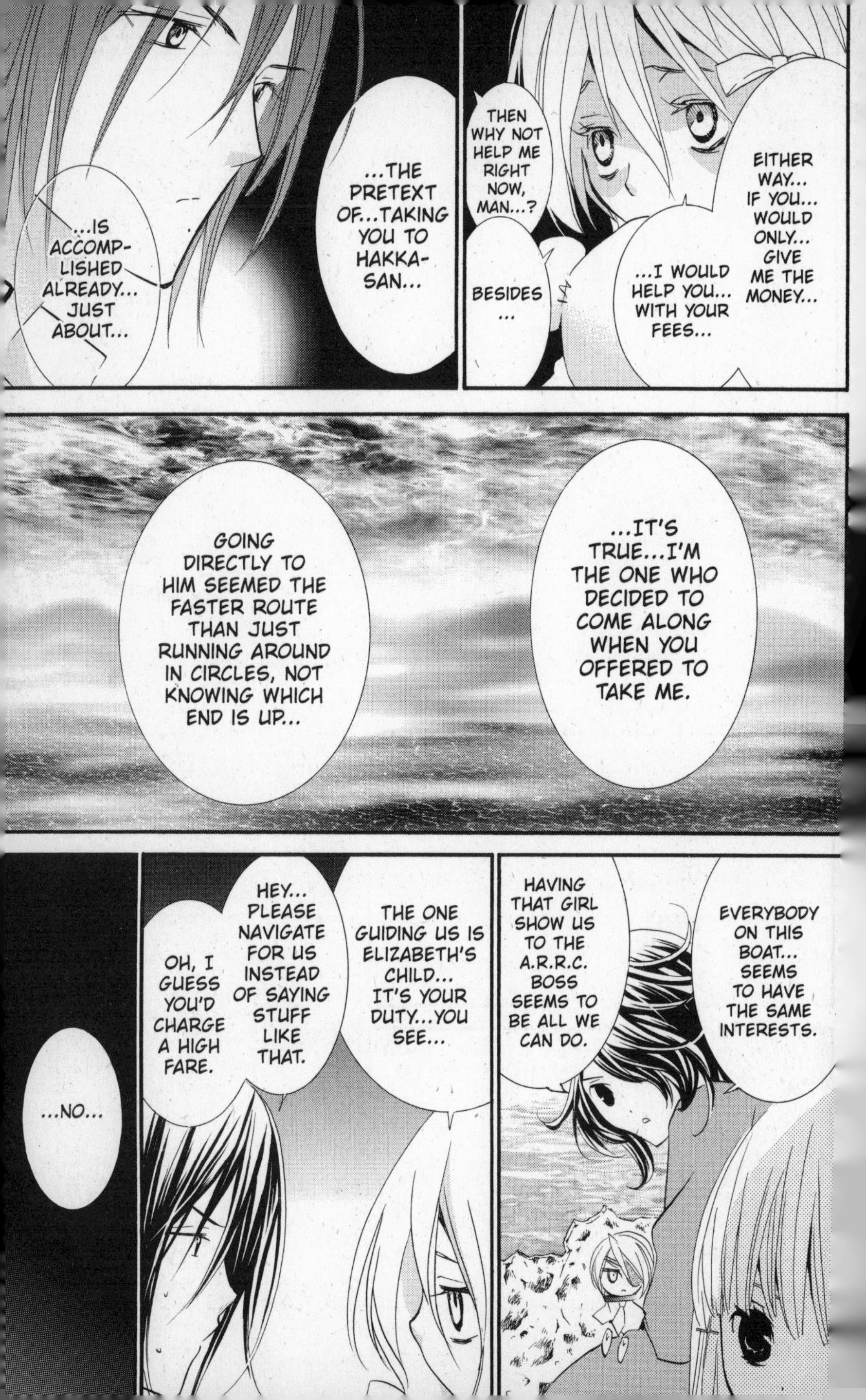
EITHER WAY... IF YOU... WOULD ONLY... GIVE ME THE MONEY...
...I WOULD HELP YOU... WITH YOUR FEES...
THEN WHY NOT HELP ME RIGHT NOW, MAN...?
BESIDES ...
...THE PRETEXT OF...TAKING YOU TO HAKKA-SAN...
...IS ACCOMP-LISHED ALREADY... JUST ABOUT...
...IT'S TRUE...I'M THE ONE WHO DECIDED TO COME ALONG WHEN YOU OFFERED TO TAKE ME.
GOING DIRECTLY TO HIM SEEMED THE FASTER ROUTE THAN JUST RUNNING AROUND IN CIRCLES, NOT KNOWING WHICH END IS UP...
EVERYBODY ON THIS BOAT... SEEMS TO HAVE THE SAME INTERESTS.
HAVING THAT GIRL SHOW US TO THE A.R.R.C. BOSS SEEMS TO BE ALL WE CAN DO.
THE ONE GUIDING US IS ELIZABETH'S CHILD... IT'S YOUR DUTY...YOU SEE...
HEY... PLEASE NAVIGATE FOR US INSTEAD OF SAYING STUFF LIKE THAT.
OH, I GUESS YOU'D CHARGE A HIGH FARE.
...NO...

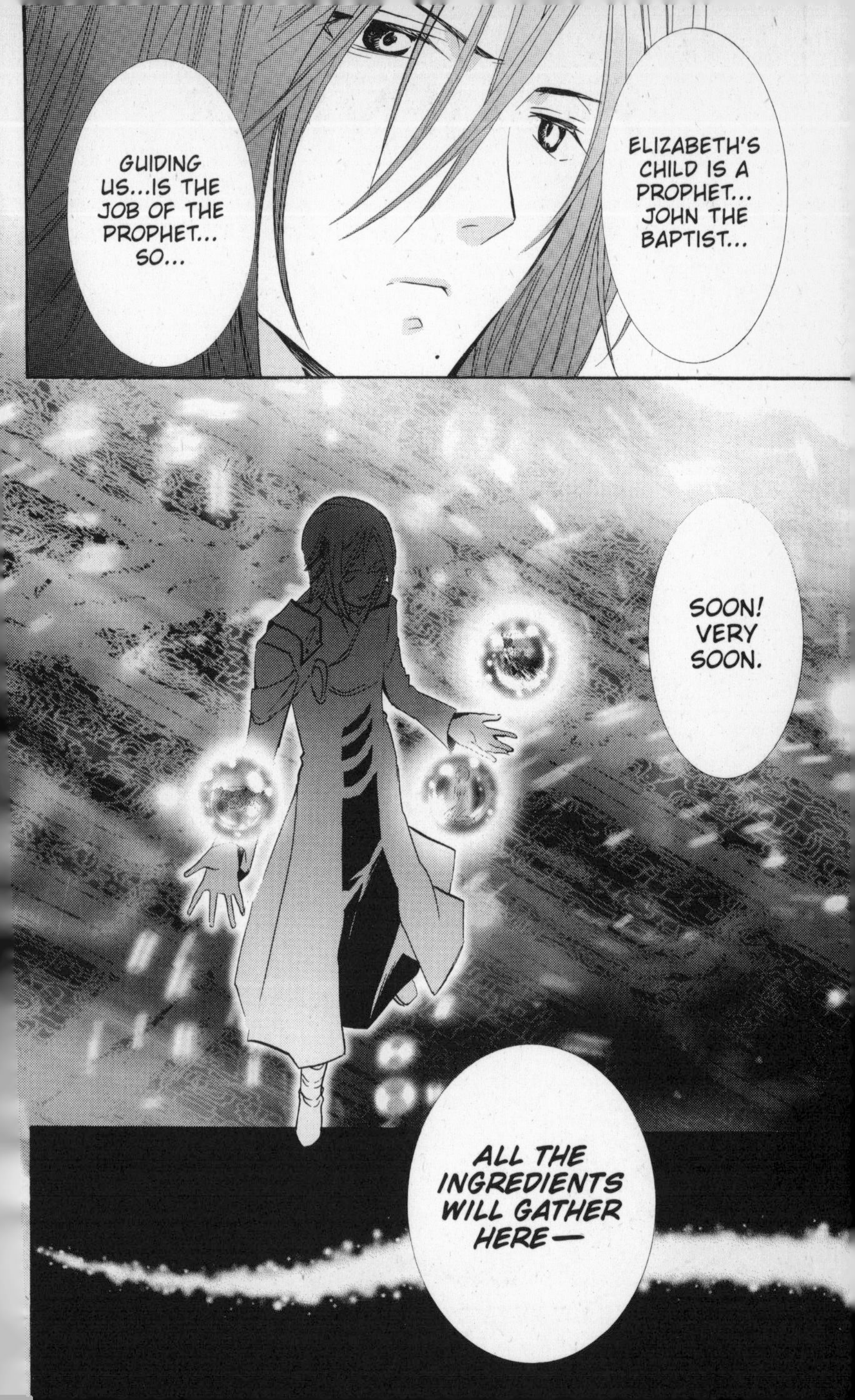
ELIZABETH'S CHILD IS A PROPHET... JOHN THE BAPTIST...
GUIDING US...IS THE JOB OF THE PROPHET... SO...
SOON! VERY SOON.
ALL THE INGREDIENTS WILL GATHER HERE—

PAYMENT:78

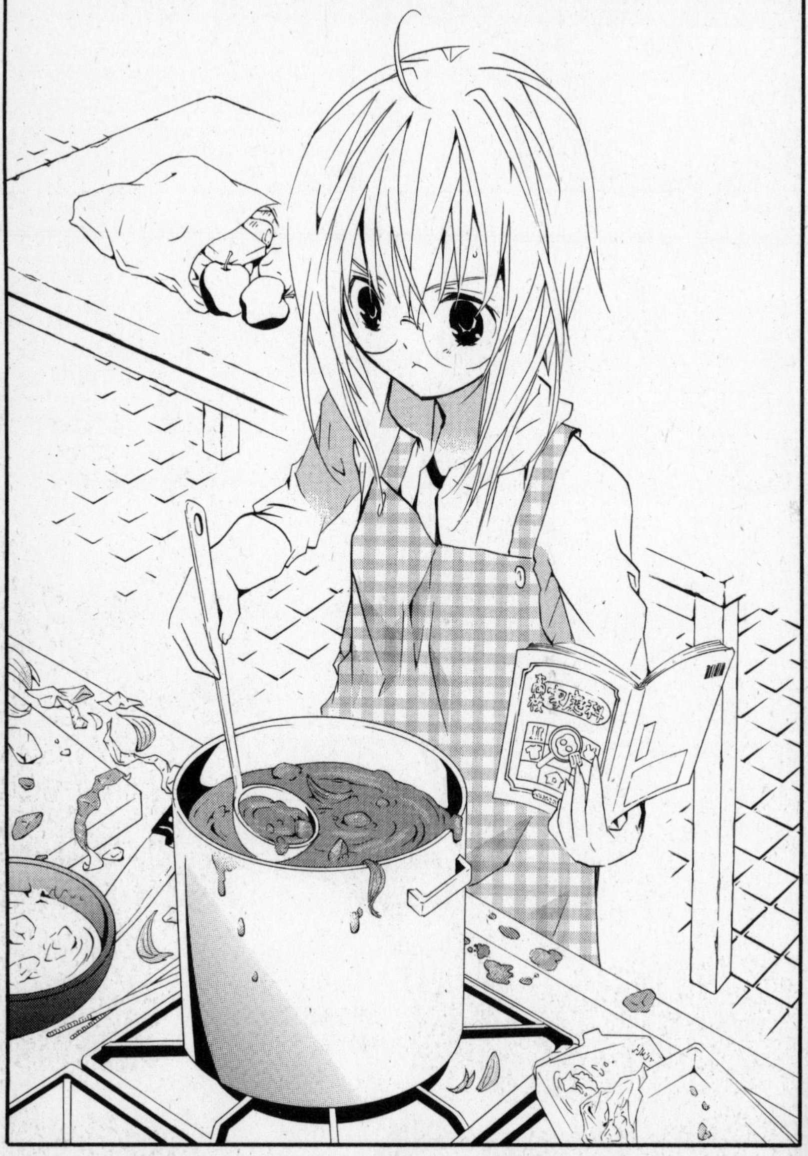

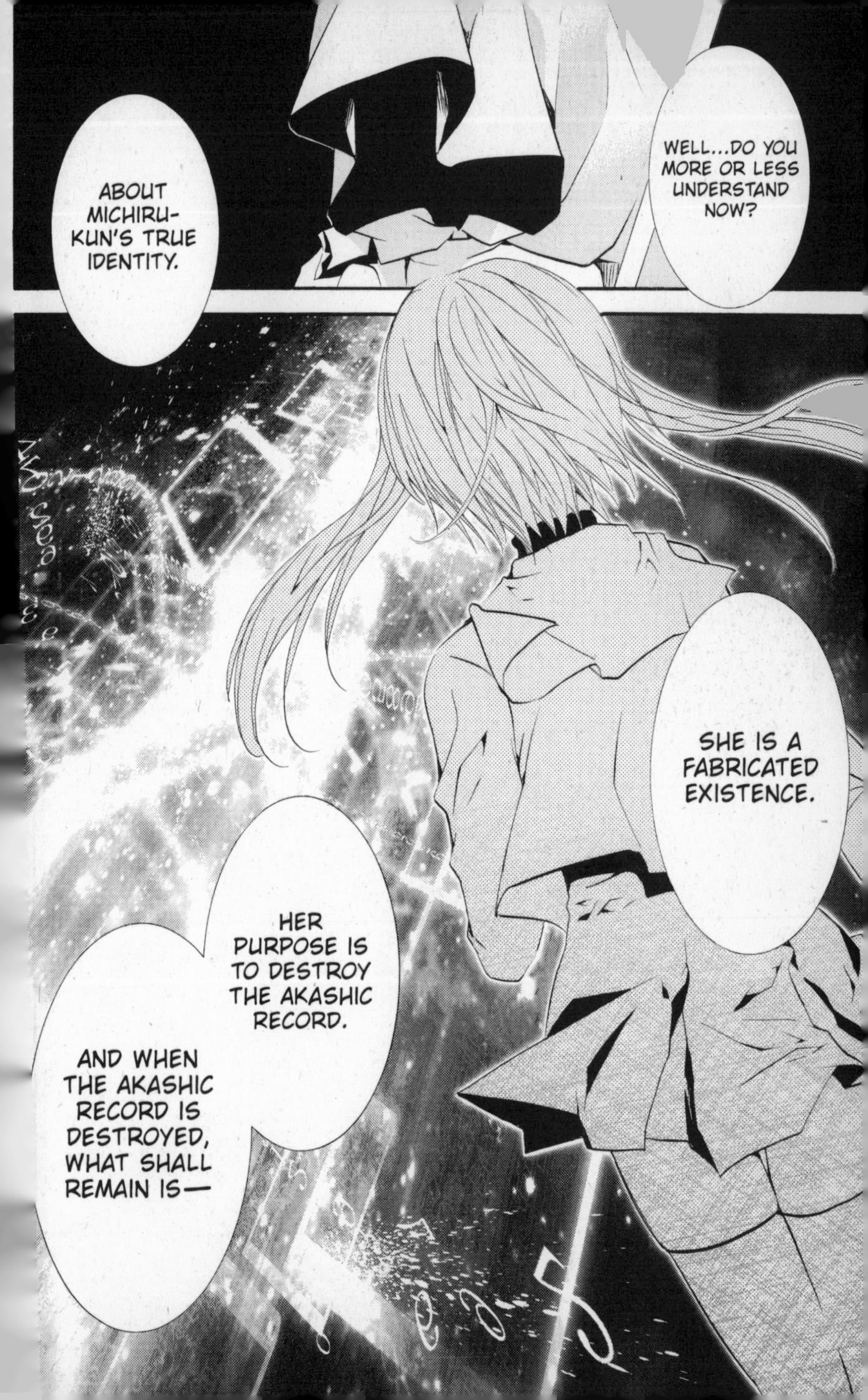
WELL...DO YOU MORE OR LESS UNDERSTAND NOW?
ABOUT MICHIRU-KUN'S TRUE IDENTITY.
SHE IS A FABRICATED EXISTENCE.
HER PURPOSE IS TO DESTROY THE AKASHIC RECORD.
AND WHEN THE AKASHIC RECORD IS DESTROYED, WHAT SHALL REMAIN IS—

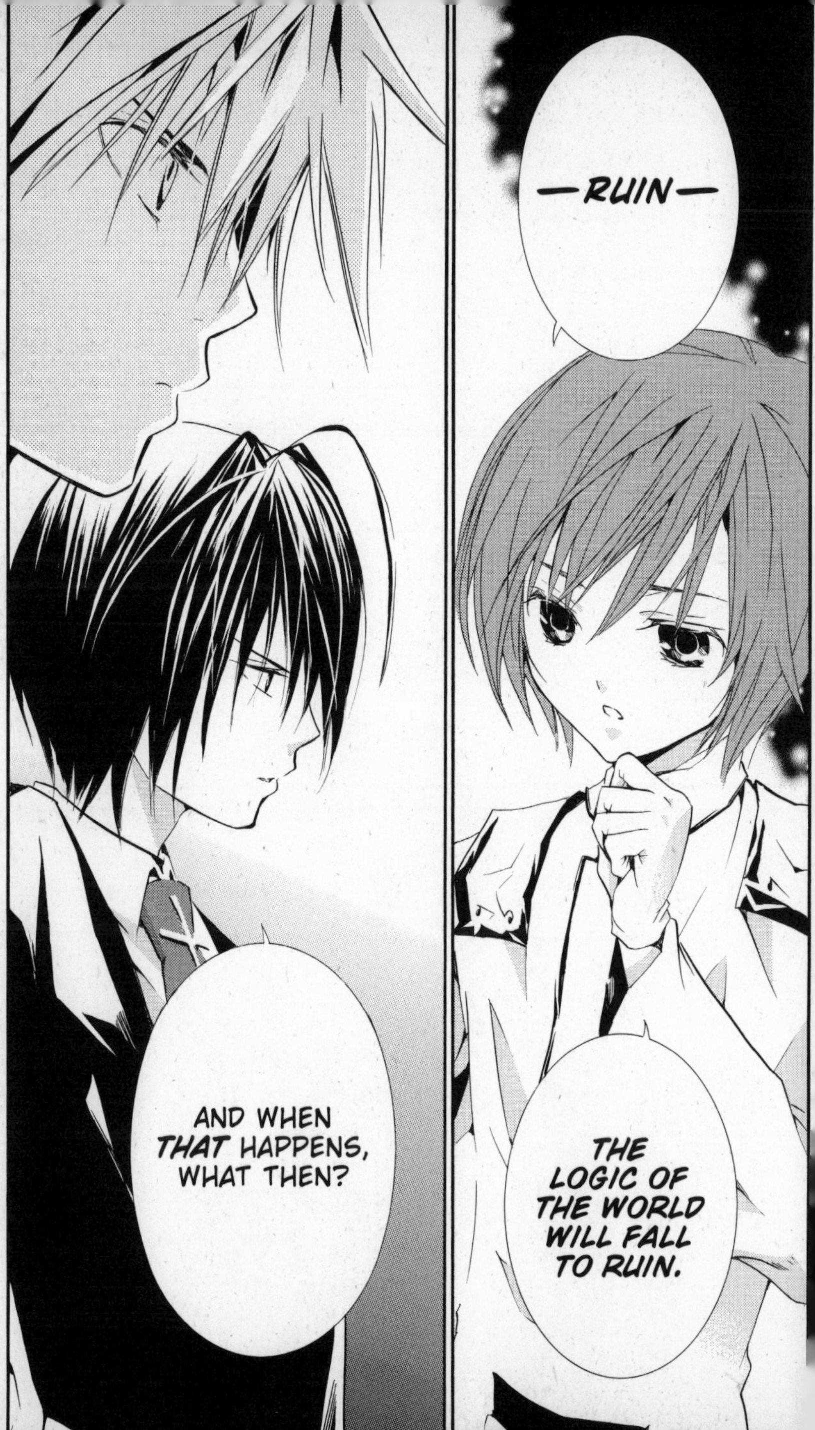
—RUIN—
THE LOGIC OF THE WORLD WILL FALL TO RUIN.
AND WHEN *THAT* HAPPENS, WHAT THEN?

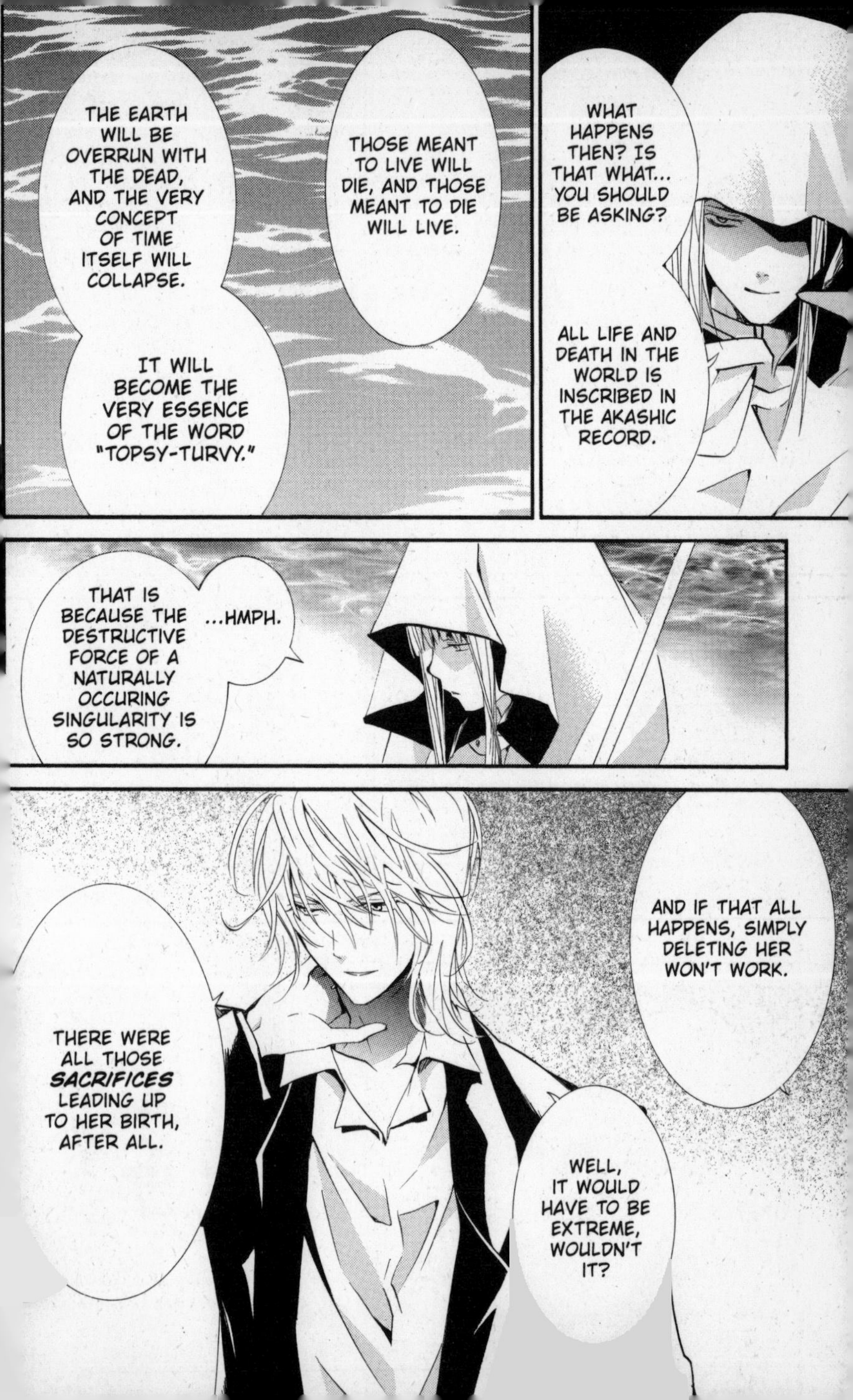
WHAT HAPPENS THEN? IS THAT WHAT... YOU SHOULD BE ASKING?
ALL LIFE AND DEATH IN THE WORLD IS INSCRIBED IN THE AKASHIC RECORD.
THOSE MEANT TO LIVE WILL DIE, AND THOSE MEANT TO DIE WILL LIVE.
THE EARTH WILL BE OVERRUN WITH THE DEAD, AND THE VERY CONCEPT OF TIME ITSELF WILL COLLAPSE.
IT WILL BECOME THE VERY ESSENCE OF THE WORD "TOPSY-TURVY."
...HMPH.
THAT IS BECAUSE THE DESTRUCTIVE FORCE OF A NATURALLY OCCURING SINGULARITY IS SO STRONG.
AND IF THAT ALL HAPPENS, SIMPLY DELETING HER WON'T WORK.
WELL, IT WOULD HAVE TO BE EXTREME, WOULDN'T IT?
THERE WERE ALL THOSE ***SACRIFICES*** LEADING UP TO HER BIRTH, AFTER ALL.

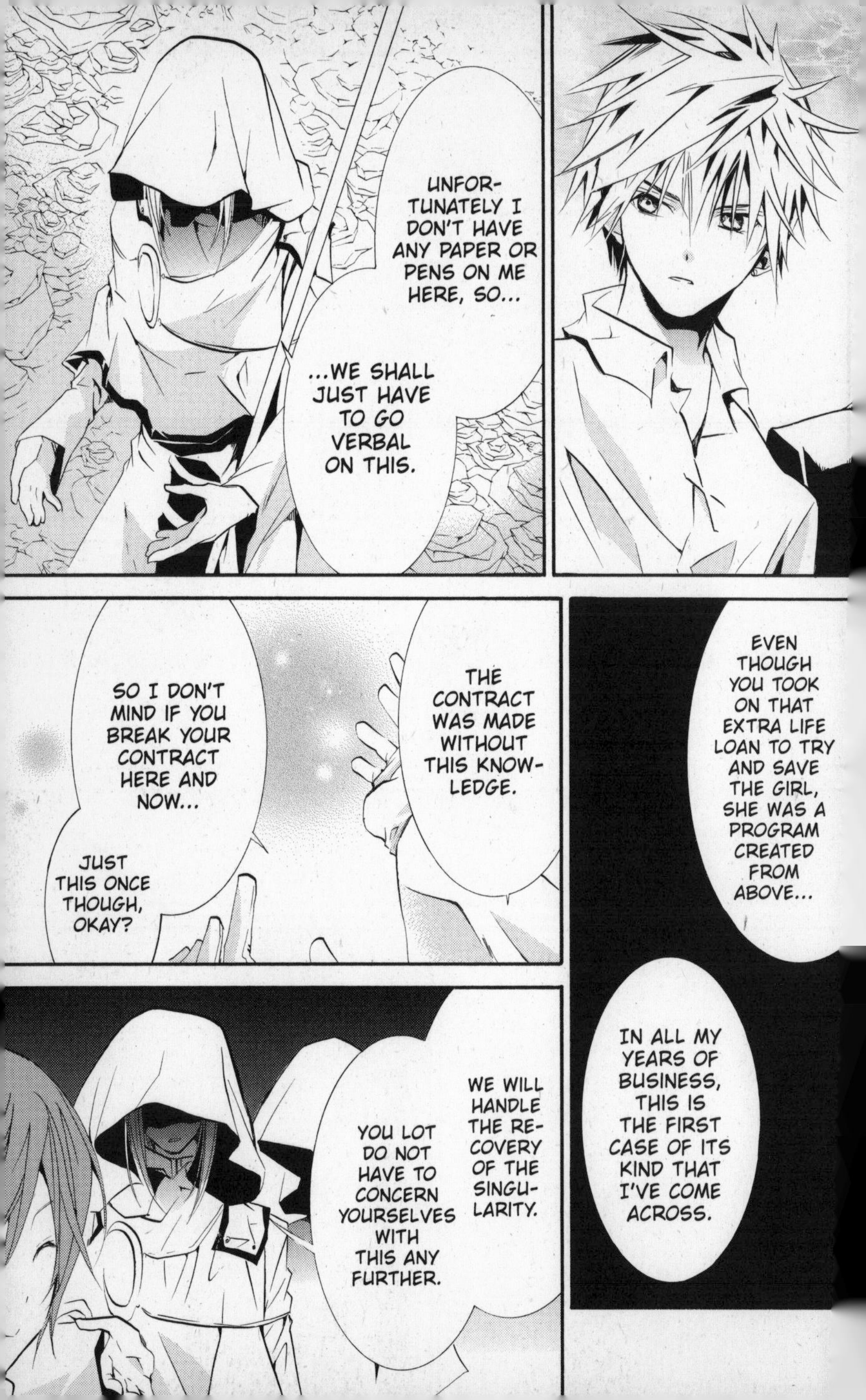
UNFOR-TUNATELY I DON'T HAVE ANY PAPER OR PENS ON ME HERE, SO...
...WE SHALL JUST HAVE TO GO VERBAL ON THIS.
EVEN THOUGH YOU TOOK ON THAT EXTRA LIFE LOAN TO TRY AND SAVE THE GIRL, SHE WAS A PROGRAM CREATED FROM ABOVE...
IN ALL MY YEARS OF BUSINESS, THIS IS THE FIRST CASE OF ITS KIND THAT I'VE COME ACROSS.
THE CONTRACT WAS MADE WITHOUT THIS KNOW-LEDGE.
SO I DON'T MIND IF YOU BREAK YOUR CONTRACT HERE AND NOW...
JUST THIS ONCE THOUGH, OKAY?
WE WILL HANDLE THE RE-COVERY OF THE SINGU-LARITY.
YOU LOT DO NOT HAVE TO CONCERN YOURSELVES WITH THIS ANY FURTHER.

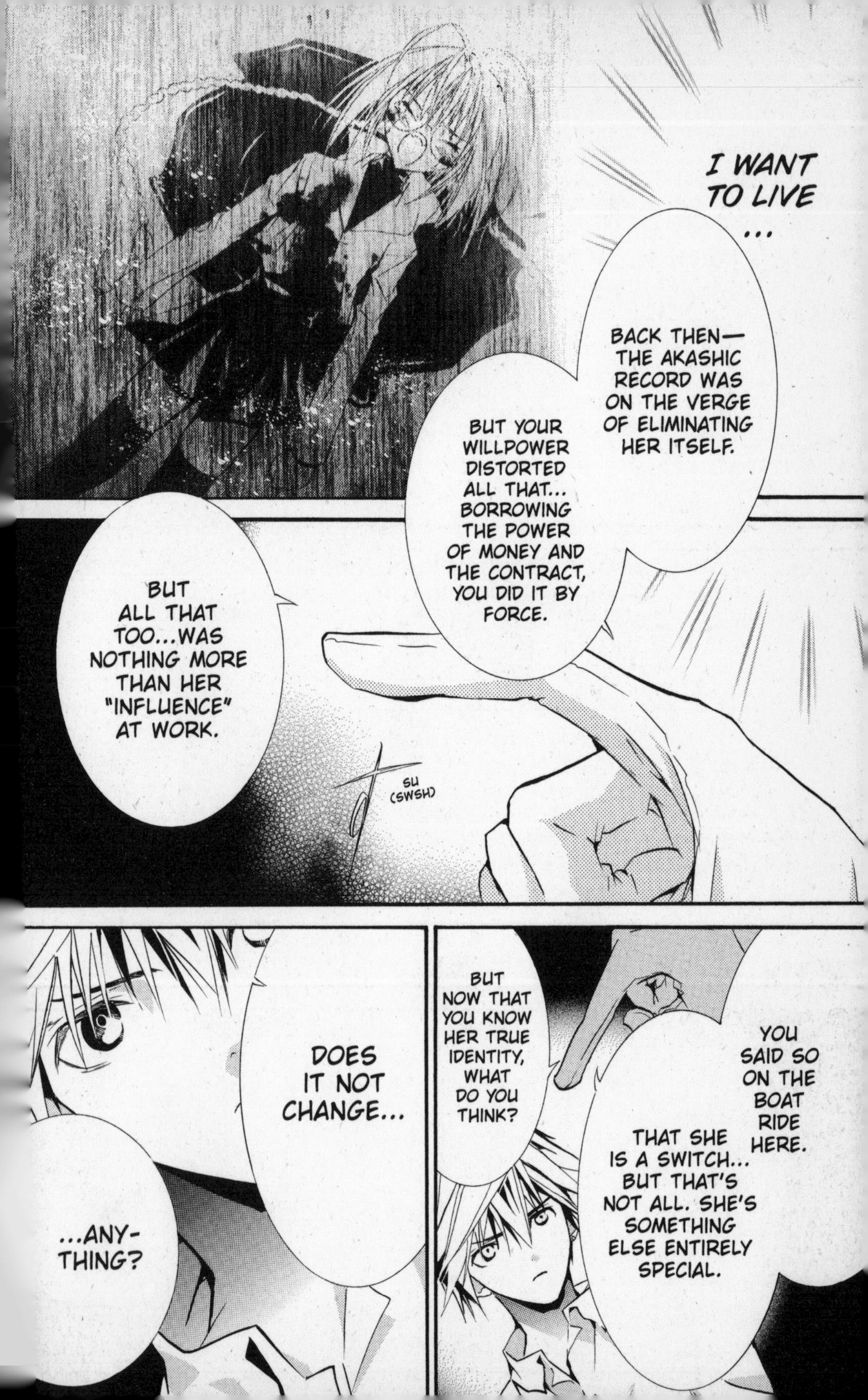
I WANT TO LIVE ...
BACK THEN— THE AKASHIC RECORD WAS ON THE VERGE OF ELIMINATING HER ITSELF.
BUT YOUR WILLPOWER DISTORTED ALL THAT... BORROWING THE POWER OF MONEY AND THE CONTRACT, YOU DID IT BY FORCE.
BUT ALL THAT TOO...WAS NOTHING MORE THAN HER "INFLUENCE" AT WORK.
SU (SWSH)
YOU SAID SO ON THE BOAT RIDE HERE.
THAT SHE IS A SWITCH... BUT THAT'S NOT ALL. SHE'S SOMETHING ELSE ENTIRELY SPECIAL.
BUT NOW THAT YOU KNOW HER TRUE IDENTITY, WHAT DO YOU THINK?
DOES IT NOT CHANGE...
...ANY-THING?

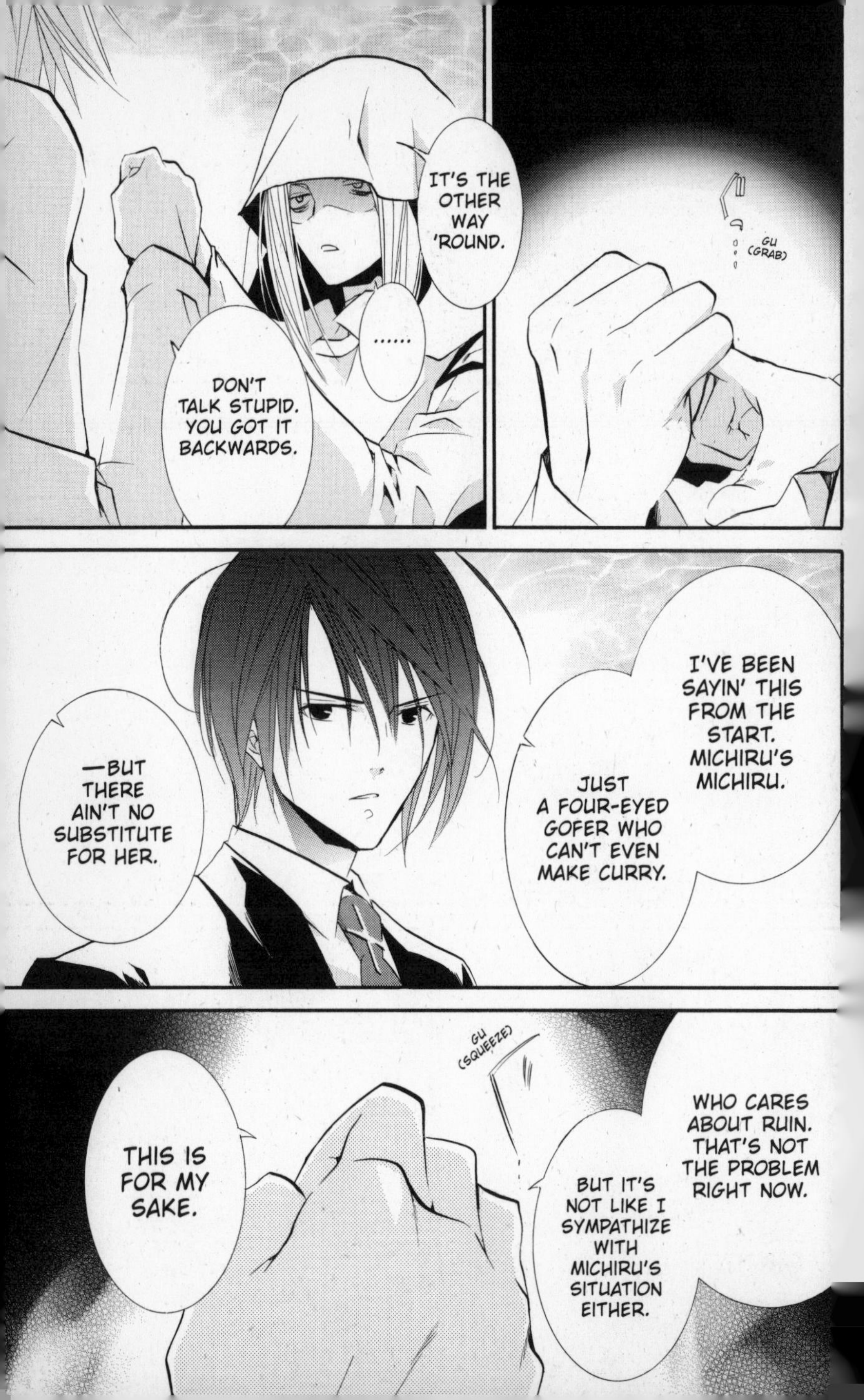
GU (GRAB)
IT'S THE OTHER WAY 'ROUND.
......
DON'T TALK STUPID. YOU GOT IT BACKWARDS.
I'VE BEEN SAYIN' THIS FROM THE START. MICHIRU'S MICHIRU.
JUST A FOUR-EYED GOFER WHO CAN'T EVEN MAKE CURRY.
—BUT THERE AIN'T NO SUBSTITUTE FOR HER.
WHO CARES ABOUT RUIN. THAT'S NOT THE PROBLEM RIGHT NOW.
BUT IT'S NOT LIKE I SYMPATHIZE WITH MICHIRU'S SITUATION EITHER.
GU (SQUEEZE)
THIS IS FOR MY SAKE.

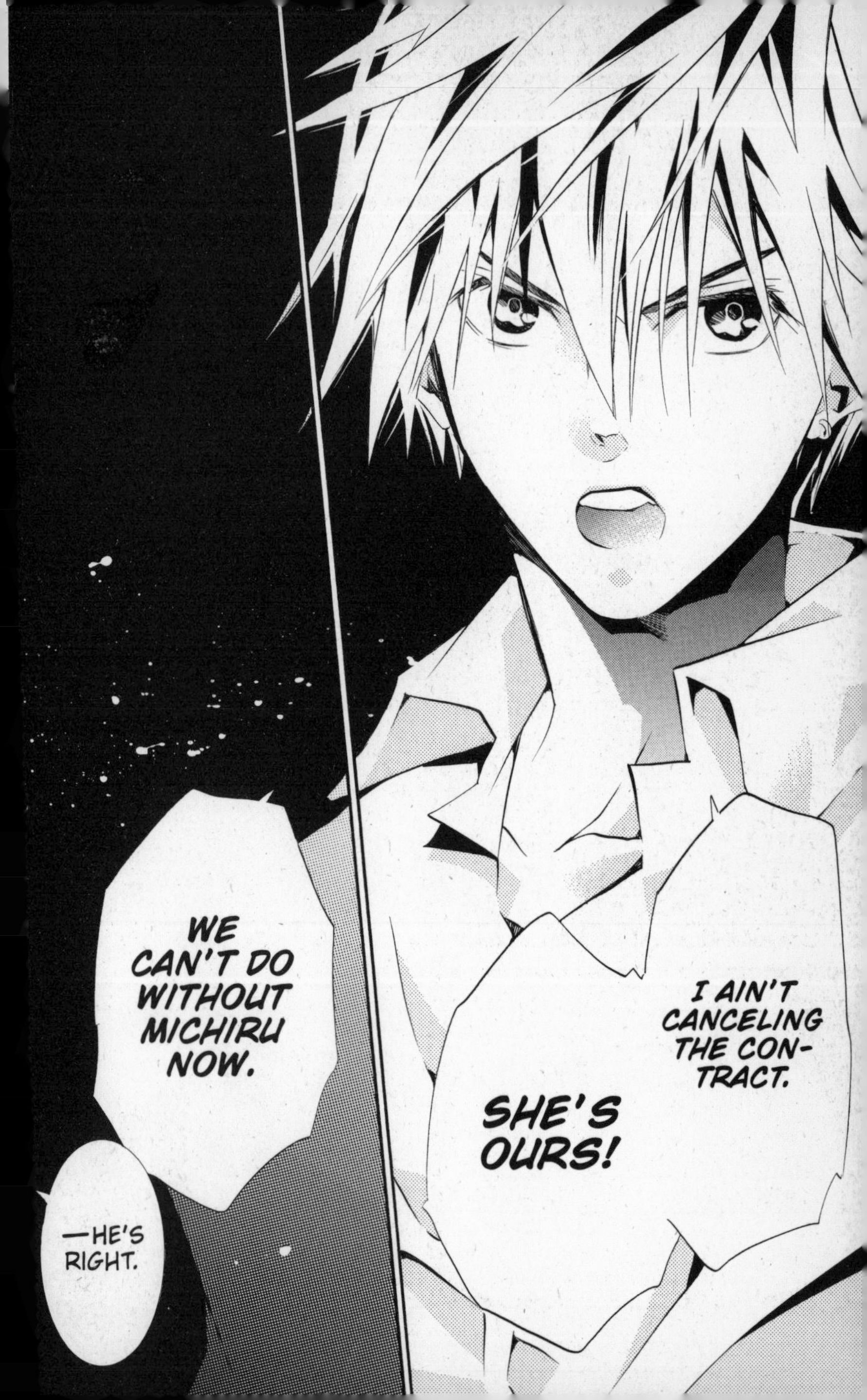
I AIN'T CANCELING THE CONTRACT.
SHE'S OURS!
WE CAN'T DO WITHOUT MICHIRU NOW.
—HE'S RIGHT.

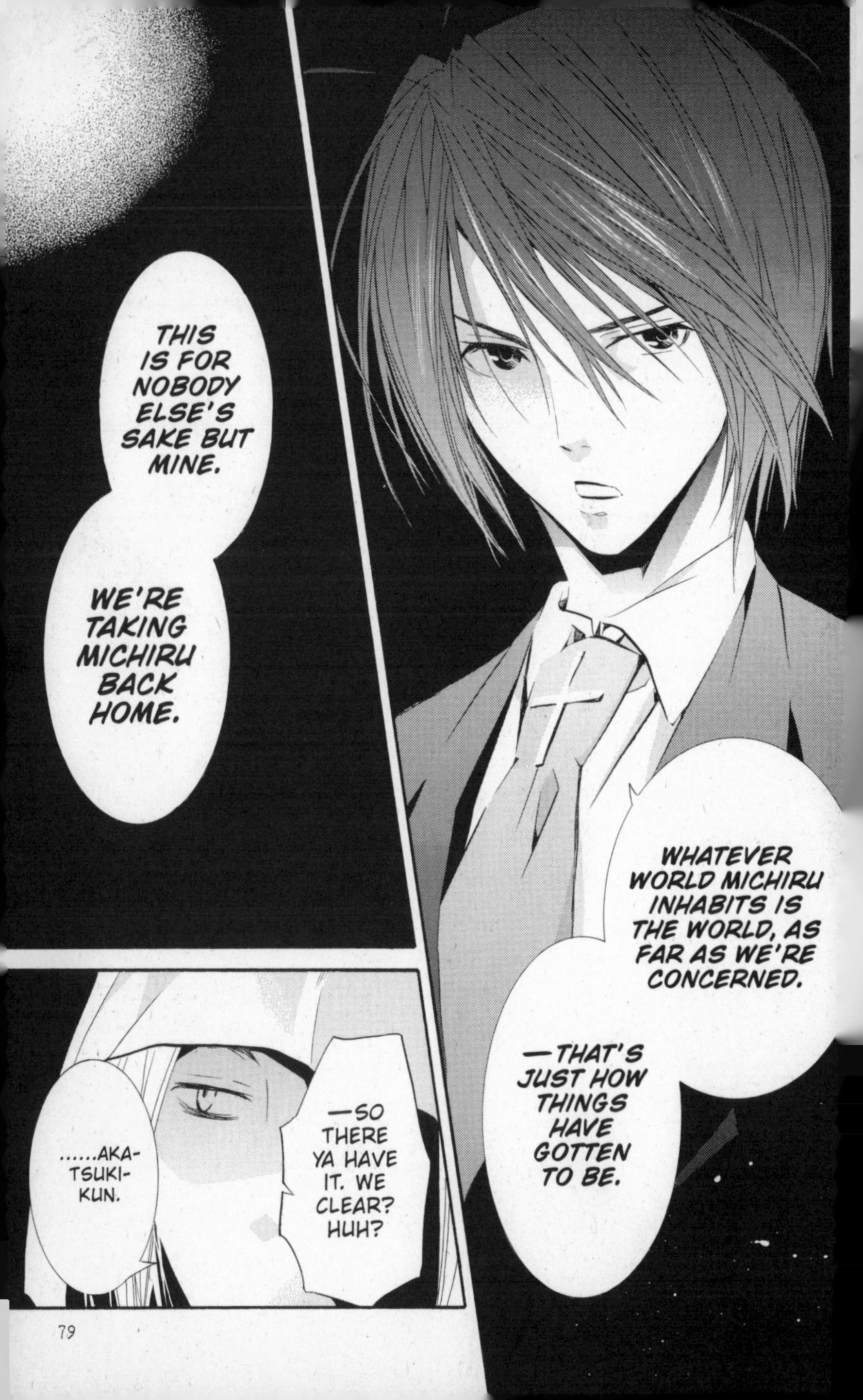
WHATEVER WORLD MICHIRU INHABITS IS THE WORLD, AS FAR AS WE'RE CONCERNED.
—THAT'S JUST HOW THINGS HAVE GOTTEN TO BE.
THIS IS FOR NOBODY ELSE'S SAKE BUT MINE.
WE'RE TAKING MICHIRU BACK HOME.
—SO THERE YA HAVE IT. WE CLEAR? HUH?
......AKA-TSUKI-KUN.

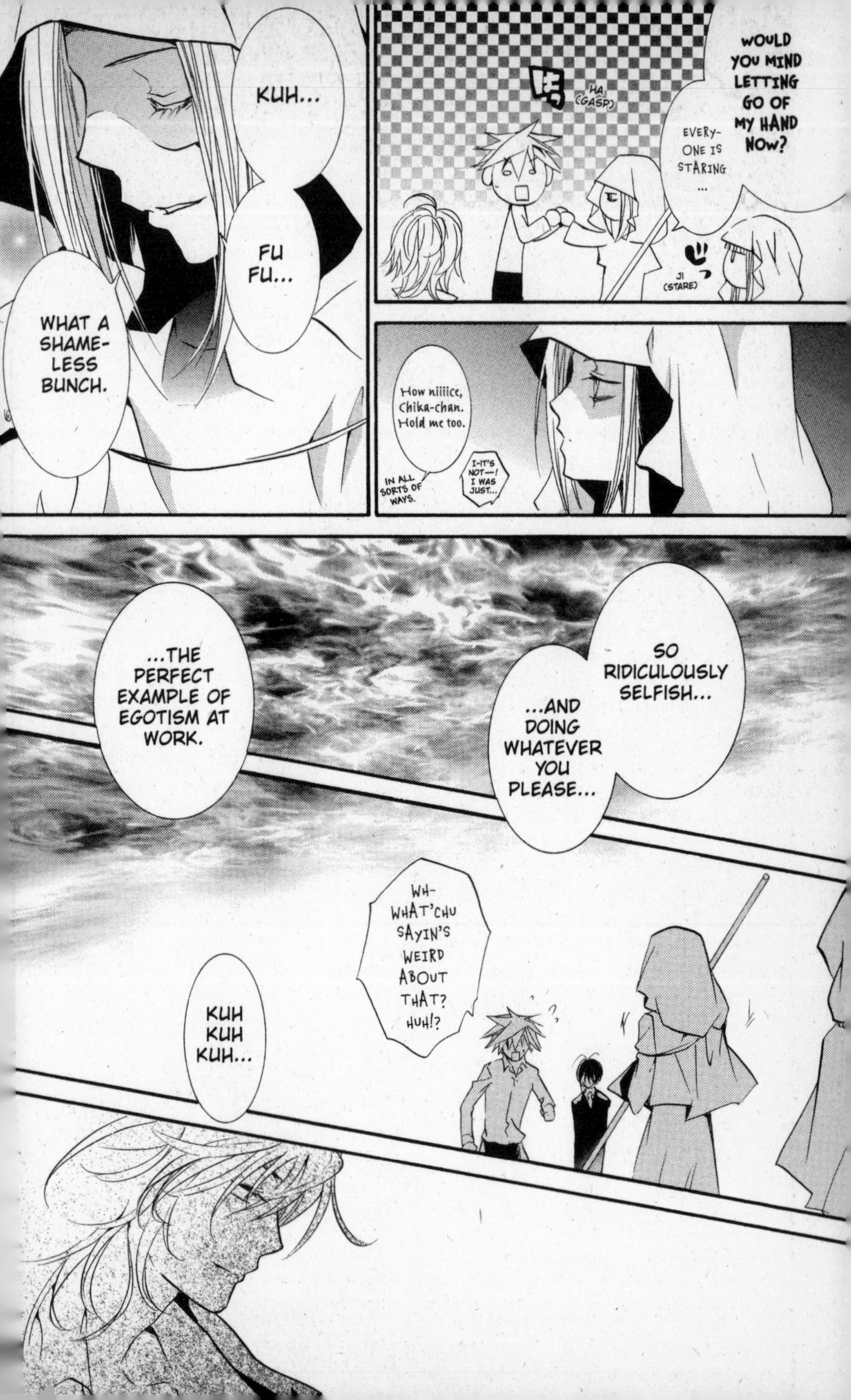

WOULD YOU MIND LETTING GO OF MY HAND NOW?
EVERY-ONE IS STARING...
HA (GASP)
JI (STARE)
How niiiice, Chika-chan. Hold me too.
IN ALL SORTS OF WAYS.
I-IT'S NOT—! I WAS JUST...
KUH...
FU FU...
WHAT A SHAME-LESS BUNCH.
SO RIDICULOUSLY SELFISH...
...AND DOING WHATEVER YOU PLEASE...
...THE PERFECT EXAMPLE OF EGOTISM AT WORK.
WH-WHAT'CHU SAYIN'S WEIRD ABOUT THAT? HUH!?
KUH KUH KUH...

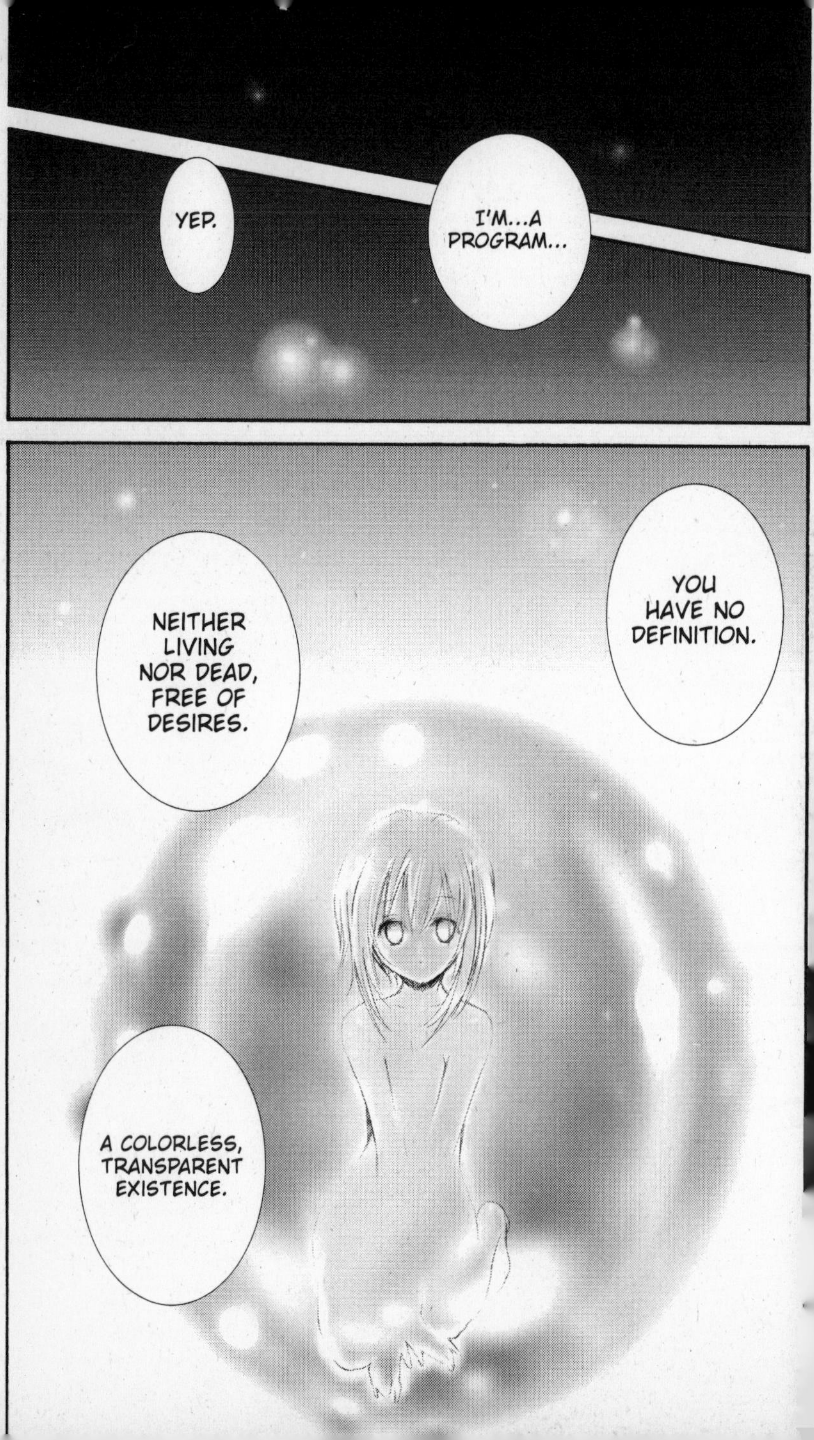
I'M...A PROGRAM...
YEP.
YOU HAVE NO DEFINITION.
NEITHER LIVING NOR DEAD, FREE OF DESIRES.
A COLORLESS, TRANSPARENT EXISTENCE.

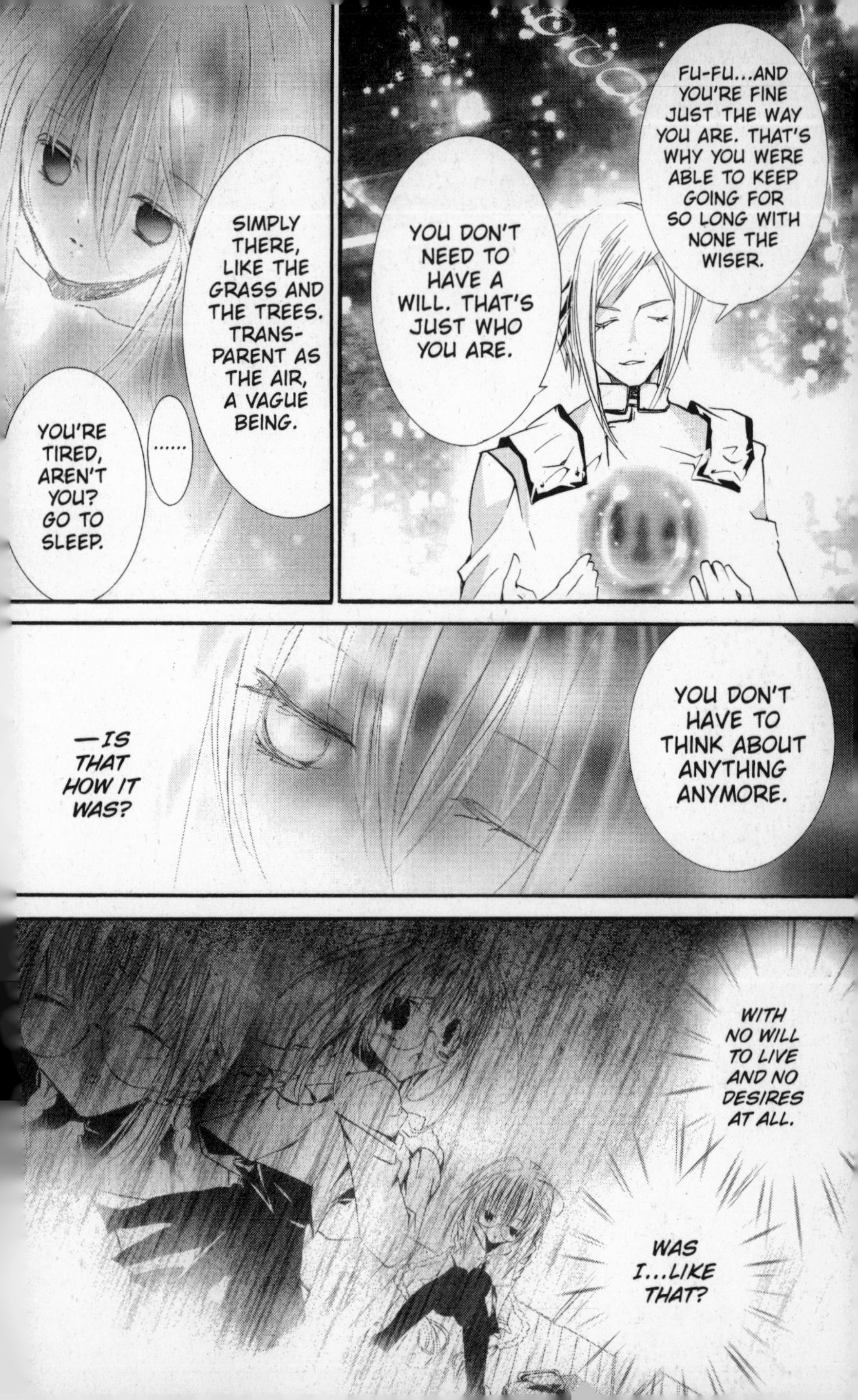
FU-FU...AND YOU'RE FINE JUST THE WAY YOU ARE. THAT'S WHY YOU WERE ABLE TO KEEP GOING FOR SO LONG WITH NONE THE WISER.
YOU DON'T NEED TO HAVE A WILL. THAT'S JUST WHO YOU ARE.
SIMPLY THERE, LIKE THE GRASS AND THE TREES. TRANS-PARENT AS THE AIR, A VAGUE BEING.
......
YOU'RE TIRED, AREN'T YOU? GO TO SLEEP.
YOU DON'T HAVE TO THINK ABOUT ANYTHING ANYMORE.
—IS THAT HOW IT WAS?
WITH NO WILL TO LIVE AND NO DESIRES AT ALL.
WAS I...LIKE THAT?

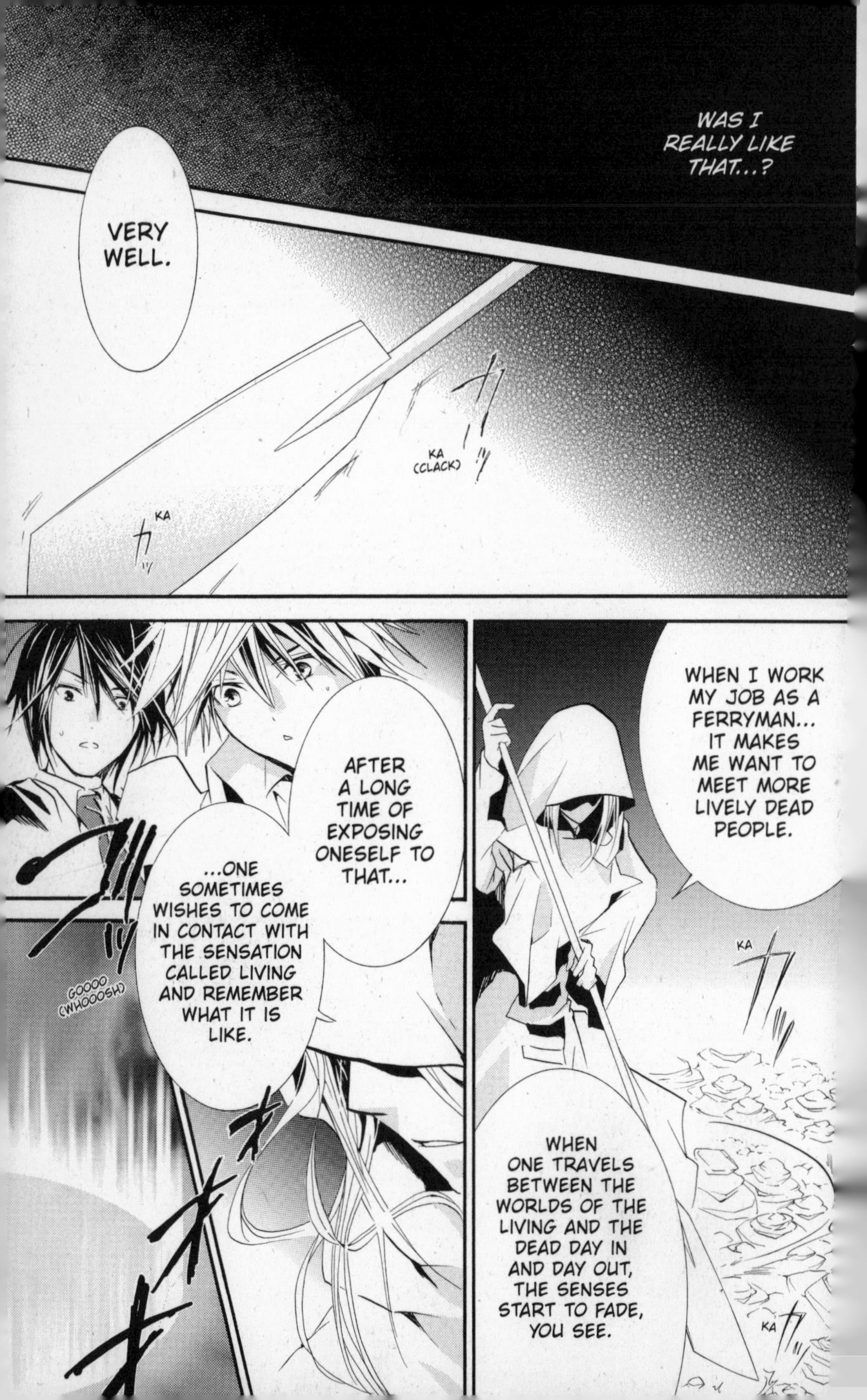
WAS I REALLY LIKE THAT...?
VERY WELL.
KA (CLACK)
KA
WHEN I WORK MY JOB AS A FERRYMAN... IT MAKES ME WANT TO MEET MORE LIVELY DEAD PEOPLE.
KA
WHEN ONE TRAVELS BETWEEN THE WORLDS OF THE LIVING AND THE DEAD DAY IN AND DAY OUT, THE SENSES START TO FADE, YOU SEE.
KA
AFTER A LONG TIME OF EXPOSING ONESELF TO THAT...
...ONE SOMETIMES WISHES TO COME IN CONTACT WITH THE SENSATION CALLED LIVING AND REMEMBER WHAT IT IS LIKE.
GOOOO (WHOOOSH)

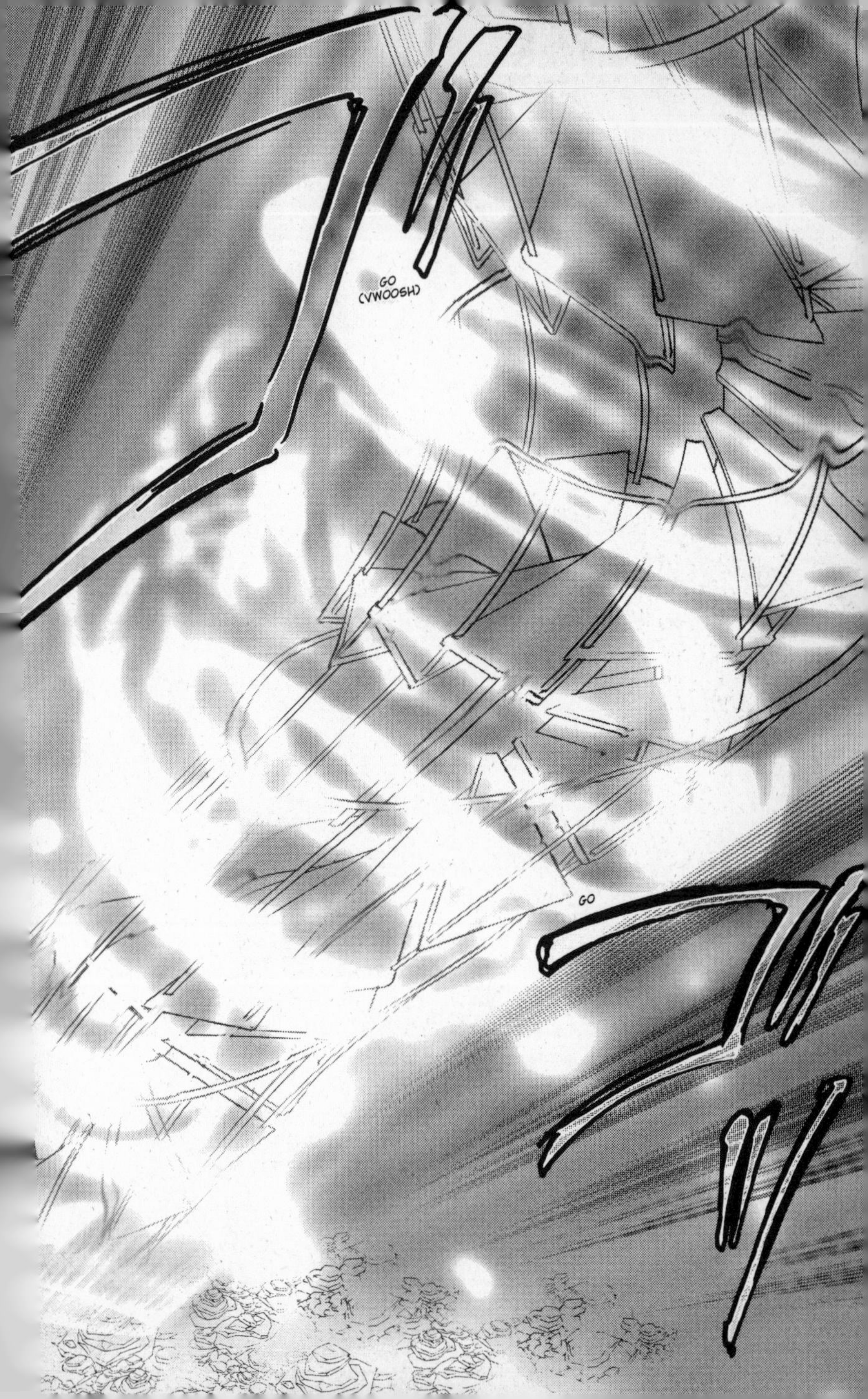
GO
(VWOOSH)
GO

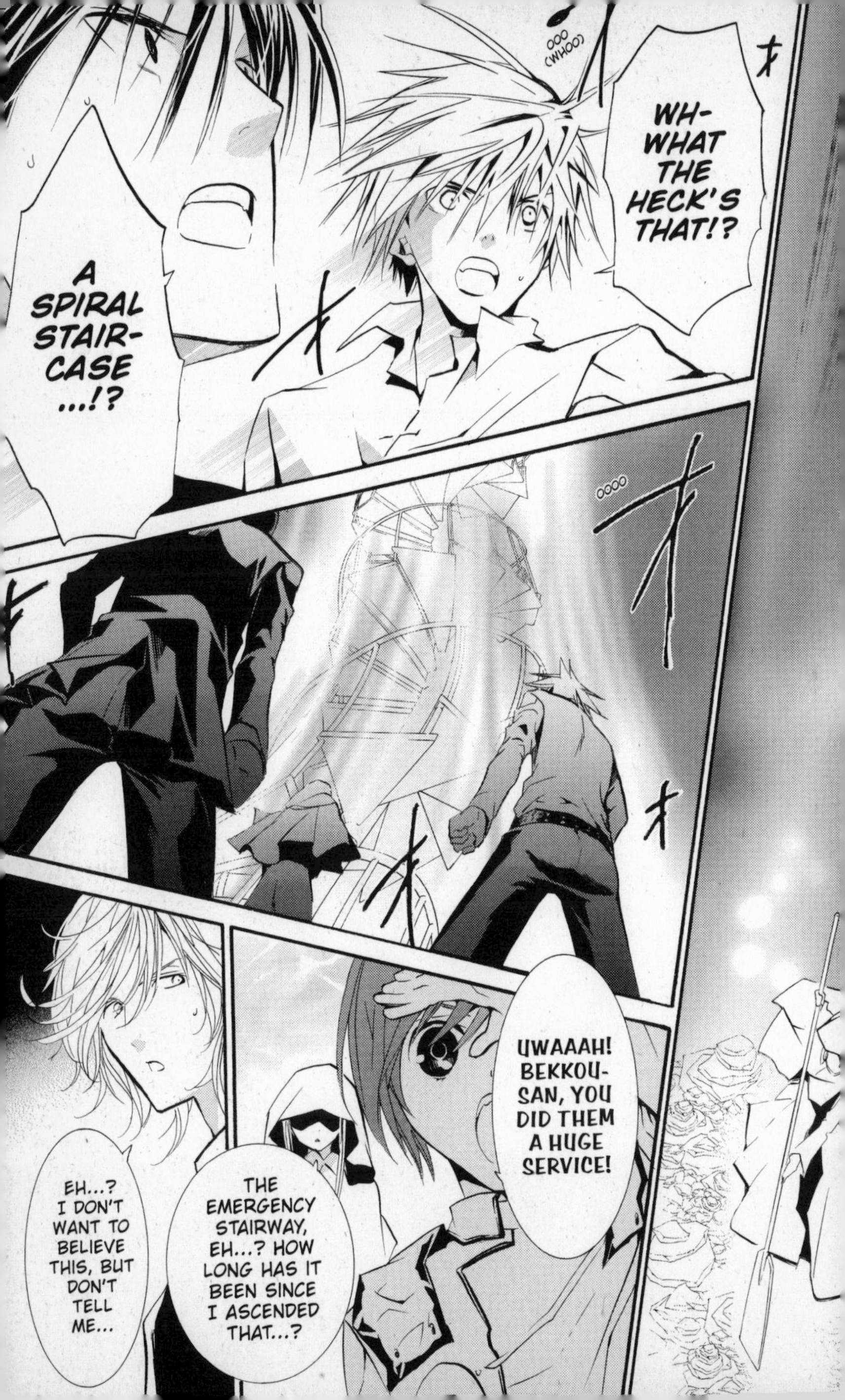
OOO (WHOO)
WH- WHAT THE HECK'S THAT!?
A SPIRAL STAIR-CASE ...!?
OOOO
UWAAAH! BEKKOU-SAN, YOU DID THEM A HUGE SERVICE!
THE EMERGENCY STAIRWAY, EH...? HOW LONG HAS IT BEEN SINCE I ASCENDED THAT...?
EH...? I DON'T WANT TO BELIEVE THIS, BUT DON'T TELL ME...

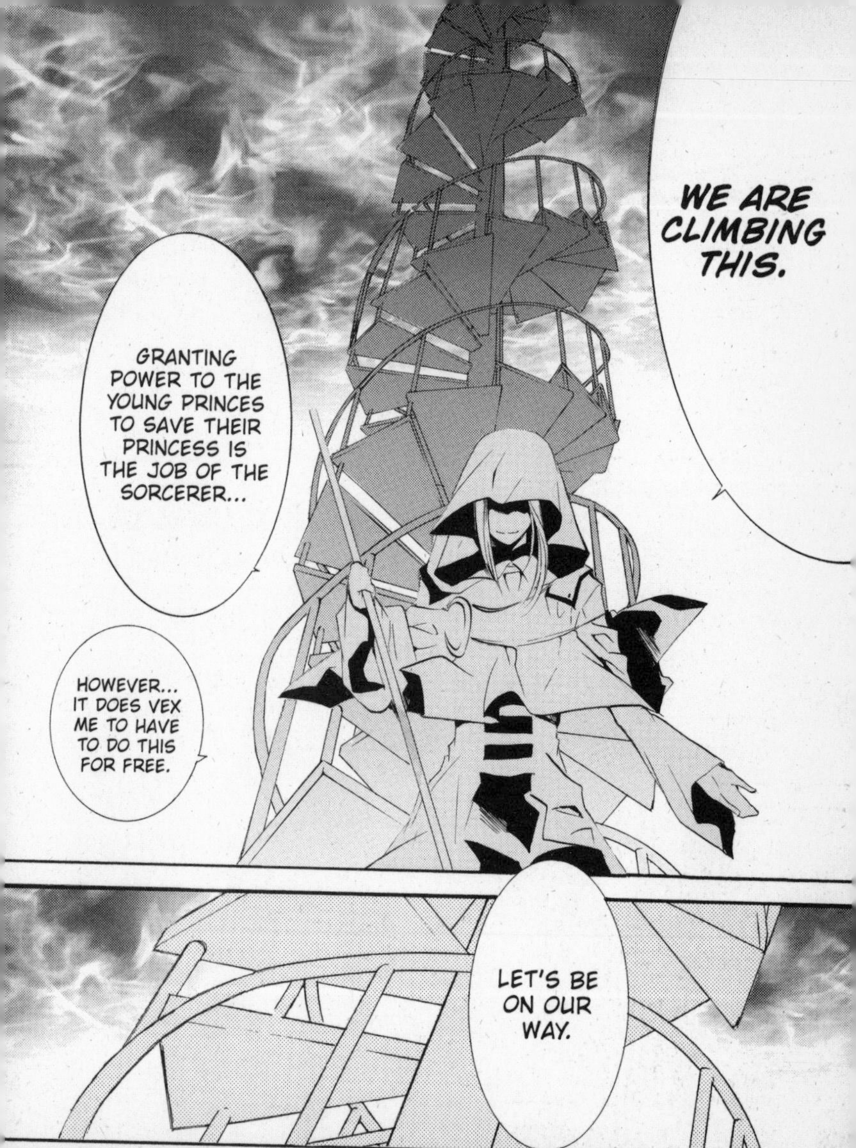
WE ARE CLIMBING THIS.
GRANTING POWER TO THE YOUNG PRINCES TO SAVE THEIR PRINCESS IS THE JOB OF THE SORCERER...
HOWEVER... IT DOES VEX ME TO HAVE TO DO THIS FOR FREE.
LET'S BE ON OUR WAY.

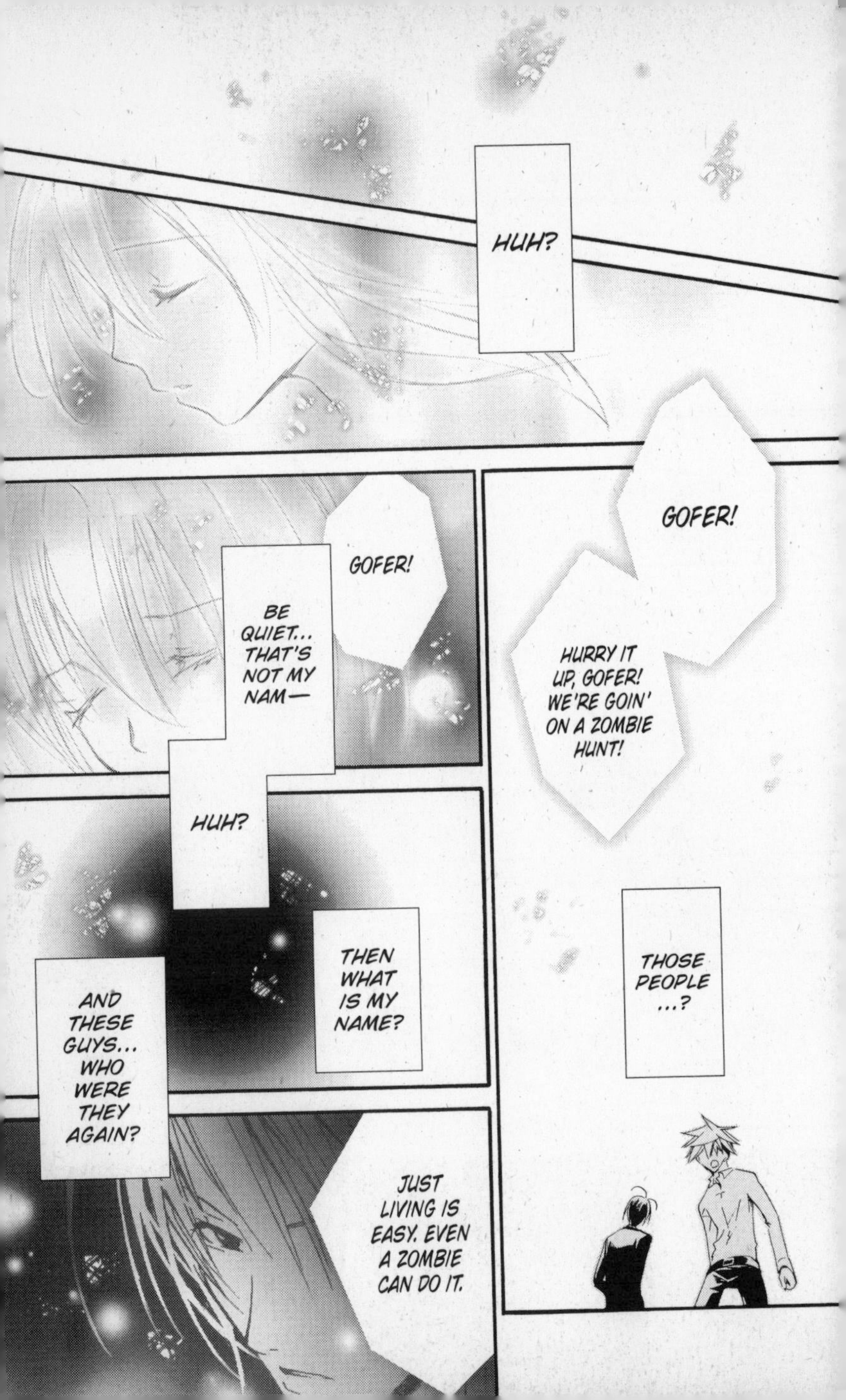
HUH?
GOFER!
HURRY IT UP, GOFER! WE'RE GOIN' ON A ZOMBIE HUNT!
THOSE PEOPLE ...?
GOFER!
BE QUIET... THAT'S NOT MY NAM—
HUH?
THEN WHAT IS MY NAME?
AND THESE GUYS... WHO WERE THEY AGAIN?
JUST LIVING IS EASY. EVEN A ZOMBIE CAN DO IT.

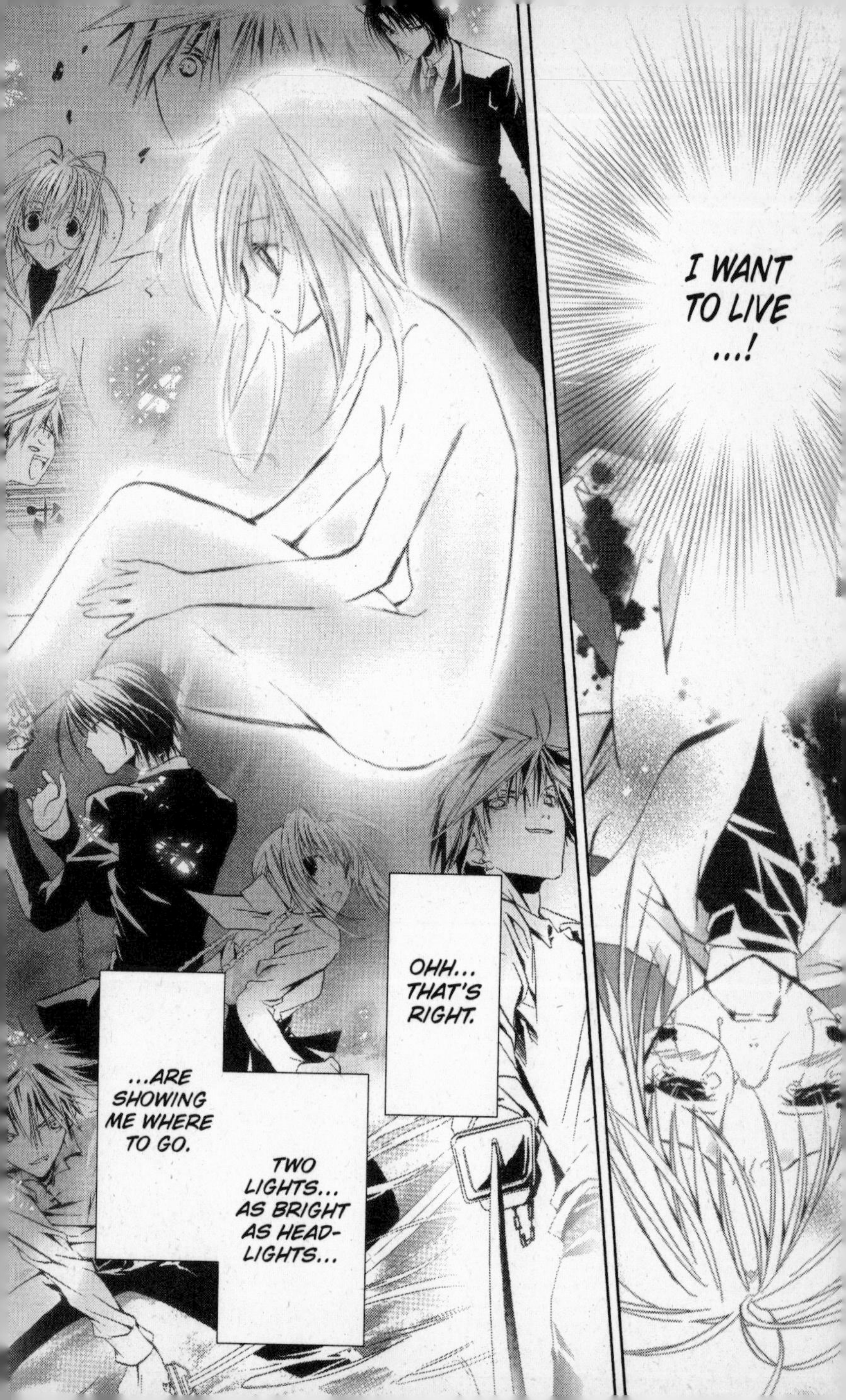
I WANT TO LIVE ...!
OHH... THAT'S RIGHT.
TWO LIGHTS... AS BRIGHT AS HEAD-LIGHTS...
...ARE SHOWING ME WHERE TO GO.

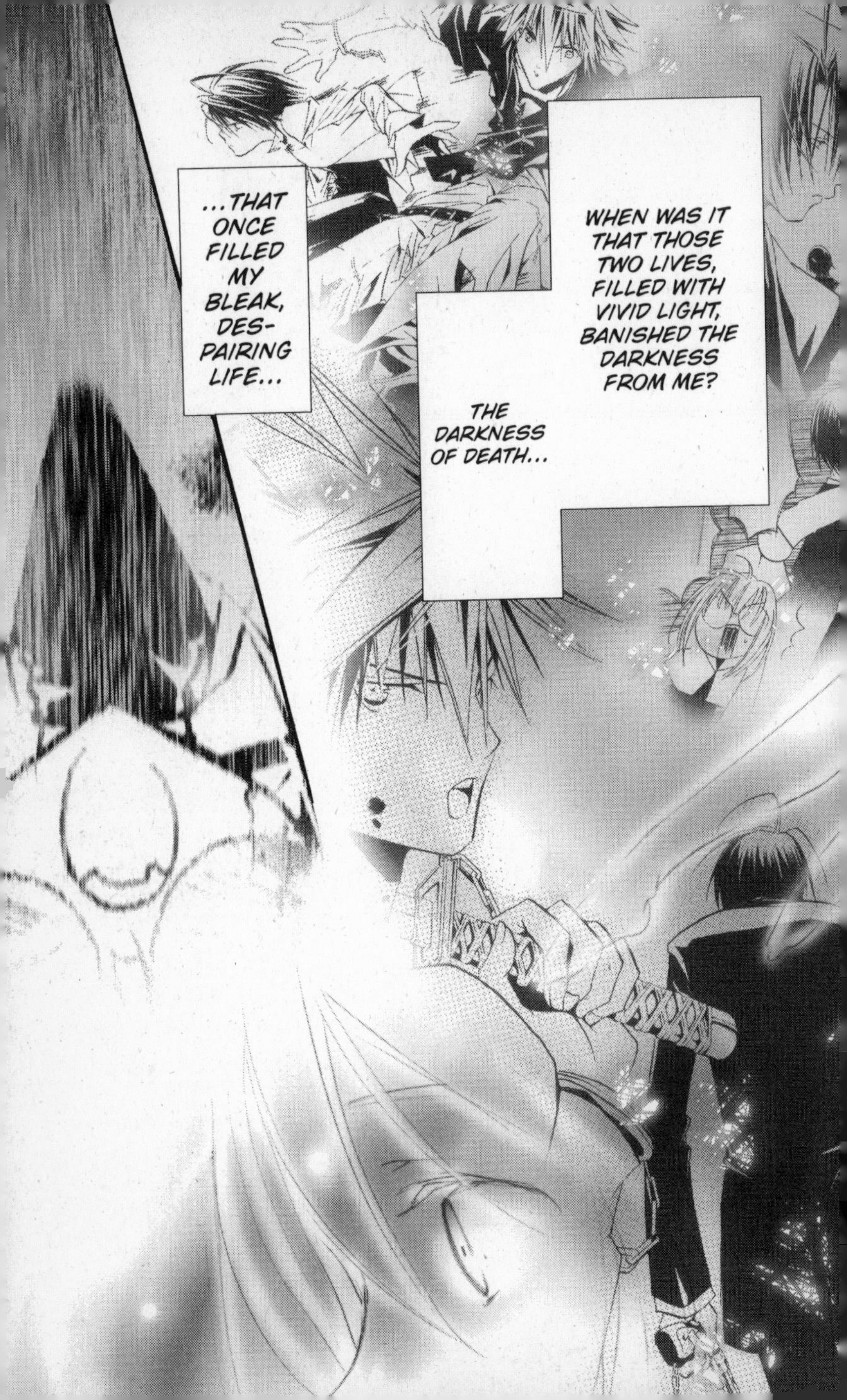
WHEN WAS IT THAT THOSE TWO LIVES, FILLED WITH VIVID LIGHT, BANISHED THE DARKNESS FROM ME?
THE DARKNESS OF DEATH...
...THAT ONCE FILLED MY BLEAK, DES-PAIRING LIFE...

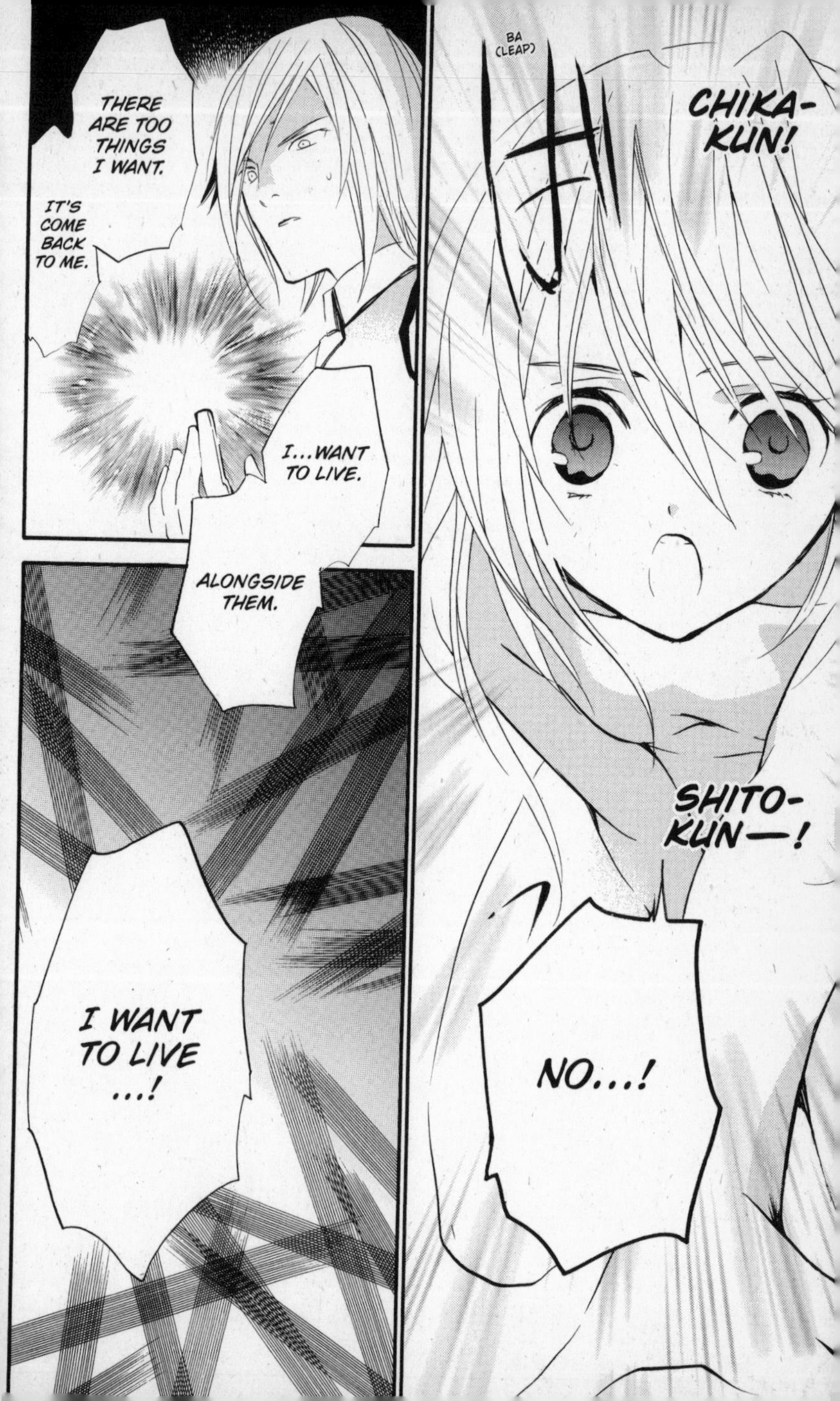
BA (LEAP)
CHIKA-KUN!
SHITO-KUN—!
NO...!
THERE ARE TOO THINGS I WANT.
IT'S COME BACK TO ME.
I...WANT TO LIVE.
ALONGSIDE THEM.
I WANT TO LIVE ...!

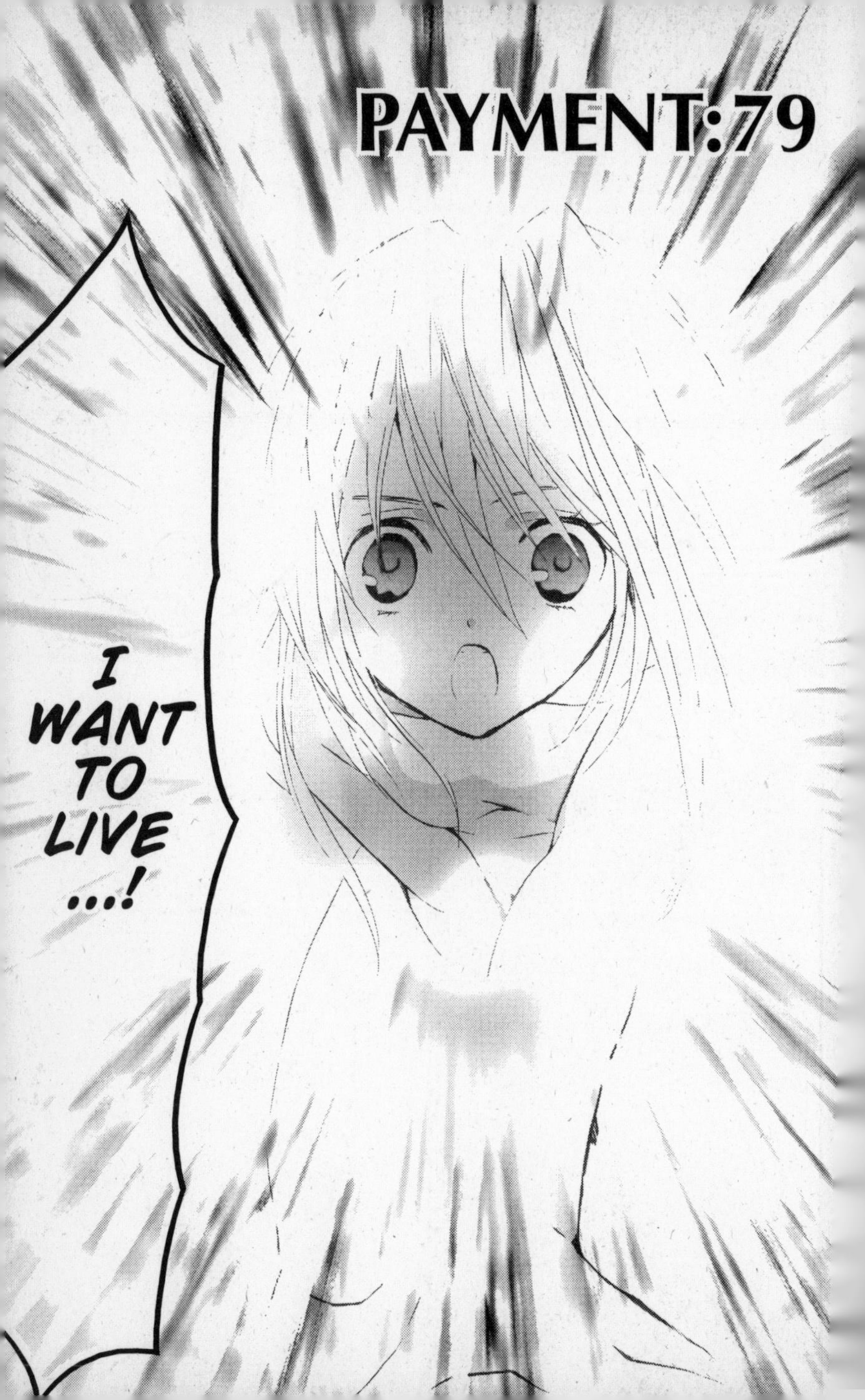
PAYMENT: 79
I WANT TO LIVE ...!

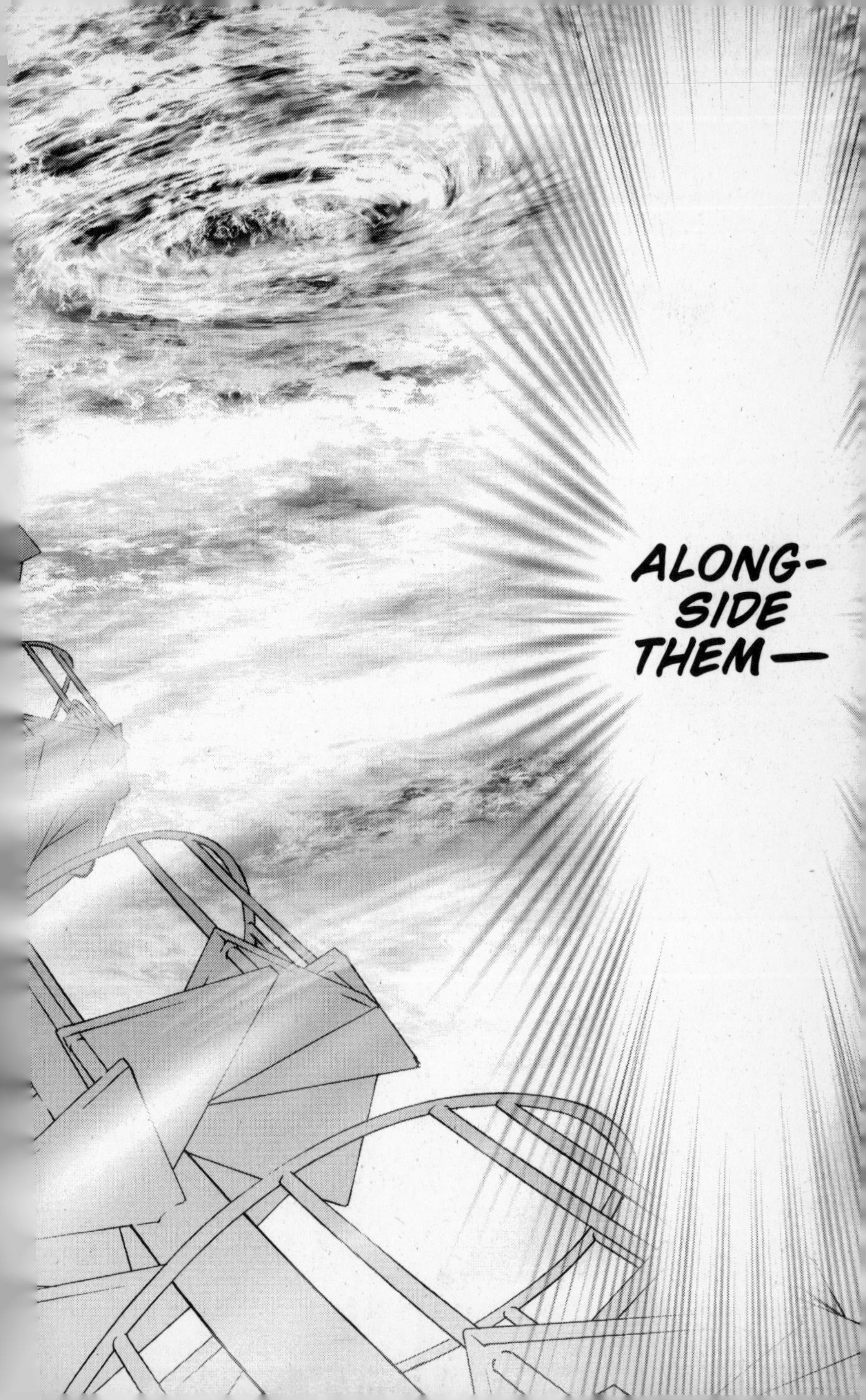
ALONG-
SIDE
THEM—

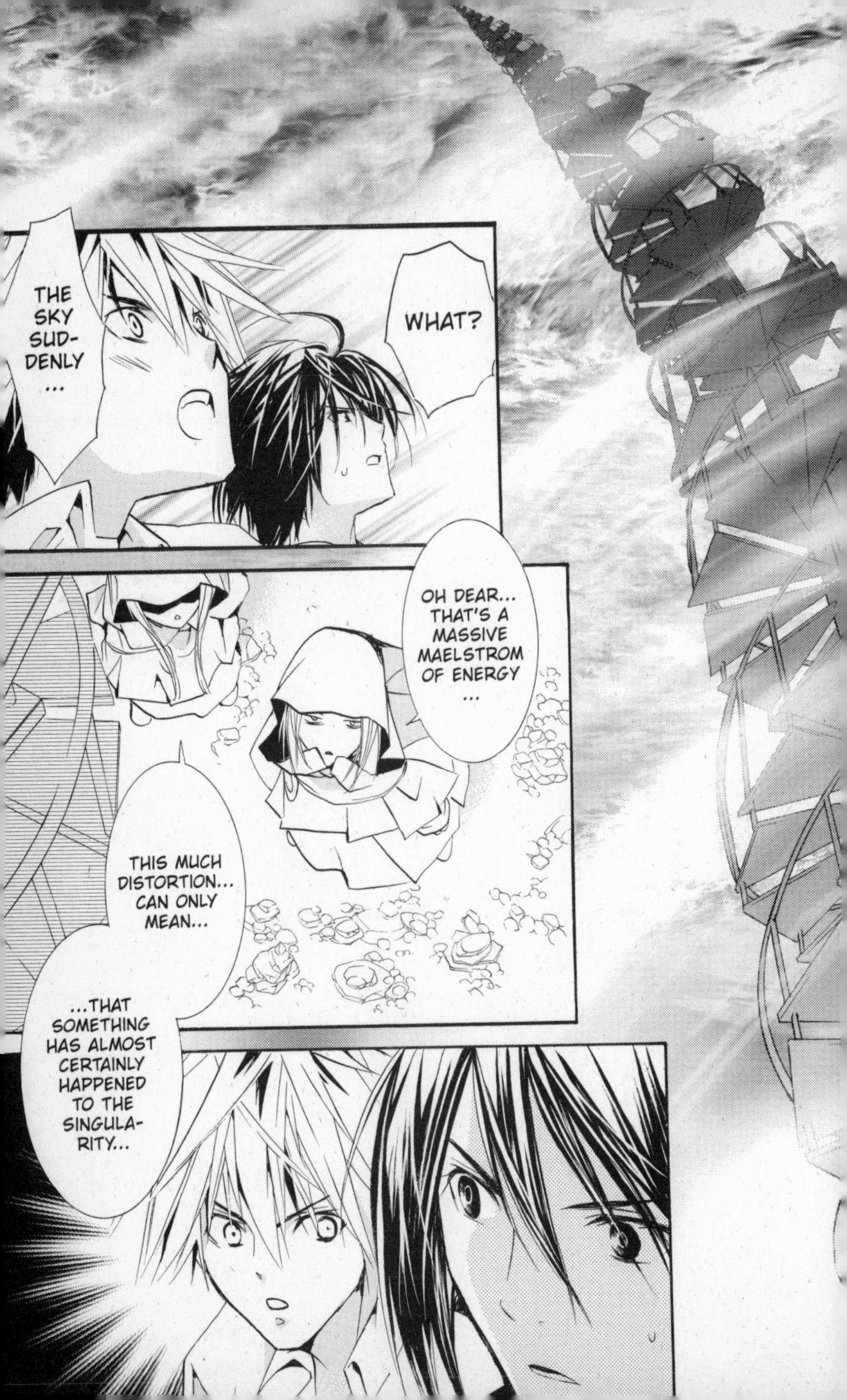
WHAT?
THE SKY SUDDENLY...
OH DEAR... THAT'S A MASSIVE MAELSTROM OF ENERGY...
THIS MUCH DISTORTION... CAN ONLY MEAN...
...THAT SOMETHING HAS ALMOST CERTAINLY HAPPENED TO THE SINGULARITY...

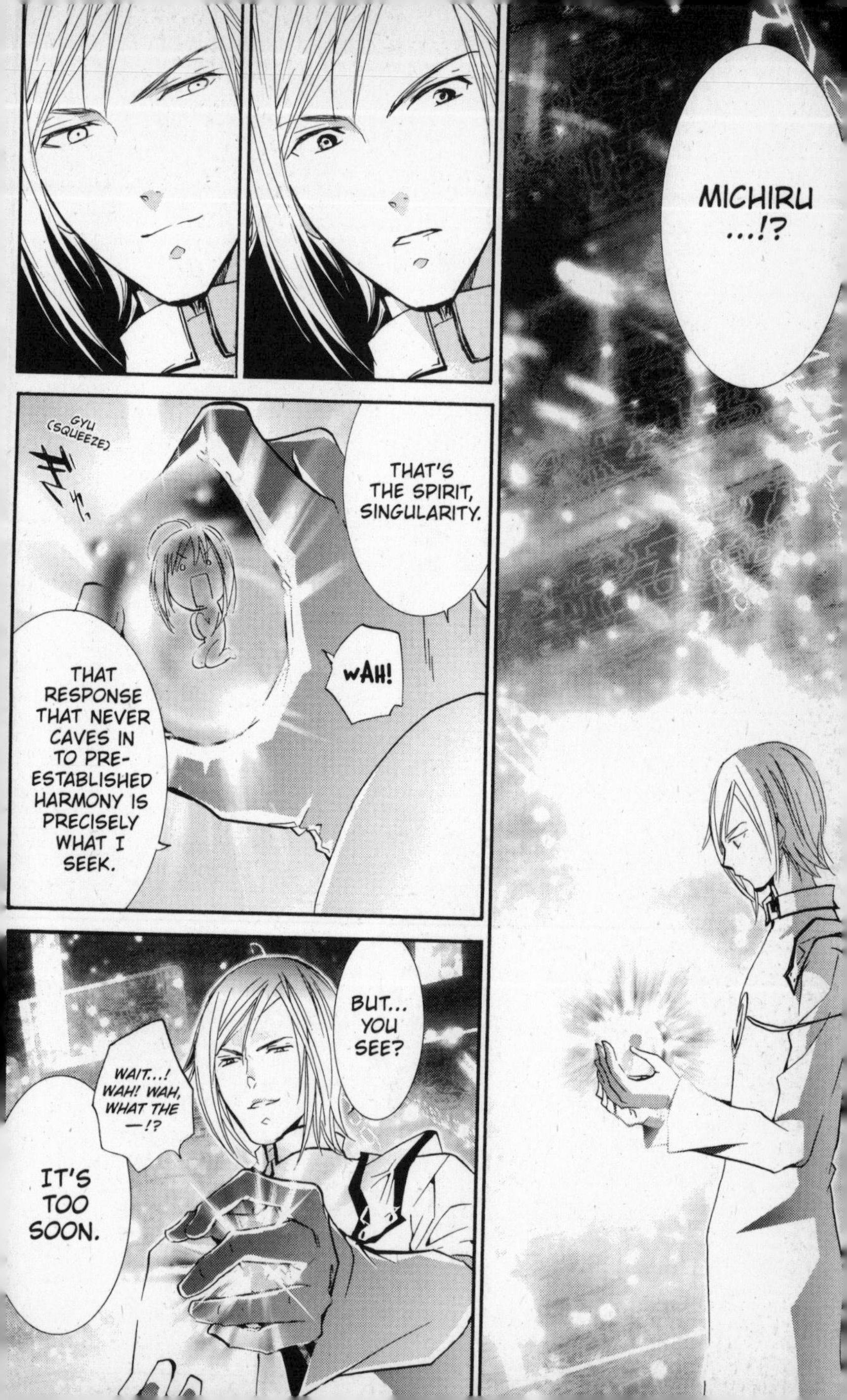
MICHIRU ...!?
THAT'S THE SPIRIT, SINGULARITY.
GYU (SQUEEZE)
WAH!
THAT RESPONSE THAT NEVER CAVES IN TO PRE-ESTABLISHED HARMONY IS PRECISELY WHAT I SEEK.
BUT... YOU SEE?
WAIT...! WAH! WAH, WHAT THE —!?
IT'S TOO SOON.

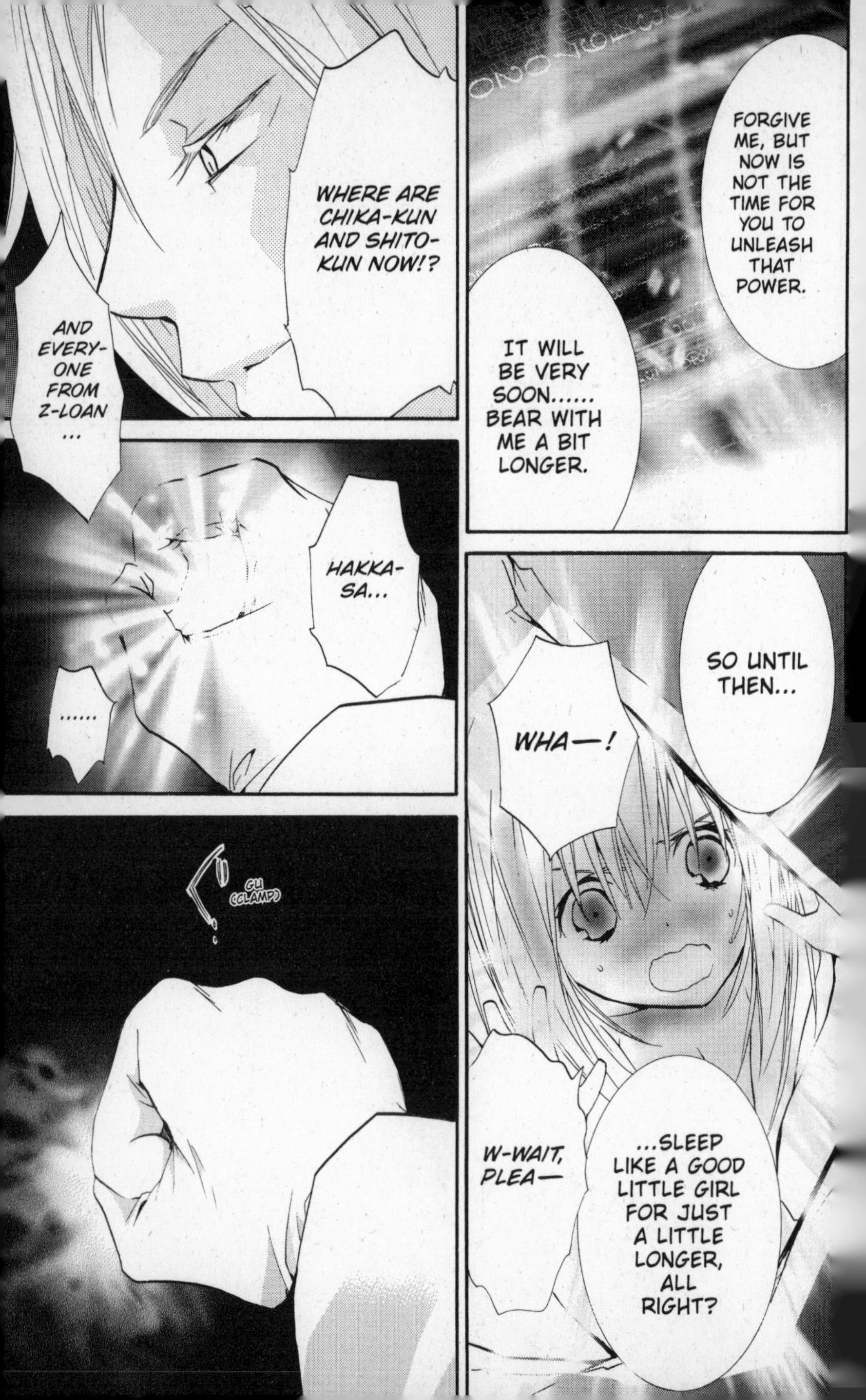
FORGIVE ME, BUT NOW IS NOT THE TIME FOR YOU TO UNLEASH THAT POWER.
IT WILL BE VERY SOON...... BEAR WITH ME A BIT LONGER.
WHERE ARE CHIKA-KUN AND SHITO-KUN NOW!?
AND EVERY-ONE FROM Z-LOAN ...
SO UNTIL THEN...
WHA—!
...SLEEP LIKE A GOOD LITTLE GIRL FOR JUST A LITTLE LONGER, ALL RIGHT?
W-WAIT, PLEA—
HAKKA-SA...
......
GU (CLAMP)

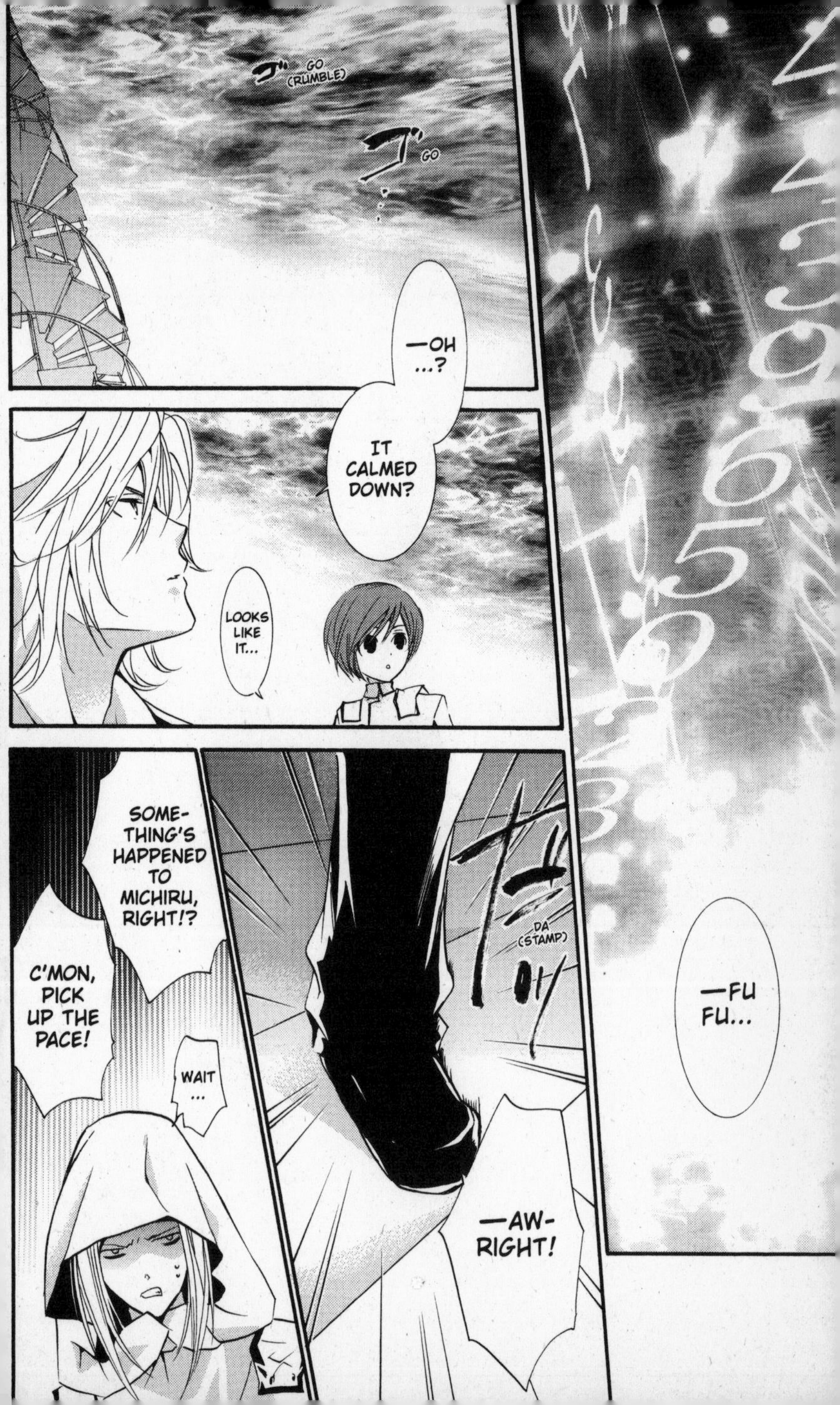
—FU FU...
ゴ
GO (RUMBLE)
ゴ
GO
—OH ...?
IT CALMED DOWN?
LOOKS LIKE IT...
DA (STAMP)
—AW-RIGHT!
SOME-THING'S HAPPENED TO MICHIRU, RIGHT!?
C'MON, PICK UP THE PACE!
WAIT ...

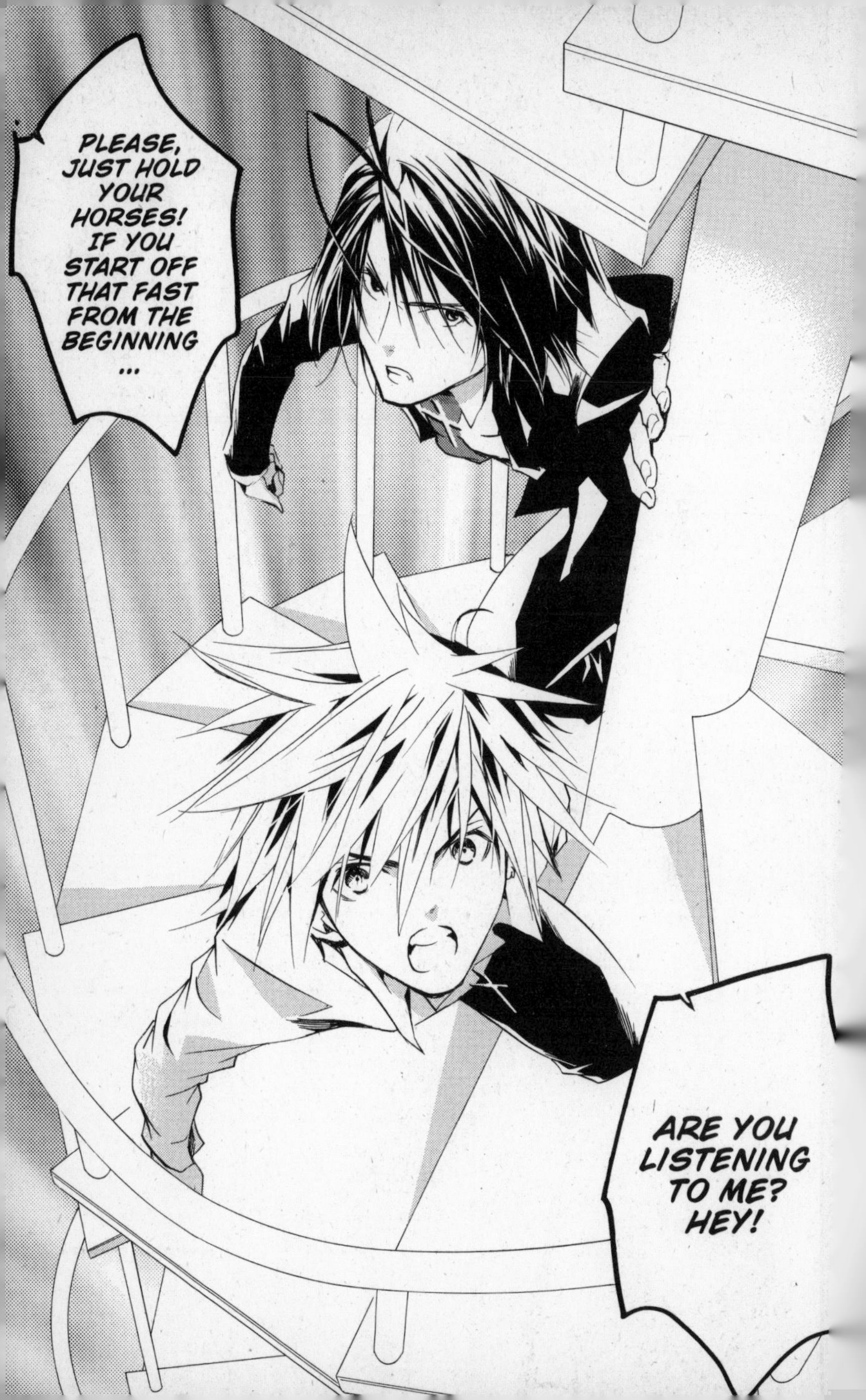
PLEASE, JUST HOLD YOUR HORSES! IF YOU START OFF THAT FAST FROM THE BEGINNING ...
ARE YOU LISTENING TO ME? HEY!

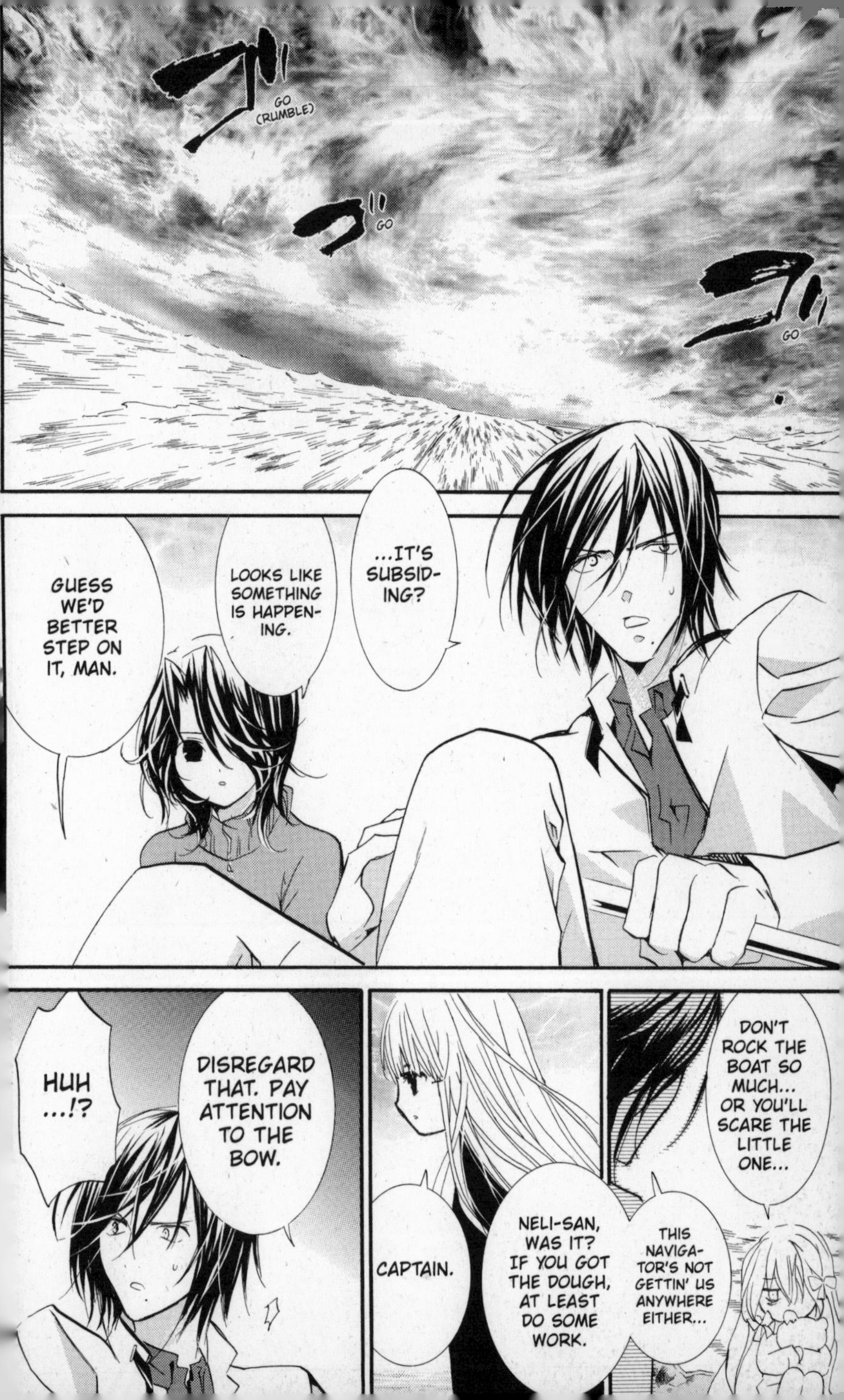
GO (RUMBLE)
GO
GO
...IT'S SUBSID-ING?
LOOKS LIKE SOMETHING IS HAPPEN-ING.
GUESS WE'D BETTER STEP ON IT, MAN.
DON'T ROCK THE BOAT SO MUCH... OR YOU'LL SCARE THE LITTLE ONE...
THIS NAVIGA-TOR'S NOT GETTIN' US ANYWHERE EITHER...
NELI-SAN, WAS IT? IF YOU GOT THE DOUGH, AT LEAST DO SOME WORK.
CAPTAIN.
DISREGARD THAT. PAY ATTENTION TO THE BOW.
HUH ...!?

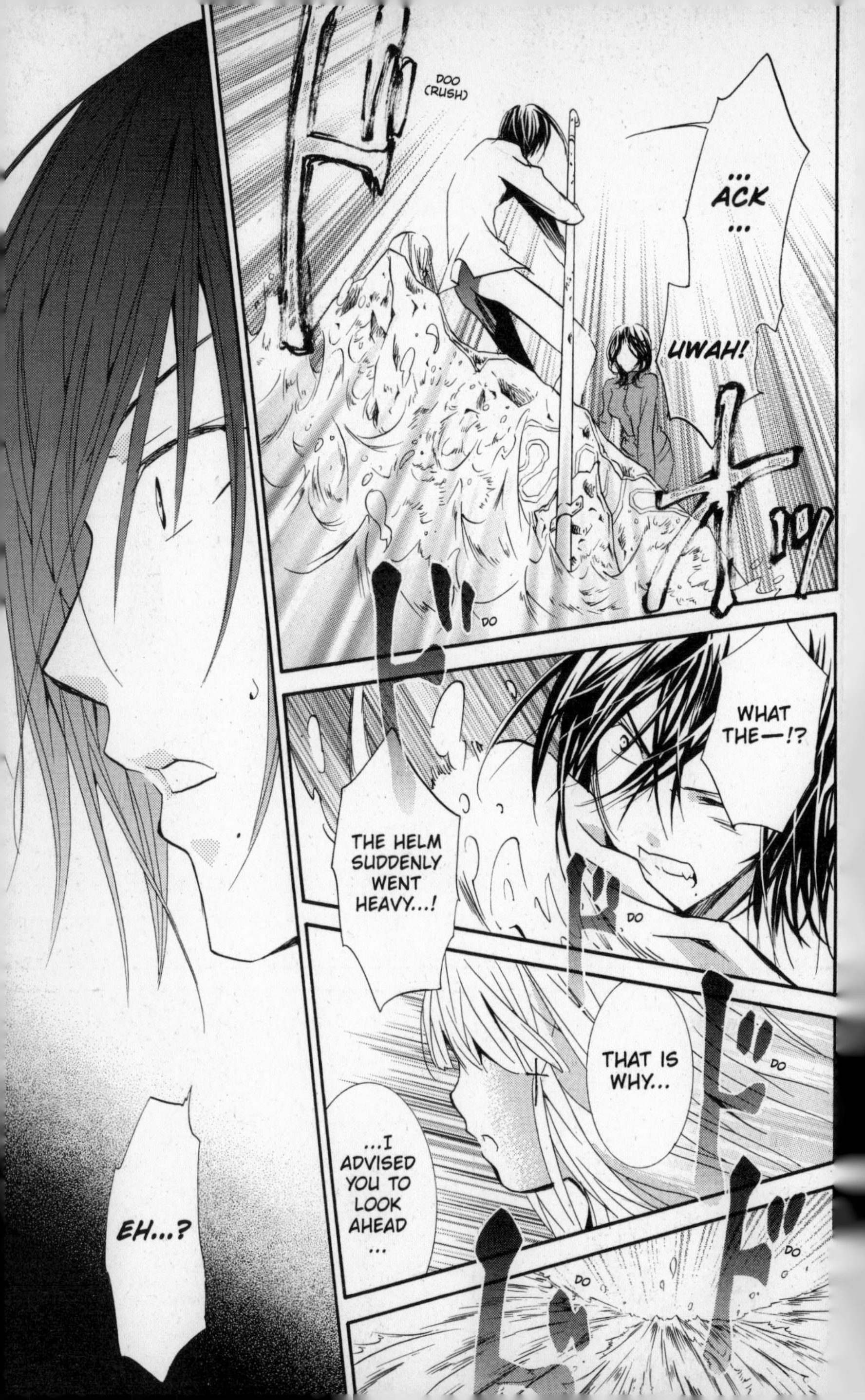

... ACK ...
UWAH!
DOO (RUSH)
DO
WHAT THE—!?
THE HELM SUDDENLY WENT HEAVY...!
DO
THAT IS WHY...
DO
...I ADVISED YOU TO LOOK AHEAD ...
DO
DO
EH...?

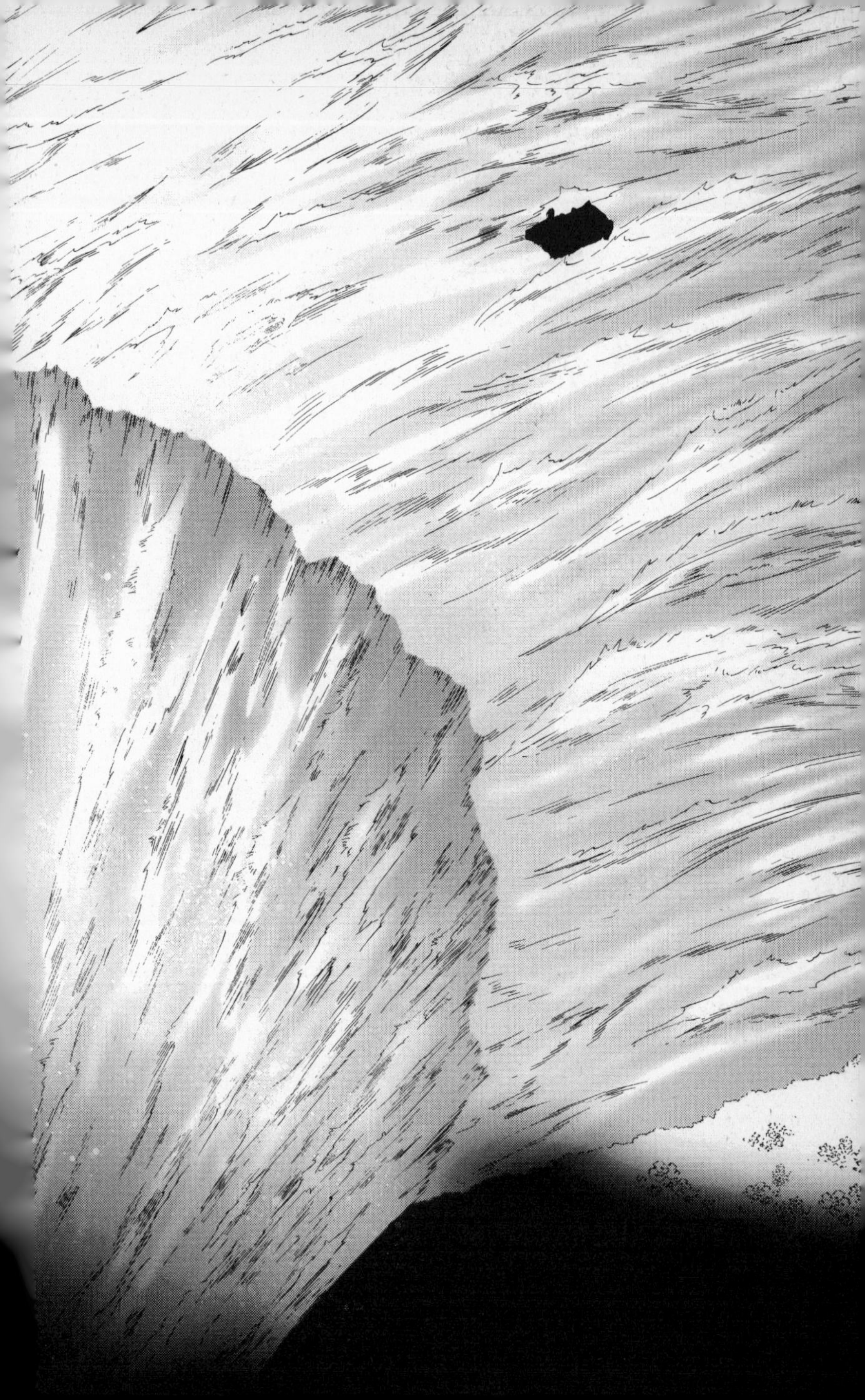

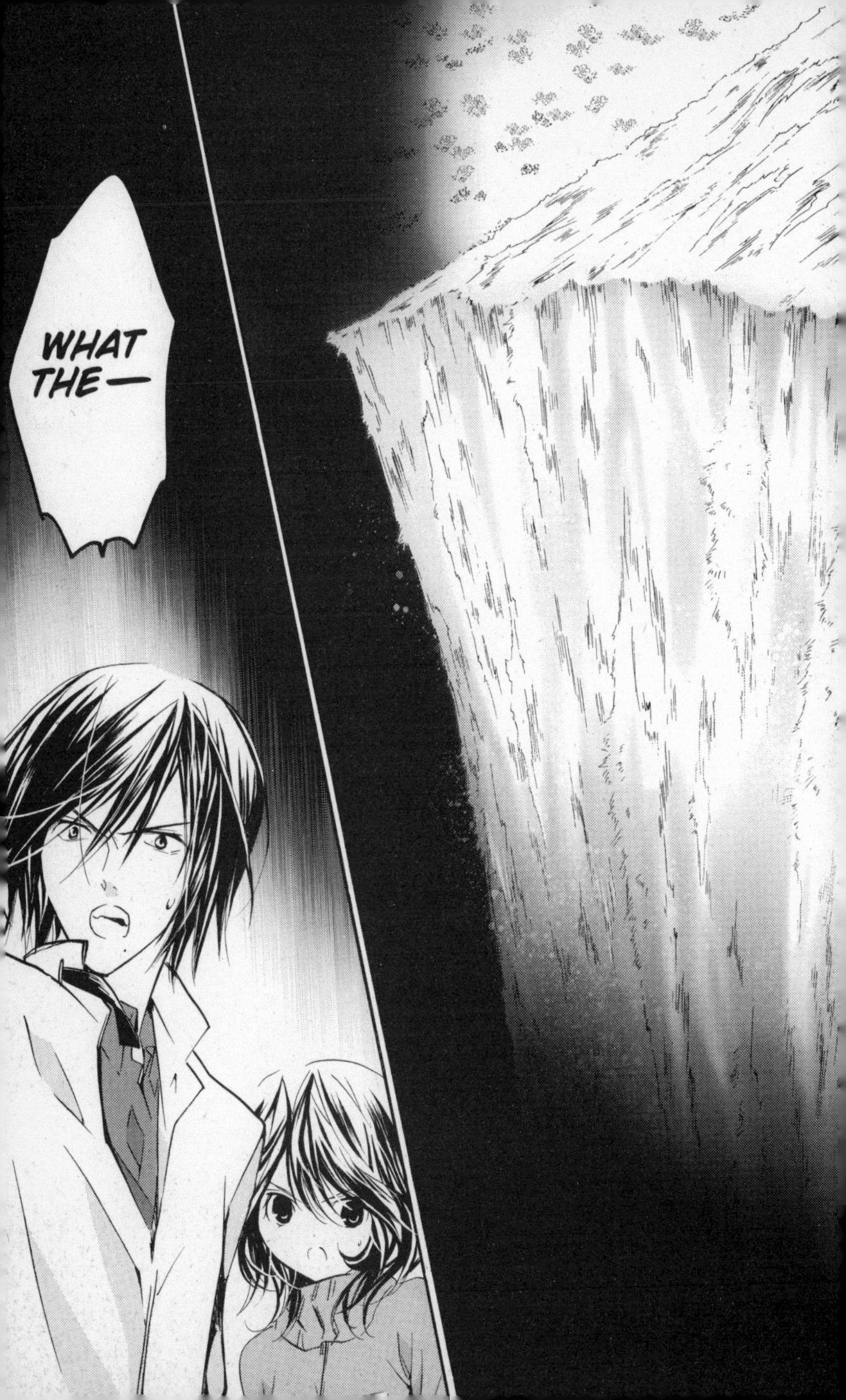
WHAT THE—

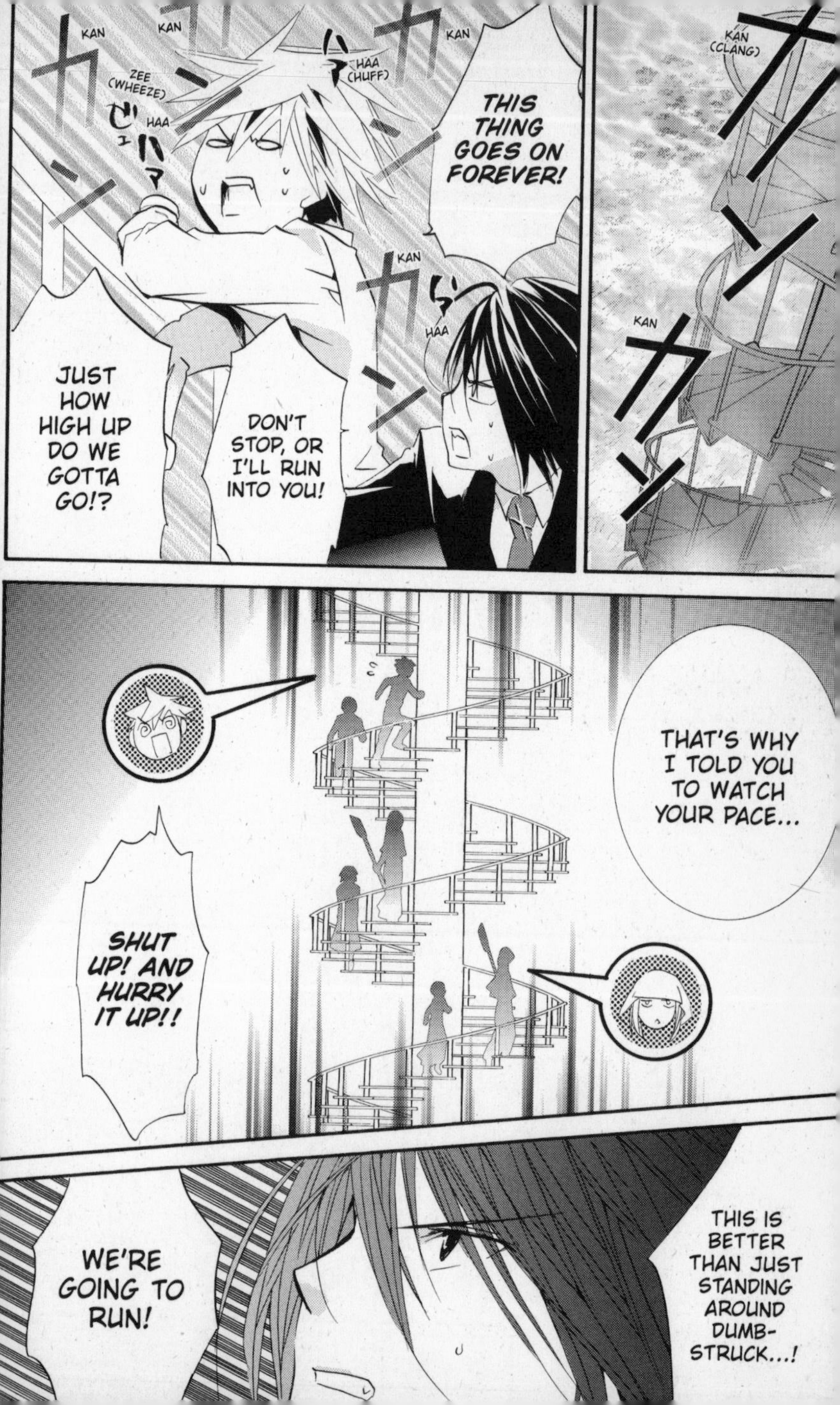
KAN (CLANG)
KAN
KAN
THIS THING GOES ON FOREVER!
HAA (HUFF)
KAN
KAN
ZEE (WHEEZE)
HAA
KAN
HAA
DON'T STOP, OR I'LL RUN INTO YOU!
JUST HOW HIGH UP DO WE GOTTA GO!?
THAT'S WHY I TOLD YOU TO WATCH YOUR PACE...
SHUT UP! AND HURRY IT UP!!
THIS IS BETTER THAN JUST STANDING AROUND DUMB-STRUCK...!
WE'RE GOING TO RUN!

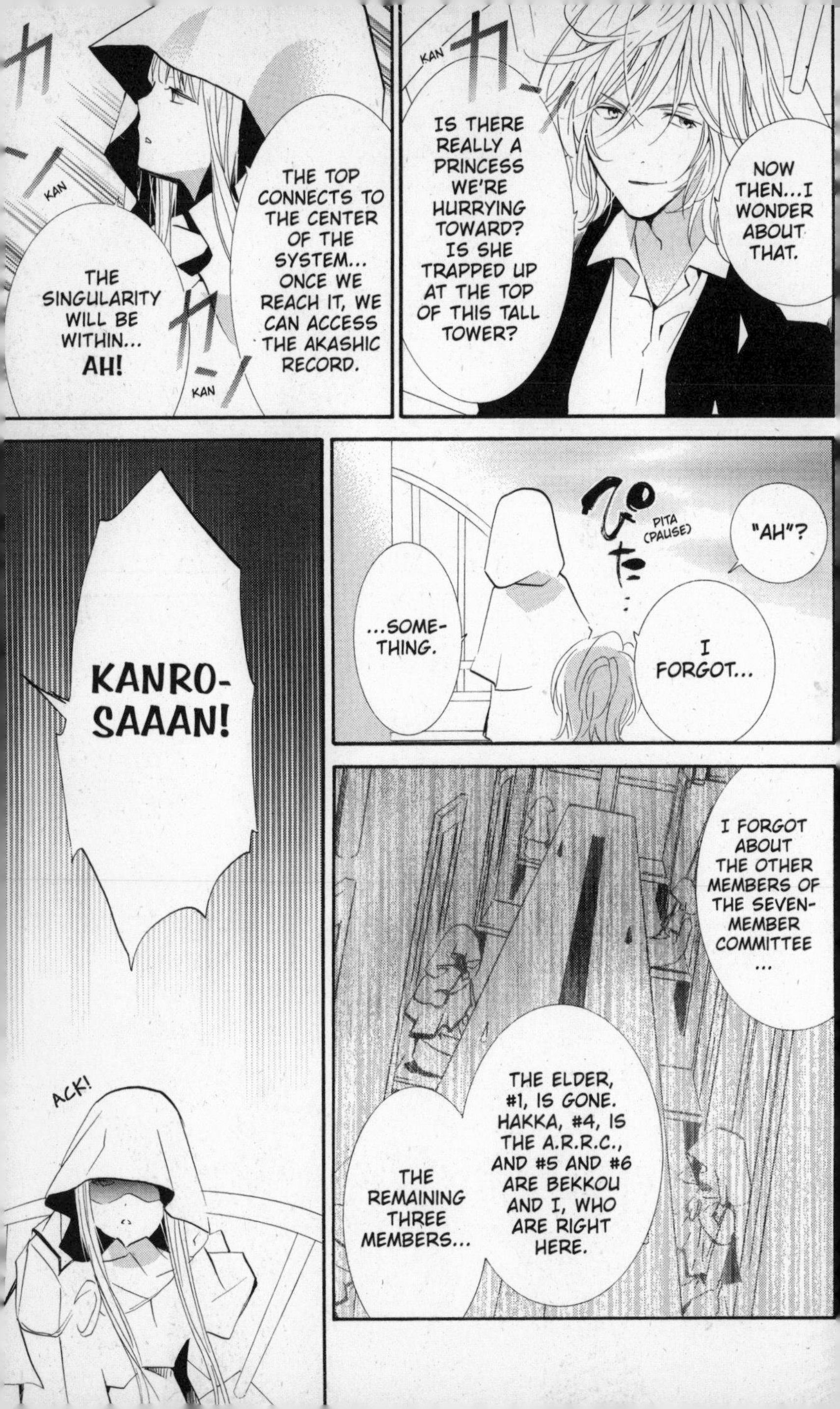
KAN
NOW THEN...I WONDER ABOUT THAT.
IS THERE REALLY A PRINCESS WE'RE HURRYING TOWARD? IS SHE TRAPPED UP AT THE TOP OF THIS TALL TOWER?
THE TOP CONNECTS TO THE CENTER OF THE SYSTEM... ONCE WE REACH IT, WE CAN ACCESS THE AKASHIC RECORD.
KAN
THE SINGULARITY WILL BE WITHIN... **AH!**
KAN
"AH"?
PITA (PAUSE)
I FORGOT...
...SOME-THING.
I FORGOT ABOUT THE OTHER MEMBERS OF THE SEVEN-MEMBER COMMITTEE...
THE ELDER, #1, IS GONE. HAKKA, #4, IS THE A.R.R.C., AND #5 AND #6 ARE BEKKOU AND I, WHO ARE RIGHT HERE.
THE REMAINING THREE MEMBERS...
KANRO-SAAAN!
ACK!

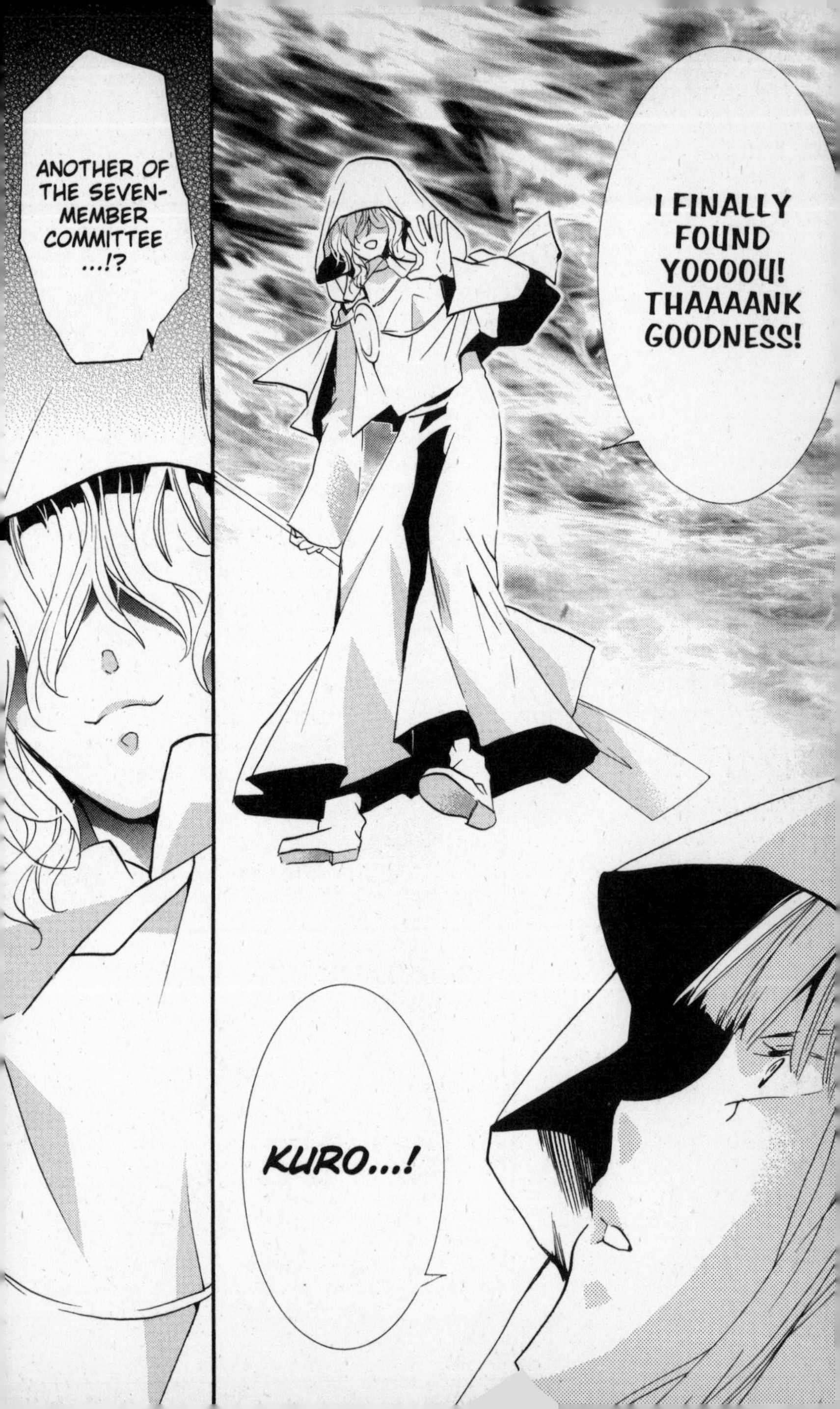
I FINALLY FOUND YOOOOU! THAAAANK GOODNESS!
KURO...!
ANOTHER OF THE SEVEN-MEMBER COMMITTEE ...!?

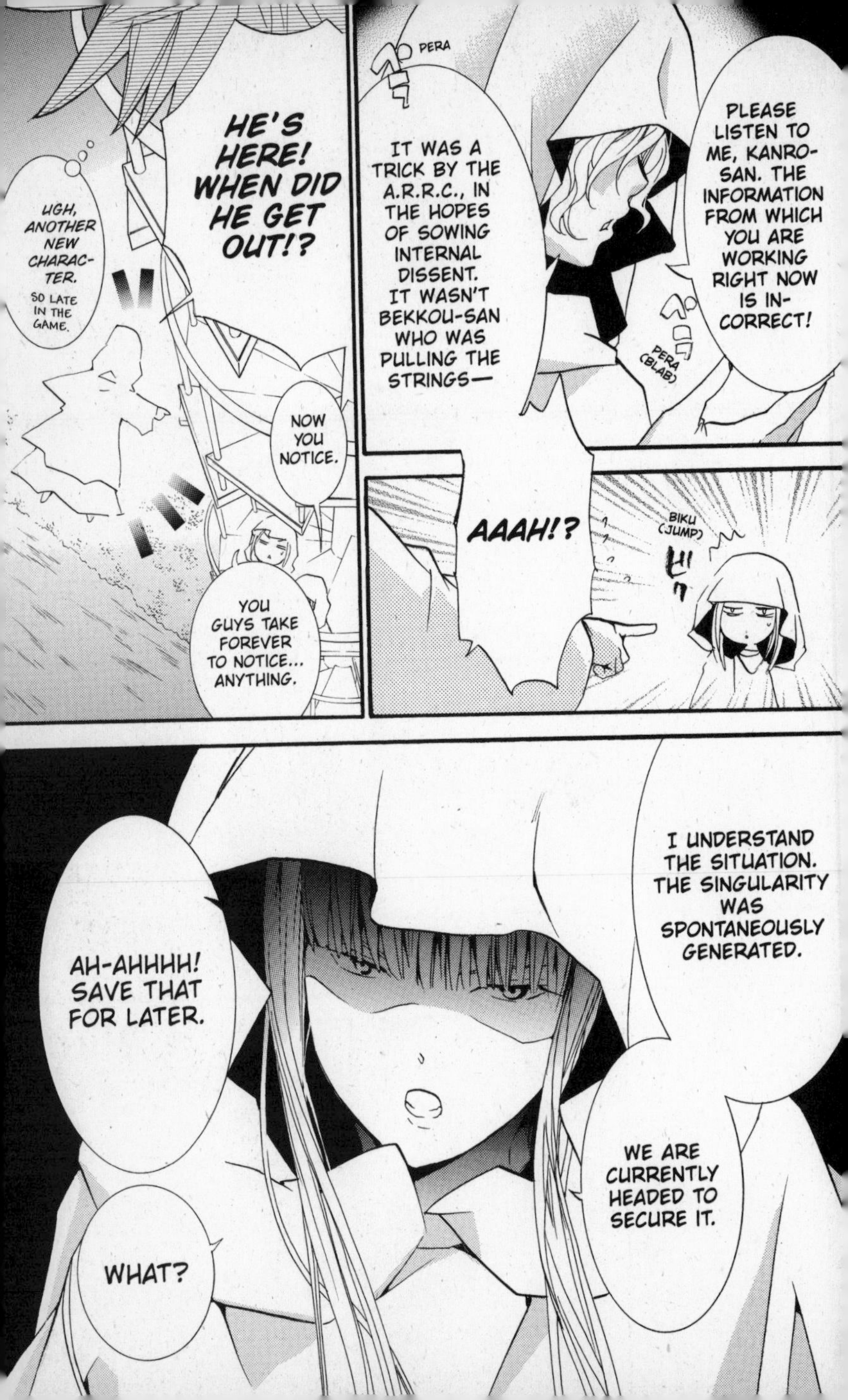
PLEASE LISTEN TO ME, KANRO-SAN. THE INFORMATION FROM WHICH YOU ARE WORKING RIGHT NOW IS IN-CORRECT!
PERA (BLAB)
PERA
IT WAS A TRICK BY THE A.R.R.C., IN THE HOPES OF SOWING INTERNAL DISSENT. IT WASN'T BEKKOU-SAN WHO WAS PULLING THE STRINGS—
BIKU (JUMP)
AAAH!?
HE'S HERE! WHEN DID HE GET OUT!?
UGH, ANOTHER NEW CHARAC-TER.
SO LATE IN THE GAME.
NOW YOU NOTICE.
YOU GUYS TAKE FOREVER TO NOTICE... ANYTHING.
I UNDERSTAND THE SITUATION. THE SINGULARITY WAS SPONTANEOUSLY GENERATED.
AH-AHHHH! SAVE THAT FOR LATER.
WE ARE CURRENTLY HEADED TO SECURE IT.
WHAT?

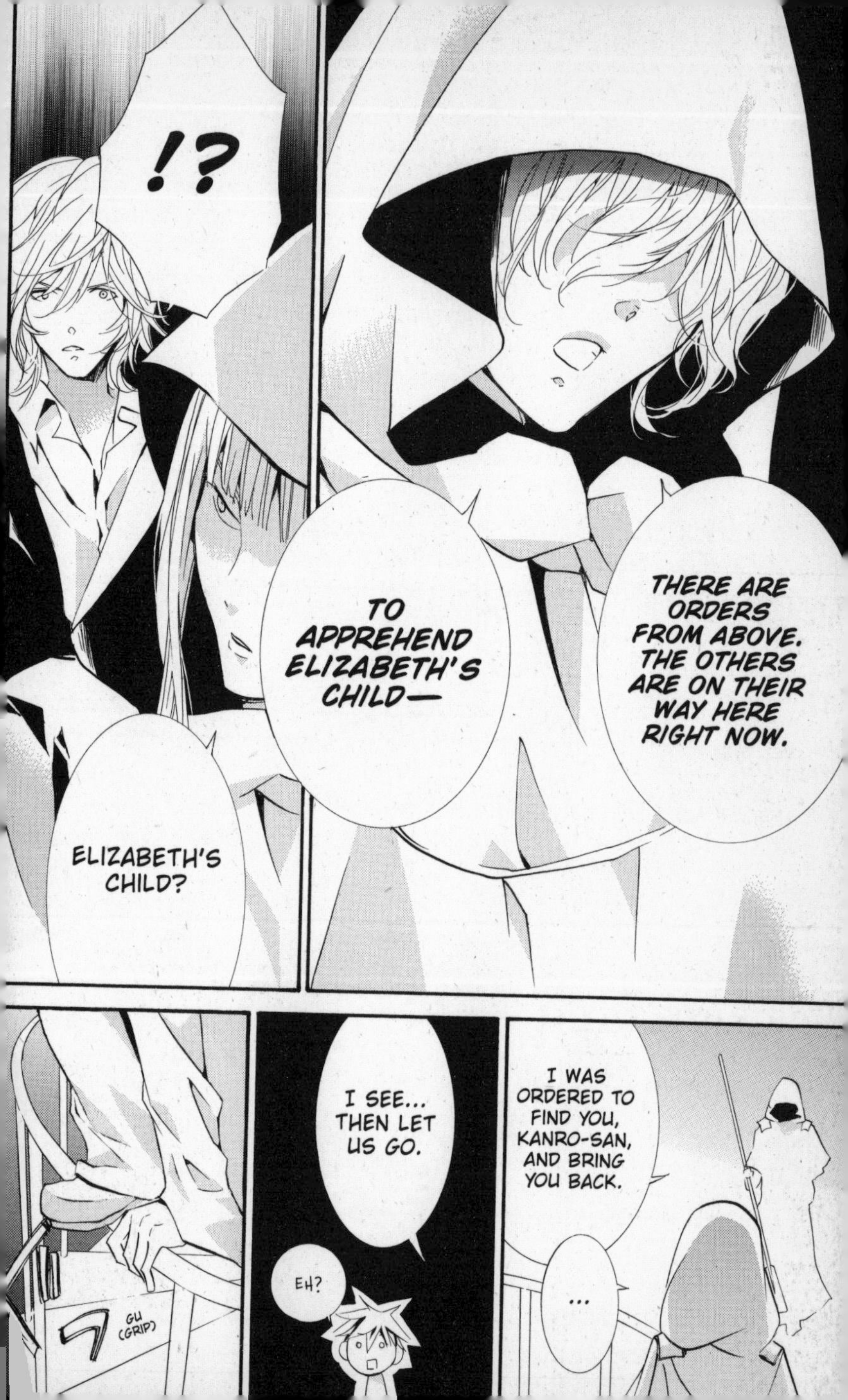
THERE ARE ORDERS FROM ABOVE. THE OTHERS ARE ON THEIR WAY HERE RIGHT NOW.
TO APPREHEND ELIZABETH'S CHILD—
!?
ELIZABETH'S CHILD?
I WAS ORDERED TO FIND YOU, KANRO-SAN, AND BRING YOU BACK.
...
I SEE... THEN LET US GO.
EH?
GU (GRIP)

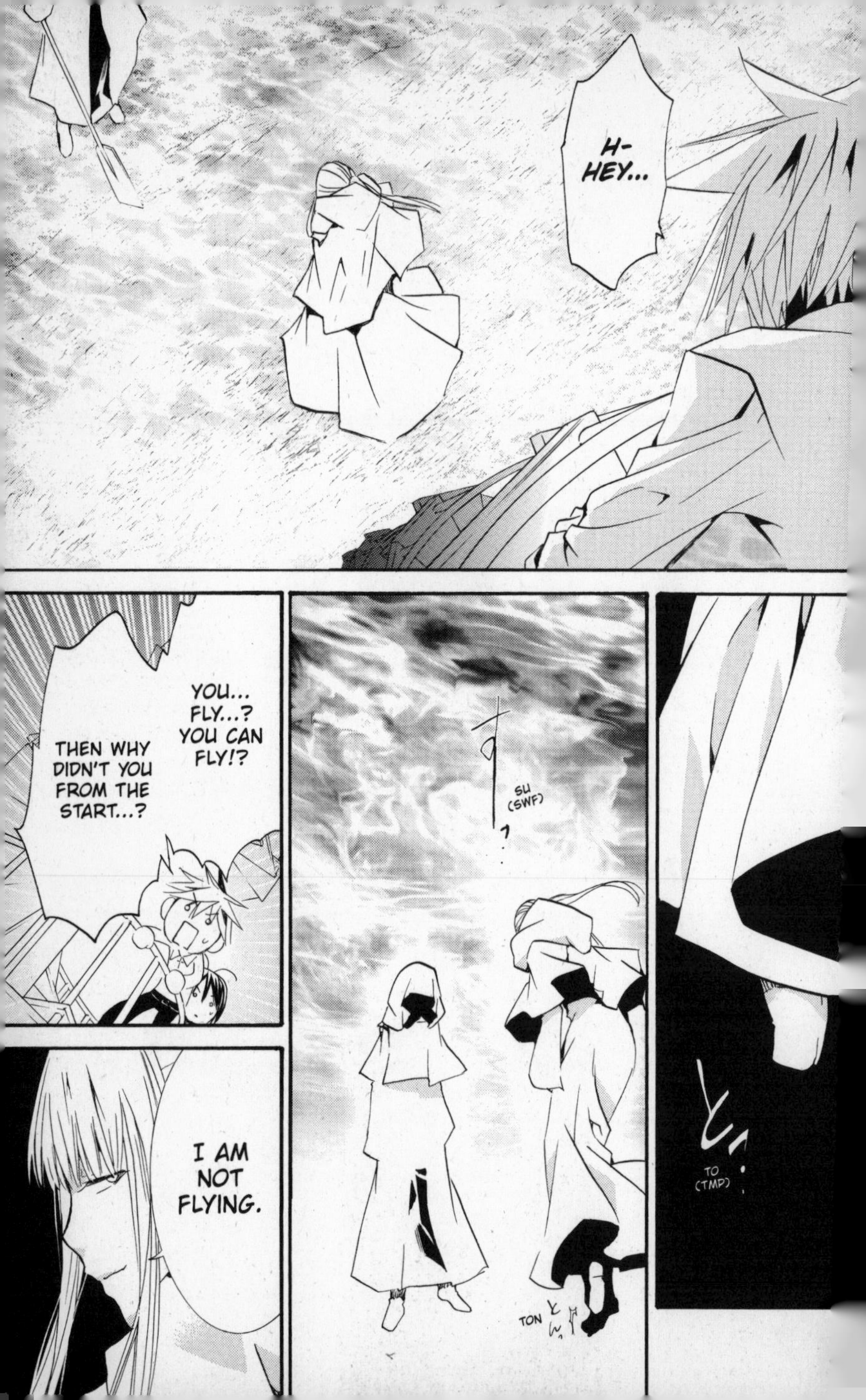
H-
HEY...
TO
(TMP)
SU
(SWF)
TON
YOU...
FLY...?
YOU CAN
FLY!?
THEN WHY
DIDN'T YOU
FROM THE
START...?
I AM
NOT
FLYING.

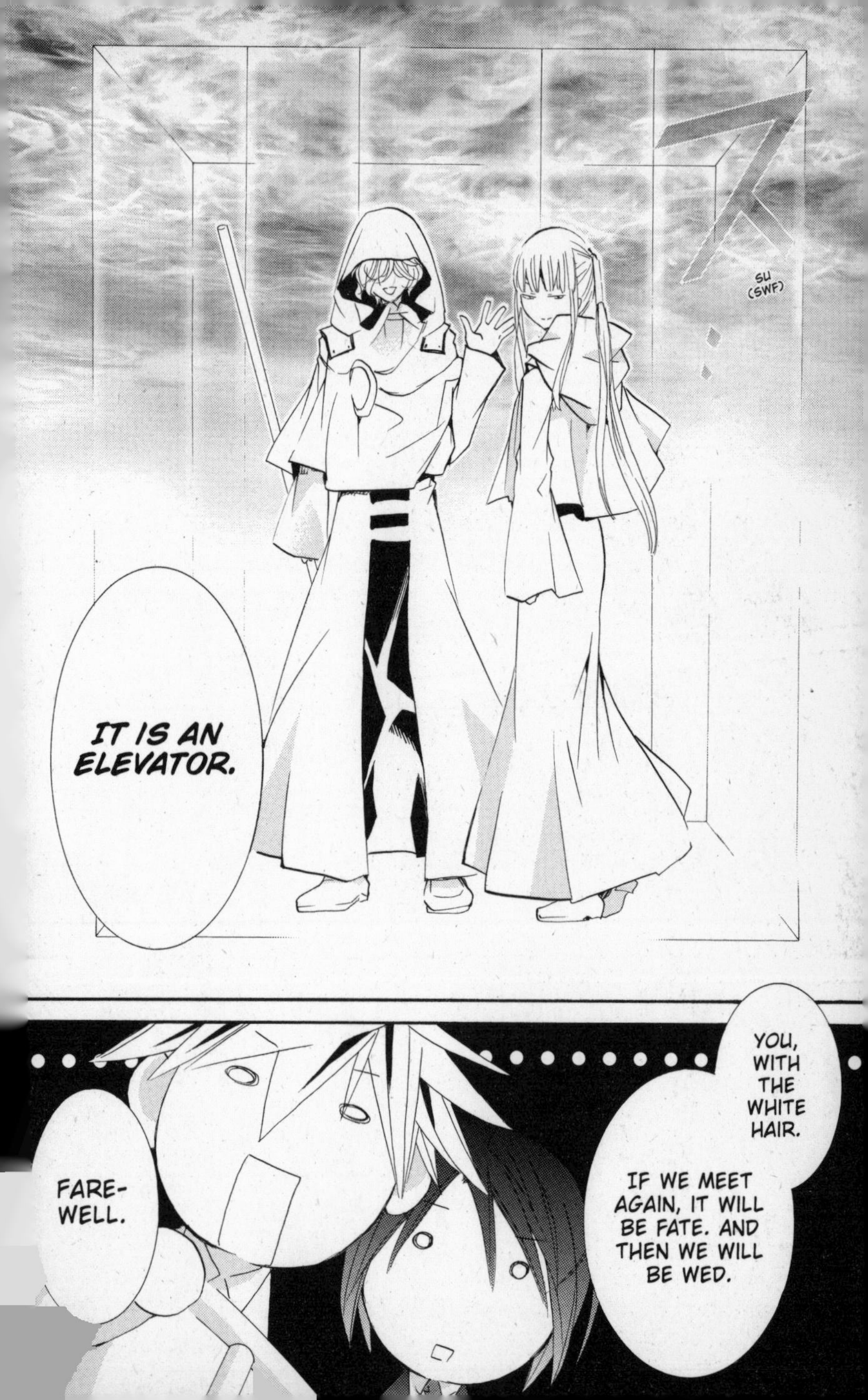
SU (SWF)
IT IS AN ELEVATOR.
YOU, WITH THE WHITE HAIR.
IF WE MEET AGAIN, IT WILL BE FATE. AND THEN WE WILL BE WED.
FARE-WELL.

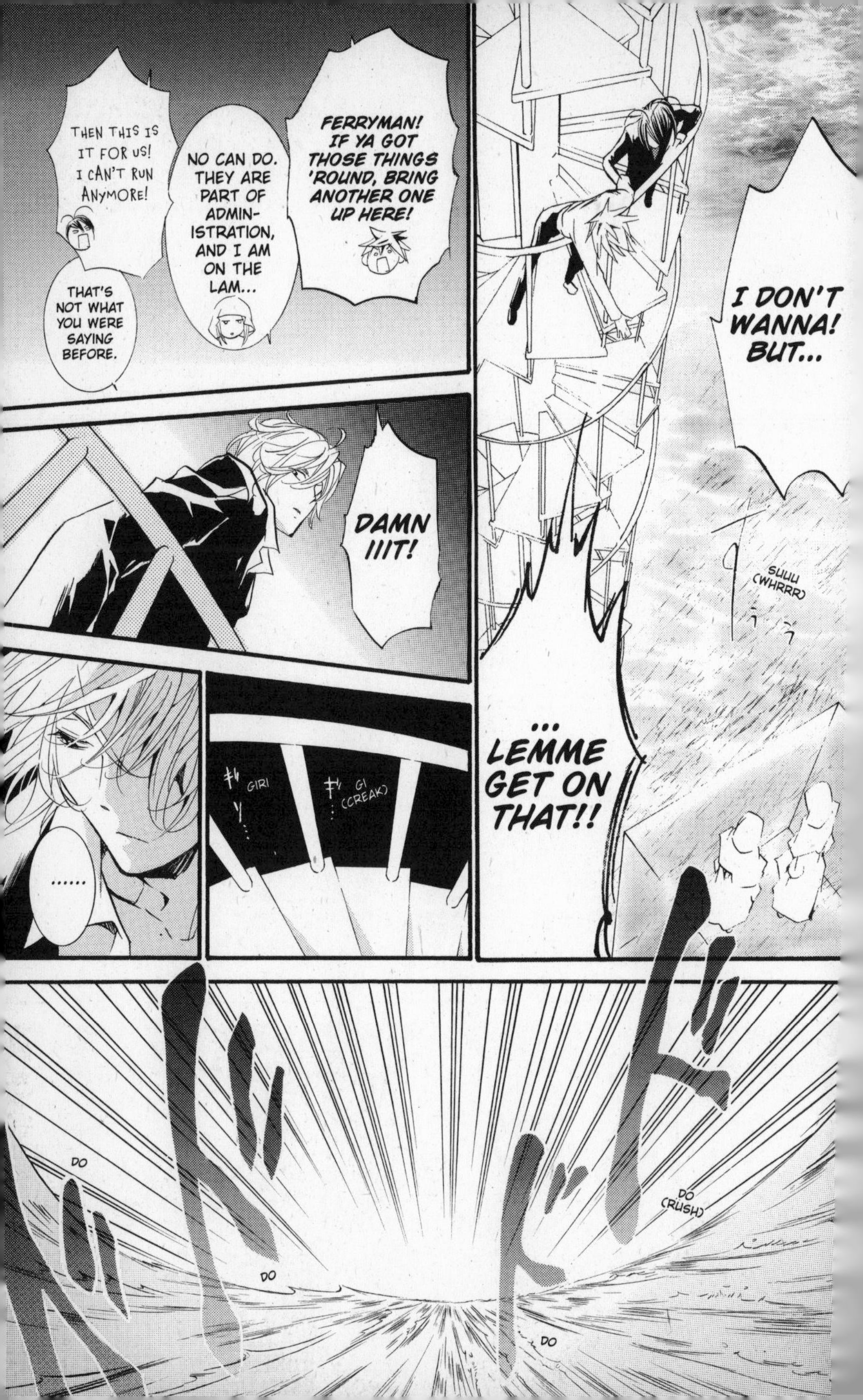
I DON'T WANNA! BUT...
SUUU (WHRRR)
...LEMME GET ON THAT!!
FERRYMAN! IF YA GOT THOSE THINGS 'ROUND, BRING ANOTHER ONE UP HERE!
NO CAN DO. THEY ARE PART OF ADMIN-ISTRATION, AND I AM ON THE LAM...
THEN THIS IS IT FOR US! I CAN'T RUN ANYMORE!
THAT'S NOT WHAT YOU WERE SAYING BEFORE.
DAMN IIIT!
GI (CREAK)
GIRI
......
DO (RUSH)
DO
DO
DO

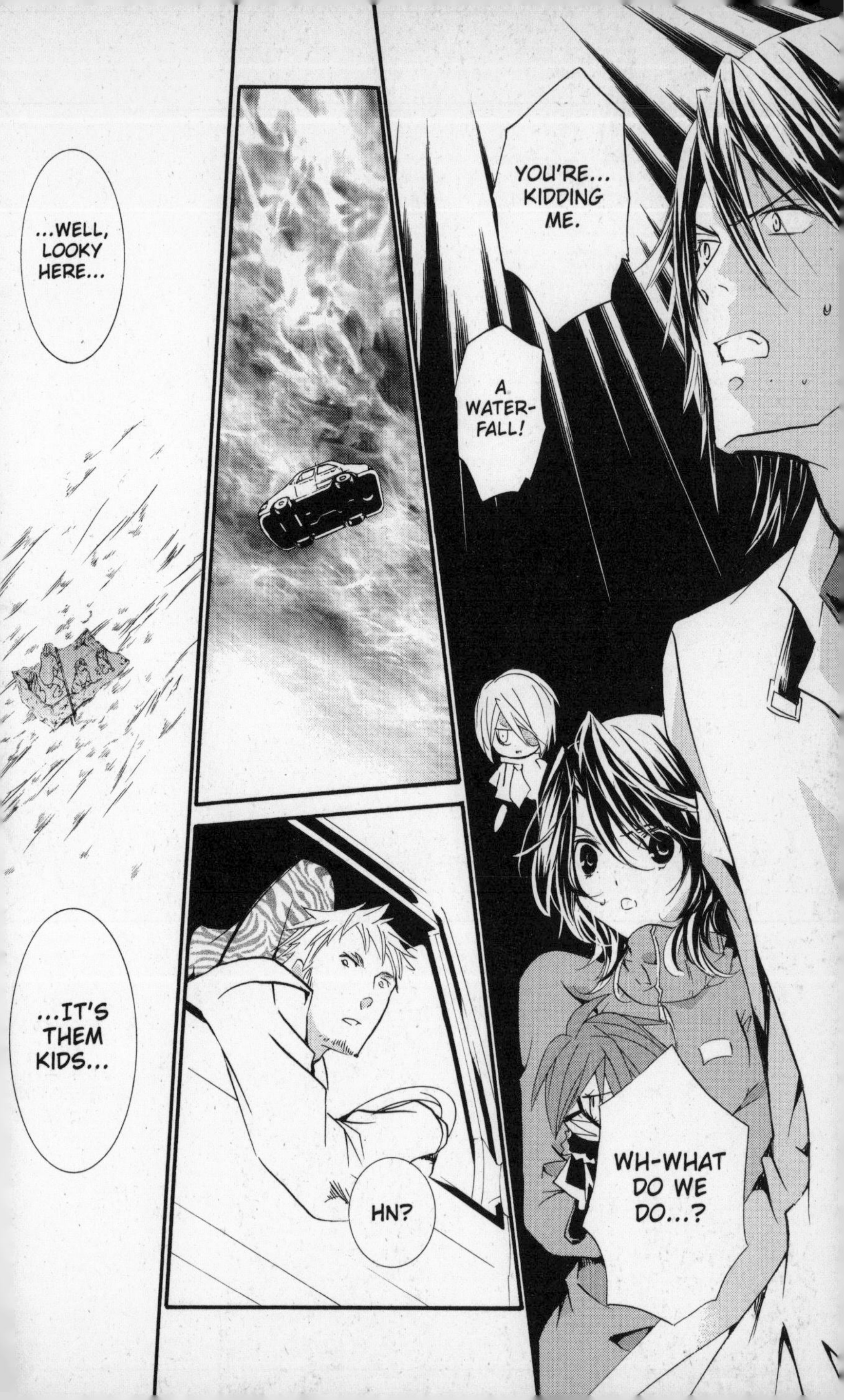
YOU'RE... KIDDING ME.
A WATER-FALL!
WH-WHAT DO WE DO...?
HN?
...WELL, LOOKY HERE...
...IT'S THEM KIDS...

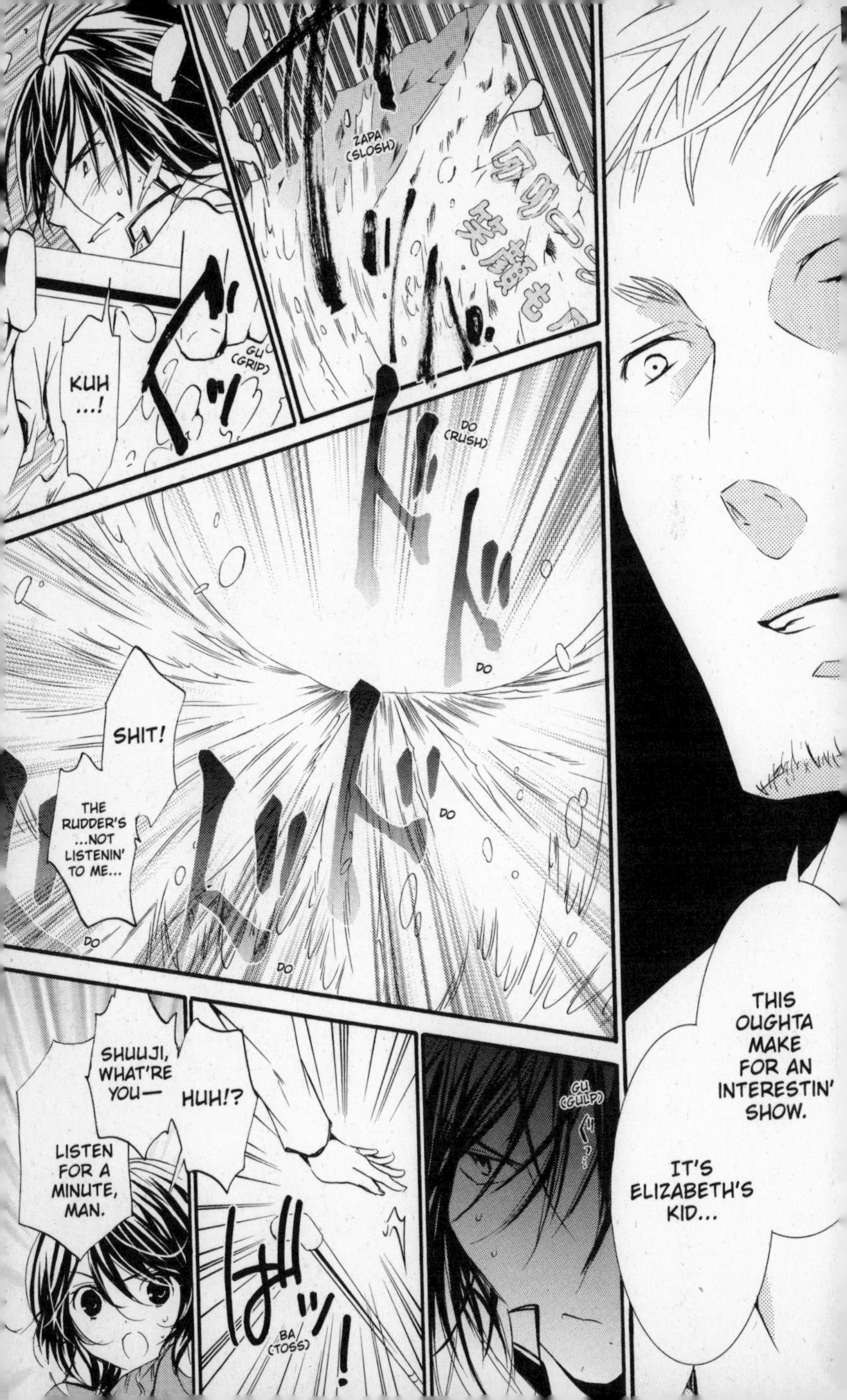
THIS OUGHTA MAKE FOR AN INTERESTIN' SHOW.
IT'S ELIZABETH'S KID...
ZAPA (SLOSH)
GU (GRIP)
KUH ...!
DO (RUSH)
DO
DO
SHIT!
THE RUDDER'S ...NOT LISTENIN' TO ME...
DO
DO
GU (GULP)
SHUUJI, WHAT'RE YOU—
HUH!?
LISTEN FOR A MINUTE, MAN.
BA (TOSS)

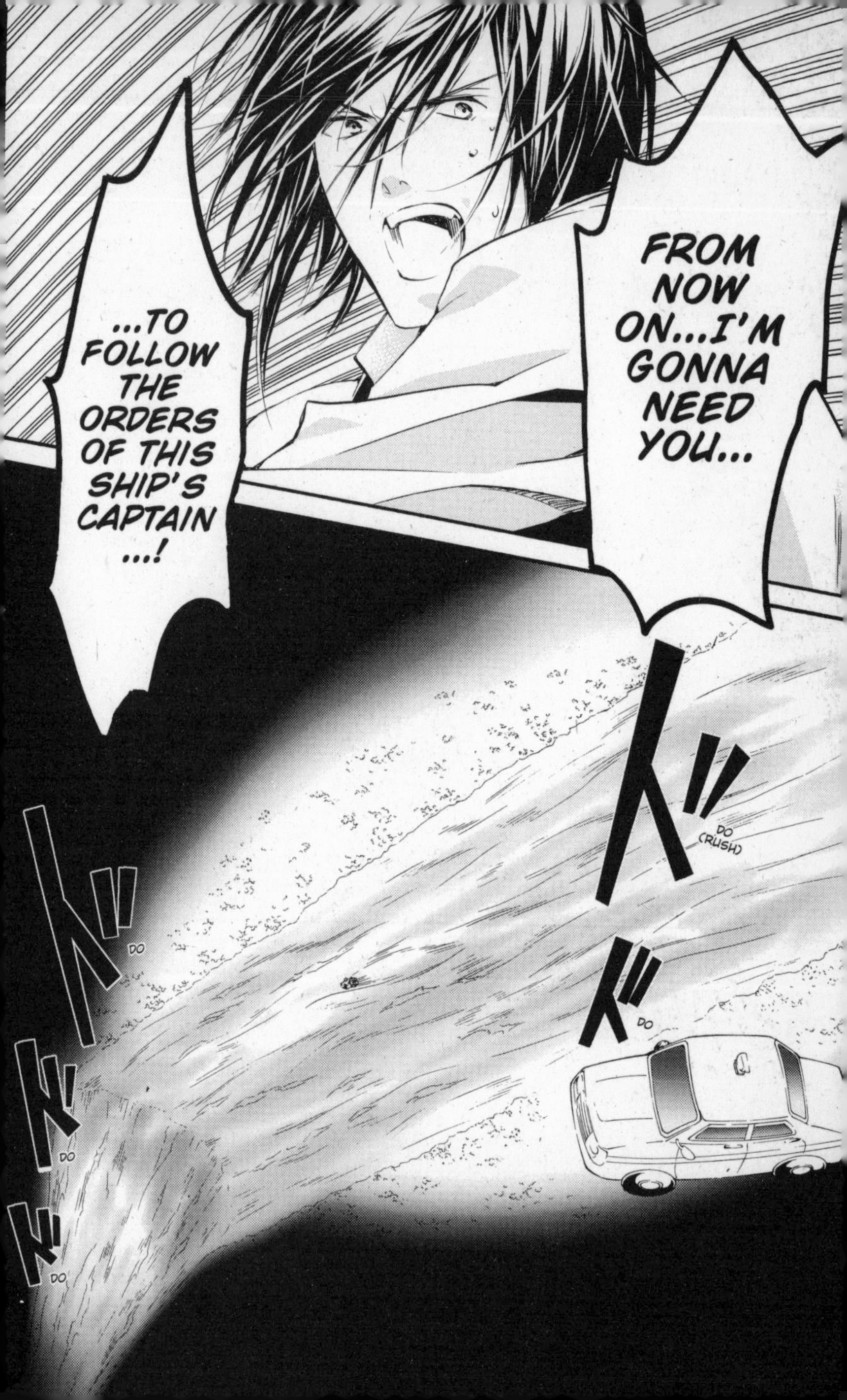
FROM NOW ON...I'M GONNA NEED YOU...
...TO FOLLOW THE ORDERS OF THIS SHIP'S CAPTAIN...!
DO (RUSH)
DO
DO
DO
DO

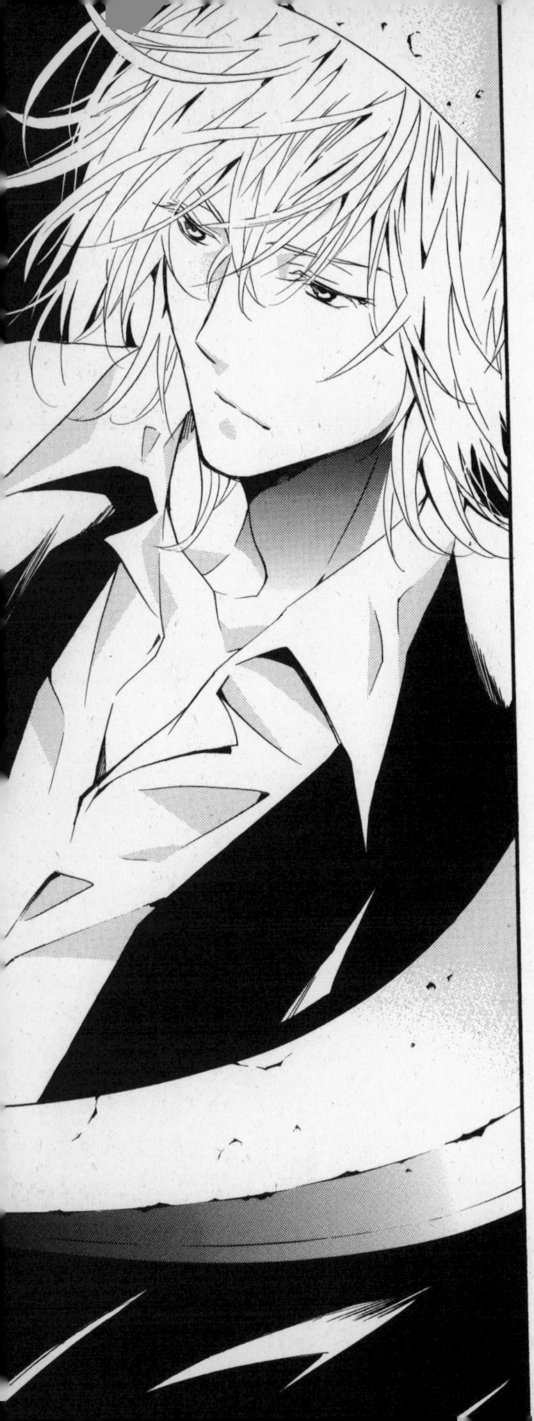

PAYMENT:80

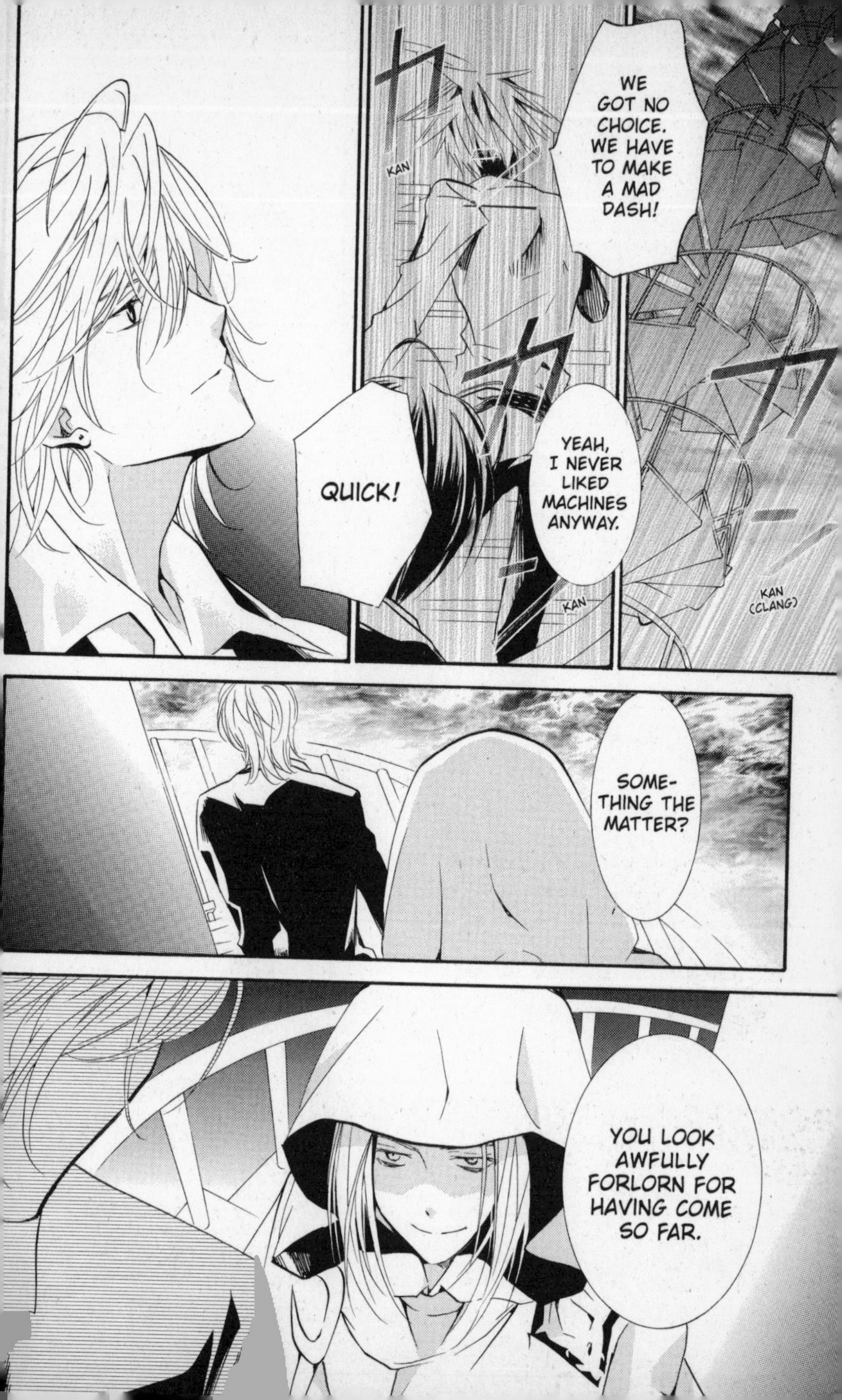
WE GOT NO CHOICE. WE HAVE TO MAKE A MAD DASH!
KAN (CLANG)
KAN
YEAH, I NEVER LIKED MACHINES ANYWAY.
KAN
QUICK!
SOME-THING THE MATTER?
YOU LOOK AWFULLY FORLORN FOR HAVING COME SO FAR.

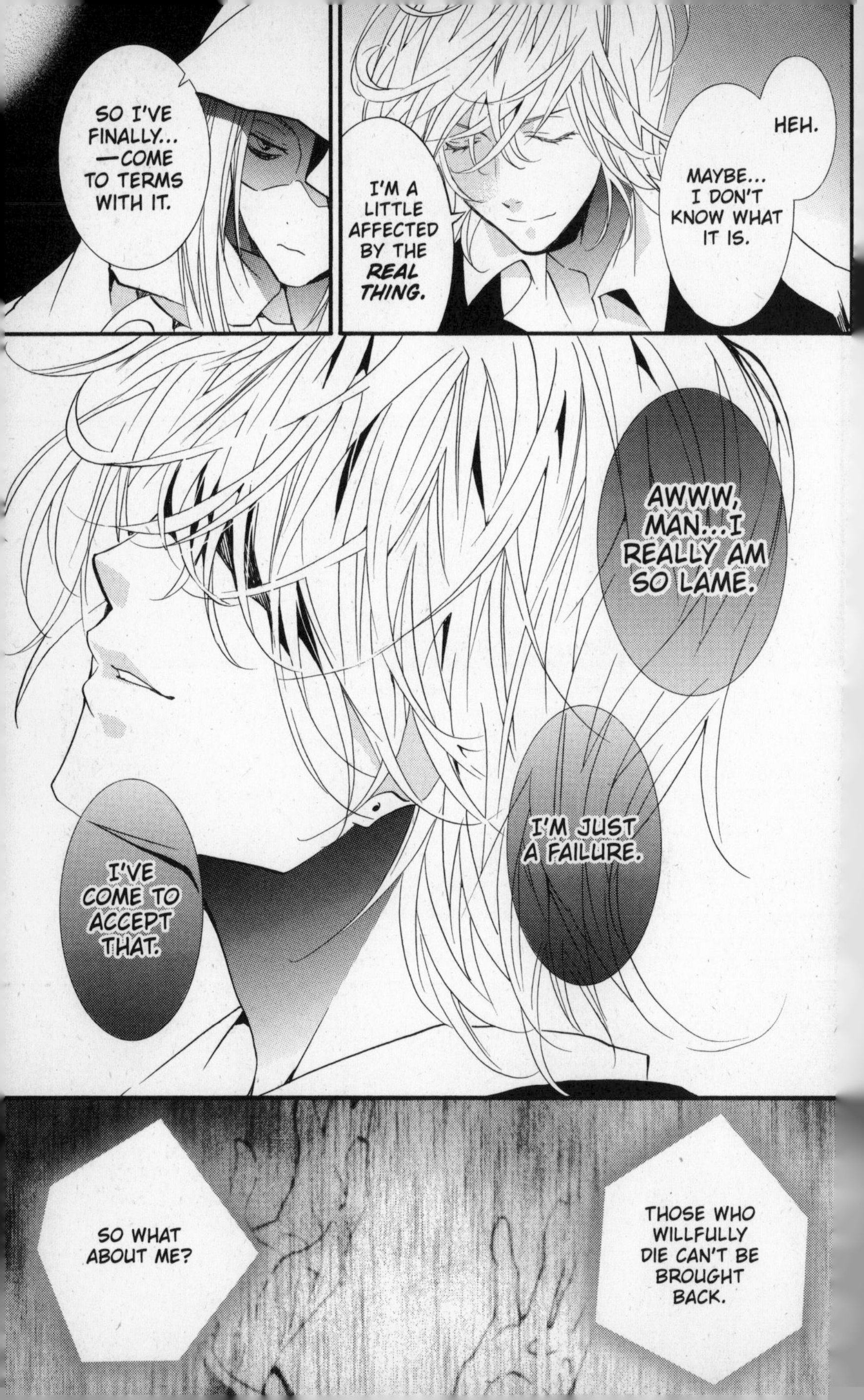
HEH.
MAYBE... I DON'T KNOW WHAT IT IS.
I'M A LITTLE AFFECTED BY THE *REAL THING.*
SO I'VE FINALLY... —COME TO TERMS WITH IT.
AWWW, MAN...I REALLY AM SO LAME.
I'M JUST A FAILURE.
I'VE COME TO ACCEPT THAT.
THOSE WHO WILLFULLY DIE CAN'T BE BROUGHT BACK.
SO WHAT ABOUT ME?

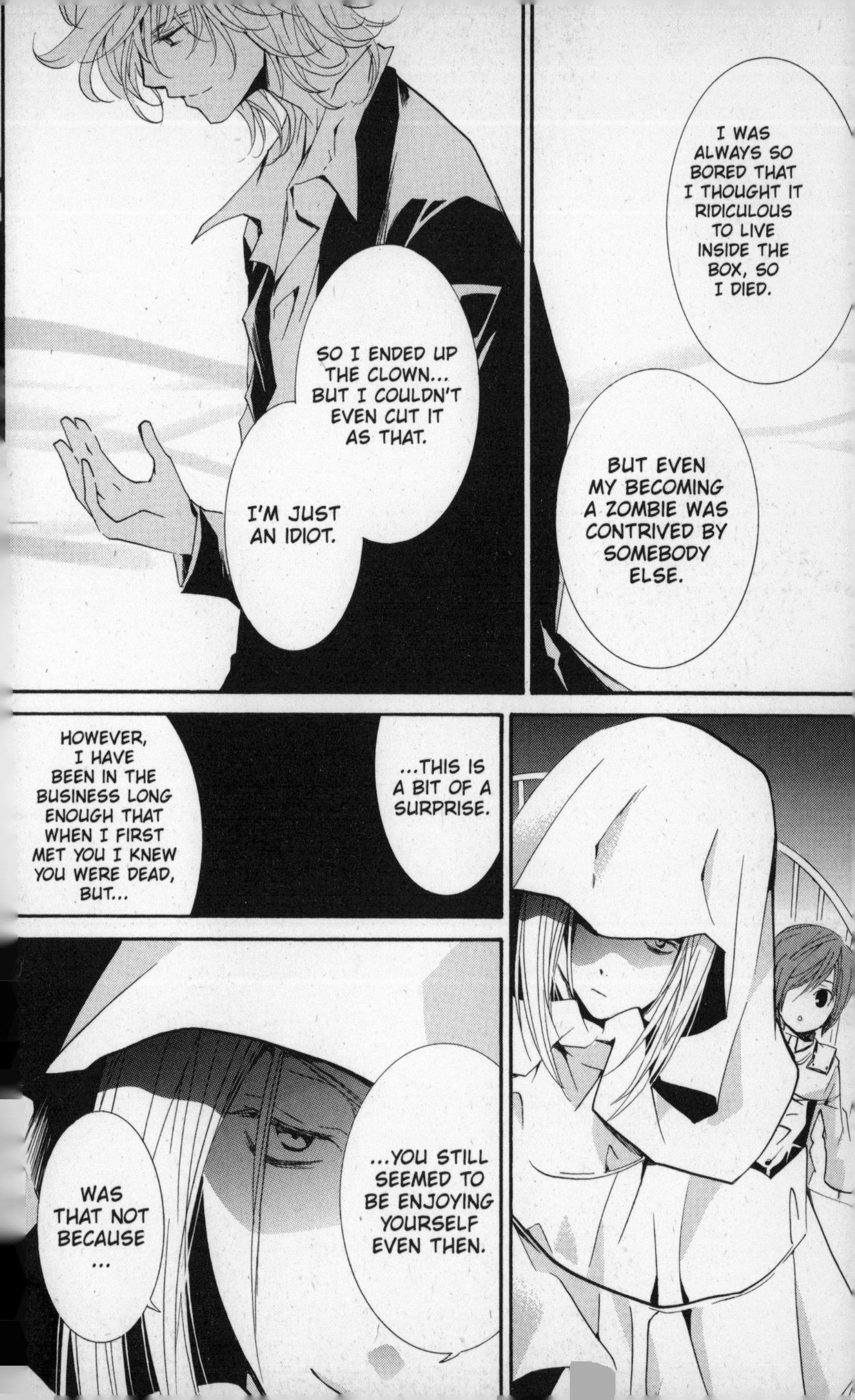

I WAS ALWAYS SO BORED THAT I THOUGHT IT RIDICULOUS TO LIVE INSIDE THE BOX, SO I DIED.
BUT EVEN MY BECOMING A ZOMBIE WAS CONTRIVED BY SOMEBODY ELSE.
SO I ENDED UP THE CLOWN... BUT I COULDN'T EVEN CUT IT AS THAT.
I'M JUST AN IDIOT.
...THIS IS A BIT OF A SURPRISE.
HOWEVER, I HAVE BEEN IN THE BUSINESS LONG ENOUGH THAT WHEN I FIRST MET YOU I KNEW YOU WERE DEAD, BUT...
...YOU STILL SEEMED TO BE ENJOYING YOURSELF EVEN THEN.
WAS THAT NOT BECAUSE ...

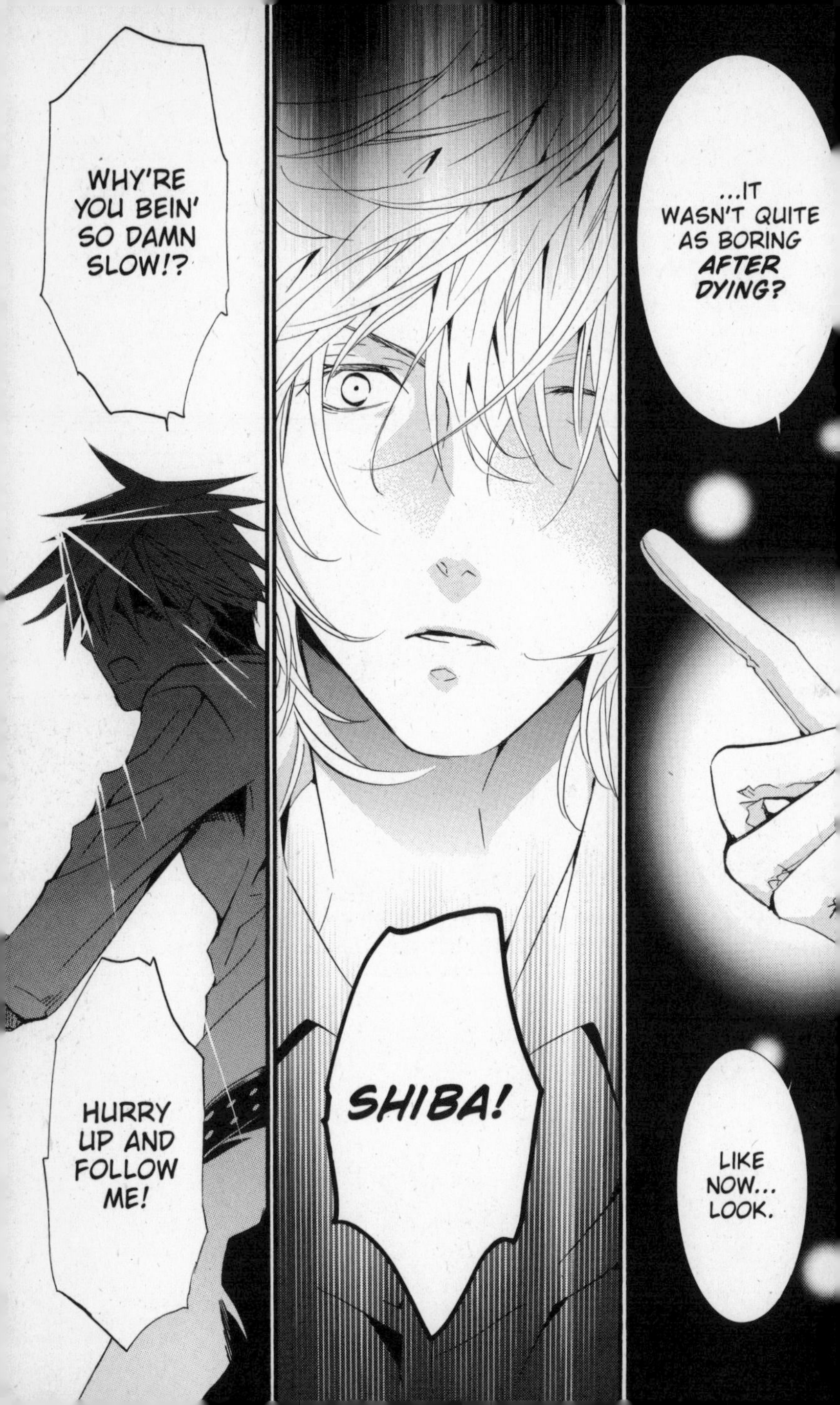
...IT WASN'T QUITE AS BORING AFTER DYING?
LIKE NOW... LOOK.
SHIBA!
WHY'RE YOU BEIN' SO DAMN SLOW!?
HURRY UP AND FOLLOW ME!

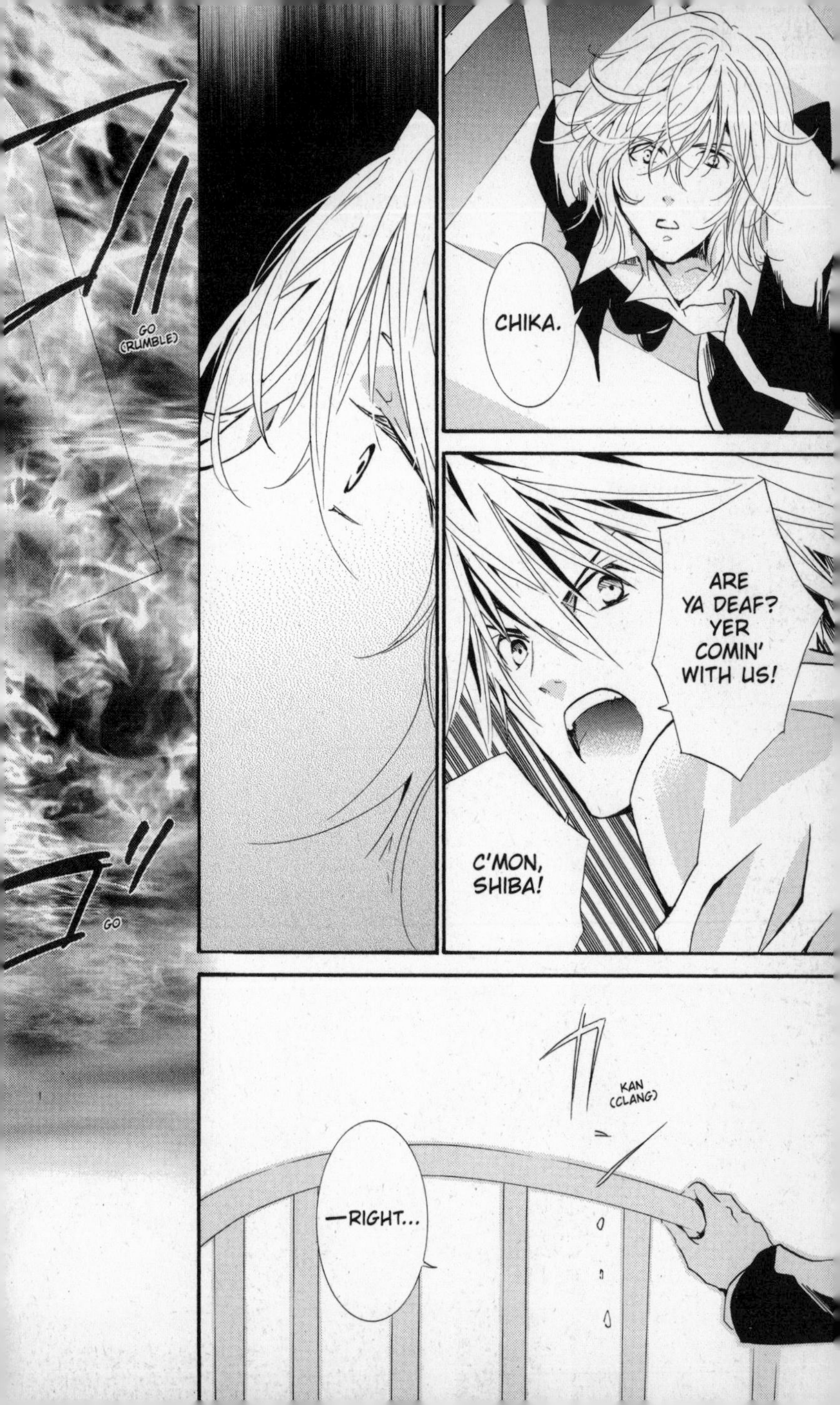
CHIKA.
ARE YA DEAF? YER COMIN' WITH US!
C'MON, SHIBA!
KAN (CLANG)
—RIGHT...
GO (RUMBLE)
GO

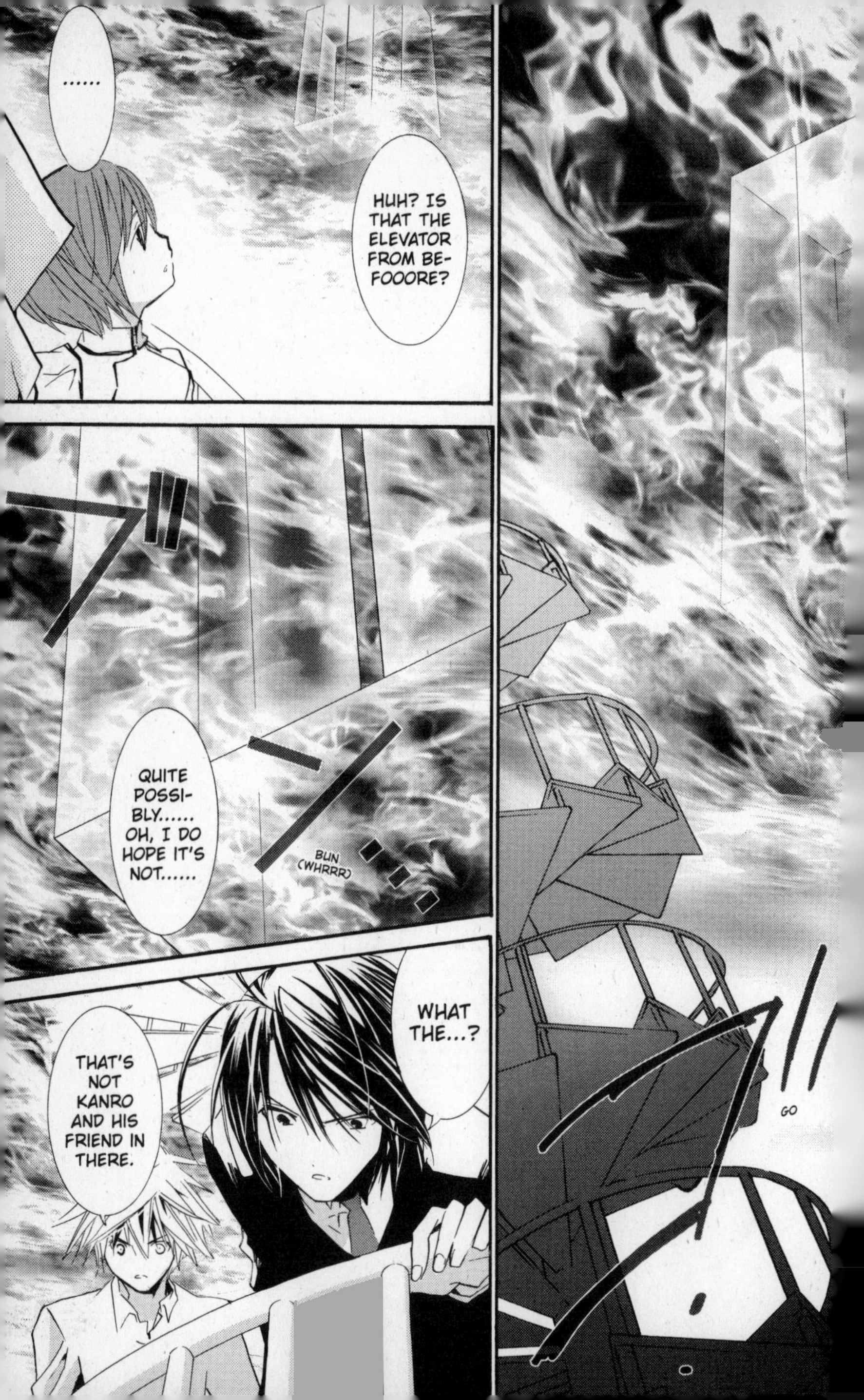
GO
......
HUH? IS THAT THE ELEVATOR FROM BE-FOOORE?
QUITE POSSIBLY...... OH, I DO HOPE IT'S NOT......
BUN (WHRRR)
WHAT THE...?
THAT'S NOT KANRO AND HIS FRIEND IN THERE.

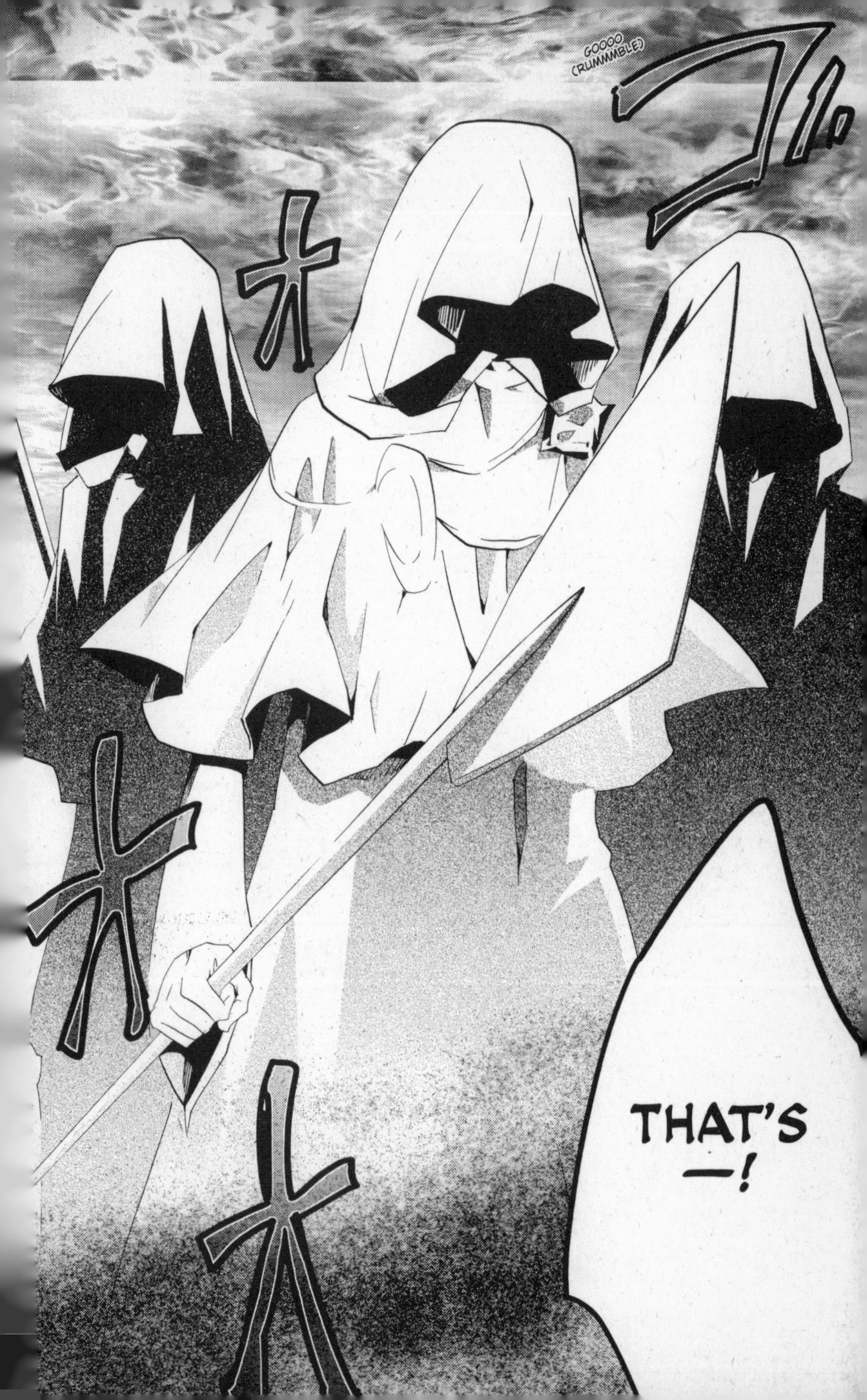
GOOOO
(RUMMMBLE)
THAT'S
—!

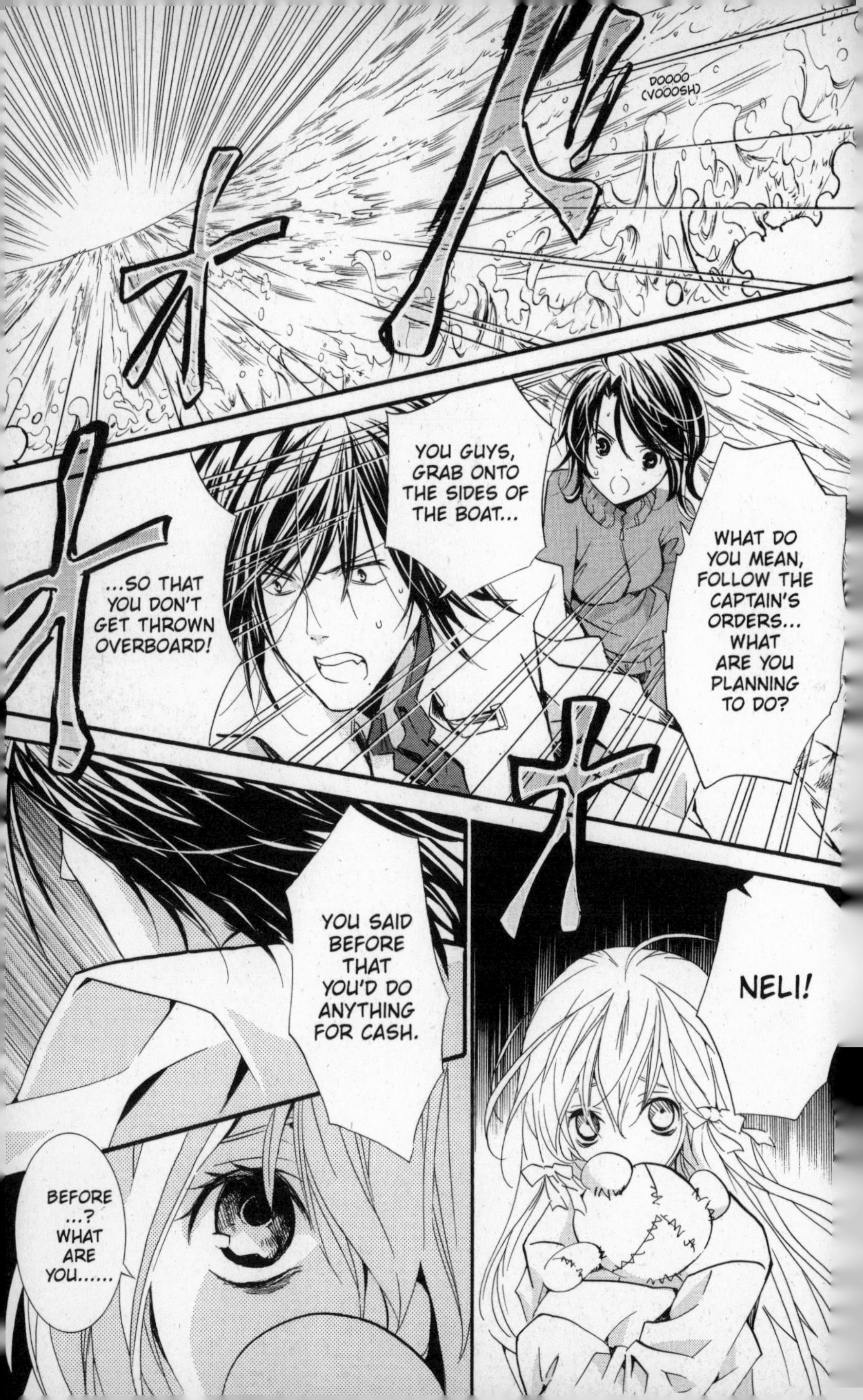
DOOOO (VOOOSH)
YOU GUYS, GRAB ONTO THE SIDES OF THE BOAT...
...SO THAT YOU DON'T GET THROWN OVERBOARD!
WHAT DO YOU MEAN, FOLLOW THE CAPTAIN'S ORDERS... WHAT ARE YOU PLANNING TO DO?
NELI!
YOU SAID BEFORE THAT YOU'D DO ANYTHING FOR CASH.
BEFORE ...? WHAT ARE YOU......

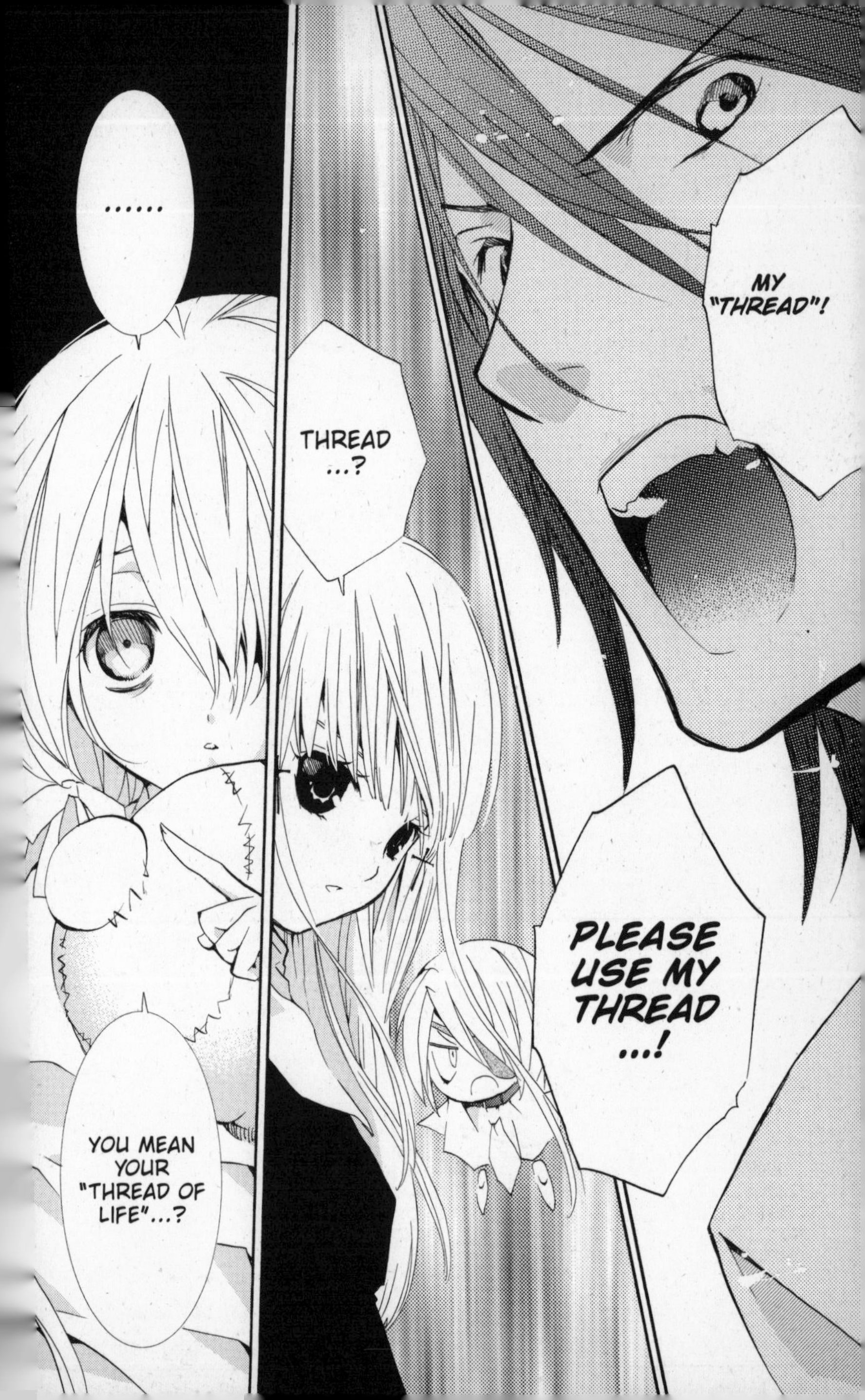
MY "THREAD"!
PLEASE USE MY THREAD ...!
THREAD ...?
......
YOU MEAN YOUR "THREAD OF LIFE"...?

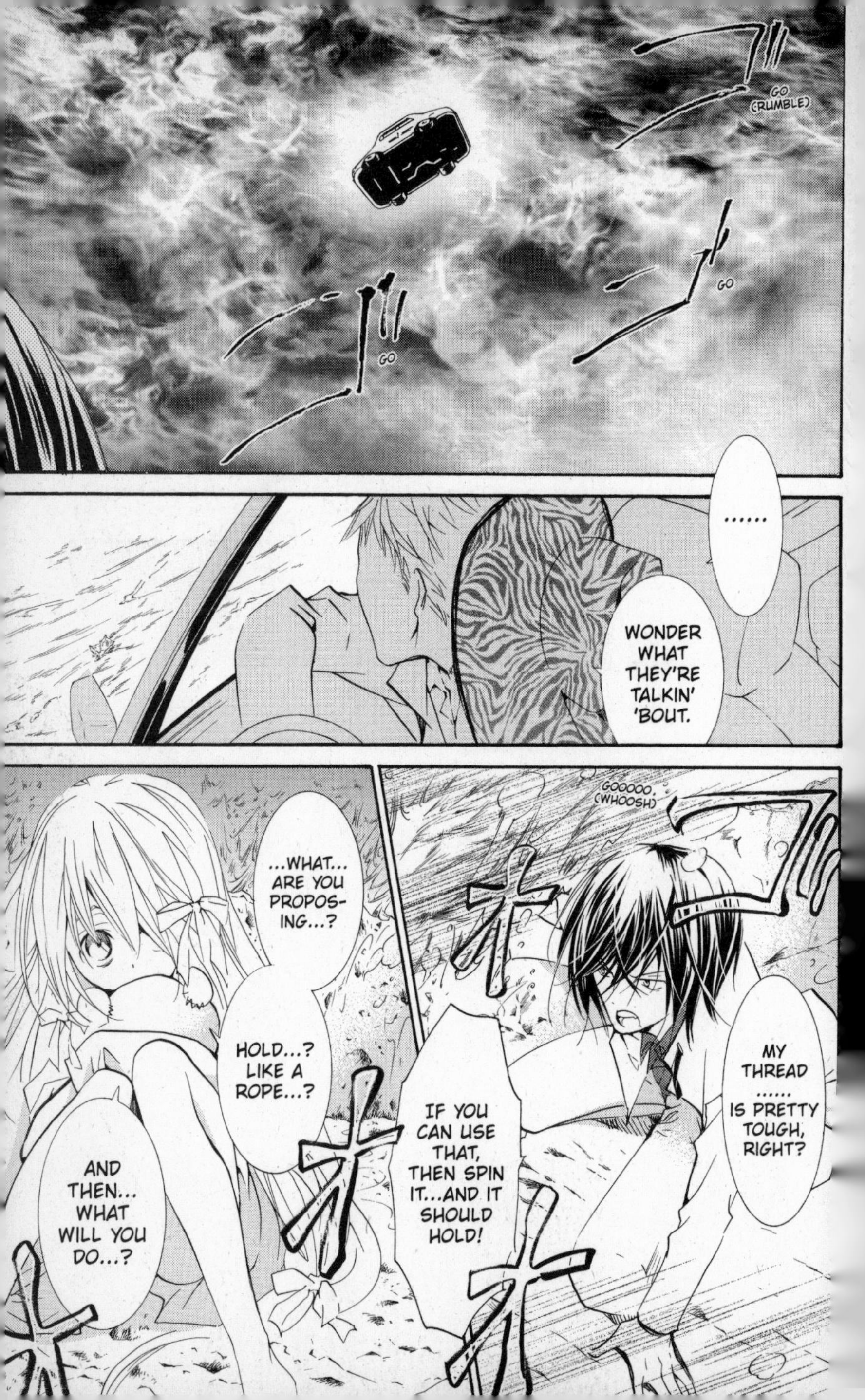
GO (RUMBLE)
GO
GO
......
WONDER WHAT THEY'RE TALKIN' 'BOUT.
GOOOOO (WHOOSH)
MY THREAD ...... IS PRETTY TOUGH, RIGHT?
...WHAT... ARE YOU PROPOS-ING...?
HOLD...? LIKE A ROPE...?
IF YOU CAN USE THAT, THEN SPIN IT...AND IT SHOULD HOLD!
AND THEN... WHAT WILL YOU DO...?

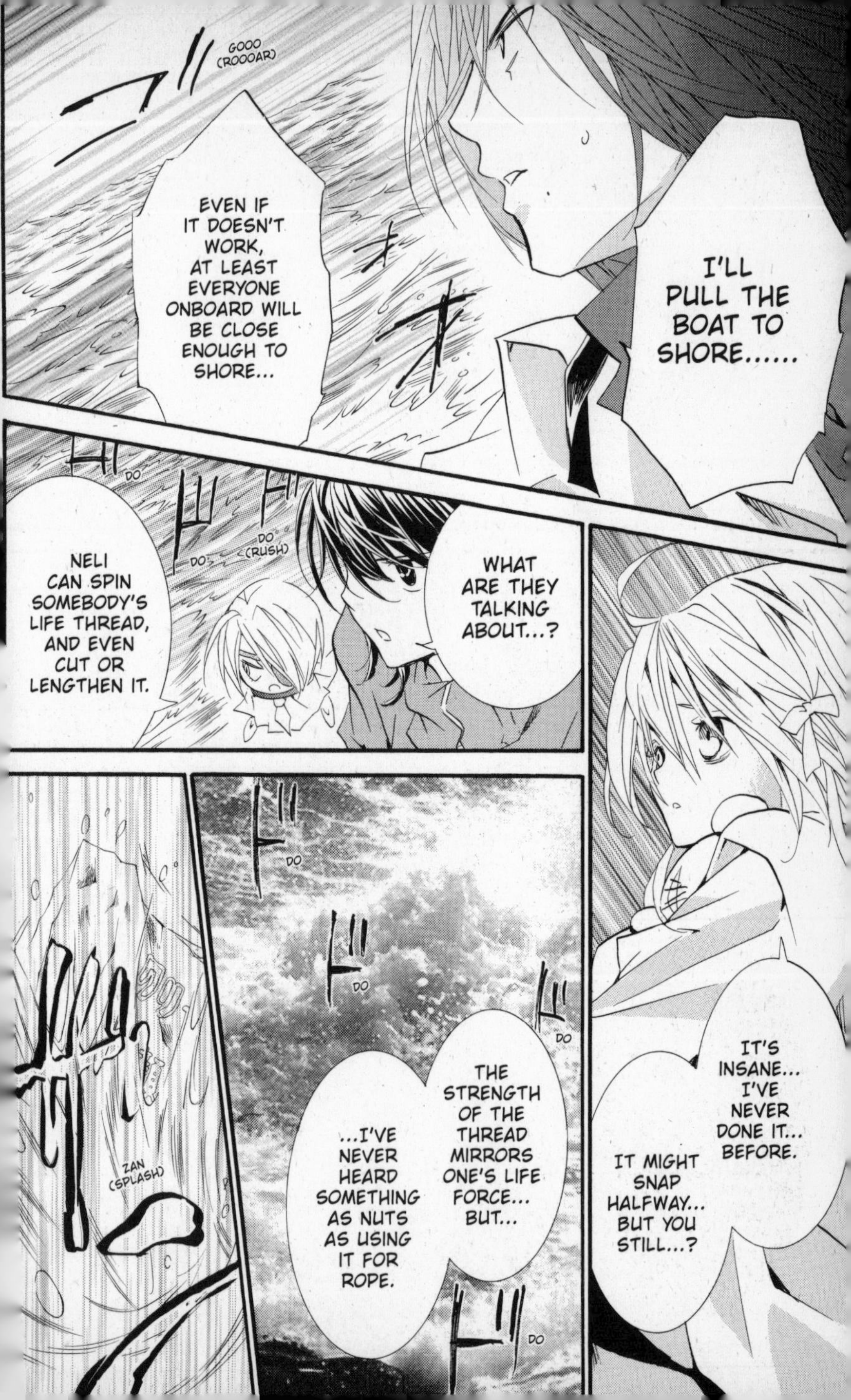
I'LL PULL THE BOAT TO SHORE......
EVEN IF IT DOESN'T WORK, AT LEAST EVERYONE ONBOARD WILL BE CLOSE ENOUGH TO SHORE...
GOOO (ROOOAR)
IT'S INSANE... I'VE NEVER DONE IT... BEFORE.
IT MIGHT SNAP HALFWAY... BUT YOU STILL...?
WHAT ARE THEY TALKING ABOUT...?
DO (RUSH)
DO
DO
NELI CAN SPIN SOMEBODY'S LIFE THREAD, AND EVEN CUT OR LENGTHEN IT.
DO
DO
DO
THE STRENGTH OF THE THREAD MIRRORS ONE'S LIFE FORCE... BUT...
...I'VE NEVER HEARD SOMETHING AS NUTS AS USING IT FOR ROPE.
DO
ZAN (SPLASH)

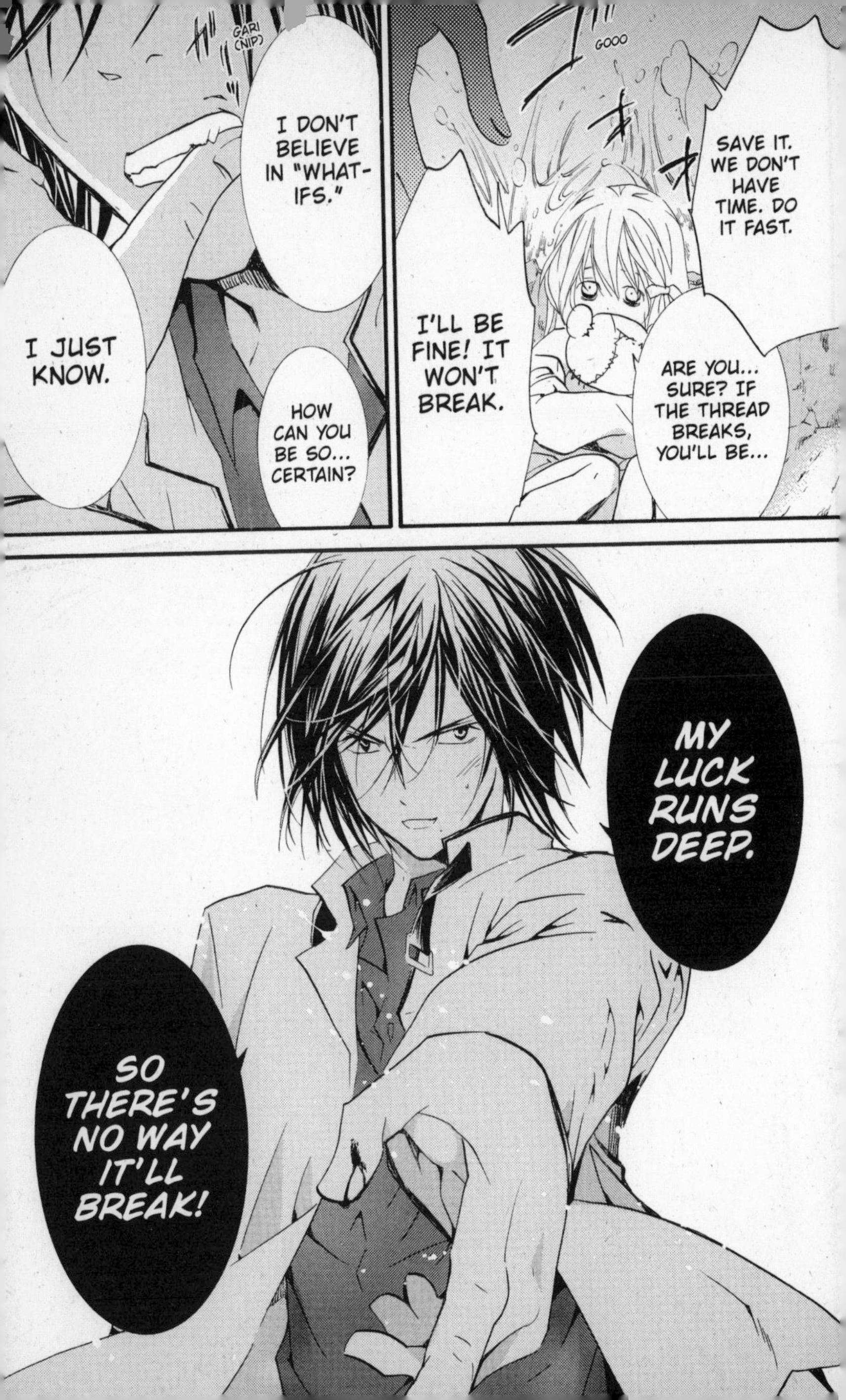

GOOO
SAVE IT. WE DON'T HAVE TIME. DO IT FAST.
ARE YOU... SURE? IF THE THREAD BREAKS, YOU'LL BE...
I'LL BE FINE! IT WON'T BREAK.
GARI (NIP)
I DON'T BELIEVE IN "WHAT-IFS."
HOW CAN YOU BE SO... CERTAIN?
I JUST KNOW.
MY LUCK RUNS DEEP.
SO THERE'S NO WAY IT'LL BREAK!

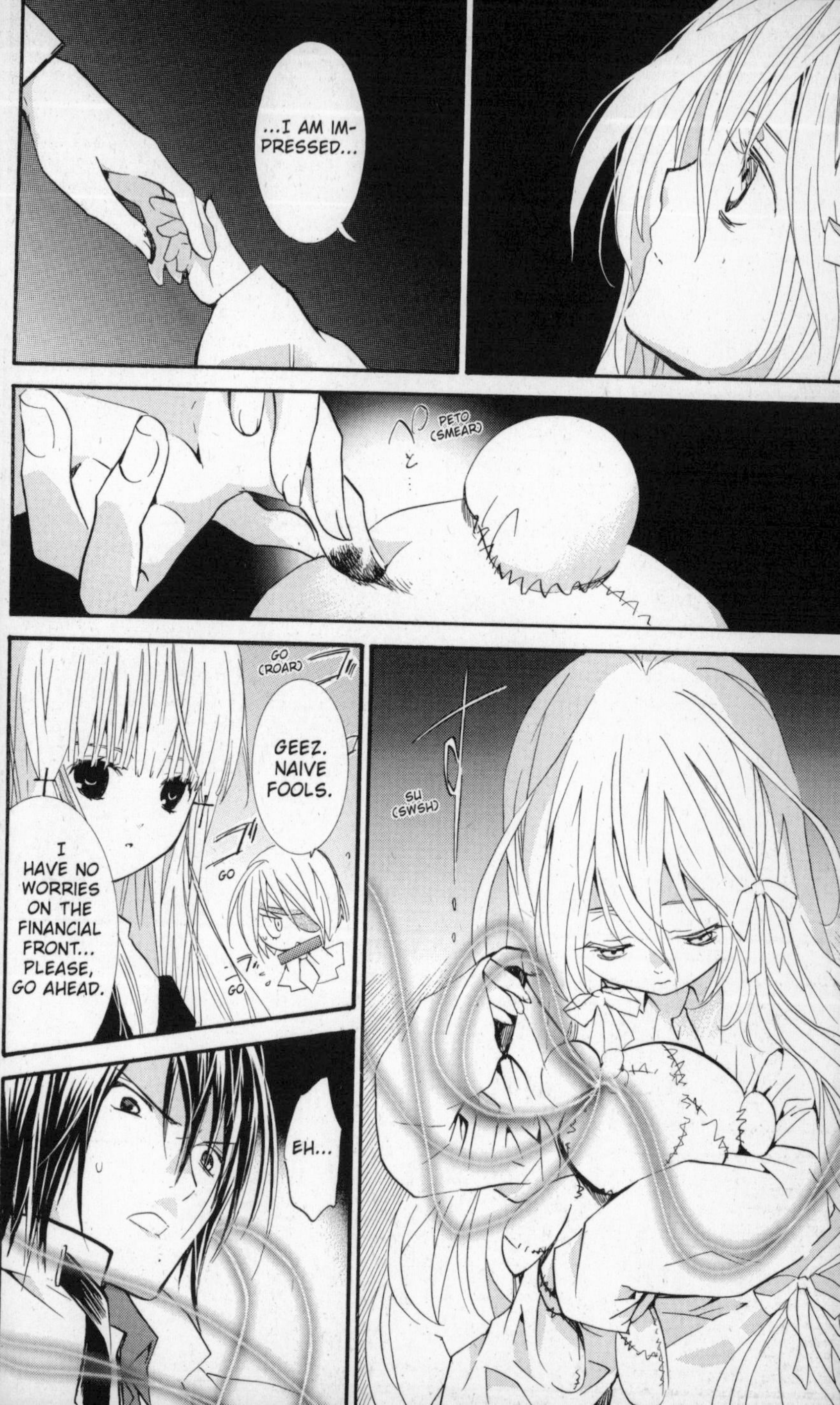
...I AM IM-PRESSED...
PETO (SMEAR)
SU (SWSH)
GO (ROAR)
GEEZ. NAIVE FOOLS.
GO
GO
I HAVE NO WORRIES ON THE FINANCIAL FRONT... PLEASE, GO AHEAD.
EH...

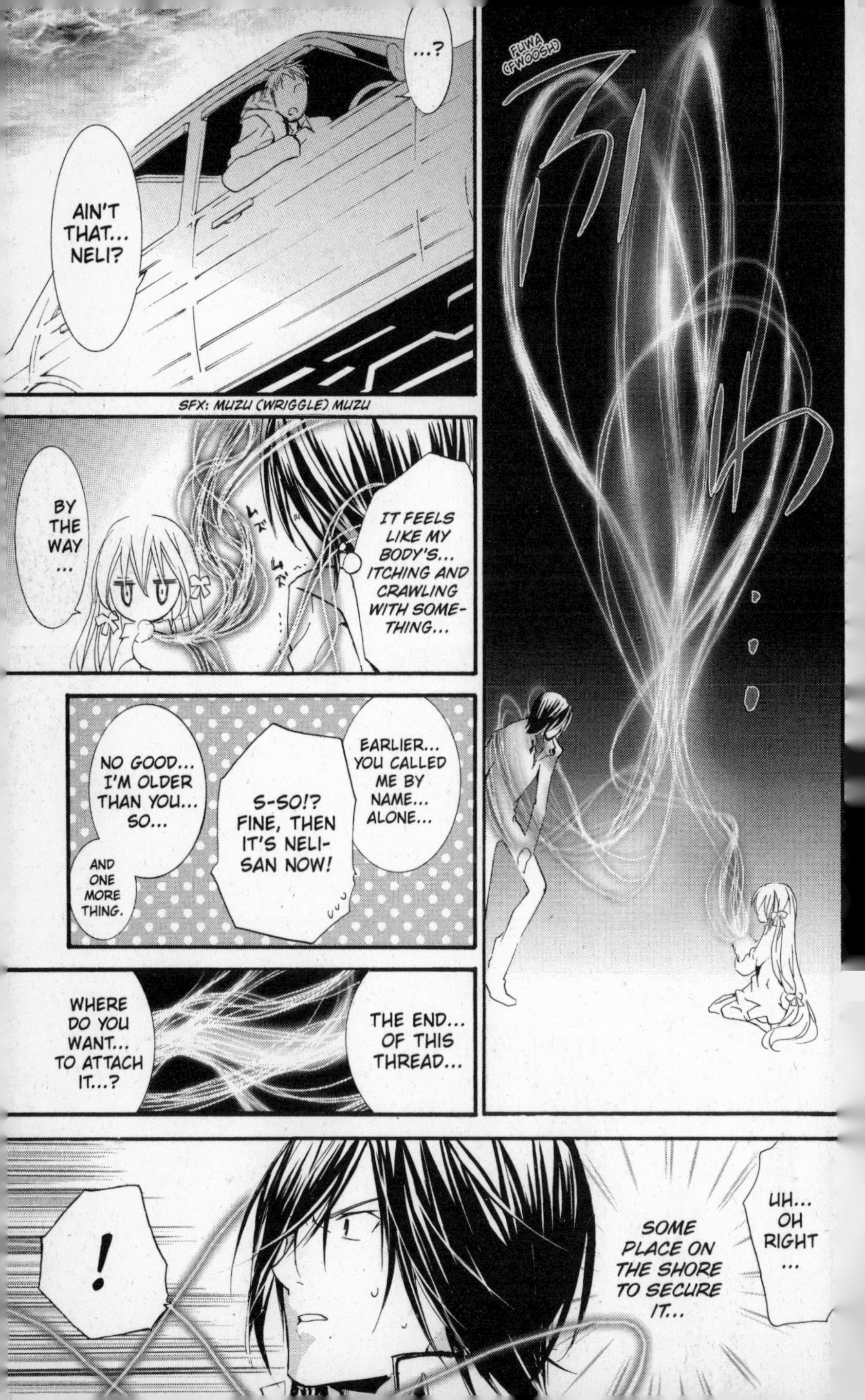
FUWA (FWOOSH)
...?
AIN'T THAT... NELI?
SFX: MUZU (WRIGGLE) MUZU
IT FEELS LIKE MY BODY'S... ITCHING AND CRAWLING WITH SOMETHING...
BY THE WAY...
EARLIER... YOU CALLED ME BY NAME... ALONE...
S-SO!? FINE, THEN IT'S NELI-SAN NOW!
NO GOOD... I'M OLDER THAN YOU... SO...
AND ONE MORE THING.
THE END... OF THIS THREAD...
WHERE DO YOU WANT... TO ATTACH IT...?
UH... OH RIGHT...
SOME PLACE ON THE SHORE TO SECURE IT...
!

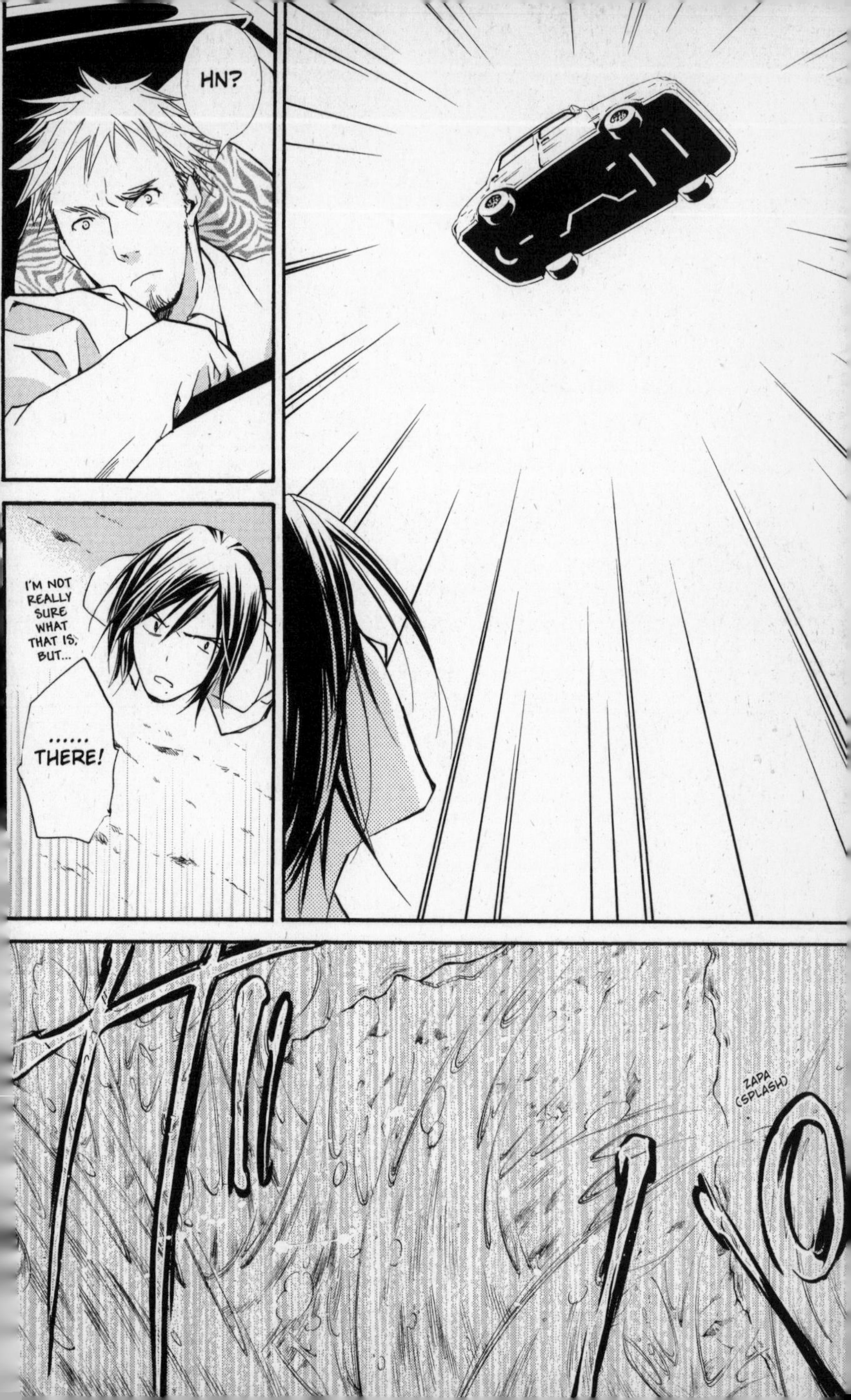
HN?
I'M NOT REALLY SURE WHAT THAT IS, BUT...
......THERE!
ZAPA (SPLASH)

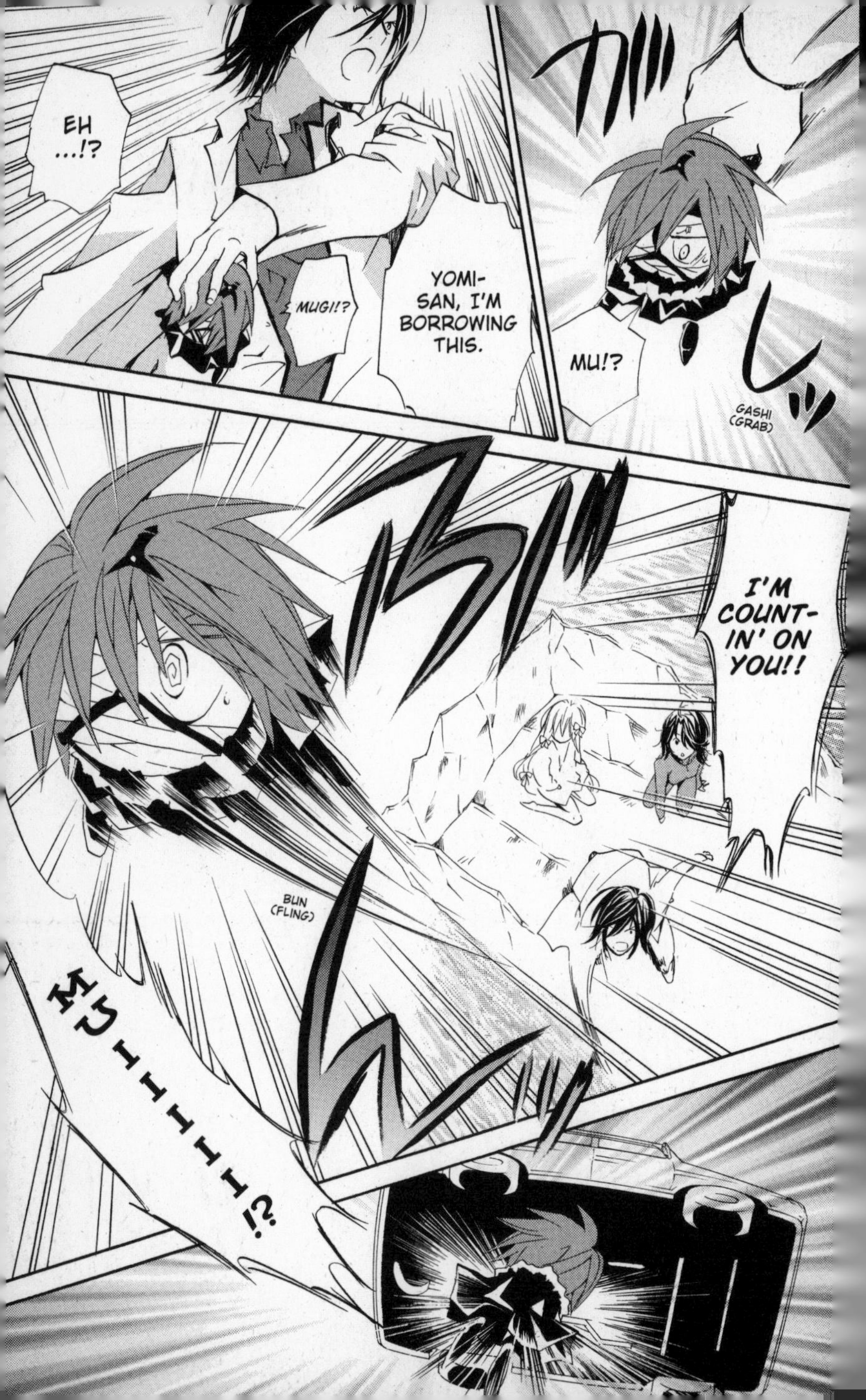
MU!?
GASHI (GRAB)
EH ...!?
YOMI-SAN, I'M BORROWING THIS.
MUGI!?
I'M COUNTIN' ON YOU!!
BUN (FLING)
MUIIIIII!?

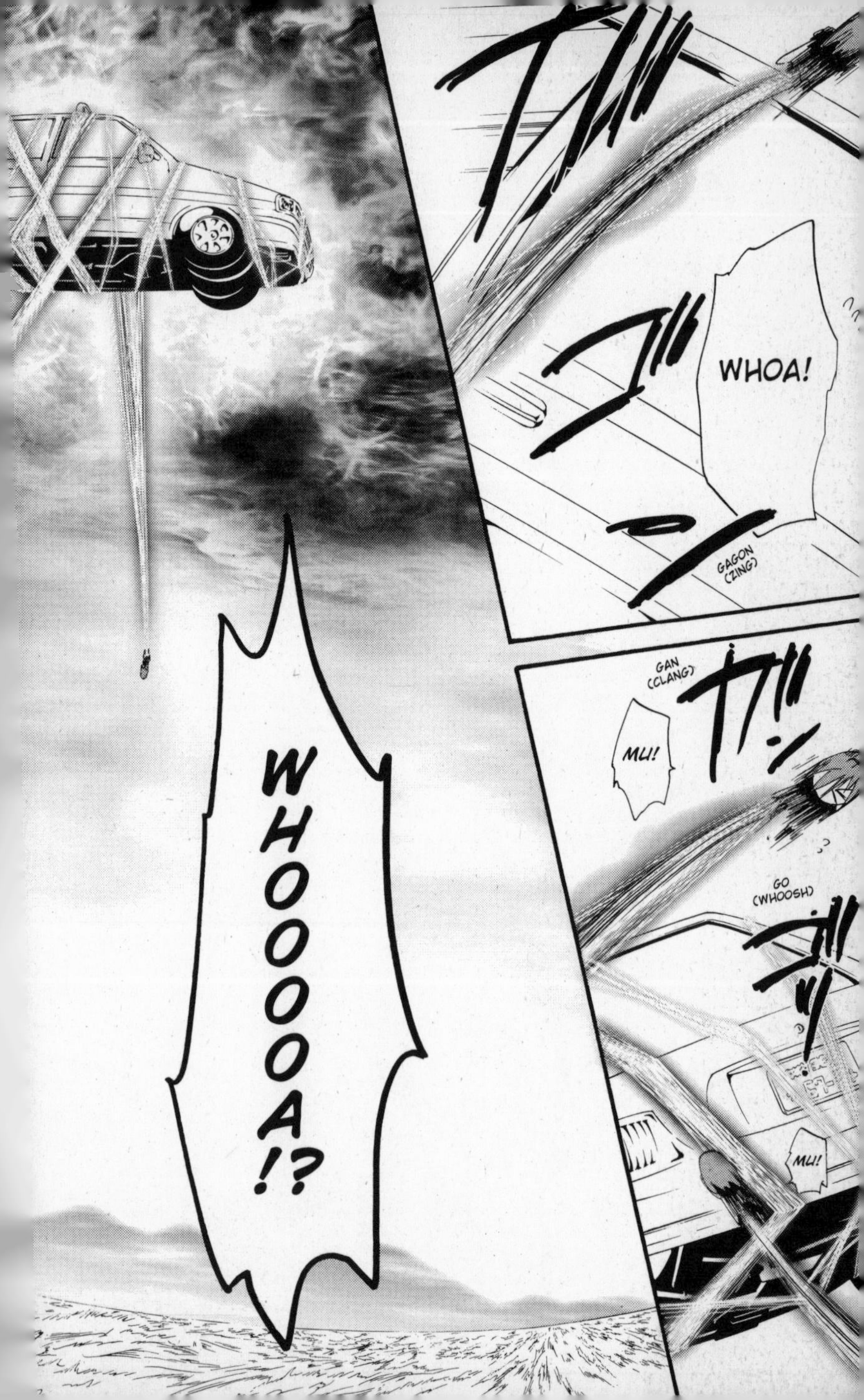
WHOA!
GAGON (ZING)
GAN (CLANG)
MU!
GO (WHOOSH)
MU!
WHOOOOA!?

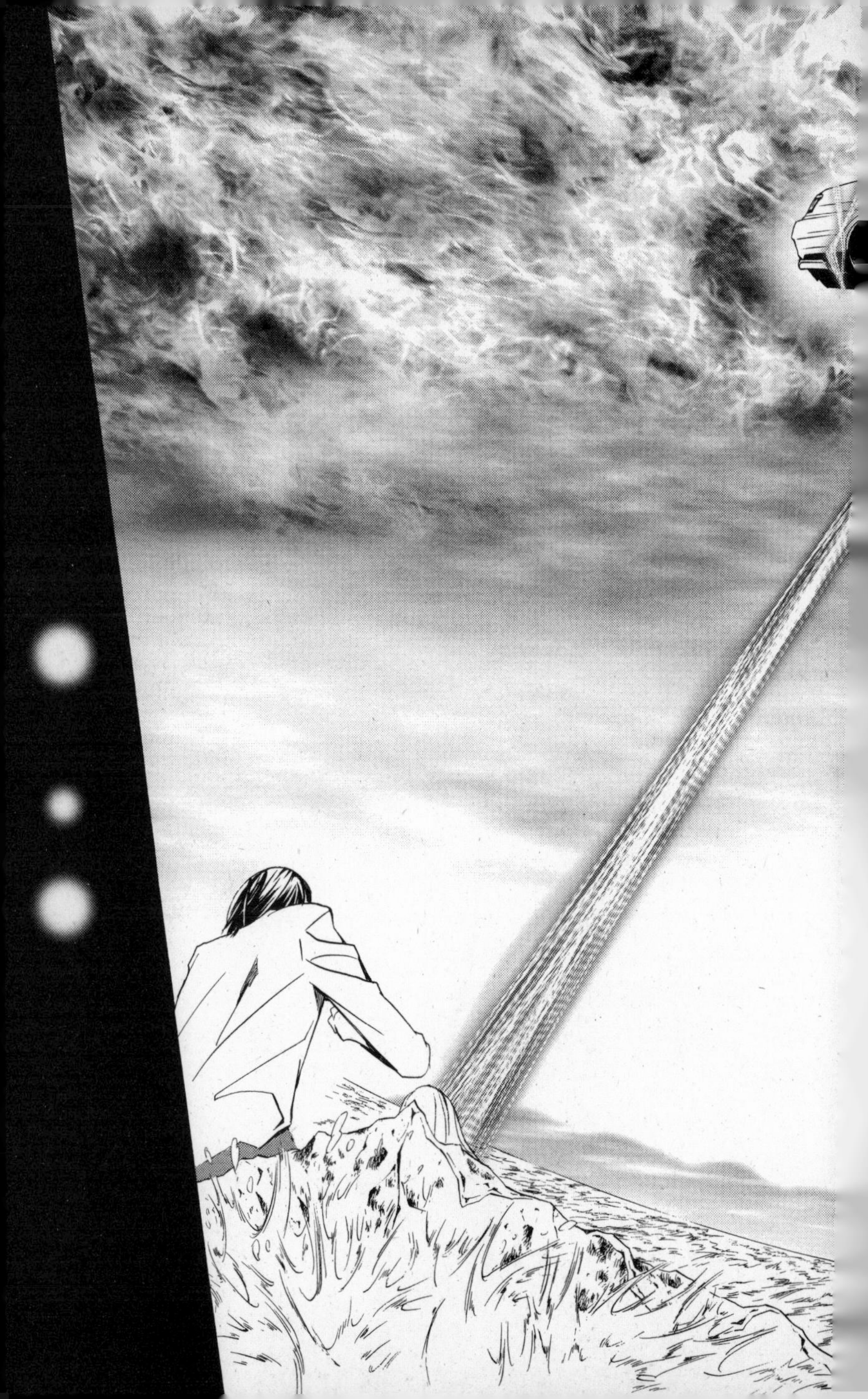

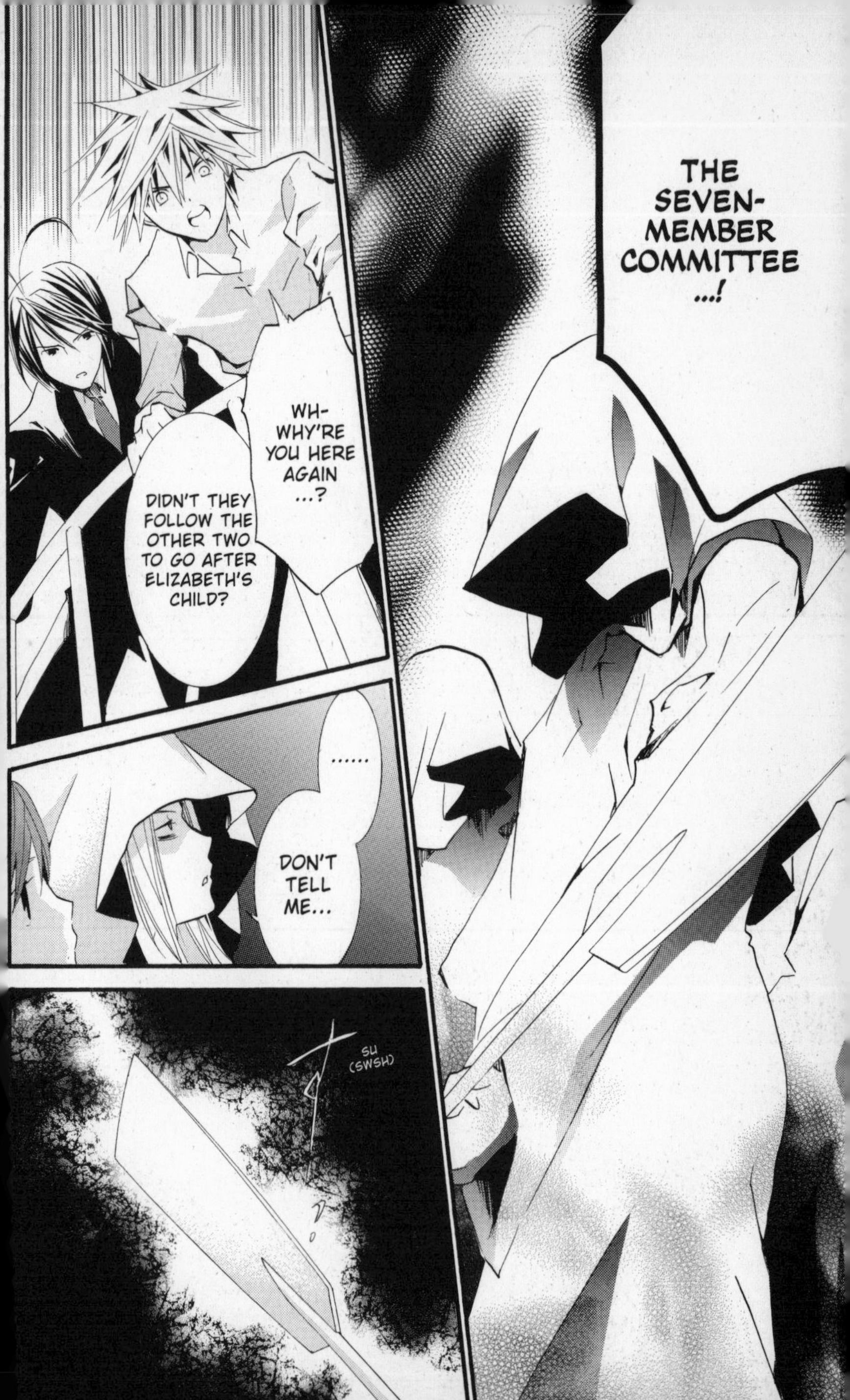
THE SEVEN-MEMBER COMMITTEE ...!
WH-WHY'RE YOU HERE AGAIN ...?
DIDN'T THEY FOLLOW THE OTHER TWO TO GO AFTER ELIZABETH'S CHILD?
......
DON'T TELL ME...
SU (SWSH)

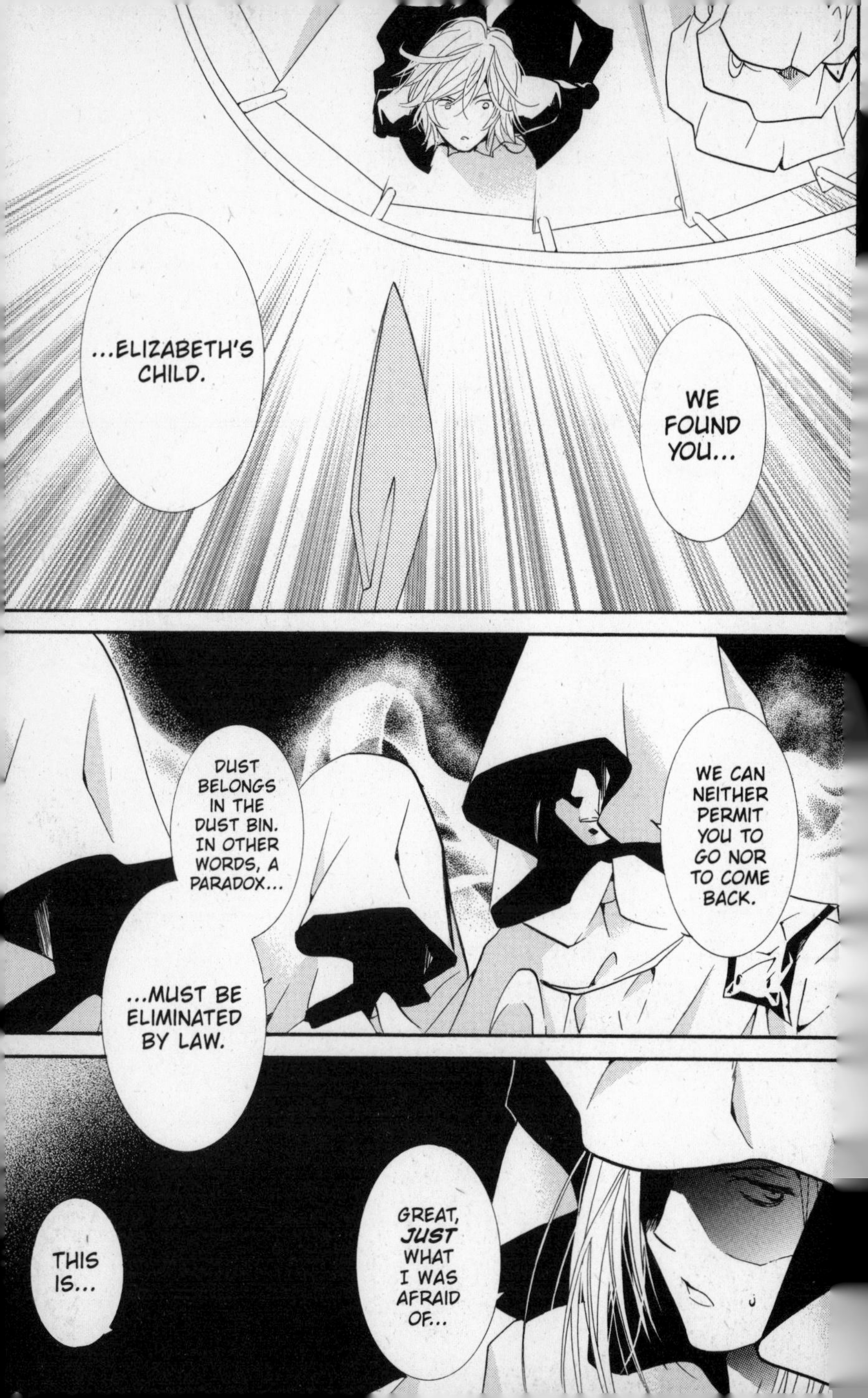
WE FOUND YOU...
...ELIZABETH'S CHILD.
WE CAN NEITHER PERMIT YOU TO GO NOR TO COME BACK.
DUST BELONGS IN THE DUST BIN. IN OTHER WORDS, A PARADOX...
...MUST BE ELIMINATED BY LAW.
GREAT, *JUST* WHAT I WAS AFRAID OF...
THIS IS...

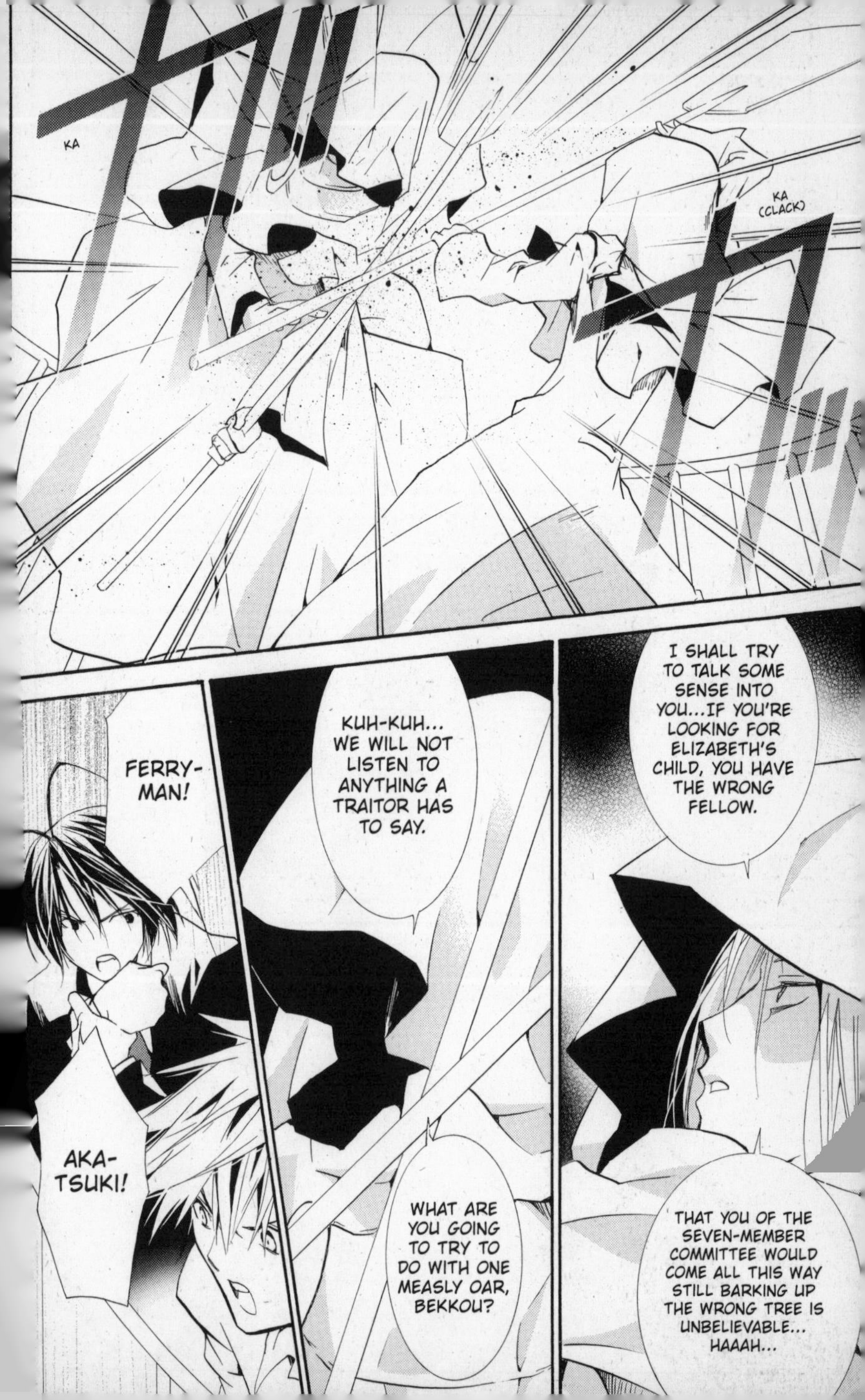
KA (CLACK)
KA
I SHALL TRY TO TALK SOME SENSE INTO YOU...IF YOU'RE LOOKING FOR ELIZABETH'S CHILD, YOU HAVE THE WRONG FELLOW.
THAT YOU OF THE SEVEN-MEMBER COMMITTEE WOULD COME ALL THIS WAY STILL BARKING UP THE WRONG TREE IS UNBELIEVABLE... HAAAH...
KUH-KUH... WE WILL NOT LISTEN TO ANYTHING A TRAITOR HAS TO SAY.
WHAT ARE YOU GOING TO TRY TO DO WITH ONE MEASLY OAR, BEKKOU?
FERRY-MAN!
AKA-TSUKI!

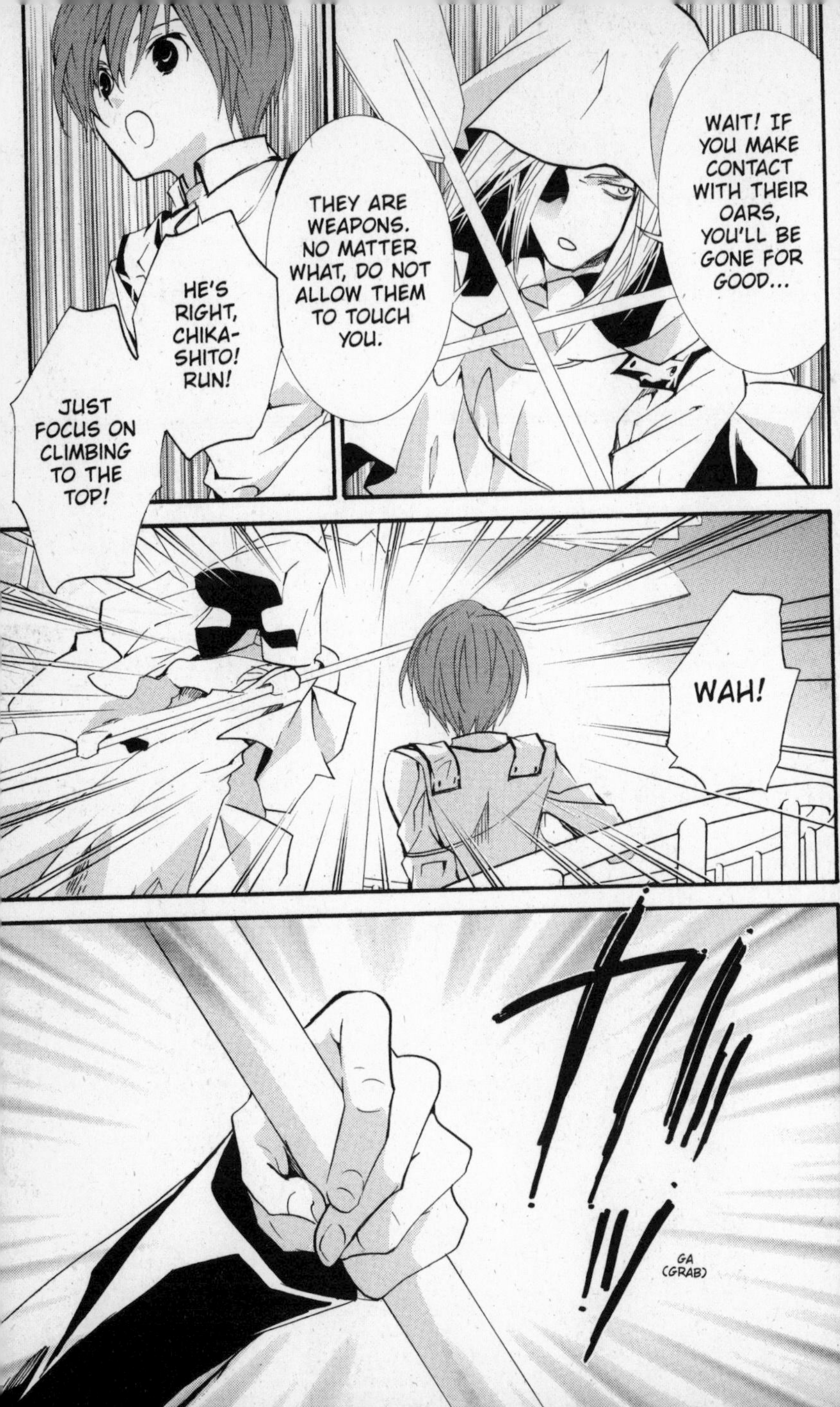
WAIT! IF YOU MAKE CONTACT WITH THEIR OARS, YOU'LL BE GONE FOR GOOD...
THEY ARE WEAPONS. NO MATTER WHAT, DO NOT ALLOW THEM TO TOUCH YOU.
HE'S RIGHT, CHIKA-SHITO! RUN!
JUST FOCUS ON CLIMBING TO THE TOP!
WAH!
GA (GRAB)

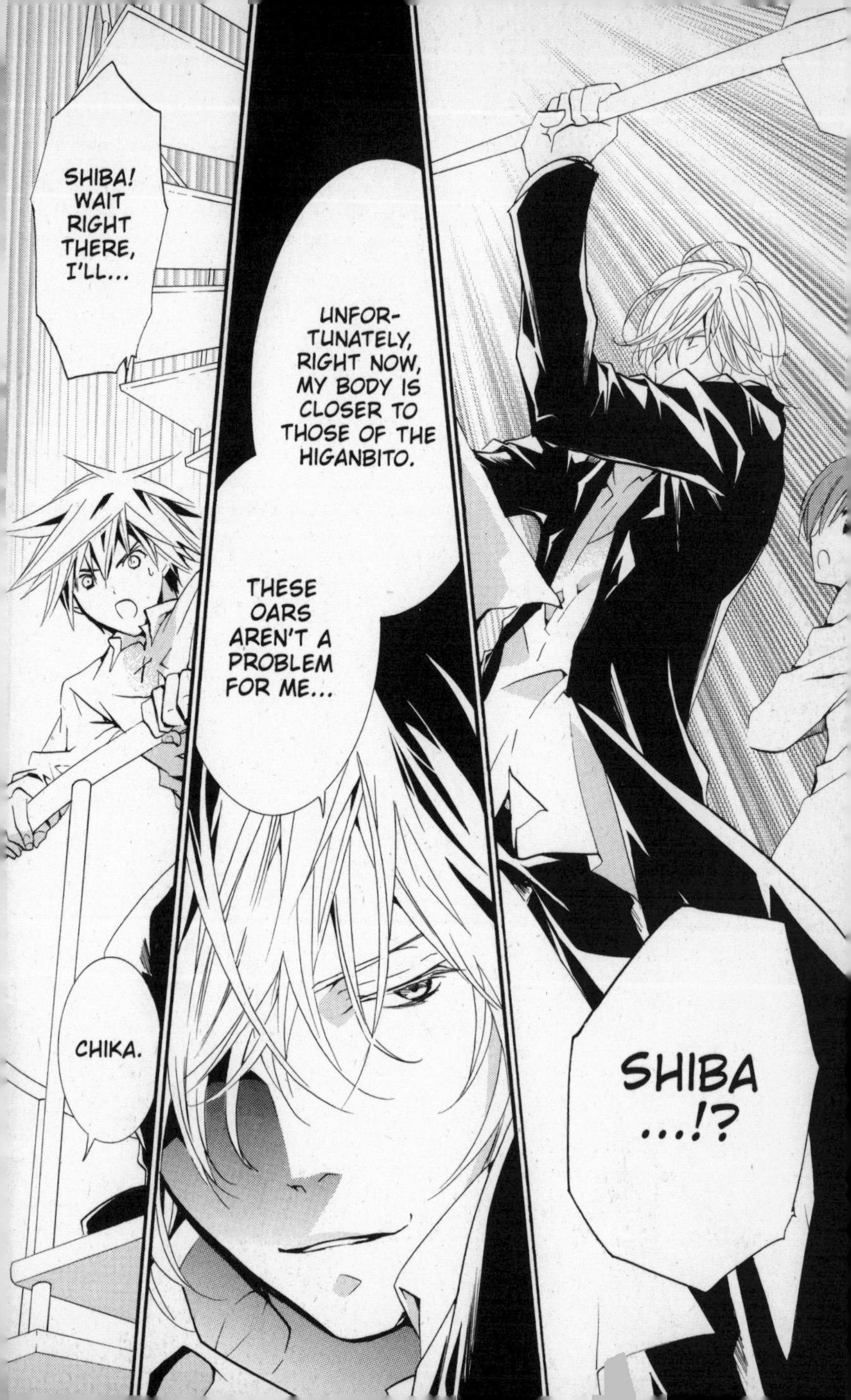
SHIBA ...!?
UNFORTUNATELY, RIGHT NOW, MY BODY IS CLOSER TO THOSE OF THE HIGANBITO.
THESE OARS AREN'T A PROBLEM FOR ME...
SHIBA! WAIT RIGHT THERE, I'LL...
CHIKA.

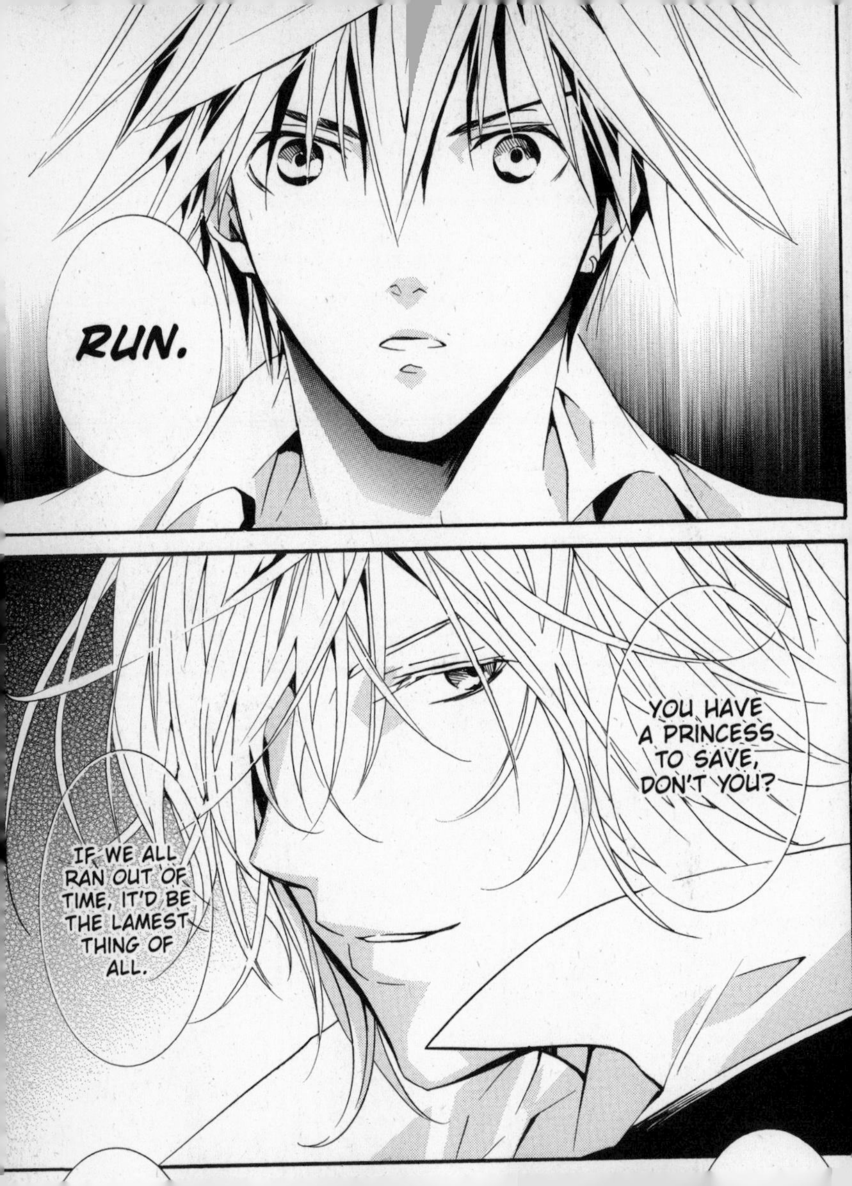
RUN.
YOU HAVE A PRINCESS TO SAVE, DON'T YOU?
IF WE ALL RAN OUT OF TIME, IT'D BE THE LAMEST THING OF ALL.

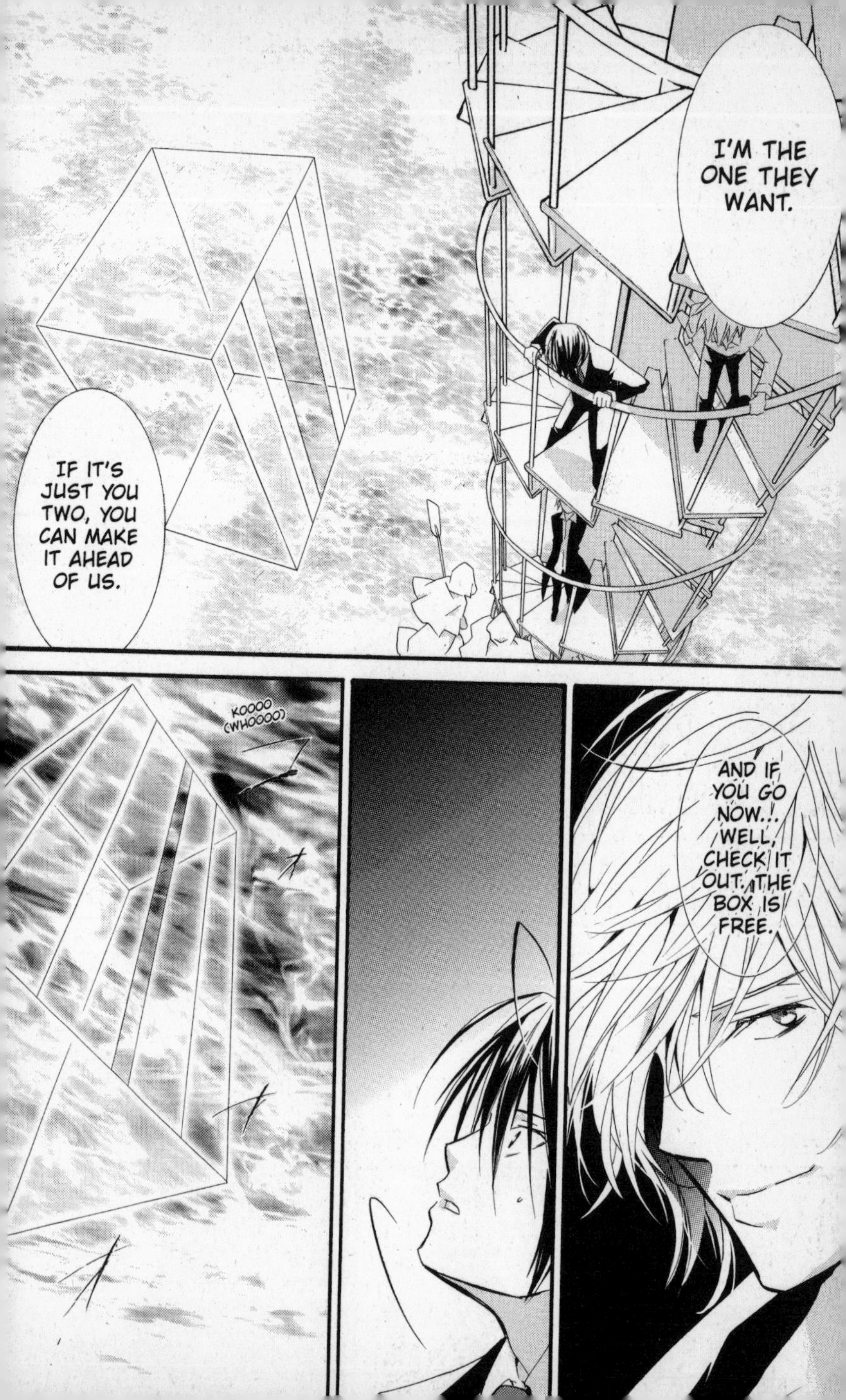
I'M THE ONE THEY WANT.
IF IT'S JUST YOU TWO, YOU CAN MAKE IT AHEAD OF US.
AND IF YOU GO NOW... WELL, CHECK IT OUT. THE BOX IS FREE.
KOOOO (WHOOOO)

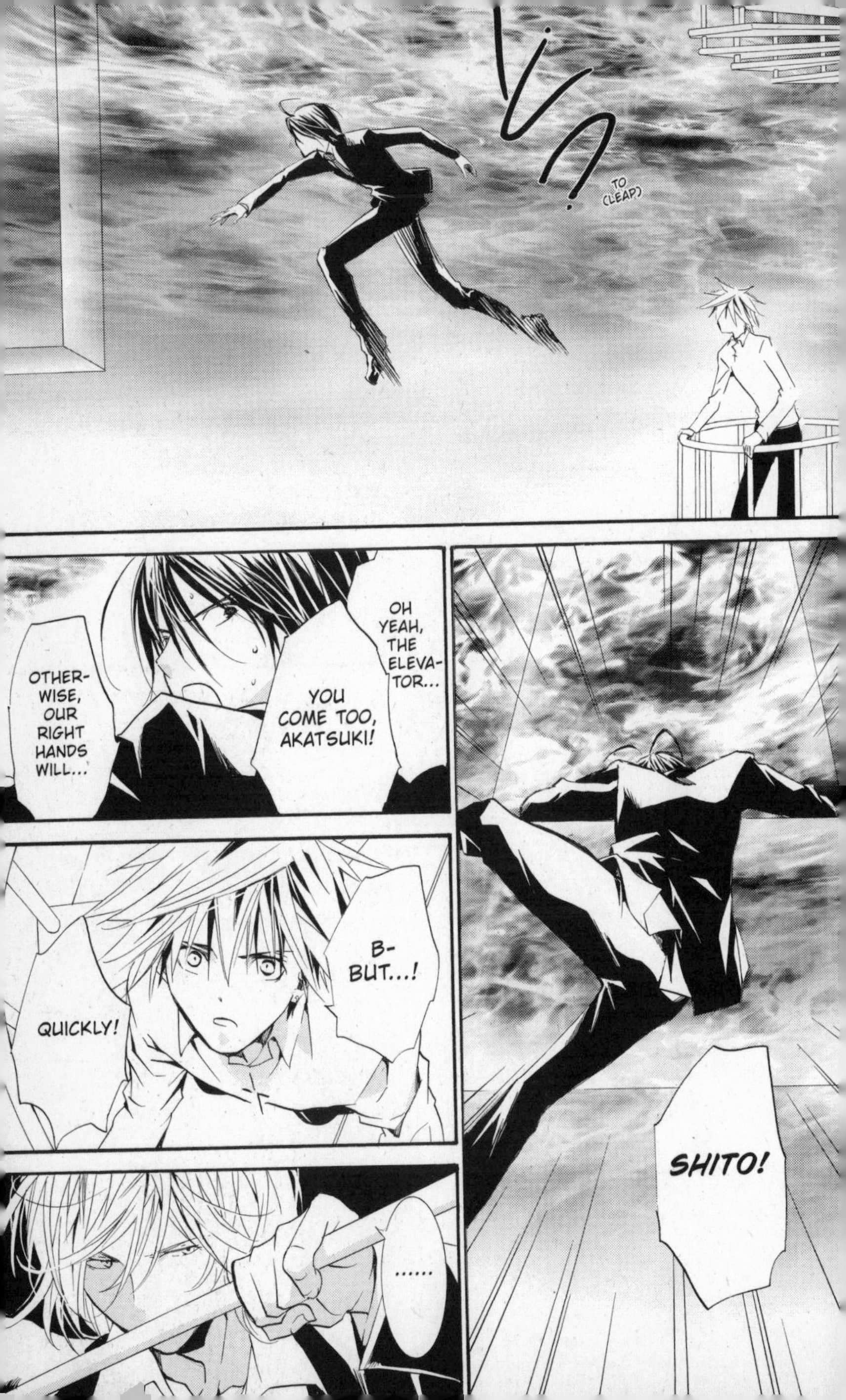
TO (LEAP)
SHITO!
OH YEAH, THE ELEVATOR...
YOU COME TOO, AKATSUKI!
OTHER-WISE, OUR RIGHT HANDS WILL...
B-BUT...!
QUICKLY!
......

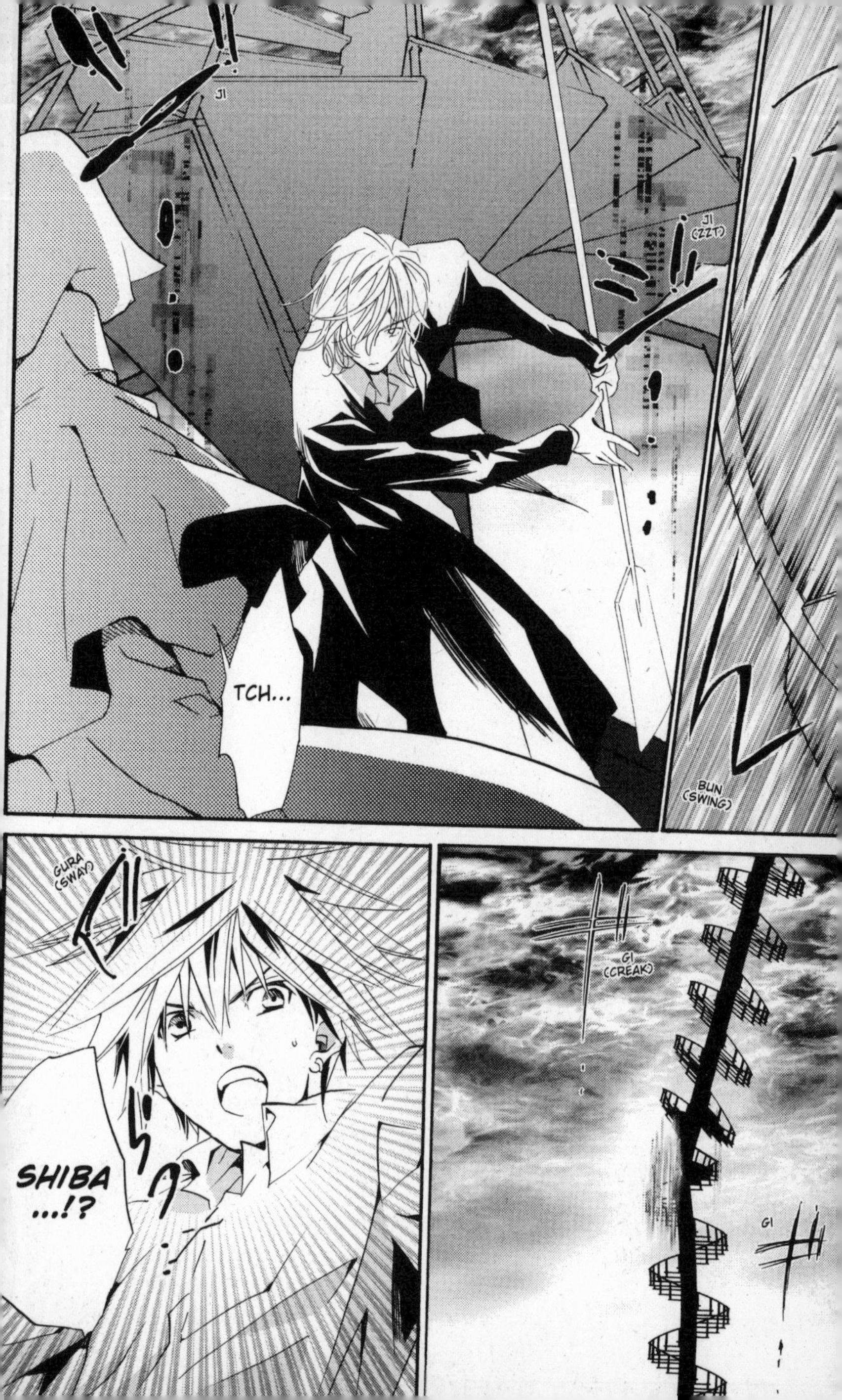
JI
JI
(ZZT)
TCH...
BUN
(SWING)
GI
(CREAK)
GI
GURA
(SWAY)
SHIBA
...!?

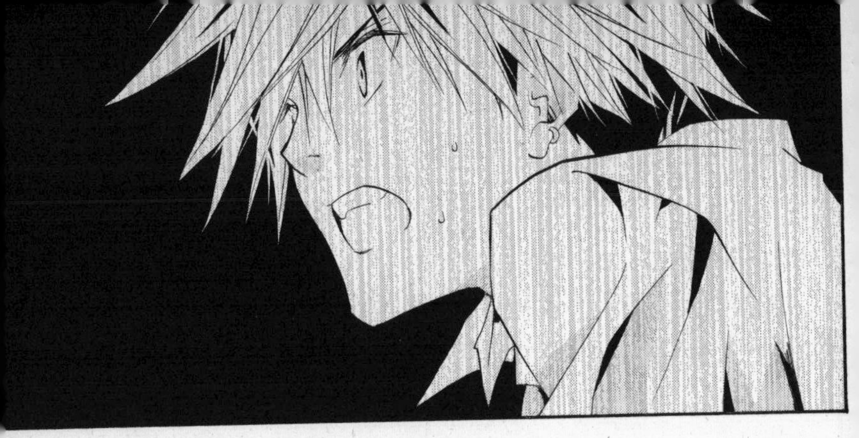

PAYMENT:81

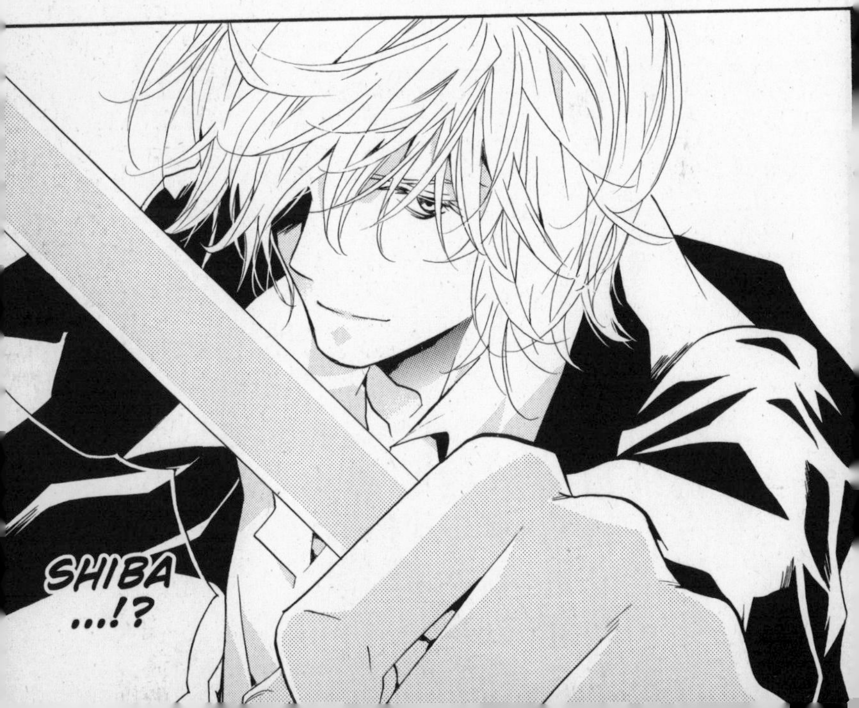
SHIBA ...!?

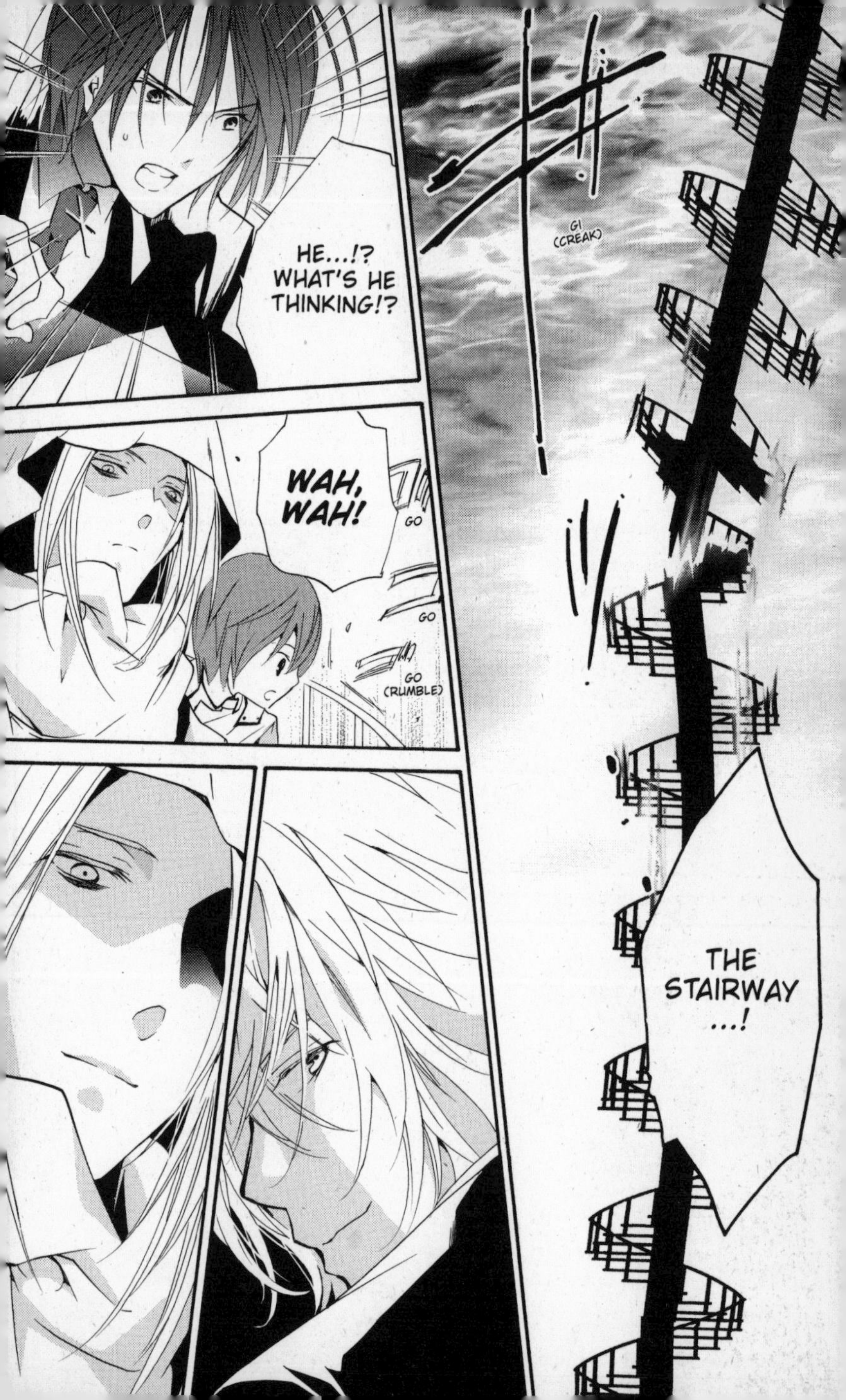
GI (CREAK)
THE STAIRWAY ...!
HE...!? WHAT'S HE THINKING!?
WAH, WAH!
GO
GO
GO (RUMBLE)

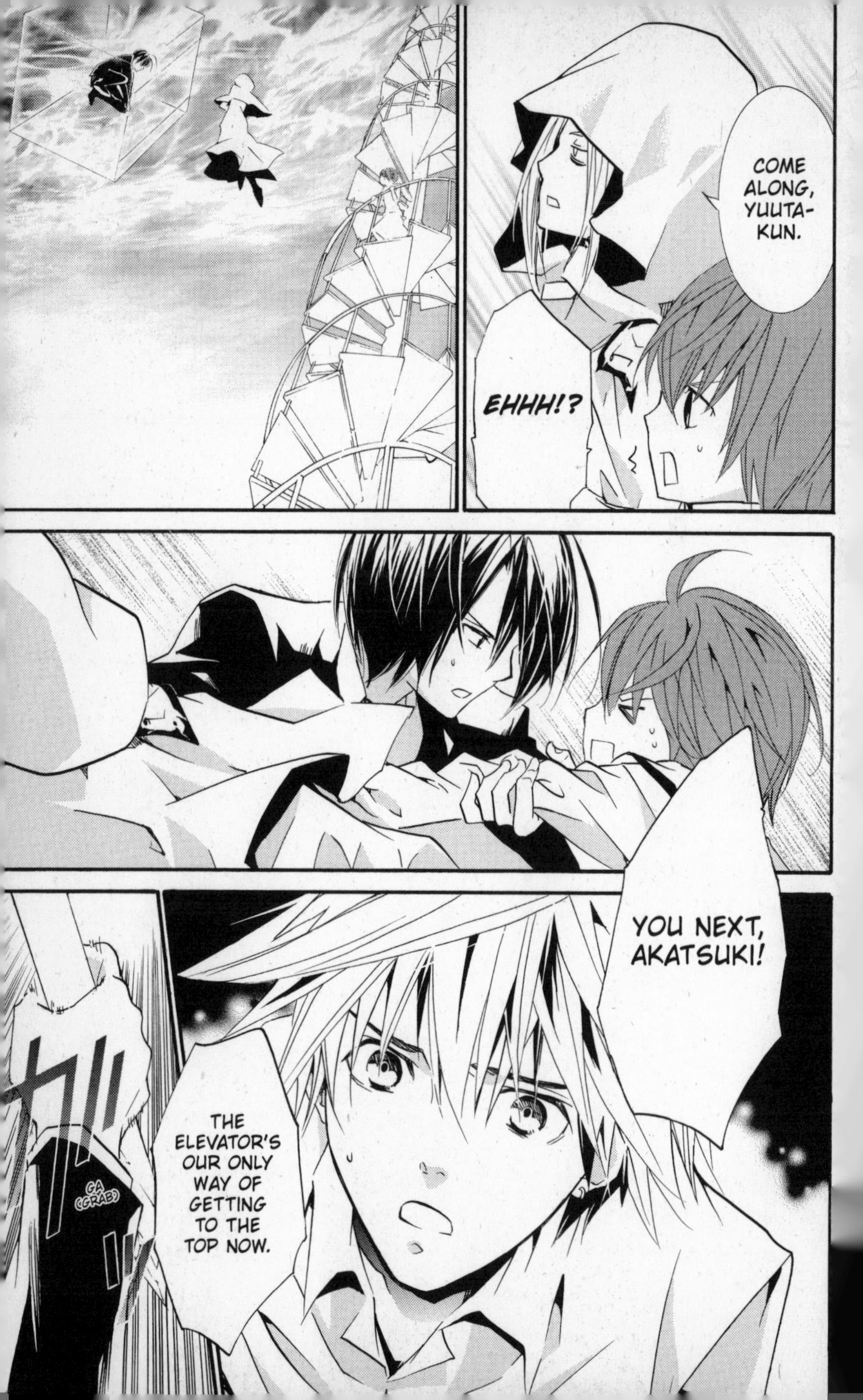
COME ALONG, YUUTA-KUN.
EHHH!?
YOU NEXT, AKATSUKI!
THE ELEVATOR'S OUR ONLY WAY OF GETTING TO THE TOP NOW.
GA (GRAB)

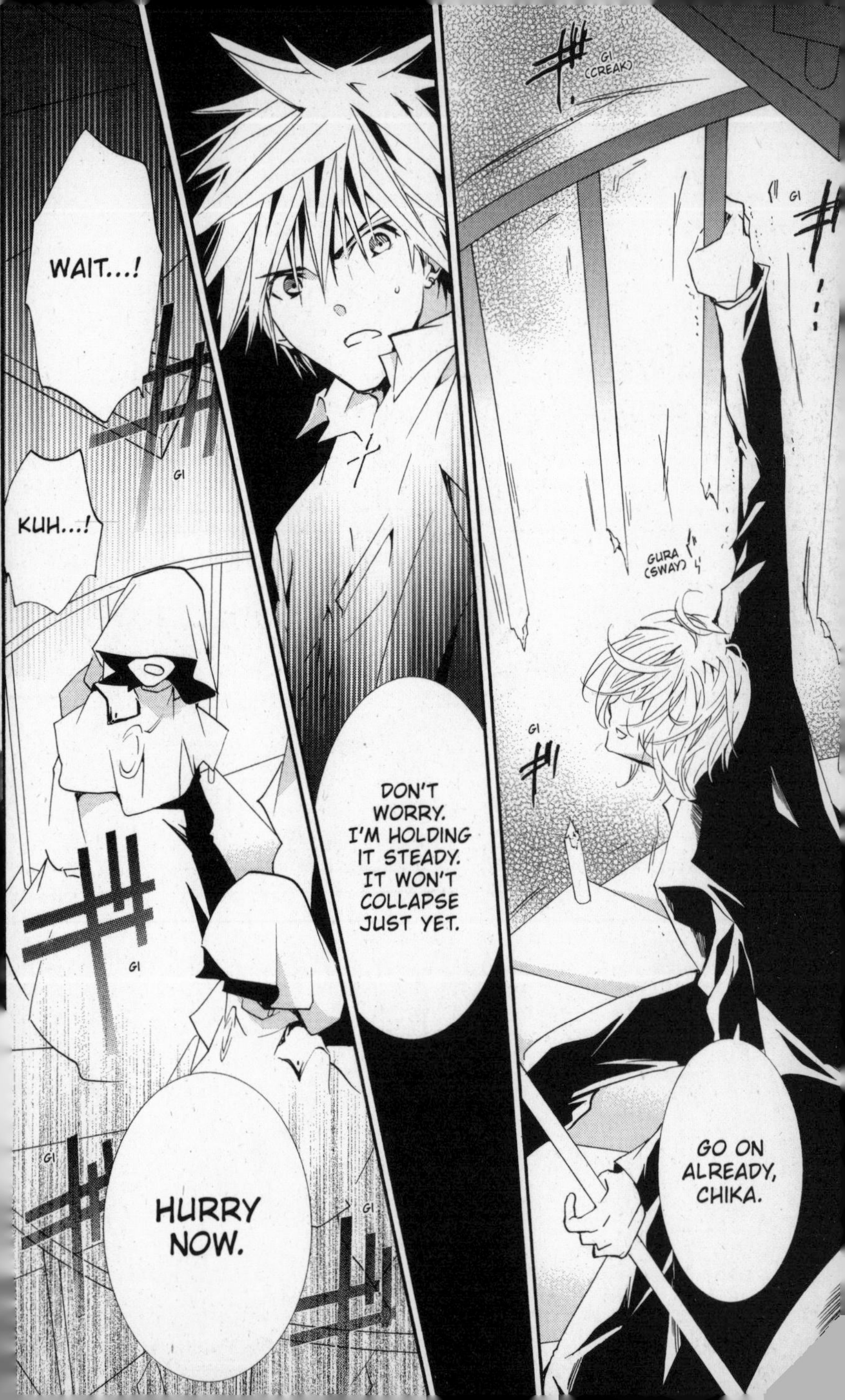
GI
(CREAK)
GI
GURA
(SWAY)
GI
GO ON ALREADY, CHIKA.
DON'T WORRY. I'M HOLDING IT STEADY. IT WON'T COLLAPSE JUST YET.
WAIT...!
GI
KUH...!
GI
GI
HURRY NOW.
GI

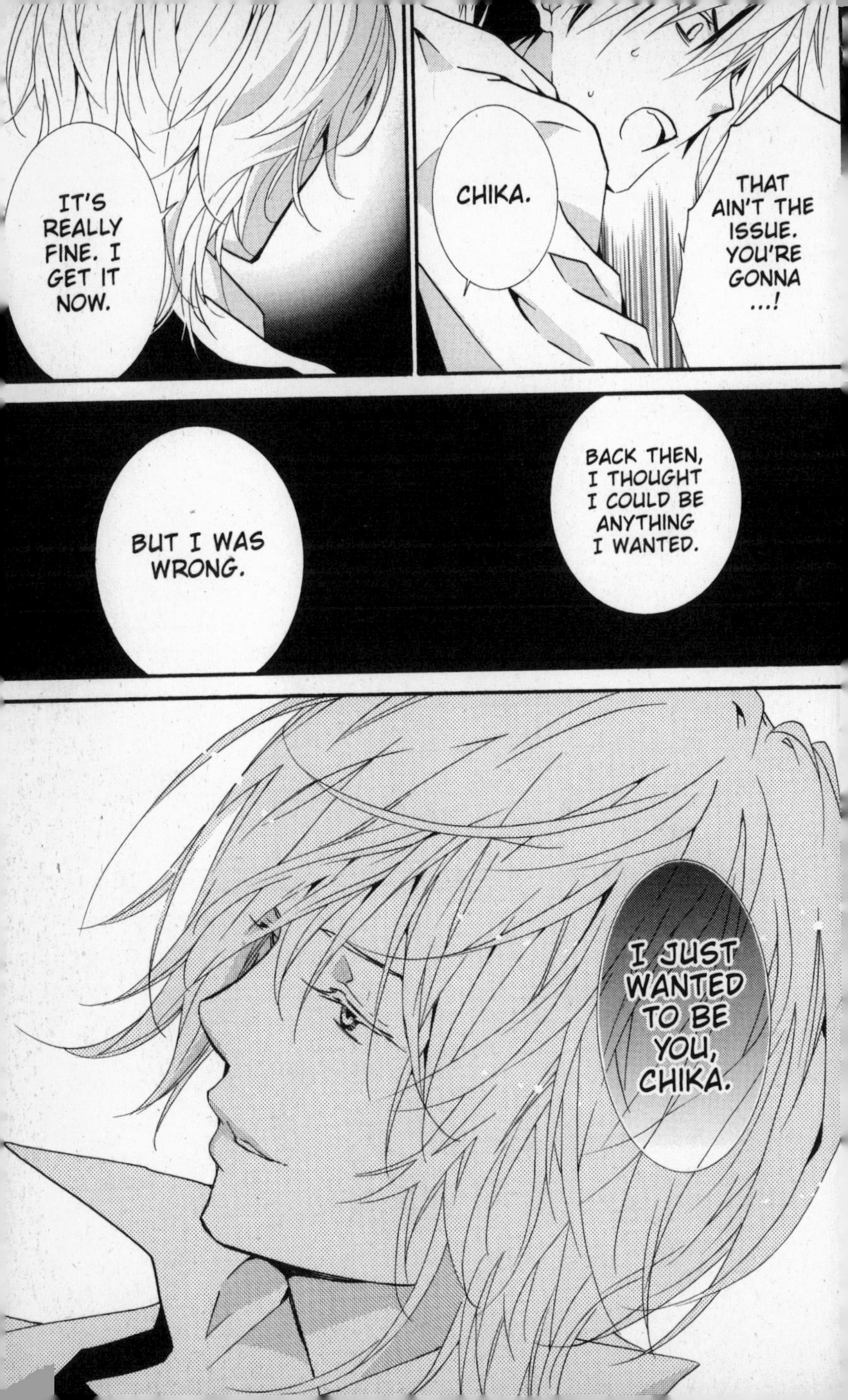
THAT AIN'T THE ISSUE. YOU'RE GONNA ...!
CHIKA.
IT'S REALLY FINE. I GET IT NOW.
BACK THEN, I THOUGHT I COULD BE ANYTHING I WANTED.
BUT I WAS WRONG.
I JUST WANTED TO BE YOU, CHIKA.

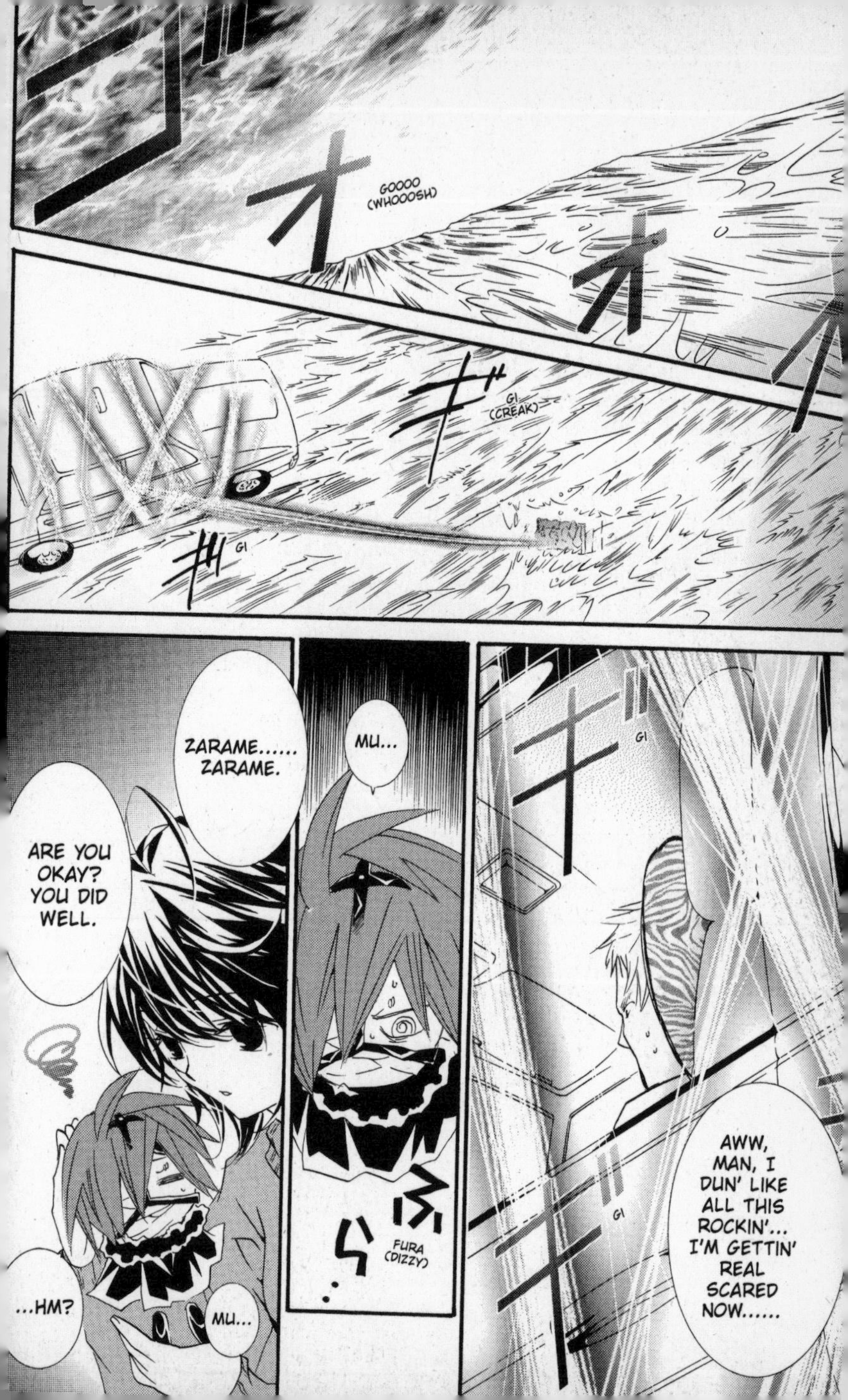
GOOOO (WHOOOSH)
GI (CREAK)
GI
GI
AWW, MAN, I DUN' LIKE ALL THIS ROCKIN'... I'M GETTIN' REAL SCARED NOW......
GI
MU...
FURA (DIZZY)
ZARAME...... ZARAME.
ARE YOU OKAY? YOU DID WELL.
MU...
...HM?

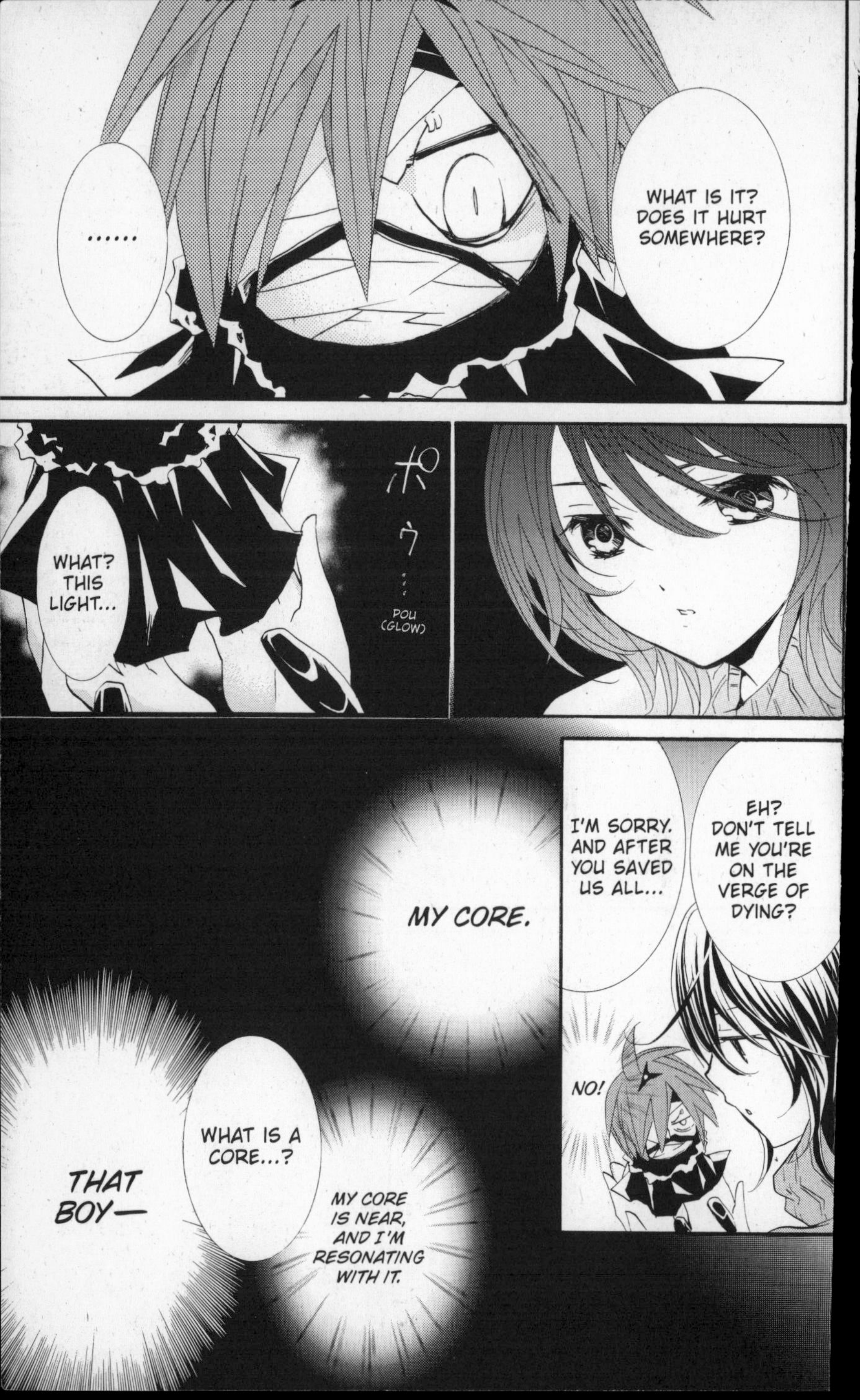
WHAT IS IT? DOES IT HURT SOMEWHERE?
......
ポウ…
POU (GLOW)
WHAT? THIS LIGHT...
EH? DON'T TELL ME YOU'RE ON THE VERGE OF DYING?
I'M SORRY. AND AFTER YOU SAVED US ALL...
NO!
MY CORE.
WHAT IS A CORE...?
MY CORE IS NEAR, AND I'M RESONATING WITH IT.
THAT BOY—

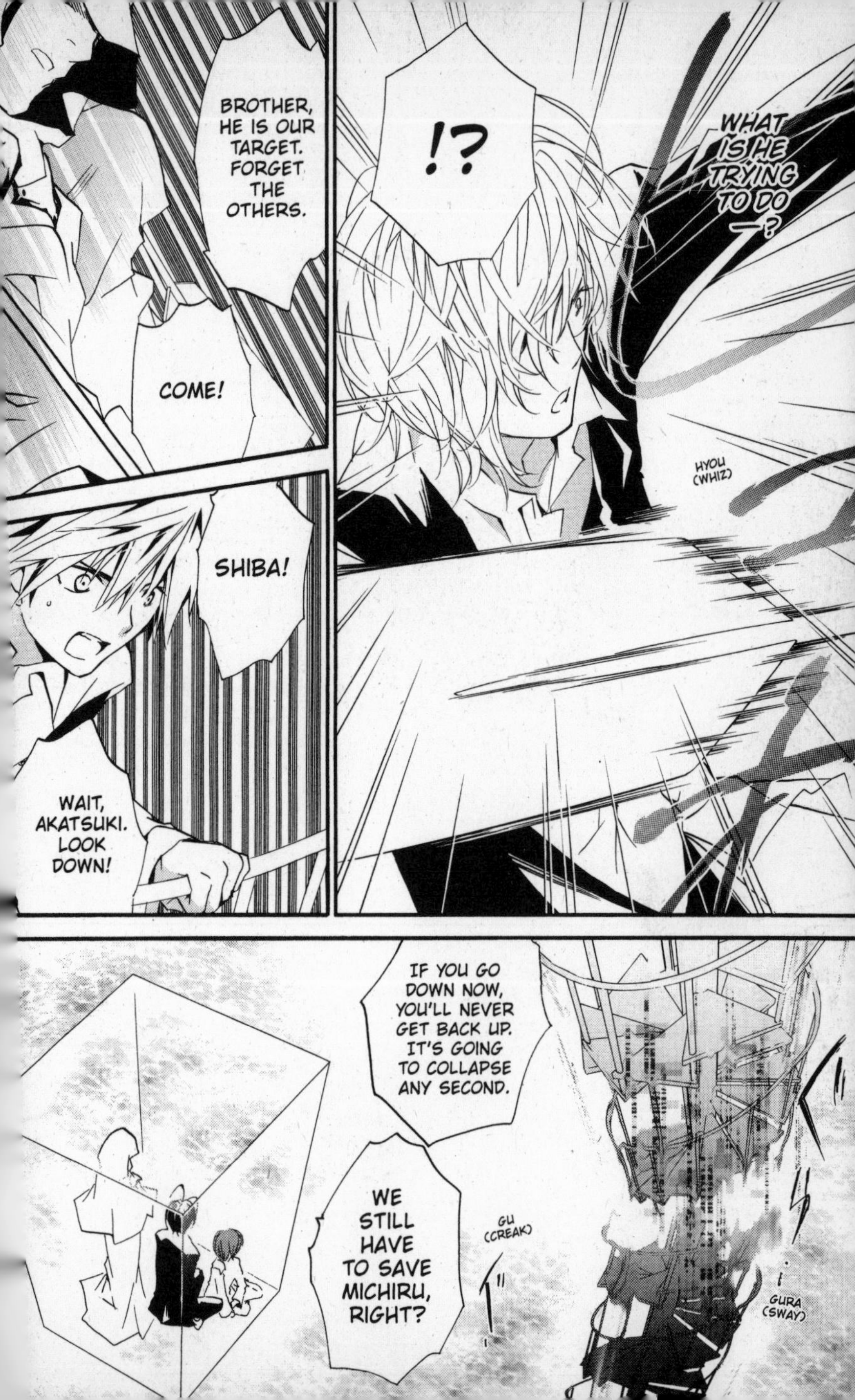
WHAT IS HE TRYING TO DO—?
!?
HYOU (WHIZ)
BROTHER, HE IS OUR TARGET. FORGET THE OTHERS.
COME!
SHIBA!
WAIT, AKATSUKI. LOOK DOWN!
IF YOU GO DOWN NOW, YOU'LL NEVER GET BACK UP. IT'S GOING TO COLLAPSE ANY SECOND.
GURA (SWAY)
GU (CREAK)
WE STILL HAVE TO SAVE MICHIRU, RIGHT?

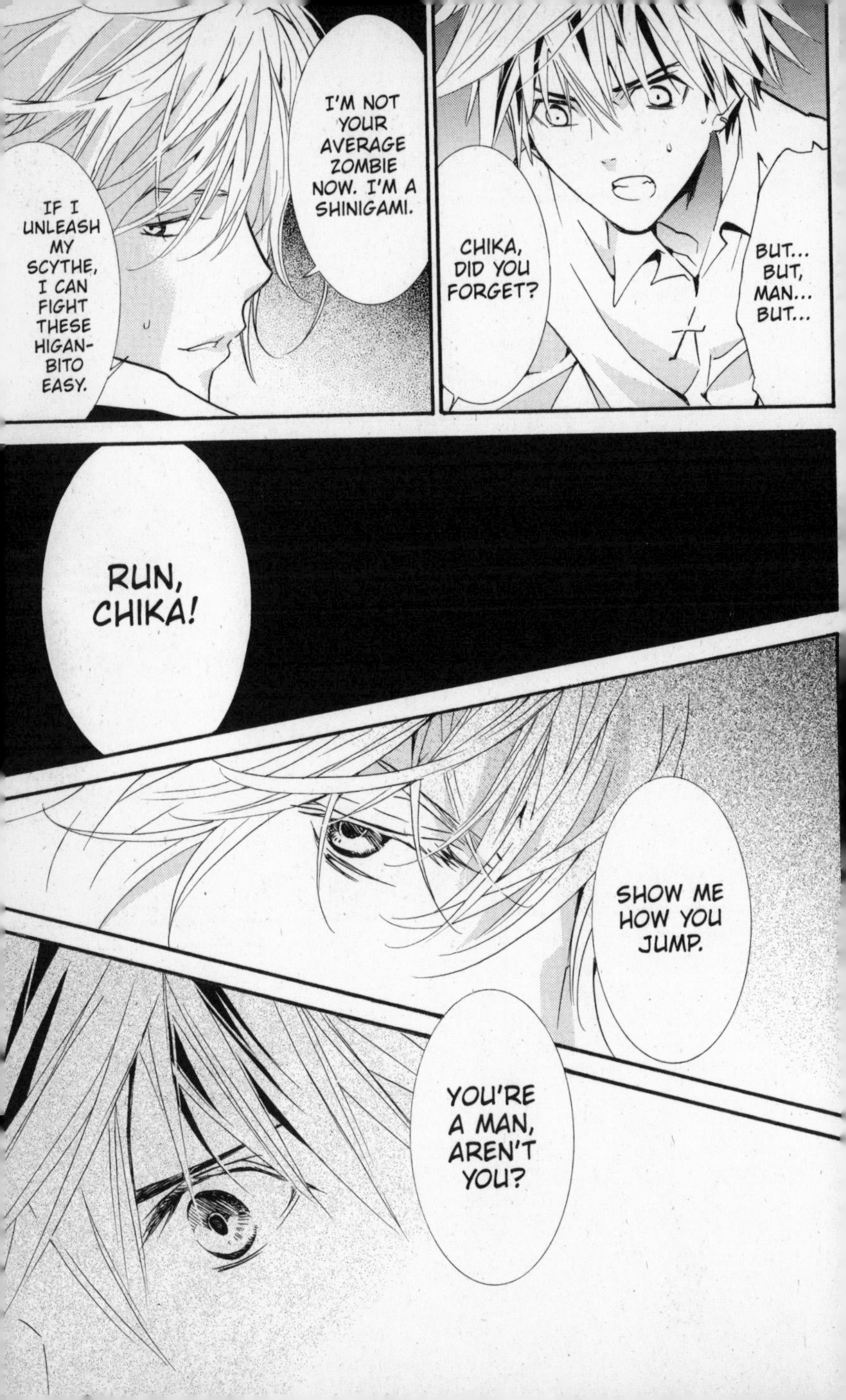
BUT... BUT, MAN... BUT...
CHIKA, DID YOU FORGET?
I'M NOT YOUR AVERAGE ZOMBIE NOW. I'M A SHINIGAMI.
IF I UNLEASH MY SCYTHE, I CAN FIGHT THESE HIGAN-BITO EASY.
RUN, CHIKA!
SHOW ME HOW YOU JUMP.
YOU'RE A MAN, AREN'T YOU?

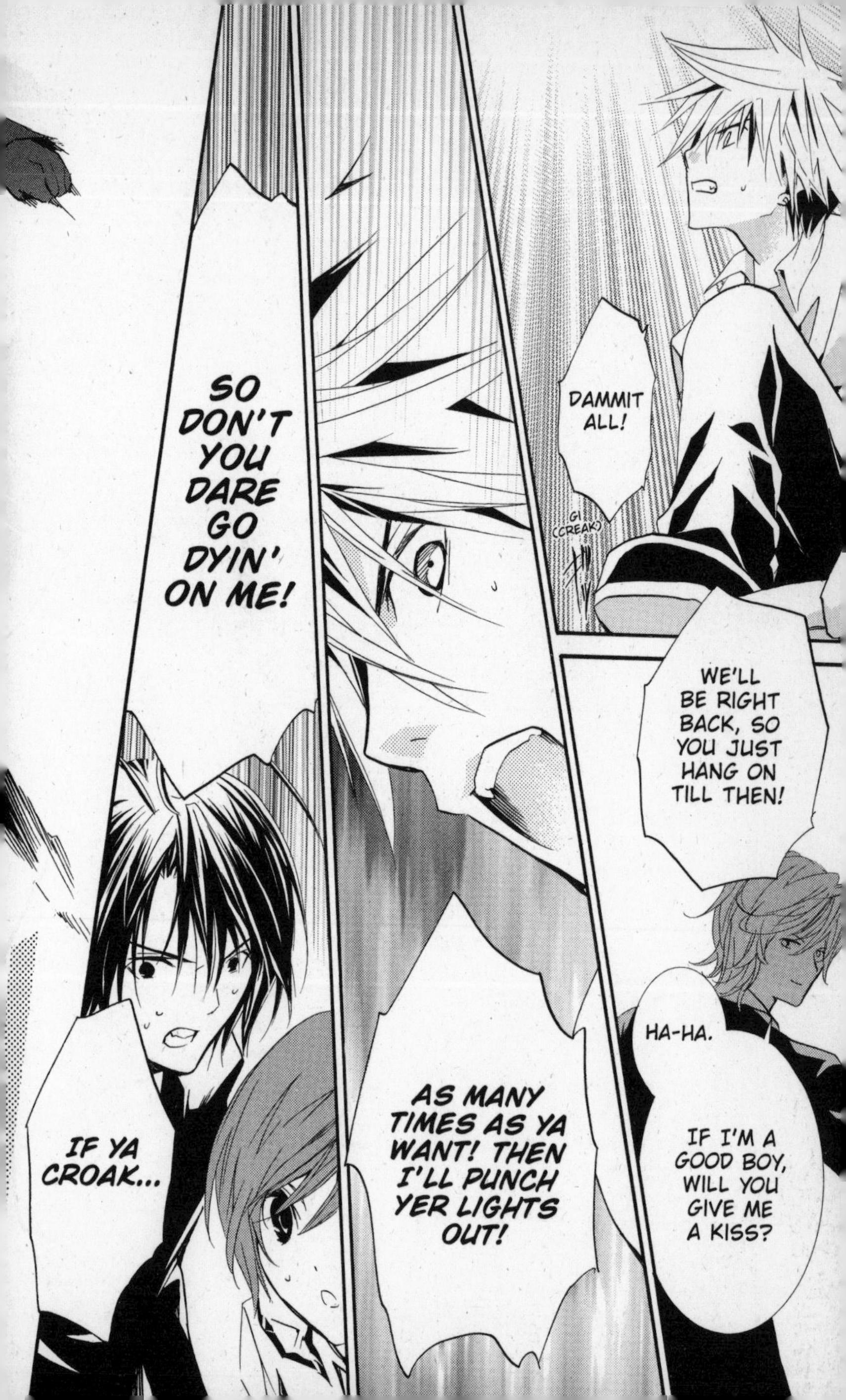
DAMMIT ALL!
GI (CREAK)
WE'LL BE RIGHT BACK, SO YOU JUST HANG ON TILL THEN!
HA-HA.
IF I'M A GOOD BOY, WILL YOU GIVE ME A KISS?
AS MANY TIMES AS YA WANT! THEN I'LL PUNCH YER LIGHTS OUT!
SO DON'T YOU DARE GO DYIN' ON ME!
IF YA CROAK...

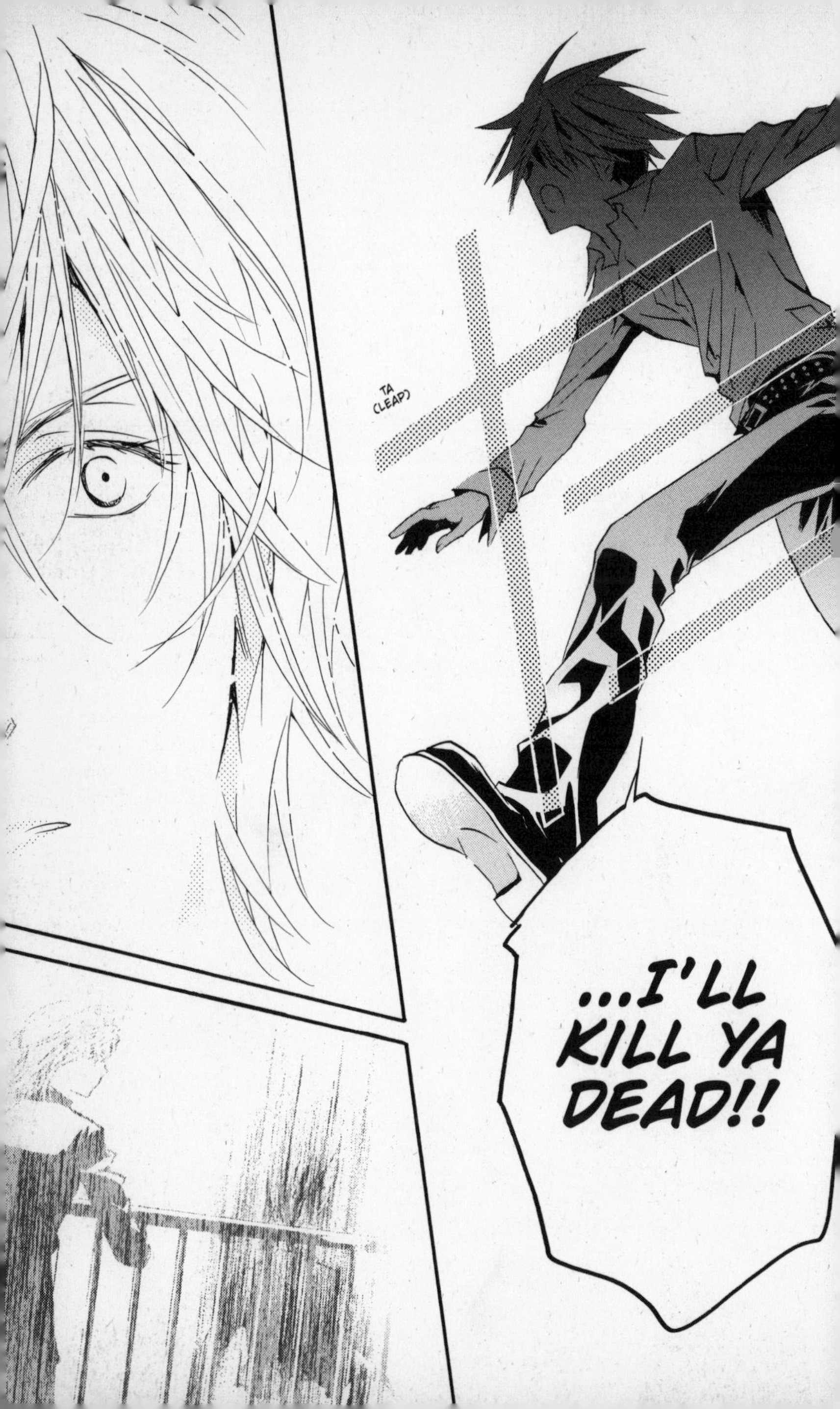
TA
(LEAP)
...I'LL KILL YA DEAD!!

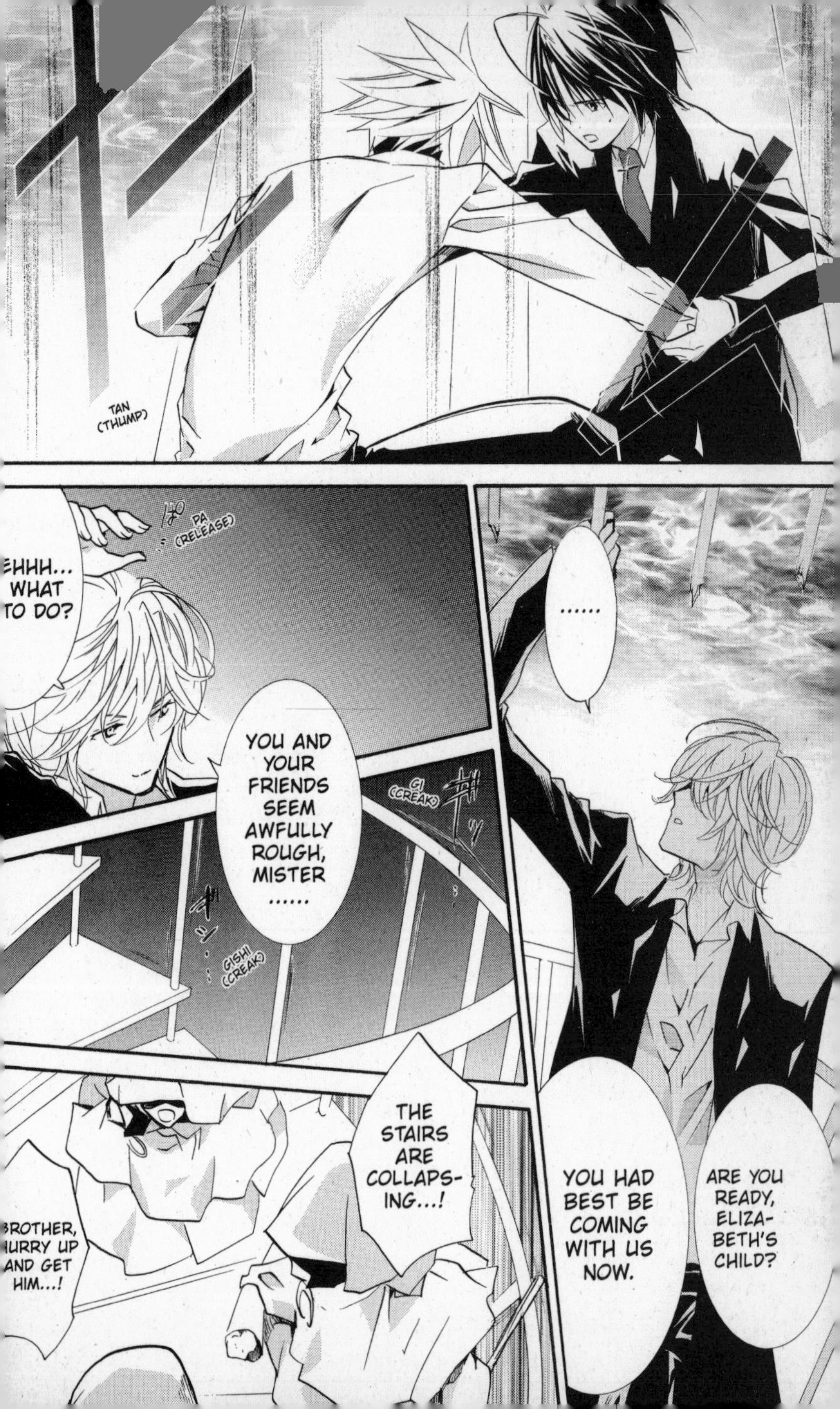
TAN (THUMP)
......
ARE YOU READY, ELIZABETH'S CHILD?
YOU HAD BEST BE COMING WITH US NOW.
PA (RELEASE)
YOU AND YOUR FRIENDS SEEM AWFULLY ROUGH, MISTER ......
EHHH... WHAT TO DO?
GI (CREAK)
GISHI (CREAK)
THE STAIRS ARE COLLAPSING...!
BROTHER, HURRY UP AND GET HIM...!

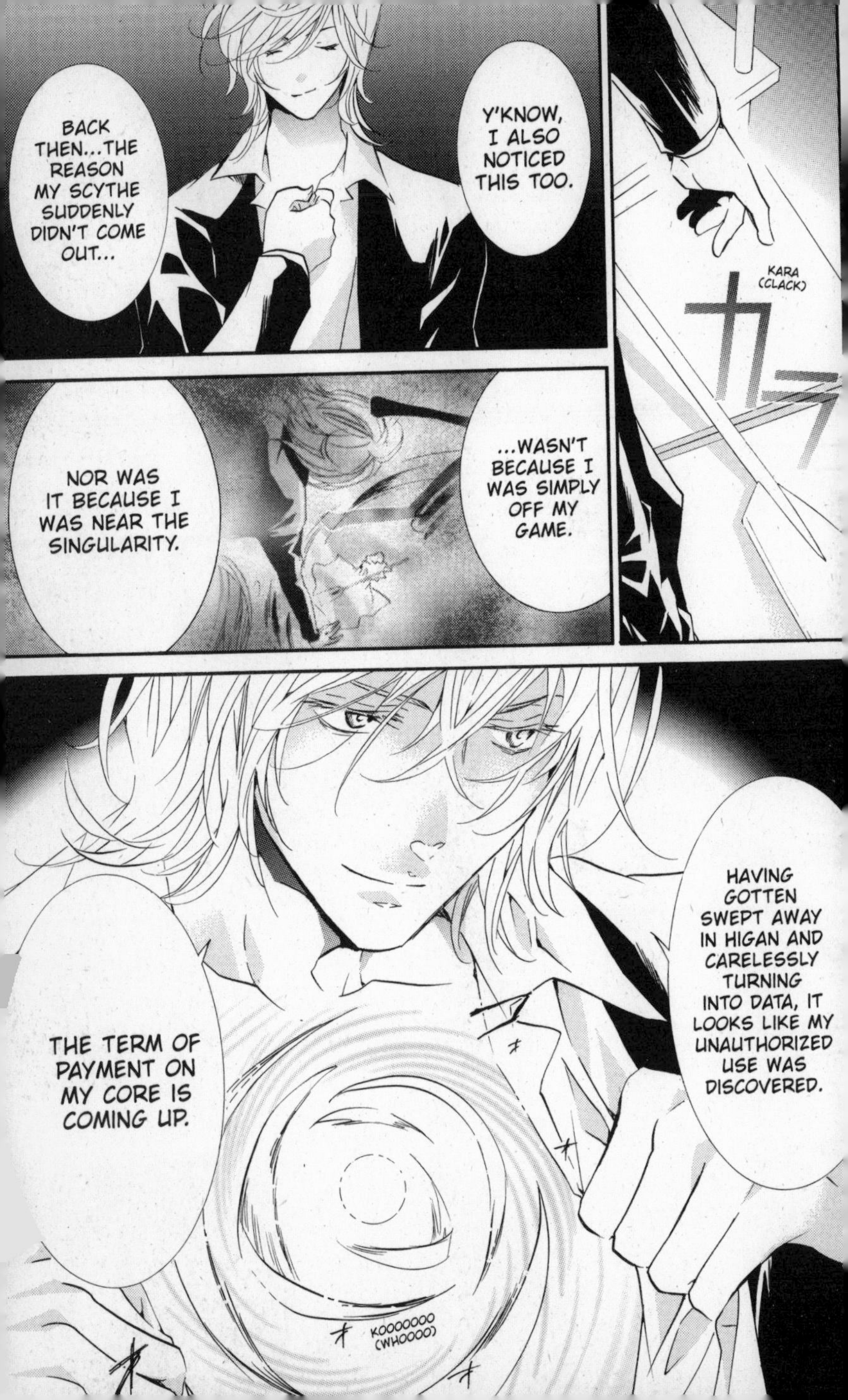
KARA (CLACK)
Y'KNOW, I ALSO NOTICED THIS TOO.
BACK THEN...THE REASON MY SCYTHE SUDDENLY DIDN'T COME OUT...
...WASN'T BECAUSE I WAS SIMPLY OFF MY GAME.
NOR WAS IT BECAUSE I WAS NEAR THE SINGULARITY.
HAVING GOTTEN SWEPT AWAY IN HIGAN AND CARELESSLY TURNING INTO DATA, IT LOOKS LIKE MY UNAUTHORIZED USE WAS DISCOVERED.
THE TERM OF PAYMENT ON MY CORE IS COMING UP.
KOOOOOOO (WHOOOO)

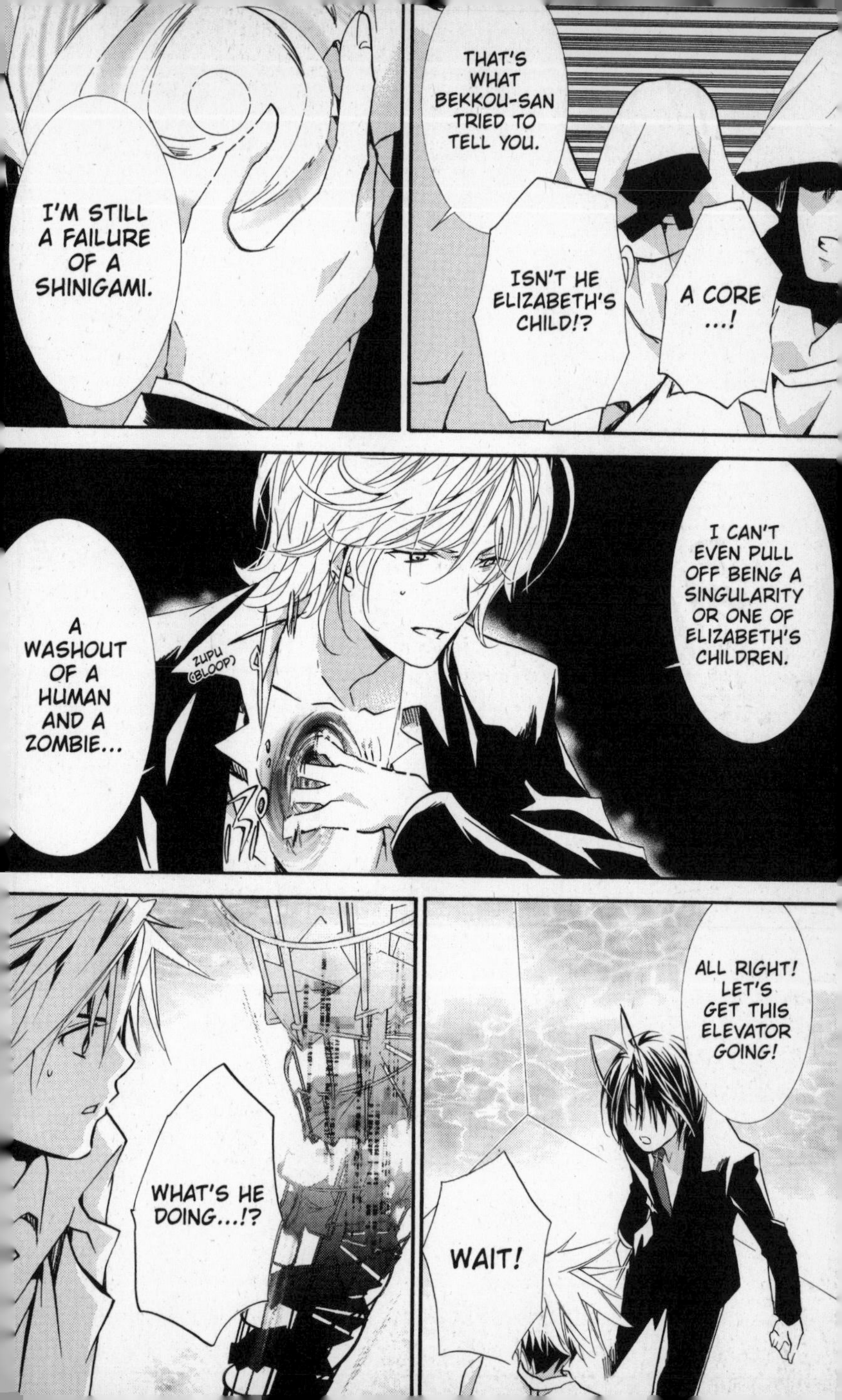
THAT'S WHAT BEKKOU-SAN TRIED TO TELL YOU.
A CORE ...!
ISN'T HE ELIZABETH'S CHILD!?
I'M STILL A FAILURE OF A SHINIGAMI.
I CAN'T EVEN PULL OFF BEING A SINGULARITY OR ONE OF ELIZABETH'S CHILDREN.
ZUPU (BLOOP)
A WASHOUT OF A HUMAN AND A ZOMBIE...
ALL RIGHT! LET'S GET THIS ELEVATOR GOING!
WAIT!
WHAT'S HE DOING...!?

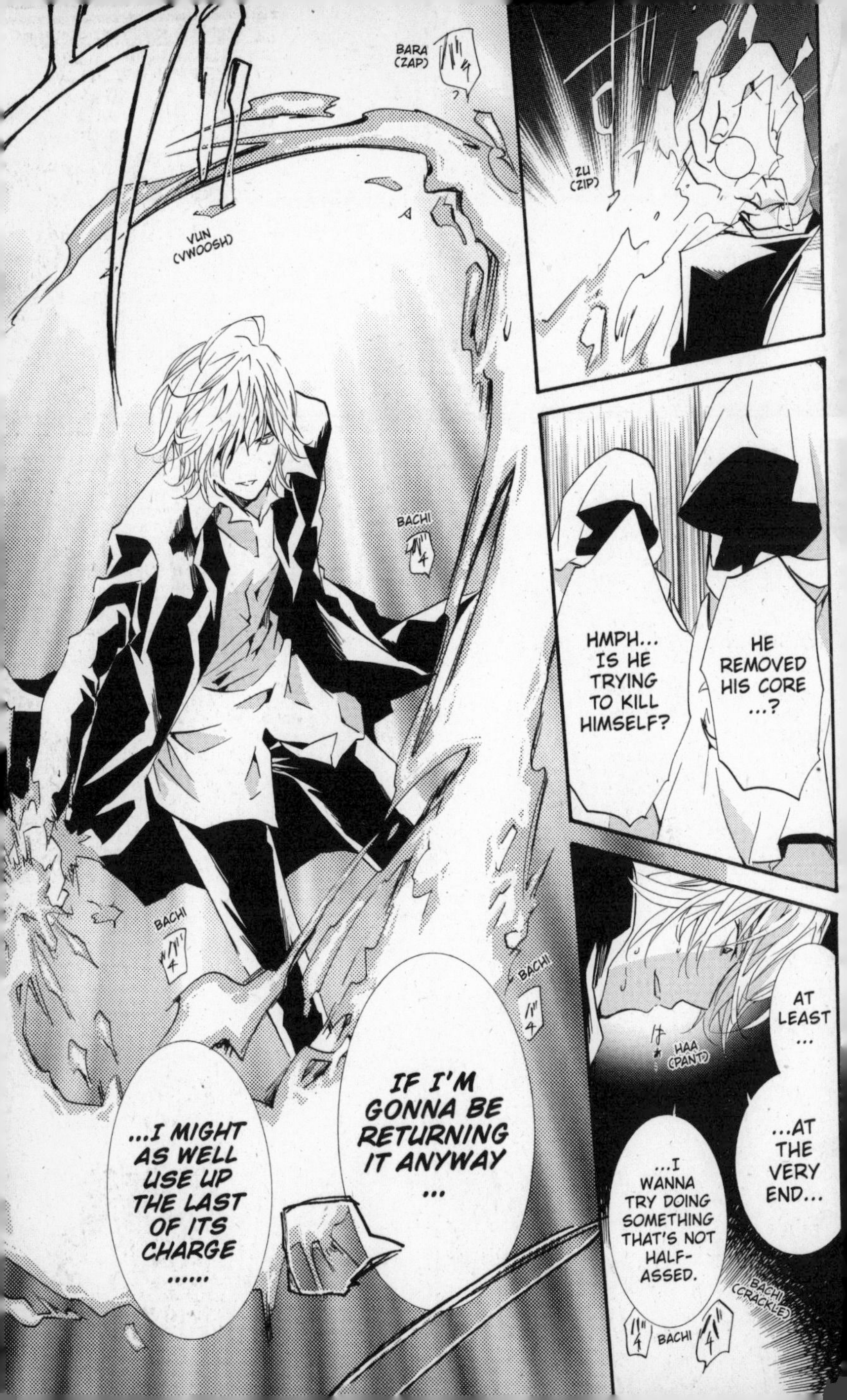
ZU
(ZIP)
HE REMOVED HIS CORE ...?
HMPH... IS HE TRYING TO KILL HIMSELF?
AT LEAST ...
HAA
(PANT)
...AT THE VERY END...
...I WANNA TRY DOING SOMETHING THAT'S NOT HALF-ASSED.
BACHI
(CRACKLE)
BACHI
BARA
(ZAP)
VUN
(VWOOSH)
BACHI
BACHI
BACHI
IF I'M GONNA BE RETURNING IT ANYWAY ...
...I MIGHT AS WELL USE UP THE LAST OF ITS CHARGE ......

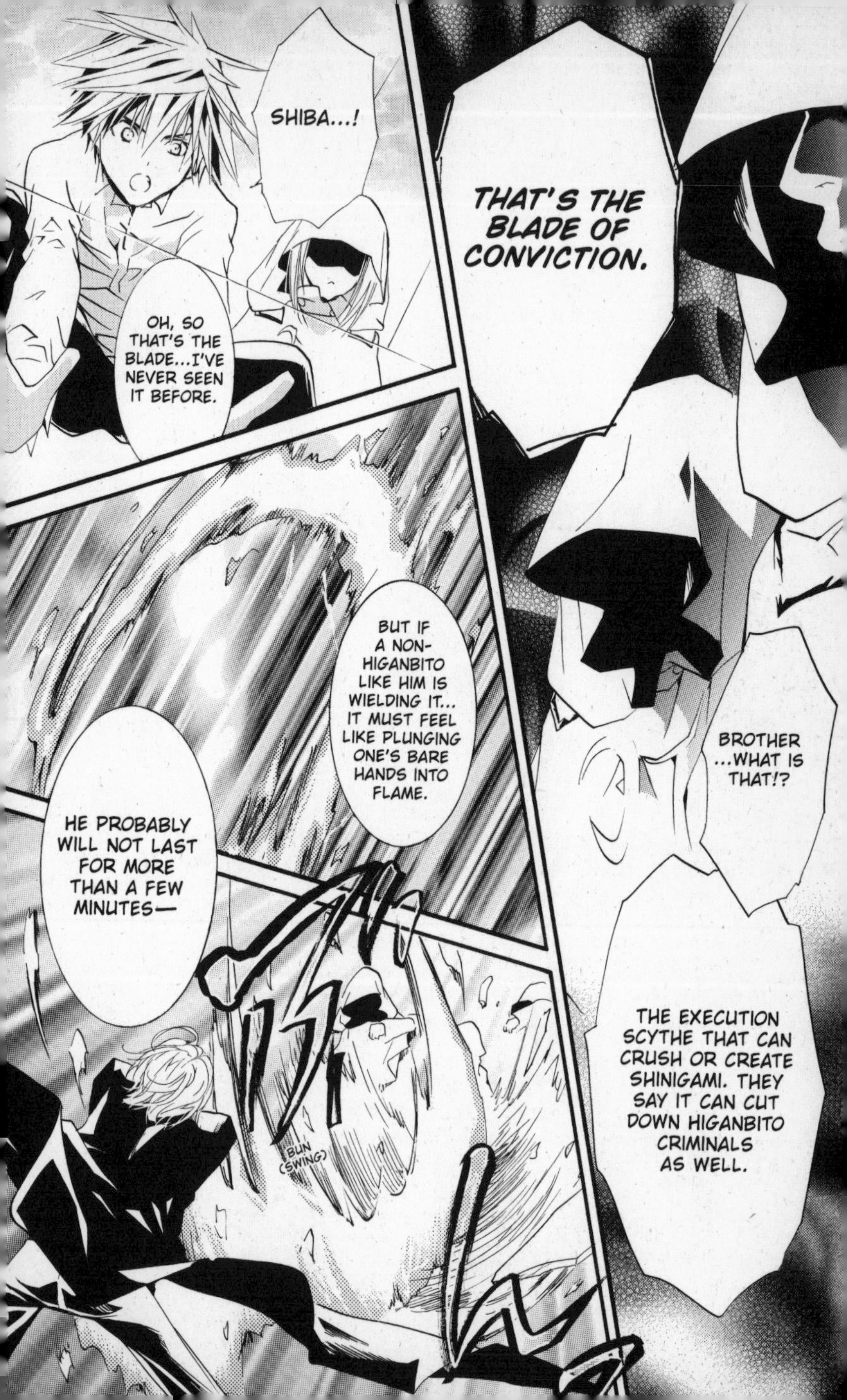
THAT'S THE BLADE OF CONVICTION.
BROTHER ...WHAT IS THAT!?
THE EXECUTION SCYTHE THAT CAN CRUSH OR CREATE SHINIGAMI. THEY SAY IT CAN CUT DOWN HIGANBITO CRIMINALS AS WELL.
SHIBA...!
OH, SO THAT'S THE BLADE...I'VE NEVER SEEN IT BEFORE.
BUT IF A NON-HIGANBITO LIKE HIM IS WIELDING IT... IT MUST FEEL LIKE PLUNGING ONE'S BARE HANDS INTO FLAME.
HE PROBABLY WILL NOT LAST FOR MORE THAN A FEW MINUTES—
BUN (SWING)

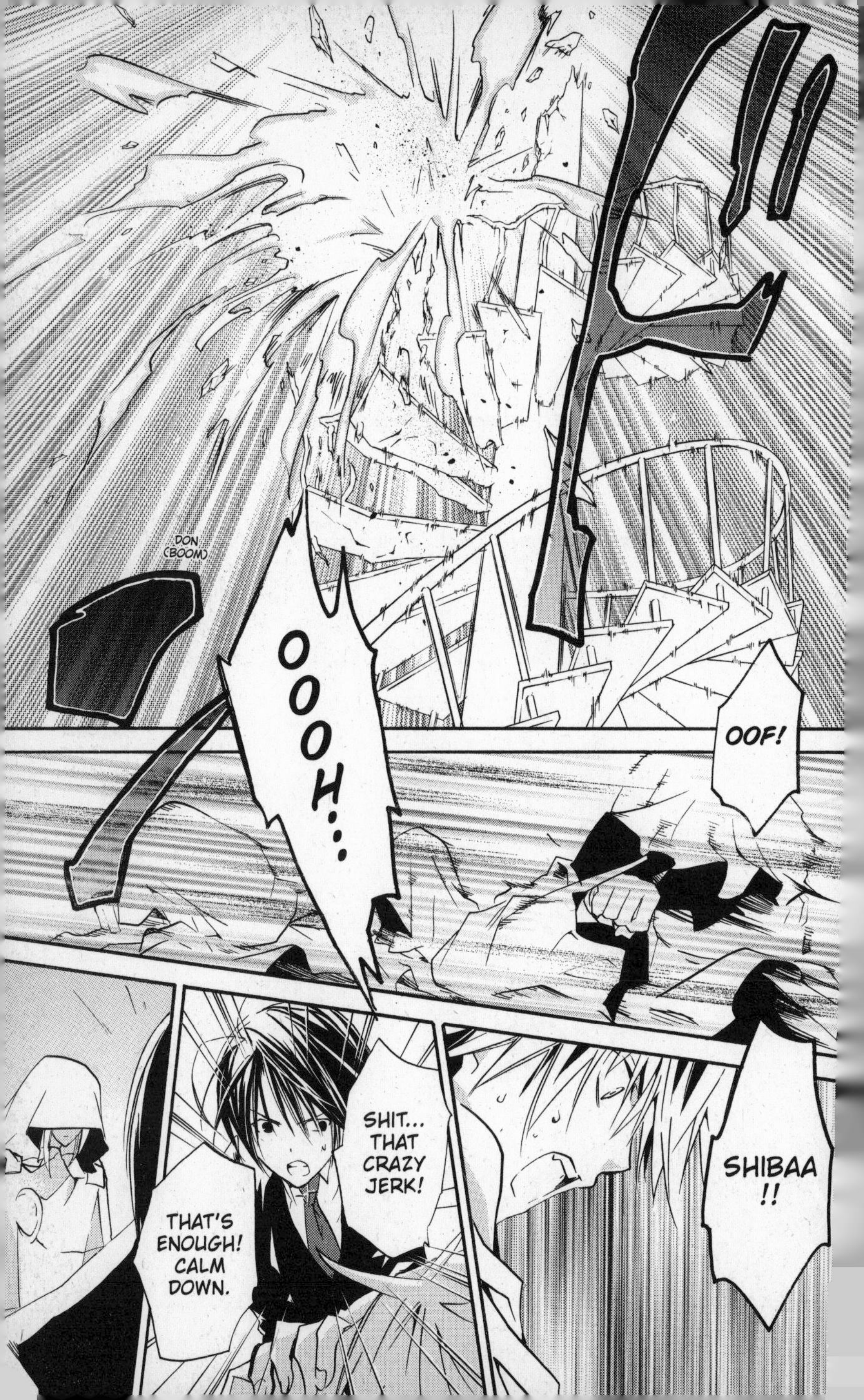
DON (BOOM)
OOOOH...
OOF!
SHIBAA!!
SHIT... THAT CRAZY JERK!
THAT'S ENOUGH! CALM DOWN.

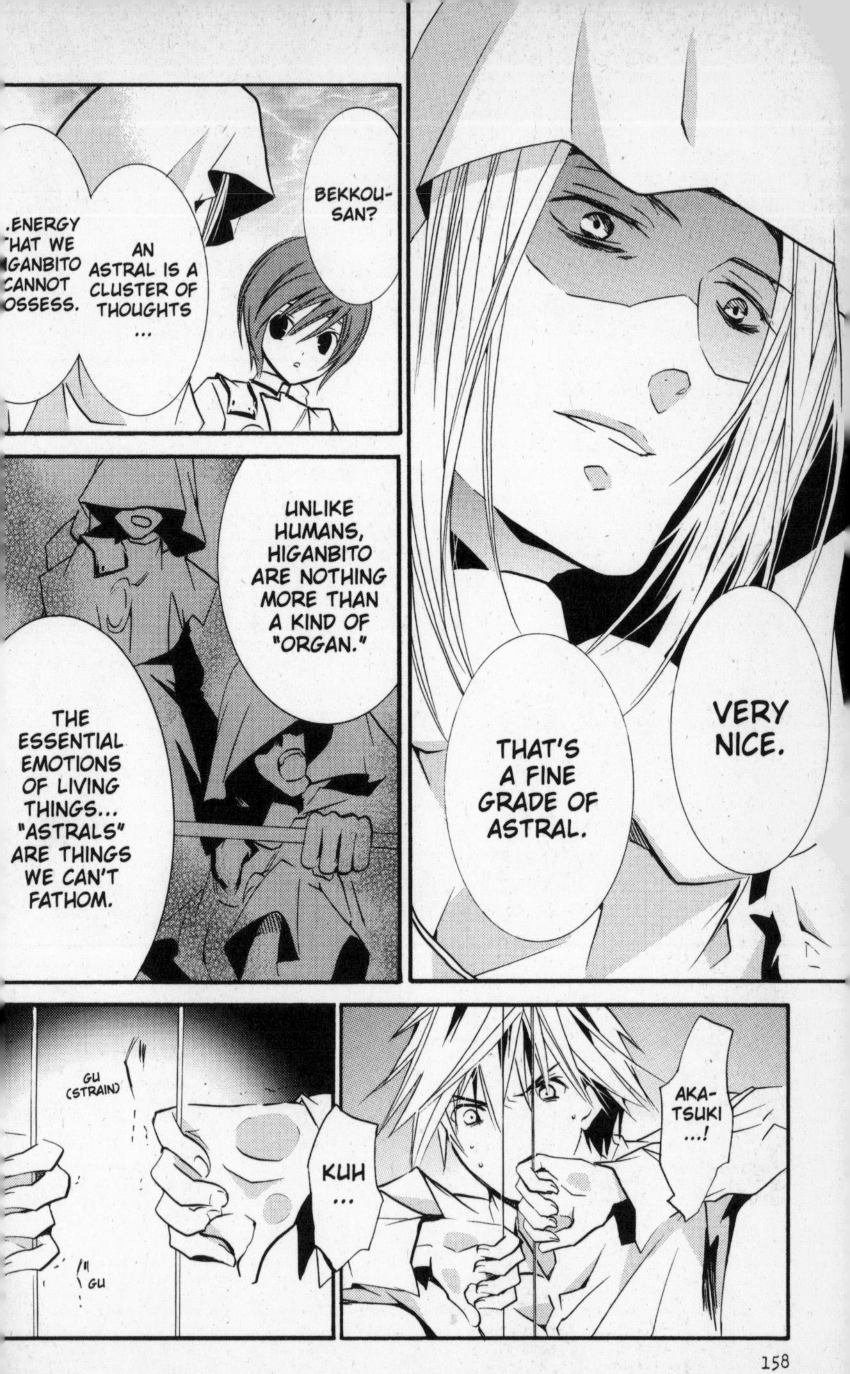
VERY NICE.
THAT'S A FINE GRADE OF ASTRAL.
BEKKOU-SAN?
AN ASTRAL IS A CLUSTER OF THOUGHTS...
.ENERGY THAT WE IGANBITO CANNOT OSSESS.
UNLIKE HUMANS, HIGANBITO ARE NOTHING MORE THAN A KIND OF "ORGAN."
THE ESSENTIAL EMOTIONS OF LIVING THINGS... "ASTRALS" ARE THINGS WE CAN'T FATHOM.
AKA-TSUKI...!
KUH...
GU (STRAIN)
GU

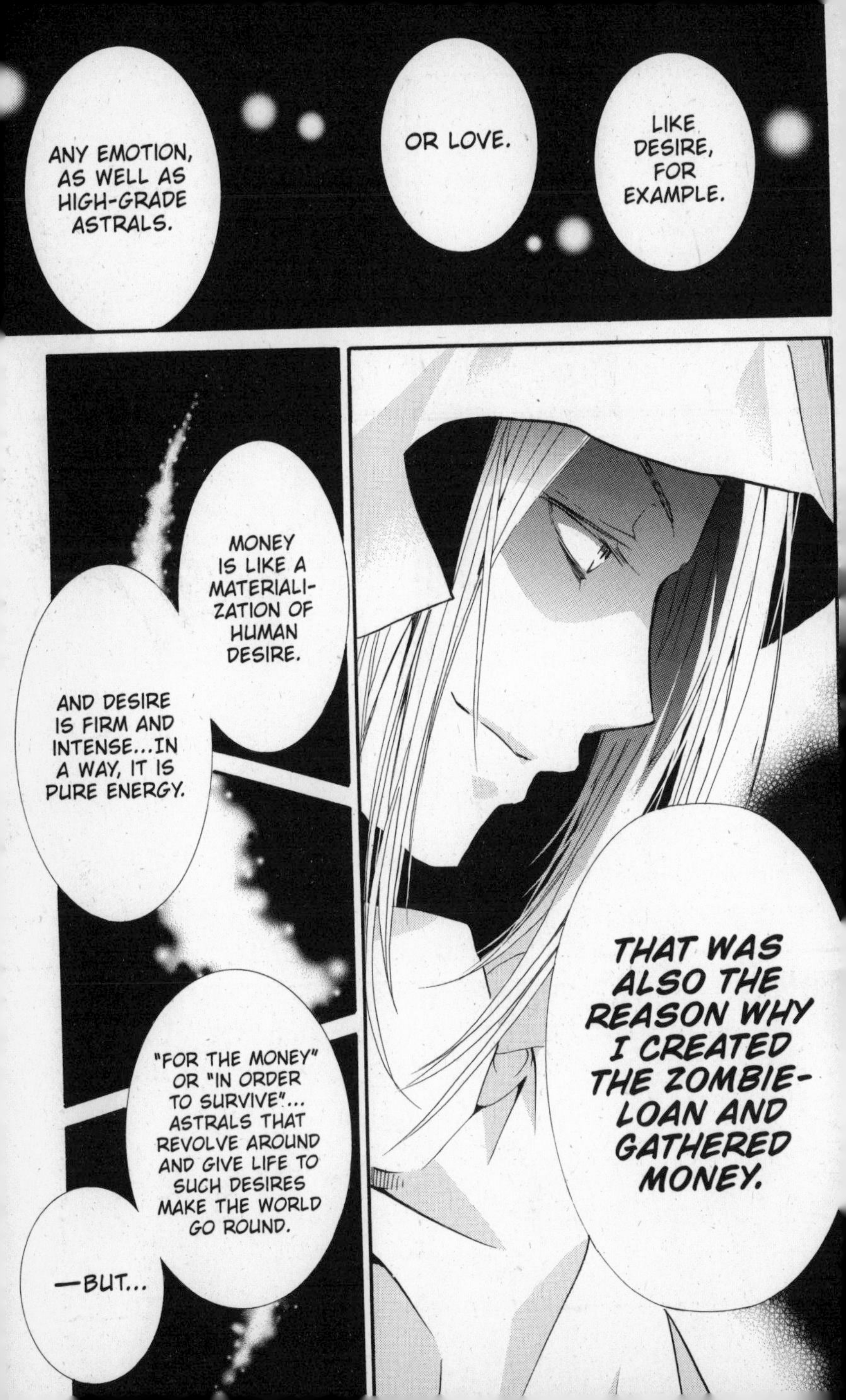

LIKE DESIRE, FOR EXAMPLE.
OR LOVE.
ANY EMOTION, AS WELL AS HIGH-GRADE ASTRALS.
THAT WAS ALSO THE REASON WHY I CREATED THE ZOMBIE-LOAN AND GATHERED MONEY.
MONEY IS LIKE A MATERIALIZATION OF HUMAN DESIRE.
AND DESIRE IS FIRM AND INTENSE...IN A WAY, IT IS PURE ENERGY.
"FOR THE MONEY" OR "IN ORDER TO SURVIVE"... ASTRALS THAT REVOLVE AROUND AND GIVE LIFE TO SUCH DESIRES MAKE THE WORLD GO ROUND.
—BUT...

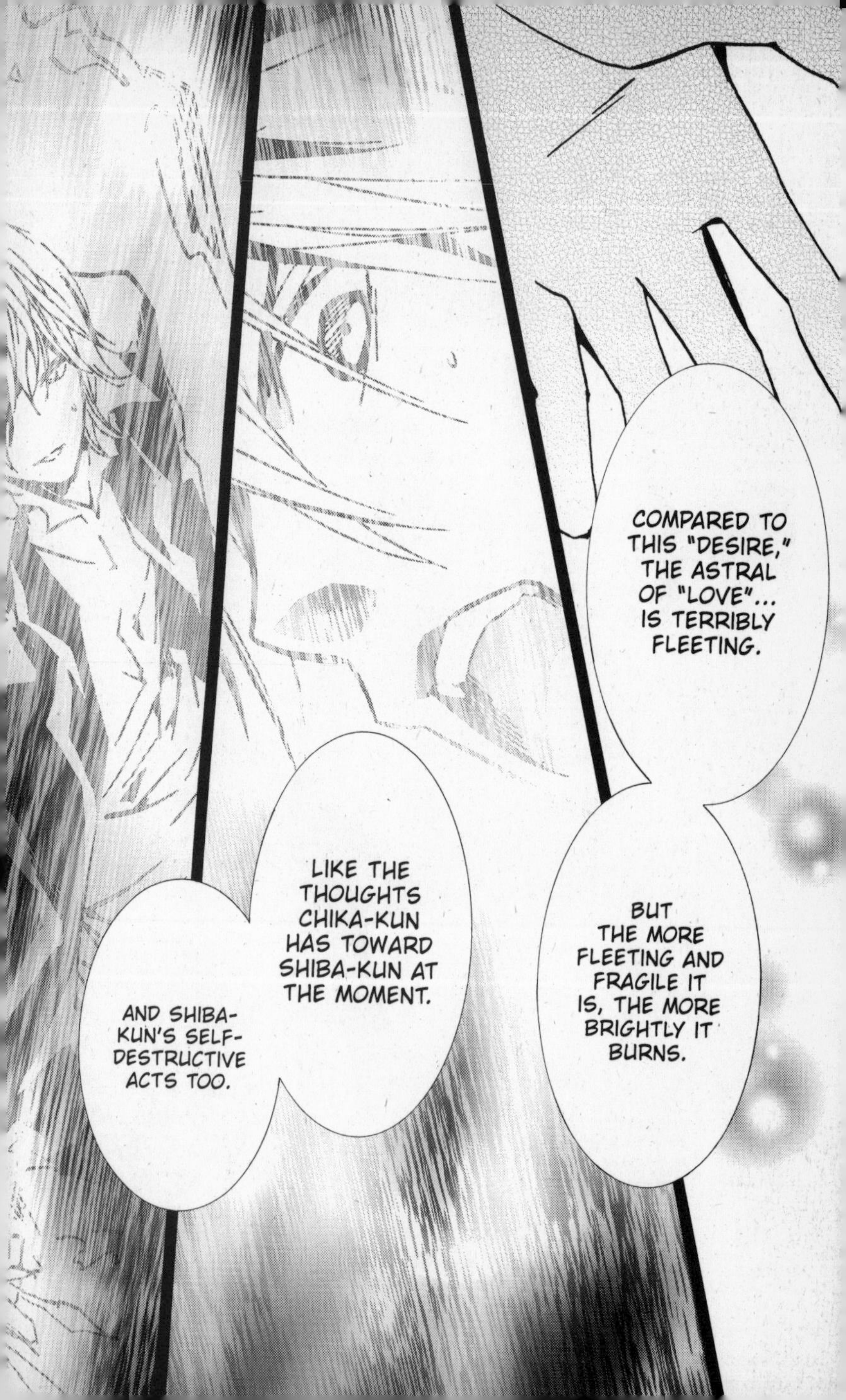
COMPARED TO THIS "DESIRE," THE ASTRAL OF "LOVE"... IS TERRIBLY FLEETING.
BUT THE MORE FLEETING AND FRAGILE IT IS, THE MORE BRIGHTLY IT BURNS.
LIKE THE THOUGHTS CHIKA-KUN HAS TOWARD SHIBA-KUN AT THE MOMENT.
AND SHIBA-KUN'S SELF-DESTRUCTIVE ACTS TOO.

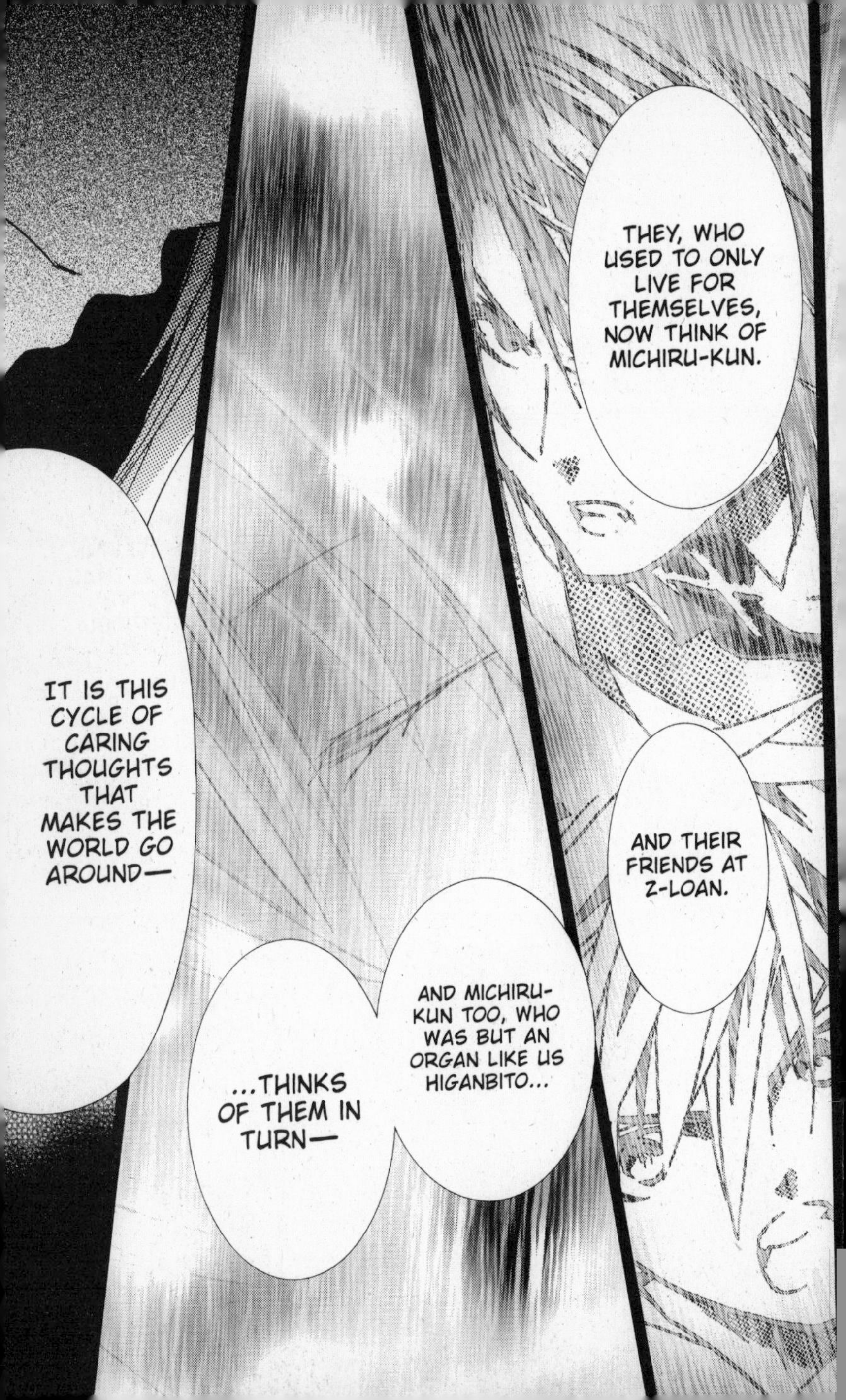
THEY, WHO USED TO ONLY LIVE FOR THEMSELVES, NOW THINK OF MICHIRU-KUN.
AND THEIR FRIENDS AT Z-LOAN.
AND MICHIRU-KUN TOO, WHO WAS BUT AN ORGAN LIKE US HIGANBITO...
...THINKS OF THEM IN TURN—
IT IS THIS CYCLE OF CARING THOUGHTS THAT MAKES THE WORLD GO AROUND—

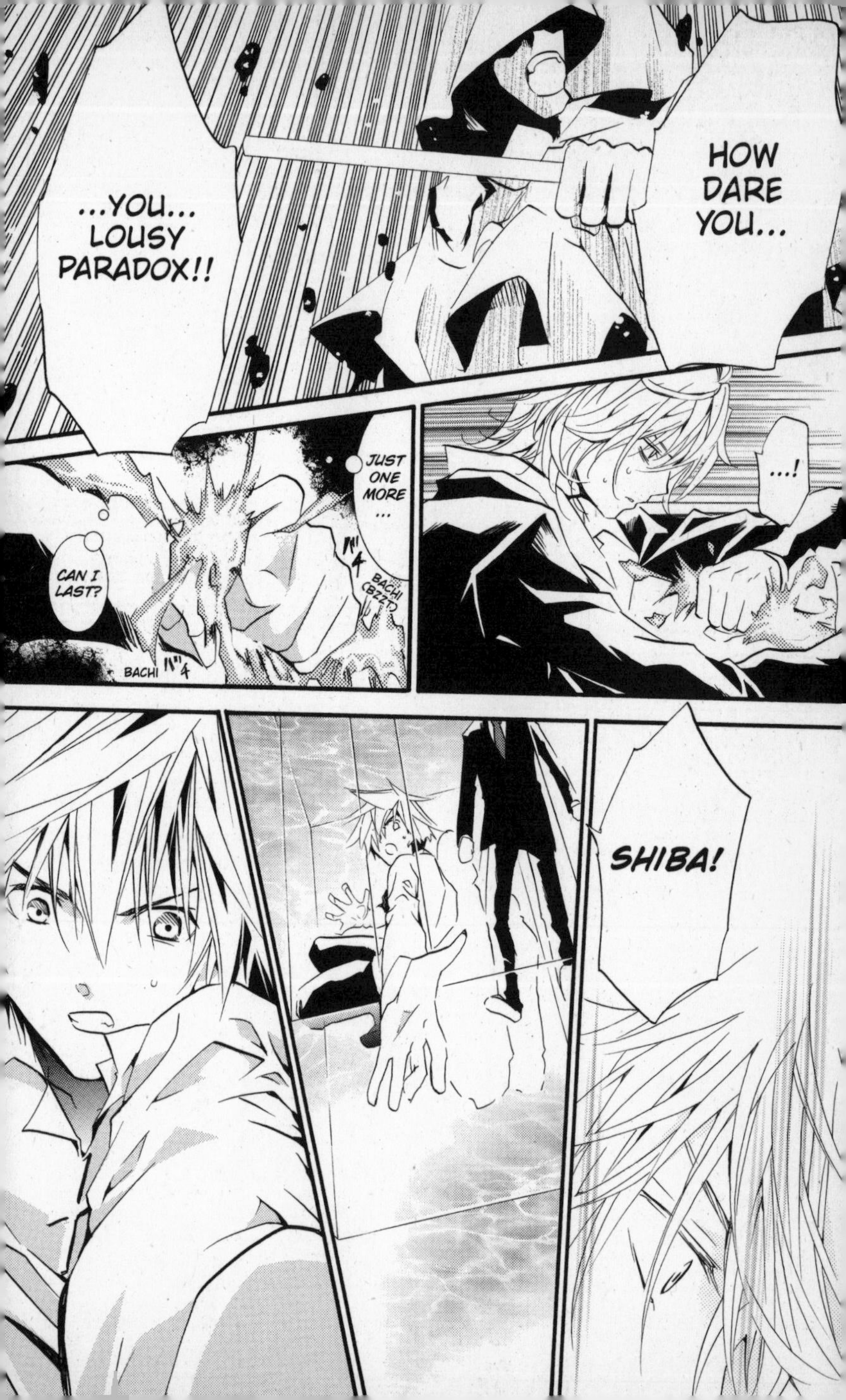
HOW DARE YOU...
...YOU... LOUSY PARADOX!!
...!
JUST ONE MORE ...
バチ
BACHI (BZZT)
CAN I LAST?
BACHI バチ
SHIBA!

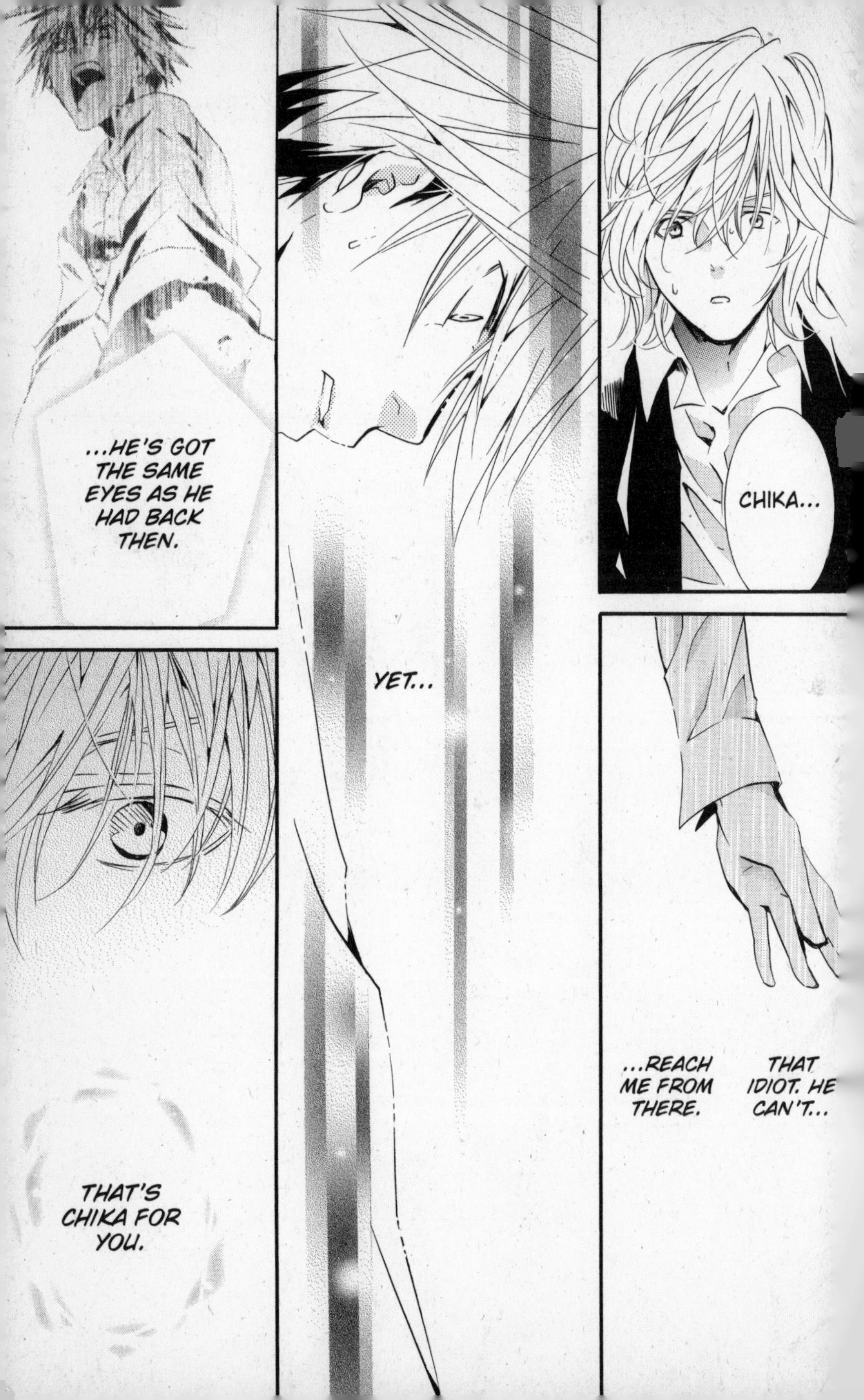
CHIKA...
THAT IDIOT. HE CAN'T...
...REACH ME FROM THERE.
YET...
...HE'S GOT THE SAME EYES AS HE HAD BACK THEN.
THAT'S CHIKA FOR YOU.

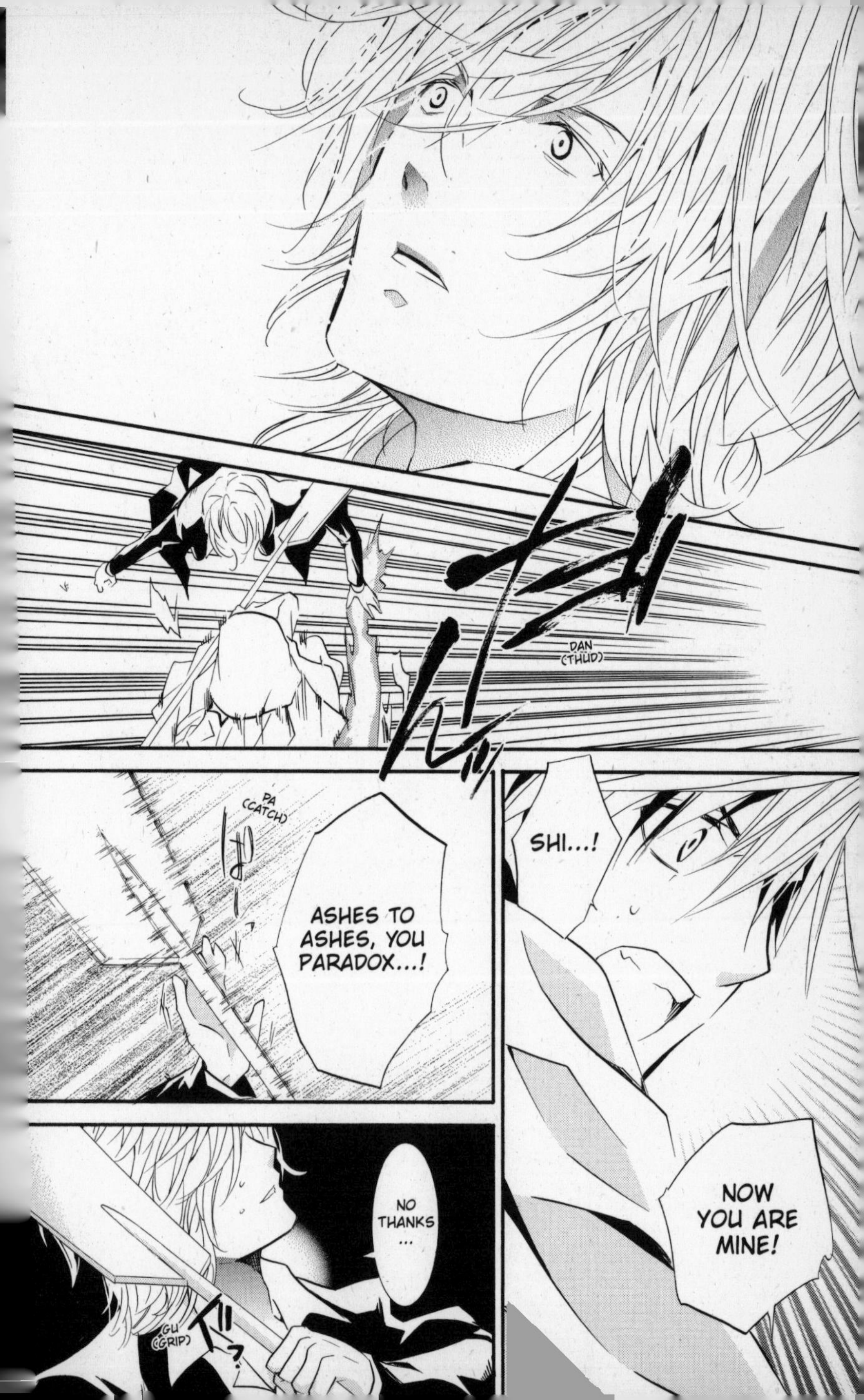
DAN (THUD)
SHI...!
NOW YOU ARE MINE!
PA (CATCH)
ASHES TO ASHES, YOU PARADOX...!
NO THANKS ...
GU (GRIP)

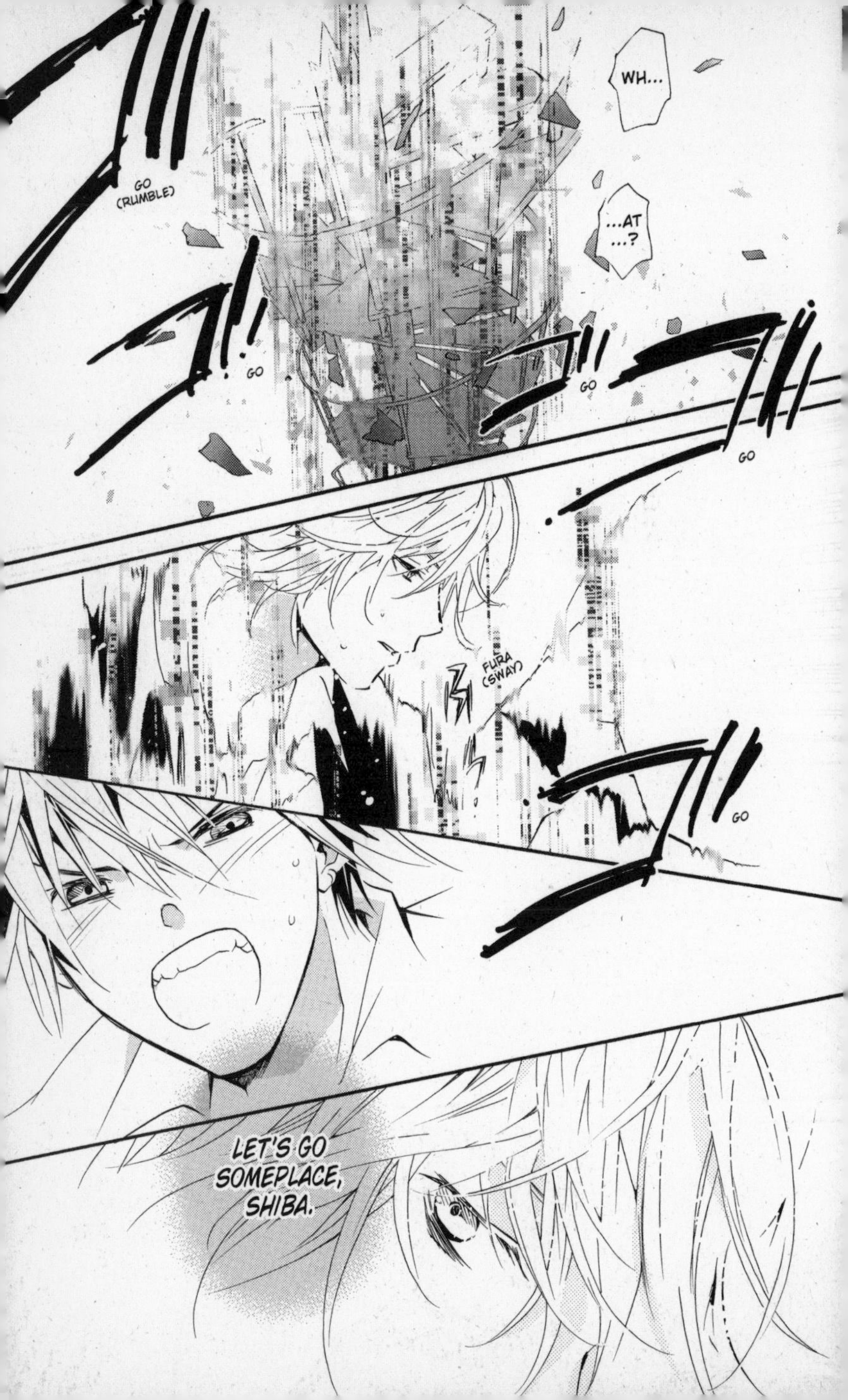
WH...
...AT ...?
GO
GO
GO
GO (RUMBLE)
FURA (SWAY)
GO
LET'S GO SOMEPLACE, SHIBA.

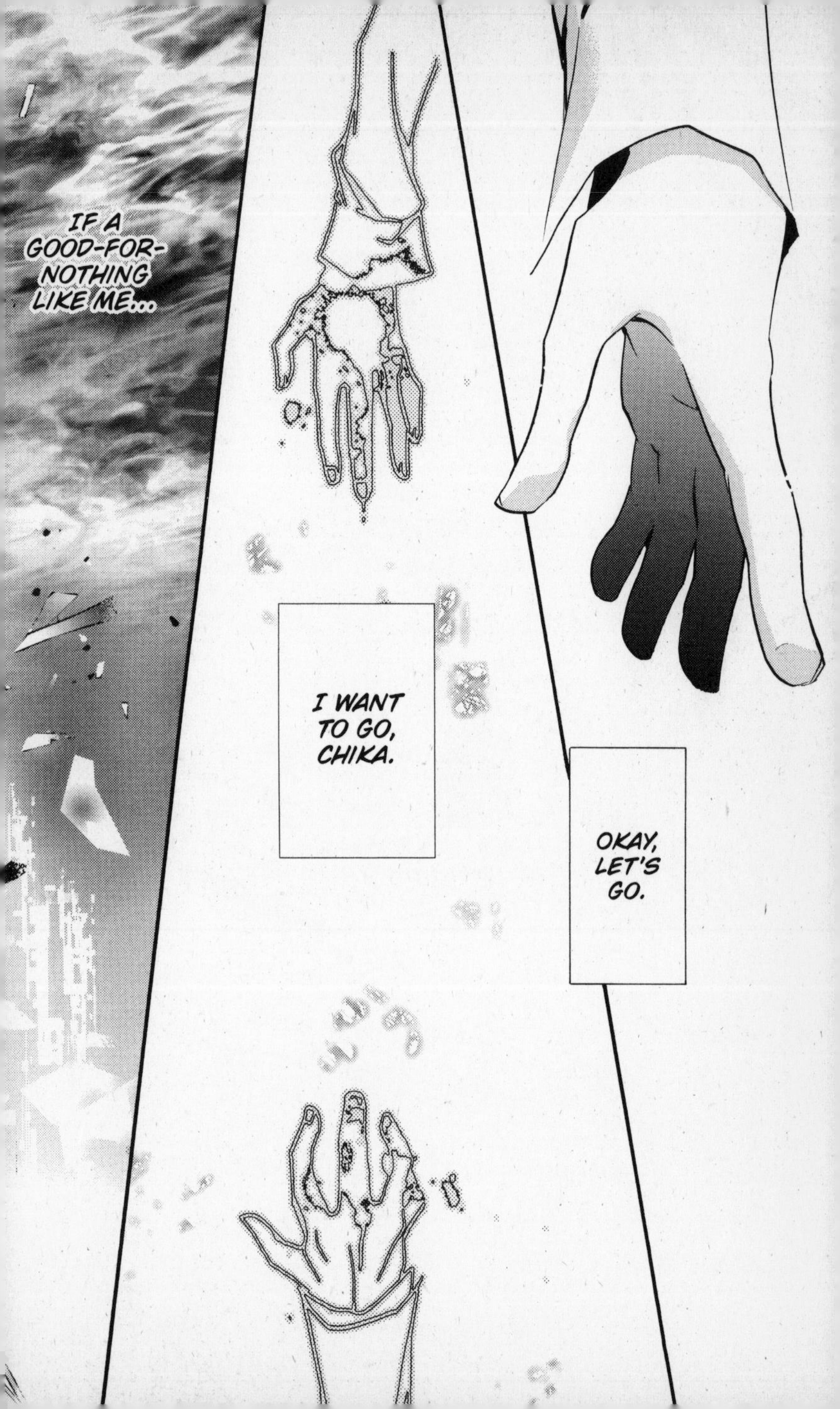
OKAY, LET'S GO.
I WANT TO GO, CHIKA.
IF A GOOD-FOR-NOTHING LIKE ME...

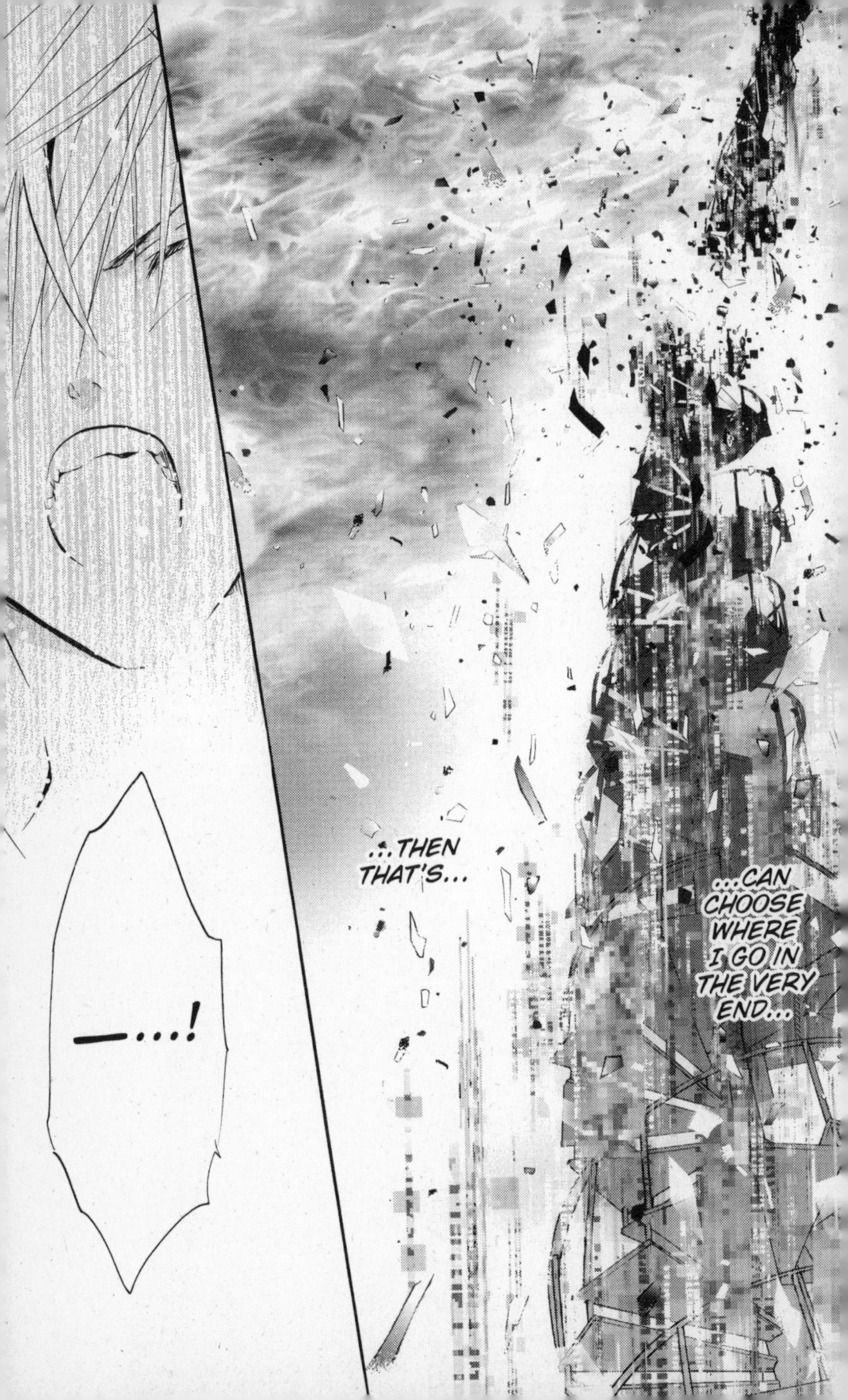
...CAN CHOOSE WHERE I GO IN THE VERY END...
...THEN THAT'S...
—...!

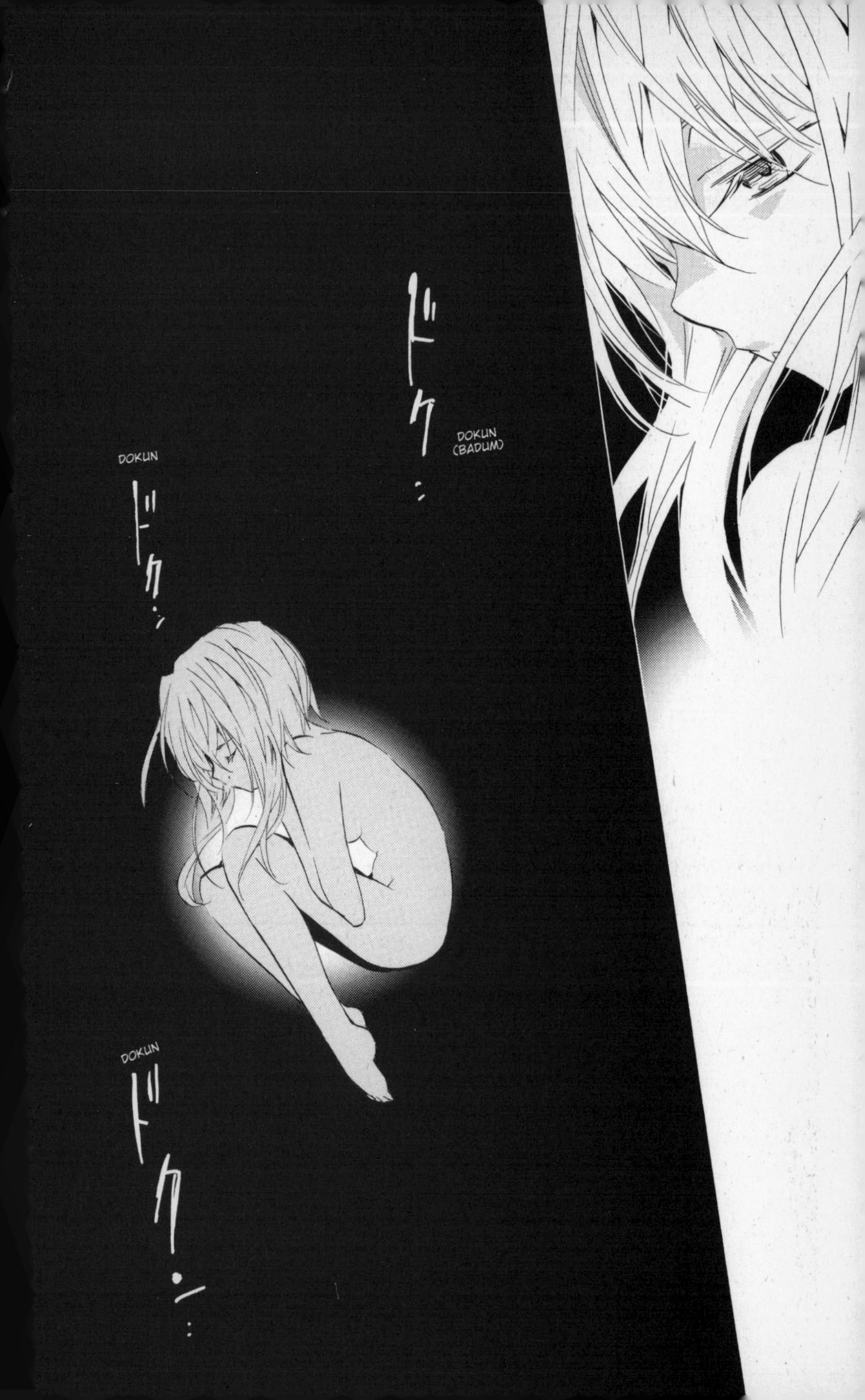
ドクン
DOKUN (BADUM)
ドクン
DOKUN
ドクン
DOKUN

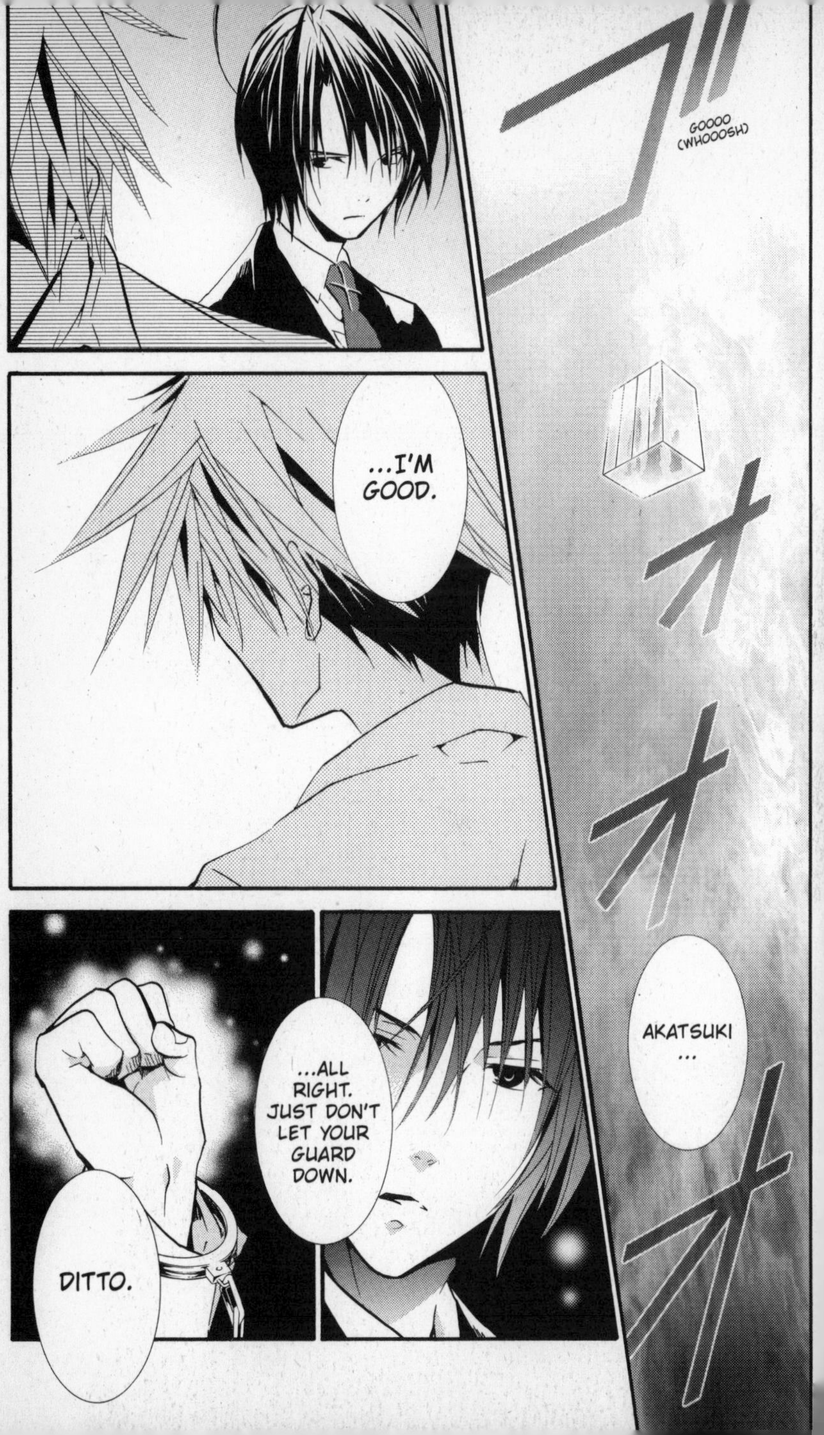
GOOOO (WHOOOSH)
AKATSUKI ...
...I'M GOOD.
...ALL RIGHT. JUST DON'T LET YOUR GUARD DOWN.
DITTO.

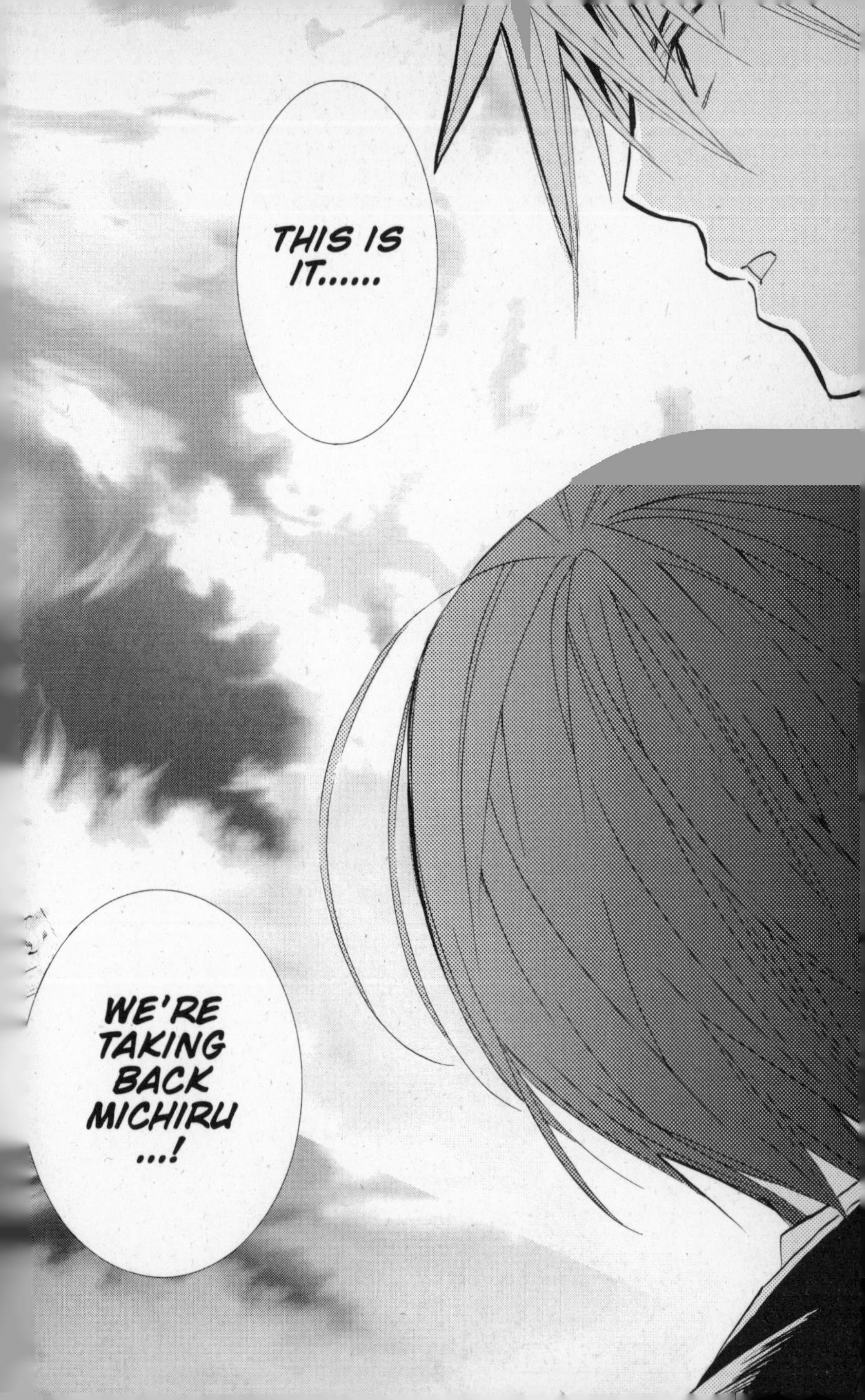
THIS IS IT......
WE'RE TAKING BACK MICHIRU ...!

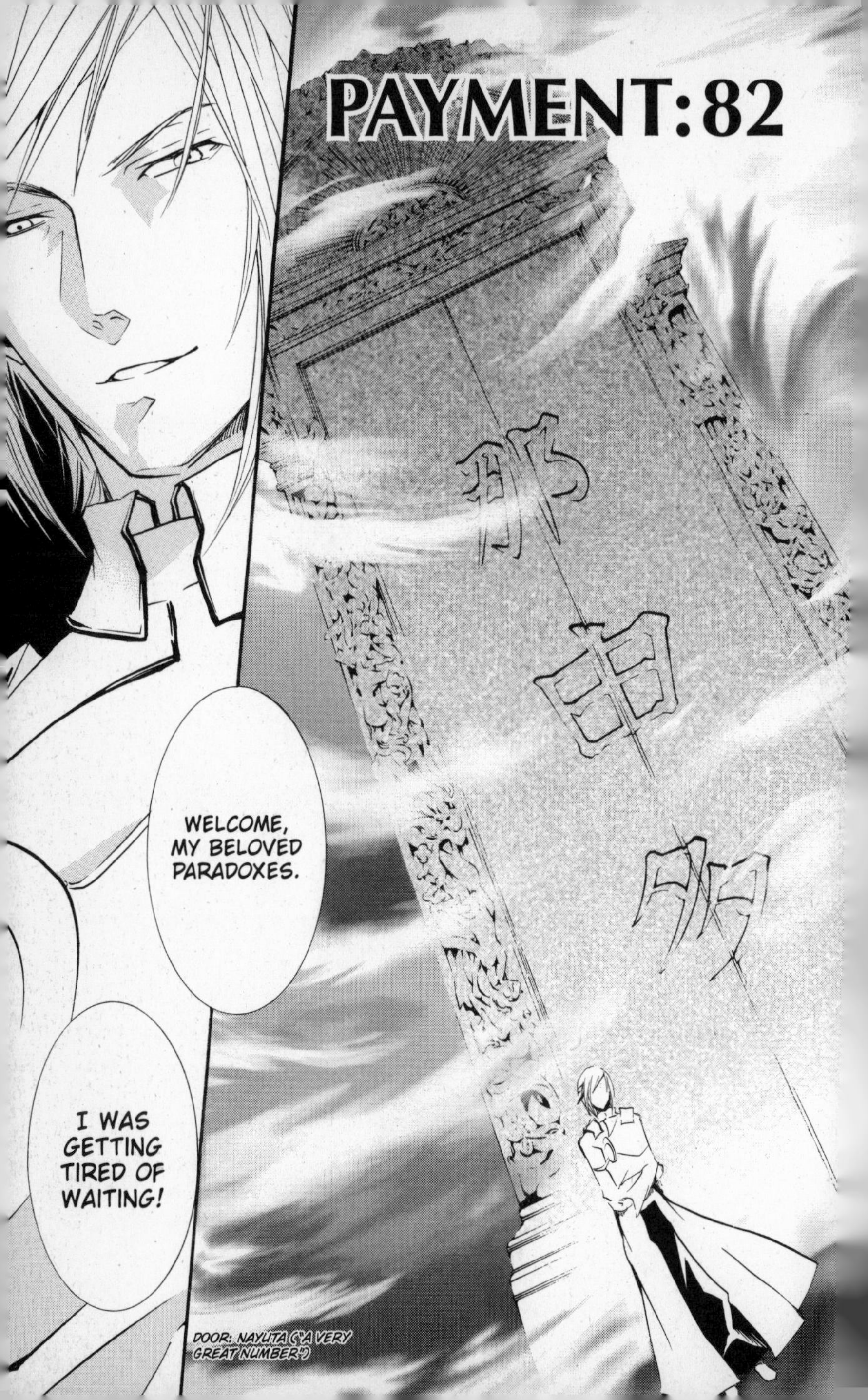
PAYMENT: 82
WELCOME, MY BELOVED PARADOXES.
I WAS GETTING TIRED OF WAITING!
DOOR: NAYUTA ("A VERY GREAT NUMBER")

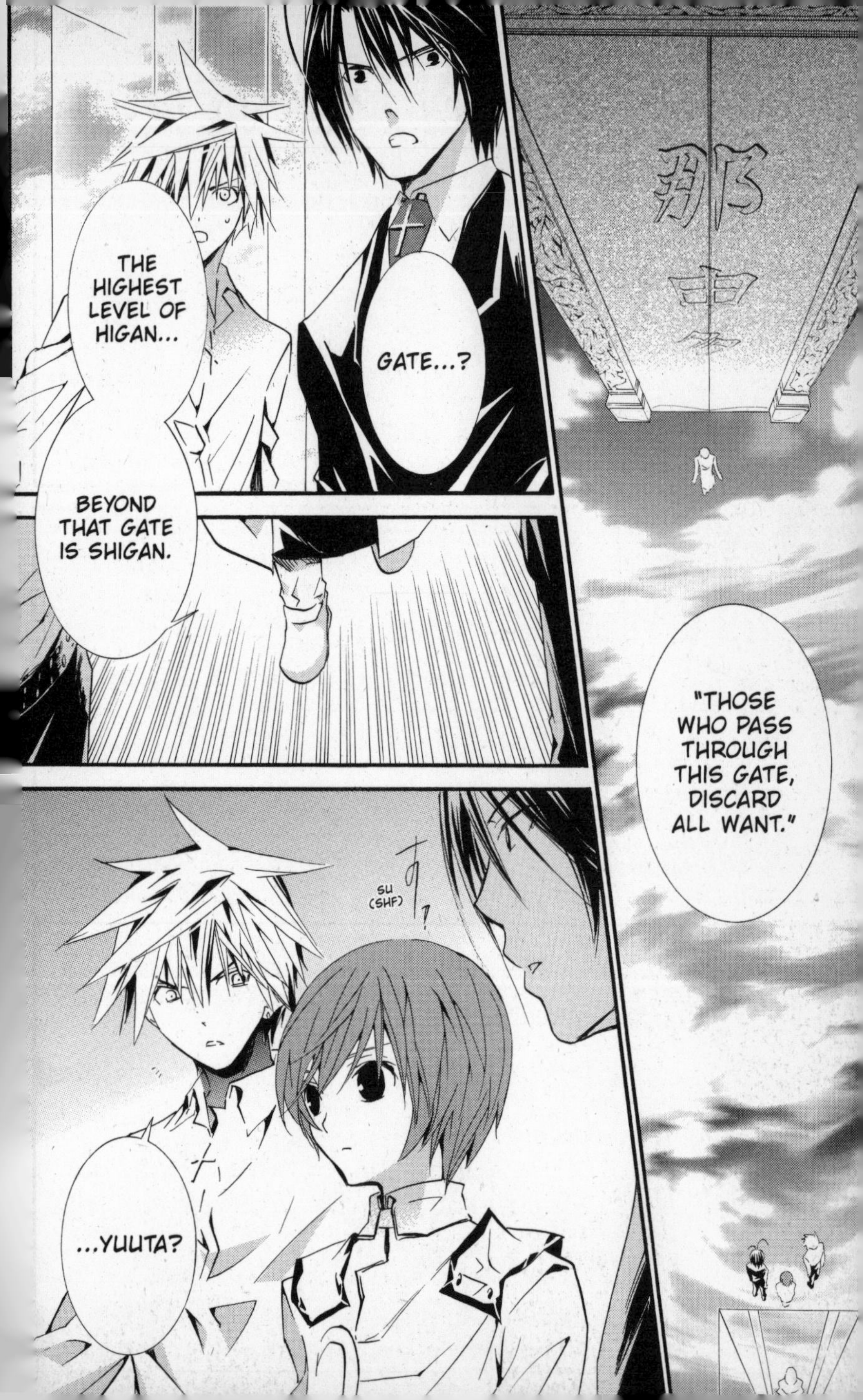
"THOSE WHO PASS THROUGH THIS GATE, DISCARD ALL WANT."
GATE...?
THE HIGHEST LEVEL OF HIGAN...
BEYOND THAT GATE IS SHIGAN.
SU (SHF)
...YUUTA?

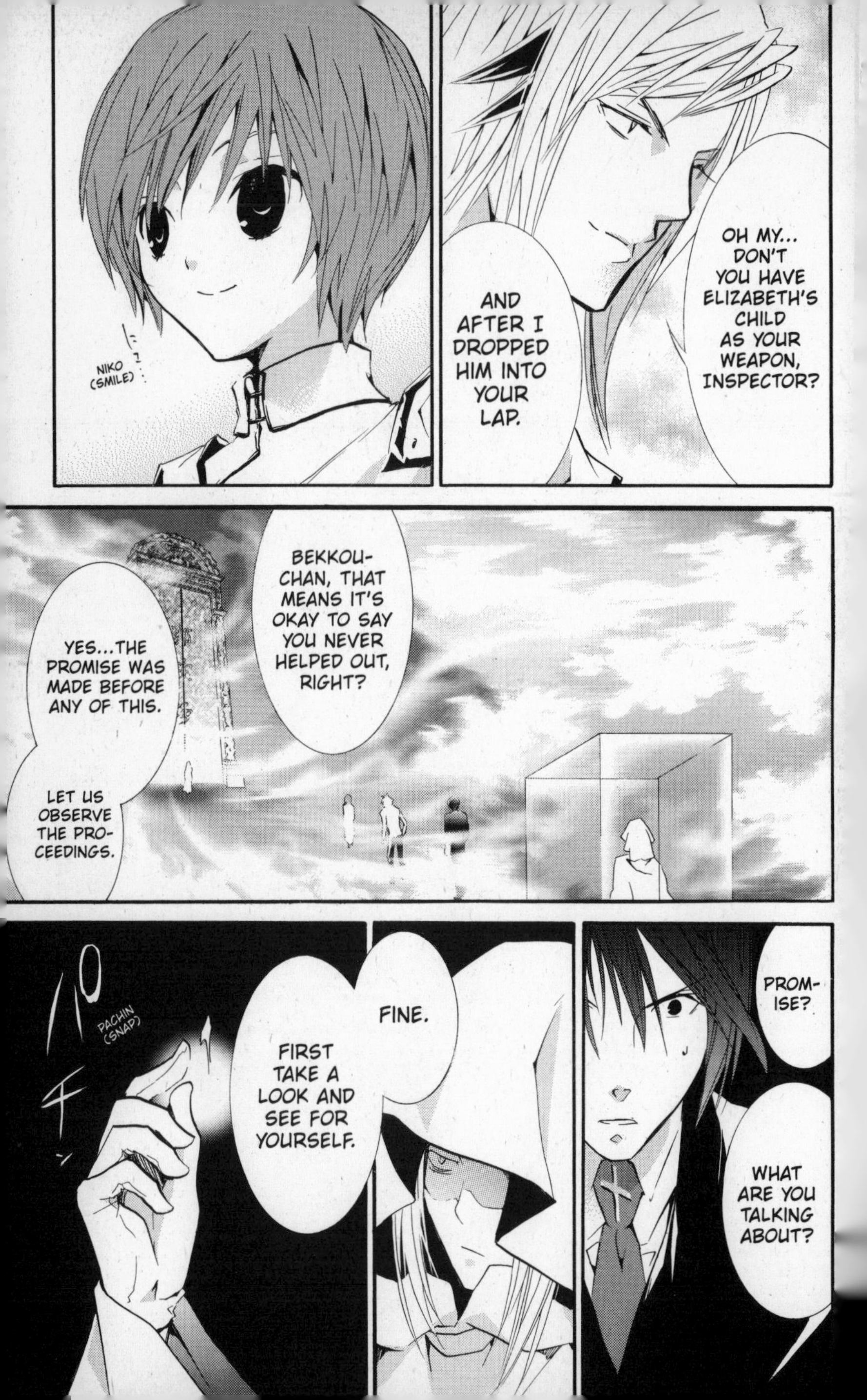
OH MY... DON'T YOU HAVE ELIZABETH'S CHILD AS YOUR WEAPON, INSPECTOR?
AND AFTER I DROPPED HIM INTO YOUR LAP.
NIKO (SMILE)
BEKKOU-CHAN, THAT MEANS IT'S OKAY TO SAY YOU NEVER HELPED OUT, RIGHT?
YES...THE PROMISE WAS MADE BEFORE ANY OF THIS.
LET US OBSERVE THE PRO-CEEDINGS.
PROM-ISE?
WHAT ARE YOU TALKING ABOUT?
FINE.
FIRST TAKE A LOOK AND SEE FOR YOURSELF.
PACHIN (SNAP)

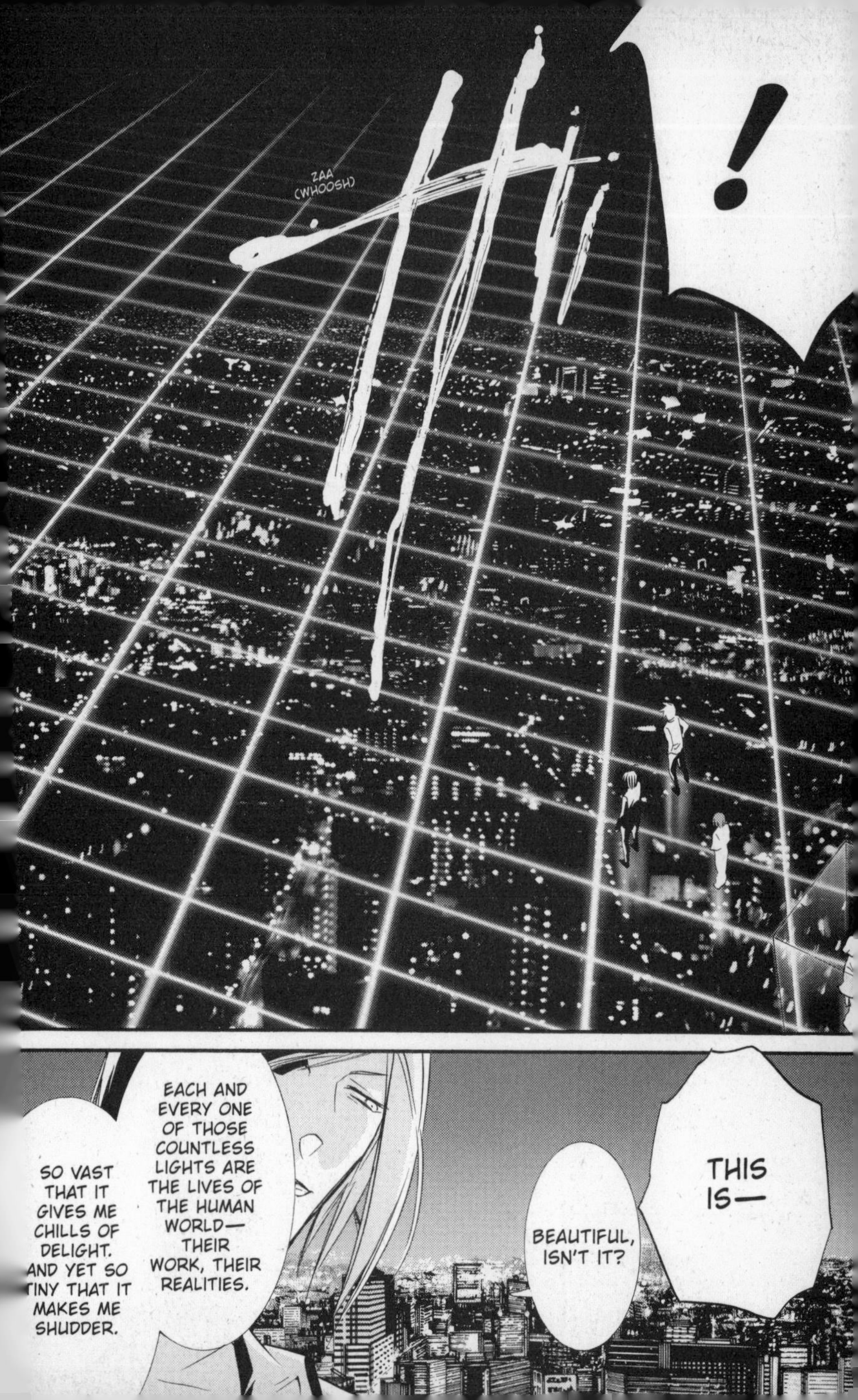
!
ZAA (WHOOSH)
THIS IS—
BEAUTIFUL, ISN'T IT?
EACH AND EVERY ONE OF THOSE COUNTLESS LIGHTS ARE THE LIVES OF THE HUMAN WORLD—THEIR WORK, THEIR REALITIES.
SO VAST THAT IT GIVES ME CHILLS OF DELIGHT. AND YET SO TINY THAT IT MAKES ME SHUDDER.

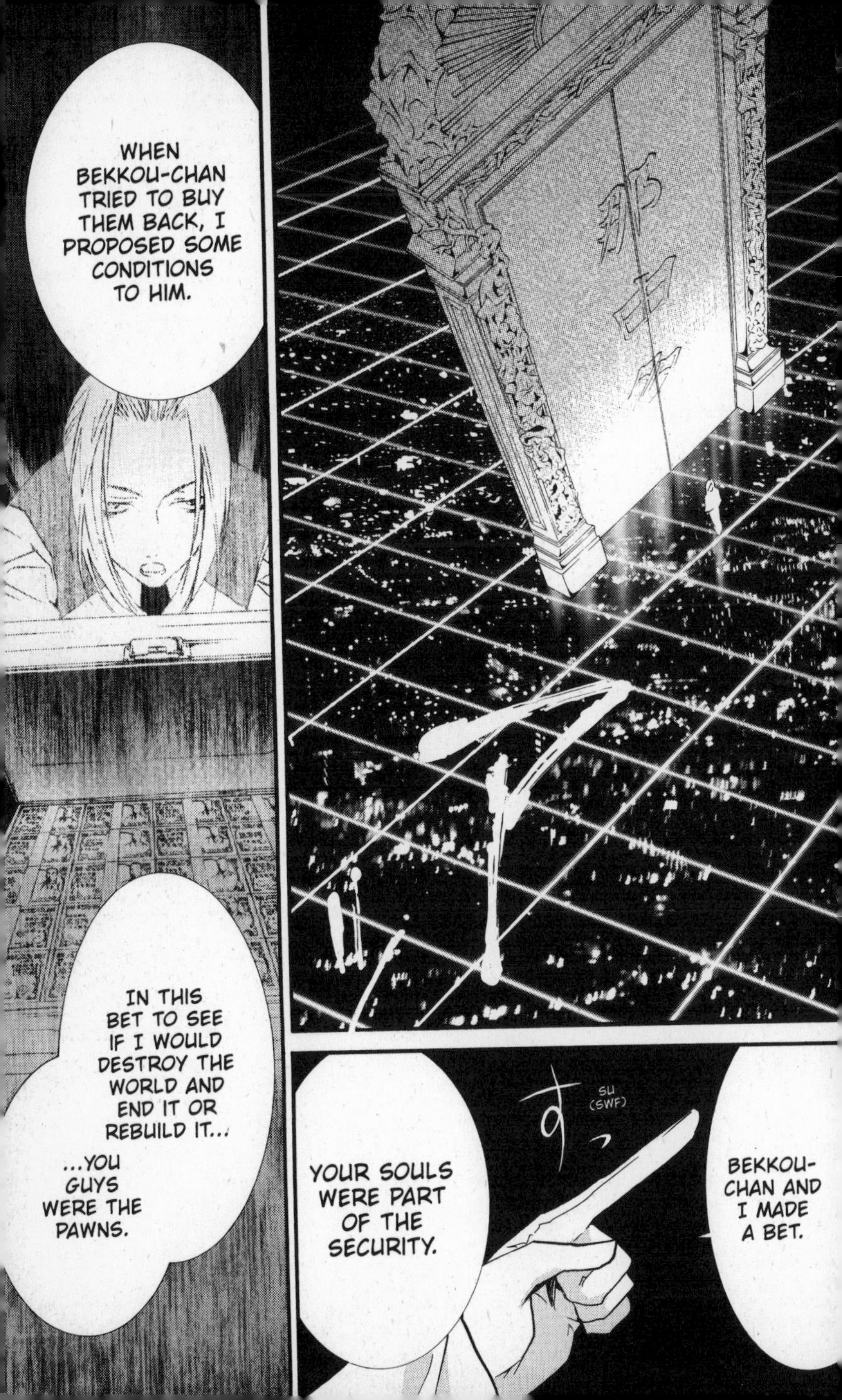
BEKKOU-CHAN AND I MADE A BET.
す
SU (SWF)
YOUR SOULS WERE PART OF THE SECURITY.
WHEN BEKKOU-CHAN TRIED TO BUY THEM BACK, I PROPOSED SOME CONDITIONS TO HIM.
IN THIS BET TO SEE IF I WOULD DESTROY THE WORLD AND END IT OR REBUILD IT...
...YOU GUYS WERE THE PAWNS.

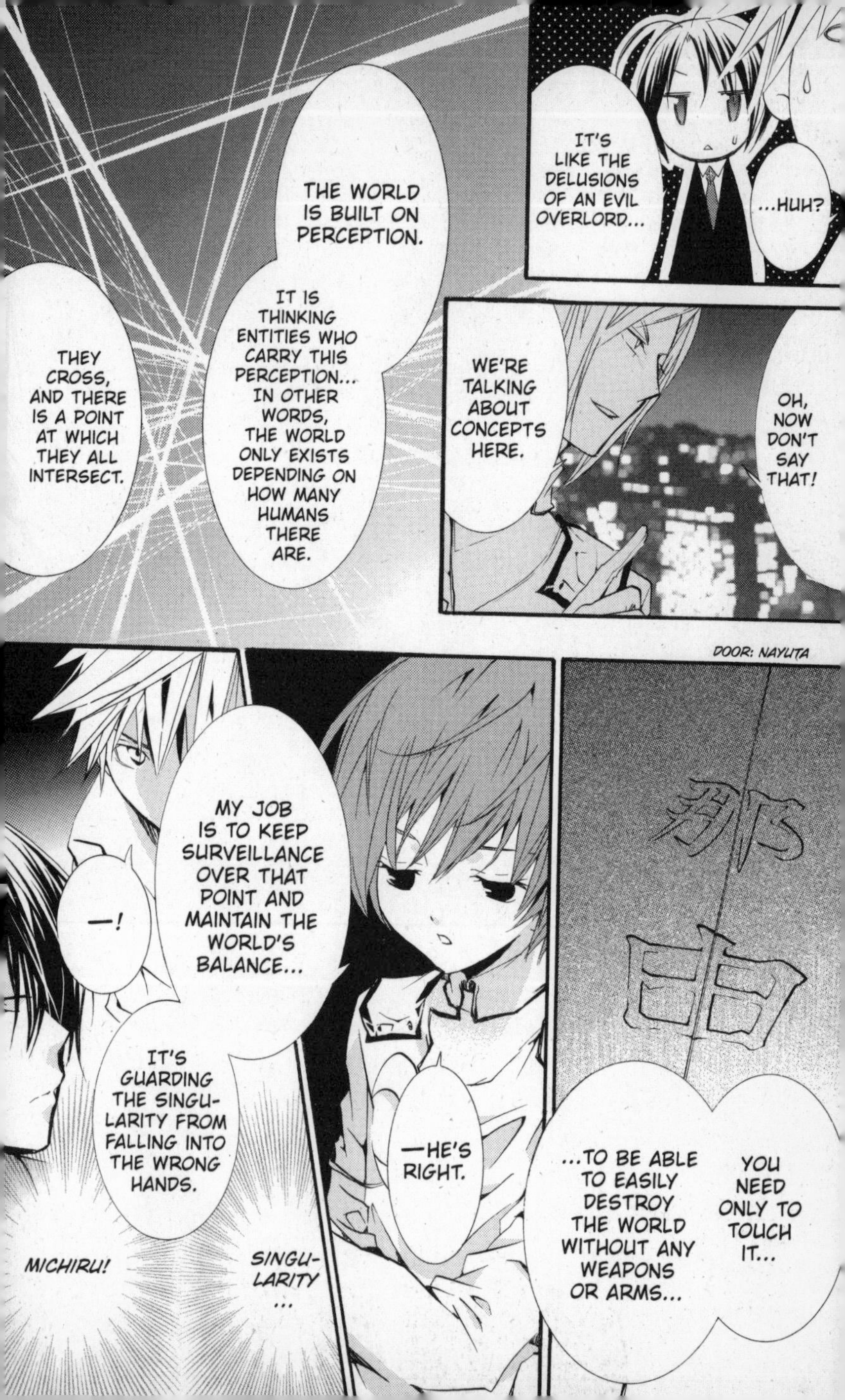
...HUH?
IT'S LIKE THE DELUSIONS OF AN EVIL OVERLORD...
OH, NOW DON'T SAY THAT!
WE'RE TALKING ABOUT CONCEPTS HERE.
THE WORLD IS BUILT ON PERCEPTION.
IT IS THINKING ENTITIES WHO CARRY THIS PERCEPTION... IN OTHER WORDS, THE WORLD ONLY EXISTS DEPENDING ON HOW MANY HUMANS THERE ARE.
THEY CROSS, AND THERE IS A POINT AT WHICH THEY ALL INTERSECT.
DOOR: NAYUTA
YOU NEED ONLY TO TOUCH IT...
...TO BE ABLE TO EASILY DESTROY THE WORLD WITHOUT ANY WEAPONS OR ARMS...
—HE'S RIGHT.
SINGU-LARITY ...
MY JOB IS TO KEEP SURVEILLANCE OVER THAT POINT AND MAINTAIN THE WORLD'S BALANCE...
—!
IT'S GUARDING THE SINGU-LARITY FROM FALLING INTO THE WRONG HANDS.
MICHIRU!

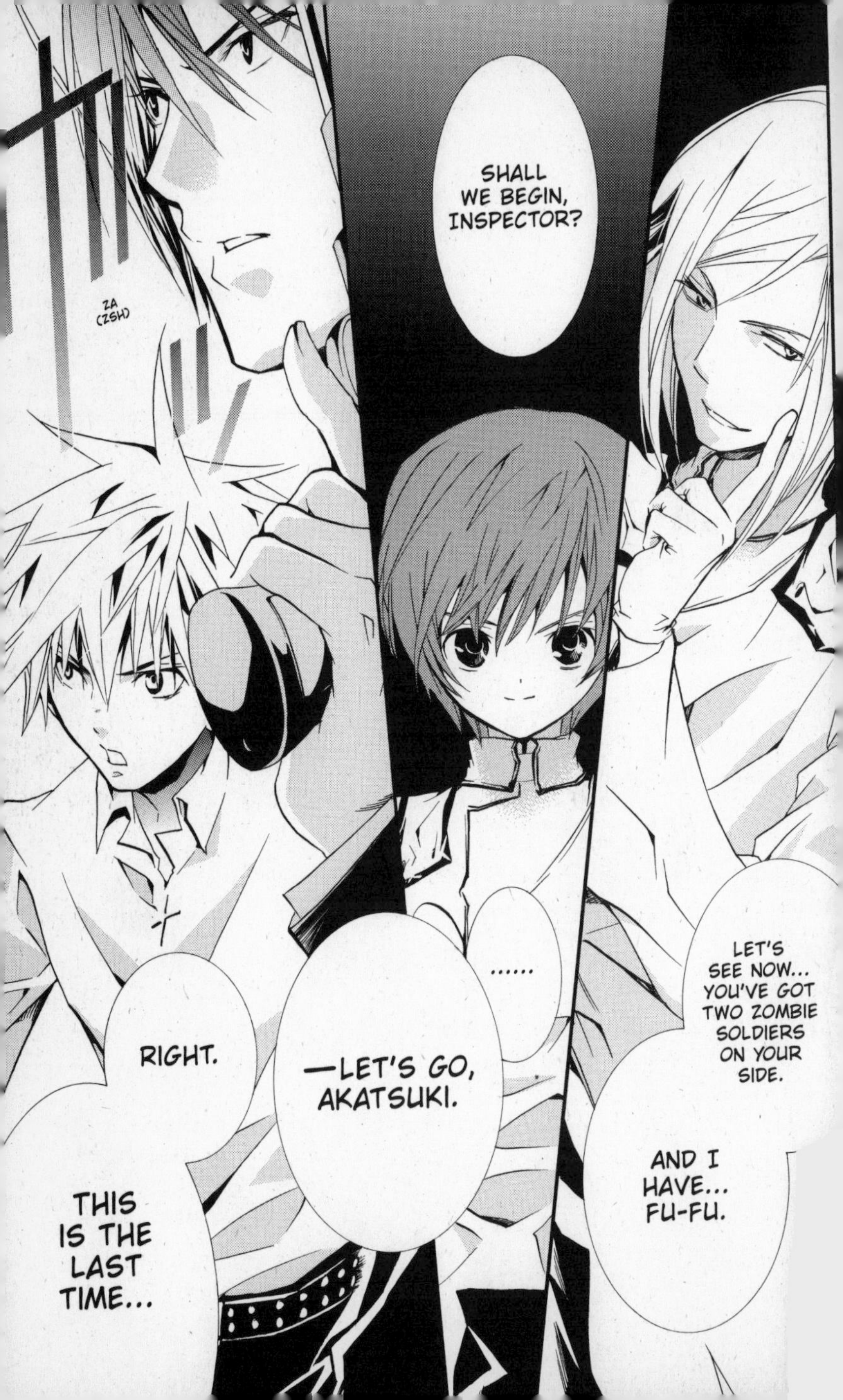
SHALL WE BEGIN, INSPECTOR?
LET'S SEE NOW... YOU'VE GOT TWO ZOMBIE SOLDIERS ON YOUR SIDE.
AND I HAVE... FU-FU.
......
—LET'S GO, AKATSUKI.
ZA (ZSH)
RIGHT.
THIS IS THE LAST TIME...

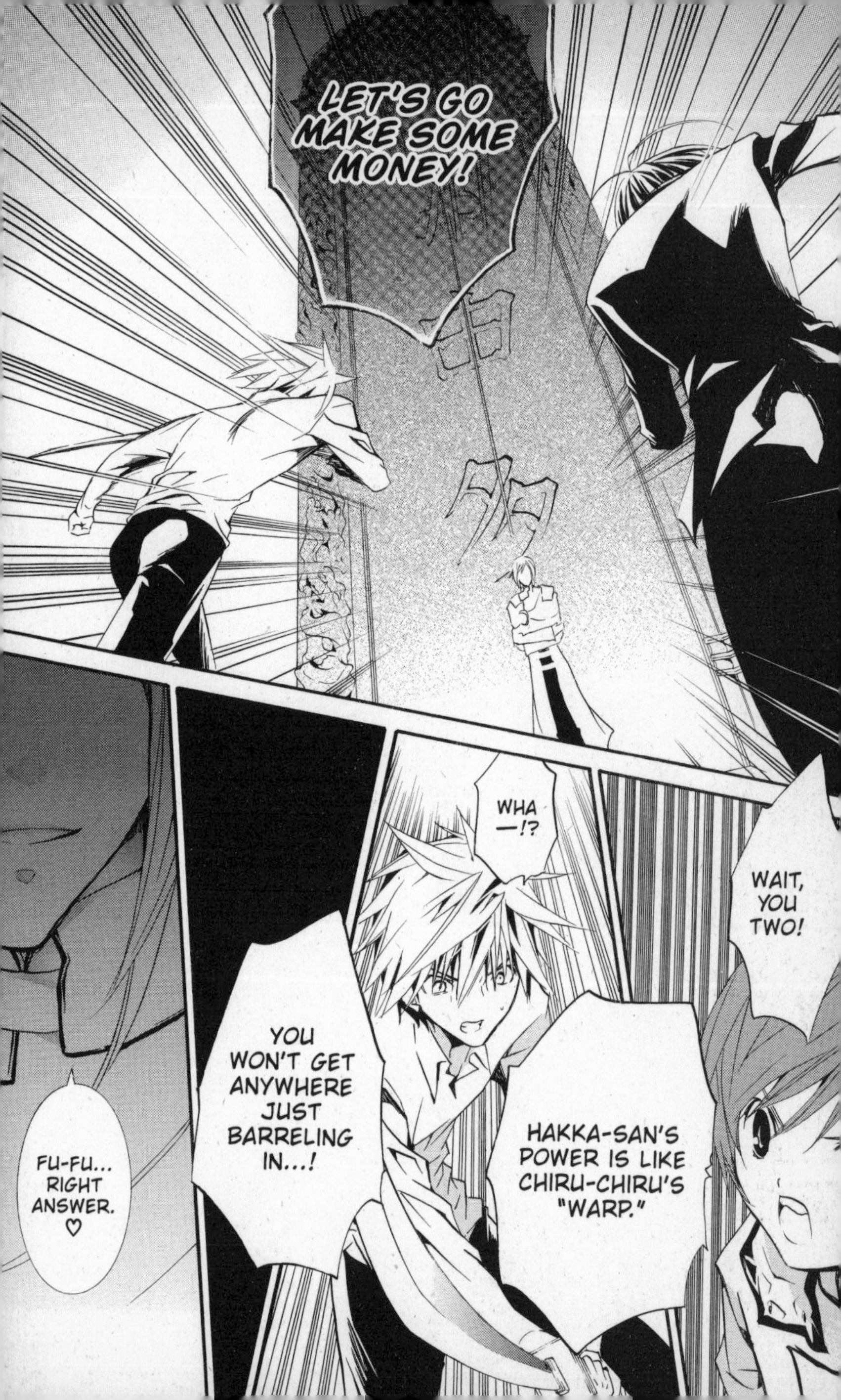
LET'S GO MAKE SOME MONEY!
WAIT, YOU TWO!
WHA—!?
HAKKA-SAN'S POWER IS LIKE CHIRU-CHIRU'S "WARP."
YOU WON'T GET ANYWHERE JUST BARRELING IN...!
FU-FU... RIGHT ANSWER. ♡

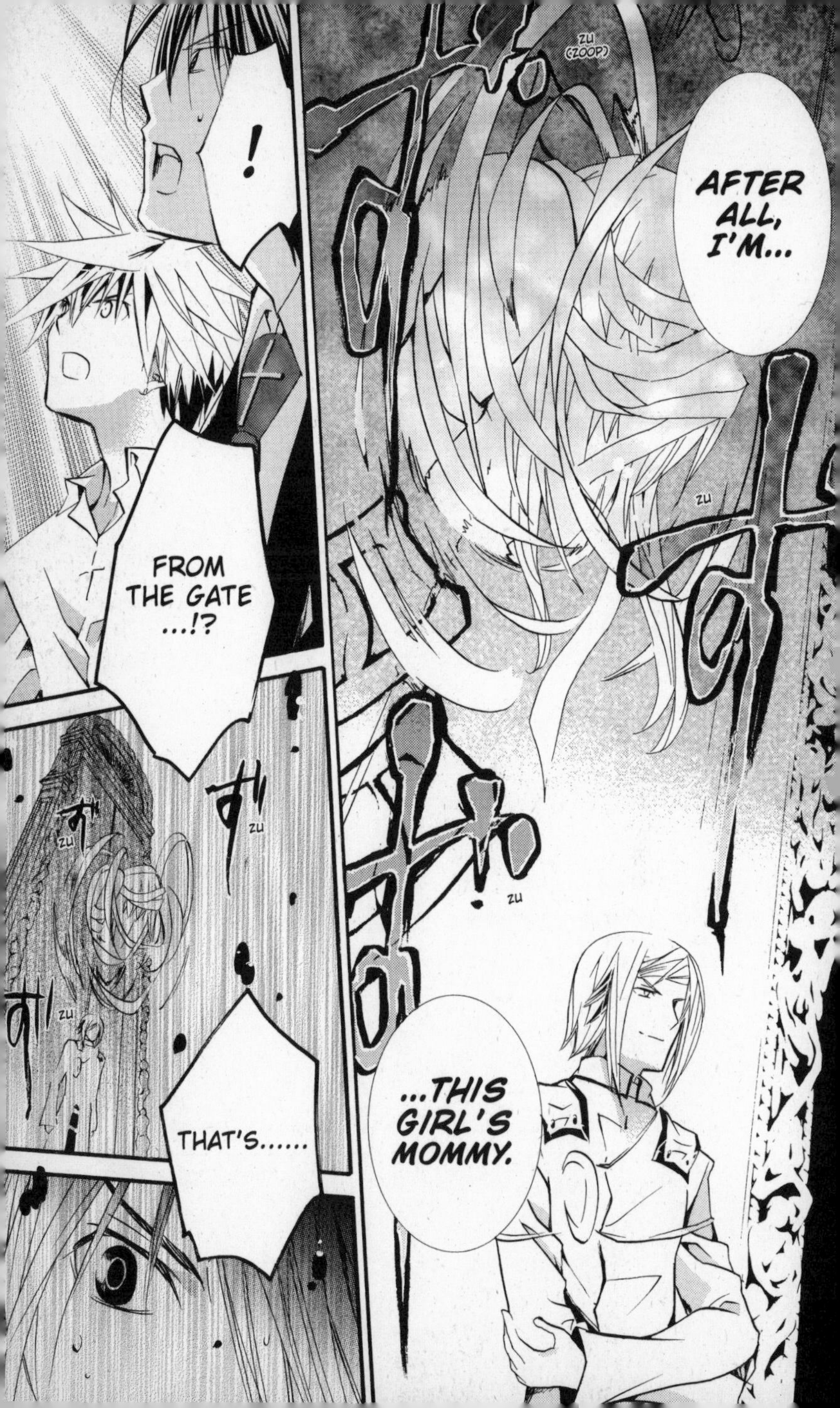
ZU (ZOOP)
AFTER ALL, I'M...
ZU
ZU
...THIS GIRL'S MOMMY.
!
FROM THE GATE ...!?
ZU
ZU
ZU
THAT'S......

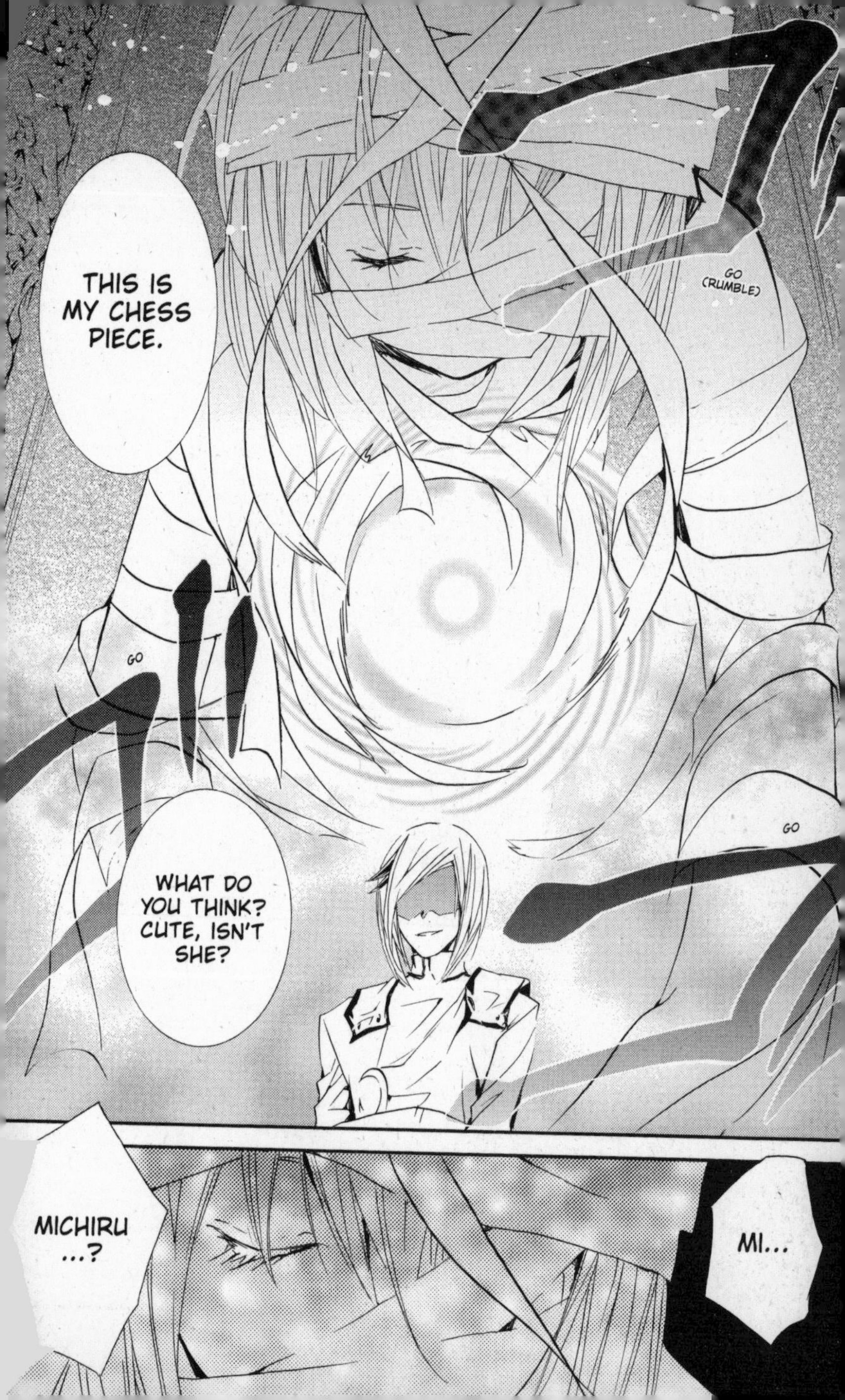
GO (RUMBLE)
THIS IS MY CHESS PIECE.
GO
GO
WHAT DO YOU THINK? CUTE, ISN'T SHE?
MI...
MICHIRU ...?

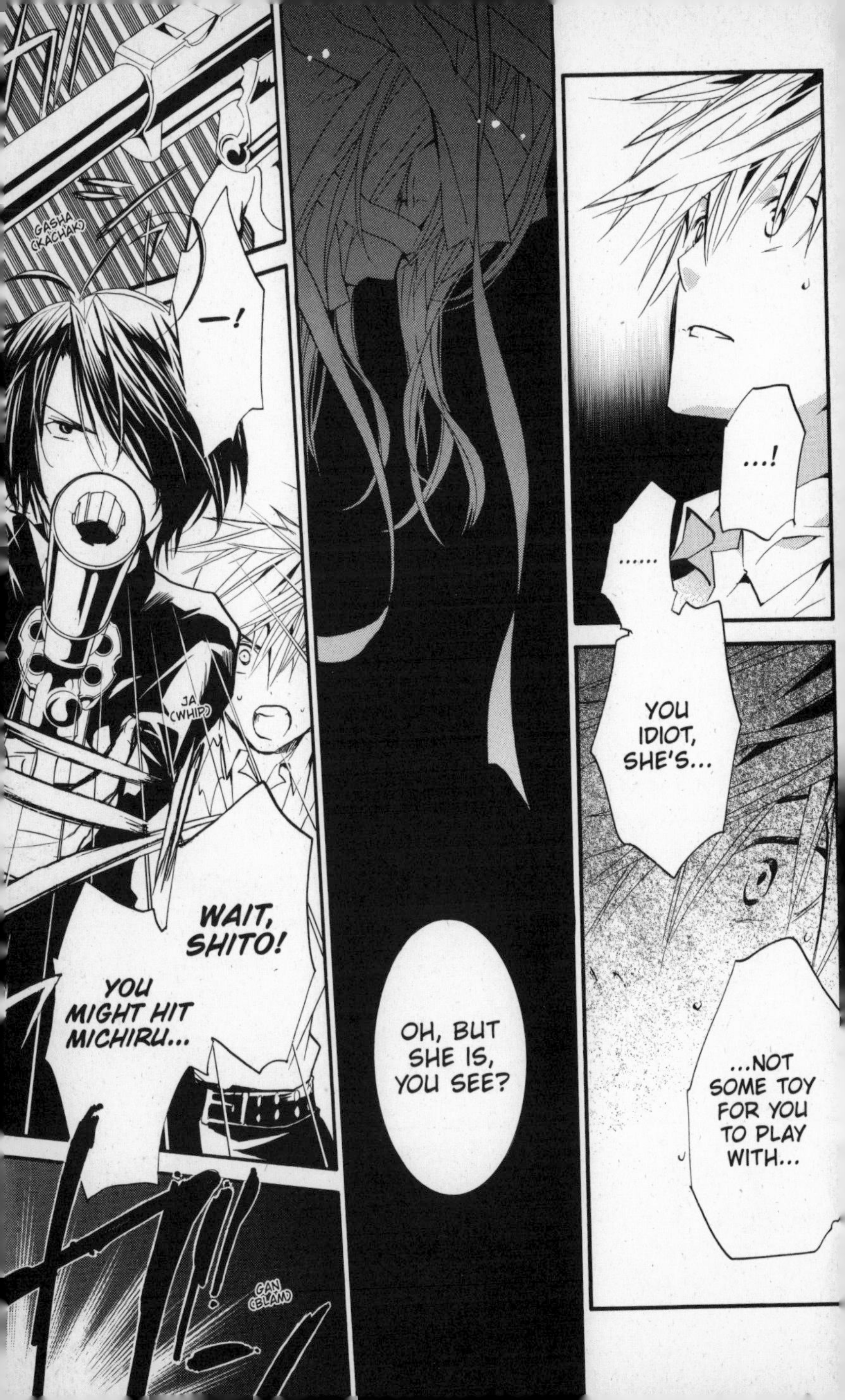
...!
......
YOU IDIOT, SHE'S...
...NOT SOME TOY FOR YOU TO PLAY WITH...
OH, BUT SHE IS, YOU SEE?
GASHA (KACHAK)
—!
JA (WHIP)
WAIT, SHITO!
YOU MIGHT HIT MICHIRU...
GAN (BLAM)

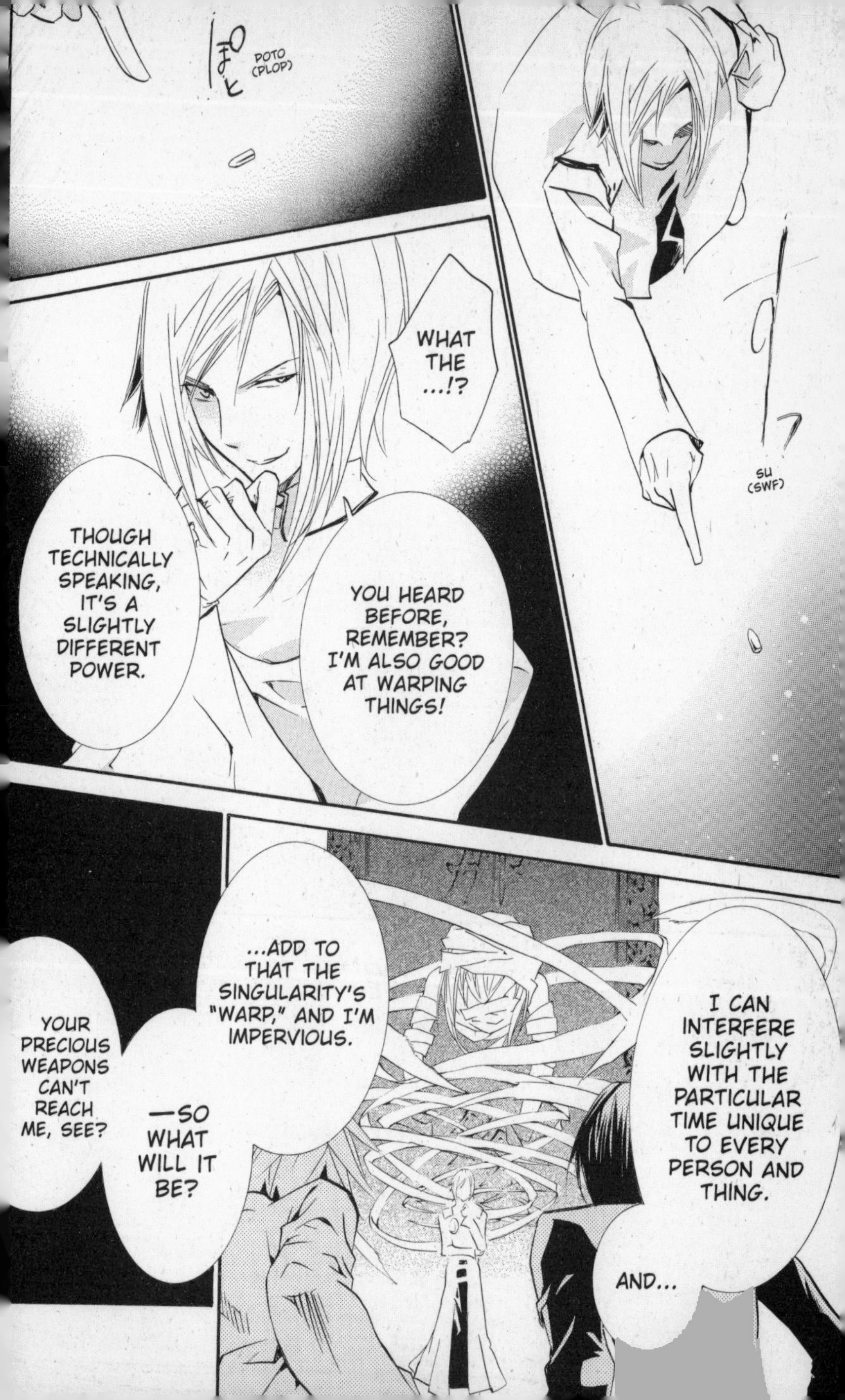
SU (SWF)
ぽと
POTO (PLOP)
WHAT THE ...!?
YOU HEARD BEFORE, REMEMBER? I'M ALSO GOOD AT WARPING THINGS!
THOUGH TECHNICALLY SPEAKING, IT'S A SLIGHTLY DIFFERENT POWER.
I CAN INTERFERE SLIGHTLY WITH THE PARTICULAR TIME UNIQUE TO EVERY PERSON AND THING.
AND...
...ADD TO THAT THE SINGULARITY'S "WARP," AND I'M IMPERVIOUS.
YOUR PRECIOUS WEAPONS CAN'T REACH ME, SEE?
—SO WHAT WILL IT BE?

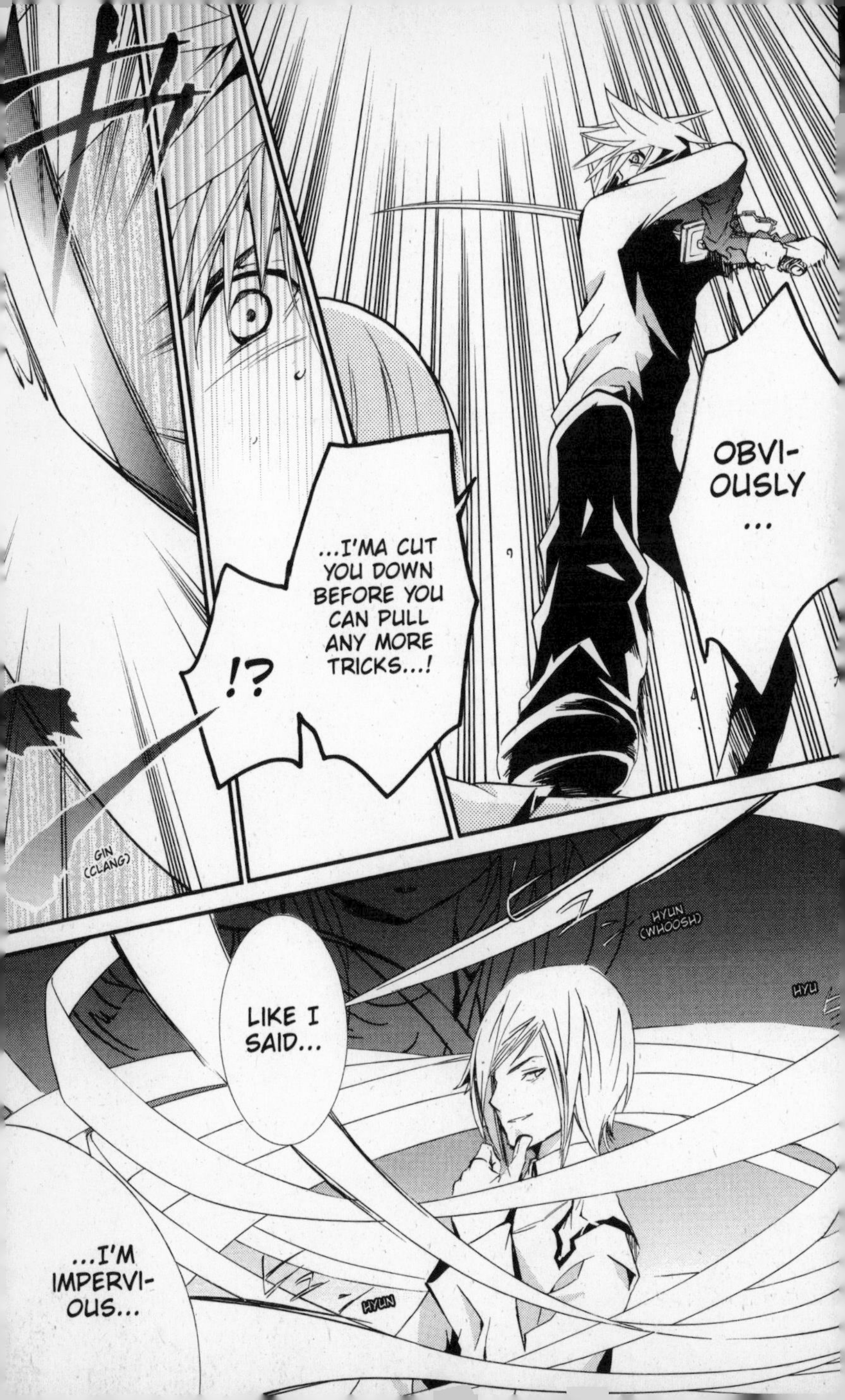
OBVI-OUSLY ...
...I'MA CUT YOU DOWN BEFORE YOU CAN PULL ANY MORE TRICKS...!
!?
GIN (CLANG)
HYUN (WHOOSH)
HYU
LIKE I SAID...
...I'M IMPERVI-OUS...
HYUN

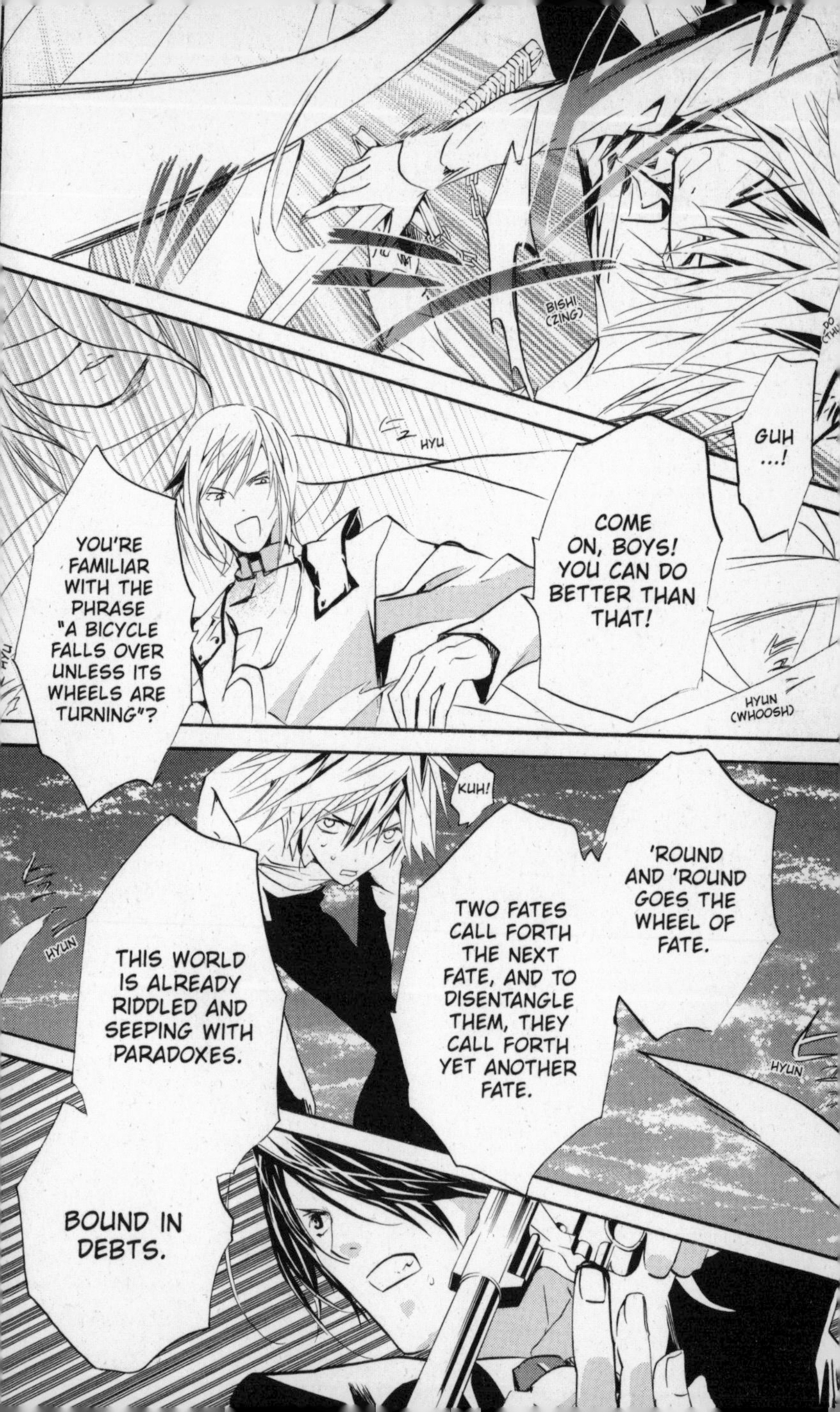
DO (THU
BISHI (ZING)
GUH ...!
HYUN (WHOOSH)
COME ON, BOYS! YOU CAN DO BETTER THAN THAT!
HYU
YOU'RE FAMILIAR WITH THE PHRASE "A BICYCLE FALLS OVER UNLESS ITS WHEELS ARE TURNING"?
HYU
HYUN
'ROUND AND 'ROUND GOES THE WHEEL OF FATE.
KUH!
TWO FATES CALL FORTH THE NEXT FATE, AND TO DISENTANGLE THEM, THEY CALL FORTH YET ANOTHER FATE.
THIS WORLD IS ALREADY RIDDLED AND SEEPING WITH PARADOXES.
HYUN
BOUND IN DEBTS.

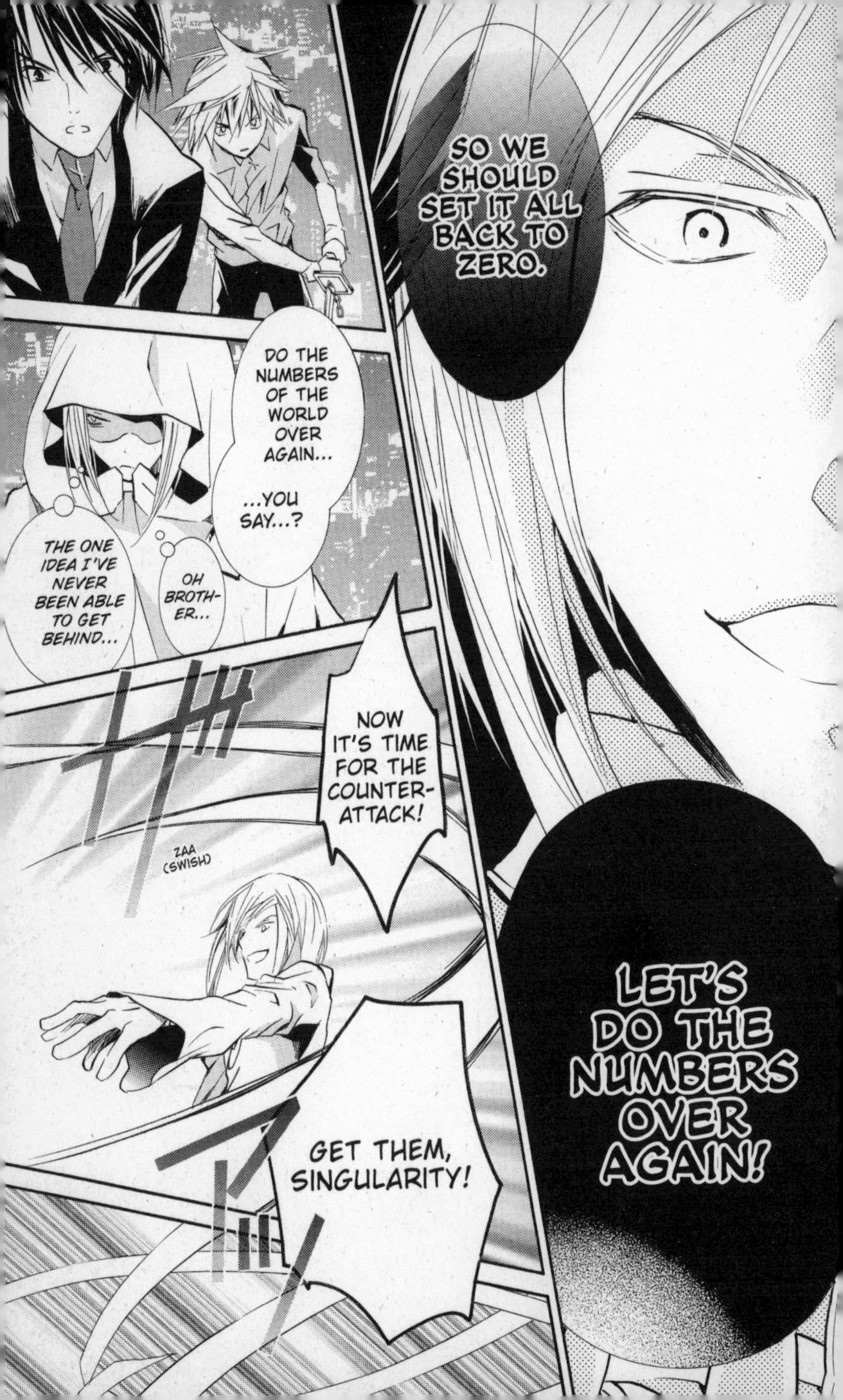
SO WE SHOULD SET IT ALL BACK TO ZERO.
LET'S DO THE NUMBERS OVER AGAIN!
DO THE NUMBERS OF THE WORLD OVER AGAIN...
...YOU SAY...?
OH BROTHER...
THE ONE IDEA I'VE NEVER BEEN ABLE TO GET BEHIND...
NOW IT'S TIME FOR THE COUNTER-ATTACK!
ZAA (SWISH)
GET THEM, SINGULARITY!

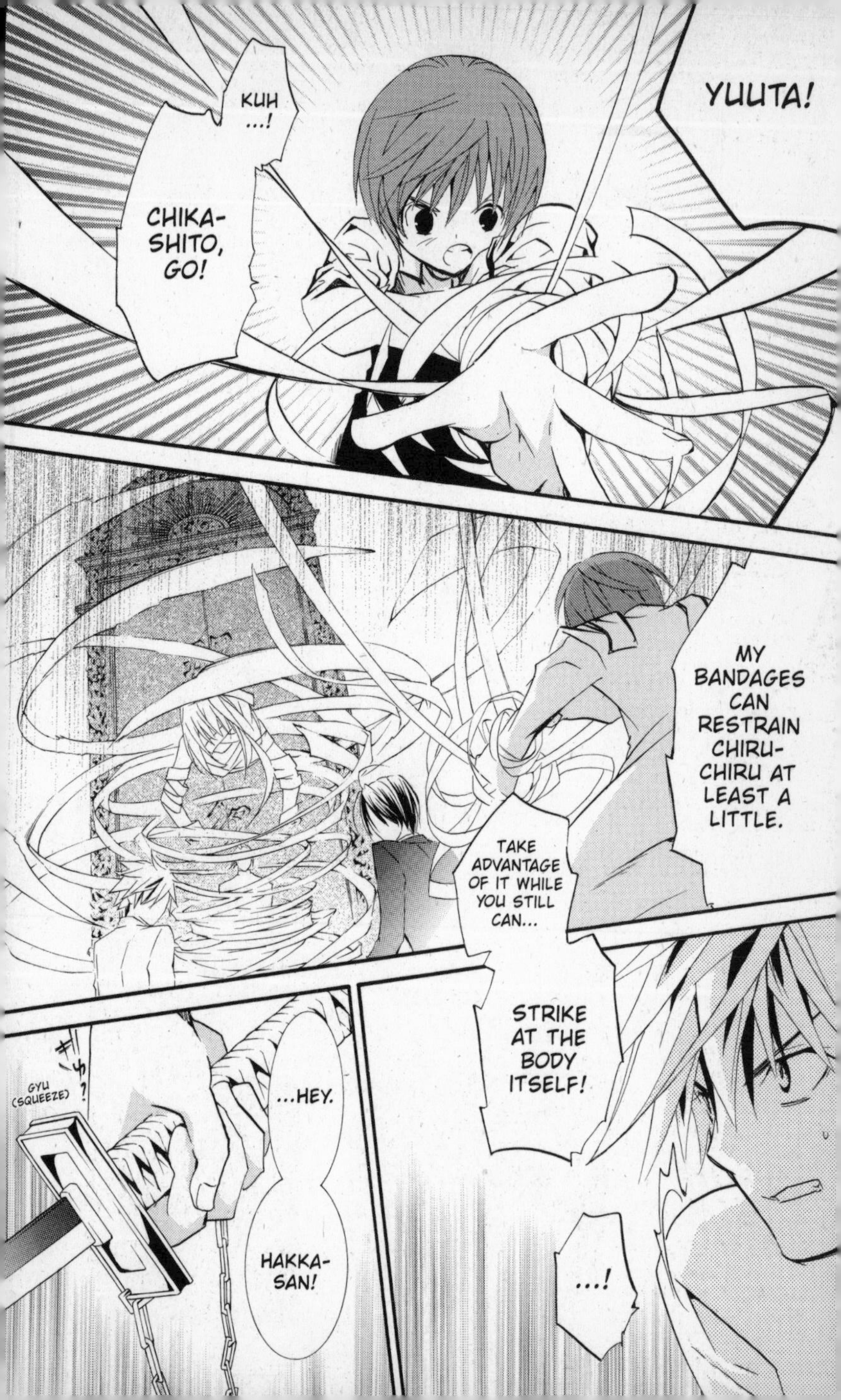
YUUTA!
KUH ...!
CHIKA-SHITO, GO!
MY BANDAGES CAN RESTRAIN CHIRU-CHIRU AT LEAST A LITTLE.
TAKE ADVANTAGE OF IT WHILE YOU STILL CAN...
STRIKE AT THE BODY ITSELF!
...!
...HEY.
HAKKA-SAN!
GYU (SQUEEZE)

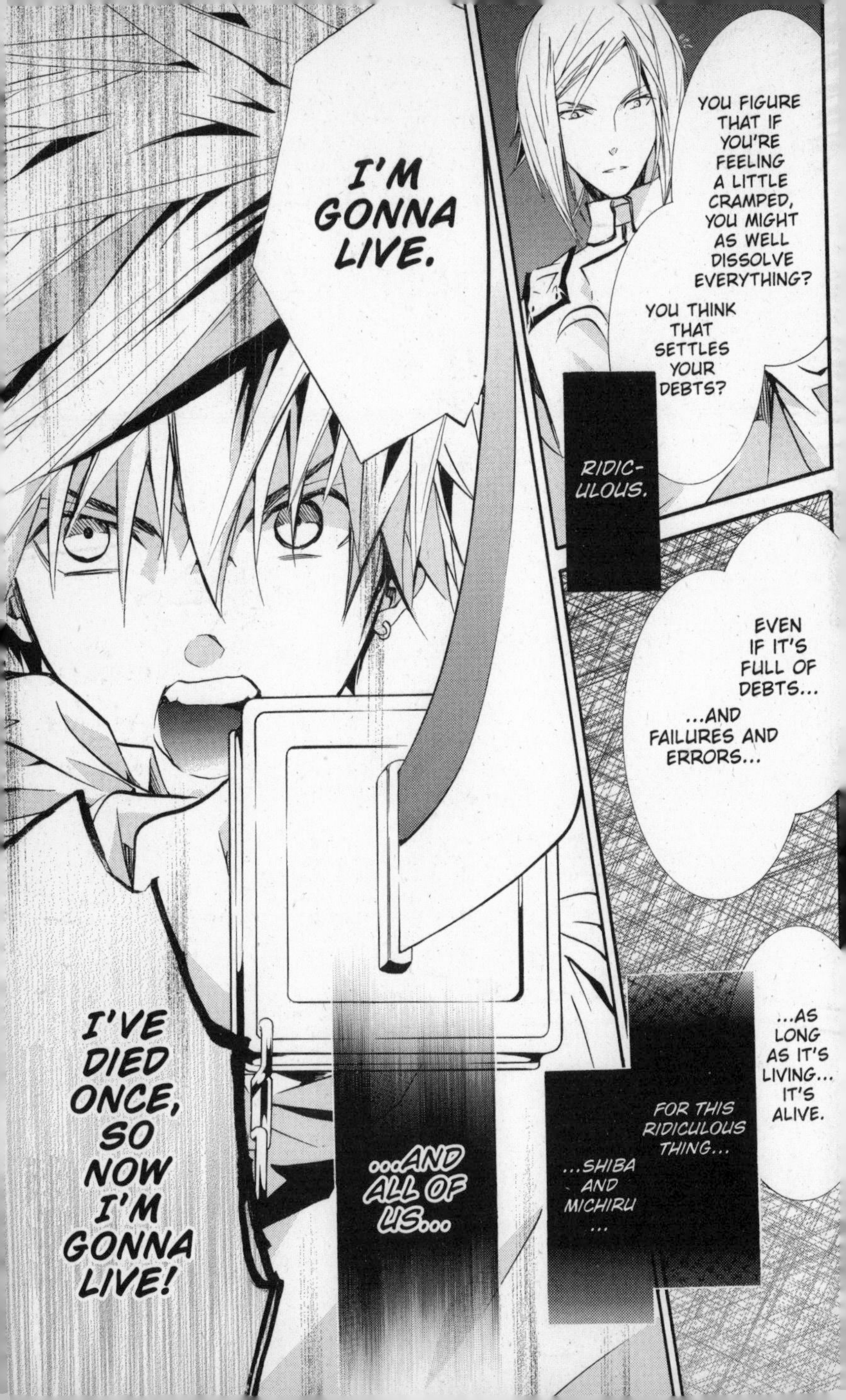
YOU FIGURE THAT IF YOU'RE FEELING A LITTLE CRAMPED, YOU MIGHT AS WELL DISSOLVE EVERYTHING?
YOU THINK THAT SETTLES YOUR DEBTS?
RIDIC-ULOUS.
EVEN IF IT'S FULL OF DEBTS...
...AND FAILURES AND ERRORS...
...AS LONG AS IT'S LIVING... IT'S ALIVE.
FOR THIS RIDICULOUS THING...
...SHIBA AND MICHIRU ...
...AND ALL OF US...
I'M GONNA LIVE.
I'VE DIED ONCE, SO NOW I'M GONNA LIVE!

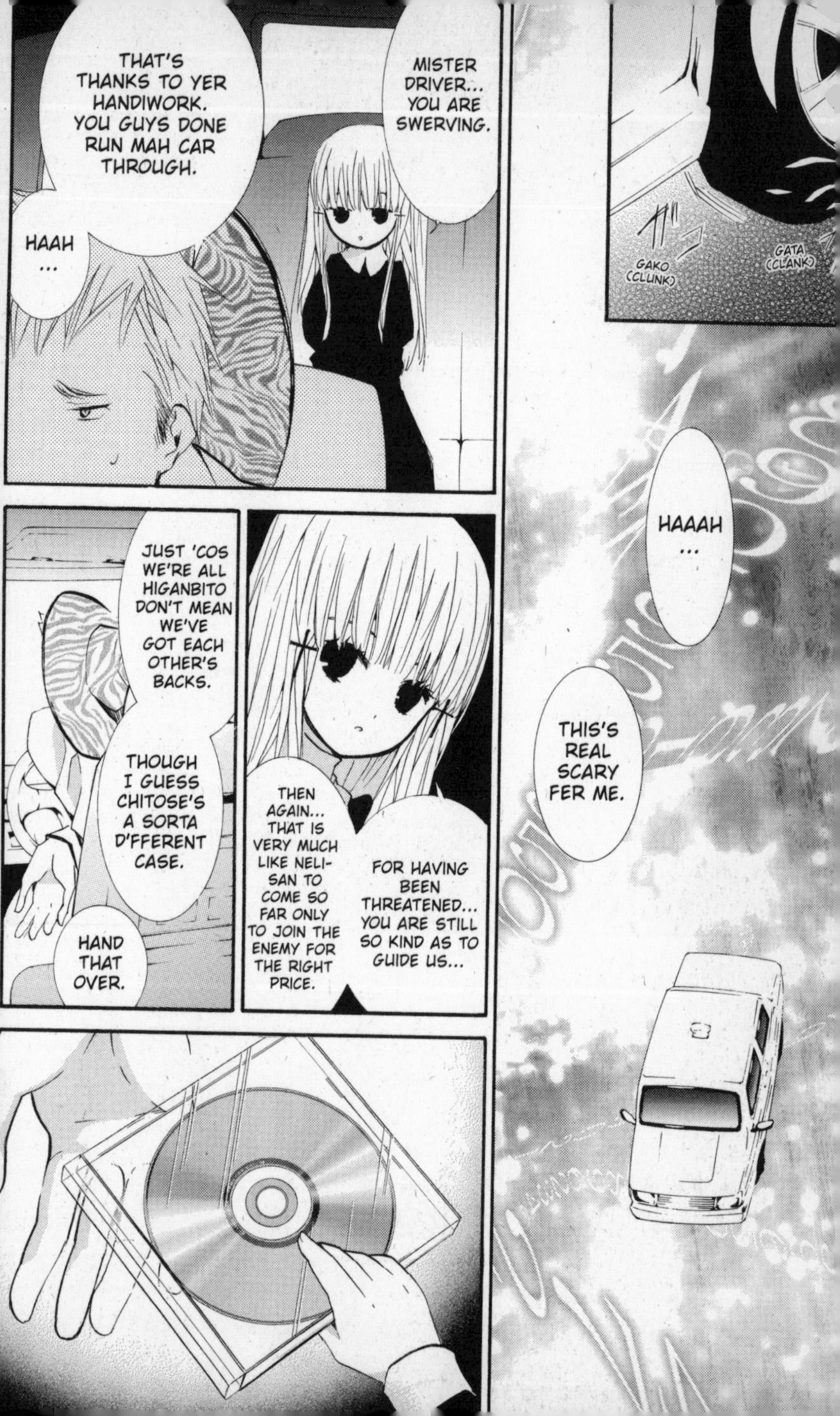
GATA (CLANK)
GAKO (CLUNK)
HAAAH ...
THIS'S REAL SCARY FER ME.
MISTER DRIVER... YOU ARE SWERVING.
THAT'S THANKS TO YER HANDIWORK. YOU GUYS DONE RUN MAH CAR THROUGH.
HAAH ...
FOR HAVING BEEN THREATENED... YOU ARE STILL SO KIND AS TO GUIDE US...
THEN AGAIN... THAT IS VERY MUCH LIKE NELI-SAN TO COME SO FAR ONLY TO JOIN THE ENEMY FOR THE RIGHT PRICE.
JUST 'COS WE'RE ALL HIGANBITO DON'T MEAN WE'VE GOT EACH OTHER'S BACKS.
THOUGH I GUESS CHITOSE'S A SORTA D'FFERENT CASE.
HAND THAT OVER.

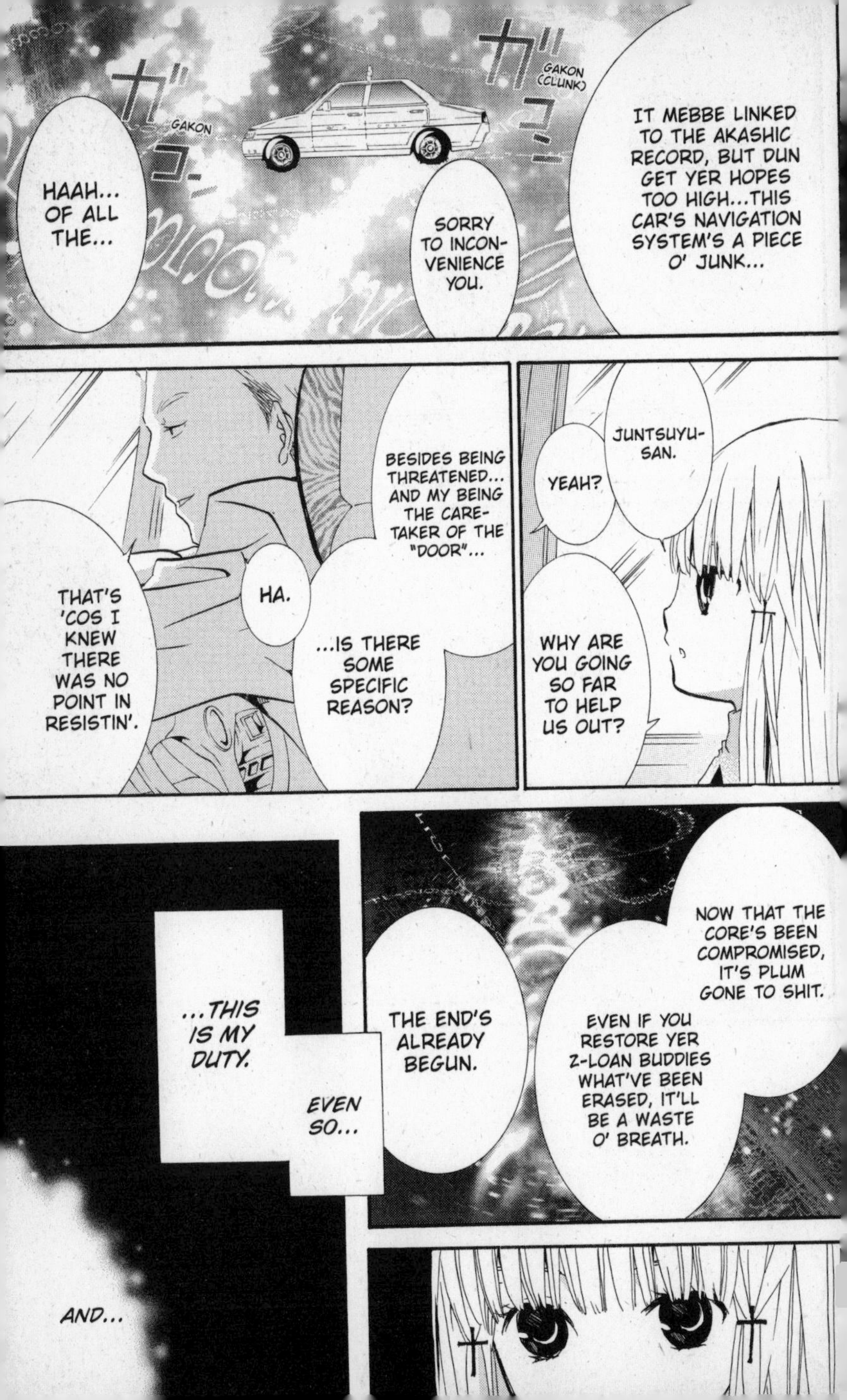
IT MEBBE LINKED TO THE AKASHIC RECORD, BUT DUN GET YER HOPES TOO HIGH...THIS CAR'S NAVIGATION SYSTEM'S A PIECE O' JUNK...
GAKON (CLUNK)
SORRY TO INCONVENIENCE YOU.
GAKON
HAAH... OF ALL THE...
JUNTSUYU-SAN.
YEAH?
WHY ARE YOU GOING SO FAR TO HELP US OUT?
BESIDES BEING THREATENED... AND MY BEING THE CARETAKER OF THE "DOOR"...
...IS THERE SOME SPECIFIC REASON?
HA.
THAT'S 'COS I KNEW THERE WAS NO POINT IN RESISTIN'.
NOW THAT THE CORE'S BEEN COMPROMISED, IT'S PLUM GONE TO SHIT.
EVEN IF YOU RESTORE YER Z-LOAN BUDDIES WHAT'VE BEEN ERASED, IT'LL BE A WASTE O' BREATH.
THE END'S ALREADY BEGUN.
EVEN SO...
...THIS IS MY DUTY.
AND...

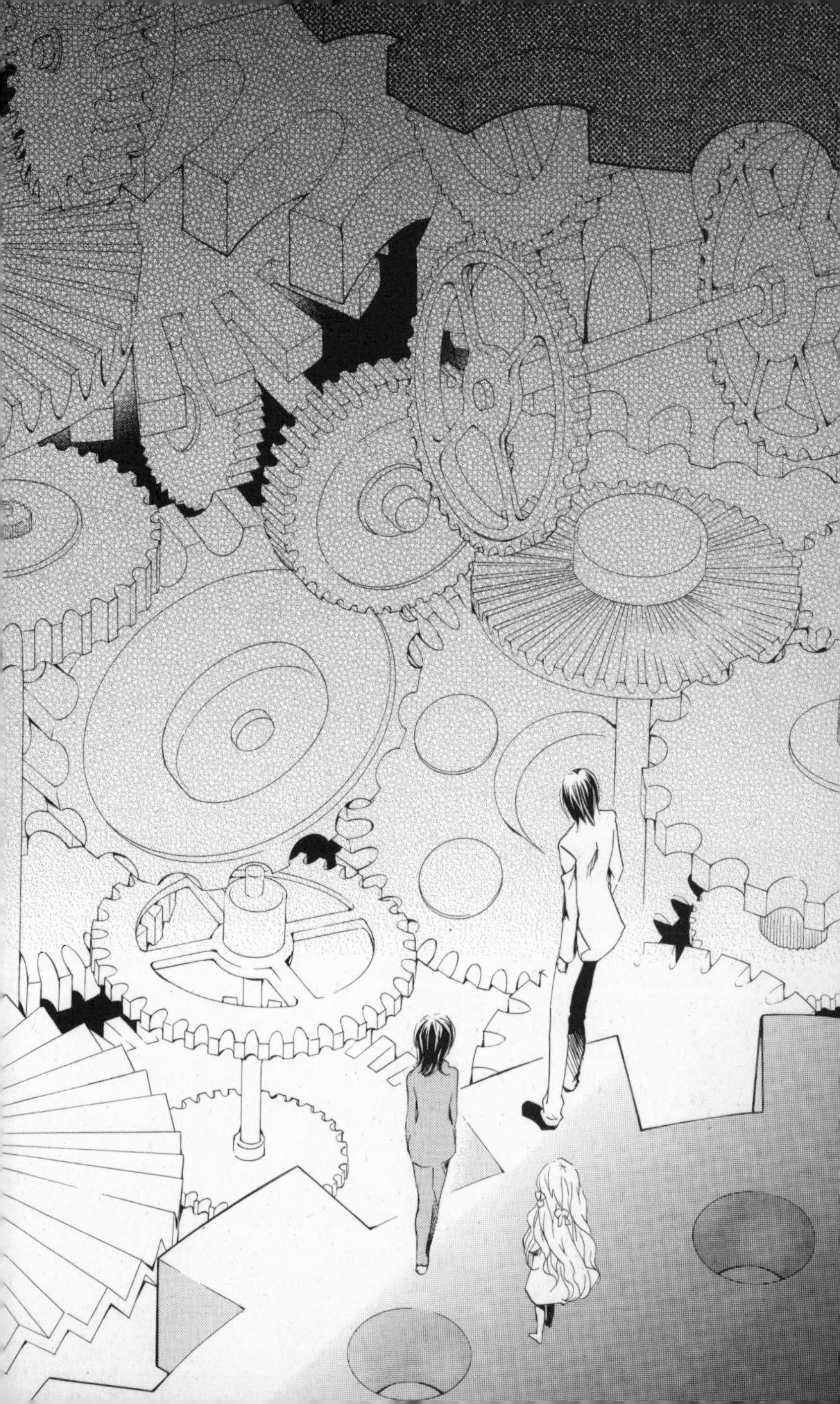

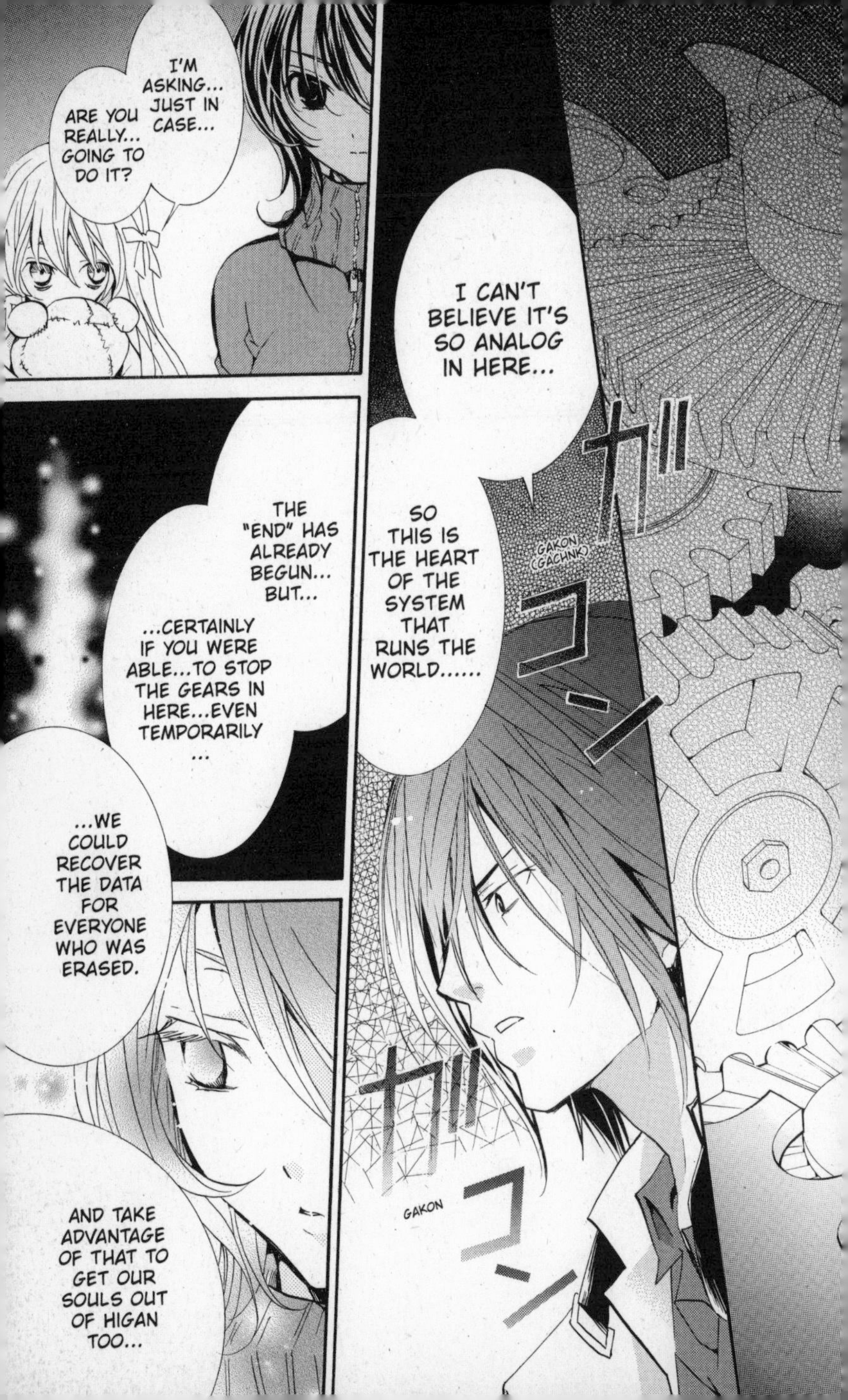

I CAN'T BELIEVE IT'S SO ANALOG IN HERE...
SO THIS IS THE HEART OF THE SYSTEM THAT RUNS THE WORLD......
ガコーン
GAKON (GACHNK)
ガコーン
GAKON
I'M ASKING... JUST IN CASE...
ARE YOU REALLY... GOING TO DO IT?
THE "END" HAS ALREADY BEGUN... BUT...
...CERTAINLY IF YOU WERE ABLE...TO STOP THE GEARS IN HERE...EVEN TEMPORARILY ...
...WE COULD RECOVER THE DATA FOR EVERYONE WHO WAS ERASED.
AND TAKE ADVANTAGE OF THAT TO GET OUR SOULS OUT OF HIGAN TOO...

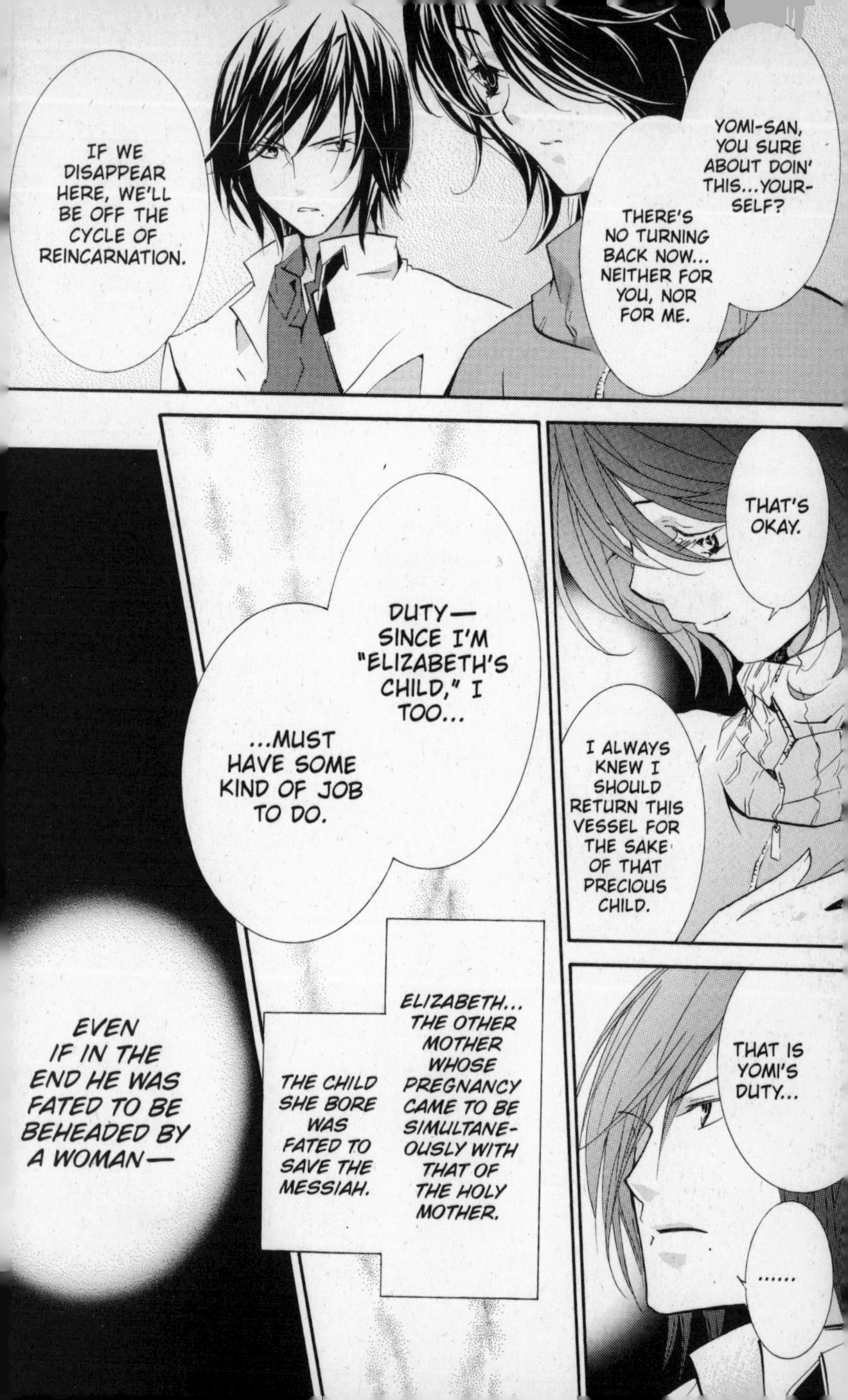
YOMI-SAN, YOU SURE ABOUT DOIN' THIS...YOURSELF?
THERE'S NO TURNING BACK NOW... NEITHER FOR YOU, NOR FOR ME.
IF WE DISAPPEAR HERE, WE'LL BE OFF THE CYCLE OF REINCARNATION.
THAT'S OKAY.
I ALWAYS KNEW I SHOULD RETURN THIS VESSEL FOR THE SAKE OF THAT PRECIOUS CHILD.
THAT IS YOMI'S DUTY...
......
DUTY—SINCE I'M "ELIZABETH'S CHILD," I TOO...
...MUST HAVE SOME KIND OF JOB TO DO.
ELIZABETH... THE OTHER MOTHER WHOSE PREGNANCY CAME TO BE SIMULTANEOUSLY WITH THAT OF THE HOLY MOTHER.
THE CHILD SHE BORE WAS FATED TO SAVE THE MESSIAH.
EVEN IF IN THE END HE WAS FATED TO BE BEHEADED BY A WOMAN—

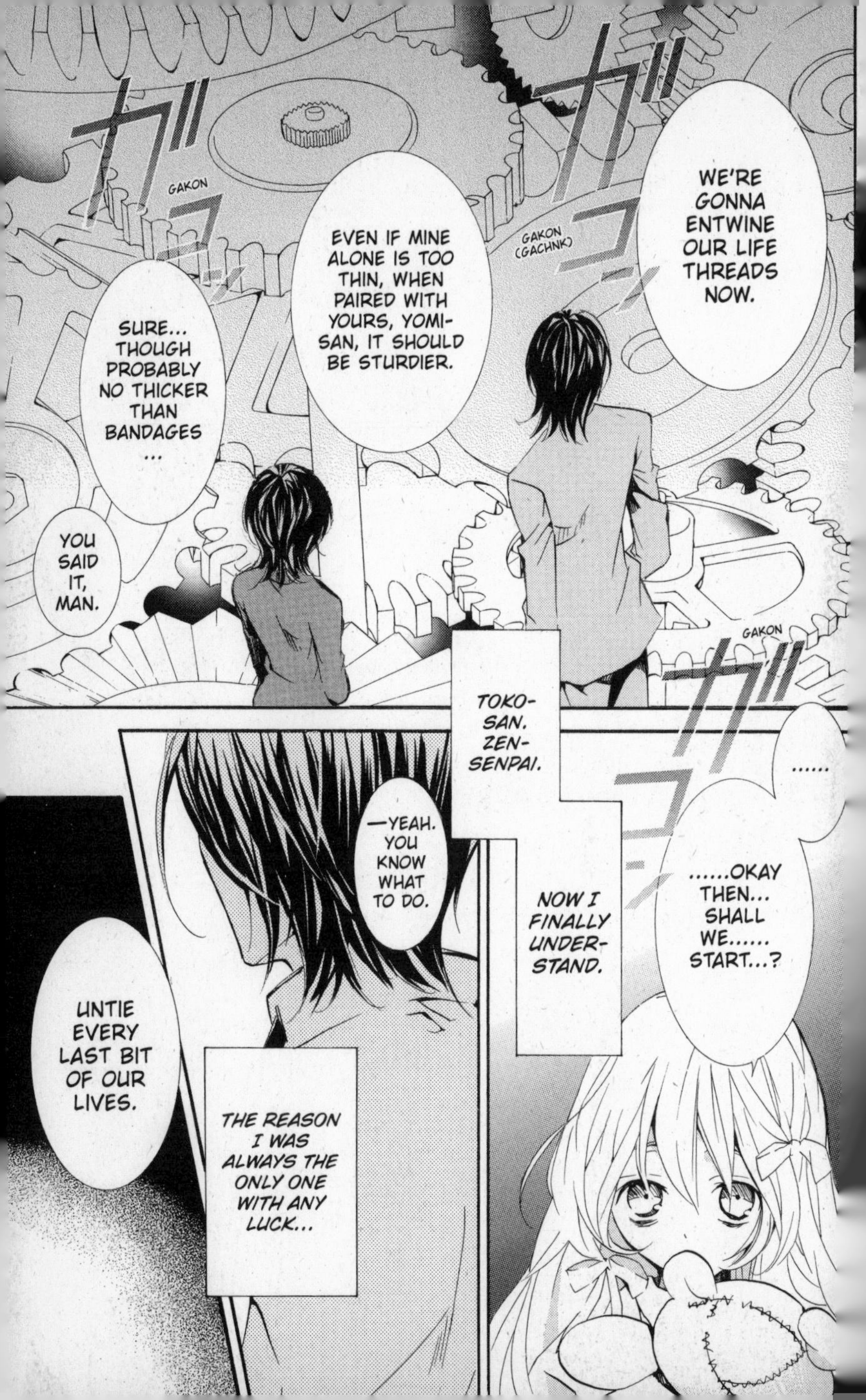
WE'RE GONNA ENTWINE OUR LIFE THREADS NOW.
GAKON (GACHNK)
EVEN IF MINE ALONE IS TOO THIN, WHEN PAIRED WITH YOURS, YOMI-SAN, IT SHOULD BE STURDIER.
GAKON
SURE... THOUGH PROBABLY NO THICKER THAN BANDAGES ...
YOU SAID IT, MAN.
GAKON
......
......OKAY THEN... SHALL WE...... START...?
TOKO-SAN. ZEN-SENPAI.
NOW I FINALLY UNDER-STAND.
—YEAH. YOU KNOW WHAT TO DO.
UNTIE EVERY LAST BIT OF OUR LIVES.
THE REASON I WAS ALWAYS THE ONLY ONE WITH ANY LUCK...

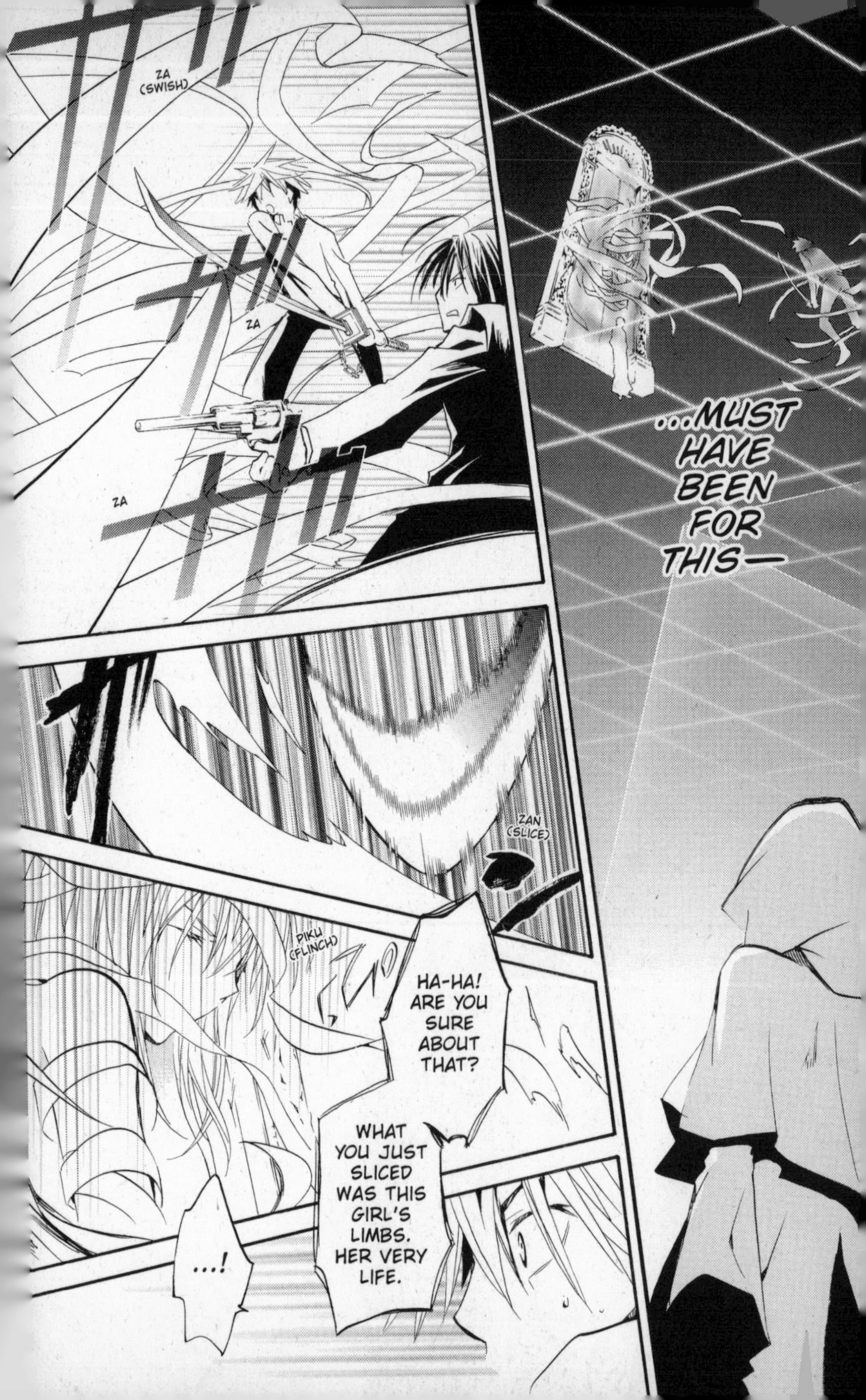
...MUST HAVE BEEN FOR THIS—
ZA (SWISH)
ZA
ZA
ZAN (SLICE)
PIKU (FLINCH)
HA-HA! ARE YOU SURE ABOUT THAT?
WHAT YOU JUST SLICED WAS THIS GIRL'S LIMBS. HER VERY LIFE.
...!

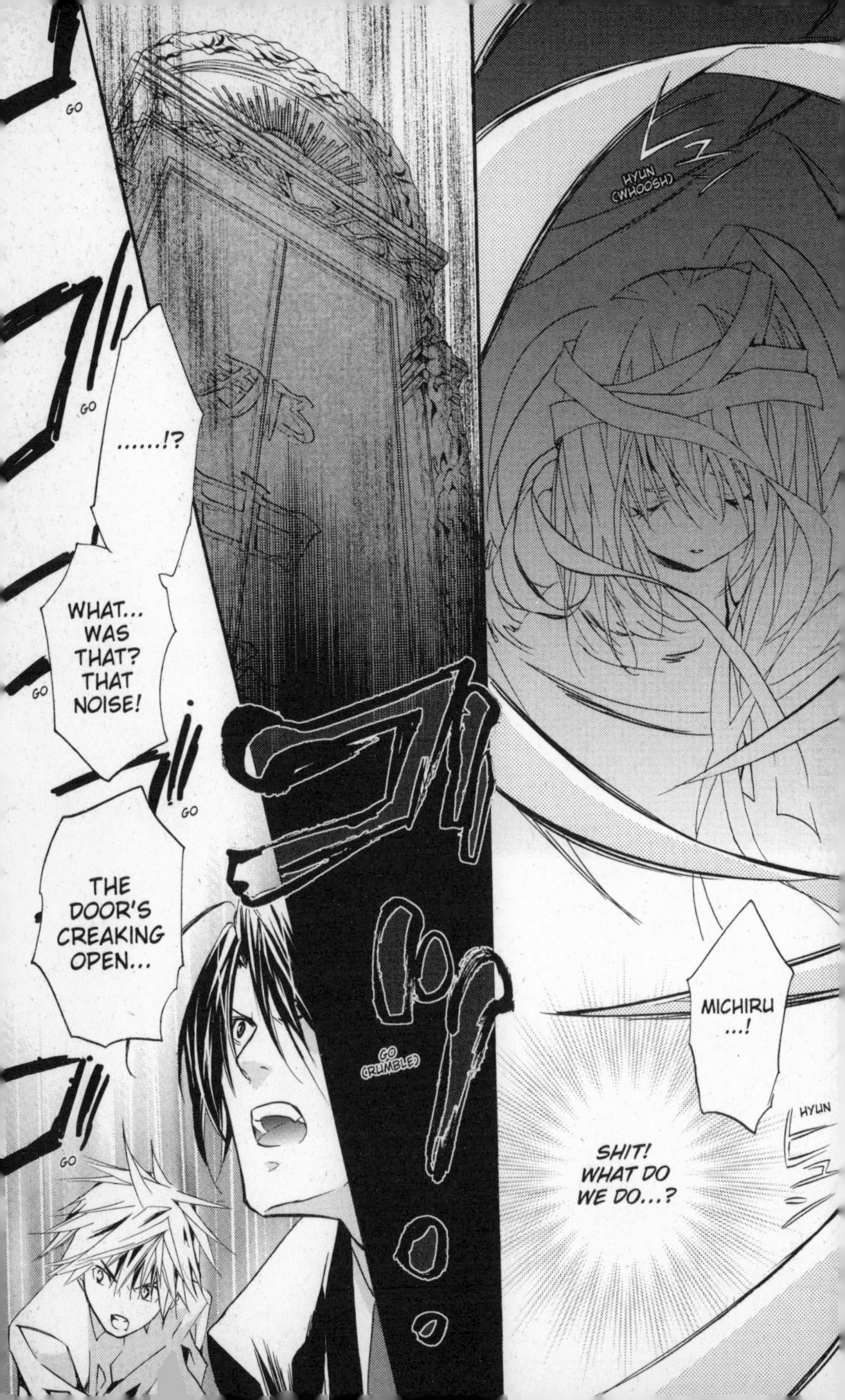
HYUN (WHOOSH)
MICHIRU ...!
HYUN
SHIT! WHAT DO WE DO...?
GO
GO
......!?
WHAT... WAS THAT? THAT NOISE!
GO
GO
THE DOOR'S CREAKING OPEN...
GO (RUMBLE)
GO

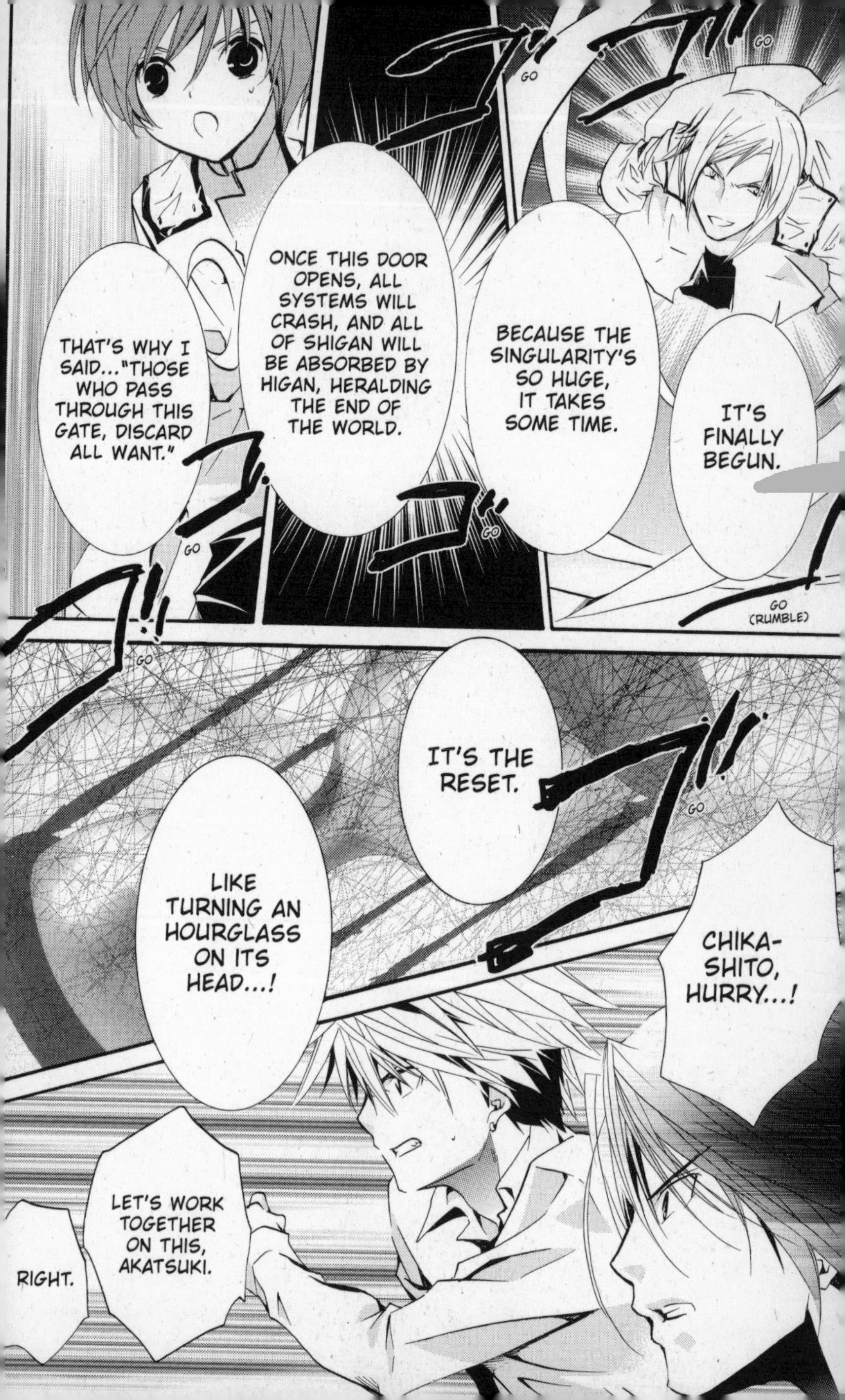
GO
GO
IT'S FINALLY BEGUN.
BECAUSE THE SINGULARITY'S SO HUGE, IT TAKES SOME TIME.
GO (RUMBLE)
ONCE THIS DOOR OPENS, ALL SYSTEMS WILL CRASH, AND ALL OF SHIGAN WILL BE ABSORBED BY HIGAN, HERALDING THE END OF THE WORLD.
GO
THAT'S WHY I SAID..."THOSE WHO PASS THROUGH THIS GATE, DISCARD ALL WANT."
GO
GO
GO
IT'S THE RESET.
LIKE TURNING AN HOURGLASS ON ITS HEAD...!
CHIKA-SHITO, HURRY...!
LET'S WORK TOGETHER ON THIS, AKATSUKI.
RIGHT.

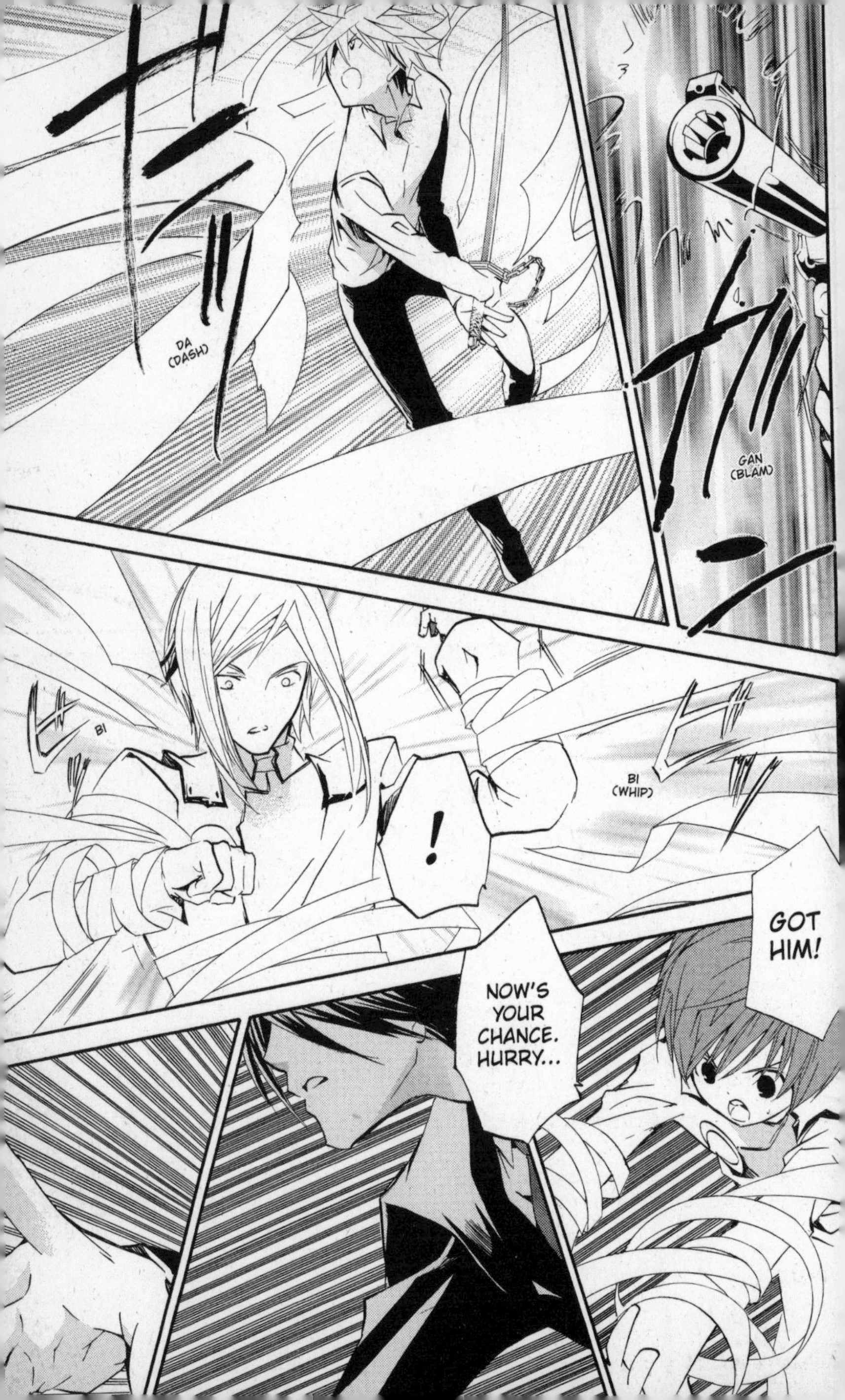
GAN
(BLAM)
DA
(DASH)
BI
(WHIP)
!
BI
GOT HIM!
NOW'S YOUR CHANCE. HURRY...

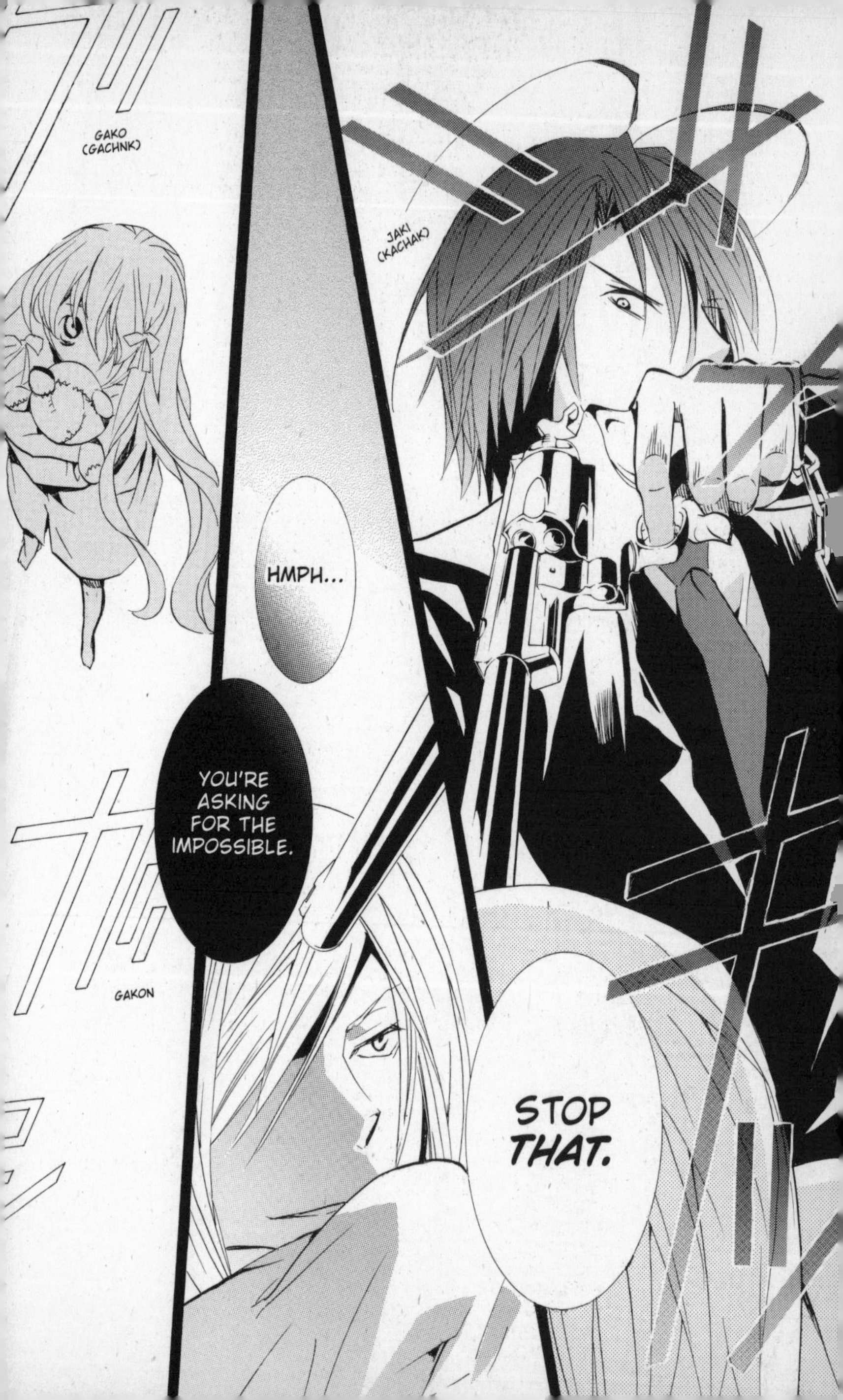
JAKI (KACHAK)
HMPH...
YOU'RE ASKING FOR THE IMPOSSIBLE.
STOP THAT.
GAKO (GACHNK)
GAKON

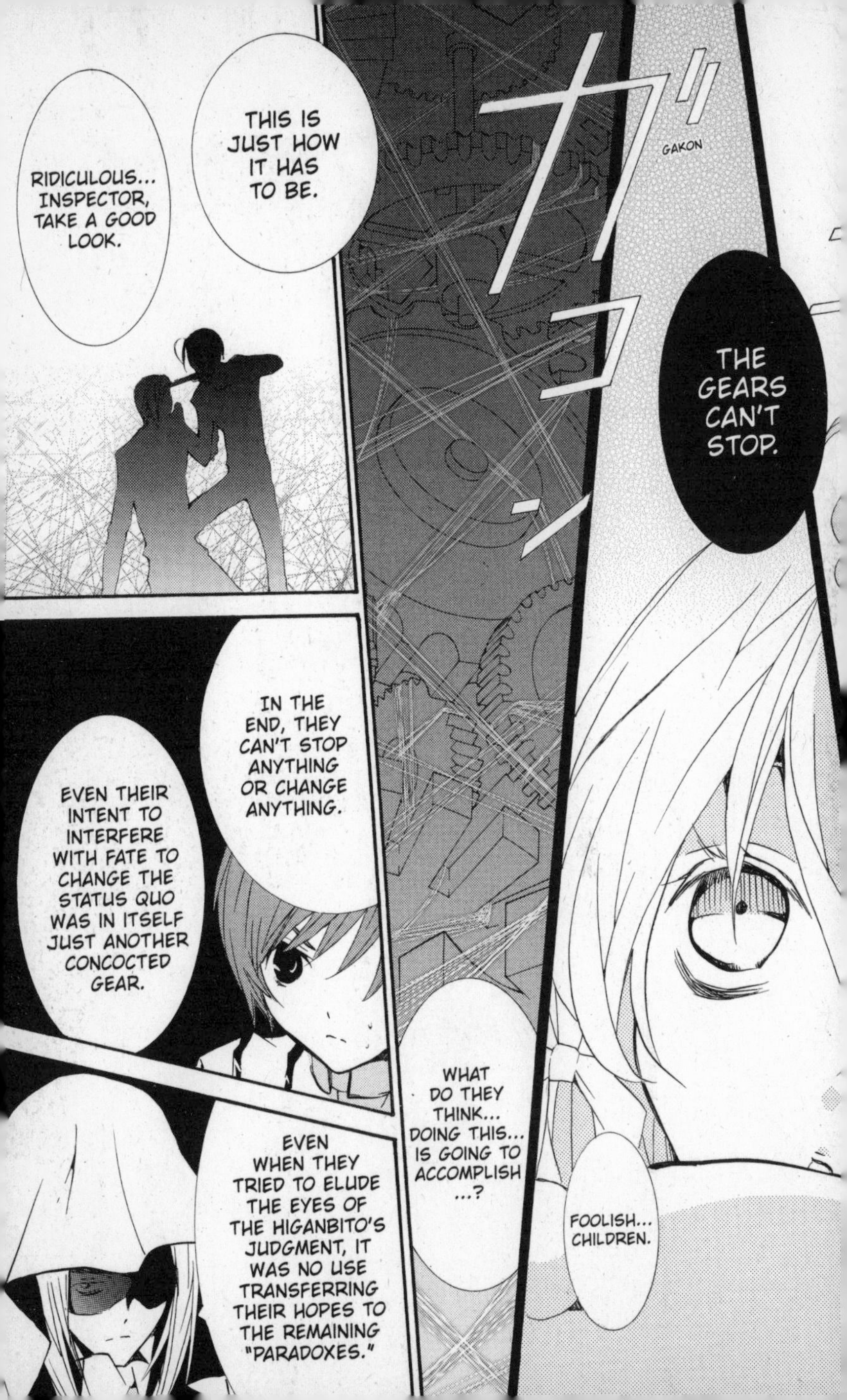

GAKON
THE GEARS CAN'T STOP.
FOOLISH... CHILDREN.
WHAT DO THEY THINK... DOING THIS... IS GOING TO ACCOMPLISH ...?
THIS IS JUST HOW IT HAS TO BE.
RIDICULOUS... INSPECTOR, TAKE A GOOD LOOK.
IN THE END, THEY CAN'T STOP ANYTHING OR CHANGE ANYTHING.
EVEN THEIR INTENT TO INTERFERE WITH FATE TO CHANGE THE STATUS QUO WAS IN ITSELF JUST ANOTHER CONCOCTED GEAR.
EVEN WHEN THEY TRIED TO ELUDE THE EYES OF THE HIGANBITO'S JUDGMENT, IT WAS NO USE TRANSFERRING THEIR HOPES TO THE REMAINING "PARADOXES."

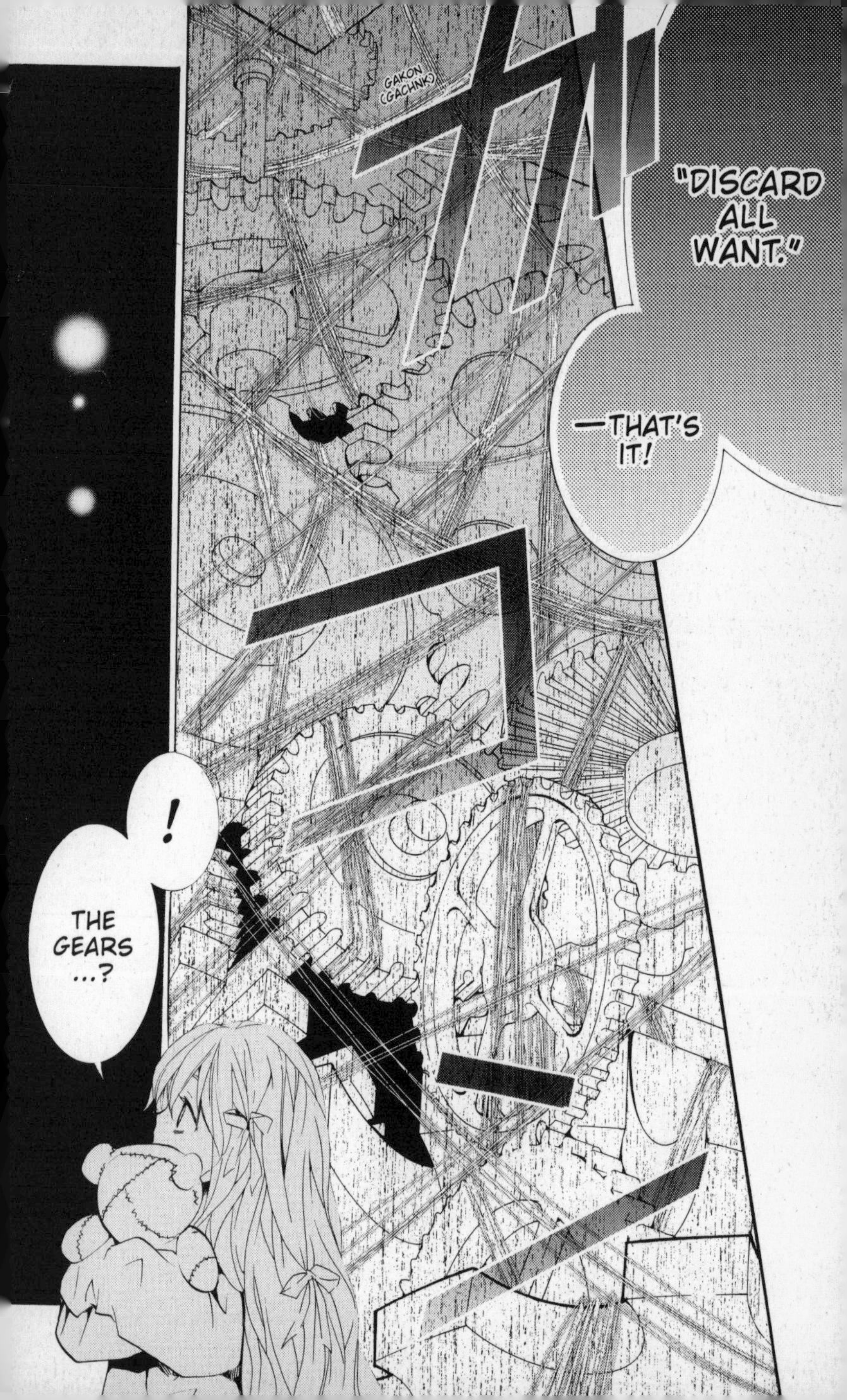
"DISCARD ALL WANT."
GAKON (GACHNK)
—THAT'S IT!
!
THE GEARS ...?

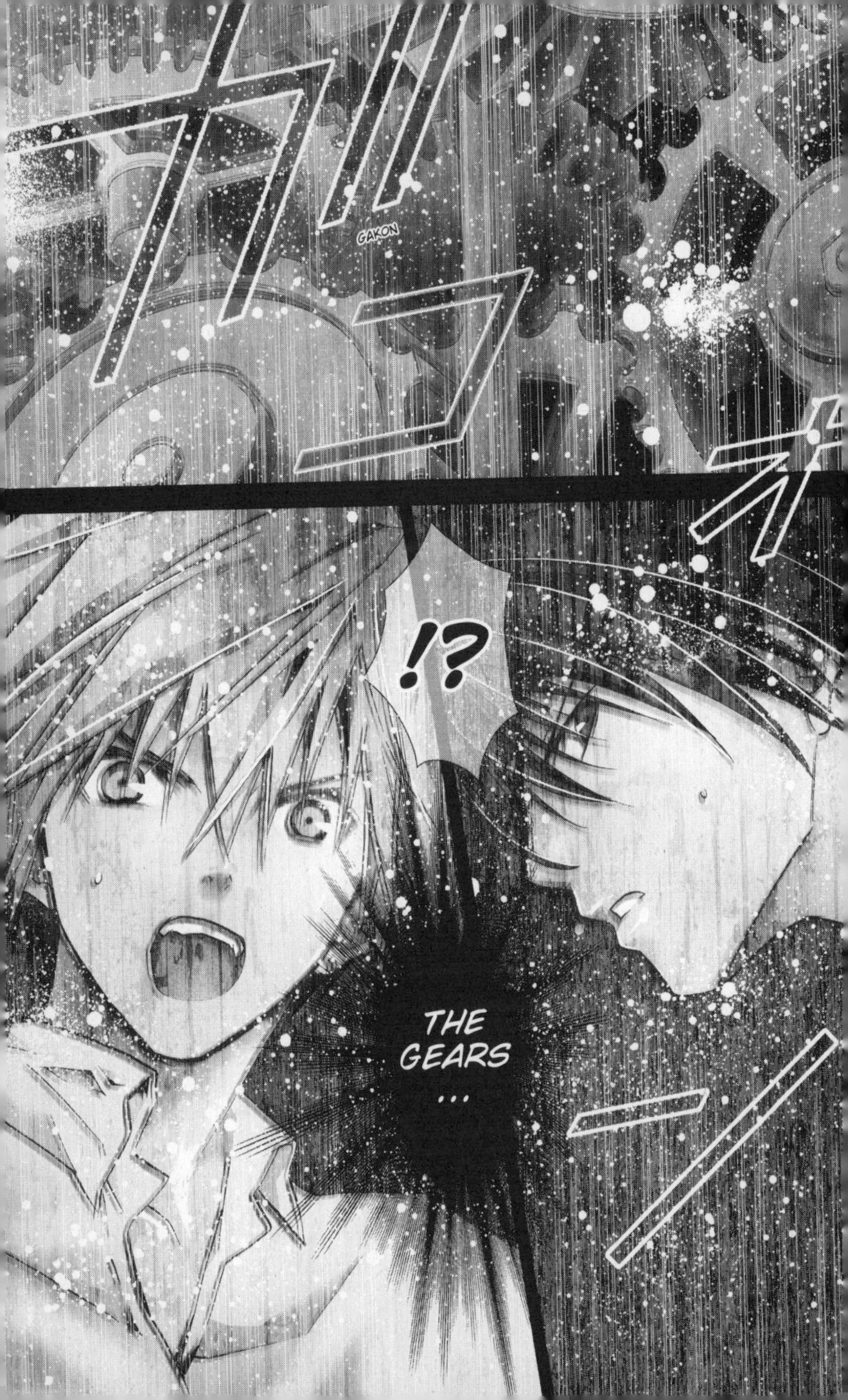
GAKON
!?
THE GEARS ...

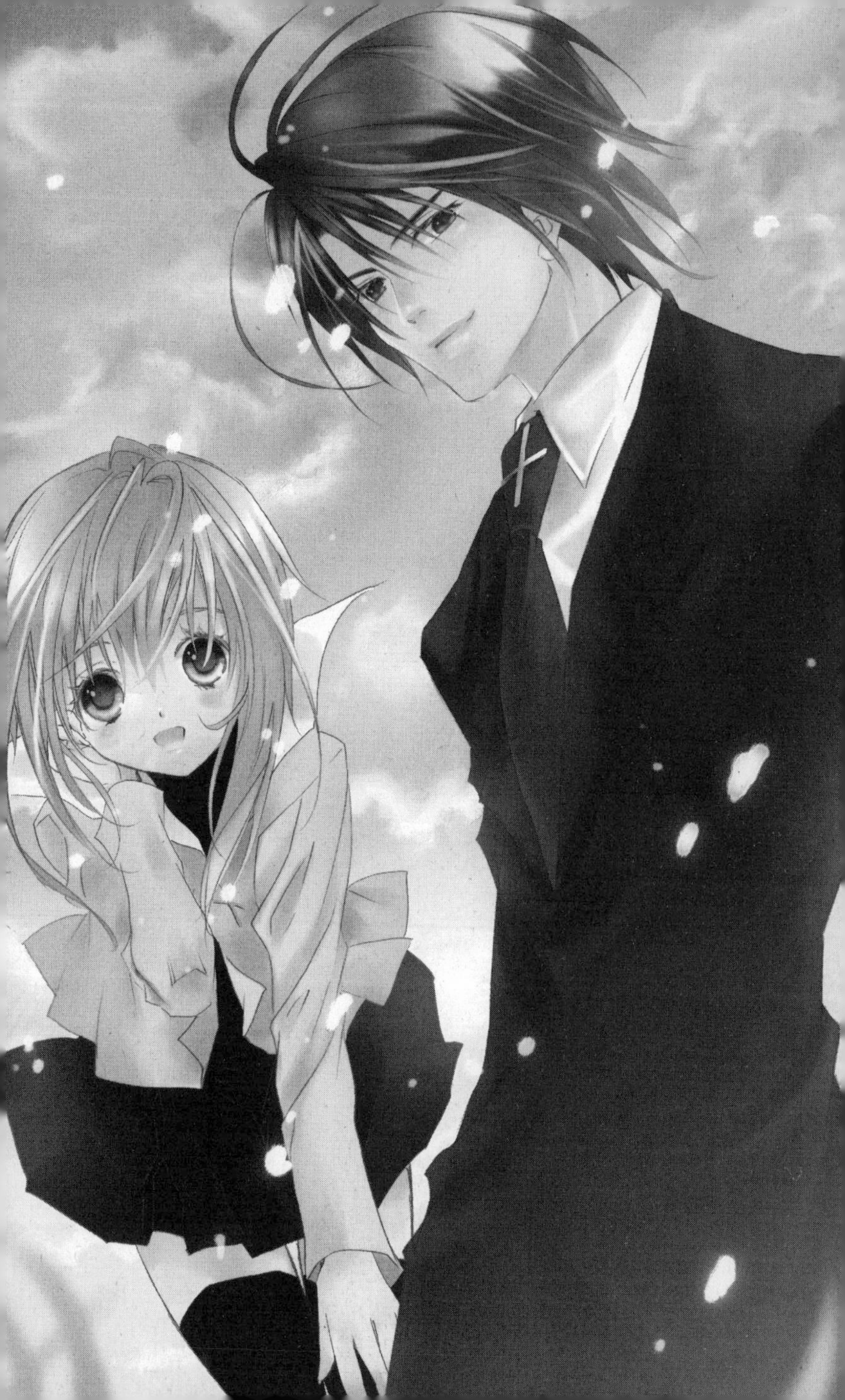

PAYMENT:FINAL

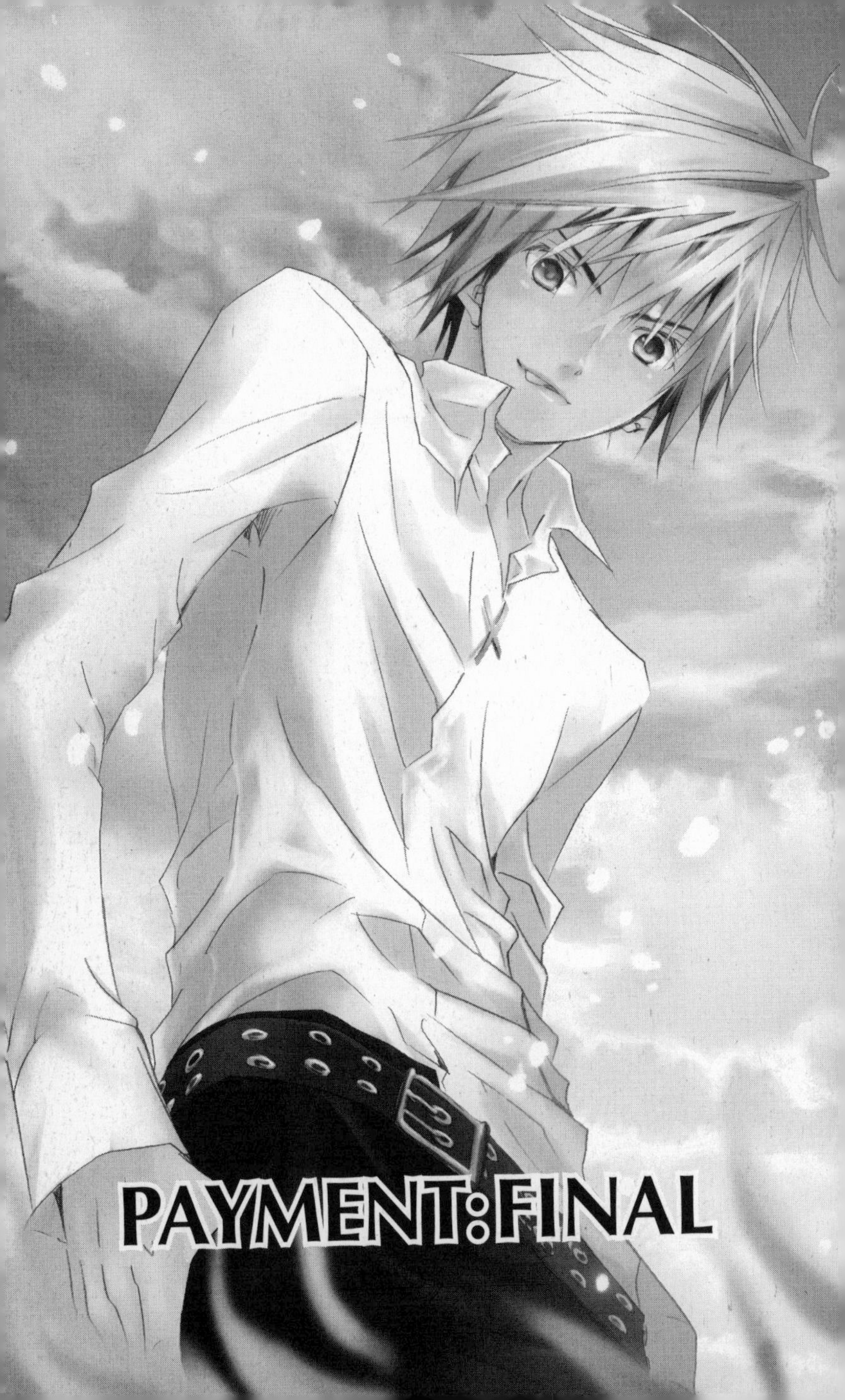

ZOMBIE-LOAN

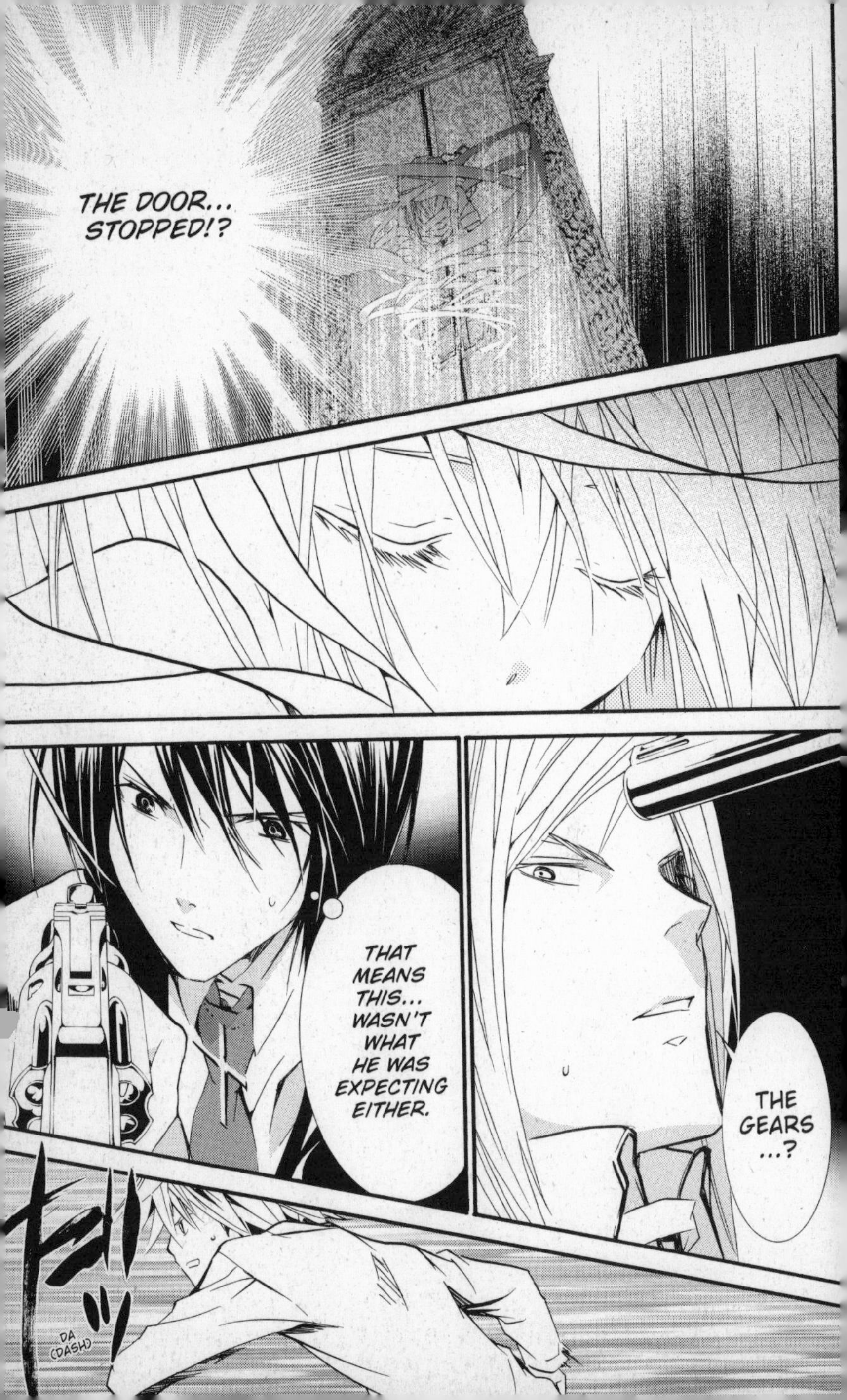
THE DOOR... STOPPED!?
THE GEARS ...?
THAT MEANS THIS... WASN'T WHAT HE WAS EXPECTING EITHER.
DA (DASH)

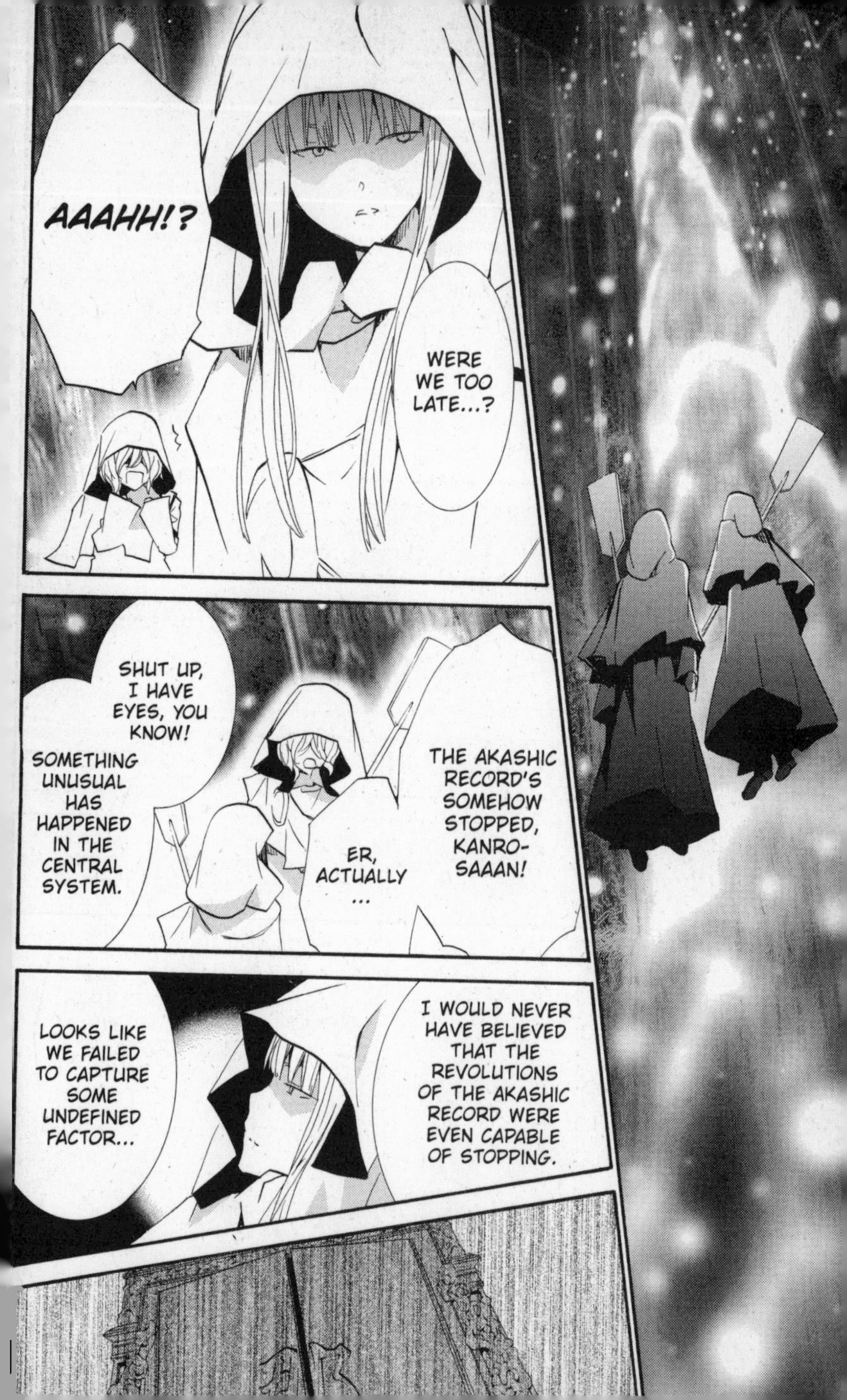
WERE WE TOO LATE...?
AAAHH!?
THE AKASHIC RECORD'S SOMEHOW STOPPED, KANRO-SAAAN!
ER, ACTUALLY...
SHUT UP, I HAVE EYES, YOU KNOW!
SOMETHING UNUSUAL HAS HAPPENED IN THE CENTRAL SYSTEM.
I WOULD NEVER HAVE BELIEVED THAT THE REVOLUTIONS OF THE AKASHIC RECORD WERE EVEN CAPABLE OF STOPPING.
LOOKS LIKE WE FAILED TO CAPTURE SOME UNDEFINED FACTOR...

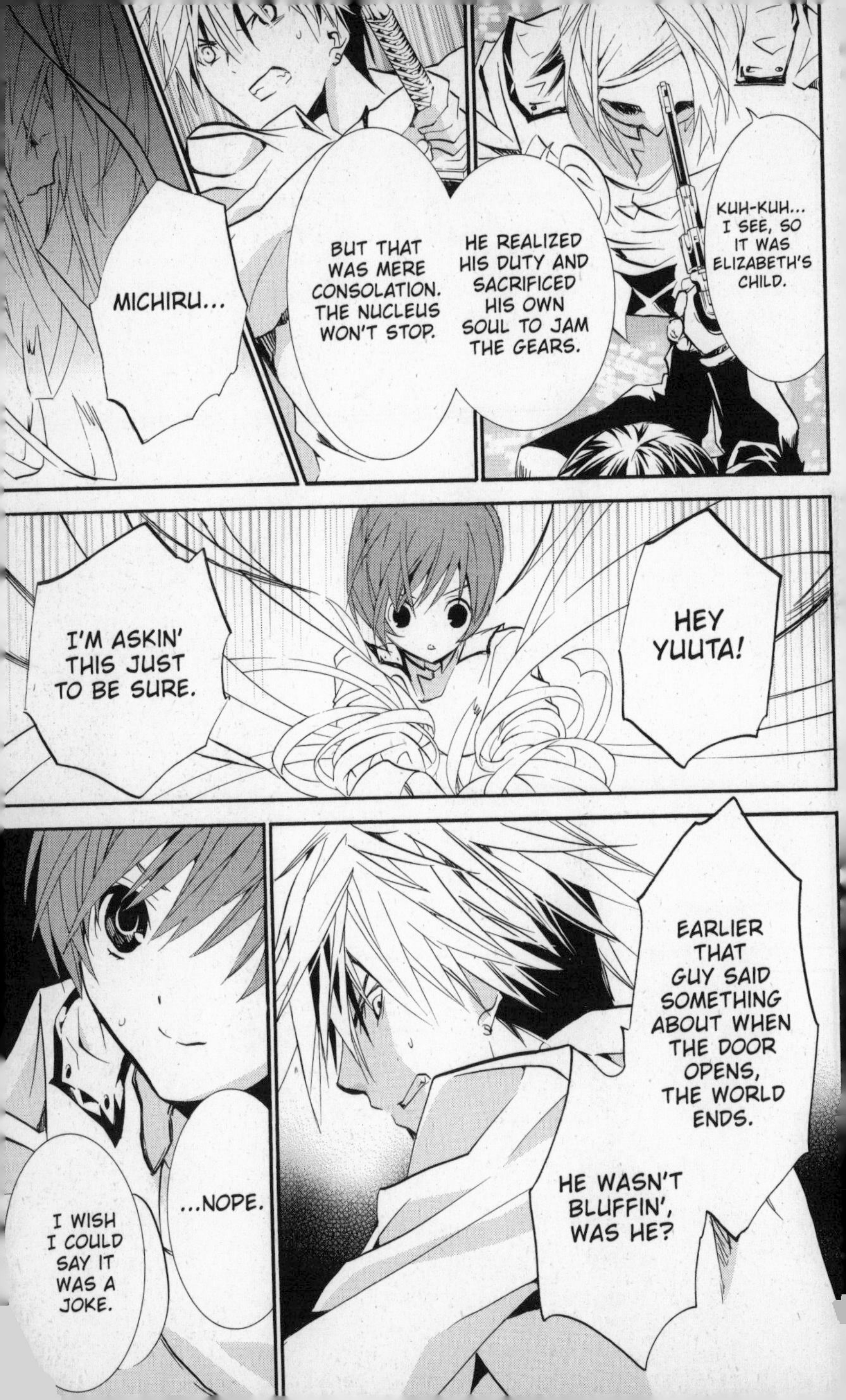
KUH-KUH... I SEE, SO IT WAS ELIZABETH'S CHILD.
HE REALIZED HIS DUTY AND SACRIFICED HIS OWN SOUL TO JAM THE GEARS.
BUT THAT WAS MERE CONSOLATION. THE NUCLEUS WON'T STOP.
MICHIRU...
HEY YUUTA!
I'M ASKIN' THIS JUST TO BE SURE.
EARLIER THAT GUY SAID SOMETHING ABOUT WHEN THE DOOR OPENS, THE WORLD ENDS.
HE WASN'T BLUFFIN', WAS HE?
...NOPE.
I WISH I COULD SAY IT WAS A JOKE.

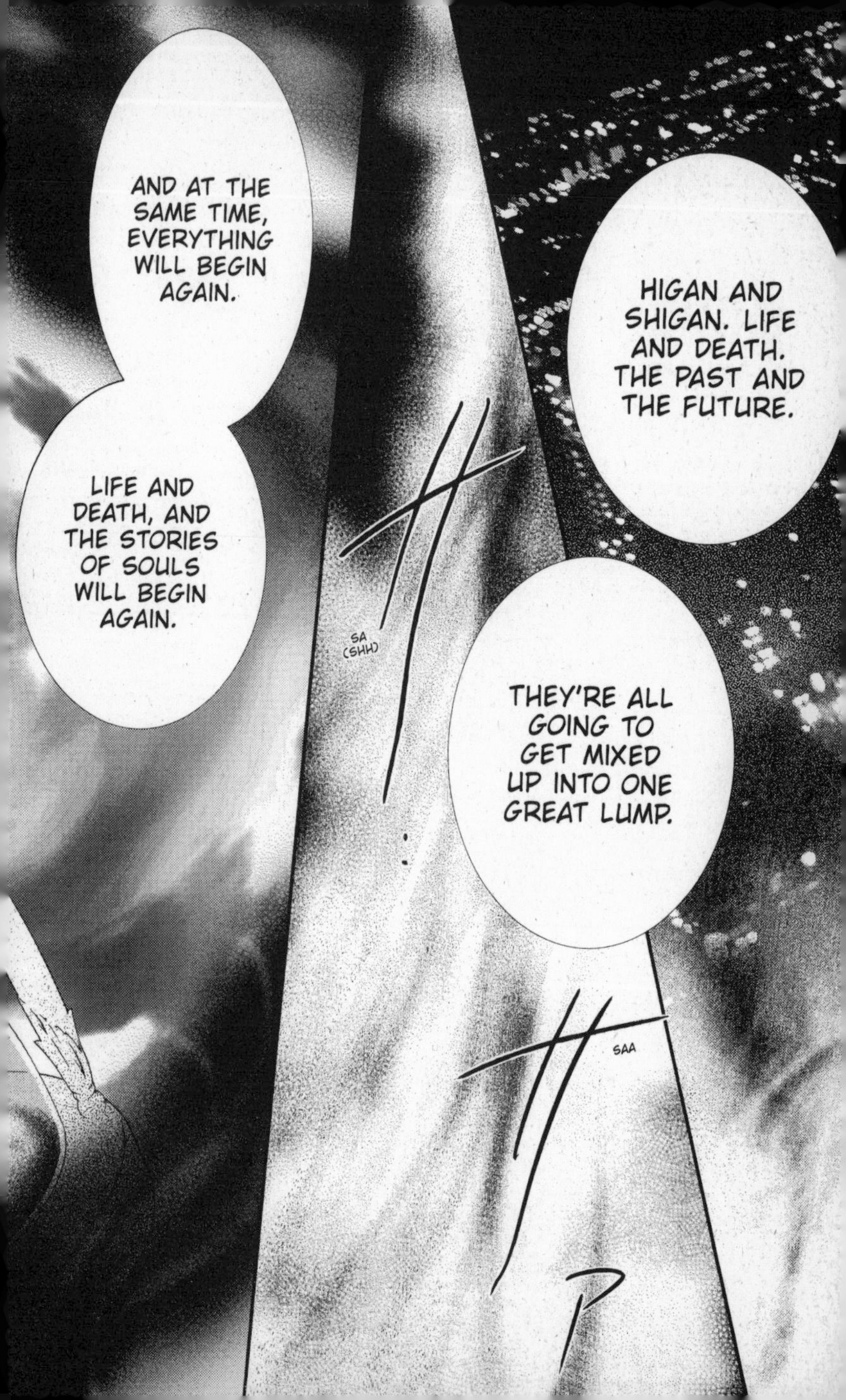
HIGAN AND SHIGAN. LIFE AND DEATH. THE PAST AND THE FUTURE.
THEY'RE ALL GOING TO GET MIXED UP INTO ONE GREAT LUMP.
SAA
SA (SHH)
AND AT THE SAME TIME, EVERYTHING WILL BEGIN AGAIN.
LIFE AND DEATH, AND THE STORIES OF SOULS WILL BEGIN AGAIN.

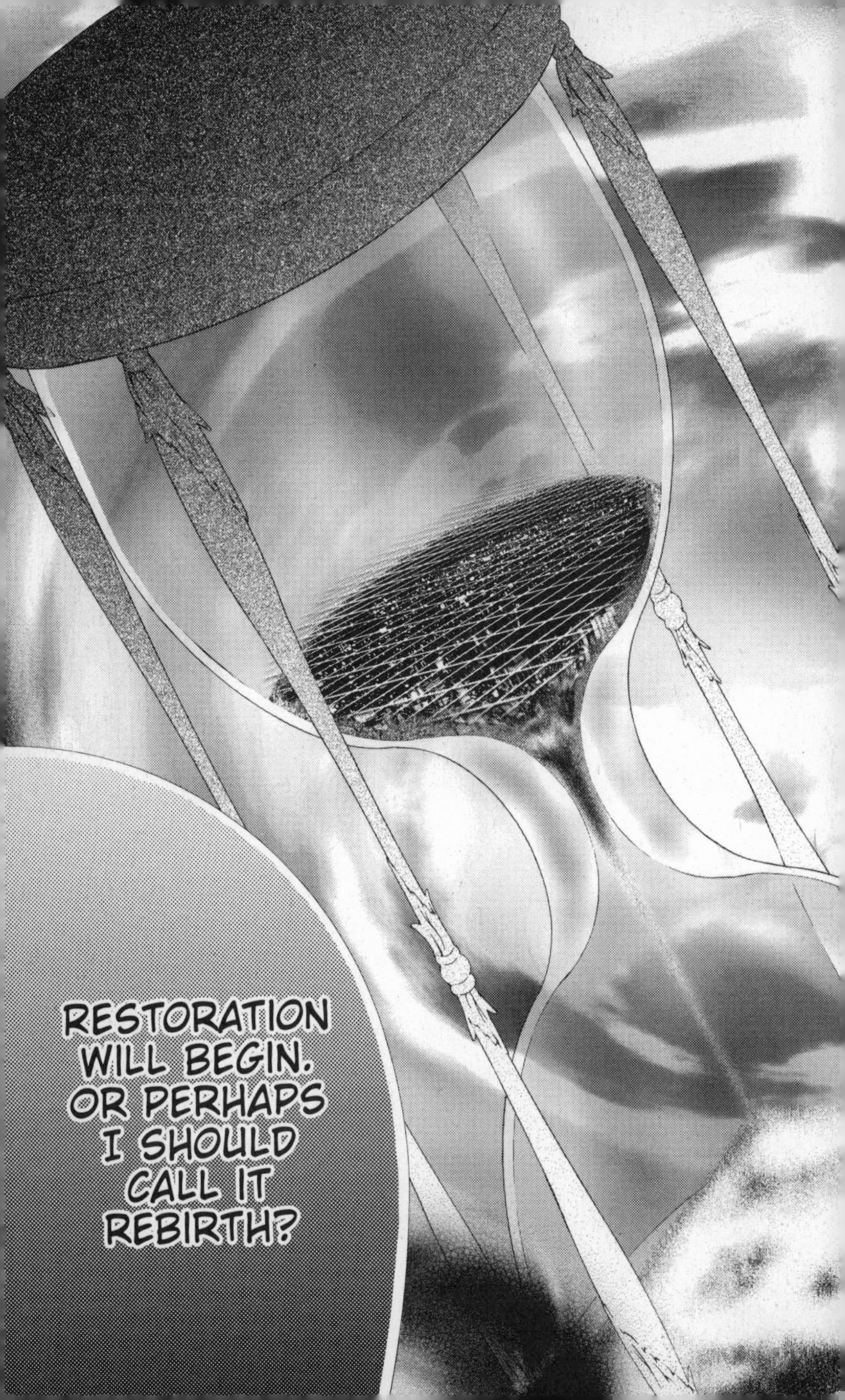
RESTORATION WILL BEGIN. OR PERHAPS I SHOULD CALL IT REBIRTH?

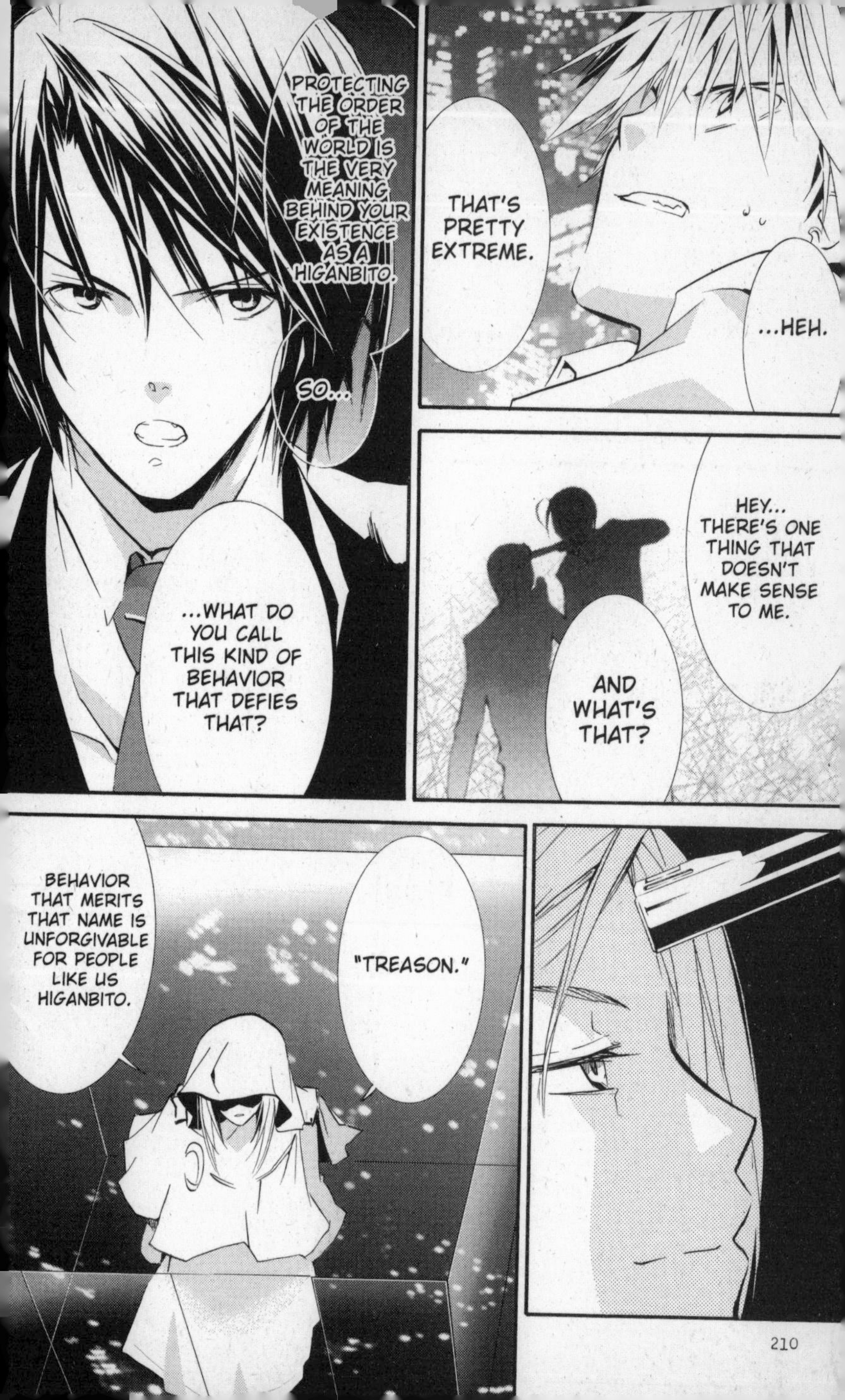
...HEH.
THAT'S PRETTY EXTREME.
HEY... THERE'S ONE THING THAT DOESN'T MAKE SENSE TO ME.
AND WHAT'S THAT?
PROTECTING THE ORDER OF THE WORLD IS THE VERY MEANING BEHIND YOUR EXISTENCE AS A HIGANBITO.
SO...
...WHAT DO YOU CALL THIS KIND OF BEHAVIOR THAT DEFIES THAT?
"TREASON."
BEHAVIOR THAT MERITS THAT NAME IS UNFORGIVABLE FOR PEOPLE LIKE US HIGANBITO.

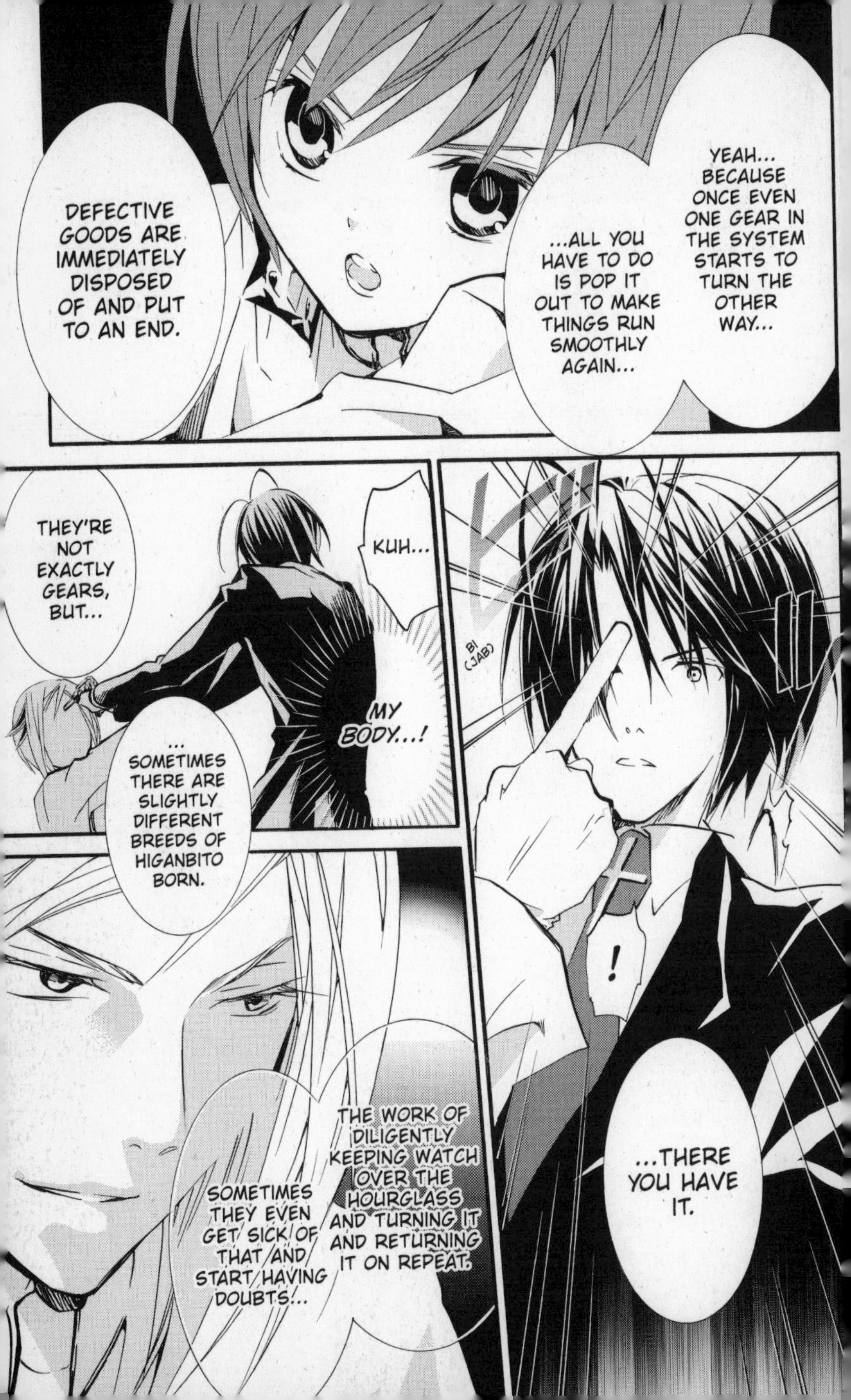
YEAH... BECAUSE ONCE EVEN ONE GEAR IN THE SYSTEM STARTS TO TURN THE OTHER WAY...
...ALL YOU HAVE TO DO IS POP IT OUT TO MAKE THINGS RUN SMOOTHLY AGAIN...
DEFECTIVE GOODS ARE IMMEDIATELY DISPOSED OF AND PUT TO AN END.
BI (JAB)
!
...THERE YOU HAVE IT.
KUH...
THEY'RE NOT EXACTLY GEARS, BUT...
MY BODY...!
...SOMETIMES THERE ARE SLIGHTLY DIFFERENT BREEDS OF HIGANBITO BORN.
THE WORK OF DILIGENTLY KEEPING WATCH OVER THE HOURGLASS AND TURNING IT AND RETURNING IT ON REPEAT.
SOMETIMES THEY EVEN GET SICK OF THAT AND START HAVING DOUBTS...

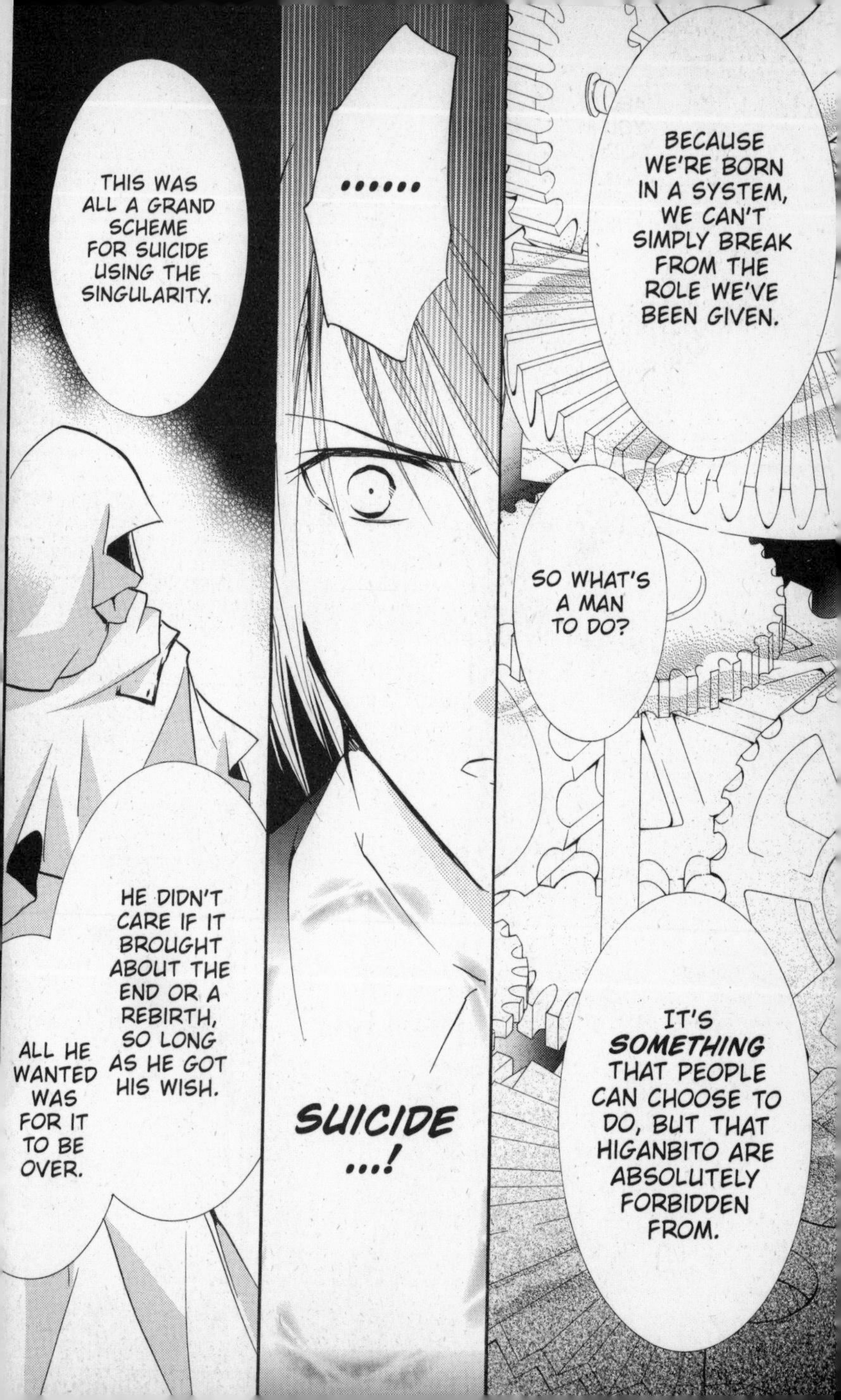
BECAUSE WE'RE BORN IN A SYSTEM, WE CAN'T SIMPLY BREAK FROM THE ROLE WE'VE BEEN GIVEN.
SO WHAT'S A MAN TO DO?
IT'S *SOMETHING* THAT PEOPLE CAN CHOOSE TO DO, BUT THAT HIGANBITO ARE ABSOLUTELY FORBIDDEN FROM.
......
SUICIDE ...!
THIS WAS ALL A GRAND SCHEME FOR SUICIDE USING THE SINGULARITY.
HE DIDN'T CARE IF IT BROUGHT ABOUT THE END OR A REBIRTH, SO LONG AS HE GOT HIS WISH.
ALL HE WANTED WAS FOR IT TO BE OVER.

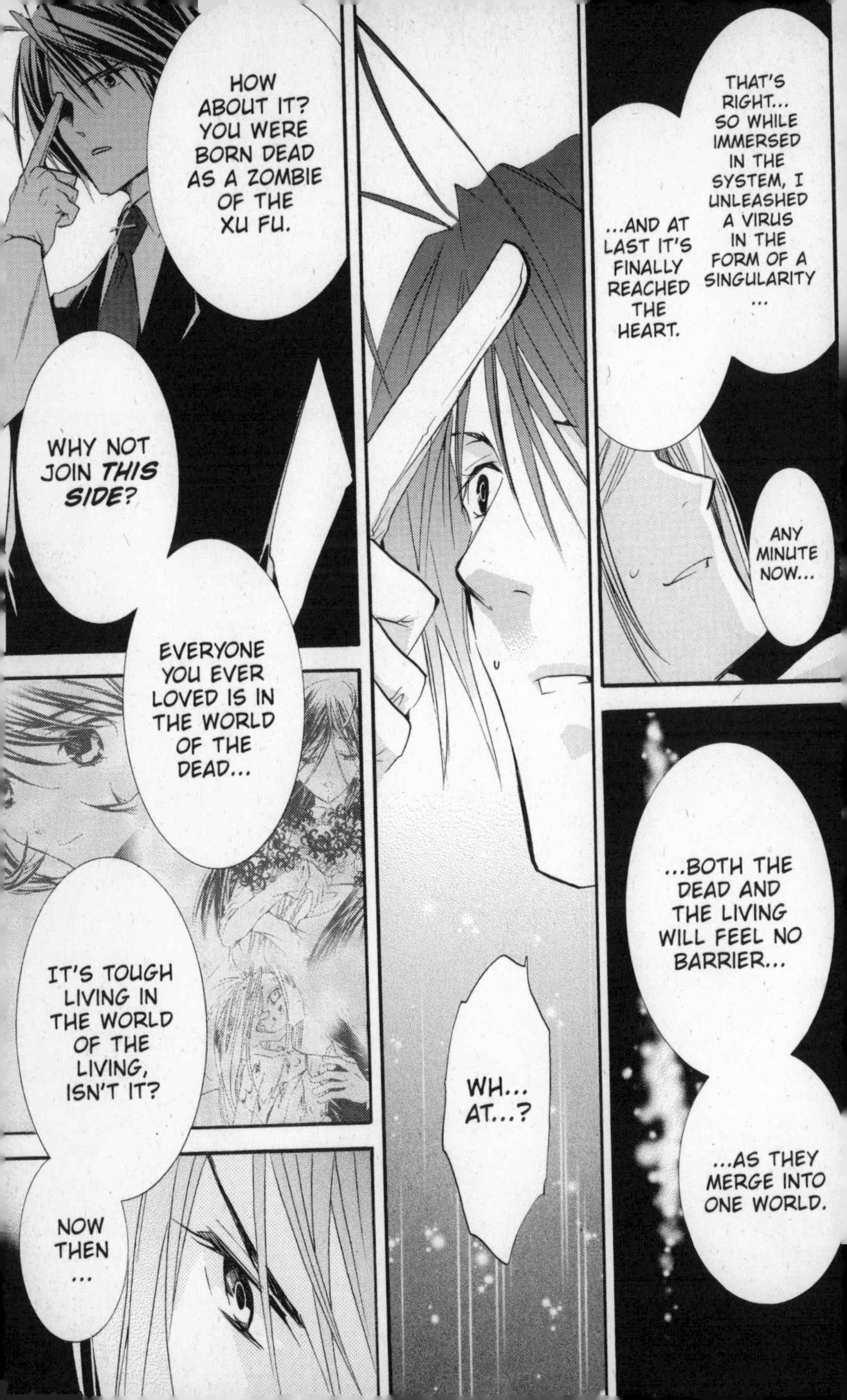
THAT'S RIGHT... SO WHILE IMMERSED IN THE SYSTEM, I UNLEASHED A VIRUS IN THE FORM OF A SINGULARITY ...
...AND AT LAST IT'S FINALLY REACHED THE HEART.
ANY MINUTE NOW...
...BOTH THE DEAD AND THE LIVING WILL FEEL NO BARRIER...
...AS THEY MERGE INTO ONE WORLD.
WH... AT...?
HOW ABOUT IT? YOU WERE BORN DEAD AS A ZOMBIE OF THE XU FU.
WHY NOT JOIN *THIS SIDE*?
EVERYONE YOU EVER LOVED IS IN THE WORLD OF THE DEAD...
IT'S TOUGH LIVING IN THE WORLD OF THE LIVING, ISN'T IT?
NOW THEN ...

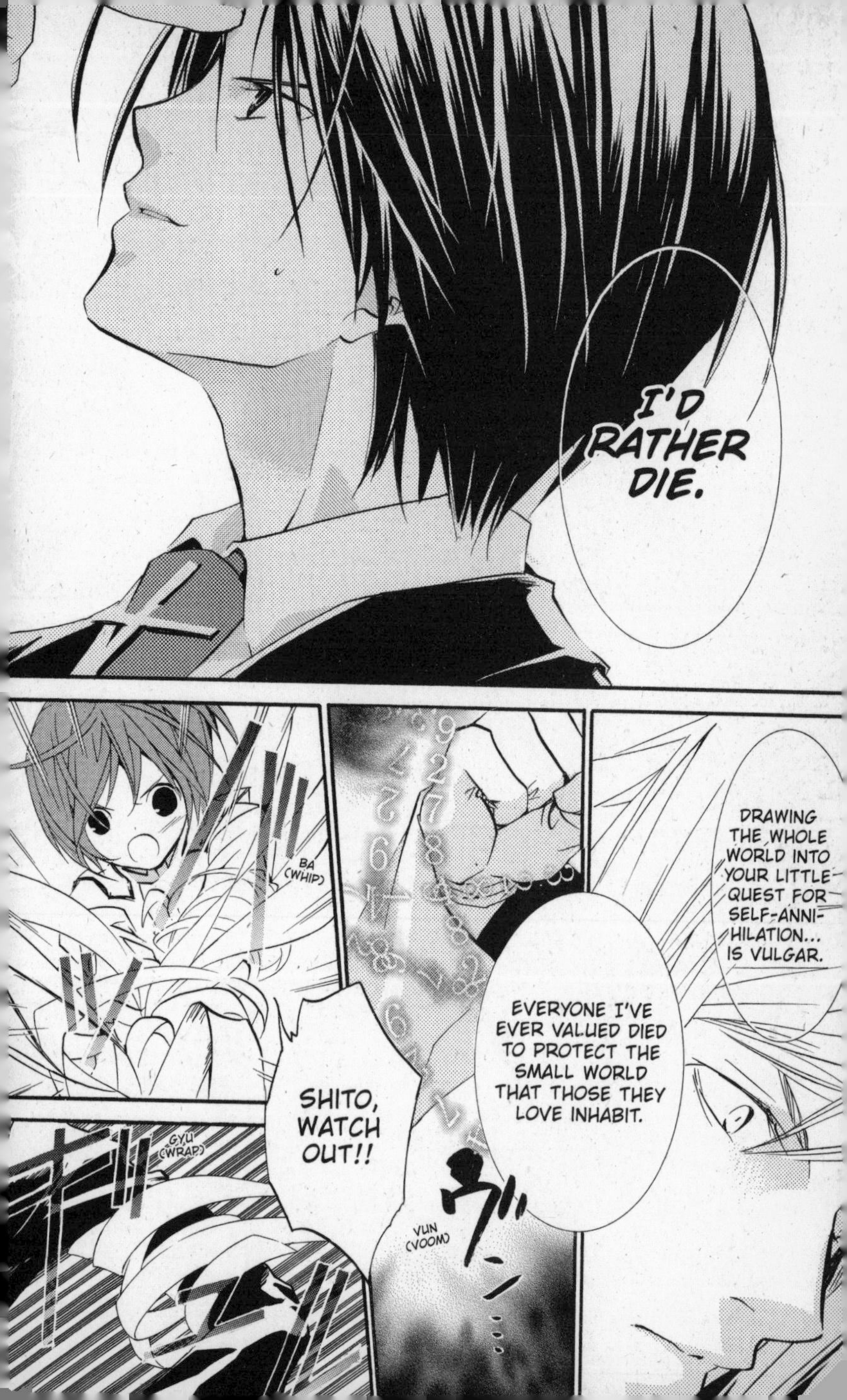
I'D RATHER DIE.
DRAWING THE WHOLE WORLD INTO YOUR LITTLE QUEST FOR SELF-ANNIHILATION... IS VULGAR.
EVERYONE I'VE EVER VALUED DIED TO PROTECT THE SMALL WORLD THAT THOSE THEY LOVE INHABIT.
BA (WHIP)
VUN (VOOM)
SHITO, WATCH OUT!!
GYU (WRAP)

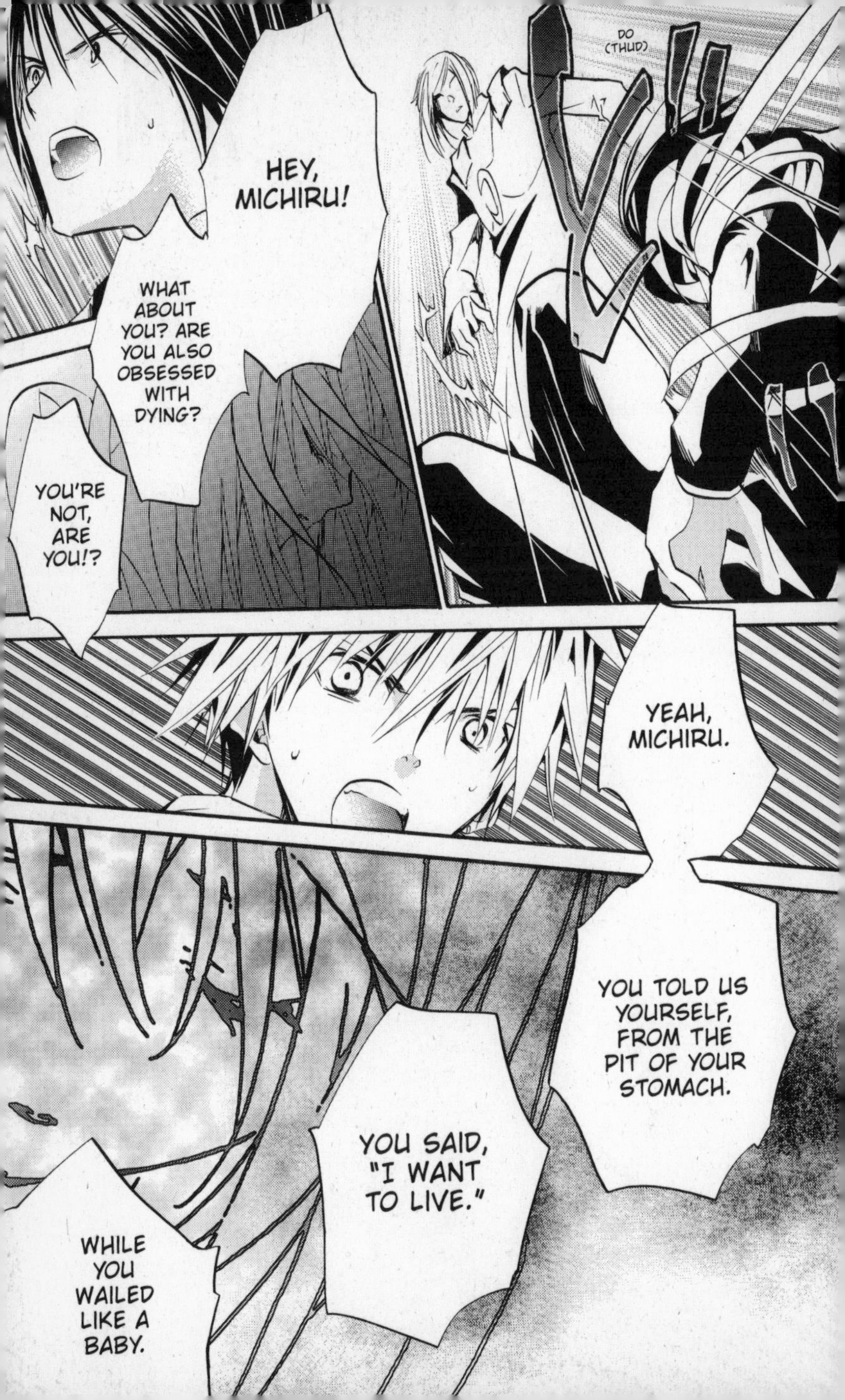
DO (THUD)
HEY, MICHIRU!
WHAT ABOUT YOU? ARE YOU ALSO OBSESSED WITH DYING?
YOU'RE NOT, ARE YOU!?
YEAH, MICHIRU.
YOU TOLD US YOURSELF, FROM THE PIT OF YOUR STOMACH.
YOU SAID, "I WANT TO LIVE."
WHILE YOU WAILED LIKE A BABY.

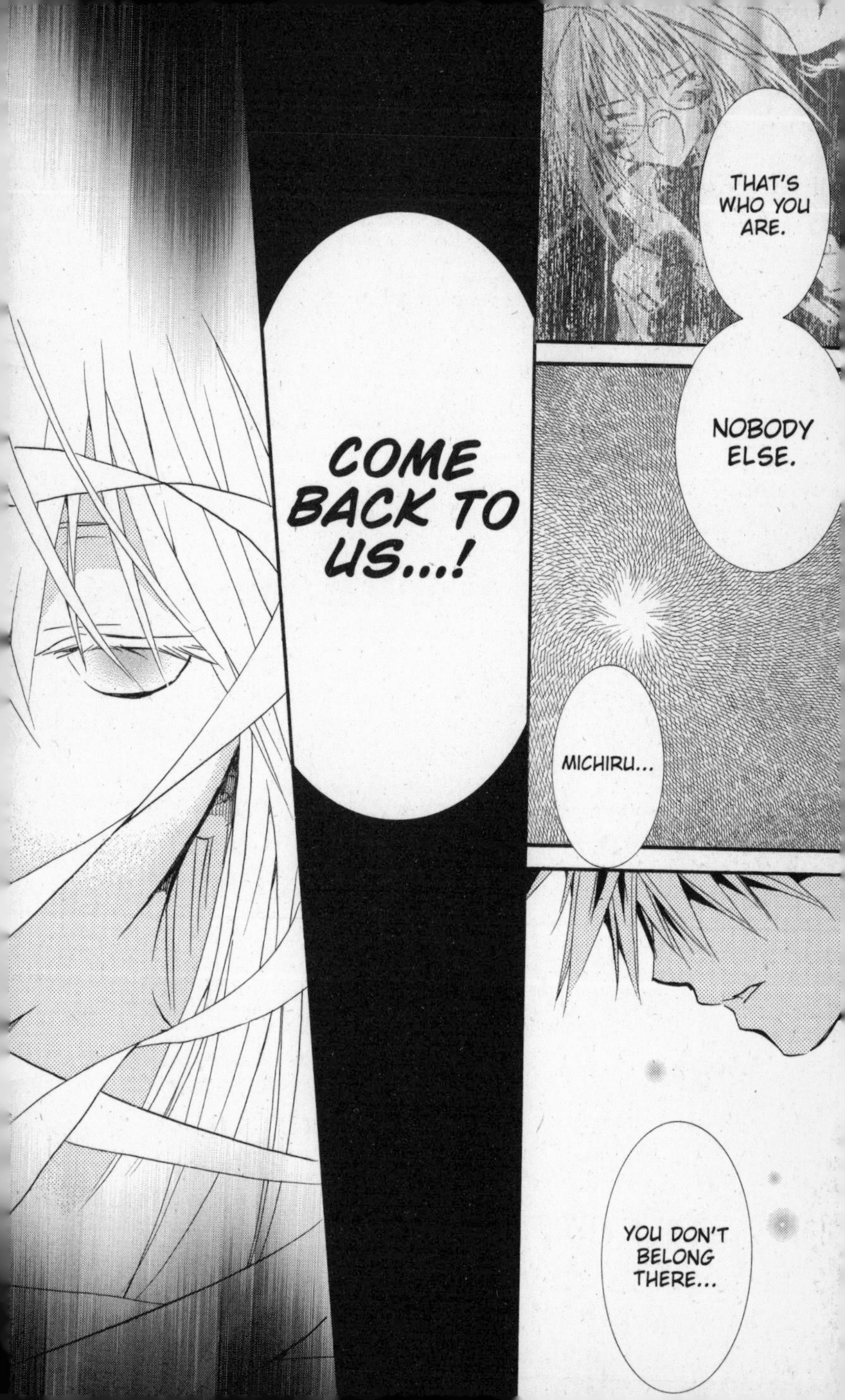
THAT'S WHO YOU ARE.
NOBODY ELSE.
MICHIRU...
YOU DON'T BELONG THERE...
COME BACK TO US...!

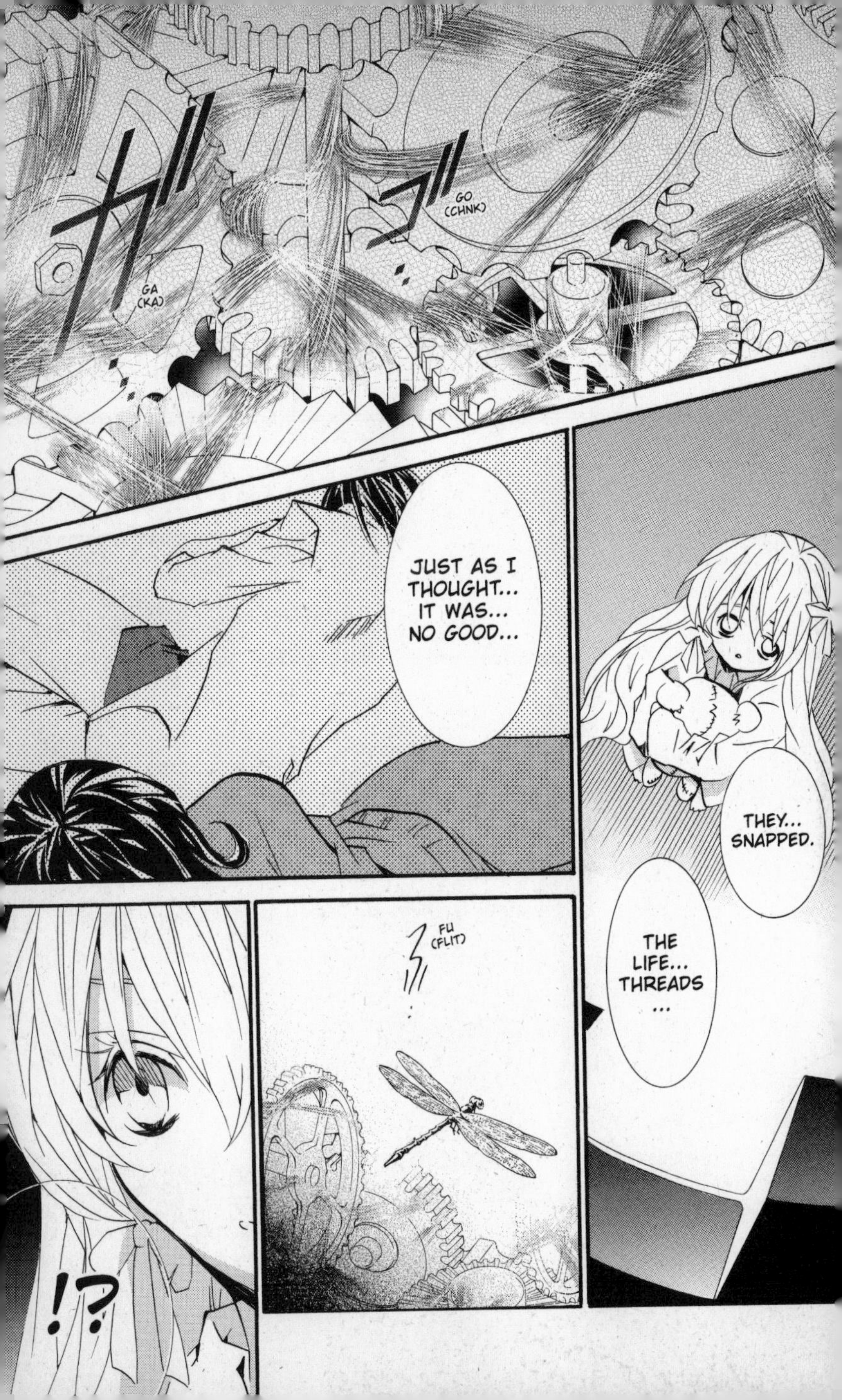
GO
(CHNK)
GA
(KA)
THEY... SNAPPED.
THE LIFE... THREADS ...
JUST AS I THOUGHT... IT WAS... NO GOOD...
FU
(FLIT)
!?

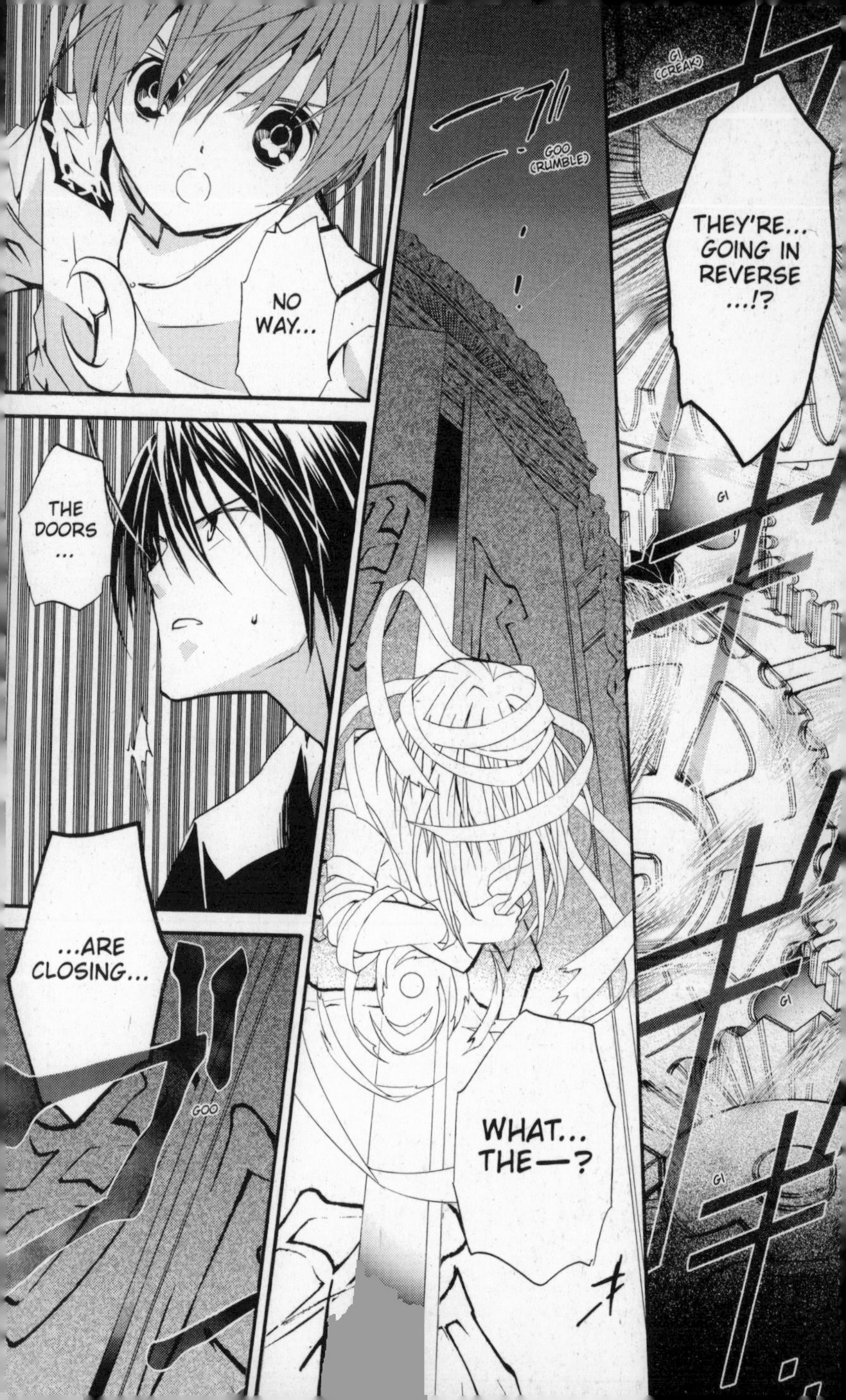
GI (CREAK)
THEY'RE... GOING IN REVERSE ...!?
GI
GI
GI
GOO (RUMBLE)
!
WHAT... THE—?
NO WAY...
THE DOORS ...
...ARE CLOSING...
GOO

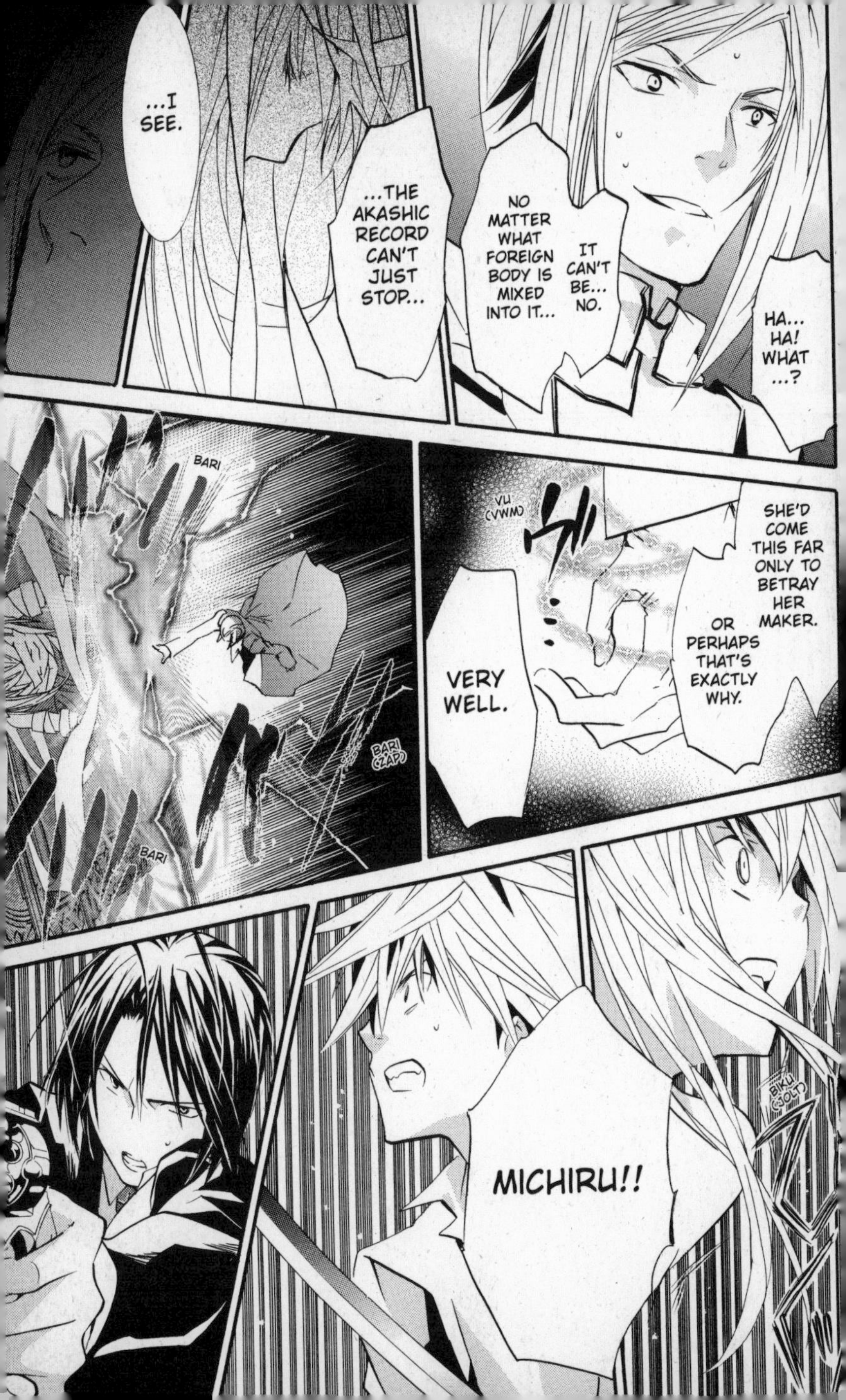
HA... HA! WHAT ...?
IT CAN'T BE... NO.
NO MATTER WHAT FOREIGN BODY IS MIXED INTO IT...
...THE AKASHIC RECORD CAN'T JUST STOP...
...I SEE.
VU (VWM)
SHE'D COME THIS FAR ONLY TO BETRAY HER MAKER.
OR PERHAPS THAT'S EXACTLY WHY.
VERY WELL.
BARI
BARI (ZAP)
BARI
BIKU (JOLT)
MICHIRU!!

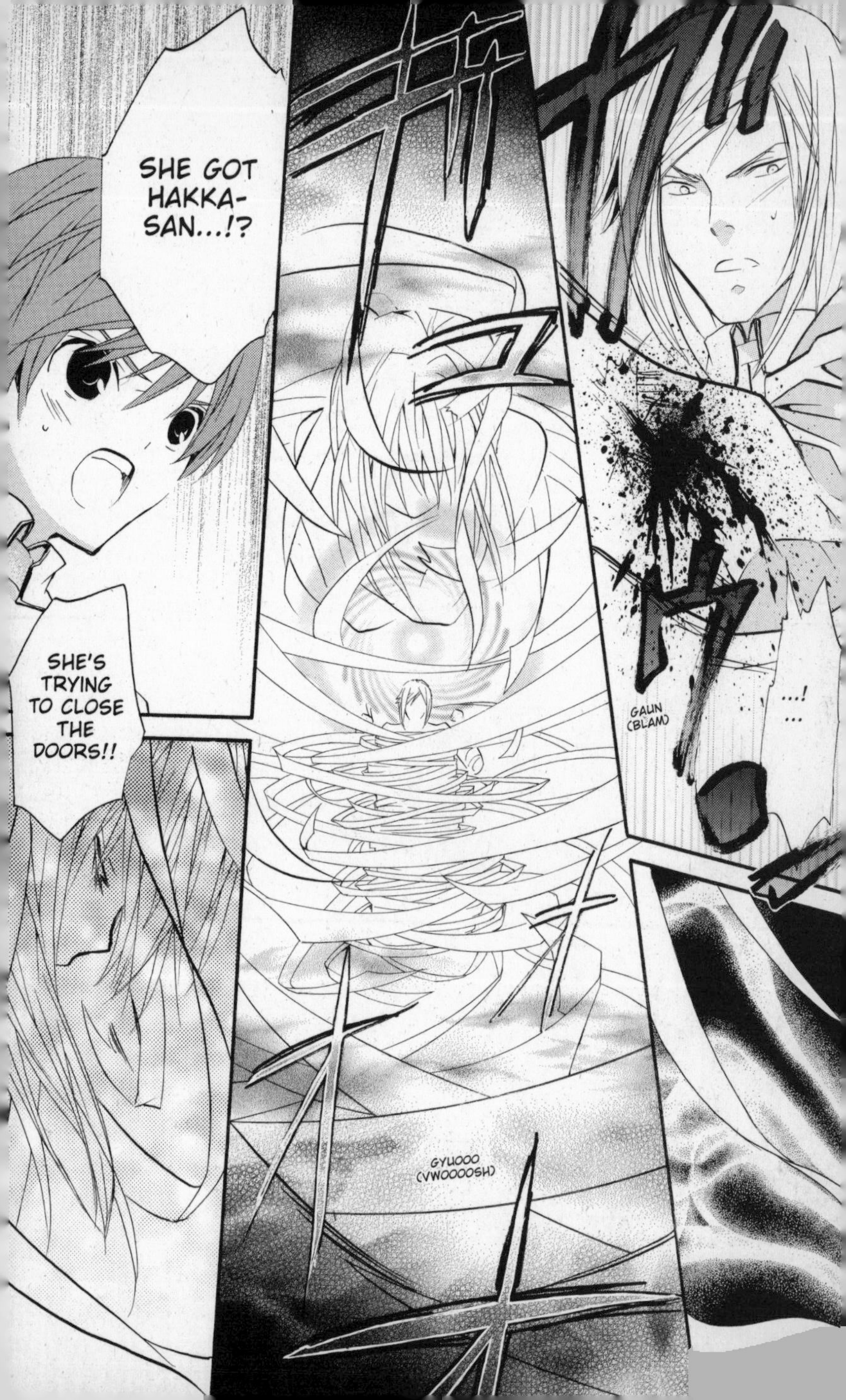
GAUN (BLAM)
...!
...
GYUOOO (VWOOOOSH)
SHE GOT HAKKA-SAN...!?
SHE'S TRYING TO CLOSE THE DOORS!!

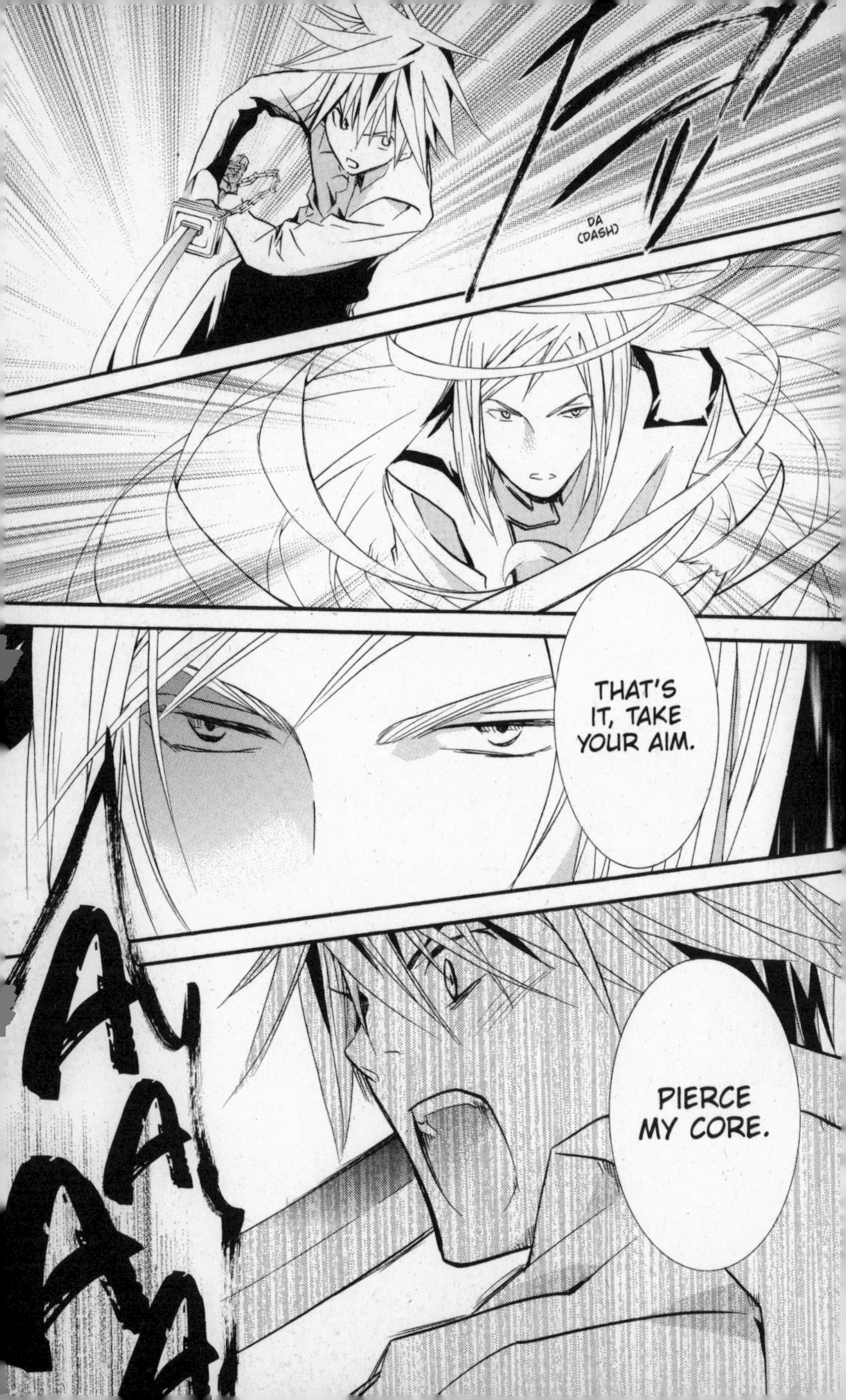
DA
(DASH)
THAT'S IT, TAKE YOUR AIM.
PIERCE MY CORE.

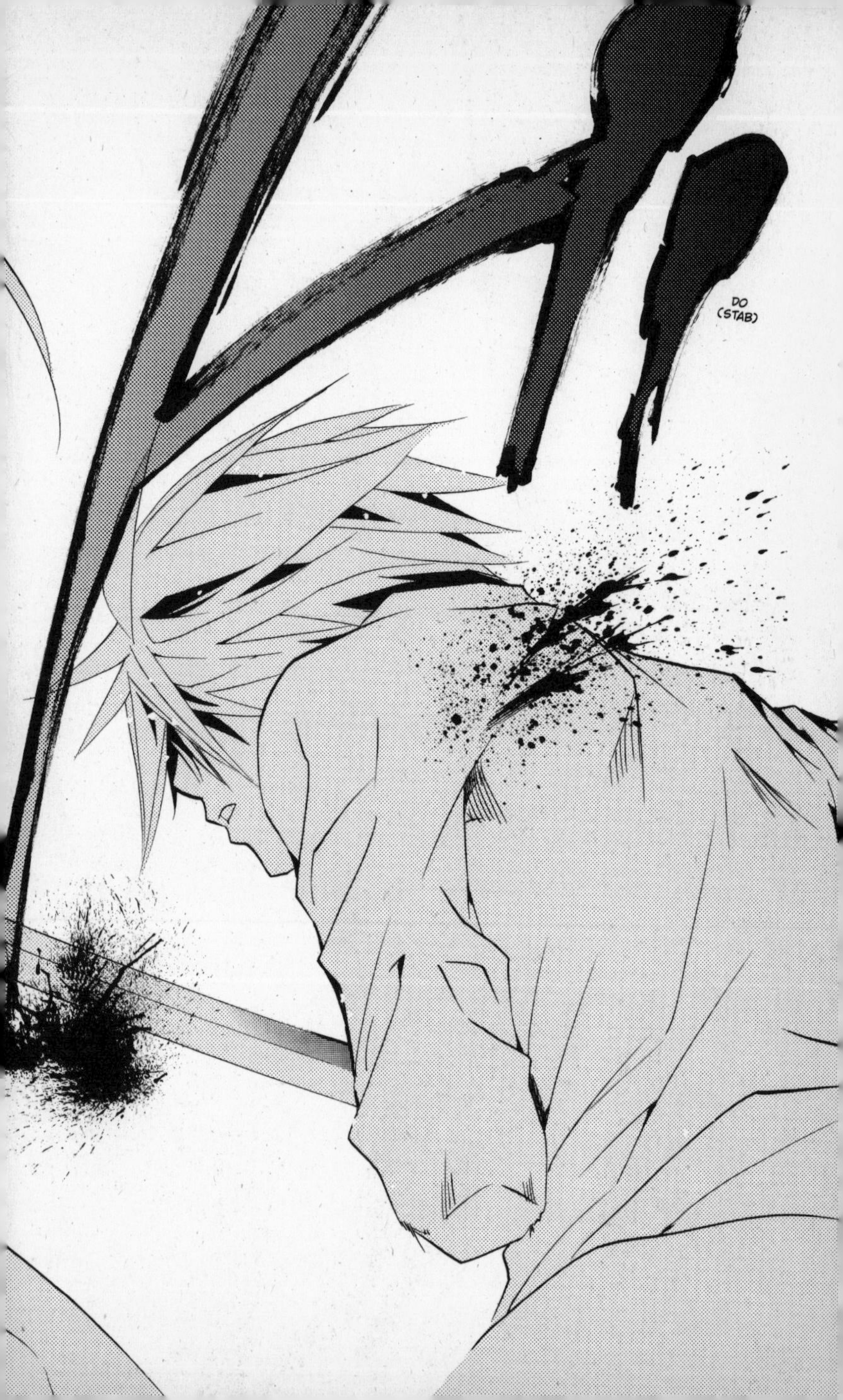
DO
(STAB)

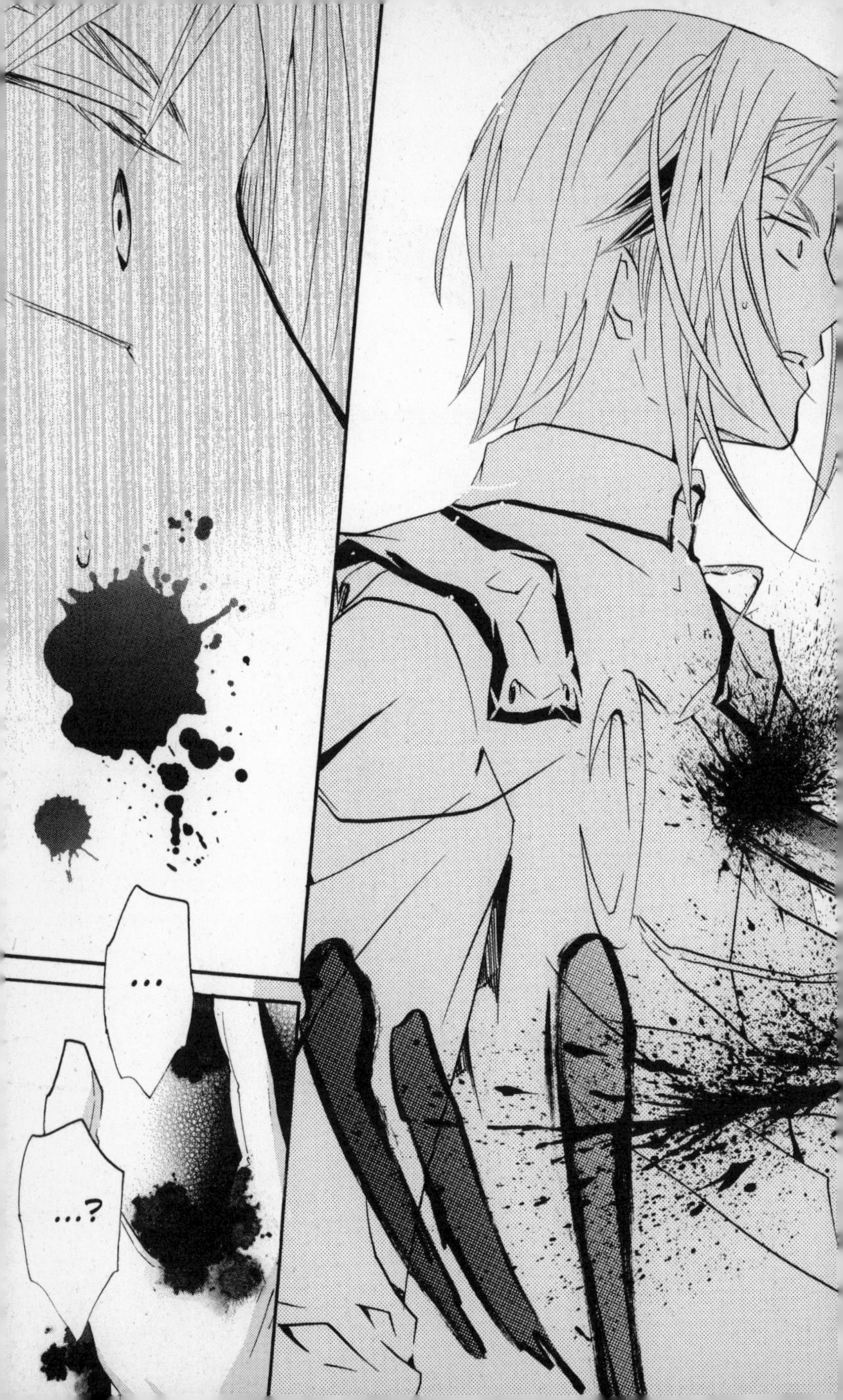
...
...?

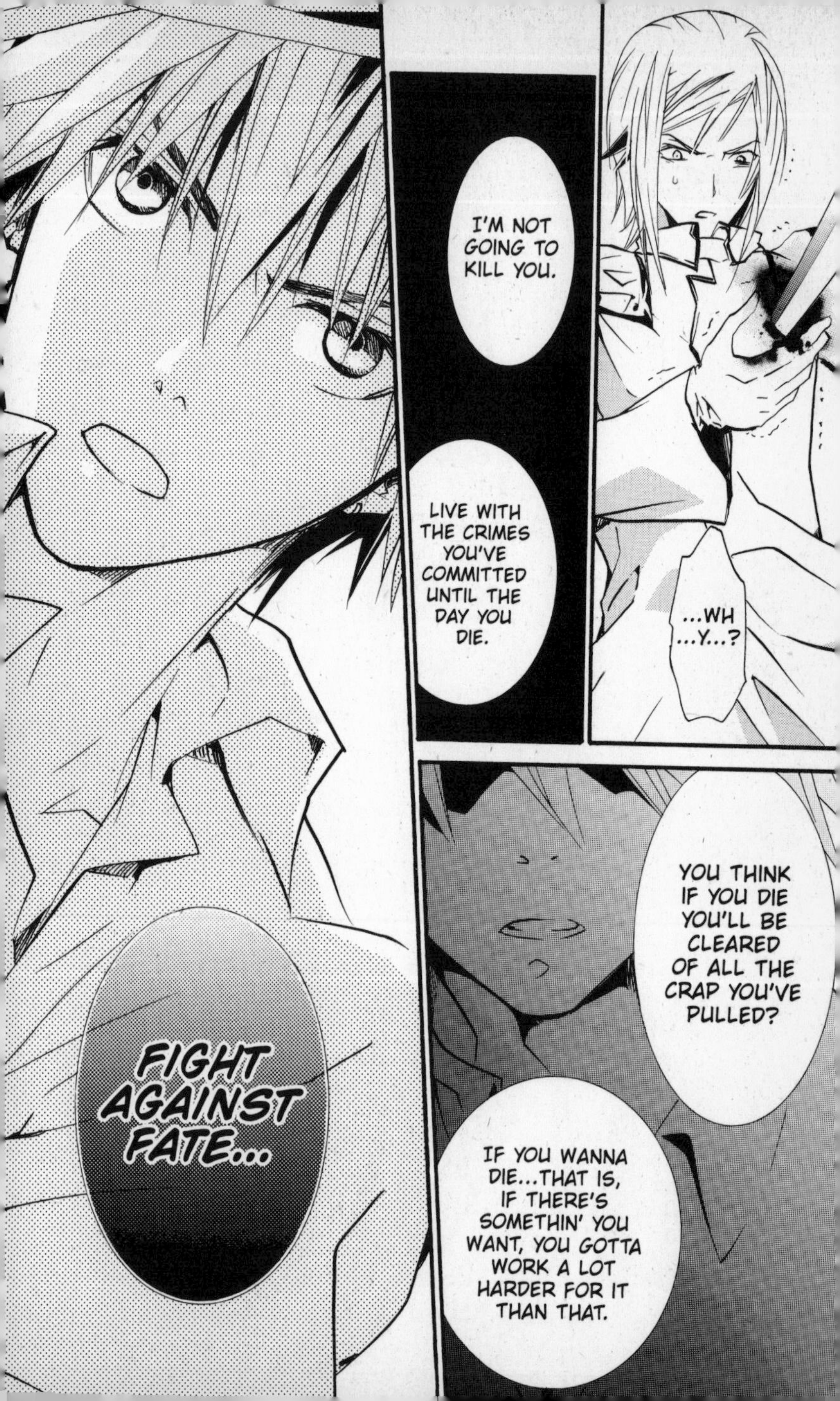
...WH ...Y...?
I'M NOT GOING TO KILL YOU.
LIVE WITH THE CRIMES YOU'VE COMMITTED UNTIL THE DAY YOU DIE.
YOU THINK IF YOU DIE YOU'LL BE CLEARED OF ALL THE CRAP YOU'VE PULLED?
IF YOU WANNA DIE...THAT IS, IF THERE'S SOMETHIN' YOU WANT, YOU GOTTA WORK A LOT HARDER FOR IT THAN THAT.
FIGHT AGAINST FATE...

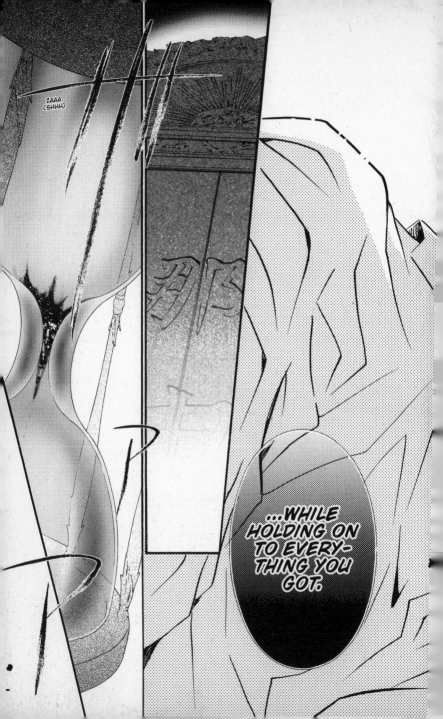

ZAAA
(SHHH)

...WHILE HOLDING ON TO EVERY-THING YOU GOT.

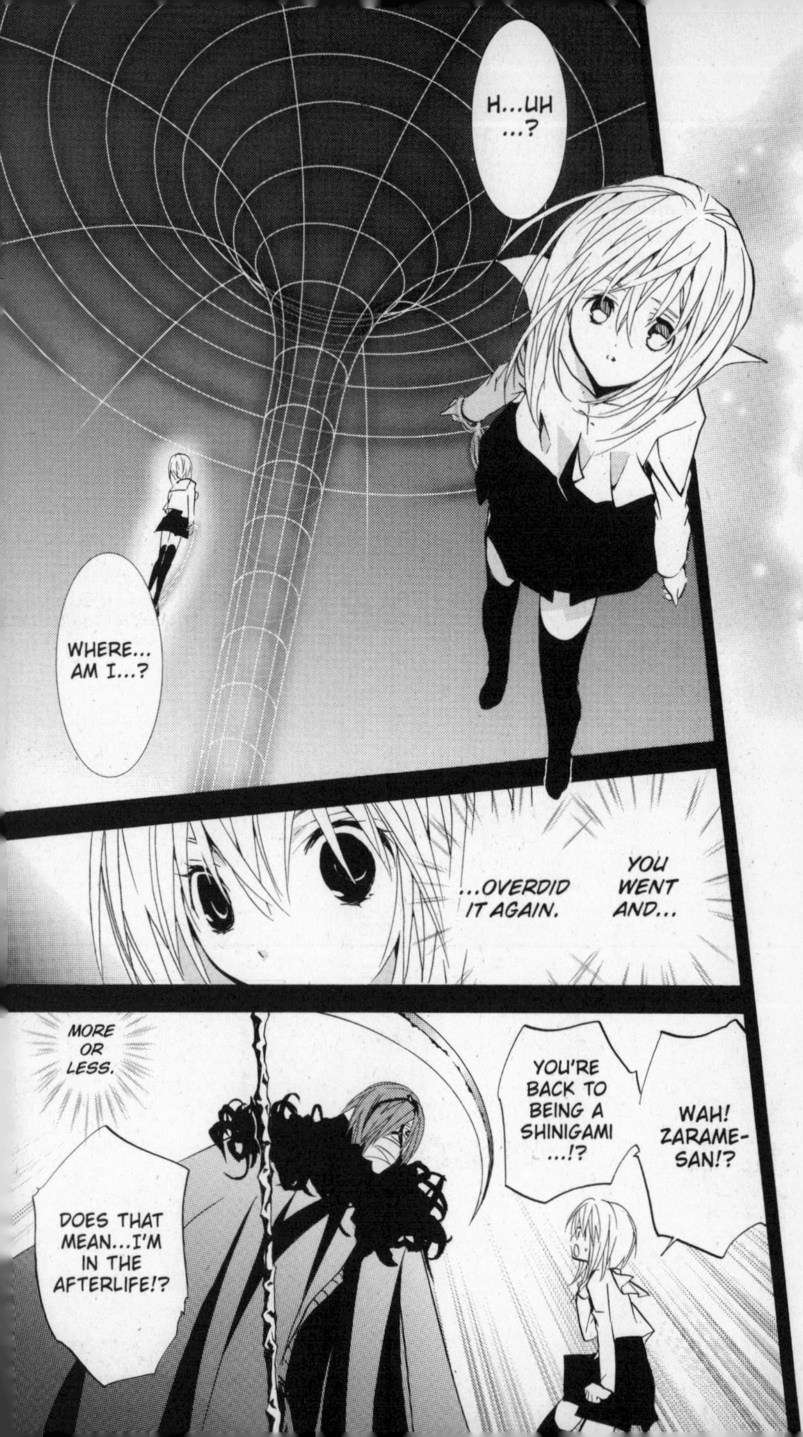
H...UH ...?
WHERE... AM I...?
YOU WENT AND...
...OVERDID IT AGAIN.
WAH! ZARAME-SAN!?
YOU'RE BACK TO BEING A SHINIGAMI ...!?
MORE OR LESS.
DOES THAT MEAN...I'M IN THE AFTERLIFE!?

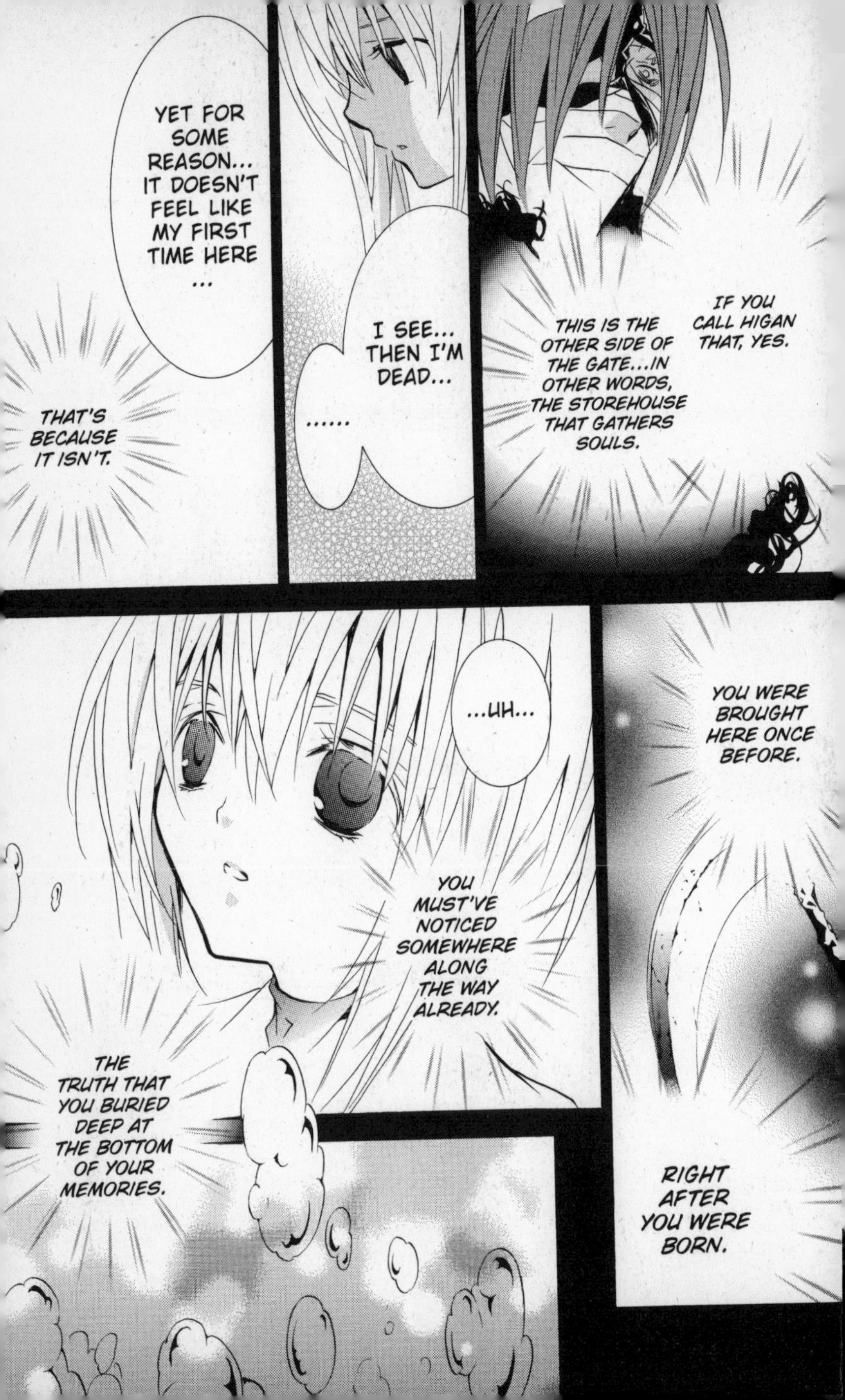
IF YOU CALL HIGAN THAT, YES.
THIS IS THE OTHER SIDE OF THE GATE...IN OTHER WORDS, THE STOREHOUSE THAT GATHERS SOULS.
I SEE... THEN I'M DEAD...
......
YET FOR SOME REASON... IT DOESN'T FEEL LIKE MY FIRST TIME HERE ...
THAT'S BECAUSE IT ISN'T.
YOU WERE BROUGHT HERE ONCE BEFORE.
RIGHT AFTER YOU WERE BORN.
...UH...
YOU MUST'VE NOTICED SOMEWHERE ALONG THE WAY ALREADY.
THE TRUTH THAT YOU BURIED DEEP AT THE BOTTOM OF YOUR MEMORIES.

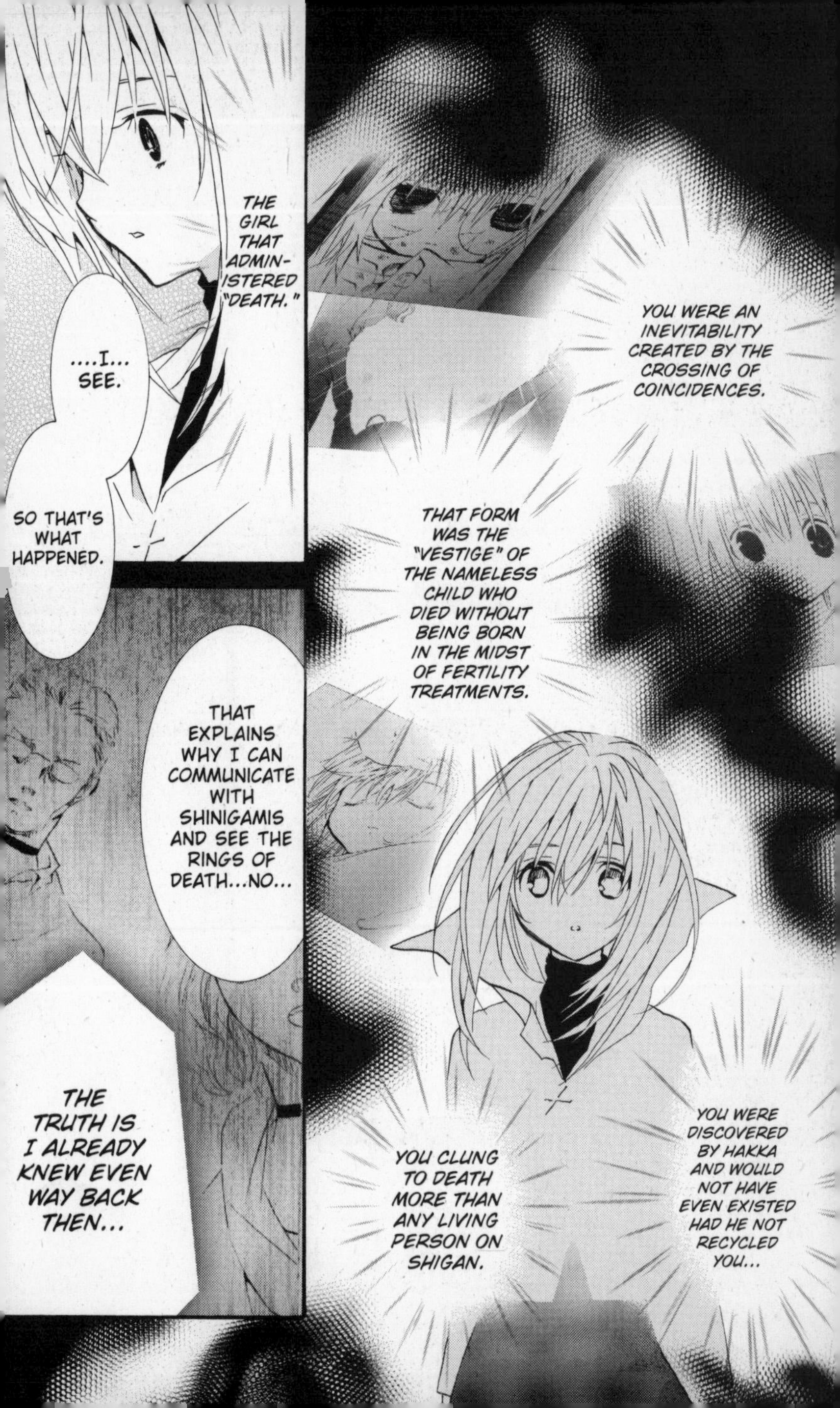
YOU WERE AN INEVITABILITY CREATED BY THE CROSSING OF COINCIDENCES.
THAT FORM WAS THE "VESTIGE" OF THE NAMELESS CHILD WHO DIED WITHOUT BEING BORN IN THE MIDST OF FERTILITY TREATMENTS.
YOU WERE DISCOVERED BY HAKKA AND WOULD NOT HAVE EVEN EXISTED HAD HE NOT RECYCLED YOU...
YOU CLUNG TO DEATH MORE THAN ANY LIVING PERSON ON SHIGAN.
THE GIRL THAT ADMIN-ISTERED "DEATH."
....I... SEE.
SO THAT'S WHAT HAPPENED.
THAT EXPLAINS WHY I CAN COMMUNICATE WITH SHINIGAMIS AND SEE THE RINGS OF DEATH...NO...
THE TRUTH IS I ALREADY KNEW EVEN WAY BACK THEN...

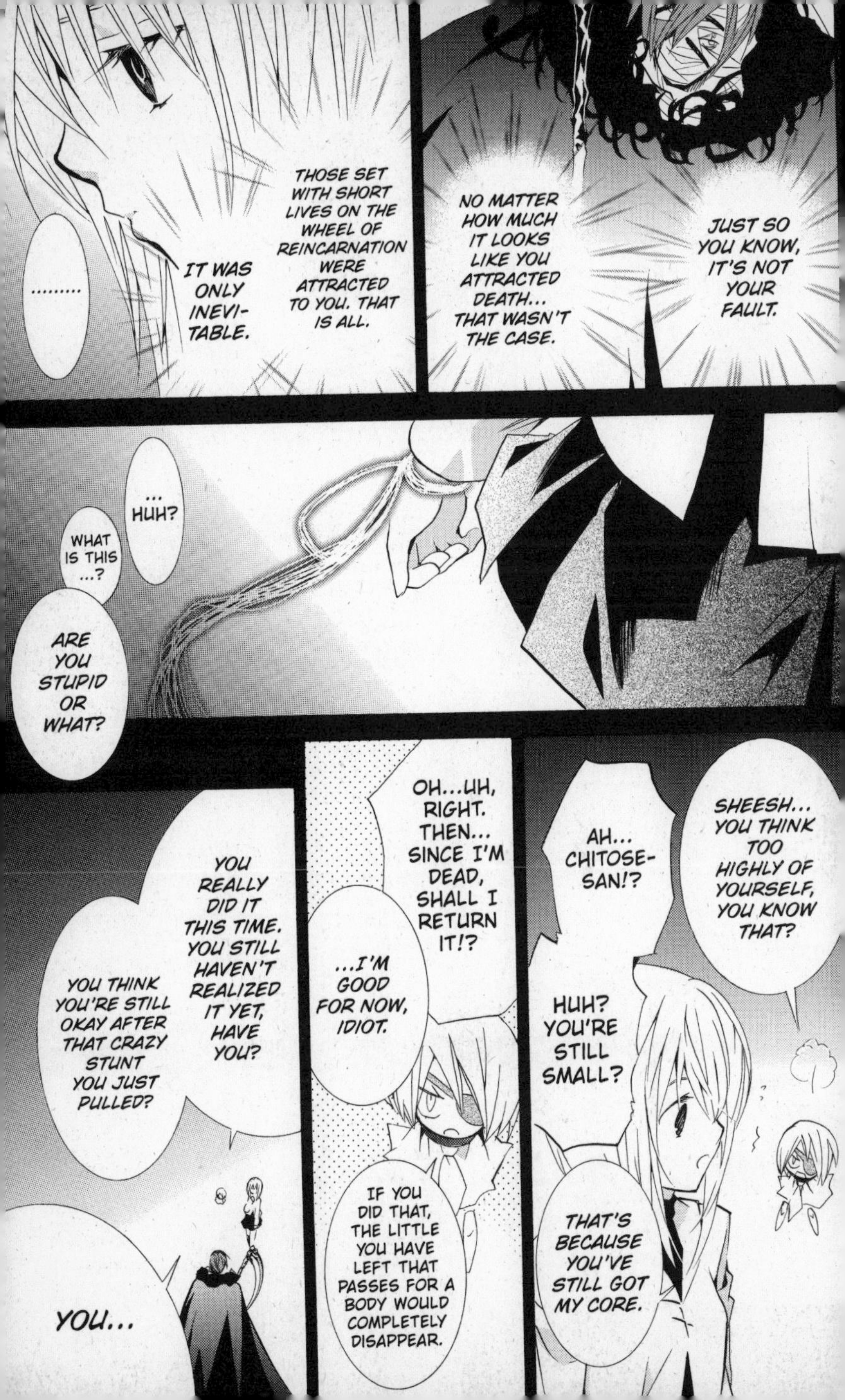
JUST SO YOU KNOW, IT'S NOT YOUR FAULT.
NO MATTER HOW MUCH IT LOOKS LIKE YOU ATTRACTED DEATH... THAT WASN'T THE CASE.
THOSE SET WITH SHORT LIVES ON THE WHEEL OF REINCARNATION WERE ATTRACTED TO YOU. THAT IS ALL.
IT WAS ONLY INEVI-TABLE.
....
...HUH?
WHAT IS THIS ...?
ARE YOU STUPID OR WHAT?
SHEESH... YOU THINK TOO HIGHLY OF YOURSELF, YOU KNOW THAT?
AH... CHITOSE-SAN!?
HUH? YOU'RE STILL SMALL?
THAT'S BECAUSE YOU'VE STILL GOT MY CORE.
OH...UH, RIGHT. THEN... SINCE I'M DEAD, SHALL I RETURN IT!?
...I'M GOOD FOR NOW, IDIOT.
IF YOU DID THAT, THE LITTLE YOU HAVE LEFT THAT PASSES FOR A BODY WOULD COMPLETELY DISAPPEAR.
YOU REALLY DID IT THIS TIME. YOU STILL HAVEN'T REALIZED IT YET, HAVE YOU?
YOU THINK YOU'RE STILL OKAY AFTER THAT CRAZY STUNT YOU JUST PULLED?
YOU...

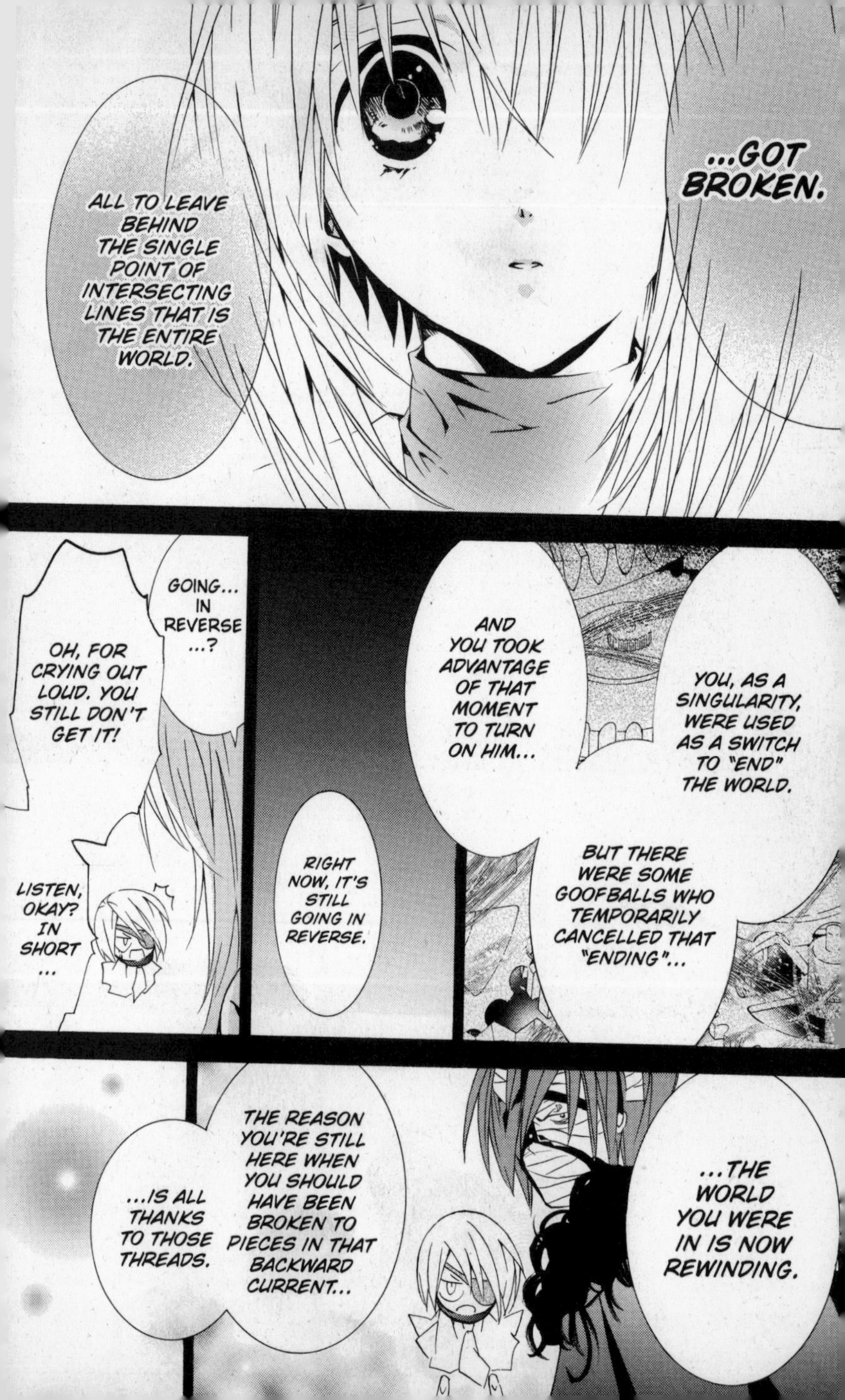
...GOT BROKEN.
ALL TO LEAVE BEHIND THE SINGLE POINT OF INTERSECTING LINES THAT IS THE ENTIRE WORLD.
YOU, AS A SINGULARITY, WERE USED AS A SWITCH TO "END" THE WORLD.
AND YOU TOOK ADVANTAGE OF THAT MOMENT TO TURN ON HIM...
BUT THERE WERE SOME GOOFBALLS WHO TEMPORARILY CANCELLED THAT "ENDING"...
RIGHT NOW, IT'S STILL GOING IN REVERSE.
GOING... IN REVERSE...?
OH, FOR CRYING OUT LOUD. YOU STILL DON'T GET IT!
LISTEN, OKAY? IN SHORT...
...THE WORLD YOU WERE IN IS NOW REWINDING.
THE REASON YOU'RE STILL HERE WHEN YOU SHOULD HAVE BEEN BROKEN TO PIECES IN THAT BACKWARD CURRENT...
...IS ALL THANKS TO THOSE THREADS.

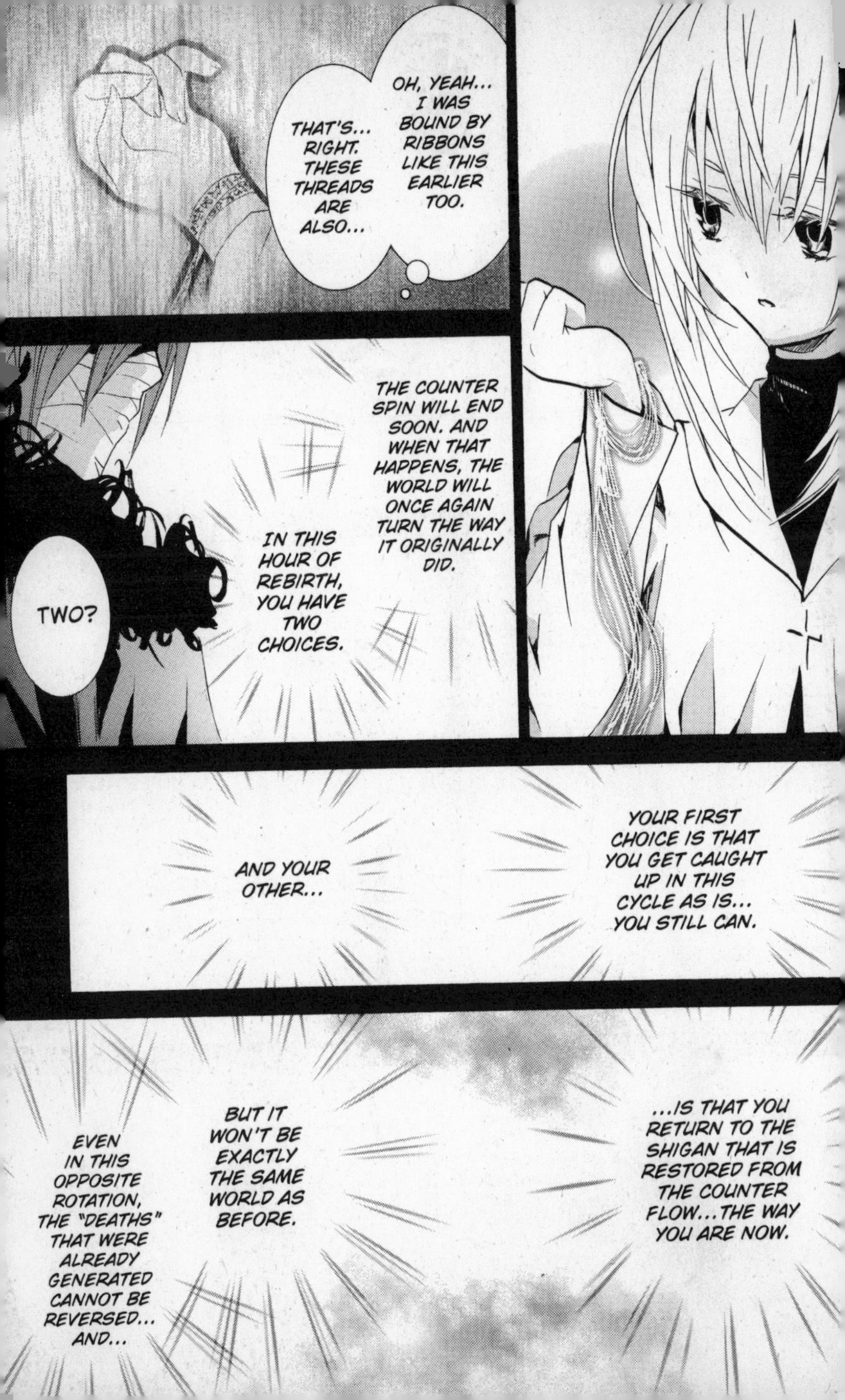
OH, YEAH... I WAS BOUND BY RIBBONS LIKE THIS EARLIER TOO.
THAT'S... RIGHT. THESE THREADS ARE ALSO...
THE COUNTER SPIN WILL END SOON. AND WHEN THAT HAPPENS, THE WORLD WILL ONCE AGAIN TURN THE WAY IT ORIGINALLY DID.
IN THIS HOUR OF REBIRTH, YOU HAVE TWO CHOICES.
TWO?
YOUR FIRST CHOICE IS THAT YOU GET CAUGHT UP IN THIS CYCLE AS IS... YOU STILL CAN.
AND YOUR OTHER...
...IS THAT YOU RETURN TO THE SHIGAN THAT IS RESTORED FROM THE COUNTER FLOW...THE WAY YOU ARE NOW.
BUT IT WON'T BE EXACTLY THE SAME WORLD AS BEFORE.
EVEN IN THIS OPPOSITE ROTATION, THE "DEATHS" THAT WERE ALREADY GENERATED CANNOT BE REVERSED... AND...

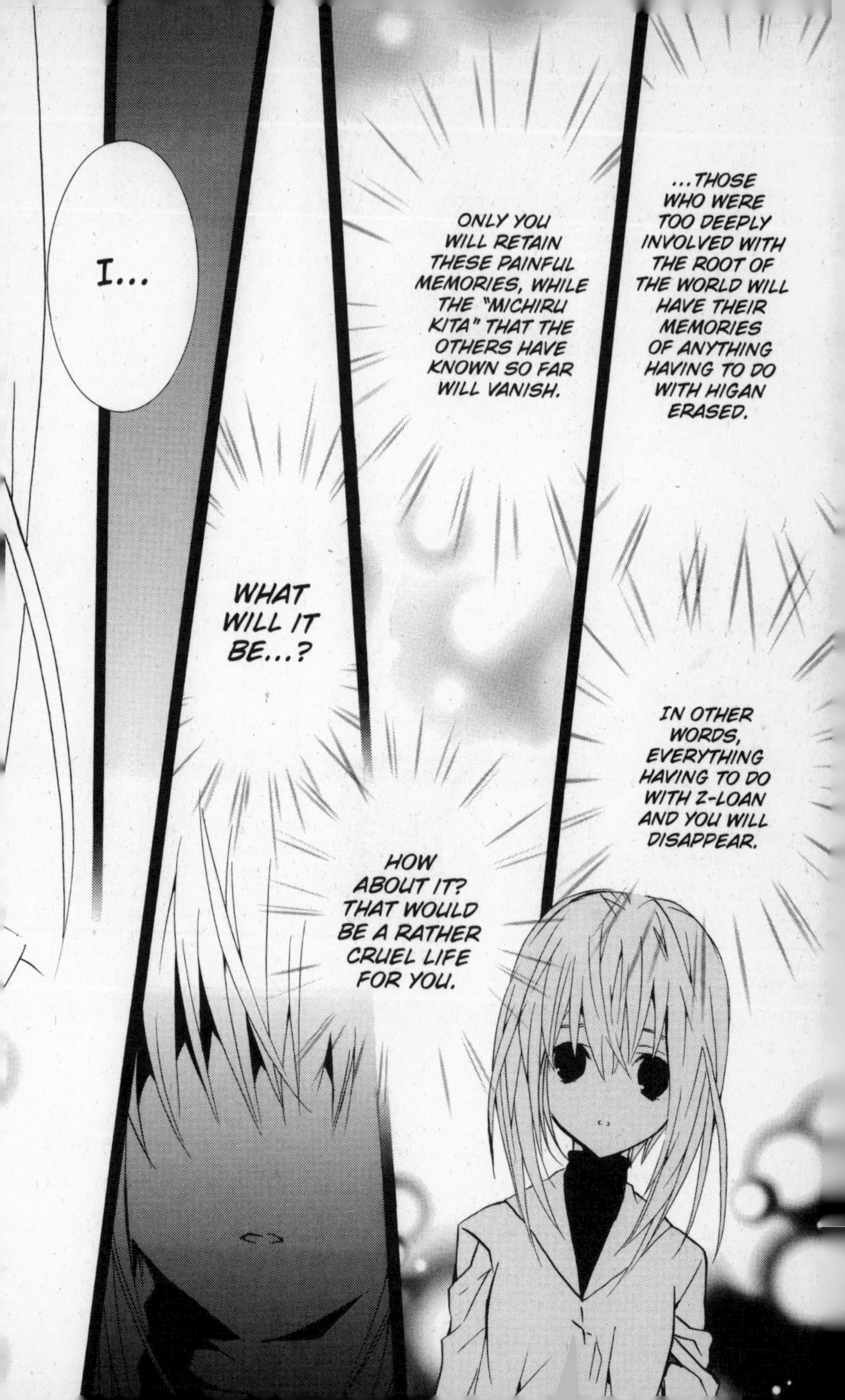
...THOSE WHO WERE TOO DEEPLY INVOLVED WITH THE ROOT OF THE WORLD WILL HAVE THEIR MEMORIES OF ANYTHING HAVING TO DO WITH HIGAN ERASED.
IN OTHER WORDS, EVERYTHING HAVING TO DO WITH Z-LOAN AND YOU WILL DISAPPEAR.
ONLY YOU WILL RETAIN THESE PAINFUL MEMORIES, WHILE THE "MICHIRU KITA" THAT THE OTHERS HAVE KNOWN SO FAR WILL VANISH.
HOW ABOUT IT? THAT WOULD BE A RATHER CRUEL LIFE FOR YOU.
WHAT WILL IT BE...?
I...

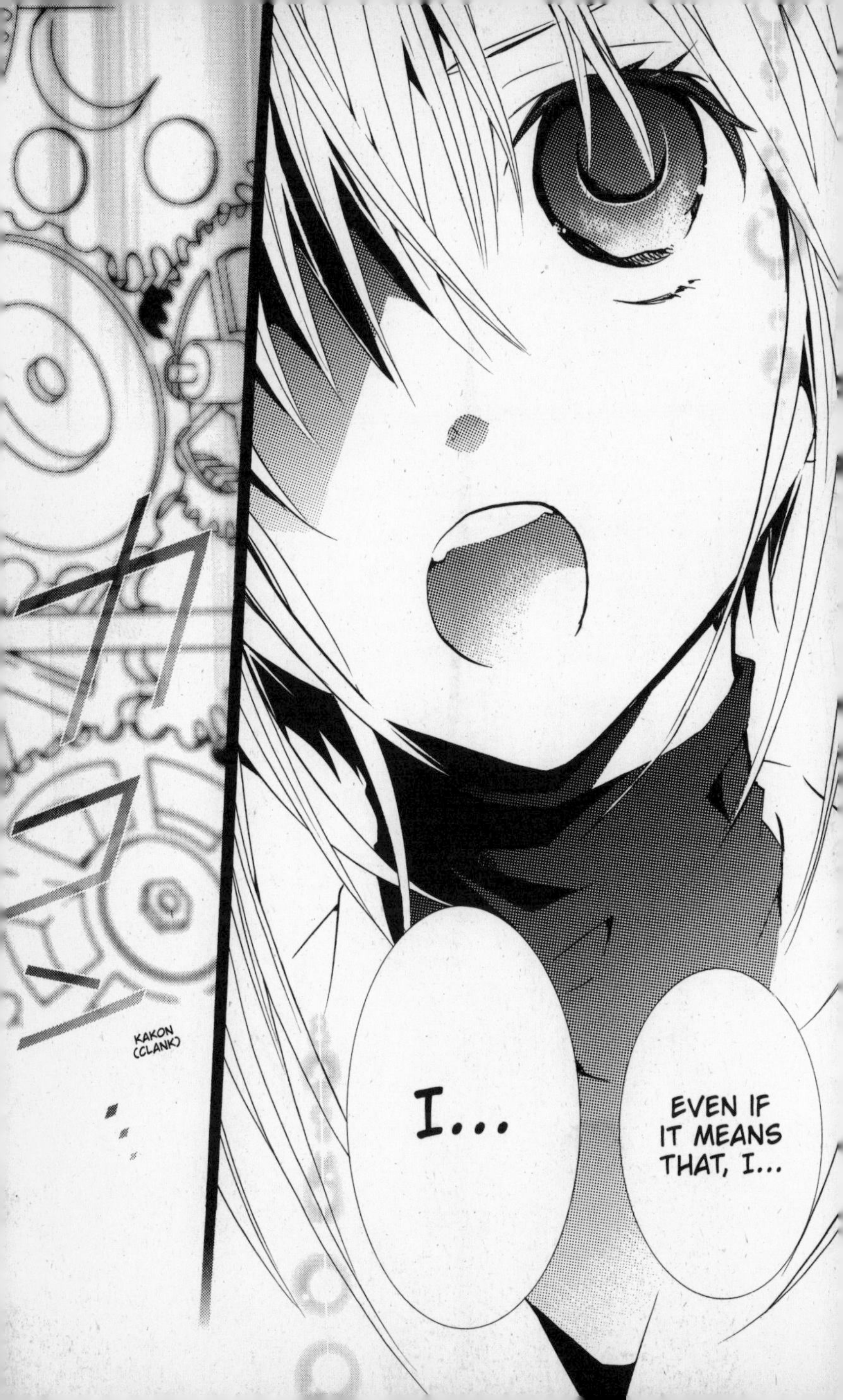
EVEN IF IT MEANS THAT, I...
I...
KAKON (CLANK)

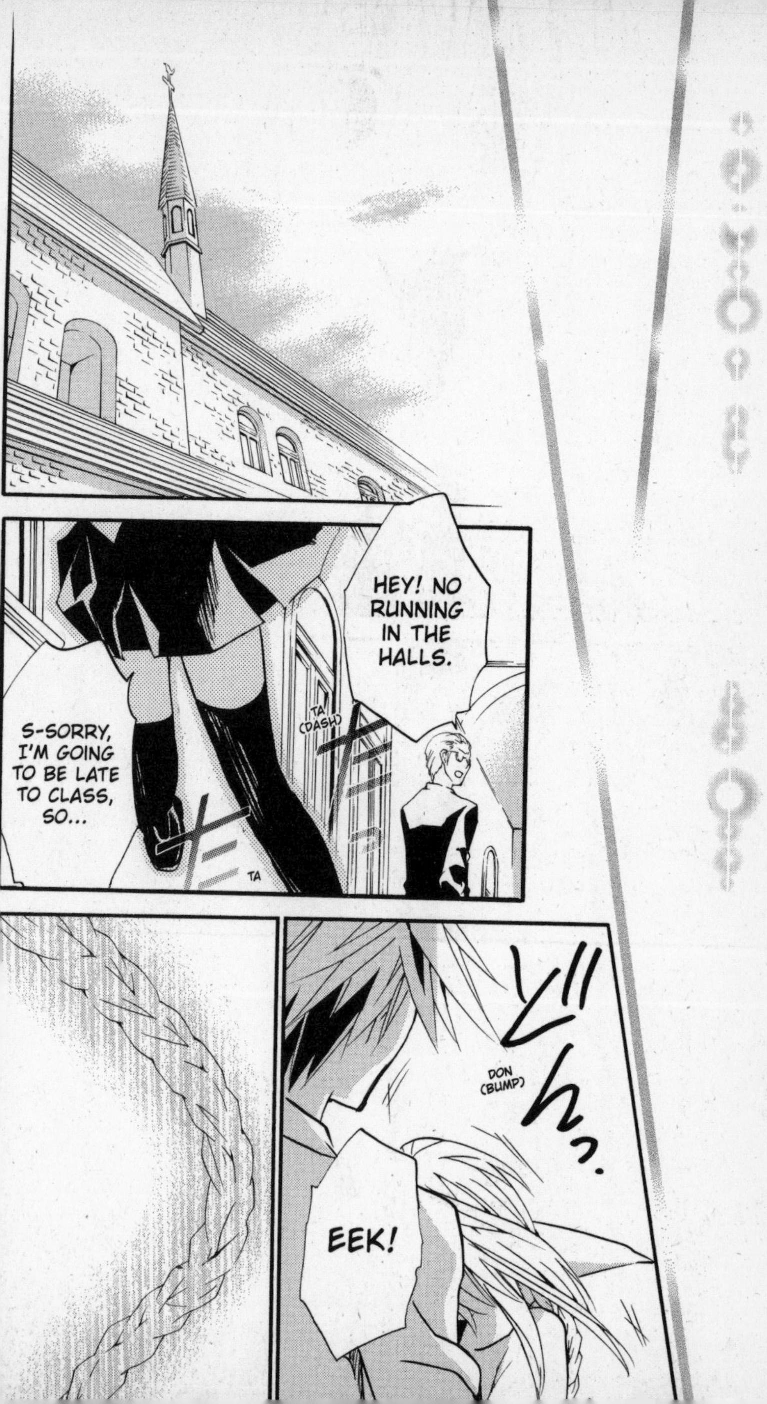
HEY! NO RUNNING IN THE HALLS.
TA (DASH)
S-SORRY, I'M GOING TO BE LATE TO CLASS, SO...
TA
DON (BUMP)
EEK!

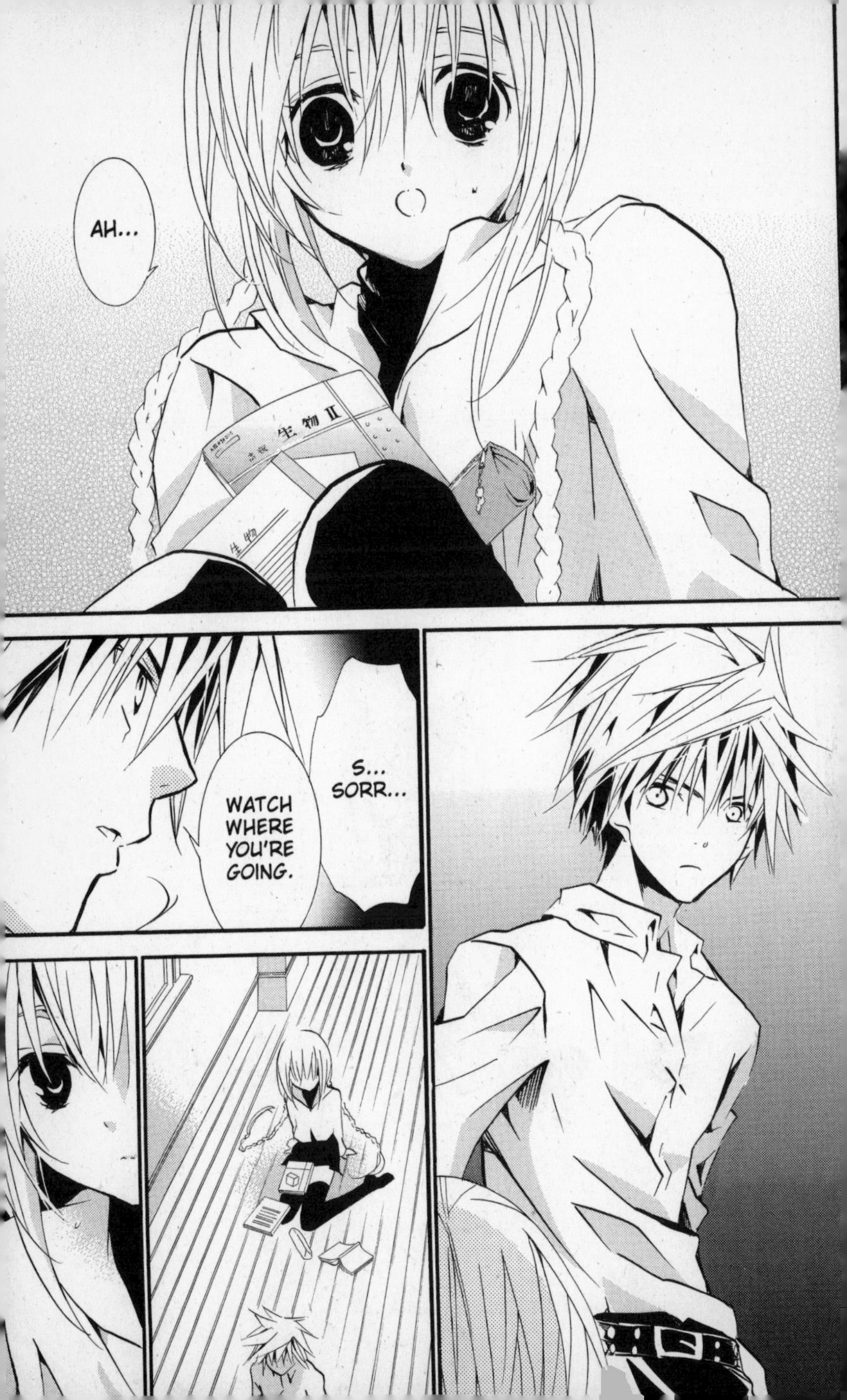
AH...
S... SORR...
WATCH WHERE YOU'RE GOING.

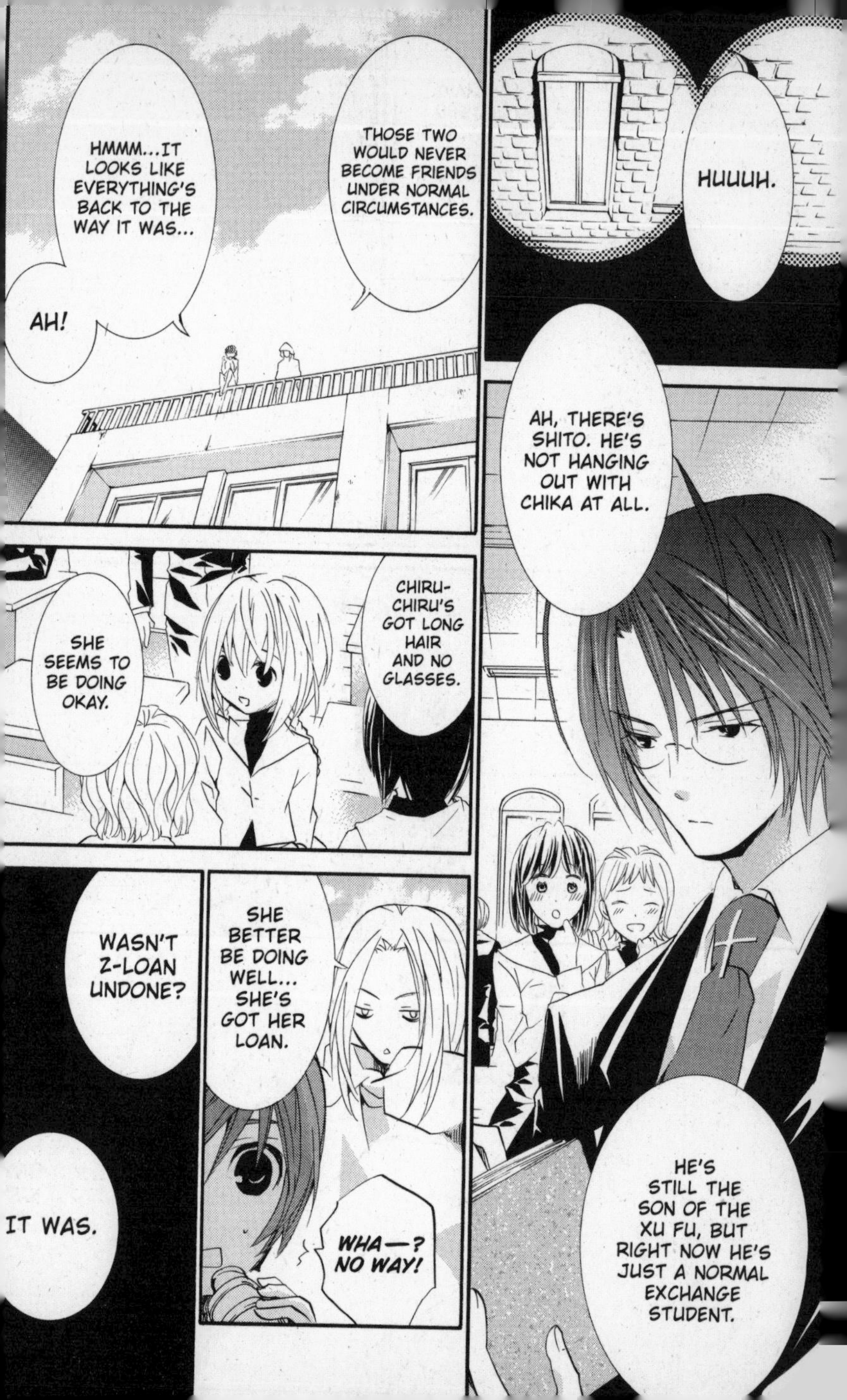
HUUUH.
THOSE TWO WOULD NEVER BECOME FRIENDS UNDER NORMAL CIRCUMSTANCES.
HMMM...IT LOOKS LIKE EVERYTHING'S BACK TO THE WAY IT WAS...
AH!
AH, THERE'S SHITO. HE'S NOT HANGING OUT WITH CHIKA AT ALL.
HE'S STILL THE SON OF THE XU FU, BUT RIGHT NOW HE'S JUST A NORMAL EXCHANGE STUDENT.
CHIRU-CHIRU'S GOT LONG HAIR AND NO GLASSES.
SHE SEEMS TO BE DOING OKAY.
SHE BETTER BE DOING WELL... SHE'S GOT HER LOAN.
WHA—? NO WAY!
WASN'T Z-LOAN UNDONE?
IT WAS.

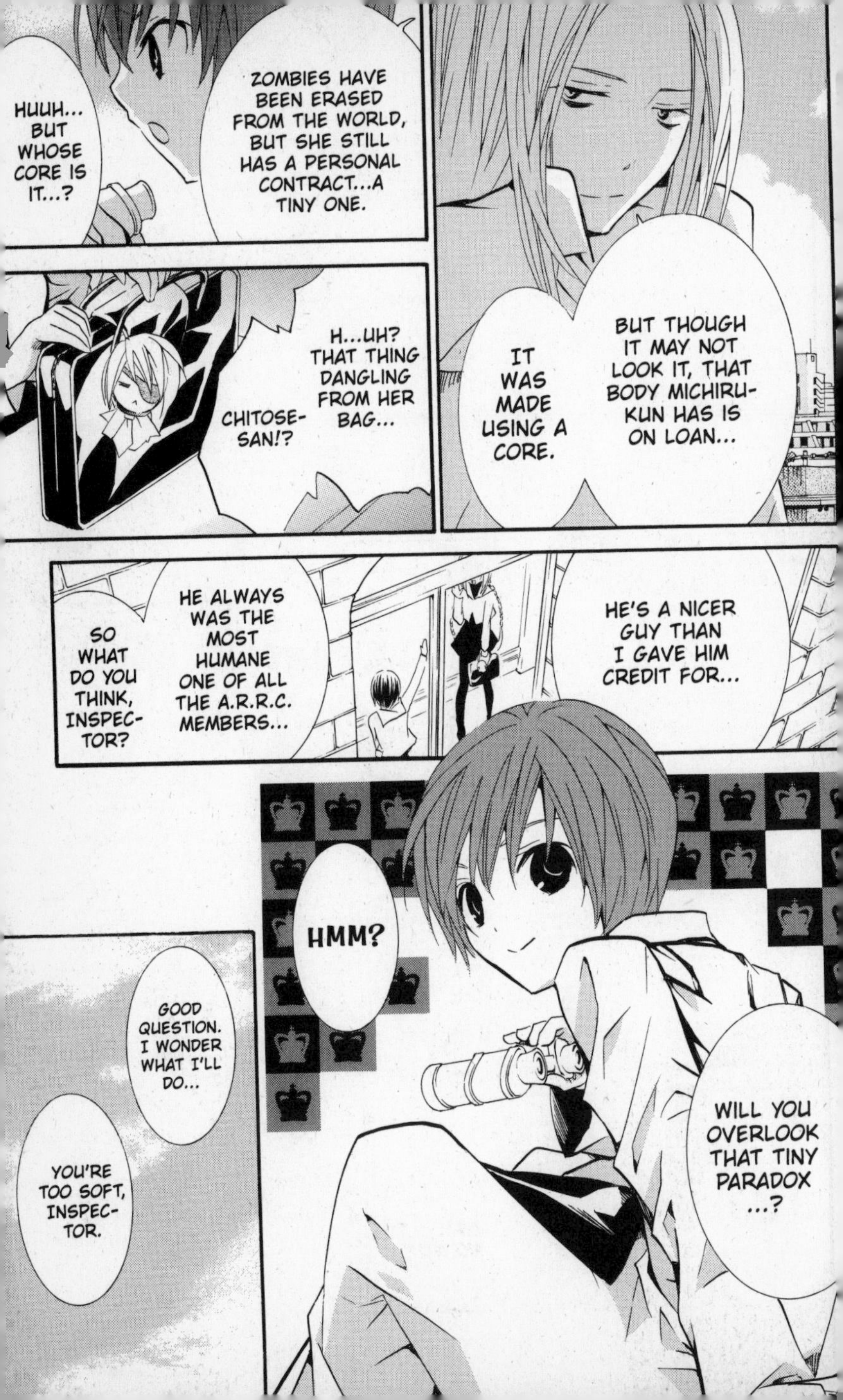
BUT THOUGH IT MAY NOT LOOK IT, THAT BODY MICHIRU-KUN HAS IS ON LOAN...
IT WAS MADE USING A CORE.
ZOMBIES HAVE BEEN ERASED FROM THE WORLD, BUT SHE STILL HAS A PERSONAL CONTRACT...A TINY ONE.
HUUH... BUT WHOSE CORE IS IT...?
H...UH? THAT THING DANGLING FROM HER BAG...
CHITOSE-SAN!?
HE'S A NICER GUY THAN I GAVE HIM CREDIT FOR...
HE ALWAYS WAS THE MOST HUMANE ONE OF ALL THE A.R.R.C. MEMBERS...
SO WHAT DO YOU THINK, INSPECTOR?
WILL YOU OVERLOOK THAT TINY PARADOX ...?
HMM?
GOOD QUESTION. I WONDER WHAT I'LL DO...
YOU'RE TOO SOFT, INSPECTOR.

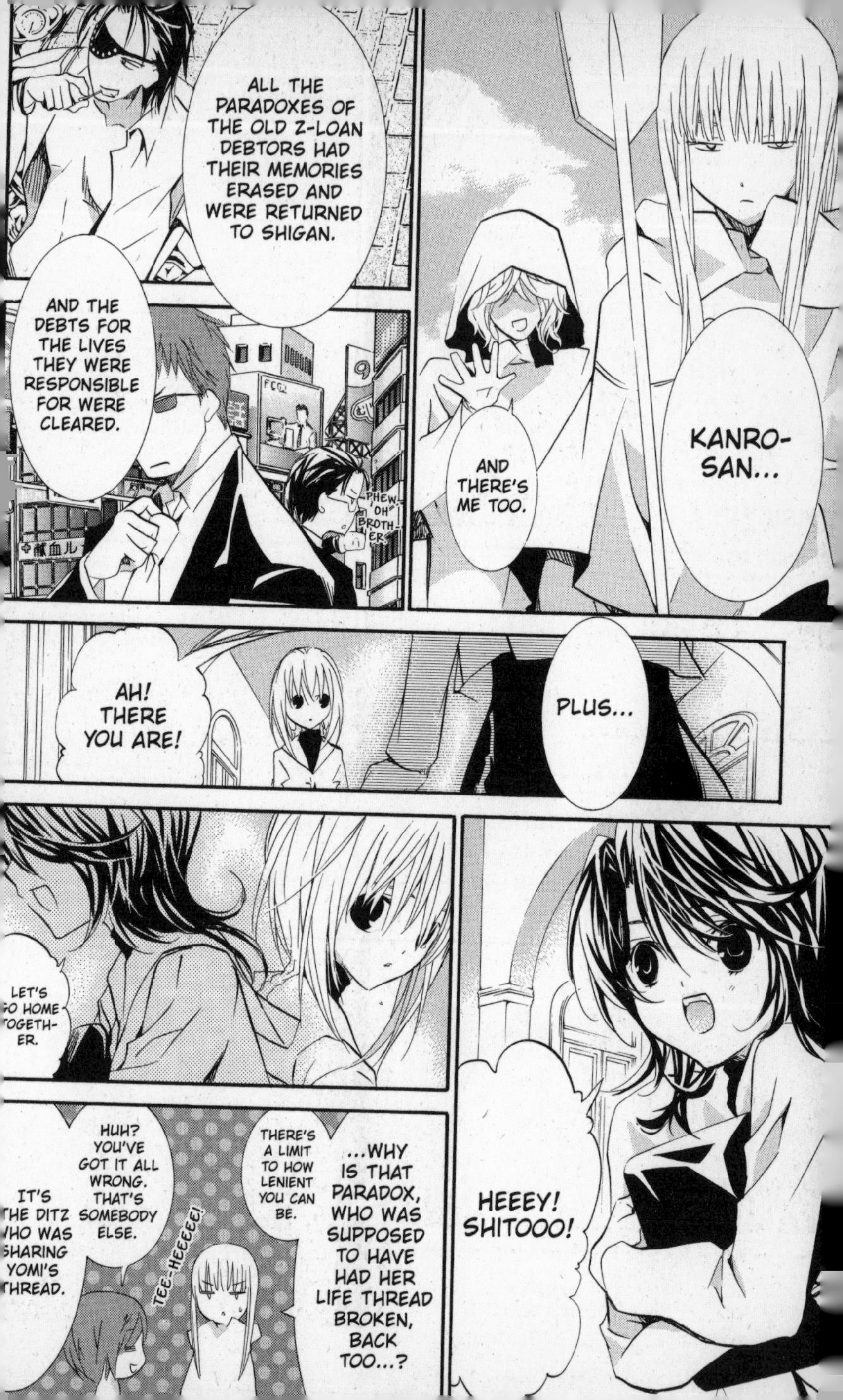
KANRO-SAN...
AND THERE'S ME TOO.
ALL THE PARADOXES OF THE OLD Z-LOAN DEBTORS HAD THEIR MEMORIES ERASED AND WERE RETURNED TO SHIGAN.
AND THE DEBTS FOR THE LIVES THEY WERE RESPONSIBLE FOR WERE CLEARED.
PHEW OH BROTHER
PLUS...
AH! THERE YOU ARE!
HEEEY! SHITOOO!
LET'S GO HOME TOGETH-ER.
...WHY IS THAT PARADOX, WHO WAS SUPPOSED TO HAVE HAD HER LIFE THREAD BROKEN, BACK TOO...?
THERE'S A LIMIT TO HOW LENIENT YOU CAN BE.
HUH? YOU'VE GOT IT ALL WRONG. THAT'S SOMEBODY ELSE.
IT'S THE DITZ WHO WAS SHARING YOMI'S THREAD.
TEE-HEEEEE!

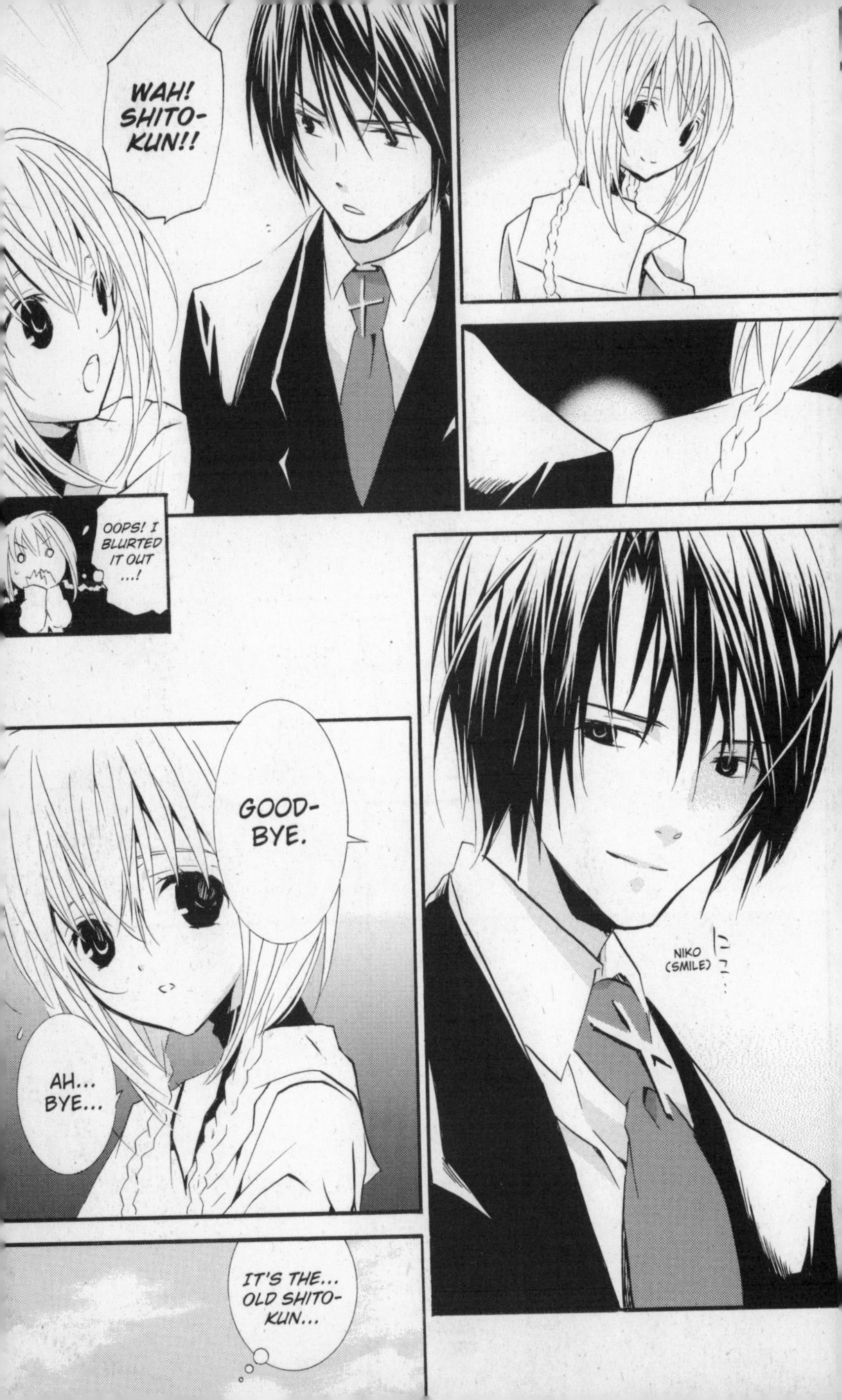
WAH! SHITO-KUN!!
NIKO (SMILE)
OOPS! I BLURTED IT OUT ...!
GOOD-BYE.
AH... BYE...
IT'S THE... OLD SHITO-KUN...

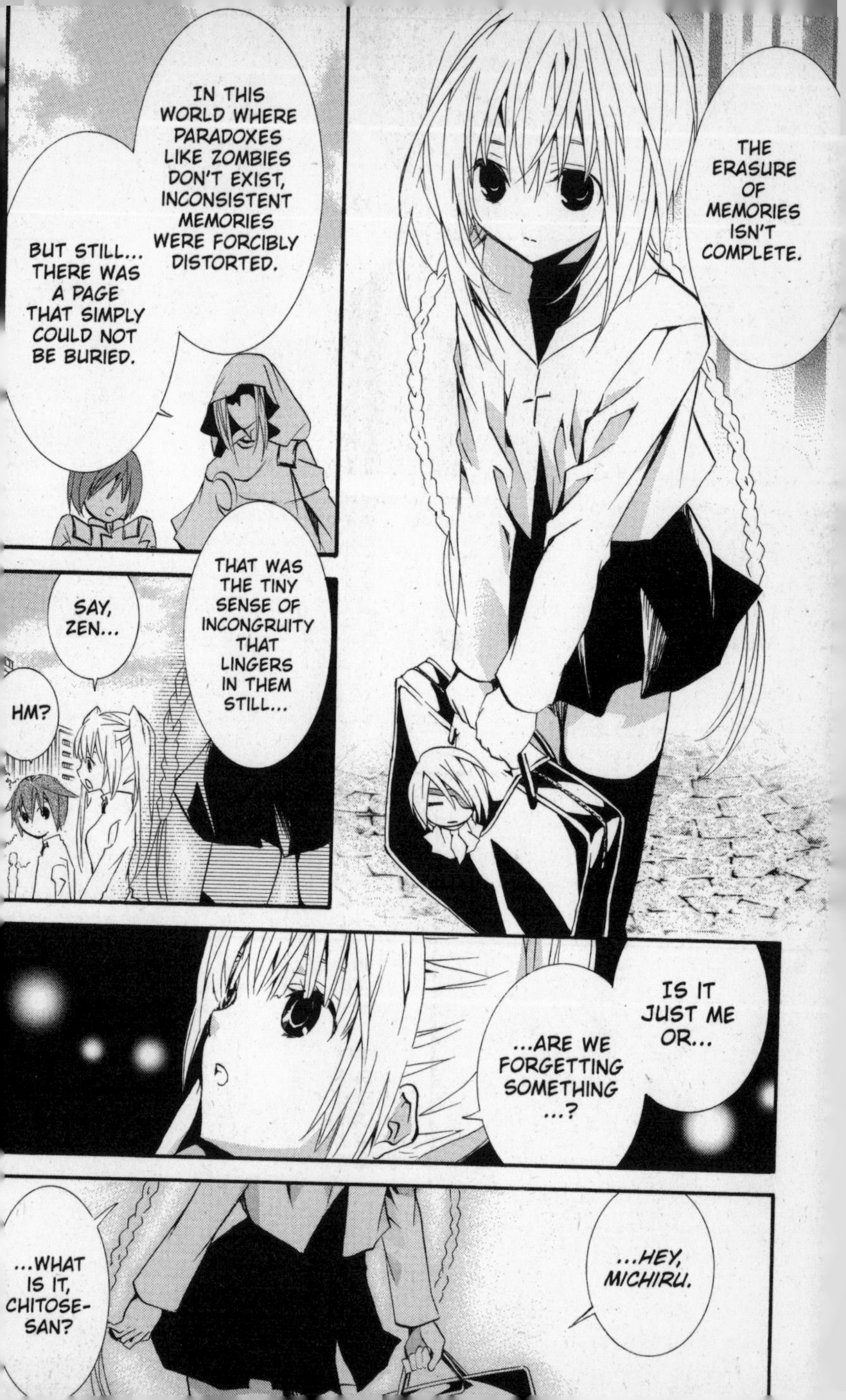
THE ERASURE OF MEMORIES ISN'T COMPLETE.
IN THIS WORLD WHERE PARADOXES LIKE ZOMBIES DON'T EXIST, INCONSISTENT MEMORIES WERE FORCIBLY DISTORTED.
BUT STILL... THERE WAS A PAGE THAT SIMPLY COULD NOT BE BURIED.
THAT WAS THE TINY SENSE OF INCONGRUITY THAT LINGERS IN THEM STILL...
SAY, ZEN...
HM?
IS IT JUST ME OR...
...ARE WE FORGETTING SOMETHING ...?
...HEY, MICHIRU.
...WHAT IS IT, CHITOSE-SAN?

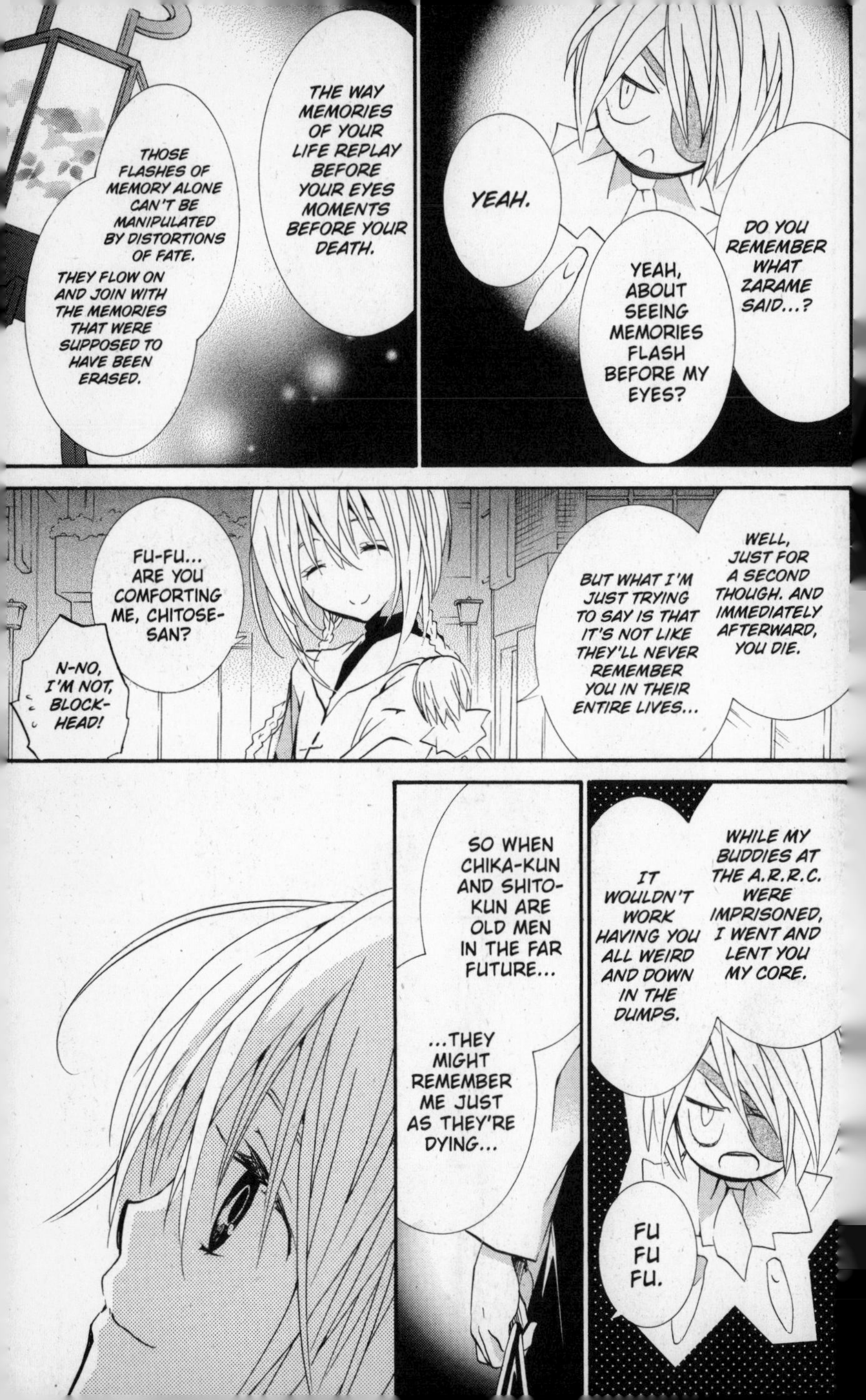
DO YOU REMEMBER WHAT ZARAME SAID...?
YEAH.
YEAH, ABOUT SEEING MEMORIES FLASH BEFORE MY EYES?
THE WAY MEMORIES OF YOUR LIFE REPLAY BEFORE YOUR EYES MOMENTS BEFORE YOUR DEATH.
THOSE FLASHES OF MEMORY ALONE CAN'T BE MANIPULATED BY DISTORTIONS OF FATE.
THEY FLOW ON AND JOIN WITH THE MEMORIES THAT WERE SUPPOSED TO HAVE BEEN ERASED.
WELL, JUST FOR A SECOND THOUGH. AND IMMEDIATELY AFTERWARD, YOU DIE.
BUT WHAT I'M JUST TRYING TO SAY IS THAT IT'S NOT LIKE THEY'LL NEVER REMEMBER YOU IN THEIR ENTIRE LIVES...
FU-FU... ARE YOU COMFORTING ME, CHITOSE-SAN?
N-NO, I'M NOT, BLOCK-HEAD!
WHILE MY BUDDIES AT THE A.R.R.C. WERE IMPRISONED, I WENT AND LENT YOU MY CORE.
IT WOULDN'T WORK HAVING YOU ALL WEIRD AND DOWN IN THE DUMPS.
FU FU FU.
SO WHEN CHIKA-KUN AND SHITO-KUN ARE OLD MEN IN THE FAR FUTURE...
...THEY MIGHT REMEMBER ME JUST AS THEY'RE DYING...

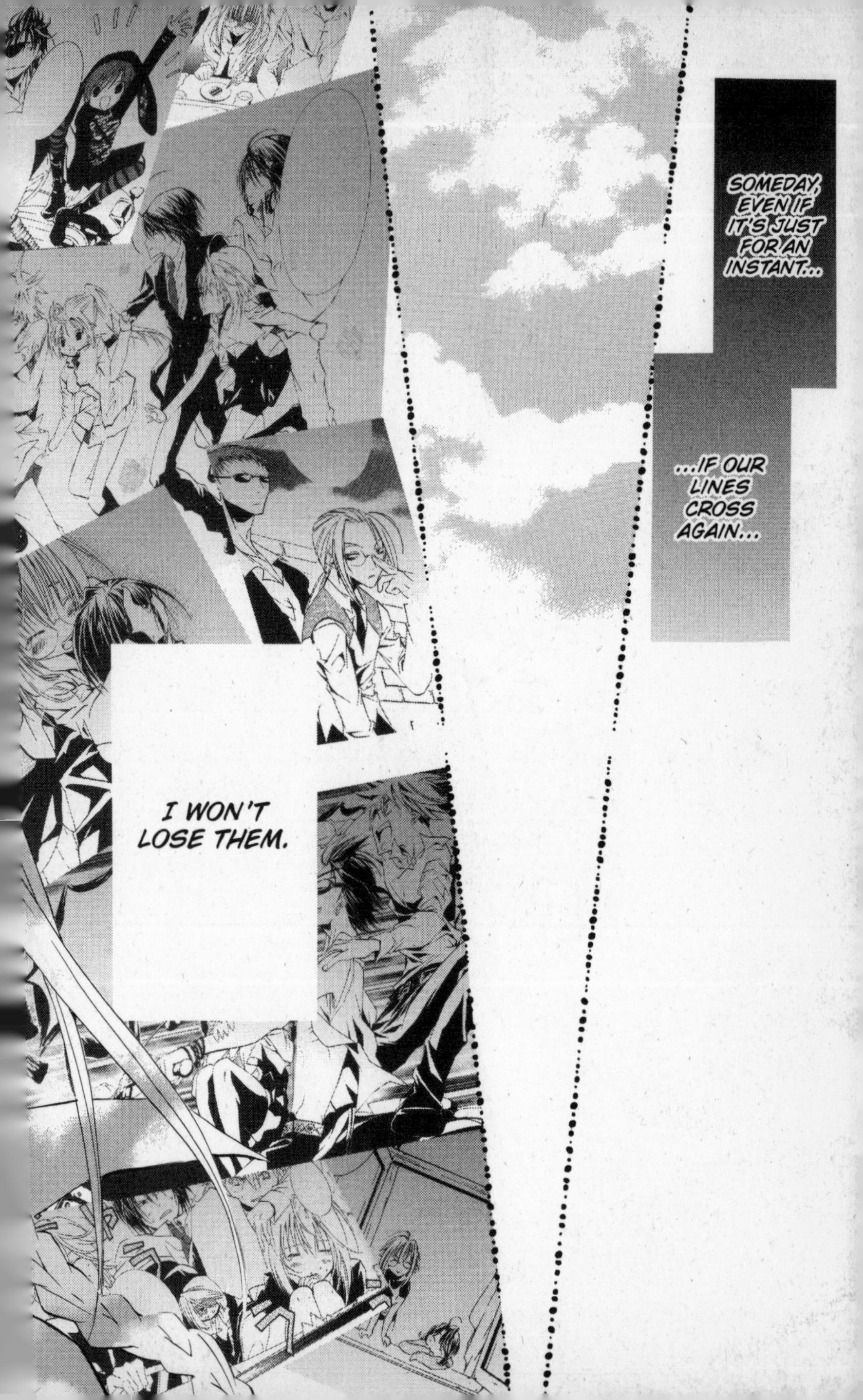
SOMEDAY, EVEN IF IT'S JUST FOR AN INSTANT...
...IF OUR LINES CROSS AGAIN...
I WON'T LOSE THEM.

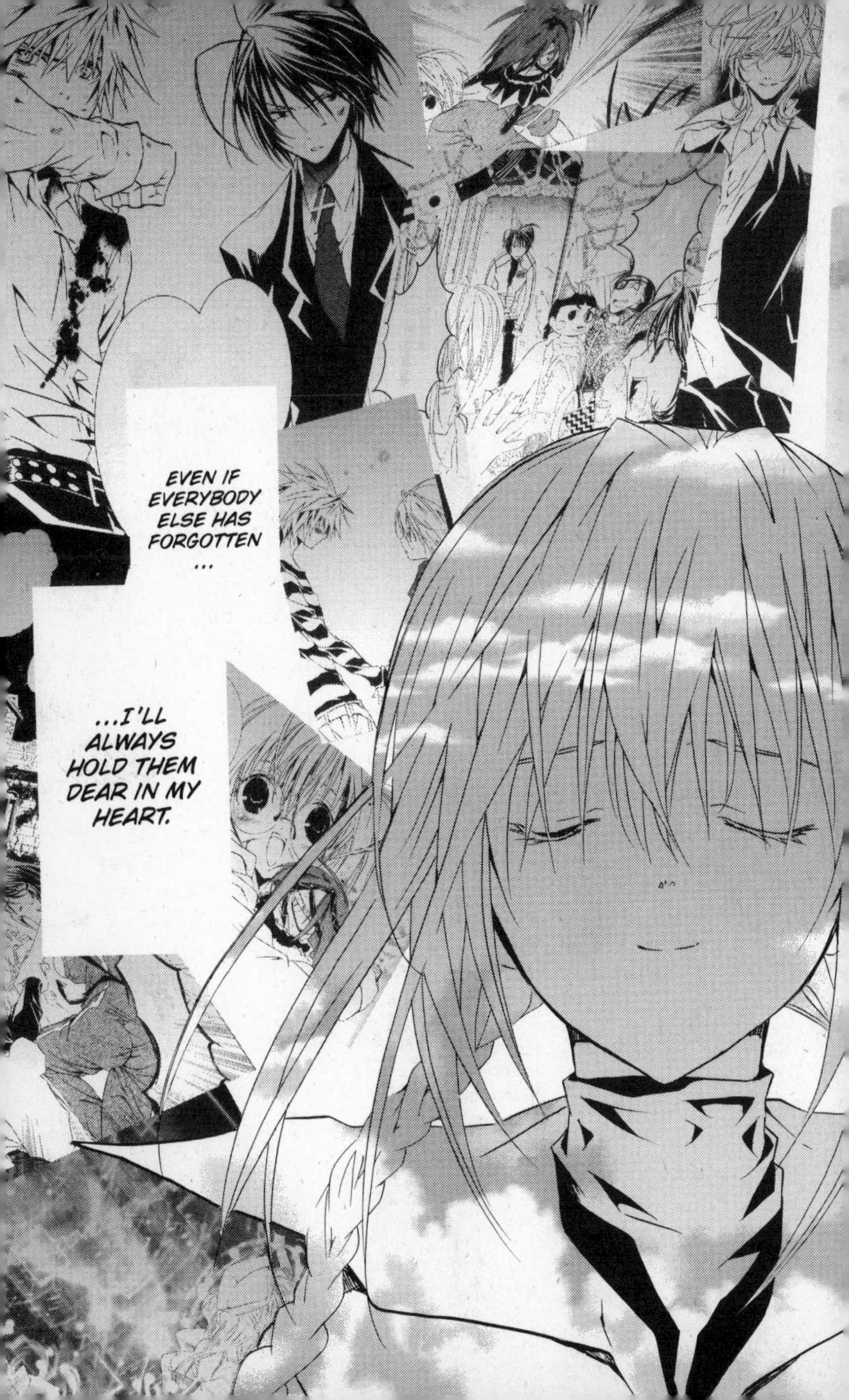
EVEN IF EVERYBODY ELSE HAS FORGOTTEN ...
...I'LL ALWAYS HOLD THEM DEAR IN MY HEART.

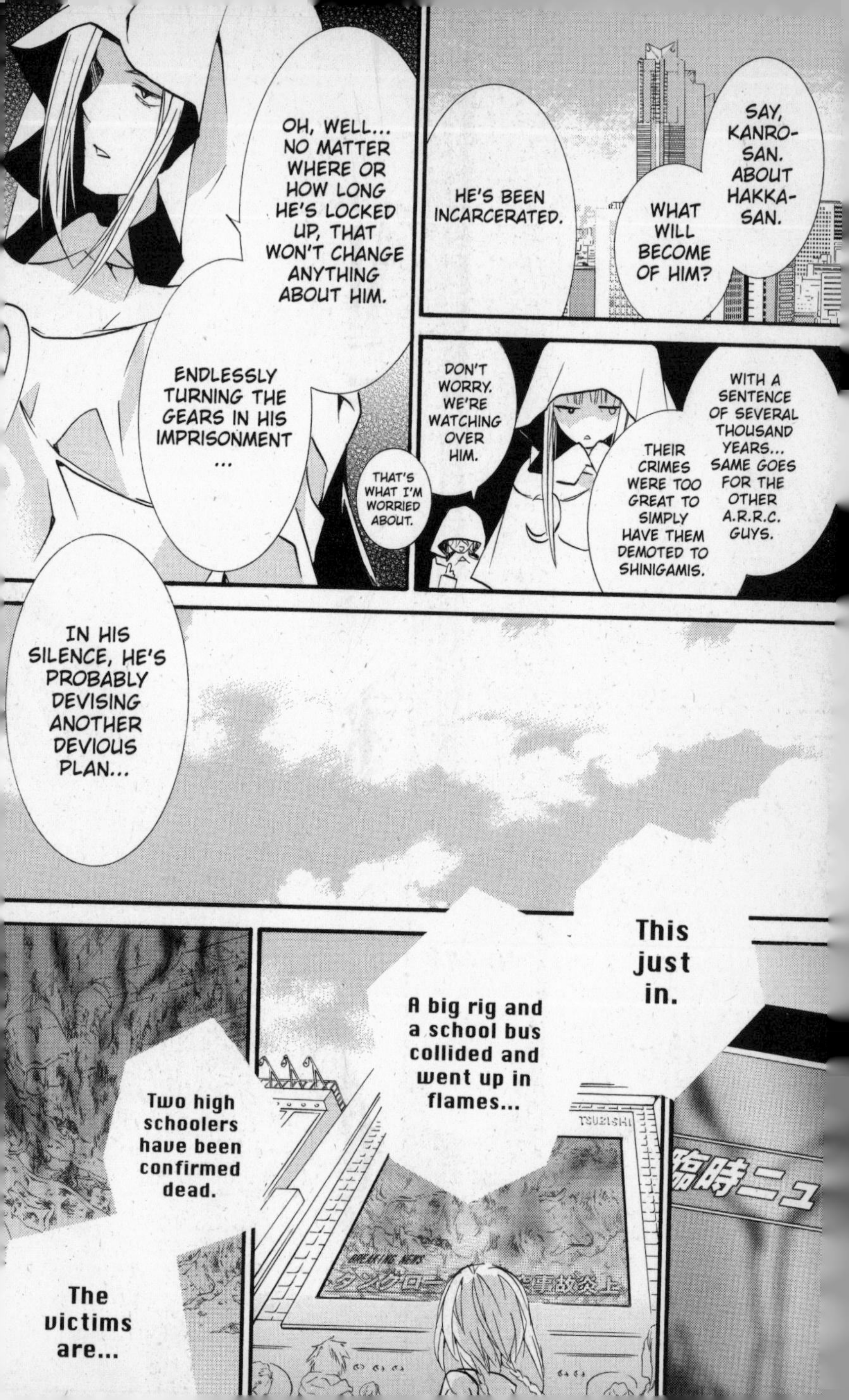
SAY, KANRO-SAN. ABOUT HAKKA-SAN.
WHAT WILL BECOME OF HIM?
HE'S BEEN INCARCERATED.
WITH A SENTENCE OF SEVERAL THOUSAND YEARS... SAME GOES FOR THE OTHER A.R.R.C. GUYS.
THEIR CRIMES WERE TOO GREAT TO SIMPLY HAVE THEM DEMOTED TO SHINIGAMIS.
DON'T WORRY. WE'RE WATCHING OVER HIM.
THAT'S WHAT I'M WORRIED ABOUT.
OH, WELL... NO MATTER WHERE OR HOW LONG HE'S LOCKED UP, THAT WON'T CHANGE ANYTHING ABOUT HIM.
ENDLESSLY TURNING THE GEARS IN HIS IMPRISONMENT...
IN HIS SILENCE, HE'S PROBABLY DEVISING ANOTHER DEVIOUS PLAN...
This just in.
A big rig and a school bus collided and went up in flames...
TSUBISHI
臨時ニュ
BREAKING NEWS
Two high schoolers have been confirmed dead.
The victims are...

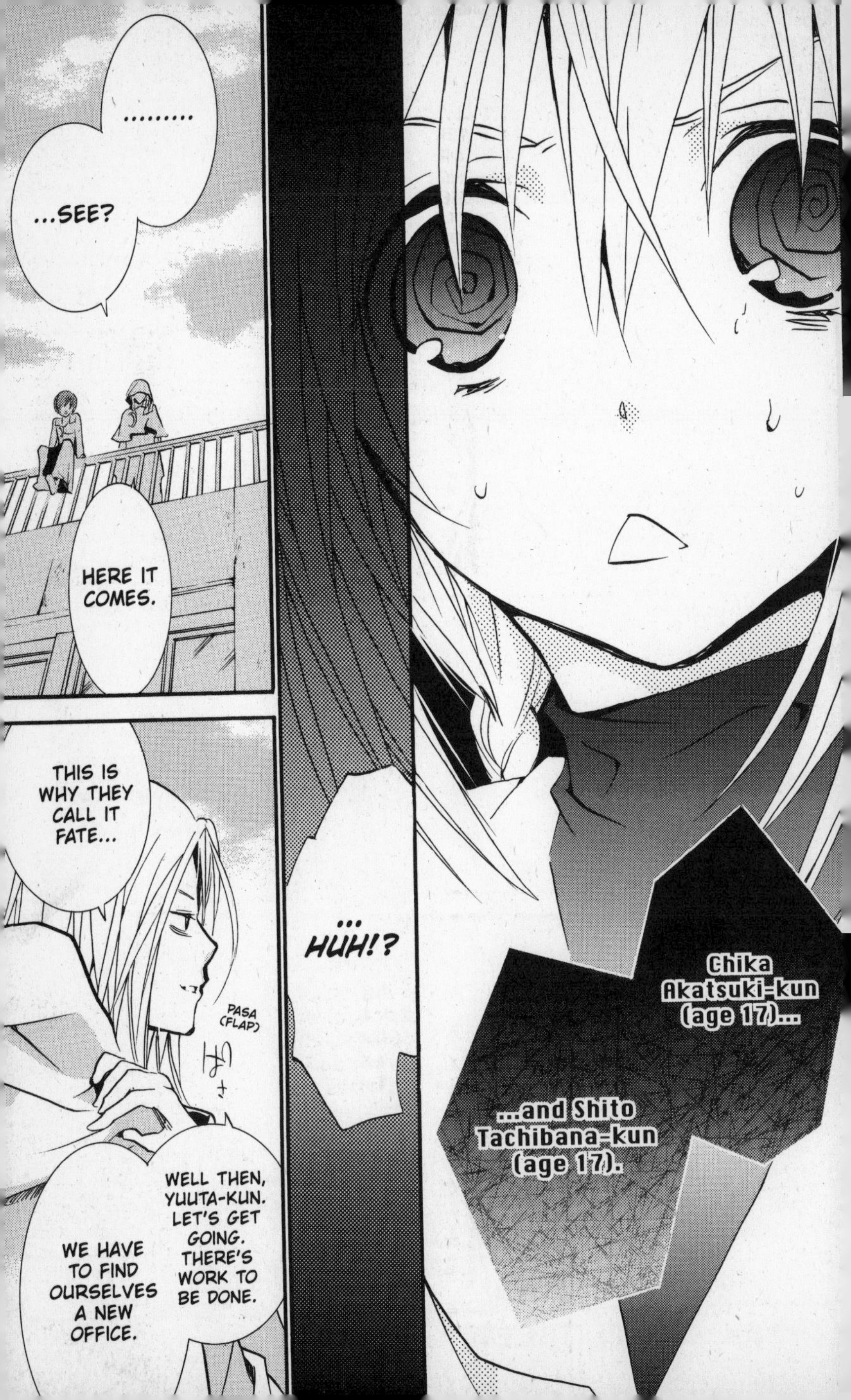

...HÜH!?
Chika Akatsuki-kun (age 17)...
...and Shito Tachibana-kun (age 17).
....
...SEE?
HERE IT COMES.
THIS IS WHY THEY CALL IT FATE...
PASA (FLAP)
WELL THEN, YUUTA-KUN. LET'S GET GOING. THERE'S WORK TO BE DONE.
WE HAVE TO FIND OURSELVES A NEW OFFICE.

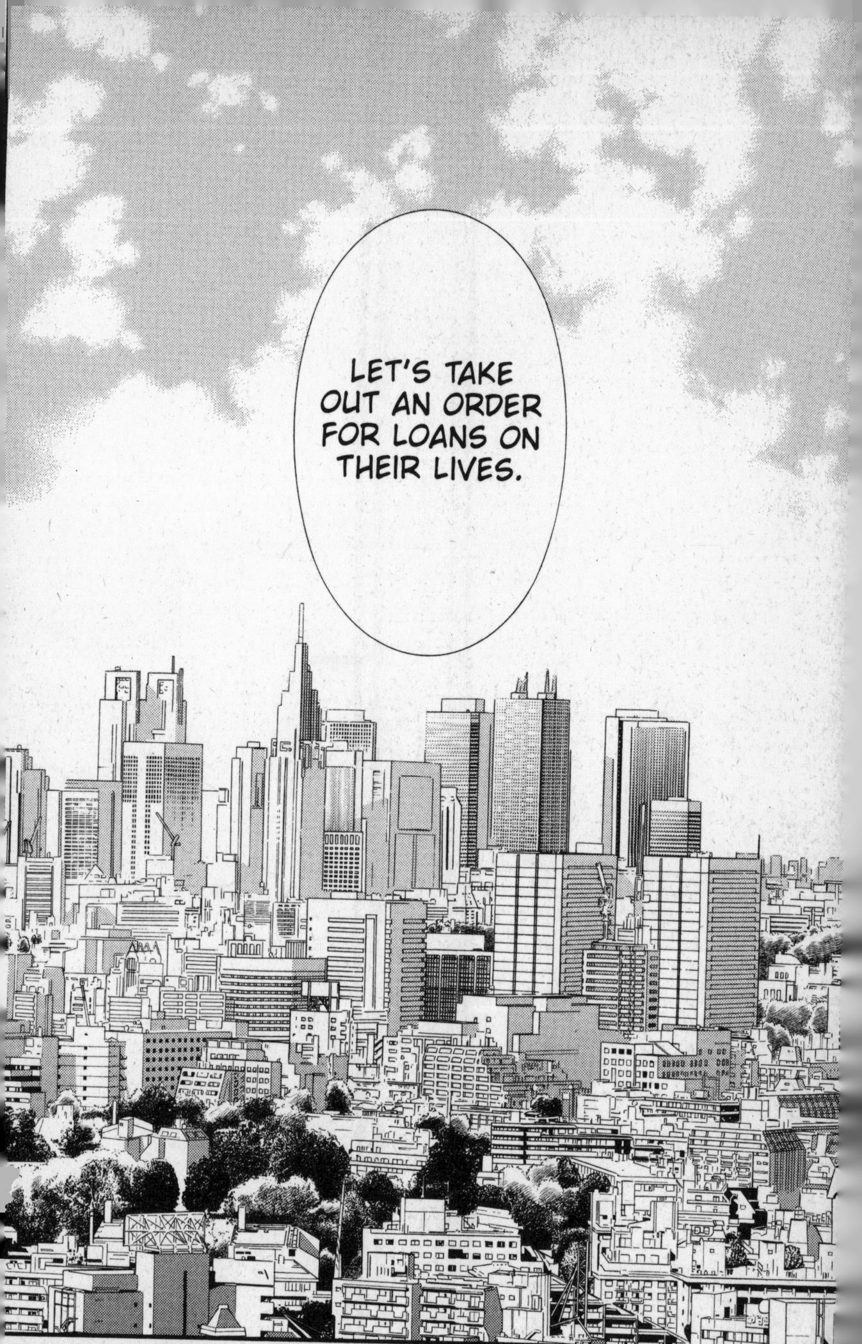
LET'S TAKE OUT AN ORDER FOR LOANS ON THEIR LIVES.

ZOMBIE-LOAN 13 THE END

ZOMBIE-LOAN

http://p-pit.net/

And so we draw the curtain on "ZOMBIE-LOAN."
We really appreciate you having read it so lovingly for its long run.

This work first started its serialization right after
PEACH-PIT officially became a creator team, and
we initially didn't expect it to run for so long.
By the time we realized it, it had been running for nearly
eight years. And though it was slowly paced, the only
reason we were able to continue writing it for this long is
thanks to the support of you readers and you alone.
There was so much that we, as the creators, gained during the
writing of this, and it sustained us for a long time. Thanks to
everyone's encouragement, it even expanded into the fields
of an anime and a radio drama, making it a very joyful piece
of work that we were able to enjoy on several levels.
Being as long as it was, looking back on it now, it is very clear
to us that it is riddled with many instances of amateur decisions,
and there were a lot of times we wish we could have improved the
pacing on such-and-such...or drawn such-and-such in a different
style...etc, etc. There's no end to the thoughts it provokes in us,
but one thing is for sure: for being as amateur as we were, we did
the best we could at that time and put all our energy into it.
It may have been an unrefined and unshapely piece of
work, but it is this "ZOMBIE-LOAN" that comes out first
and foremost in my mind when I think of what the "core"
of PEACH-PIT is as we continue creating works.
There is no greater a joy for us, as its creators, to be accepted
by all you readers and to enjoy the story alongside you.

We hope to see you again some time.

All produced by
PEACH-PIT
BanriSendou : ShibukoEbara

Staff
Nao
Kinomin
Yu.H
Hitomi.I
Mai.T
Shirayuki
Tomohiro.I
Zaki

Special thanks
T.Kuma

Thank you for your reading

ZOMBIE-LOAN

13

by PEACH-PIT

Translation: Christine Dashiell
Lettering: Alexis Eckerman

ZOMBIE-LOAN Vol. 13 © 2011 PEACH-PIT / SQUARE ENIX. All rights reserved. First published in Japan in 2011 by SQUARE ENIX CO., LTD. English translation rights arranged with SQUARE ENIX CO., LTD. and Hachette Book Group through Tuttle-Mori Agency, Inc. Translation © 2012 by SQUARE ENIX CO., LTD.

Yen Press
Hachette Book Group
237 Park Avenue, New York, NY 10017

www.HachetteBookGroup.com
www.YenPress.com

Yen Press is an imprint of Hachette Book Group, Inc. The Yen Press name and logo are trademarks of Hachette Book Group, Inc.

First Yen Press Edition: January 2012

ISBN: 978-0-316-20468-2

10 9 8 7 6 5 4 3 2 1

BVG

Printed in the United States of America